Great Lives from History

Latinos

Great Lives from History

Latinos

Volume I

José Aceves – Tomás Estrada Palma

Editors

Carmen Tafolla

University of Texas - San Antonio

and

Martha P. Cotera

University of Texas - San Antonio

SALEM PRESS

Ipswich, Massachusetts Hackensack, New Jersey

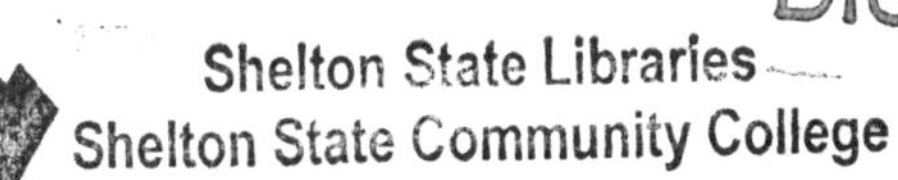

Cover Photos (pictured left to right, from top left): César Chávez (Geoff Hansen/Getty Images); Ricardo Montalbán (Michael Ochs Archives/Getty Images); Jennifer Lopez (Frederick M. Brown/Getty Images); Sonia Sotomayor (AP Photo); Carmen Miranda (Silver Screen Collection/Getty Images); Roberto Clemente (Focus on Sport/Getty Images).

The paper used in these volumes conforms to the American National Standard for Permanence of Paper for Printed Library Materials, X39.48-1992 (R1997).

Library of Congress Cataloging-in-Publication Data

Great lives from history. Latinos / Carmen Tafolla, Martha P. Cotera, editors.
p. cm.
ISBN 978-1-58765-810-5 (set) — ISBN 978-1-58765-811-2 (vol. 1) — ISBN 978-1-58765-812-9 (vol. 2) — ISBN 978-1-58765-813-6 (vol. 3)
1. Hispanic Americans—Biography—Encyclopedias. I. Tafolla, Carmen, 1951- II. Cotera, Martha.
III. Title: Latinos.
E184.S75G75 2012
920.009268—dc23
[B]

2011043168

Printed in the United States of America

Contents

Publisher's Note .ix
Contributors .xiii
Key to Pronunciation .xix
Complete List of Contents .xxi

José Aceves 1
Daniel Acosta 2
Mercedes de Acosta 4
Oscar Zeta Acosta 6
Edna Acosta-Belén 9
Rodolfo F. Acuña 10
Alma Flor Ada 12
Aristídes Agramonte 14
Jessica Alba 15
Pedro Albizu Campos 17
Olga Albizu 19
Lalo Alcaraz 21
John F. Alderete 23
Fernando Alegría 25
Luis Alfaro 26
Miguel Algarín 28
Isabel Allende 30
Mel Almada 32
Roberto Alomar 33
Sandy Alomar, Jr. 35
María Conchita Alonso 37
Felipe Alou 38
Ignacio Manuel Altamirano 40
Alurista 42
Juan Bautista Alvarado 44
Linda Alvarado 46
Anne Maino Alvarez 48
Julia Alvarez 49
Luis W. Alvarez 52
Mabel Alvarez 55
Ralph Alvarez 57
Walter Alvarez 59
Ralph Amado 60
Rudolfo Anaya 61
Toney Anaya 64
Joaquín Andújar 65
Gloria Anzaldúa 67
Luis Aparicio 69
Jerry Apodaca 71
Art Aragon 72
Marie Arana 74
Julio Arce 75
Reinaldo Arenas 77
Ron Arias 79
Desi Arnaz 80
Claudio Arrau 83
Alfredo M. Arreguín 85
Gus Arriola 86
Carlos Arroyo 88
Elizabeth Avellán 90
Bobby Ávila 91
Joaquín G. Avila 93
Francisco Ayala 95

Elfego Baca 98
Jimmy Santiago Baca 99
Judith F. Baca 101
Catherine Bach 103
Herman Badillo 105
Albert V. Baez 107
Joan Baez 108
Lourdes G. Baird 111
Román Baldorioty de Castro 113
José Celso Barbosa 114
Gertrudis Barceló 116
Ray Barretto 117
Raymond Barrio 119
Gregg Barrios 120
Ruth Behar 122
Pura Belpré 124
Baruj Benacerraf 127
Santos Benavides 129
Roy Benavidez 130
Wilfred Benitez 132
Joe J. Bernal 134
Martha Bernal 136
Teresa Bernardez 138
Rubén Berríos 140
Rolando Blackman 142
Rubén Blades 143
Jorge Bolet 146
Bobby Bonilla 147
Juan Boza 149

Giannina Braschi . . . 150
Benjamin Bratt . . . 152
Monica Brown . . . 154
Juan Bruce-Novoa . . . 155
Tedy Bruschi . . . 157
Fernando Bujones . . . 159
José Antonio Burciaga . . . 161
Julia de Burgos . . . 162
Cruz Bustamante . . . 164

Lydia Cabrera . . . 167
Miguel Cabrera . . . 169
José Canseco . . . 171
Mario Cantú . . . 173
Norma Elia Cantú . . . 175
Norma V. Cantú . . . 176
José Raúl Capablanca . . . 178
Luisa Capetillo . . . 181
José A. Cárdenas . . . 182
Reyes Cárdenas . . . 184
Manuel Cardona . . . 185
David Cardús . . . 187
Rod Carew . . . 189
Mariah Carey . . . 191
Richard Henry Carmona . . . 193
Vikki Carr . . . 195
Barbara Carrasco . . . 197
Leo Carrillo . . . 198
Lynda Carter . . . 200
Lourdes Casal . . . 202
Rosie Casals . . . 203
Oscar Cásares . . . 205
Carlos Castaneda . . . 206
Carlos E. Castañeda . . . 209
Ana Castillo . . . 211
George Castro . . . 212
Joaquín Castro . . . 214
Julián Castro . . . 216
Eduardo Catalano . . . 217
Lauro Cavazos . . . 219
Richard E. Cavazos . . . 220
César Cedeño . . . 222
Orlando Cepeda . . . 224
Lorna Dee Cervantes . . . 226
Willie Champion . . . 227
Franklin Ramón Chang-Díaz . . . 229
César Chávez . . . 231
Denise Chávez . . . 234
Dennis Chavez . . . 236
Fray Angélico Chávez . . . 239
Helen Fabela Chávez . . . 241
Linda Chavez . . . 243
Guillermo B. Cintron . . . 245
Evelyn Cisneros . . . 246
Henry G. Cisneros . . . 248
Sandra Cisneros . . . 251
Roberto Clemente . . . 253
Oscar Collazo . . . 255
Margarita Colmenares . . . 257
Jesús Colón . . . 259
Miriam Colón . . . 261
Willie Colón . . . 262
Dave Concepción . . . 264
Laura Contreras-Rowe . . . 266
Angel Cordero, Jr. . . . 267
France Anne Córdova . . . 269
Lucha Corpi . . . 271
Gregorio Cortez . . . 273
Juan Cortina . . . 274
Juan Estanislao Cotera . . . 276
Martha P. Cotera . . . 277
Linda Cristal . . . 279
Celia Cruz . . . 280
Nicky Cruz . . . 283
Victor Hernández Cruz . . . 285

Francisco Dallmeier . . . 287
Nicholas Dante . . . 288
Angela de Hoyos . . . 290
Eligio de la Garza II . . . 292
Oscar De La Hoya . . . 294
Oscar de la Renta . . . 296
Jane L. Delgado . . . 298
Dolores del Río . . . 300
Daniel DeSiga . . . 302
Donna de Varona . . . 303
Cameron Diaz . . . 305
Gwendolyn Díaz . . . 307
Henry F. Díaz . . . 308
Junot Díaz . . . 310
Justino Díaz . . . 312
José de Diego . . . 313
Paquito D'Rivera . . . 315

Sheila E. . . . 317
Hector Elizondo . . . 319
Virgilio Elizondo . . . 320
Gaspar Enríquez . . . 322

Jaime Escalante 323
Sixto Escobar 325
Martín Espada 327
Gloria Estefan 329
Luis R. Esteves 331
Emilio Estevez 332
Leobardo Estrada 334
Tomás Estrada Palma 336

Publisher's Note

Great Lives from History: Latinos (3 vols.) joins the *Great Lives* series, which provides in-depth critical essays on important men and women in all areas of achievement, from around the world and throughout history. The series was initiated in 2004 with *The Ancient World, Prehistory-476 C.E.* (2 vols.) and was followed in 2005 by *The Middle Ages, 477-1453* (2 vols.) and *The Renaissance & Early Modern Era, 1454-1600* (2 vols.); in 2006 by *The 17th Century, 1601-1700* (2 vols.) and *The 18th Century, 1701-1800* (2 vols.); in 2007 by *The 19th Century, 1801-1900* (4 vols.) and *Notorious Lives* (3 vols.); in 2008 by *The 20th Century, 1901-2000* (10 vols.); in 2010 by *Inventors & Inventions* (4 vols.); and in 2011 by *The Incredibly Wealthy* (3 vols.), *Jewish Americans* (4 vols.), and *African Americans* (5 vols.). With this new installment, the entire series extends to 46 volumes, covering more than 7,200 lives.

Online Access

Salem provides access to its award-winning content both in traditional, printed form and online. Any school or library that purchases this three-volume set is entitled to free, complimentary access to Salem's online version of the content through our Salem History Database. Access is available through a code printed on the inside cover of this first volume, and that access is unlimited and immediate. Our online customer service representatives, at (800) 221-1592, are happy to help with any questions.

The advantages are clear:

- Complimentary with print purchase
- Fully supported
- Unlimited users at your library
- Full access from home or dorm rooms
- Immediate access via online registration
- A simple, intuitive interface
- User profile areas for students and patrons
- Sophisticated search functionality
- Complete content, including appendixes
- Integrated searches with any other Salem Press product you already have on the Salem History platform.

E-books are also available.

Scope of Coverage

Great Lives from History: Latinos features 514 essays covering 514 people. The vast majority of the individuals included in this set have never been covered in this series before. Many of these individuals—from artists and business giants to religious and political leaders, scientists, inventors, philosophers, and social activists—are not covered in other biographical reference works of this magnitude.

Each one of these essays has been specially written for this set. The subjects of the essays are Latinos whose achievements and contributions are essential to any well-rounded liberal arts curriculum. The editors' criteria for including these individuals in this publication took into account their historical significance; their representation from a wide range of fields of endeavor; their relevance to class curricula; and their interest to high school, undergraduate, and general readers.

Essay Length and Format

Each essay is from 1,000 to 2,000 words in length (approximately 2 to 4 pages) and displays standard ready reference top matter offering easy access to the following biographical information:

- The **name** by which the subject is best known.
- A succinct **identification** that signals the person's occupation.
- A **synopsis** highlighting the individual's historical or social importance.
- **Born** and **Died** lines that list the most complete dates of birth and death available, followed by the most precise locations available, as well as an indication of when these data are unknown, only probable, or only approximate.
- **Also known as**, a listing of other versions of the individual's name, including full names, birth names, alternative spellings, pseudonyms, and nicknames.
- The **Areas of Achievement** with which the subject is most closely identified.

The body of each essay, which also includes a byline for the contributing writer-scholar, is divided into the following three parts:

- **Early Life** provides facts about the individual's upbringing and the environment in which the subject was reared. This section also provides the pronunciation of the profiled subject's full name upon first mention. Where little is known about the person's early life, historical context is provided.
- **Life's Work**, the heart of the essay, consists of a straightforward, generally chronological account of how the individual gained recognition in his or her chosen field, emphasizing the most significant achievements in the figure's life and career.
- **Significance** provides an overview of the long-range importance of the individual's accomplishments, emphasizing the impact on American history, business, culture, sports or other areas of endeavor. This section sums up why it is important to study this individual.

The end matter of each essay includes the following resources:

- **Further Reading**, an annotated bibliography, provides a starting point for further research.
- **See Also**, a list of cross-references to other essays in the set covering other individuals who have had similar careers or whose lives intersect that of the subject of the essay.

Special Features

Several features distinguish this set:

- **Key to Pronunciation**: A key to in-text pronunciation of unfamiliar names appears in all volumes. Pronunciation guidelines for difficult-to-pronounce names are provided in the first paragraph of the essay's "Early Life" section.
- **Complete List of Contents**: This alphabetical list of contents appears in all three volumes.
- **Sidebars:** A key feature of 314 of the essays in this publication is a sidebar on a particularly important or ancillary aspect of the individual's life.
- **Photographs:** More than 400 photographs illustrate the essays.

The back matter to Volume 3 includes these appendixes:

- **Chronological List of Entries**, by year of birth
- **Mediagraphy**
- **Literary Bibliography**
- **Organizations and Societies**
- **Research Centers and Libraries**
- **Bibliography**
- **Web Site Directory**

Finally, Volume 3 ends with three useful indexes:

- **Category Index:** Profiled figures by area of achievement.
- **Geographic Index:** A listing of each person by his or her country of origin or heritage.
- **Subject Index:** A comprehensive index including personages, professions, concepts, terms, other topics of discussion.

Contributors

Salem Press would like to extend its appreciation to all involved in the development and production of this work. The essays have been written and signed by scholars of history, humanities, the sciences, and other disciplines related to the essays' topics.Without these expert contributions, a project of this nature would not be possible. A full list of the contributors' names and affiliations appears in the front matter of this volume.

Special thanks go to Carmen Tarfolla and Martha P. Cotera, the set's editors, without whose guidance and creative vision this publication would not have been possible. They developed the contents list and sidebar topics, as well as contributed significantly to this work. An internationally noted educator, scholar and poet, and one of the most highly anthologized of Latina writers, Dr. Carmen Tafolla has been published in more than 300 anthologies, magazines, journals, readers, textbooks, kindergarten Big Books, and in the Poetry-in-Motion series installed on city buses. Recognized by the National Association for Chicano Studies for work which "gives voice to the peoples and cultures of this land," Tafolla has received numerous recognitions, including the 1999 Art of Peace Award for work which contributes to peace, justice, and human understanding; the prestigious Charlotte Zolotow Award for best children's picture-book writing; two Tomas Rivera Book Awards; the Américas Award, given at the Library of Congress; and induction into the Texas Institute of Letters.

Activist, educator, and historian Martha P. Cotera has authored groundbreaking studies that defined the pivotal role of women in Chicano political and cultural history in both Mexico and America. Among the works she has authored are *The Chicana Feminist*, *Diosa y hembra: The History and Heritage of Chicanas in the U.S.*, *Chicanas in Politics and Public Life*, and *Dona*

Doormat No Esta Aqui: An Assertiveness and Communications Skills Manual for Hispanic Women. She also distinguished herself within Texas's Latino community by her passionate defense of civil rights and her advocacy of expanded educational opportunities for women and minorities.

Contributors

Randy Abbott
University of Evansville

Michael Adams
CUNY Graduate Center

Richard Adler
University of Michigan, Dearborn

Emily Alward
College of Southern Nevada

Carolyn Anderson
University of Massachusetts Amherst

Madeline Archer
Duquesne University

Gustavo Aybar
University of Missouri, Kansas City

Christine Ayorinde
London, UK

Anita Baker-Blocker
Ann Arbor, MI

Leigh Barkley
Yale University

David Barratt
Montreat College

Cordelia Barrera
Texas Tech University

Melissa Barton
Westminster, CO

Yvette Benavides
Our Lady of the Lake University

Raymond Benge Jr.
Tarrant County College, Northeast Campus

Michael Bennett
High Point University

Alvin Benson
Utah Valley University

Janet Berman
Temple University School of Medicine

Ernesto Bernal
Texas A&M University, San Antonio

Nicholas Birns
Eugene Lang College, The New School

Margaret Birns
New York University

Kyle Bluth
Charlotte, NC

Pegge Bochynski
Beverly, MA

Michael Buratovich
Spring Arbor University

Alison Burke
Southern Oregon University

Leon Bynum
Columbia University

Michelle Camacho
University of San Diego

Jennifer Campbell
Lycoming College

Adolfo Campoy-Cubillo
Oakland University

Cordelia Candelaria
Arizona State University

Margaret Cantu
University of Texas at San Antonio

Russell Carney
Missouri State University

Josef Castaneda-Liles
University of California, Santa Barbara

Tamela Chambers
University of Illinois at Urbana-Champaign

Tina Chan
Syracuse University Library

Frederick Chary
Indiana University Northwest

Dennis Cheek
University of Pennsylvania

Chinchilla-Gonzalez
University of Minnesota

Mary Christianakis
Occidental College

Esperanza Cintron
Wayne County Community College

John Clark Jr.
Connecticut College

Michael Conklin
The College of New Jersey

Brett Conway
Hansung University

Kevin-Khristian Cosgriff-Hernandez
Texas A&M University

Richard Costa
Texas A&M University

Michael Cummings Jr.
Madonna University

Steven Danver
Mesa Verde Publishing

Anita Davis
Converse College

Caprice de Lorm
Lake Forest, CA

Mark DeStephano
Saint Peter's College

James Deutsch
Smithsonian Institution

Joseph Dewey
University of Pittsburgh

Jonathan Dinneen
Bridgewater, MA

Marcia Dinneen
Bridgewater State University

Yolanda Doub
California State University, Fresno

Thomas Drucker
University of Wisconsin, Whitewater

Thomas Du Bose
Louisiana State University, Shreveport

Victor Duran
University of South Carolina

Robert Ellis
Northborough Historical Society

Mauricio Espinoza-Quesada
The Ohio State University

Jack Ewing
Boise, ID

Sandra Fallon-Ludwig
Brandeis University

Michael Faucette
Caldwell Community College and Technical Institute

Doug Feldmann
Northern Kentucky University

Maria Felix-Ortiz
University of the Incarnate Word

Thomas Feller
Nashville, TN

Gabriel Fernandez
Texas A&M University, Kingsville

Susan Filler
Chicago, IL

Paul Finnicum
Arkansas State University

George Flynn
SUNY—Plattsburgh

Anthony Fonseca
Nicholls State University

Macey Freudensprung
University of Texas at San Antonio

Marlene Galvan
University of Texas, Pan American

Gary Galvan
LaSalle University

Enrique Garcia
Middlebury College

Karen Garvin
American Military University

Thomas Genova
University of California, Santa Cruz

Yolanda Godsey
University of Houston

Sheldon Goldfarb
University of British Columbia

Bonnye Good
Seymour, IN

Matthew Goodwin
University of Massachusetts Amherst

Scot Guenter
San Jose State University

Kristina Gutierrez
University of Texas at San Antonio

Michael Hall
Armstrong Atlantic State University

Fusako Hamao
Santa Monica, CA

Monica Hanna
Los Angeles, CA

C. Alton Hassell
Baylor University

P. Graham Hatcher
University of Alabama

Pilar Herrera
University of Texas at El Paso

Teri Herron
Delta State University

KaaVonia Hinton-Johnson
Old Dominion University

Michael Hix
Troy University

Mary Hurd
East Tennessee State University

Aida Hurtado
University of California, Santa Barbara

Raymond Hylton
Virginia Union University

Robin Imhof
University of the Pacific Library

Derrick Jenkins Sr.
University of Cincinnati

Bruce Johansen
University of Nebraska at Omaha

Jeffrey Jones
University of Kentucky

George Kauffman
California State University, Fresno

Marylane Koch
University of Memphis

David Kopel
Indepndence Institute

P. Huston Ladner
University of Hawaii

Timothy Lane
Louisville, KY

Sandra Leconte
Chicago Public Schools

Sonia Lee
University of Illinois at Urbana-Champaign

Gabriela Lemmons
University of Kansas

Alyson Lerma
Oak Ridge High School; Lincoln Memorial University

Norma Lewis
Byron Center, MI

Thomas Lewis
St. Cloud Technical and Community College

Roy Liebman
California State University, Los Angeles

Victoria Linchong
New York, NY

Victor Lindsey
East Central University

Lisa Locascio
University of Southern California

Bernadette Low
Community College of Baltimore County, Dundalk

M. Philip Lucas
Cornell College

Eric Luft
SUNY Upstate Medical University

R. C. Lutz
CII Group

Mary Markland
Argosy University

Rebecca Marrall
University of Hawaii at Manoa

Sonya Mason
New School University

Roxanne McDonald
Wilmot, NH

Alesia McFadden-Williams
Washington, D.C.

Robert McFarland
Southern Historical Consultants

Scott Merriman
Troy University

Julia Meyers
Duquesne University

Michael Meyers
Pfeiffer University

Itzcoatl Meztli
Slippery Rock University

Seth Michelson
University of Southern California

Matthew Mihalka
University of Minnesota, Twin Cities

Karie Mize
Western Oregon University

Monica Montelongo
University of Texas-Pan American

Fawn-Amber Montoya
Colorado State University

Richard Mora
Occidental College

Mario Morelli
Western Illinois University

Norma Mouton
University of Houston

Pamela Mueller-Anderson
Indiana University School of Law, Indianapolis

Salvador Murguia
Miyazaki International College

B. Keith Murphy
Fort Valley State University

John Myers
Bard College at Simon's Rock

Jeff Naidoo
University of Kentucky

Jamie Naidoo
University of Alabama

Jennifer Najera
University of California, Riverside

Leslie Neilan
Virginia Polytechnic Institute and State University

Erika Noguera
Mattie Rhodes Center

Norma Noonan
Augsburg College

Olivia Olivares
Saint Cloud State University

Jose Ortal
McKenzie River Insights

Arsenio Orteza
WORLD Magazine

Fernando Ortiz
Gonzaga University

Shannon Oxley
University of Leeds

William Paquette
Tidewater Community College

Robert Paradowski
Rochester Institute of Technology

Erin Parrish
St. Paul, MN

Alyson Payne
University of California, Riverside

Amada Perez
University of California, Santa Barbara

Mark Perry
North Georgia College & State University

Barbara Peterson
University of Hawaii

Anastasia Pike
Columbia University, Teachers College

Michael Polley
Columbia College of Missouri

David Porter
William Penn University

Brooke Posley
Clarion University

Moumin Quazi
Tarleton State University

Erin Ranft
University of Texas at San Antonio

John Rausch Jr.
West Texas A&M University

Erin Redmond
Alfred University

Tammy Reedy-Strother
University of Kentucky

Kevin Reid
Henderson Community College

Rosemary Reisman
Sonoma, CA

Robert Ridinger
Northern Illinois University

Edward Riedinger
Ohio State University

Linda Rodriguez
Kansas City, MO

Sandra Rothenberg
Framingham State University

Michael Royster
Prairie View A&M University

Virginia Salmon
Northeast State Community College

Timothy Sawicki
Canisius College

Richard Sax
Lake Erie College

Jean Schaefer
University of Wyoming

Elizabeth Schafer
Loachapoka, AL

Mary Schons
Hammond Public Library

Basilio Serrano
SUNY College at Old Westbury

Maria Silva
Universidad Finis Terrae, Chile

Amy Sisson
Houston Community College

Stacey Sowards
University of Texas at El Paso

Jan Statman
Longview, TX

David Steffens
Oklahoma City University

Willette Stinson
Wilberforce University

Eric Strother
University of Kentucky

Cynthia Svoboda
Bridgewater State University

William Teipe Jr.
North Orange County Community College District

John Thorburn Jr.
Waco, TX

Maria Trillo
Western New Mexico University

J. Jehriko Turner
City College of New York (CUNY)

Gloria Vando
Midwest Center for the Literary Arts, Inc.

Charles Vigue
University of New Haven

Jan Voogd
New York, NY

Mary Ware
SUNY, College at Cortland

Shawncey Webb
Taylor University

Latanya West
Education Writers Association

Winifred Whelan
St. Bonaventure University

Nancy Wilson
Texas State University

Sharon Wilson
Fort Hays State University

Crystal Wolfe
Larwill, IN

Scott Wright
University of St. Thomas

Lisa Wroble
Edison State College

KEY TO PRONUNCIATION

Many of the names of personages covered in *Great Lives from History: Latinos* may be unfamiliar to students and general readers. For difficult-to-pronounce names, guidelines to pronounciation have been provided upon first mention of the name in each essay. These guidelines do not purport to achieve the subleties of all languages but will offer readers a rough equivalent of how English speakers may approximate the proper pronunciation.

Vowel Sounds

Symbol	**Spelled (Pronounced)**
a	answer (AN-suhr), laugh (laf), sample (SAM-puhl), that (that)
ah	father (FAH-thur), hospital (HAHS-pih-tuhl)
aw	awful (AW-fuhl), caught (kawt)
ay	blaze (blayz), fade (fayd), waiter (WAYT-ur), weigh (way)
eh	bed (behd), head (hehd), said (sehd)
ee	believe (bee-LEEV), cedar (SEE-dur), leader (LEED-ur), liter (LEE-tur)
ew	boot (bewt), lose (lewz)
i	buy (bi), height (hit), lie (li), surprise (sur-PRIZ)
ih	bitter (BIH-tur), pill (pihl)
o	cotton (KO-tuhn), hot (hot)
oh	below (bee-LOH), coat (koht), note (noht), wholesome (HOHL-suhm)
oo	good (good), look (look)
ow	couch (kowch), how (how)
oy	boy (boy), coin (koyn)
uh	about (uh-BOWT), butter (BUH-tuhr), enough (ee-NUHF), other (UH-thur).

Consonant Sounds

Symbol	**Spelled (Pronounced)**
ch	beach (beech), chimp (chihmp)
g	beg (behg), disguise (dihs-GIZ), get (geht)
j	digit (DIH-juht), edge (ehj), jet (jeht)
k	cat (kat), kitten (KIH-tuhn), hex (hehks)
s	cellar (SEHL-ur), save (sayv), scent (sehnt)
sh	champagne (sham-PAYN), issue (IH-shew), shop (shop)
ur	birth (burth), disturb (dihs-TURB), earth (urth), letter (LEH-tur)
y	useful (YEWS-fuhl), young (yuhng)
z	business (BIHZ-nehs), zest (zehst)
zh	vision (VIH-zhuhn)

Complete List of Contents

Volume 1

Contents . . . v
Publisher's Note . . . ix
Contributors . . . xiii
Key to Pronunciation . . . xix

José Aceves . . . 1
Daniel Acosta . . . 2
Mercedes de Acosta . . . 4
Oscar Zeta Acosta . . . 6
Edna Acosta-Belén . . . 9
Rodolfo F. Acuña . . . 10
Alma Flor Ada . . . 12
Aristídes Agramonte . . . 14
Jessica Alba . . . 15
Pedro Albizu Campos . . . 17
Olga Albizu . . . 19
Lalo Alcaraz . . . 21
John F. Alderete . . . 23
Fernando Alegría . . . 25
Luis Alfaro . . . 26
Miguel Algarín . . . 28
Isabel Allende . . . 30
Mel Almada . . . 32
Roberto Alomar . . . 33
Sandy Alomar, Jr. . . . 35
María Conchita Alonso . . . 37
Felipe Alou . . . 38
Ignacio Manuel Altamirano . . . 40
Alurista . . . 42
Juan Bautista Alvarado . . . 44
Linda Alvarado . . . 46
Anne Maino Alvarez . . . 48
Julia Alvarez . . . 49
Luis W. Alvarez . . . 52
Mabel Alvarez . . . 55
Ralph Alvarez . . . 57
Walter Alvarez . . . 59
Ralph Amado . . . 60
Rudolfo Anaya . . . 61
Toney Anaya . . . 64
Joaquín Andújar . . . 65
Gloria Anzaldúa . . . 67
Luis Aparicio . . . 69
Jerry Apodaca . . . 71
Art Aragon . . . 72
Marie Arana . . . 74
Julio Arce . . . 75
Reinaldo Arenas . . . 77
Ron Arias . . . 79
Desi Arnaz . . . 80
Claudio Arrau . . . 83
Alfredo M. Arreguín . . . 85
Gus Arriola . . . 86
Carlos Arroyo . . . 88
Elizabeth Avellán . . . 90
Bobby Ávila . . . 91
Joaquín G. Avila . . . 93
Francisco Ayala . . . 95

Elfego Baca . . . 98
Jimmy Santiago Baca . . . 99
Judith F. Baca . . . 101
Catherine Bach . . . 103
Herman Badillo . . . 105
Albert V. Baez . . . 107
Joan Baez . . . 108
Lourdes G. Baird . . . 111
Román Baldorioty de Castro . . . 113
José Celso Barbosa . . . 114
Gertrudis Barceló . . . 116
Ray Barretto . . . 117
Raymond Barrio . . . 119
Gregg Barrios . . . 120
Ruth Behar . . . 122
Pura Belpré . . . 124
Baruj Benacerraf . . . 127
Santos Benavides . . . 129
Roy Benavidez . . . 130
Wilfred Benitez . . . 132
Joe J. Bernal . . . 134
Martha Bernal . . . 136
Teresa Bernardez . . . 138

Rubén Berríos . . . 140
Rolando Blackman . . . 142
Rubén Blades . . . 143
Jorge Bolet . . . 146
Bobby Bonilla . . . 147
Juan Boza . . . 149
Giannina Braschi . . . 150
Benjamin Bratt . . . 152
Monica Brown . . . 154
Juan Bruce-Novoa . . . 155
Tedy Bruschi . . . 157
Fernando Bujones . . . 159
José Antonio Burciaga . . . 161
Julia de Burgos . . . 162
Cruz Bustamante . . . 164

Lydia Cabrera . . . 167
Miguel Cabrera . . . 169
José Canseco . . . 171
Mario Cantú . . . 173
Norma Elia Cantú . . . 175
Norma V. Cantú . . . 176
José Raúl Capablanca . . . 178
Luisa Capetillo . . . 181
José A. Cárdenas . . . 182
Reyes Cárdenas . . . 184
Manuel Cardona . . . 185
David Cardús . . . 187
Rod Carew . . . 189
Mariah Carey . . . 191
Richard Henry Carmona . . . 193
Vikki Carr . . . 195
Barbara Carrasco . . . 197
Leo Carrillo . . . 198
Lynda Carter . . . 200
Lourdes Casal . . . 202
Rosie Casals . . . 203
Oscar Cásares . . . 205
Carlos Castaneda . . . 206
Carlos E. Castañeda . . . 209
Ana Castillo . . . 211
George Castro . . . 212
Joaquín Castro . . . 214
Julián Castro . . . 216
Eduardo Catalano . . . 217
Lauro Cavazos . . . 219
Richard E. Cavazos . . . 220
César Cedeño . . . 222
Orlando Cepeda . . . 224
Lorna Dee Cervantes . . . 226
Willie Champion . . . 227
Franklin Ramón Chang-Díaz . . . 229
César Chávez . . . 231
Denise Chávez . . . 234
Dennis Chavez . . . 236
Fray Angélico Chávez . . . 239
Helen Fabela Chávez . . . 241
Linda Chavez . . . 243
Guillermo B. Cintron . . . 245
Evelyn Cisneros . . . 246
Henry G. Cisneros . . . 248
Sandra Cisneros . . . 251
Roberto Clemente . . . 253
Oscar Collazo . . . 255
Margarita Colmenares . . . 257
Jesús Colón . . . 259
Miriam Colón . . . 261
Willie Colón . . . 262
Dave Concepción . . . 264
Laura Contreras-Rowe . . . 266
Angel Cordero, Jr. . . . 267
France Anne Córdova . . . 269
Lucha Corpi . . . 271
Gregorio Cortez . . . 273
Juan Cortina . . . 274
Juan Estanislao Cotera . . . 276
Martha P. Cotera . . . 277
Linda Cristal . . . 279
Celia Cruz . . . 280
Nicky Cruz . . . 283
Victor Hernández Cruz . . . 285

Francisco Dallmeier . . . 287
Nicholas Dante . . . 288
Angela de Hoyos . . . 290
Eligio de la Garza II . . . 292
Oscar De La Hoya . . . 294
Oscar de la Renta . . . 296
Jane L. Delgado . . . 298
Dolores del Río . . . 300
Daniel DeSiga . . . 302
Donna de Varona . . . 303
Cameron Diaz . . . 305
Gwendolyn Díaz . . . 307
Henry F. Díaz . . . 308
Junot Díaz . . . 310
Justino Díaz . . . 312
José de Diego . . . 313
Paquito D'Rivera . . . 315

Sheila E. 317
Hector Elizondo 319
Virgilio Elizondo. 320
Gaspar Enríquez 322
Jaime Escalante. 323
Sixto Escobar 325
Martín Espada. 327
Gloria Estefan 329
Luis R. Esteves 331
Emilio Estevez 332
Leobardo Estrada 334
Tomás Estrada Palma 336

Volume 2

Contents v
Key to Pronunciation vii
Complete List of Contents ix

Mimi Fariña 339
David G. Farragut 341
José Feliciano 343
Gigi Fernández 345
Joseph A. Fernández 347
Manny Fernández 348
Royes Fernández. 350
Tony Fernandez. 351
Jose Alberto Fernandez-Pol 353
Luis A. Ferré 355
Rosario Ferré. 356
José Ferrer. 359
Mel Ferrer 361
America Ferrera 363
Ricardo Flores Magón. 364
Patrick Flores 366
Tom Flores 368
Maria Irene Fornes 370
Julio Franco. 372
Coco Fusco 373

Guy Gabaldon 376
Andrés Galarraga 378
Ernesto Galarza. 379
Rudy Galindo 381
Andy Garcia 383
Cristina García 385
Gus C. Garcia 386
Héctor García 389
Jeff Garcia. 391
Jerry Garcia. 393
José D. García. 395
Carmen Lomas Garza 397
Oralia Garza de Cortés 398
John Gavin 400
Fabiola Cabeza de Baca Gilbert 402
Manu Ginóbili. 404
Isaac Goldemberg 406
Scott Gomez 408
Arturo Gómez-Pompa. 409
Paul Gonsalves 411
Alberto Gonzales 413
Corky Gonzáles. 414
Pancho Gonzales. 417
Elma González 419
Henry Barbosa González 421
Rigoberto González 424
Tony Gonzalez 425
Martín Gramática 428
Pedro Guerrero 430
Nicolás Guillén 432
Ozzie Guillén 434
José Ángel Gutiérrez. 436
Luis Gutiérrez 438
Sidney M. Gutierrez 440

Rita Hayworth. 442
Antonia Hernández 444
Joseph Marion Hernández. 446
Juano Hernández. 448
Rafael Hernández 450
Willie Hernández 452
Aurelio Herrera 454
Carolina Herrera 455
María Herrera-Sobek 457
Edward Hidalgo 459
Hilda Hidalgo 461
Oscar Hijuelos. 463
Maria Hinojosa 465
Rolando Hinojosa 467
Lorenzo Homar. 469
Eugenio María de Hostos 471
Dolores Huerta 472

Julio Iglesias 475
Arturo Islas 477

Cleofas Martinez Jaramillo 479
Marí-Luci Jaramillo 481
Flaco Jiménez 483
Francisco Jiménez 486
Luis Alfonso Jiménez, Jr. 488
Raúl Juliá 489
Katy Jurado 491

Eugenia Kalnay 494
Nicolás Kanellos 496
Joe Kapp 498
Gary D. Keller 502

Tony Labat 504
Fernando Lamas 506
Octaviano Larrazolo 508
Luis Leal 510
Lolita Lebrón 512
John Leguizamo 514
José Arcadio Limón 516
Vicente José Llamas 518
Rebecca Lobo 519
Eva Longoria 521
George Lopez 523
Jennifer Lopez 525
Nancy Lopez 528
Rafael López 530
Ramon E. Lopez 531
Trini López 533
Yolanda M. López 535
Frank Lorenzo 537
Manuel Luján, Jr. 539

Eduardo Machado 542
Arturo Madrid 544
Sonia Manzano 545
Michael A. Mares 548
Juan Marichal 549
Cheech Marín 552
Marisol 554
José Martí 556
Ricky Martin 558
Antonio José Martínez 560
Dennis Martínez 562
Elizabeth Martínez 564
Mel Martínez 566
Narciso Martínez 568

Pedro Martinez 571
Robert Martinez 573
Vilma Socorro Martínez 575
María Martínez-Cañas 577
Norma Martinez-Rogers 579
Jorge Mas Canosa 581
Eduardo Mata 583
Harold Medina 586
Bill Melendez 588
Margarita Bradford Melville 590
José Méndez 592
Ana Mendieta 594
Louis Mendoza 595
Lydia Mendoza 597
Amalia Mesa-Bains 598
Minnie Minoso 600
Carmen Miranda 602
Nicholasa Mohr 604
Gloria Molina 606
Mario Molina 608
Amalia Mondríguez 610
Carolina Monsivaís 612
Ricardo Montalbán 613
Diana Montes de Oca Lopez 616
María Montez 617
José Montoya 619
Joseph M. Montoya 621
Pat Mora 623
Cherríe Moraga 625
Alejandro Morales 627
Esai Morales 629
Noro Morales 630
Sylvia Morales 632
Yuyi Morales 633
Arte Moreno 635
Rita Moreno 637
Carlos Morton 640
Anthony Muñoz 641
Luis Muñoz Marín 644
Luis Muñoz Rivera 646
Joaquín Murieta 648

Eduardo Nájera 650
Julian Nava 652
Sandy Nava 654
José Antonio Navarro 656
Beatriz Noloesca 658
Carlos Noriega 659
Ramón Novarro 661
Antonia Novello 663

Soledad O'Brien . . . 665
Adriana C. Ocampo . . . 667
Ellen Ochoa. . . . 668
Esteban Ochoa . . . 670
Severo Ochoa . . . 671
Tony Oliva . . . 674
Francisco Oller . . . 676
Edward James Olmos . . . 677
Lupe Ontiveros . . . 679
Antonio Orendain . . . 681
Felipe de Ortego y Gasca . . . 682
David Ortiz . . . 683
Judith Ortiz Cofer . . . 685
Miguel Antonio Otero. . . . 687

Volume 3

Contents . . . v
Key to Pronunciation . . . vii
Complete List of Contents . . . ix

Eduardo Padrón. . . . 689
Rafael Palmeiro. . . . 691
Charlie Palmieri . . . 692
Américo Paredes. . . . 694
Cesar Pelli. . . . 696
Elizabeth Peña. . . . 697
Federico Peña . . . 699
Alonso Perales . . . 701
James Perez. . . . 703
Rosie Pérez . . . 704
Victor Perez-Mendez . . . 706
Ástor Piazzolla . . . 707
Pío Pico. . . . 709
Sacramento Pimentel . . . 711
Laffit Pincay, Jr. . . . 713
Miguel Piñero . . . 715
Jim Plunkett . . . 718
Mary Helen Ponce. . . . 720
Liliana Porter . . . 721
Estela Portillo Trambley . . . 723
Freddie Prinze. . . . 724
Tito Puente . . . 727
Albert Pujols . . . 729

Anthony Quinn . . . 731

Gregory Rabassa. . . . 734
Manny Ramirez. . . . 736
Samuel A. Ramirez, Sr. . . . 738
Sara Estela Ramírez . . . 739
Ángel Ramos. . . . 741
Manuel Ramos Otero . . . 743
Irma Rangel. . . . 744
John Rechy . . . 746
Evaristo Ribera Chevremont. . . . 748
Bill Richardson . . . 749
Felisa Rincón de Gautier. . . . 751
Alberto Ríos . . . 754
Marian Lucy Rivas . . . 755
Maggie Rivas-Rodriguez . . . 757
Chita Rivera . . . 759
Geraldo Rivera . . . 761
Horacio Rivera, Jr. . . . 766
Tomás Rivera . . . 764
Francisco Rodón . . . 768
Alex Rodriguez. . . . 770
Chi Chi Rodriguez . . . 772
José Policarpo Rodríguez . . . 774
Luis J. Rodríguez . . . 775
Narciso Rodriguez . . . 778
Paul Rodríguez . . . 779
Rich Rodriguez. . . . 782
Richard Rodriguez . . . 783
Robert Rodriguez . . . 786
Lola Rodríguez de Tió . . . 788
Fernando E. Rodríguez Vargas . . . 790
Gilbert Roland. . . . 792
César Romero . . . 793
George Romero. . . . 796
Oscar I. Romo. . . . 798
Tony Romo . . . 800
Linda Ronstadt . . . 801
Ileana Ros-Lehtinen . . . 804
Edward R. Roybal. . . . 806

David Domingo Sabatini. . . . 809
Eddie Saenz. . . . 810
Ken Salazar . . . 812
Rubén Salazar . . . 814
Zoë Saldana. . . . 817
Raúl R. Salinas . . . 818
Julian Samora . . . 821

Olga San Juan 822
Félix Sánchez 824
Freddy Sanchez 826
George I. Sánchez 827
Loretta Sánchez 829
Luis Rafael Sánchez 831
Poncho Sánchez 833
Jesús María Sanromá 835
Carlos Santana 836
Johan Santana 838
George Santayana 840
Esmeralda Santiago 843
John Phillip Santos 845
José Sarria 847
Lalo Schifrin 848
Arturo Alfonso Schomburg 850
Jon Secada 852
Juan Seguin 854
Selena 856
Charlie Sheen 858
Martin Sheen 860
Jimmy Smits 862
Hilda L. Solis 864
Lionel Sosa 866
Sammy Sosa 868
Gary Soto 870
Pedro Juan Soto 872
Sonia Sotomayor 873
Clemente Soto Vélez 875
Claudio Spies 877
Virgil Suárez 878

Carmen Tafolla 881
Leo Tanguma 883
Yolanda Tarango 885
Nina Tassler 886
Diana Taurasi 888
Miguel Tejada 889
Piri Thomas 891
Luis Tiant 893
Reies López Tijerina 895
Juan Tizol 897
Danny Trejo 900
Jesse Treviño 901
Lee Trevino 903
Félix Trinidad 905

Joseph A. Unanue 907
Luis Alberto Urrea 909
Teresa Urrea 910

Alisa Valdes-Rodriguez 913
Luis Miguel Valdez 915
Ritchie Valens 918
Angela Valenzuela 920
Fernando Valenzuela 921
Ismael Valenzuela 923
Liliana Valenzuela 925
Roberto Valero 926
Rima de Vallbona 928
Pedro del Valle 929
Leticia Van de Putte 931
Erasmo Vando 933
Tiburcio Vásquez 934
Jaci Velasquez 936
Loreta Janeta Velázquez 938
Lupe Velez 940
Elena Verdugo 942
Bob Vila 944
Alma Villanueva 946
Danny Villanueva 947
Antonio Villaraigosa 949
José Antonio Villarreal 952
Victor Villaseñor 954
Helena María Viramontes 956

Raquel Welch 958
William Carlos Williams 960

Vicente Martinez Ybor 963
Jose Yglesias 964
Raul Yzaguirre 966

Bernice Zamora 969
Carmen Zapata 971
Patricia Zavella 973

Appendixes

Chronological List of Entries 977
Mediagraphy 983
Literary Works 988
Organizations and Societies 1002
Research Centers and Libraries 1006
Bibliography 1013
Web Site Directory 1022

Indexes

Category Index 1027
Geographical Index 1035
Subject Index 1037

Great Lives from History

Latinos

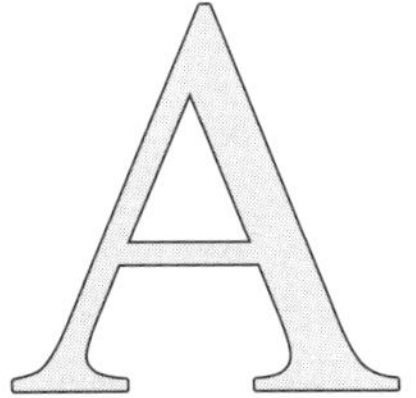

José Aceves

Mexican-born artist

Aceves was a leading member of the El Paso art community known for his public murals and colorful paintings of desert landscapes and themes from frontier history.

Latino heritage: Mexican

Born: December 22, 1909; Chihuahua, Mexico

Died: August 13, 1968; El Paso, Texas

Area of achievement: Art

Early Life

José Aceves (ah-SEH-vehs) was born in Chihuahua, Mexico, on December 22, 1901. He and his family immigrated to the United States in 1915 to avoid the turbulence of the Mexican Revolution. One of ten children, he attended public school in El Paso. There, he discovered a natural talent for drawing. While learning to draw and paint, he won several art prizes in his school; his preferred subjects were landscapes and themes from Western history.

To further his training, Aceves went to the home of the established landscape painter Audley Dean Nicols (who had come to El Paso for his health in 1919) and asked him questions about his work. Nicols recognized Aceves's talent and became his professional mentor, informally teaching the younger artist color techniques as well as the practical aspects of art. The two often went out to the desert to paint, creating distinctive and vivid compositions. Another local artist and illustrator, Tom Lea, also served as a source of critical assessment and influence on Aceves's growth. By 1930, Aceves had developed his own artistic style, beginning a career marked by the interweaving of themes from his Hispanic heritage and images from the visual language of the American West.

Life's Work

In 1937, Aceves was one of a group of seven Texas muralists hired by the Treasury Department's Section of Painting and Sculpture (created in October, 1934) to decorate public buildings with works of art emphasizing characters and events from pioneer history. The program—part of President Franklin D. Roosevelt's New Deal—was created by painter George Biddle, who believed that supporting the work of artists was just as vital to society as supporting tradesmen or farmers. His inspiration was a similar program implemented successfully by the Mexican government during the 1920's.

Prior to the creation of the Section of Painting and Sculpture, Aceves had become part of a group of artists working in El Paso who were interested in promoting the production and sale of handmade artworks historically associated with Mexican life on the frontier. In 1934, an exhibition of their work was held at the Hotel Paso del Norte. One year later, the Club Femenil in El Paso held a second art exhibition, from November 23 to 28, 1935, in which Aceves's work was shown. That year, he also completed a study for a mural depicting stagecoach travel titled *Westward Ho*. Aceves's work next was exhibited from June 6 to November 29, 1936, at the Texas Centennial Exposition in Dallas. He painted a series of murals depicting the history of Mexico, which was displayed in the show windows of a central El Paso business, and two murals showing horsemen at sunset, burros, and Mexican figures in a landscape of sandhills for the headquarters of the El Paso del Norte Arts and Crafts Guild

In July, 1938, Aceves was asked by Edward Rowan, assistant chief of the Section of Painting and Sculpture, to design a mural for the post office at Borger, Texas. Aceves's design was accepted in August, 1938, and he was given 180 days to complete the work. He selected the theme of the importance of mail delivery in a small town; the resulting mural, *Big City News*, completed in early 1939, depicts Borger's early wooden buildings and citizens' excitement at arriving mail. A second mural for the post office in Mart, Texas, *McLennan Looking for a Home* (1939), depicted the arrival of the founder of the county and his family. Aceves's experience with these projects helped him win a mural commission from the Banco Commercial in Chihuahua, Mexico. This mural, *La nueva industria de la ganadería en el estado de Chihuahua* (1940), depicts the founding of the Chihuahua livestock industry. He also created two detailed color studies for murals depicting the capture and abuse of native leaders by the conquistadors.

When World War II began, Aceves enlisted in the U.S. Navy and served three years, working as an illustrator. After the war he used his G.I. Bill benefits to attend El Paso Technical College and then the American Academy of Art in Chicago. Upon graduation, he returned to El Paso and created a mural and ten paintings for the Hotel Paso del Norte in El Paso, fulfilling a prewar commission. Aceves died on August 13, 1968, and was buried in the Fort Bliss National Cemetery.

Significance

Aceves was one of the first Latino painters to reinterpret the standard landscape form of nineteenth century paintings of the American West into a direct and vivid vehicle for the transmission and preservation of traditional cultures of the Southwest. The historical themes of his government-commissioned murals depict important events in the daily life of the frontier and reflect the heritage of the region. His work also depicted and celebrated the Hispanic past of the Southwest.

Robert B. Ridinger

Further Reading

Gonzales, Manuel G. *Mexicanos: A History of Mexicans in the United States*. Bloomington: Indiana University Press, 1999. Discusses Aceves's work in the context of Mexican and Mexican American art and mural traditions.

Parisi, Philip. *The Texas Post Office Murals: Art for the People.* College Station: Texas A&M University Press, 2004. The only extant history of the massive artistic project carried out in Texas during the 1930's under the aegis of the New Deal. Aceves's murals in Borger and Mart are shown in full color with details on the process of their creation.

Price, Carol Ann. *Early El Paso Artists*. El Paso: Texas Western Press, 1983. Useful resource on the history of the city's artistic community.

See also: José Antonio Burciaga; Leo Tanguma; Jesse Treviño.

Daniel Acosta

American pharmacist and researcher

Acosta is a pharmacist who researches drug toxicity, specifically of the cardiovascular system, through cell cultures. He is the first Hispanic dean of the University of Cincinnati and the first Hispanic dean of any national research-focused pharmacology school.

Latino heritage: Mexican

Born: March 25, 1945; El Paso, Texas

Also known as: Daniel Acosta, Jr.

Areas of achievement: Science and technology; medicine; education

Early Life

Daniel Acosta, Jr. (ah-CAHS-tah) was born in El Paso, Texas, on March 25, 1945. He completed his secondary education at Austin High School and majored in prepharmacy at the University of Texas at El Paso (1963-1965) before transferring to the University of Texas at Austin to complete a bachelor of science degree in pharmacy. He graduated first in his class in 1968.

Acosta spent two years in the United States Army as a pharmacist before becoming a research assistant in the Department of Pharmacology/Toxicology at the University of Kansas in 1972. He subsequently earned his doctorate from the same program in 1974. Acosta received a National Science Foundation Traineeship while there as well.

Life's Work

After finishing his training in 1974, Acosta accepted a position as assistant professor of pharmacology and toxicology through the College of Pharmacy at the University of Texas at Austin. He completed further post-graduate studies through a Ford Foundation Postdoctoral Fellowship from the National Chicano Council on Higher Education in 1978-1979. Acosta was promoted to associate professor in 1979 and full professor in 1983. He remained on the university's faculty for a total of twenty-two years. Acosta also concurrently served as associate head of the department and head of the biochemical toxicology drug dynamics program from 1985 to 1996. He became director of the toxicology training program in 1990. During his tenure at the school, Acosta served as the first director of a nationally ranked program of toxicology.

In 1996, Acosta was named dean of the College of Pharmacy at the University of Cincinnati. The appointment made him the first Hispanic dean at the university and the first Hispanic dean of any national research-focused pharmacology school. In 2000, Acosta created a four-year pharmacy doctoral program and a master of science program in drug development. He also has led international pharmacy courses in Dubai and Abu Dhabi and was chair of three international panels that reviewed pharmacy curriculums in the United Arab Emirates.

Acosta researches drug toxicity, specifically with regard to the liver and cardiovascular systems. His lab uses cell cultures as model systems for drug toxicity in order to reduce the need for animal testing and has created in vitro cell cultures for many organs, including the heart, kidney, liver, eyes, and skin. Acosta has published his research extensively in scientific journals. By 2011, he had published more than 125 peer-reviewed articles and 30 book chapters and had edited three textbooks. Acosta also is editor of the journal *Toxicology in Vitro* and associate editor of the journal *In Vitro Cellular and Developmental Biology*.

Acosta has received several awards and honors, including the Pharmaceutical Research and Manufacturers of America Foundation's Excellence of Pharmacology/Toxicology Award (2006) and the Society of Toxicology's Enhancement of Animal Welfare Award (2005). He was named Colgate Palmolive Visiting Professor in In Vitro Toxicology (1996-1997) and the Burroughs Welcome Toxicology Scholar (1986-1991). Acosta has served on several professional boards and committees as well; he was named president of the International Union of Toxicology in 2010, was a member of the Committee on Toxicology Testing and Assessment of Environmental Agents for the National Academy of Sciences (2007-2008), chaired the Federal Drug Administration (FDA) Scientific Advisory Board for the National Center for Toxicology Research (2003-2007), is a past president of the Society of Toxicology (2000-2001), and was a member of the Expert Committee on Toxicology and Biocompatibility of the United States Pharmacopoeia (2000-2005). Acosta was the first Hispanic president of the Society of Toxicology. He also is a consultant to the Minority Biomedical Support Program of the National Institutes of Health. Acosta and his wife, Pat, have three daughters.

Significance

Acosta's research is not only scientifically significant but also ethically important, as he continues to find methods of researching drug toxicity that do not require the use of animals as test subjects. His groundbreaking work with cell cultures has led the field of research to shift gears and follow his lead, as evidenced by the recommendations of the National Academy of Sciences report of 2007 on toxicity testing in the twenty-first century. He is a role model for the Hispanic community; through several publicly and privately awarded grants Acosta had mentored minority high school, undergraduate, and graduate students and encouraged them to enter the fields of medical research and pharmacology.

Janet Ober Berman

Further Reading

Acosta, Daniel, ed. *Cardiovascular Toxicology*. 4th ed. Cincinnati, Ohio: University of Cincinnati, 2008. This textbook, edited by Acosta, is highly regarded in the pharmacology world as an essential source for toxicology information.

_______. "An Introduction to Toxicology and Its Methodologies." In *An Introduction to Toxicology and Its Methodologies, in Computational Toxicology: Risk Assessment for Pharmaceutical and Environmental Chemicals*, edited by S. Ekins. Hoboken, N.J.: John Wiley & Sons, 2006. Acosta's chapter serves as the background for basic understanding of the field of toxicology.

Flannery, Michael A., and Dennis B. Worthen. *Pharmaceutical Education in the Queen City: 150 Years of Service 1850-2000*. Binghamton, N.Y.: Haworth Press, 2001. Details Acosta's role in creating new master's degree and doctorate programs for pharmacy students.

Krewski, D., et al. "Toxicity Testing in the Twenty-first Century: A Vision and a Strategy." *Journal of Toxicology and Environmental Health. Part B, Critical Reviews* 13, nos. 2-4. (February, 2010): 51-138. Implications and recommendations for the future of the toxicology field based on the hallmark report by the National Academy of Sciences in 2007.

Whitman, Sylvia. "Hazards of Cures." *The Alcalde* 76, no. 4 (March/April, 1988): 11. Description of Acosta's laboratory research on cell cultures in drug toxicology.

See also: Richard Henry Carmona; Jose Alberto Fernandez-Pol; Antonia Novello.

Mercedes de Acosta

American writer

Although Acosta's fame predominantly rests on her intimate relationships with some of the most celebrated women in art, film, and theater, she had literary success in her own right by publishing her controversial autobiography, Here Lies the Heart *(1960).*

Latino heritage: Cuban and Spanish

Born: March 1, 1893; New York, New York

Died: May 9, 1968; New York, New York

Areas of achievement: Theater; literature; poetry; screenwriting

Early Life

Mercedes de Acosta (mur-SAY-deez dee ah-COS-tah) was the youngest of eight children born to a Cuban father and a Spanish mother. Acosta was proud of her heritage and emphasizes in her memoir that both sides of her family had Castilian lineage. Acosta's father, Ricardo, was born in Cuba after his parents migrated from Spain to establish a coffee plantation in La Jagua. According to Acosta's dramatic account, her father led an uprising against Spanish forces in Cuba, escaped a firing squad, and ended up in the United States, where he met and married Micaela Hernandez de Alba y de Alba, who had inherited a significant family fortune. This fortune allowed the Acostas to reside in New York City's fashionable Park Avenue district.

Acosta's sister, Rita Lydig, was a prominent socialite noted for her stunning beauty and innovative fashion sense. She had her portrait painted by several famous artists of the time, including John Singer Sargeant. It was Rita who introduced Acosta to the Modernist art circles in Paris that included Igor Stravinsky, Pablo Picasso, and Sarah Bernhardt.

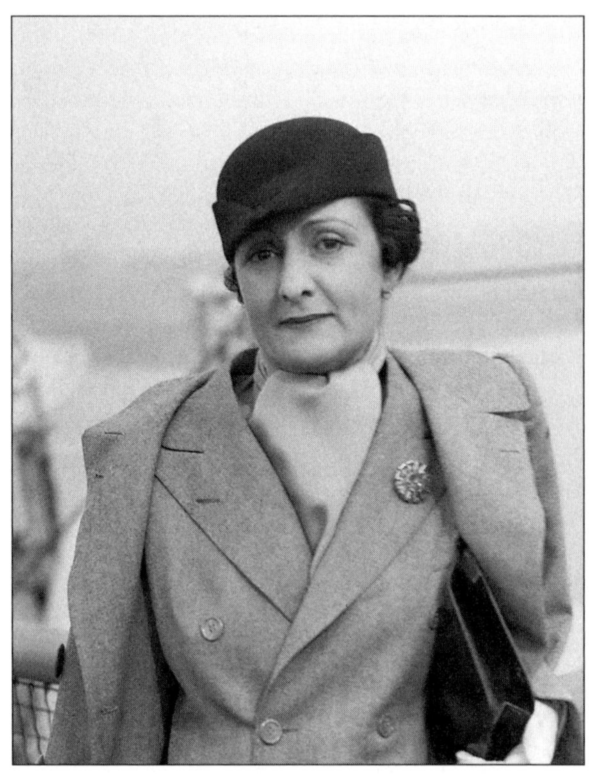

Mercedes de Acosta. (©Bettmann/Corbis)

During World War I, Acosta was active in the Censorship Bureau and the Red Cross. She was a committed suffragette and fought for women's right to vote. She admired Isadora Duncan's attempt to liberate women from restricting corsets and other constricting styles of clothing. Until the age of seven, Acosta thought she was a boy and referred to herself as "Raphael." This sexual ambiguity would be a source of continued reflection and expression throughout her life. Acosta married Army captain and artist Abram Poole in 1920 but insisted on keeping her maiden name to retain her independence. While married, Acosta had passionate affairs with women, which she chronicled in her autobiography. She and Poole divorced in 1935. Although Acosta was raised in a strict Spanish-Catholic tradition, she developed an interest in Eastern spirituality that lasted the rest of her life. Her exploration included adopting vegetarianism and traveling to India to meet Ramana Maharshi, a revered Hindu sage to whom her autobiography is dedicated.

Life's Work

Early in her career, Acosta fell in love with the theater and tried her hand as a playwright. She wrote and produced two plays as vehicles for her then-lover, Eva Le Gallienne. *Sandro Bottocelli* (1923) premiered in New York and *Jehanne d'Arc* (1925) premiered in Paris, because Acosta wanted the play to open in her heroine's own country. *Jacob Slovak*, a play about anti-Semitism, opened in 1927 to generally favorable reviews. Acosta also published three collections of poetry—*Moods: Prose Poems* (1920), *Archways of Life* (1921), and *Streets and Shadows* (1922)—and two novels, *Wind Chaff* (1920) and *Until the Day Break* (1928). However, she was unable to achieve a successful career as a poet and novelist. Critical reception to these works was generally disappointing.

Acosta had a short-lived career in Hollywood in the early 1930's under the legendary producer Irving Thalberg. An idea for her lover Greta Garbo to appear in a film wearing boy's clothes was quickly nixed (although Garbo's androgyny would be featured prominently in the 1933 film *Queen Christina*). While writing the screenplay for a film on the life of Rasputin, Acosta was asked by Thalberg to include a scene that had no basis in historical fact. She refused and was fired. None of the screenplays Acosta wrote during her time in Hollywood were produced.

After publishing her memoirs in 1960, Acosta sold her letters, photographs, and other ephemera to the Rosenbach Library and Museum in Philadelphia. Her letters from Garbo came with the stipulation that they not be made public until ten years after the death of the last surviving correspondent. The letters were released to the public in April, 2000, ten years after Garbo's death, and disappointed observers who had hoped to find among them an explicit love letter from Garbo to Acosta. Because Acosta moved in the various artistic circles of Modernist thought in the United States and Europe, her correspondents made up a veritable who's who of art, dance, film, literary, and theater worlds.

Nearly destitute at the end of her life, Acosta lived in a small two-room apartment in New York City and suffered from a variety of ailments. She felt snubbed by former lovers and friends who never forgave her for "outing" them in her autobiography. Acosta died in 1968 and is buried in Trinity Cemetery with her mother and sister.

Significance

Critics agree that Acosta never fulfilled her early promise as a writer. Her greatest literary success came with the publication of her memoir, *Here Lies the Heart* (1960), which received enthusiastic reviews although it cost her

The Controversy Surrounding *Here Lies the Heart*

In 1960, at the age of sixty-seven, Mercedes de Acosta published her autobiography, *Here Lies the Heart.* While the book makes no explicit reference to lesbianism, many of those who were intimate with Acosta (Greta Garbo included) never spoke to her again after its appearance. Eva Le Gallienne, who was never comfortable with her own sexual orientation, supposedly referred to the book as "Here the Heart Lies" as a way to distance herself from Acosta. In spite of those who protested that Acosta had exaggerated the nature of their relationships, much of the information Acosta revealed has been substantiated through personal correspondence and testimony from various insiders. While she often has been depicted as a predatory lesbian, there is ample evidence that Acosta also was pursued as an object of desire. Despite some inaccuracies that Robert A. Schanke noted in his biography of Acosta, *Here Lies the Heart* remains an important chronicle of same-sex female relationships during the era before Stonewall. It was reprinted in the mid-1970's and enjoyed great success, giving Acosta a renewed popularity, albeit more for her love affairs than for any of her literary accomplishments.

dearly in terms of her relationships. Acosta's reputation today primarily rests on the sensationalism of the celebrity women she bedded, rather than her broader role in advancing the cause of women's rights. Her forthrightness about her lifestyle during a time when the stigma of lesbianism was so pervasive is truly remarkable.

Her striking fashion sense (she favored capes, tricorn hats, and silver-buckled shoes) earned her the nickname "Black & White." Acosta continues to inspire generations of artists and writers interested in lesbian history. In a fitting tribute to Acosta's aspirations as a playwright and her cultural heritage, Odalys Nanín, founder of Mujeres Advancing Culture History and Art (MACHA), wrote and starred in *Garbo's Cuban Lover* (2001), a play chronicling Acosta's tempestuous relationship with the elusive Hollywood star. *The Advocate* magazine listed it among the ten best plays of 2001.

Robin Imhof

FURTHER READING

Acosta, Mercedes de. *Here Lies the Heart*. New York: William Morrow, 1960. Acosta's famous and controversial memoir.

Cohen, Lisa. "Fame Fatale." *Out* 8, no. 4 (October, 1999): 76. Lively account of Acosta's life and loves from a homosexual perspective.

Schanke, Robert A. *"That Furious Lesbian": The Story of Mercedes de Acosta*. Carbondale: Southern Illinois University Press, 2003. Schanke's scholarship calls into question some of the claims made by Acosta in her autobiography but nevertheless provides ample evidence that Acosta was much more than a mere seducer of famous women.

_______, ed. *Women in Turmoil: Six Plays by Mercedes de Acosta*. Carbondale: Southern Illinois University, 2003. Published as a companion work to the biography, Schanke, a professor of theater, rescued these plays from oblivion (only two were produced). A strong autobiographical thread runs through this collection as the female characters grapple with unfulfilling marriages and thwarted desires.

Vickers, Hugo. *Loving Garbo: The Story of Greta Garbo, Cecil Beaton, and Mercedes de Acosta*. New York: Random House, 1994. Vickers, as Cecil Beaton's official biographer and literary executor, relies on extant letters to situate this unlikely triumvirate of complicated and frustrating relationships.

See also: Gloria Anzaldúa; Ana Castillo; Denise Chávez; Cherríe Moraga; Sara Estela Ramírez.

OSCAR ZETA ACOSTA

American writer, lawyer, and activist

Acosta was one of the most significant figures of the Chicano movement in the late 1960's and early 1970's. Along with his work as a lawyer and political activist, Acosta produced two of the most important Chicano texts of the era: The Autobiography of a Brown Buffalo *(1972) and* The Revolt of the Cockroach People *(1973).*

Latino heritage: Mexican
Born: April 8, 1935; El Paso, Texas
Disappeared: 1974; Mexico
Also known as: Oscar Acosta; Brown Buffalo; Buffalo Z. Brown; Zeta
Areas of achievement: Literature; law; activism

EARLY LIFE

Oscar Zeta Acosta (SEH-tah ah-COHS-tah) was born on April 8, 1935, in El Paso, Texas. His parents, Manuel Mercado Acosta and Juana Fierro Acosta, were born in Mexico and moved to El Paso before their son was born. In 1940, the Acosta family moved to Riverbank, a small town near Modesto in the Central Valley of California, where the family earned a living by harvesting peaches. Acosta's father, originally from the Mexican state of Durango, earned his U.S. citizenship as a result of serving in the Navy during World War II. Acosta describes Riverbank as a town with strict social divisions between Mexicans and whites. According to Acosta, these racial divisions torpedoed his early romantic relationships with Anglo girls whose parents were unwilling to accept him.

After graduating from high school in 1952, Acosta joined the Air Force, serving as a clarinetist in the band. During his time in the military, Acosta, who was raised Catholic, converted; while stationed in Panama, he was a Baptist missionary and minister before renouncing

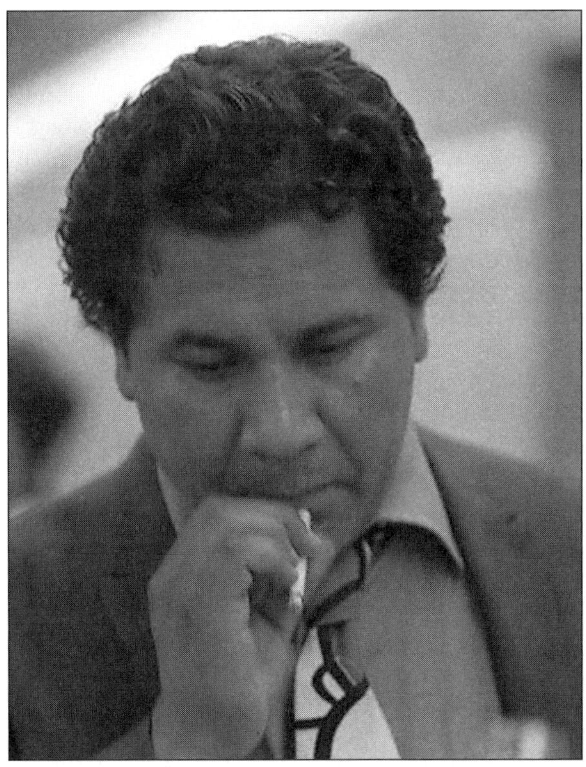

Oscar Zeta Acosta. (© Bettmann/Corbis)

the faith. After his honorable discharge in 1956, Acosta studied French and creative writing at Modesto Junior College. He finished his studies in mathematics and creative writing at San Francisco State University.

In 1956, Acosta married Betty Daves who gave birth to their son, Marco, in 1959. In his published work, Acosta does not discuss his relationship with Daves, whom he divorced in 1963; their son, Marco; or his second wife, Socorro Aguiniga, to whom he was married from 1969 to 1971. However, correspondence between Acosta and Daves, dated from 1956 to 1971, has been preserved at the University of California at Santa Barbara in the Oscar Zeta Acosta Papers archive.In 1957, Acosta began to receive psychiatric care from Dr. William Serbin, and he continued to receive treatment until 1967. Acosta completed his legal studies at San Francisco Law School, where he attended evening courses while working for *The San Francisco Examiner*, and passed the California bar exam in 1966.

Life's Work

Acosta documents his life in *The Autobiography of a Brown Buffalo* (1972) and *The Revolt of the Cockroach People* (1973). Although mostly autobiographical, these two books contain fictionalized elements, including pseudonyms for real historical figures, the conflation of time, the omission of certain details, and unrealistic scenes.

The Autobiography of a Brown Buffalo focuses on the second half of 1967, but throughout the text, Acosta also describes key moments in his adolescence. The book opens in 1967 with Acosta abruptly leaving his unfulfilling first job as a legal aid attorney in Oakland, firing his psychiatrist, and leaving San Francisco on a road trip with an uncertain destination. Acosta's travels took him through Idaho, Colorado (where he met writer Hunter S. Thompson), Texas, Los Angeles, and Mexico. A major element of Acosta's journey was his desire to comprehend his identity as a Mexican American. Although Acosta rejected popular counterculture figures such as Allen Ginsberg and Timothy Leary, *The Autobiography of a Brown Buffalo* extensively chronicles Acosta's use of various drugs, including peyote and lysergic acid diethylamide (LSD), throughout his travels. Upon his return to El Paso, Acosta planned to travel to Guatemala to participate in that country's revolution; however, his brother Bob suggested that Acosta instead focus on the East Los Angeles Brown Power movement. Acosta was electrified to learn of the uprising of "brown buffalos," a term he uses to refer to Chicanos as a group of people that had survived mass slaughter. At the end of the book, Acosta arrives in Los Angeles, ready to "start the last revolution."

The Revolt of the Cockroach People explores Acosta's experiences in Los Angeles from 1968 to 1971 as a lawyer and activist working in the Chicano movement. Acosta stated that he came to Los Angeles prepared to leave behind his legal career to launch his literary career. Despite his initial skepticism, however, Acosta was persuaded to provide legal help to movement organizers in part because of an inspirational meeting with César Chávez in Delano in 1968, while Chávez was on a hunger strike. Acosta's experiences in Los Angeles caused him to seek a stronger connection to his ethnic identity, and he began to improve his Spanish. During this time, Acosta adopted the name "Zeta."Acosta was involved in key events of the Chicano movement, including the Chicano walkouts (also called blowouts) in 1968, during which students walked out of their high schools to protest the poor quality of public education in East Los Angeles. Acosta participated in the legal defense of the "East L.A. Thirteen," the walkout leaders who were charged with conspiring to disturb the peace.

In protest of the criminal justice system, Acosta became a La Raza Unida Party candidate for sheriff of

Acosta's Association with Hunter S. Thompson

Oscar Zeta Acosta's friendship with journalist Hunter S. Thompson began in Colorado in 1967 and has been documented in the work of both writers. "Karl King" in *The Autobiography of a Brown Buffalo* (1972) and "Stonewall" in *The Revolt of the Cockroach People* (1973) are characters based on Thompson, while Acosta appears as "Dr. Gonzo," the "300-pound Samoan" attorney in Thompson's *Fear and Loathing in Las Vegas: A Savage Journey to the Heart of the American Dream* (1971). Thompson often is considered the founder of "gonzo" journalism, the style employed by his 1971 book, although in a 1973 letter to *Playboy*, Acosta claimed that the two writers learned about the term and its methodology together.

Although not discussed in *Fear and Loathing in Las Vegas*, one reason that Thompson and Acosta first traveled to Las Vegas together was their need to get away from Los Angeles to speak freely about the killing of journalist Rubén Salazar during the Chicano Moratorium. Thompson published an article based on his research into the Chicano Moratorium, titled "Strange Rumblings in Aztlán," in *Rolling Stone* magazine in 1971.

Los Angeles County in 1970, earning more than 100,000 votes. He announced his candidacy on the radio to Rubén Salazar, the news reporter who was killed by a sheriff's deputy during the Chicano Moratorium on August 29, 1970. Acosta also took part in the defense of criminal cases involving the "Saint Basil Twenty-one," the "Biltmore Seven," and Rodolfo "Corky" Gonzalez, a founding leaders of the Chicano movement, who was accused of crossing state lines to incite a riot because of his role in the Chicano Moratorium. As a lawyer, Acosta pushed the boundaries, attempting to expose what he saw as inherent racism within the U.S. legal system. He stopped practicing law in 1972 to devote himself to writing.

Acosta disappeared in 1974 while traveling in Mexico. His last known conversation was with his son, Marco, in May, 1974; he is believed to have boarded a boat and disappeared off the coast of Mazatlán. Acosta was legally declared dead in December, 1986.

Significance

Acosta was an influential figure in the areas of literature, the law, and Chicano political activism. He played a key role in the Chicano movement as a lawyer and activist but also was important for his iconoclasm. In his autobiographical writings, Acosta documented the tension he felt between his commitment to social justice and his fierce embrace of his own individuality and freedom. He challenged numerous types of institutions and identifications, refusing to embrace any dogmas, even those of the Chicano movement itself. Acosta's body of literary work has had a profound impact on Chicano literature. Acosta's friend Hunter S. Thompson was much better known in the mainstream as a "gonzo" journalist; nonetheless, in his autobiographical writings Acosta also used a "gonzo" style, characterized by an emphasis on the subjectivity and participation of the chronicler, a sense of immediacy that tends to reject much editing, and, in Acosta's words, the practice of "reporting under fire and drugs." Acosta's work also pushed the boundaries of the autobiography genre, blurring the distinction between author and narrator, truth and imagination.

Monica Hanna

Further Reading

Acosta, Oscar Zeta. *Oscar "Zeta" Acosta: The Uncollected Works*. Edited by Ilan Stavans. Houston: Arte Público Press, 1996. This collection includes autobiographical writing, poetry, fiction, letters, political writing, and a teleplay by Acosta. The volume also includes a bibliography of Acosta's work and a chronology of important events in Acosta's life and Chicano history.

Bracher, Philip. "Writing the Fragmented Self in Oscar Zeta Acosta's *Autobiography of a Brown Buffalo*." In *Ethnic Life Writing and Histories: Genres, Performance, and Culture*, edited by Rocío David, Jaume Aurell i Cardona, and Ana Beatriz Delgado. Berlin: Lit Verlag, 2007. In this chapter, Bracher argues against the traditional view of Acosta's autobiography as one in which Acosta embraces his ethnic identity. Bracher instead emphasizes the carnivalesque elements of *The Autobiography of a Brown Buffalo*, focusing on the "polyphonic consciousness" of the identity envisioned by Acosta.

Stavans, Ilan. *Bandido: The Death and Resurrection of Oscar "Zeta" Acosta*. 2d ed. Evanston, Ill.: Northwestern University Press, 2003. This book is partly a biography of Acosta and partly Stavans's examination and discussion of the legacy of the Chicano movement. The author ruminates on Acosta's biography and, especially, the lasting significance of Acosta's body of work.

Thompson, Hunter S. *Fear and Loathing in Las Vegas: A Savage Journey to the Heart of the American Dream*. New York: Random House, 1971. Thompson's most famous book is a fictionalized representation of two trips he took with Acosta to Las Vegas in 1971. "Dr. Gonzo," a character based on Acosta, accompanies narrator and protagonist Raoul Duke, a stand-in for Thompson, on a trip to Las Vegas. It is considered one of the most important texts about the aftereffects of the 1960's counterculture era in the United States.

See also: César Chávez; Corky Gonzáles; José Ángel Gutiérrez; Reies López Tijerina.

Edna Acosta-Belén

Puerto Rican-born educator and writer

Acosta-Belén is a distinguished professor of Latin American, Caribbean, and U.S. Latino and women's studies at the State University of New York at Albany. Born to a working-class family in Puerto Rico, she has achieved high honors for her writing and teaching and is well known among students of Latin American studies.

Latino heritage: Puerto Rican

Born: January 14, 1948; Hormigueros, Puerto Rico

Areas of achievement: Education; scholarship; social issues; women's rights

Early Life

Edna Acosta-Belén (ah-COS-tah beh-LEHN) was born in Hormigueros, a small town in the western part of Puerto Rico. Encouraged and supported by parents who had not had the advantage of a college education, Acosta-Belén and her brother, Carlos David, graduated from high school with high honors.

Acosta-Belén began her undergraduate work at the University of Puerto Rico-Río Pedras (UPR) in 1965. There she began to understand the consequences of colonialism as Puerto Rico experienced it. After her sophomore year, she obtained a scholarship to study in the United States at the State University of New York (SUNY) at Albany. Upon her arrival there in 1967, Acosta-Belén experienced first hand the Civil Rights and women's liberation movements. These movements influenced her social consciousness and have been the topic of her many books and articles. At SUNY, Acosta-Belén deepened her understanding of the dynamics of colonial oppression, socioeconomic inequalities, and how racism, sexism, and heterosexism have affected the lives of people in Latin America, the Caribbean, and other parts of the world, including the United States. She graduated cum laude with a bachelor of arts degree in 1969. She continued her studies at SUNY Albany to earn a master's degree in 1971, then went to Columbia University in New York for her Ph.D, which she completed in 1977. Acosta-Belén took on postdoctoral fellowships at Princeton and Yale.

Life's Work

In 1970, Acosta-Belén became a part-time instructor at SUNY Albany, then in the following years was appointed lecturer and, later, assistant professor. In 1971, she was instrumental in starting a Puerto Rican studies program. From 1974 to 1981 she taught in the departments

Edna Acosta-Belén. (© Joan Heffler)

of Puerto Rican studies and Hispanic and Italian studies, at which time she was promoted to associate professor. Among other awards, she received a grant from the National Endowment for the Humanities, which she used to document the status and contributions of Puerto Rican women both in their home country and in the United States. The department of Latin American, Caribbean and U.S. Latino studies, which she has chaired, is one of the major centers in the United States for the study of the Puerto Rican and U.S. Latino experience.

Acosta-Belén also has been a pioneer in ethnic and women's studies movements among college professors. She earned a promotion to distinguished professor, the highest professorial rank at SUNY Albany, because of her outstanding record of scholarship and service to the institution, the community, the profession and the nation. In 1979, Acosta-Belén published *The Puerto Rican Woman: Perspectives on Culture, History, and Society*. She reminds her readers that before the Spaniards took over the island, indigenous women were active in society and held leadership positions. After colonialization, women were taught to be devoted wives, daughters, and mothers—that is, to be submissive—although some women defied those roles. Acosta-Belén is the author of many scholarly books and articles, including *Puerto Ricans in the United States: A Contemporary Portrait* (2006), *Researching Women in Latin America and the Caribbean* (1993), and *Women in the Latin American Development Process* (1995). She mentors and encourages doctoral students to do original research into the Latino experience and heritage.

Significance

Acosta-Belén and her coauthor Carlos E. Santiago have been referred to as the deans of Puerto Rican studies. Acosta-Belén consistently has worked to document and publish research on the migration of Puerto Ricans and other Latinos as well as on their music, art, literature, Spanish-language newspapers, civil rights, and other aspects of their lives.

Winifred Whelan

Further Reading

Acosta-Belén, Edna, ed. *The Puerto Rican Woman: Perspectives on Culture, History, and Society*. New York: Praeger, 1979. Acosta-Belén wrote chapter 8, a summary of women in Puerto Rican literature.

Acosta-Belén, Edna, and Carlos E. Santiago. *Puerto Ricans in the United States: A Contemporary Portrait*. Boulder, Colo.: Lynne Reinner, 2006. Examines the culture of Puerto Rico and how that experience translates to the United States. Highlights the contributions of Puerto Ricans to U.S. society.

Acosta-Belén, Edna, and Barbara R. Sjostrom. *The Hispanic Experience in the United States: Contemporary Issues and Perspectives*. Connecticut: Praeger, 1988. A book of essays by scholars who document the origins of Hispanics in the U.S., as well as how the immigration of Hispanics has affected the United States.

Bose, Christine E., and Edna Acosta-Belén, eds. *Women in the Latin American Development Process*. Philadelphia: Temple University Press, 1995. The oppression experienced by many Latin American countries has led to thousands of women entering the labor force and has impelled them to engage in protests against their governments. The oppression has taken them out of their homes, into the streets, and even to prison.

Chassen-Lopez, Francie. "From Casa to Calle: Latin American Women Transforming Patriarchal Spaces." *Journal of Women's History* 9, no. 1 (Spring, 1997): 174-191. Reviews eleven books by writers who analyze the situation of women in Latin American countries. The book by Bose and Acosta-Belén is included.

See also: Rodolfo F. Acuña; María Herrera-Sobek; Arturo Madrid; Patricia Zavella.

Rodolfo F. Acuña

American historian

Acuña is a writer and historian of the Mexican American experience. The seventh edition of his seminal work,Occupied America: A History of Chicanos (1972), was published in 2010. Considered one of the fathers of Chicano Studies movement, Acuña's enduring commitment to activism and social justice spans over forty years.

Latino heritage: Mexican

Born: May 18, 1932; Los Angeles, California

Also known as: Rodolfo Francisco Acuña; Rudy Acuña

Areas of achievement: Education; scholarship; activism; social issues

Rodolfo F. Acuña. (© Gerda Wolff/Retna Ltd./Corbis)

Early Life

In 1932, Rodolfo Francisco Acuña (ro-DOHL-foh fran-SIHS-koh ah-KOON-yah) was born into a Mexican American family in the Boyle Heights neighborhood of Los Angeles, California. His father was from Jalisco, Mexico, and his mother came from Sonora, northern Mexico. Acuña married Lupita Compeán and fathered three children: two sons, Frank and Walter, and one daughter, Angela.

Acuña taught social studies for seven years, beginning in 1958, at San Fernando Junior High and later at Cleveland High School. In 1965, he transitioned to teaching at Los Angeles Pierce College, a two-year community college. Acuña simultaneously worked toward his doctorate in history with a focus in Latin American studies at the University of Southern California. Acuña received his Ph.D. in 1968.

Acuña accepted a position as professor of history at San Fernando Valley College (which in 1972 became California State University, Northridge) at the height of the Civil Rights movement. Seeing the need for a multifaceted field of study that focused on people of Mexican ancestry, he founded the college's Chicano Studies Department in April, 1969. Acuña developed dozens of courses and recruited faculty members to help him teach about the historical, cultural, social, political, and economic context of the Chicano community. He became chairman of the department, which became the largest in the United States. Acuña received a Ford Foundation grant in1973 to launch Operation Chicano Teacher, which expanded the mission of the department to prepare teachers who work in elementary through high schools with Mexican American students.

Life's Work

Acuña's writing career began in 1972 with the first edition of his seminal book, *Occupied America: A History of Chicanos* (its original title was *Occupied America: The Chicano's Struggle Toward Liberation*). A comprehensive survey of the Mexican American experience since the Spanish conquest, the book became a staple text for Chicano studies classes. Other well-known books by Acuña include *Corridors of Migration: Odyssey of Mexican Laborers, 1600-1933* (2007), *Sometimes There Is No Other Side: Essays on Truth and Objectivity* (1998), and *Anything But Mexican: Chicanos in Contemporary Los Angeles* (1996). The latter received the Gustavus Myers Award as an outstanding book on race relations in North America.

In addition to a plethora of journal articles, chapters in edited books, book reviews, and children's books, Acuña has written for newspapers such as *The Los Angeles Times*, *The Los Angeles Herald-Examiner*, and *La Opinión*.

Community and political activism has been consistent themes of Acuña's career. He helped to write "El Plan de Santa Bárbara," which established Chicano studies as an interdisciplinary field that marries history, sociology, political science, and other areas of study that focus on the lived realities of the Mexican American community. Helping to inspire students toward political and social action, Acuña served as the adviser for the CSU Northridge chapter of MEChA (Movimiento Estudiantil Chicanos de Aztlán), a student group that promotes equality for the Mexican American community and other marginalized groups. In 1996, Acuña served as the keynote speaker at the national MEChA conference.

Acuña also used his personal experience to confront ethnic and racial discrimination. When he applied to teach at the University of California at Santa Barbara (UCSB), his research and professional efforts were discredited and his application was rejected. Acuña partnered with the American Civil Liberties Union (ACLU) to challenge the University of California's hiring practices. A 1995 decision awarded Acuña a $325,000 settlement, which he used to create a foundation that offers funds to nascent scholars who need legal aid. His lawsuit established an important precedent against race- and age-based discrimination.

For decades, Acuña has remained vigilant about calling attention to inequalities that affect ethnic minorities in general and the Mexican American community in particular. He was a vocal opponent of California's Proposition 209 in 1996, which greatly restricted affirmative action. Acuña also spoke out against two bills passed by the Arizona legislature in 2010 to target undocumented immigrants. Senate Bill 1070 authorized police officers to request documentation of legal residency if there is "reasonable suspicion" that an offender has illegally immigrated to the United States.

House Bill 2281, passed just two days after Senate Bill 1070, prohibits public schools from offering courses that focus on a single ethnic group and was widely interpreted as an attack on the type of ethnic studies curriculum that Acuña has championed throughout his career. Acuña has written multiple articles and commentaries that explicitly connect the actions of the Arizona legislature with past acts of ethnic and racial discrimination.

For his sociopolitical and scholarly efforts, Acuña has received numerous accolades, such as the National Association for Chicana and Chicano Studies (NACCS) Scholar Award in 1989. *Black Issues in Higher Education* named him one of its "100 Most Influential Educators of the Twentieth Century." Acuña also has received the Emil Freed Award from the Southern California Social Science Library and the Liberty Hill Foundation's Founder Award. He was recognized with a lifetime achievement award by the National Hispanic Institute in 2008.

Significance

Acuña's career helped establish the social, political, and economic needs of the Chicano community as an interdisciplinary field of study and an integral part of institutions of higher education. Through his writings, speeches, and interviews, Acuña has supported numerous causes associated with the Chicano and Civil Rights movements. He has modeled activism on both personal and professional levels and created empowering contexts in which others can find their own voices. His relentless commitment to social justice for the Mexican American community forged a path that other Chicanos will continue to follow.

Karie Mize

Further Reading

Acuña, Rodolfo. *Occupied America: The Chicano's Struggle Toward Liberation.* San Francisco: Canfield Press, 1972. The first edition of Acuña's landmark work on Mexican American history, society, and culture.

Alaniz, Yolanda, and Megan Cornish. *Viva la Raza: A History of Chicano Identity and Resistance.* Foreword by Rodolfo Acuña. Seattle: Red Letter Press, 2008. In the foreword, Acuña situates the struggles for Chicano, gay, and women's rights in a broader historical and sociopolitical context.

Diaz Soto, Lourdes, ed. *The Praeger Handbook of Latino Education in the U.S.* Vol. 1. Westport, Conn.: Praeger, 2007. Acuña's seminal work, *Occupied America*, is cited in this comprehensive text that summarizes the educational issues that impact Latino communities.

See also: María Herrera-Sobek; Arturo Madrid; Patricia Zavella.

Alma Flor Ada

Cuban-born writer, poet, and educator

Ada has written children's books in Spanish and English to demonstrate the value of using the arts—particularly literature—to teach language acquisition. Her pedagogical studies and model programs have presented strategies for teaching literacy to Spanish-speaking immigrants and migrant workers.

Latino heritage: Cuban

Born: January 3, 1938; Camagüey, Cuba

Areas of achievement: Literature; poetry; education

Early Life

Alma Flor Ada (AH-duh) was born in the small town of Camagüey, Cuba, on January 3, 1938. She lived with her extended family in a large, old house called La Quita Simoni that had been built by an Italian family when Cuba was a colony of Spain (prior to 1898). Although Cuba was a place of sharp contrasts between rich and poor, her family was neither rich nor impoverished. All of her relatives were educated, professional, ambitious, energetic, and entrepreneurial. For years, they shared this large house owned by Ada's maternal grandparents, and all of the adults contributed to its upkeep.

Ada's grandmother, a forward-thinking educator, ran a school in the house for children during the day and for working adults in the evening. She taught Ada to read when she was three years old and encouraged her love of poetry, introducing her to the poems of Cuban poet José Martí. Ada's father, a surveyor, often took his daughter along when he plotted land and property. Her mother studied at night to become a certified public accountant, then kept the books for several small businesses at their home.

While Ada was in elementary school, her grandmother died, and her aunts and uncles moved away. Her mother sold the house she had inherited and purchased a business in town. After completing early schooling in town, Ada attended the Universidad Complutense de Madrid studying Spanish writers and philosophers and earning a diploma in 1959; she earned a doctorate from Pontificia Universidad Católica del Perú in 1965, writing a dissertation on Spanish poet Pedro Salinas and later publishing a scholarly study of his work.

Life's Work

As she began her career teaching Spanish, Ada's scholarly interests in Spanish literature and philosophy, teaching challenges, and life experiences came together to shape what became her life's mission. Teaching at Colegio Alexander von Humboldt in Lima, Peru, and later at Mercy College in Detroit, Michigan, where her students were mostly African American, she developed strategies that employed the arts, especially literature and story-writing, to help students acquire language. She met and was strongly influenced by Brazilian educator and thinker Paulo Freire and his educational treatise, *Pedagogy of the Oppressed* (1970), which presented strategies for educating indigenous and minority populations as a means of empowerment. Watching with fascination her own four children as they learned and explored also shaped her theories of learning, including the importance of storytelling.

Interested in issues of education for the lower classes, Ada and her students at Mercy College embraced the cause of César Chávez in the early 1970's as he supported the migrant workers of California. She then transitioned from teaching Spanish language and literature to teaching education and directing the Center for Multicultural Literature for Children and Young Adults at the University of San Francisco. The university had taken the lead in educating minorities in California, especially the Spanish-speaking immigrant and migrant-worker population. There, Ada participated in a project in which she and other team members developed a methodology for teaching migrant children and their parents to read and communicate in English. The work resulted in her book *A Magical Encounter: Spanish-Language Children's Literature in the Classroom*, published in 1994, with a second edition in 2003.

While encouraging students to tell their own stories, Ada wrote and cowrote Spanish and bilingual literature for Spanish-speaking readers. In Peru in the early 1970's, she published collections of Spanish and Latin American folktales. She subsequently created stories depicting family life and cultural traditions, always maintaining the highest standards of literary and artistic quality.

Significance

Ada's educational practices and publications have shaped pedagogical practices for teaching non-English-speaking populations. Encouraging learners to tell and write stories from their own lives, she demonstrated that using storytelling to acquire language and validate experience promotes literacy for children and parents. While working with students' stories, she began collecting folktales and writing stories for Spanish-speaking students. She has won numerous awards for children's books, including the Parents' Choice Honor Book award in 1995 for *Dear Peter Rabbit* (1994) and *The Gold Coin* (1994). She has won awards for teaching and advised many colleges in the development of bilingual education programs.

Bernadette Flynn Low

Further Reading

Ada, Alma Flor. *Where the Flame Trees Bloom*. New York: Atheneum, 1994. Stories for young readers describing family, favorite local people, and events of author's childhood in rural Cuba.

_______. *Under the Royal Palms: A Childhood in Cuba*. New York: Atheneum, 1998. Ada's second recollection of her early years in Cuba.

Ada, Alma Flor, and Josefina Villamil Tinajero, eds. *The Power of Two Languages: Literacy and Biliteracy for Spanish-Speaking Students*. New York: Macmillan/McGraw-Hill, 1993. Discusses the specific techniques that have made Ada a successful bilingual educator.

"Alma Flor Ada." In *The Oxford Companion to Fairy Tales*, edited by Jack Zipes. New York: Oxford University Press, 2000. Identifies Ada's importance in bilingual education, especially notes importance of her compilation of Spanish and Latin American folktales.

Parker-Rock, Michelle. *Alma Flor Ada: An Author Kids Love.* Berkeley Heights, N.J.: Enslow, 2009. Biography for young readers that includes a summary of Ada's achievements and quotations from the author about her work.

See also: Rodolfo F. Acuña; Julia Alvarez; Monica Brown; Ana Castillo; Nicholasa Mohr.

Arístides Agramonte

Cuban-born physician and scientist

As a pathologist and bacteriologist, Agramonte's specialization in tropical medicine research led him to be one of four men appointed to the Yellow Fever Commission, where he confirmed that mosquitoes are the transmitting agents for the disease yellow fever.

Latino heritage: Cuban

Born: June 3, 1868; Puerto Príncipe (now Camagüey), Cuba

Died: August 17, 1931; New Orleans, Louisiana

Also known as: Arístides Agramonte y Simoni

Areas of achievement: Medicine; science and technology

Early Life

Arístides Agramonte y Simoni (ahr-ee-STEE-days ah-grah-MOHN-tay ee see-MOHN-ee) emigrated to the United States from Cuba in 1870 at three years of age with his mother, Matilde Argilagos Simoni. His father, General Eduardo Agramonte Piña, was killed in the first Cuban war for independence. In addition to serving in the military, his father was a prominent physician.Agramonte earned his bachelor's degree at the City College of New York and subsequently attended medical school at Columbia University. He graduated with honors from Columbia's College of Physicians and Surgeons in 1892.

Life's Work

Upon graduation from medical school, Agramonte remained in New York City, where he was hired as an assistant bacteriologist in the health department. In 1898 Agramonte was made acting assistant surgeon of the United States Army Medical Corps. The United States recently had taken control of Cuba, which had been liberated from Spain in the Spanish-American War. Agramonte was deployed to Santiago de Cuba in southeast Cuba to study a yellow fever outbreak in the U.S. Army. He was thought to be immune to the disease because of his assumed exposure as a child in Cuba. Prior research by Italian bacteriologist Giuseppe Sanarelli suggested the bacteria *Bacillus icteroides* caused yellow fever transmission. Agramonte performed autopsies on infected individuals in an attempt to verify that this bacterium was linked to yellow fever. In fact, Agramonte's work disputed Sanarelli and found no evidence that *Bacillus icteroides* was the causative agent for yellow fever.

In 1900, Agramonte assumed leadership of the laboratory at Military Hospital Number One in Havana, Cuba. During the same year, U.S. Army Surgeon General George Sternberg enlisted Agramonte to again study the epidemic of yellow fever. Agramonte served as a pathologist on the Army's Yellow Fever Commission, led by Walter Reed and including two other researchers, James Carroll and Jesse Lazear. They studied exposed volunteers for six months and confirmed the *Aedes Aegypti* mosquito transmitted yellow fever. This discovery led to control over the spread of the disease and dramatically reduced disease prevalence within one year.

Agramonte and his colleagues received a Congressional Gold Medal in 1929 for this work. Although there was considerable pressure for Agramonte to be a recipient of the Nobel Prize in Medicine for this discovery, it never came to fruition. Rather, Dr. Max Theiler won the prestigious award years later for his development of a yellow fever vaccine.

In addition to yellow fever, Agramonte studied other tropical diseases such as the plague, dengue, malaria, and typhoid fever. He became a professor of experimental pathology and bacteriology at the University of Havana, Cuba, in 1901. He returned to the United States shortly before his death to serve as professor of tropical medicine at the Louisiana University Medical School, New Orleans.

In 1901, Agramonte was elected as an honorary member of the American Society of Tropical Medicine, where he served as the society's second vice president. In 1930, Agramonte was made an honorary fellow of the American Public Health Association. That same year, he published a book titled *Looking Back on Cuban Sanitary Progress*. Shortly before his death, Agramonte was elected president of the Pan-American Medical Congress.

Agramonte died at the age of sixty-three from cardiac complications. He was the last surviving member of the Yellow Fever Commission. In 1940, a Cuban park at the former site of the mosquito experiments, Camp Lazear, was created in honor of the men who worked on the commission and all volunteers from that time. A bronze medallion of Agramonte rests there in his honor.

Significance

The research of Agramonte and the entire Yellow Fever Commission now is considered inhumane but selfless, as the men exposed themselves and other volunteers to the disease and hazardous conditions. There now are scientific guidelines regarding the use of animal and human subjects in medical studies, especially in regard to informed consent. As a result of the commission's research, a vaccine for yellow fever was created; the World Health Organization has promoted its use in routine childhood vaccination programs since 1988. Some have suggested that the irradiation of yellow fever in Cuba was the first great accomplishment in the field of public health. The elimination of yellow fever also is credited with facilitating progress in other important development projects; it was a precipitating event in allowing the creation of the Panama Canal.

Janet Ober Berman

Further Reading

A. G. N. "Aristídes Agramonte." *The Canadian Medical Association Journal* 25, no. 4 (October, 1931): 460. Obituary that details the work of the Yellow Fever Commission and Agramonte's contribution.

"Biography of Aristídes Agramonte." *Military Medicine* 166, no. 9 Supplement. (September, 2001): 23. Brief story of Agramonte's early years and career accomplishments, especially with regard to his work on yellow fever.

Petri, William A. "America in the World: 100 Years of Tropical Medicine and Hygeine." *American Journal of Tropical Medicine and Hygiene* 71, no. 1 (2004): 2-16. Describes the implications of the Yellow Fever Commission's work. Article contains original study data, as well as the commission's drawings and notes regarding their findings.

Reed, Walter, et al. "The Etiology of Yellow Fever: A Preliminary Note." *Public Health Papers and Reports* 26 (1900): 37-53. Yellow Fever Commission's initial conclusions and recommendations from their historic work on the disease.

See also: Baruj Benacerraf; Severo Ochoa; Fernando E. Rodríguez Vargas; David Domingo Sabatini.

Jessica Alba

American actor

Alba began acting when she was a teenager and became well known in 2000, when she began appearing in the television series Dark Angel. Alba questions Hollywood's tendency to stereotype roles for Latina actors and strives to be a role model for Latinas and other young people.

Latino heritage: Mexican

Born: April 28, 1981; Pomona, California

Also known as: Jessica Marie Alba; Farrah Dawn Luisa Alba; Sky Angel; Albz

Areas of achievement: Acting; radio and television

Early Life

Jessica Marie Alba (AL-bah) was born Farrah Dawn Luisa Alba on April 28, 1981, the daughter of Cathy Jensen Alba, a Danish-French lifeguard, and Mark Alba, a professional tennis player who later became a U.S. Marine. Alba had a sickly childhood. She suffered from asthma and pneumonia and was hospitalized. She completed much of her schooling while in the hospital, yet she managed to ace her courses and graduate from high school when she was sixteen.

Life's Work

Alba had wanted to be an actor since she was five years old. She began acting in 1994, when she had a featured

Jessica Alba. (AP Photo)

role in the film *Camp Nowhere* and the television series *The Secret World of Alex Mack*. The following year, she joined the cast of the television series *Flipper*, which ran until 1998, and she had roles in episodes of other television series, including *Chicago Hope* (1996), *ABC Afterschool Specials* (1996), and *Brooklyn South* (1998). She rose to prominence in 2000, when she played the leading role of Max Guevera in *Dark Angel*, a popular science-fiction series that aired until 2002. This role earned her a Golden Globe nomination.

Since then, Alba has starred in numerous films, including *Honey* (2003), *Sin City* (2005), *Fantastic Four* (2005), *Fantastic Four: The Rise of the Silver Surfer* (2007), *Good Luck Chuck* (2007), *The Love Guru* (2008), *The Eye* (2008), *The Killer Inside Me* (2010), *Little Fockers* (2010), and *Valentine's Day* (2010). Alba throughly researches her characters in order to prepare for her roles. She became a certified scuba diver for her part in *Flipper*, learned to play the violin for *The Eye*, visited strip bars in order to play an exotic dancer in *Sin City*, and took Tae Bo lessons for *Honey*.

Alba has participated in the activities of the Step-Up Women's Network, a national, nonprofit organization in which professional women serve as mentors to disadvantaged teenage girls. She has worked for many other charities, including Habitat for Humanity, the National Center for Missing and Exploited Children, and the Revlon Run/Walk for Women.

Alba married Cash Warren in 2008, and the couple had a daughter, Honor Marie Warren. Alba has insisted that her daughter be bilingual because of her paternal grandfather's Mexican heritage, and she hired a Spanish teacher for Honor and herself. She has said that she loved her pregnancy, and in 2011, she and her husband announced that they were expecting a second child.

SIGNIFICANCE

Alba's success as an actor transcended the simplistic labeling of Latinas by Hollywood and society and advanced career opportunities for other Latinas and Latinos.

María Eugenia Trillo

FURTHER READING

Blackwell, Scott. *The Jessica Alba Handbook: Everything You Need to Know About Jessica Alba.* Ruislip, England: Tebbo, 2010. Comprehensive overview of Alba's life and career.

Liddell, Mark. *Exposed: Ten Years in Hollywood.* San Rafael, Calif.: Channel Photographics, 2009. This collection of the work of celebrity photographer Mark Liddell includes photographs of Alba.

People. Jessica Alba Biography. http://www.people.com/people/jessica_alba/biography. *People* magazine's Web site includes this two-page biography of Alba, illustrated with photographs.

See also: Cameron Diaz; America Ferrera; Eva Longoria; Zoë Saldana.

Pedro Albizu Campos

Puerto Rican-born activist for Puerto Rican independence

A lawyer, politician, orator, and president of the Nationalist Party from 1930 until his death in 1965, Albizu Campos emerged as the most significant (and controversial) figure in Puerto Rico's struggle to gain its independence from the United States.

Latino heritage: Puerto Rican

Born: September 12, 1891, or June 29, 1893; Ponce, Puerto Rico

Died: April 21, 1965; San Juan, Puerto Rico

Also known as: El Maestro (the Teacher); Pedro Campos

Areas of achievement: Law; social issues; government and politics

Early Life

Pedro Albizu Campos (PEH-droh ahl-BEE-sew KAHM-pohs) was born in Tenerías, a poor section of Ponce, Puerto Rico. Little is known of his parents except that his father, Alejandro Albizu Romero, known as "El Vizcaíno," was a Basque businessman from Ponce and his mother, Juliana Campos, a native of Puerto Rico, was of Taíno, Spanish, and African descent. Born out of wedlock, he used the name Pedro Campos during childhood. For unknown reasons, Albizu Campos was reared by his aunt in Ponce and barely knew his mother.

Because of the dire circumstances of his early life, Albizu Campos was not enrolled in school until he was eleven years old. He finished elementary school in four years and high school in two. He was a member of the Ponce High School debate team, which debated in English, the official language of Puerto Rico at the time. He graduated with honors in 1912 and, armed with letters of recommendation from his American principal and leaders in the community, won a scholarship to study chemical engineering at Vermont State University. A year later, he transferred to Harvard University and, in 1916, received a B.A. in liberal arts.

In 1917, Albizu Campos went to Washington, D.C., and offered his services to the Department of War, Bureau of Insular Affairs. He was sent to Ponce to organize the Home Guard, a company of 180 men. He was discharged as a first lieutenant in the U.S. Army.

On his return to Harvard in 1919, Albizu Campos was elected president of the Cosmopolitan Club. Meeting Éamon de Valera and Subhas Chandra Bose piqued his interest in Irish and Indian independence. In addition to his law degree, Albizu Campos earned degrees in literature, philosophy, chemical engineering, and military sciences. He also was fluent in many languages.

In 1922, Albizu Campos married Laura Meneses, a Peruvian he met at Harvard. According to Laura, the racial prejudice Albizu Campos encountered at Harvard and in the segregated Army fueled his resolve to fight for Puerto Rico's independence. After graduation, despite job offers in the United States, he returned to practice labor law in Puerto Rico, settling down in La Cantera, a poor section of Ponce.

Life's Work

Albizu Campos joined the Nationalist Party and became its vice president in 1924. Three years later, in an effort to gain the support of other Hispanic nations for the party's mission, he visited the West Indies and Central America. Upon his return home in 1930, he was elected president of the Nationalist Party. He formed the first Women's Nationalist Committee, based in Vieques, a barrier island of Puerto Rico that was soon

Pedro Albizu Campos. (Time & Life Pictures/Getty Images)

to be taken over by the U.S. Navy. During this time, Albizu Campos wrote articles for the newspaper *El Mundo* condemning U.S. imperialism and advocating autonomy for Puerto Rico.

In 1932, Albizu Campos was given a letter written by Dr. Cornelius P. Rhoads, a Rockefeller Institute pathologist. Rhoads described Puerto Ricans as a degenerate race that should be exterminated and boasted of killing eight patients and injecting others with cancer cells. Albizu Campos sent copies of the letter to the authorities and the media, accusing Rhoads of an "extermination plot." An investigation vindicated Rhoads, who claimed the letter was a joke, and discredited Albizu Campos. The case, reopened in 2003, caused the American Association for Cancer Research to remove Rhoads's name from its annual award.

The Nationalist Party lost the 1932 election but continued to agitate for independence. A year later, Albizu Campos led a general strike against the Puerto Rico Railway and Light and Power Company, and in 1934 he legally represented thousands of striking sugar cane workers against the U.S. sugar industry. Worried that anarchy would erupt, U.S. corporations formed the Citizens Committee of One Thousand for the Preservation of Peace and Order. They alerted President Franklin D. Roosevelt, who appointed Blanton Winship governor of Puerto Rico and dispatched Federal Bureau of Investigation (FBI) agents to monitor the Nationalists. Winship appointed Colonel Francis Riggs as police chief.

On March 5, 1936, Riggs was shot in retaliation for the killing of four Nationalists outside a university. The two men who killed Riggs were murdered while in police custody. The following month, Albizu Campos and others were arrested for seditious conspiracy to overthrow the U.S. government. After they were found not guilty by a jury of seven Puerto Ricans and five Americans, the judge called for a retrial. This time, a jury of ten Americans and two Puerto Ricans condemned the defendants to the federal penitentiary in Atlanta, Georgia. U.S. Congressman Vito Marcantonio called the decision "one of the blackest pages in the history of American jurisprudence."

On Palm Sunday, March 21, 1937, Nationalists organized a peaceful march to protest Albizu Campos's imprisonment. At the last minute, their permit was revoked. They marched anyway and were quickly surrounded by armed police officers who opened fire, killing twenty-one and wounding more than two hundred unarmed men, women, and children, many shot in the back as they tried to flee. The Massacre of Ponce was the worst in Puerto Rico's history; its repercussions continue to this day.

Aims and Goals of Puerto Rican Nationalist Party

On September 17, 1922, the Nationalist Association of Puerto Rico merged with two other parties, the Nationalist Youth and the Independence Association, to form the Puerto Rican Nationalist Party. The aim was to create a party that would aggressively pursue the goal of Puerto Rican independence. José Coll y Cuchí was elected president. Two years later, Pedro Albizu Campos joined the party and was made vice president. He and Coll y Cuchí could not agree on how to run the party and Coll y Cuchí and his followers resigned. On May 11, 1930, Albizu Campos was elected president, a position he held until his death in 1965. Under Albizu Campos's presidency the party became the largest independence movement in Puerto Rico. A lawyer, he argued that Spain had no legal right to cede Puerto Rico to the United States in 1898 since Spain had granted it autonomy in 1897. After the Nationalist Party fared poorly in elections and U.S. authorities began attacking its members, Albizu Campos issued a call to arms, citing the Boston Tea Party as legal precedent. Many bloody confrontations ensued. From 1936 to 1964, Albizu Campos was in and out of jail, as were many other Nationalists. After Albizu Campos's death in 1965, the Nationalist Party disbanded. As of 2010, most Nationalists and Independentists in Puerto Rico belong to either the Puerto Rican Independence Party (PIP) or the Puerto Rican Socialist Party (PSP).

Albizu Campos took ill while incarcerated and in 1943 was sent to New York's Columbus Hospital. He returned to Puerto Rico in 1947. To welcome him home, students at the University of Puerto Rico raised the Puerto Rican flag on campus. Their suspension led to a student strike which prompted the administration to shut down the school. The Gag Law, which criminalized acts advocating Puerto Rican independence, was enacted. As more repression followed, Albizu Campos relinquished peaceful means of achieving independence and began to advocate armed resistance.

On January 2, 1949, Luis Muñoz Marín ran on the Popular Democratic Party ticket and was elected governor of Puerto Rico. In October, 1950, revolts broke out across the island. On November 1, two men attempted to assassinate President Harry S. Truman. Albizu Campos was arrested along with three thousand supporters of independence. He was sentenced to eighty years in prison but pardoned by Muñoz Marín in 1953, a pardon that was revoked a year later when four activists attacked the United States House of Representatives.While in prison, Albizu Campos claimed he was subjected to radiation experiments. The authorities accused him of insanity, despite visible burns covering his body. His health deteriorated quickly and on November 15, 1964, Muñoz Marín pardoned him once again. Albizu Campos entered a hospital for treatment.

Albizu Campos died in Hato Rey, a barrio in San Juan, Puerto Rico, on April 21, 1965. More than seventy-five thousand people attended his funeral. Thirty years later, the United States Department of Energy disclosed that during the 1950's and 1970's, prisoners had been unwitting subjects in radiation experiments.

Significance

Albizu Campos was one of the most prominent figures in Puerto Rico's independence movement. His teachings earned him the nickname "El Maestro" (The Teacher). He argued that Spain had no legal authority to cede Puerto Rico to the United States, because Puerto Rico had been granted political and administrative autonomy in 1897 before the Treaty of Paris and thus was a sovereign independent nation under international law. The United States, however, considered Puerto Rico a strategic territory—in Albizu Campos's words, the invaders were interested in the cage, not the bird. As a result of his activism, Spanish was restored as the island's official language and the Puerto Rican flag was no longer outlawed. Albizu Campos is the subject of books, articles, and school curricula. Community centers, public schools, streets, and parks in Puerto Rico and the United States bear his name. He articulated for Puerto Rico a sense of national identity and pride.

Gloria Vando

Further Reading

Berríos Martínez, Rubén. "Independence for Puerto Rico: The Only Solution." *Foreign Affairs* 55 (April, 1977): 561-583. The author, president of the Puerto Rican Independence Party (PIP) and candidate for governor, presents arguments to support Puerto Rican independence.

Lederer, Susan E. "Porto Ricochet": Joking about Germs, Cancer, and Race Extermination in the 1930's," *American Literary History* 14, no. 4 (Winter, 2002): 720-746. An invaluable detailed account of the early use of "spin" in the corporate world and the press, as it relates to the infamous letter by Dr. Rhoads.

Maldonado-Denis, Manuel. *Puerto Rico: A Socio-Historic Interpretation*. New York: Random House, 1972. Maldonado-Denis offers a valuable overview of Puerto Rico's quest for independence.

Ramos-Zayas, Ana Y. *National Performances: The Politics of Class, Race, and Space in Puerto Rican Chicago*. Chicago: University of Chicago Press, 2003. Discusses the pros and cons of Albizu Campos's far-reaching legacy in Chicago's Puerto Rican community in the twenty-first century.

Ribes Tovar, Federico. *Albizu Campos: Puerto Rican Revolutionary*. New York: Plus Ultra Educational Publishers, 1971. The life and accomplishments of Albizu Campos, regarded by the author as the purest and most combative hero in Puerto Rico's modern history.

See also: Luisa Capetillo; José de Diego; Luis Muñoz Marín; Luis Muñoz Rivera; Felisa Rincón de Gautier.

Olga Albizu

Puerto Rican-born artist

Known for her vivid colors, Albizu was an abstract expressionist painter whose work reflects the experimentation prevalent in art during the mid-twentieth century. Her work bridged the gap between the cerebral and the commercial appearing in museums and on the cover of record albums.

Latino heritage: Puerto Rican

Born: May 31, 1924; Ponce, Puerto Rico

Died: July 30, 2005; New York, New York

Also known as: Olga Albizu Rosaly

Area of achievement: Art

Early Life

Olga Albizu Rosaly (OHL-guh ahl-BEE-sew roh-SAH-lee) was born in Ponce, the second largest city in Puerto Rico. She was the only child of Sarah Rosaly de Albizu and Luis Antonio Albizu. An uncle on her mother's side was Pedro Juan Rosaly, a wealthy banker and former mayor of Ponce. She spent her childhood in the southern city and was reared a devout Roman Catholic, a religion that she honored throughout her life.

In 1942, Albizu began studying art and literature at the Río Piedras campus of the University of Puerto Rico (UPR). While at UPR, she studied painting with famed Spanish abstract expressionist Esteban Vicente. After the Spanish Civil War (1936-1939), UPR welcomed exiled Spanish intellectuals and artists. Their presence, the growing anticolonialist fervor, and the rising social unrest on the island created a stimulating and diverse artistic atmosphere.

A faction of Albizu's generation of Puerto Rican artists embraced a populist agenda influenced by the Mexican muralist movement while another faction opted for the "universalism" of abstract art and its rejection of the representational, a movement prevalent in early-twentieth-century Europe. Albizu's art reflects the latter style. However, her angular boxes of vivid color pressed and splashed together resemble La Perla, the colorful slums of San Juan, from a distance.

After earning an Art Students' League fellowship for postgraduate work in 1948, Albizu moved to New York. There she studied with Czech modernist Vaclav Vytlacil and German abstract painter Hans Hoffman. To support herself during her early years in New York, Albizu took various jobs. Working and taking classes severely limited the time she had to paint. Nevertheless, Albizu rented space in a garage, where she spent every free moment listening to classical music as she painted.

In 1951, Albizu traveled to Europe to study at the Académie de la Grande Chaumière in Paris. The following year, she attended the Academia de Bellas Artes in Florence, Italy after which she spent a year painting in Provence, France. Albizu returned to New York in 1953. In December of 1956, a *New York Times* review of her first solo exhibit at the Panoras Gallery praised the young painter's "singing colors" and "sure strokes."

During the late 1950's and into the early 1960's, Albizu's paintings were used as the primary artwork for several album covers. The first and best known are those created for saxophonist Stan Getz, whose jazz compositions increased the popularity of bossa nova in the United States. Each of the paintings features compressed geometric shapes of a single color—cool blues, hot reds and muted yellows that reflect the mood and flow of the music.

Life's Work

Albizu was one of twenty-five artists whose work was exhibited at the Puerto Rican art exhibit of 1957, which was held at the Riverside Museum in New York. One reviewer of the somewhat infamous exhibit—which some academics say received scornful reviews because of its radical representations of class—suggested that poverty prevented many of the artists from achieving professional standards. However, he proclaimed Albizu "notable."

Later that year and again in 1958, the Ateneo Puertorriqueño (Puerto Rican Athenaeum) held solo exhibits of Albizu's work. Subsequent solo shows that featured her vibrant oils were held at galleries in New York, Washington, D.C, Kentucky, Pennsylvania, Puerto Rico, Germany, and Mexico throughout the 1960's. In the late 1990's, she experienced a resurgence of solo gallery exhibits in Puerto Rico. Albizu's canvases also were included in many group shows throughout the late twentieth century. Her paintings have appeared in exhibitions at the Museum of Modern Art in New York, the Interamerican Biennial in Mexico, and are in the permanent collection of the Museo Arte Contemporáneo de Puerto Rico. Albizu lived in New York until her death in 2005.

Significance

Albizu is considered a pioneer of abstract art in Puerto Rico. Her work hangs in galleries and private collections around the world. Several pieces have been auctioned by Sotheby's of New York. Further, her paintings have been reproduced on the covers of musical recordings; among those are album covers for the Boston Symphony Orchestra, the Toronto Symphony, and the Bill Evans Trio, and Stan Getz and Charlie Byrd's *Jazz Samba* (1962). Several of the original covers are collectors' items.

Esperanza Malavé Cintrón

Further Reading

Ashton, Dore. "Art: By Puerto Ricans." *The New York Times*, January 10, 1957, p. 45. A review of the infamous exhibit at the Riverside Museum in New York.

Báez, Myrna, and José A. Torres Martinó, eds. *Puerto Rico Art & Identity*. San Juan, P.R.: University of Puerto Rico Press, 2004. Bilingual reference on Puerto Rican art from the late 1800's to the present.

Cockcroft, Eva Sperling. "From Barrio to Mainstream: The Panorama of Latino Art." In *Handbook of Hispanic Cultures in the United States: Literature and*

Art, edited by Thomas Weaver and Claudio Esteva-Fabregat. Houston, Tex.: Arte Público Press, 1994. A historical overview of Latino art and artists from a sociopolitical perspective.
Samoza, Mary E. "Visual Language and the Puerto Rican Woman Artist." *Callaloo* 17, no. 3 (Summer, 1994): 905. Cursory discussion of Puerto Rican women artists with a nod toward linking them to more well-known female artists.

See also: Judith F. Baca; Rafael López; Yolanda M. López; Marisol; Liliana Porter.

Lalo Alcaraz

American political cartoonist

Best known as the creator of La Cucaracha, *the first nationally syndicated Latino-centered comic strip, cartoonist Alcaraz used the strip to explore, often with biting satire, political and cultural issues of particular concern to the urban Hispanic community.*

Latino heritage: Mexican
Born: 1964; San Diego, California
Also known as: Eduardo López Alcaraz
Areas of achievement: Art; social issues

Early Life

Eduardo López Alcaraz , better known as Lalo Alcaraz (LAH-loh AHL-kahr-ehs), was born in Lemon Grove, a predominantly Latino blue-collar neighborhood in San Diego, California, just north of the Mexican border. His parents, both immigrants who had come north looking for work, had met in an English language skills class. Early on, young Lalo showed a remarkable propensity for pencil sketching, and his parents encouraged his drawing.

Dedicated in the classroom, Alcaraz matriculated at nearby San Diego State University, where he majored in art and environmental design to prepare for a career as an architect. During his junior year in 1985, concerned over the often vitriolic rhetoric and partisanship of the national political discourse, Alcaraz began publishing daily editorial cartoons in the student newspaper, *The Daily Aztec*, that reflected his liberal leanings. In addition to his editorial cartoons, Alcaraz joined numerous campus activist associations, spearheading student marches in support of greater diversity in faculty hiring and curriculum development in the nascent field of ethnic studies. He also performed occasionally in a Second City-styled student comedy troupe called the Chicano Service, which performed broad satiric skits that drew on Latino stereotypes. However, what most influenced Alcaraz were the stunning murals that decorated downtown San Diego. In this vibrant and energetic street art, Alcaraz discovered a passion and a primitive aesthetic that he found not only appealing but also very much a part of his own Mexican heritage. Still intent on pursuing architecture, despite the fact that several of his university cartoons were picked up by nationally syndicated wire services, Alcaraz was admitted to the master's program in architecture at the University of California at Berkeley in 1987.

Life's Work

By the time Alcaraz graduated in 1991, the highly charged political climate of the Berkeley campus, along with his love of drawing, convinced him to pursue political cartooning, a risky career decision, as Alcaraz would later admit, given the precipitous decline in newspaper readership because of the burgeoning cable news industry and the news services provided by the Internet. He got his break in 1992, when he was asked to contribute editorial cartoons to the *L.A. Weekly*, a cutting-edge alternative weekly newspaper with a wide readership (close to 200,000) that prided itself on its street-smart writing that covered the Los Angeles popular culture scene. Still reeling from the street riots following the Rodney King verdict, the newspaper's editorial board decided to broaden the newspaper's coverage of politics and to cultivate more diverse perspectives. Alcaraz's cartoons, at once satiric and irreverent, drew attention to a range of Latino concerns in the Los Angeles area, most notably education, the drug crisis, political hypocrisy, and scarce employment opportunities for Latino youths. His cartoons became one of the most widely read parts of the newspaper, and his panels were regularly syndicated and appeared in, among other venues, *The New York Times* and *The Village Voice*, as well as a wide variety of online Hispanic outlets. Given that Alcaraz's cartoons were the only editorial cartoons dealing specifically with Latino issues, he himself became something of a celebrity, profiled in national forums, including *People* and *Rolling Stone*.

Themes in *La Cucaracha*

Like Garry Trudeau's *Doonesbury* and Darrin Bell's *Candorville*, *La Cucaracha* offered piquant political commentary that drew its plotlines from contemporary headlines. However, unlike the other cartoonists, Lalo Alcaraz used the comic format to pose provocative questions about the conditions facing contemporary urban Latinos by lampooning widely held stereotypes about Hispanic culture. The strip explored a variety of hot-button topics, among them the virulent anti-immigration campaign and the so-called border wars with Mexico; inner city education funding cuts; high school and college curricula that ignore the Hispanic culture; post-September 11, 2001, hyperpatriotism and the conservative backlash against all so-called foreigners; the losing battle for authentic diversity in the workplace; the contentious debate over bilingual education; the disproportionate percentage of minorities in the armed forces (particularly in the counterterrorist offensives launched during President George W. Bush's administration after September 11, 2001); and, most profoundly, the desperation and hopelessness among Hispanic urban youths amid the street culture of drugs and crime. Despite such a range of sobering issues, the strip was wildly funny because Alcaraz developed a wide cast of nuanced characters that became more than just position statements. They were young, laid-back, working-class, street-wise kids, each with his or her own story line, each struggling to define his or her identity in the precarious bicultural environment of the barrios of Los Angeles. Indeed, the center of the strip, a feisty cockroach, drew on an iconic insect that had long represented the embattled but resilient spirit of the Mexican people.

Restless within the strictures of political cartooning, however, in November, 2002, Alcaraz inaugurated a daily comic strip that he called *La Cucaracha*. Modeled on Garry Trudeau's iconic strip *Doonesbury*, *La Cucaracha* was an ensemble strip in which characters represented different elements of the contemporary Los Angeles Latino community, all centered on a hot-tempered, anthropomorphic cockroach named Cuco Rocha (hence the name of the strip), who was fiercely dedicated to Latino pride. *La Cucaracha*'s caustic satire, which often drew on cultural stereotypes of Chicanos, was often misperceived by casual readers as Alcaraz's personal beliefs, much to his chagrin. The edgy comic strip, although controversial and deliberately provocative, became a national phenomenon, and within four years, Universal Press Syndicate was running *La Cucaracha* in close to two hundred daily newspapers. As the national debate on immigration reform heated up during the administration of President George W. Bush, and as the Latino voting bloc emerged as a prominent factor in state and national elections, Alcaraz's strip became one of the most widely read voices in the national Latino community.

In response to his popularity, Alcaraz branched out into a variety of multimedia forums, maintaining several Web sites for his cartoons; coediting an underground satiric magazine called *Poncho*; cohosting a popular weekly radio show in Los Angeles, *The Poncho Hour of Power*, which focused on topical political commentary; and, given his striking good looks and easy charisma, devoting much time to radio and television interviews, as well as campus readings around the Los Angeles area. His work was recognized by numerous regional journalism awards, most notably four Southern California Journalism Awards, presented by the Los Angeles Press Club, for outstanding weekly cartoons. In addition, his advocacy of Hispanic issues garnered Alcaraz great recognition in the Los Angeles community, including a Latino Spirit Award from the California state legislature. In 2008, during Barack Obama's campaign for the White House, Alcaraz created one of the most controversial—and popular—campaign images: To counter conservative pundits who claimed Hispanics would never vote for an African American, Alcaraz created a campaign poster showing Obama in the revolutionary fatigues of beloved Mexican hero Emiliano Zapata. The poster, dubbed *Viva Obama*, was a phenomenal hit in the national Latino community. After Obama's election, Alcaraz further enhanced the president's reputation on the national scene by producing a striking poster in which he used digital technology to mash Obama's smiling face onto the familiar Gilbert Stuart portrait of George Washington.

Significance

Despite the moribund state of print journalism in the twenty-first century, the bold and hard-hitting editorial cartoons and strips of Lalo Alcaraz used the medium to reach a wide audience that was largely unaware of the agonies and aspirations of the contemporary urban Latino community. Seeing in the long-established genre of political cartooning a way to enlighten, provoke, and entertain a post-postmodern audience under forty, Alcaraz reclaimed the credibility and vitality of the newspaper cartoon at a time when its resiliency had been largely diminished in this demographic by the omnipresent image media, most notably television and the Internet. Although targeted by incensed readers as antiwhite and deliberately inflammatory, Alcaraz depended, as the most accomplished satirists must, on sophisticated readers able to discern that mocking ethnic stereotypes and lambasting bigotry through irony is far from endorsing those divisive views.

Joseph Dewey

Further Reading

Dewey, Donald. *The Art of Ill Will: The Story of American Political Cartoons*. New York: New York University Press, 2008. A broad look at the long historical context of the genre that defined Alcaraz. Explains the use of satire and irony as essential elements of political cartooning.

Lamb, Chris. *Drawn to Extremes: The Use and Abuse of Editorial Cartoons in the United States*. New York: Columbia University Press, 2004. A critical look at political cartoons, with particular emphasis on the decline of its influence in the last decades of the twentieth century. Illustrated.

Ochoa, Enrique C., and Gilda L. Ochoa. *Latino Los Angeles: Transformations, Communities, and Activism*. Tucson: University of Arizona Press, 2005. Careful cultural study of post-Proposition 187 Los Angeles that reviews the principal racial and ethnic issues that Alcaraz used in his strips.

Stavans, Ilan. *Latino USA: A Cartoon History*. Illustrated by Lalo Alcaraz. New York: Basic Books, 2000. A graphic work, which Alcaraz coauthored with a respected academic and cultural historian, that celebrates more than two hundred years of Latino history in America.

Walker, Brian. *Doonesbury and the Art of G. B. Trudeau*. New Haven, Conn.: Yale University Press, 2010. Landmark cultural study of the long-running political cartoon strips frequently used as a model for Alcaraz's *La Cucuracha*. Details the strategies of an ensemble comic strip and the ways that satire can effectively clarify complicated political issues.

See also: Gus Arriola; Bill Melendez.

John F. Alderete

American scientist and educator

Alderete developed the first Federal Drug Administration-approved bedside diagnostic test for the world's most common sexually transmitted disease, Trichomonas vaginalis. As one of only a handful of Mexican American microbiologists in the country, Alderete has been instrumental in recruiting minority students into the medical research field.

Latino heritage: Mexican

Born: October 28, 1950; Las Vegas, New Mexico

Areas of achievement: Science and technology; medicine; education

Early Life

John F. Alderete (AHL-deh-REH-tay) was the third of nine children born to Mexican parents who had little formal education but who wanted more for their children. The family lived in a poor town with no running water or sewer systems. As an elder child, Alderete helped to raise his younger siblings and financially contribute to the family.

He began working during sixth grade at a bakery and then at a gas station throughout high school. Alderete had a difficult junior high school experience when his parents enrolled him in a wealthier school with little minority representation, but Alderete persevered and credits this experience as instilling in him the ability to overcome other life challenges.

With the assistance of financial aid, Alderete enrolled at the New Mexico Institute of Mining and Technology (NM Tech) in 1969 in Socorro, New Mexico. Early in his collegiate career, Alderete knew he would eventually become a professor because of his teachers' passion and commitment to the classroom and scientific research. It was here that Alderete met teacher Gilbert Sanchez, his first professional Hispanic role model. Alderete graduated with a bachelor of science degree in mathematics in 1973. Although he had not been a strong high school science student, Alderete developed a passion for biology in college after a stimulating bacterial physiology course. He earned a second bachelor of science degree in biology at NM Tech in

1974. During college, Alderete's research focused on an African sleeping sickness parasite, which led to his first of two undergraduate scientific publications.

Throughout his education, Alderete continuously struggled to fit in. He battled feelings of isolation as a minority student, and he often considered dropping out of school. However, Alderete persisted and earned his doctorate in microbiology from the University of Kansas in 1978.

LIFE'S WORK

Alderete completed postdoctoral work at the University of North Carolina, Chapel Hill, where his research focused on the syphilis spirochete. Alderete joined the University of Texas Health Science Center in San Antonio, Texas (UTHSCSA), first as an assistant professor (1981) and then as a full professor (1991) of microbiology and immunology. Rather than focus on syphilis, Alderete turned his attention to another sexually transmitted disease (STD), *Trichomonas vaginalis*, the most common nonviral STD in the country and worldwide. Alderete focused on this microorganism for the remainder of his career. He published extensively and spoke frequently at national and international meetings on *Trichomonas vaginalis* in hopes that he eventually would be able to develop a diagnostic test for it that was faster than tests available at the time, which took up to one week for a result.

After a thirty-year career at UTHSCSA, Alderete accepted the positions of associate vice provost for research and professor in the School of Molecular Biosciences at Washington State University in Spokane (2008). He cofounded the biotechnology company Xenotope Diagnostics, where he serves as vice president and chief scientific officer. Drawing on Alderete's wealth of research, the company developed the first Federal Drug Administration-approved rapid test that is clinically available for diagnosing a *Trichomonas vaginalis* infection. He holds several patents for his work.

Alderete is a fellow of the American Society of Microbiology and was elected to the American Academy of Microbiology (2001). He was inducted into the Mexican Academy of Science in 2006. He also is a past president of the Society for the Advancement of Chicanos and Native Americans in the Sciences (SACNAS). Alderete is a member of the National Advisory Research Council for the National Institute of Dental and Craniofacial Research and the National Academy of Sciences in Mexico. His many awards include the prestigious Premio Encuentro Award for Science and Technology (1992) and the William A. Hinton Research Training Award from the American Society for Microbiology (2004).

In addition to scientific research, Alderete also strongly supports minority organizations and activities. He frequently speaks on cultural and educational issues. Alderete runs the Saturday Morning Science Camp for minority students, parents, and teachers. He mentors and teaches minorities from high schools and colleges and welcomes summer interns in his laboratory.

SIGNIFICANCE

Alderete's scientific and personal accomplishments led him to be named to *Hispanic* magazine's list of "100 Most Influential Hispanics" in the country. Throughout his career, Alderete has brought minorities, especially Hispanic students, into the scientific community. By teaching, mentoring, and diligence, Alderete became an influential Hispanic role model and advocate. He speaks about his personal feelings of being an isolated minority in order to help change perceptions and goals of Hispanic students. He emphasizes living by six rules: understand everything has a price; have drive; accept delayed gratification; be forward-thinking; understand culture; and have good communication skills. Alderete continues to inspire the next scientific generation towards greatness.

Janet Ober Berman

FURTHER READING

"Affirmative Action: John F. Alderete, Ph. D." *Hispanic Engineer and Information Technology* 11, no. 4 (1996): 38. Alderete is among the recipients of the magazine's 1996 Hispanic Engineer National Achievement Awards; this brief profile describes his achievements in science and his advocacy of affirmative action.

Alderete, John. "Importance of Recruitment and Retention of Minority Students to the Future of Biomedical Research." *The FASEB Journal* 23, no. 427 (2009): 1. Alderete's narrative regarding the need for greater amounts of minority students in the medical research field.

Newton, David E. "John F. Alderete." In *Latinos in Science, Math, and Professions*. New York: Facts On File, 2007. Summary of Alderete's scientific career and personal background.

See also: Richard Henry Carmona; Jose Alberto Fernandez-Pol; Marian Lucy Rivas; David Domingo Sabatini.

Fernando Alegría

Chilean-born writer and educator

Best known for his critical essays on the Latin American novel, Alegría also wrote novels and poetry and was an educator who ended his academic career as a professor of Latin American literature at Stanford University.

Latino heritage: Chilean

Born: September 26, 1918; Santiago, Chile

Died: October 29, 2005; Walnut Creek, California

Areas of achievement: Education; literature; scholarship

Early Life

Fernando Alegría (ah-leh-GREE-uh) was born on September 26, 1918, in Santiago, Chile, to Julia Alfaro Olivares and Santiago Alegría Toro. After graduating from the University of Chile, Alegría immigrated to the United States, where he earned a master's degree from Bowling Green State University in Ohio in 1941 and a doctoral degree from the University of California at Berkeley in 1947. He married Carmen Letonia Meléndez on January 29, 1943, and they had four children, Carmen, Daniel, Andrés, and Isabel.

Life's Work

From 1964 to 1967, Alegría was a professor of Latin American literature at Berkeley, and from 1967 until his retirement in 1988, he was a professor at Stanford University. For a number of years, he also was the chair of the Department of Spanish and Portuguese at this same institution and was an active member of the board of trustees at the Western Institute for Social Research. From 1970 to 1973, Alegría was the cultural attaché for Chile to the United States, under the government of Salvador Allende. He also was an active member of the North American Academy of the Spanish Language and an ardent advocate for the dissemination of Latin American literature in the United States.

Alegría also strongly and openly supported the growth and spread of Chicano and Latino literature in the United States. Throughout his academic career in the United States, he maintained strong ties with his native country, whose citizenship he kept and whose tumultuous politics he followed.

Alegría's firsthand knowledge of Hispanic American literature, especially that of Chile, allowed him to initiate its study and its teaching in universities in the United Sates. Because of his knowledge of this literature and his close acquaintance with many prominent Latin American writers, such as Pablo Neruda and Julio Cortázar, he was able to develop many new courses in Hispanic American literature and culture. Alegría also promoted the importance of Latin American literature through seminar presentations that he conducted and through many literary workshops on popular contemporary writers of Latin American literature that he led. In addition, Alegría's passion for the Spanish language and literature helped spur its popularity in the United States at a time when students at all levels were discouraged from learning any second language. He therefore was the central figure in introducing Latin American literature into the curriculum of American universities and was instrumental in forging an awareness in American students that Latin literature was not confined to the literature of Spain.

Alegría's literary production is diverse and varied. He wrote two biographies, *Recabarren* (1938) and *Lautaro, joven libertador de Arauco* (1943) about people he admired. These works were followed by novels,

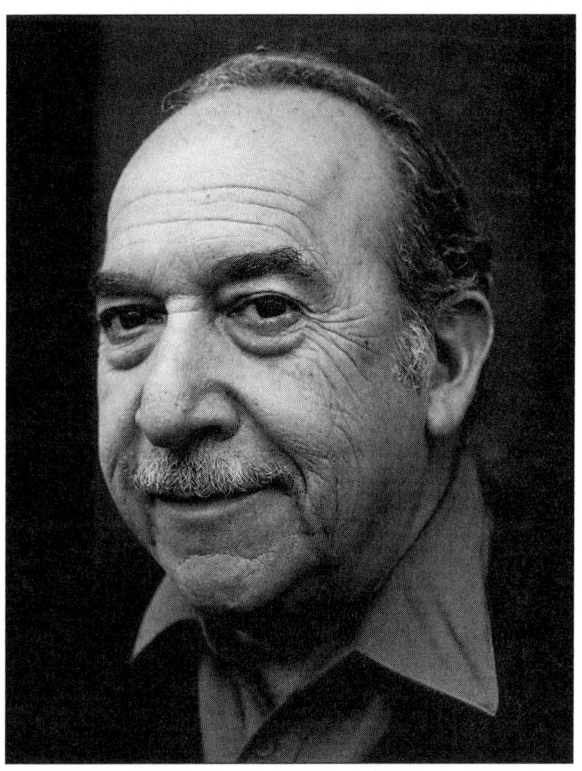

Fernando Alegría. (© Christopher Felver/Corbis)

collections of short stories, and critical essays on Latin American literature, particularly on the contemporary Latin American novel . His most famous novel, *My Horse González* (1964), is a comedic account of the adventures of a Chilean jockey who migrates to the United States. This novel placed him at the forefront of Latin American letters because of its narrative structure and his skillful use of the Spanish language. Another of his novels, *Allende, a Novel* (1993), also brought him critical acclaim for its candid and objective recounting of Salvador Allende's regime and of the military dictatorship that followed his assassination.

Alegría's poem "Viva Chile, mierda!" (1965) was very popular in Chile and was recited in many venues throughout the country during the reign of Allende. This lyrical poem was written while Alegría was teaching at Berkeley and decried social and economic stratification in his homeland.

Alegría also wrote many important essays describing the influence of North American writers such as Walt Whitman and Thomas Mann on Latin American writers. These essays were widely read in both Latin American and American universities and helped the public understand the universality of literature and literary themes. He also wrote an academic text, *Breve historia de la novela Hispanoamericana* (1959; *Brief History of the Latin American Novel*) which is widely used in Latin American literature courses. Alegría won many literary awards, among them the Latin American Prize for Literature. He died on October 29, 2005, in Walnut Creek, California.

Significance

Alegría was an activist, a scholar, and a humanitarian. His literary works embody the strength and the passions of the people and characters they depict and promote acceptance and celebration of Latin American literature. Alegría's works humanize the search for identity of marginalized people, especially Latin Americans, and depict the Spanish language as an articulate medium for expression.

Víctor Manuel Durán

Further Reading

Feinstein, Adam. *Pablo Neruda: A Passion for Life*. New York: Bloomsbury, 2004. Alegría's friendship with the poet Neruda is discussed in this biography.

Martinez Wood, Jamie. "Fernando Alegría." In *Latino Writers and Journalists*. New York: Facts On File, 2007. Comprehensive biography of Alegría covering his academic and literary contributions.

Pearson, Lon. *Chilean Literature in Exile*. Chile: Chasqui, 1985. A revealing discussion of Chilean literature produced in exile, including that of Alegría.

See also: Rodolfo F. Acuña; Juan Bruce-Novoa; Lourdes Casal; Gwendolyn Díaz; Arturo Madrid; Arturo Alfonso Schomburg.

Luis Alfaro

American playwright and activist

Alfaro's work examines intersections of sexuality, ethnicity, and poverty, the three central interests that have anchored his career as a playwright, writer, and community activist. Committed to investigating and contributing to the Los Angeles Chicano community in which he was raised, Alfaro is the recipient of many honors, including a MacArthur Foundation "genius grant."

Latino heritage: Mexican

Born: 1961; Los Angeles, California

Areas of achievement: Theater; activism; literature; gay and lesbian issues

Early Life

Luis Alfaro (ahl-FAH-roh) was born in the Pico/Union area of downtown Los Angeles in 1961. Raised by a large, devoutly Catholic Mexican American family in this diverse and impoverished neighborhood, Alfaro developed a reverence for storytelling and an appreciation for outsiders early in life. His formal schooling ended after high school, but Alfaro, a voracious reader, furthered his education through the creation of an autodidactic reading list. At eighteen, inspired by the activism of his parents, who were farmworkers, he became involved in political theater. As a member of a variety of activist groups associated with Chicano rights and the acquired immunodeficiency syndrome (AIDS) crisis, Alfaro began to design theater and performance pieces that used striking imagery to address the plight of marginalized groups, foremost among them Latinos suffering from human immunodeficiency virus (HIV) and AIDS.

Life's Work

In 1988, Alfaro founded VIVA!, a Latino gay and lesbian cultural organization (one of the first of its kind) whose multigenerational Chicano membership reflected the diversity of this long-invisible segment of the homosexual population. Using the techniques pioneered by El Teatro Campesino, the theater group affiliated with the United Farm Workers movement, Alfaro created "hit-and-run theater," in which VIVA! staged surprise performances and awareness-raising events at bars and restaurants frequented by members of the gay community in the Los Angeles area. These shows represented one of the earliest and most successful attempts at AIDS awareness and prevention education in the Latino community.

Alfaro's work is based in the tradition of Chicano activist theater, but his focus on sexuality and ethnic identity has created a new discourse in Latino theatre. Emblematic of Alfaro's career has been his refusal to define his identity simply as either "gay" or "Latino." As a result, he is considered a figure who bridges the divide between two disparate groups of political activists and cultural traditions. His early work as a playwright, notably *Downtown* (1990), explores his fascination with the Pico/Union neighborhood and its diverse shadow city of societal outcasts. Inspired by Alfaro's upbringing, family, and identification with the underside of Los Angeles, a city associated with idealized glamor, *Downtown* is a one-man show.

Luis Alfaro. (WireImage for Roberson PR /Getty Images)

The 1990's were a time of enormous professional success for Alfaro. In 1995, he was appointed codirector of the Latino Theatre Initiative at the Mark Taper Forum in Los Angeles, and in 1997, he received a John D. and Catherine T. MacArthur Foundation Fellowship (more commonly known as a "genius grant"), one of the most prestigious awards in the arts. His 1997 play *Straight As a Line*, which addresses the concept of cultural as well as physical wasting away through the suffering of a sex worker dying of AIDS, debuted at the Goodman Theatre in Chicago and went on to play in both New York and Los Angeles. Also in 1997, he wrote the screenplay for the PBS short film *Chicanismo*, which examines the lives of a group of Chicano men and women in Los Angeles and led to an Emmy nomination for Alfaro. Dedicated to depicting the emotional and metaphysical experiences of those deemed "other" by society, Alfaro found a broad audience; his plays, including *Bitter Homes and Gardens* (2000) and *Breakfast, Lunch and Dinner* (2002), have been performed across the United States and around the world.

In the early 2000's, Alfaro left the Mark Taper Forum and embarked on a series of new works that interrogated classical themes and narratives. Chief among these reexaminations, which maintained Alfaro's interest in the multifaceted topic of human identity, were *Electricidad* (2002) and *Oedipus El Rey* (2010), Chicano-themed retellings of Sophocles's classic Greek works *Electra* (418-410 B.C.E.; English translation, 1649) and *Oedipus Tyrannus* (429 B.C.E.; English translation, 1715). Alfaro's engagement with reworking classic stories also extended to his first feature-length screenplay, the 2011 film *From Prada to Nada*, which translated the plot of Jane Austen's *Sense and Sensibility* (1811) to a story about modern Latina sisters who lose their wealth and must reconsider their goals. Alfaro also became an instructor at the University of Southern California and the California Institute of the Arts.

Significance

Alfaro's forthright assertion of his identity as a gay Latino helped open new avenues of self-expression for all Latinos. This resistance to the reductive classifications of ethnicity, sexuality, and religious identity and their attendant expectations characterizes his body of work. Alfaro's commitment to serving his community through innovative forms of artistic expression and performance underscores his social importance in the landscape of modern Latino artists.

Lisa Locascio

Further Reading

Alfaro, Luis. *Downtown*. In *O Solo Homo: The New Queer Performance*, edited by Holly Hughes and David Román. New York: Grove, 1998. This is the script of Alfaro's early, groundbreaking performance piece, anthologized in an important collection of gay and lesbian writing.

_______. "Minnie Riperton Saved My Life." In *Another City: Writing From Los Angeles,* edited by David L. Uline. San Francisco: City Books, 2001. In this short essay, Alfaro reflects on the impact of music on his life as a young teenager.

Johnson, Cassandra. "*Electricidad*: Luis Alfaro Reimagines Sophocles' *Electra* for Chicano Barrio Culture." *American Theatre* 23, no. 2 (2006): 63. Discusses Alfaro's adaptation of classical tropes to modern settings and concerns.

Muñoz, José Esteban. "Queer Theater, Queer Theory: Luis Alfaro's *Cuerpo politizado*." In *The Queerest Art: Essays on Lesbian and Gay Theater*, edited by Alisa Solomon and Franji Minwalla. New York: New York University Press, 2002. Examines Alfaro's depictions and explorations of sexuality in his theater pieces.

See also: Gloria Anzaldúa; Denise Chávez; Maria Irene Fornes; Eduardo Machado; Cherríe Moraga; Luis Miguel Valdez.

Miguel Algarín

Puerto Rican-born poet

Algarín was one of the first Puerto Rican voices to be heard from the streets of New York City through his powerful poetry. Along with Pedro Piñero, Algarín is credited with coining and popularizing the term "Nuyorican," which they brought to public attention with the founding of the Nuyorican Poets' Café in 1975. Through his work as an educator and a poet, Algarín has provided several generations of Latinos with platforms from which to express their feelings and anxieties about their "otherness."

Latino heritage: Puerto Rican

Born: September 11, 1941; Santurce, Puerto Rico

Areas of achievement: Poetry; education

Early Life

Born to Miguel Algarín and María Socorro in Santurce, Puerto Rico, Miguel Algarín (ahl-gah-REEN) attended a local Catholic grammar school. His family moved to New York City to live with one of his aunts, Carmen Ana Figueras, in 1951. He continued his primary education in a New York City public school and also attended a city high school. Algarín first attended the City College of New York but transferred to the University of Wisconsin, which awarded him a bachelor's degree in Romance languages in 1963. He next enrolled in a graduate program at the Pennsylvania State University, where he earned a master's degree in English literature in 1965. Algarín began teaching English at Brooklyn College and New York University but soon was accepted into the doctoral program in comparative literature at Rutgers University, where he also worked as a teaching assistant.

Life's Work

After obtaining his doctorate, Algarín became a professor in the English Department at Rutgers University, where he has taught such subjects as the work of William Shakespeare, ethnic literature of the United States, and creative writing. As early as 1973, Algarín was meeting with poets and artists in his Manhattan apartment to share their works and discuss literary topics. By 1975, the group was so large that they decided to move to a large space on East Sixth Street in Lower Manhattan. While chatting informally on a trip, Algarín and Puerto Rican poet Pedro Piñero were discussing the nature of poetry written by "Nuyoricans"—a term combining "New Yorker" and "Puerto Rican."

Later that year, publisher William Morrow sent Algarín a contract for a forthcoming anthology of poetry written mostly by Puerto Ricans in New York. Algarín and Piñero decided that work in the new volume should be dubbed "Nuyorican" poetry and also baptized their new meeting space the Nuyorican Poets' Café. The group's first publication was *Nuyorican Poetry: An Anthology of Puerto Rican Words and Feelings* (1975) and was edited by Algarín and Piñero. Promoting the work of the Nuyorican Poets' Café became Algarín's lifelong project, and

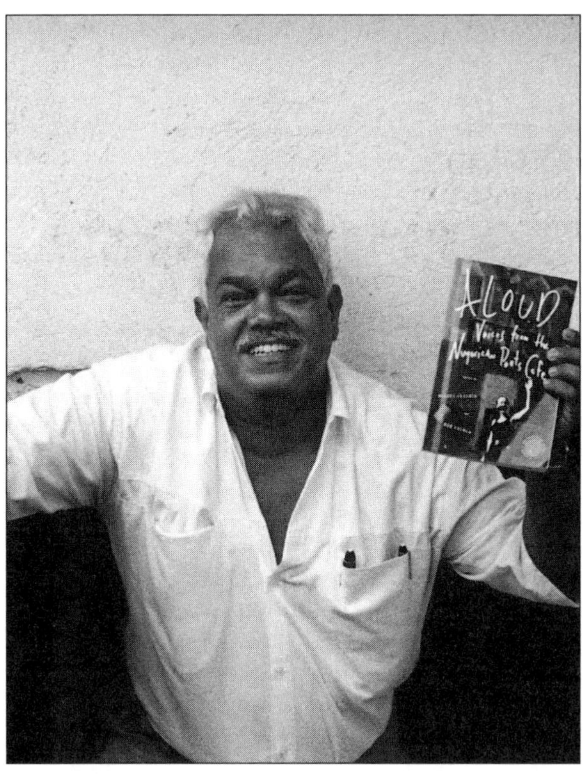

Miguel Algarín. (© Christopher Felver/Corbis)

through it he helped thousands of Latino, black, and Asian poets present their verse in an accepting environment. Many of the founders became icons of Nuyorican and Latino culture in the United States, such as Algarín, Piñero, Tato Laviera, Victor Hernández Cruz, and Piri Thomas. Numerous talented young people, such as Willie Perdomo, Martín Espada, Caridad de la Luz (la Bruja), and Edwin Torres, also found fame in the Café and began their professional careers through Algarín's inspiration.

Algarín's first published work, *Mongo Affair: Poems* (1978), is a collection of verse that spans the 1960's and 1970's. The themes of the poems include people's difficulties in establishing communication with one another, the nature of the street leader, the sense of alienation experienced by immigrants upon their arrival, and the pressures of living in a different culture than one's own. His second book of poetry, *On Call* (1980), explores the complex role of language in the process of assimilation, and also focuses on the diverse peoples who compose the American landscape. The poems of *Body Bee Calling from the 21st Century* (1982) are philosophical and ethical in nature, and question what the twenty-first-century human being will be like and how that being will act. Algarín's third book of poetry, *Time's Now/Ya es tiempo* (1985) considers the condition of the Hispanic peoples throughout the Western Hemisphere and mixes Spanish with English. After twelve years, Algarín published his highly intimate collection *Love Is Hard Work* (1997), a semiautobiographical reflection on the travails and joys of love. His book *Survival/Supervivencia* (2009) is a collection of many of Algarín's most famous works.

SIGNIFICANCE

A strong believer in the power of literature, Algarín's dedication to the Latino community, especially the Nuyorican community, led him to become one of the most prominent Puerto Rican voices in academic and cultural circles. His poetry, which is at once raw and tender, intense and endearing, embodies the struggles and sufferings of Nuyoricans who must endure poverty, discrimination, prejudice, and marginalization in their own country. Algarín was also one of the first Nuyorican writers to call attention to the plight of Latinos of African descent, whose lives were complicated by yet another dimension of prejudice.

Mark T. DeStephano

FURTHER READING

Algarín, Miguel. *Puerto Rican Voices in English: Interviews with Writers*. Interview by Carmen Dolores Hernández. Westport, Conn.: Praeger Publishers, 1997. Algarín himself offers many profound insights into his life and work as a Nuyorican poet and cultural advocate.

Algarín, Miguel, and Bob Holman, eds. *Aloud: Voices from the Nuyorican Poets' Café*. New York: Henry Holt and Company, 1994. This is the principal work of the Nuyorican Poets' Café. Algarín's excellent introduction offers many insights into his thinking and his life's work. This volume also includes a selection of several of his poems.

Flores, Juan. *The Diaspora Strikes Back*. New York: Routledge, 2009. Flores discusses Algarín's importance in the literary production of the Puerto Rican diaspora in New York.

Soto Crespo, Ramón E. *The Mainland Passage: The Cultural Anomaly of Puerto Rico*. Minneapolis: University of Minnesota Press, 2009. The author provides a good discussion of Algarín's *Mongo Affair* and discusses his understanding of the poetic art.

See also: Jimmy Santiago Baca; Giannina Braschi; Victor Hernández Cruz; Nicholasa Mohr; Judith Ortiz Cofer; Esmeralda Santiago; Piri Thomas.

Isabel Allende

Peruvian-born novelist

A prolific novelist, Allende was recognized in 2010 as the most widely read Latin American female writer of all time. Her writings are available in more than twenty languages. Her best known work is The House of the Spirits *(1982).*

Latino heritage: Chilean

Born: August 2, 1942; Lima, Peru

Also known as: Isabel Allende Llona

Areas of achievement: Literature; theater; journalism

Early Life

Isabel Allende Llona (ah-YEHN-day YOH-nah) was born on August 2, 1942, to Tomás Allende and Francisca Llona in Lima, Peru, while her father was on diplomatic duty. She is the eldest of three children. After Francisca separated from her husband in 1945, the family returned to Chile. Francisca soon met Ramon Huidobro, a diplomat whom she would accompany to his posts in Bolivia and Lebanon between 1953 and 1958. Allende's family returned to Chile in 1958 because of the Suez Canal Crisis.

In 1958, Allende met engineer Miguel Frias, whom she married in 1962. The couple had two children—Paula, born in 1963, and Nicolas, born in 1966. From 1959 to 1965, Allende worked for the United Nation's Food and Agriculture Organization. She traveled throughout Europe and lived in Switzerland and Belgium with her husband and daughter. Allende returned to Chile and began her career as a journalist in 1967 with the well-regarded magazine *Paula*.

From 1967 to 1974, as a member of the editorial team, she produced feminist articles and wrote a column of humorous content called "The Impertinent Ones." In 1973 and 1974, she wrote for children's magazine *Mampato* and penned the short stories "The Grandmother Panchita" and "Mice and Mouse" ("Lauchas y lauchones"). Also from this period are her comical articles titled "Civilize your Troglodyte." Parallel to these projects she worked as a television host for two popular Chilean programs, one based on interviews and the other on witty news commentary. In 1972, her play *The Embassador* was staged.

In 1970, Allende's uncle Salvador Allende was elected to the presidency in Chile, but he was ousted by Augusto Pinochet's coup d'état in 1973. Because of the repression in Chile under the military regime, Allende's family moved to Venezuela in 1975. There she continued her career as a reporter at *El Nacional* newspaper in Caracas. She also worked as school director from 1979 to 1982 at Morocco College in Caracas. In 1981, upon receiving news that her ninety-nine-year-old grandfather was dying in Chile, Allende decided to write him a letter. It turned out to be a long manuscript recounting memories and events related to the suffering her family had endured after the coup. This text, which was meant for her dying grandfather, became *The House of the Spirits*, Allende's first best seller, published in 1982.

Life's Work

Allende's prolific period as a novelist began with *The House of the Spirits*. This novel was translated into English in 1985 and sold millions of copies in the United States. It was adapted into a Hollywood film in 1993, starring Meryl Streep, Glenn Close, and Antonio Banderas. In 1984, Allende published *The Porcelain Fat Woman* and *Of Love and Shadows*. The latter work also

Isabel Allende. (AP Photo)

was made into a film that won second place at the Havana Film Festival in 1994. In 1987, Allende experienced both continued success and despair: her celebrated novel *Eva Luna* was published; however, she also separated from her husband, Frias.

By that time, Allende already had received many prizes and honors. In 1983, *The House of the Spirits* was named best novel of the year in her native country, and it received the Grand Prix d'Evasion in France in 1984. She also won awards for best novel in Mexico in 1986; the Quality Paperback Book Club's New Voice Award in the United States in 1986; and the Library Journal's Best Book Award in 1988. She also received a nomination for the *Los Angeles Times* Book Prize in 1987.

In 1988, Allende married Willie Gordon, an American with whom she moved to San Rafael, California. The same year, her native country restored democracy under the transitional government of Patricio Aylwin. Allende was able to return to Chile in 1990 to enjoy her country's recognition. The nation granted her the Gabriela Mistral Award for education and cultural excellence. The successful relesae of Allende's book *The Infinite Plan* in 1991 was shadowed by a family tragedy. Allende's daughter Paula suffered an attack of porphyria, a disease that put her in coma on December 6 the same year. Paula died one year later at age twenty-eight in Allende's home in California.

Tragedy was followed by immense achievements. Allende's novels continued to enjoy tremendous acceptance worldwide and most received distinctions. She published *Paula* (1994), *Aphrodite: A Memoir of the Senses* (1997), *Daughter of Fortune* (1999), *Portrait in Sepia* (2000), *City of the Beasts* (2002), and *My Invented Country: A Nostalgic Journey Through Chile* (2003). *City of the Beasts* is the first part of a trilogy whose sequels are *Kingdom of the Golden Dragon* (2004) and *Forest of the Pygmies* (2005). In 2006, she published *Inés of My Soul*, and in 2007 *The Sum of Our Days* was released. In 2009, she wrote two novels: *Island Beneath the Sea* and *Friends Are Friends*.

Allende's works continue to garner recognition around the globe. She received the Independent Foreign Fiction Award of England (1993) and the following American prizes: The Brandeis University Major Book Collection Award (1993), the Feminist of the Year Award (1994), the Critics' Choice Award (1996), the Sara Lee Foundation Award, and more than twenty other international honors. Crowing her distinctions are the 1998 Dorothy and Lillian Gish Prize for helping make the world a more beautiful place. In 2008, she received an honorary doctorate from San Francisco State University.

Allende's Ties to the United States

As a resident of San Rafael, California, since the late 1980's, Isabel Allende has contributed culturally as well as financially to the United States. She has given lectures and developed workshops to help college students improve their relationship with literature. Also, she has imparted her knowledge as visiting professor at the University of Virginia, Charlottesville; Montclair College in New Jersey; and the University of California, Berkeley. As to her financial contributions, much stems from the death of Allende's daughter, Paula, from complications of porphyria. Paula left a letter asking her mother to use her personal savings for the education of underprivileged women and children. Allende created the Isabel Allende Foundation and the Paula Scholarship Fund. These two organizations provide financial assistance to several institutions dedicated to helping marginalized individuals. Allende's motto, "We only have what we give," reflects her devotion to helping others. In the United States, her foundations support groups such as the Center for Young Women's Development in San Francisco, California; the American Porphyria Foundation in Houston, Texas; and the Children's Book Project in San Francisco.

Significance

With her writings, Allende has traversed frontiers, broadening international readers' understanding of Latin American culture and history. Allende often is compared to other Hispanic writers of her generation, and some scholars place her among what is known as the Latin American Boom that took place in the 1960's and 1970's. Others call her a post-Boom novelist because her novels began appearing in the 1980's. Although she shares techniques with both periods, she is unique in the sense that her works typically have feminist themes that appeal to a wide range of readers.

Allende's dedication to writing fiction has placed her as one of the world's most widely read novelists, and she has broadened the road for female writers in general. In 2010 she was nominated for the National Literary Prize of Chile, the most distinguished award in her country.

Maria Eugenia Silva

Further Reading

Castellucci, Karen. *Isabel Allende: A Critical Companion*. Westport, Conn.: Greenwood Press, 2003. Examines Allende's work from a cultural and historical perspective.

Correa Zapata, Celia. *Isabel Allende: Life and Spirit*. Houston, Tex.: Arte Público Press, 2002. Discusses the personal life of Allende, exposing the author's states of mind at different stages of her life.

Feal, Rosemary G., and Ivette E. Miller, eds. *Isabel Allende Today: An Anthology of Essays*. Pittsburgh, Pa.: Latin American Literary Review Press, 2002. The essays compiled in this text explain Allende's techniques and the feminist configurations present in her novels.

See also: Julia Alvarez; Marie Arana; Denise Chávez; Sandra Cisneros.

Mel Almada

Mexican-born baseball player

Almada was the first Mexican-born Major League Baseball player. He signed with the Boston Red Sox in 1933, then played for the Washington Senators, St. Louis Browns, and the Brooklyn Dodgers. After his playing career was over, he managed baseball teams.

Latino heritage: Mexican and Spanish

Born: February 7, 1913; Huatabampo, Mexico

Died: August 13, 1988; Caborca, Mexico

Also known as: Baldomero Melo Almada Quiros; Melo

Area of achievement: Baseball

Early Life

Baldomero Melo Almada Quiros, better known as Mel Almada (ahl-MAH-dah), was born February 7, 1913, in Huatabampo, located in northwestern Mexico along the Gulf of California. He was one of the eight children of Baldomero Almada and Amelia Quiros Almada, wealthy upper-class landowners. Baldomero was a descendant of conquistadors and Amelia from Spanish nobility. Baldomero was appointed governor of Baja California but the previous governor, Esteban Cantu, refused to give up the position. Hoping to escape the turmoil and violence of the Mexican Revolution, the family moved to Los Angeles, California, in 1914.

Almada and his older brother José Luis began playing baseball at an early age. Educated in the Los Angeles public school system, Almada was a star of the local baseball, football, and track teams. He was a pitcher and center fielder who threw and batted left-handed. After graduating from high school, Almada followed José Luis into semiprofessional baseball. He was signed by the Seattle Indians, part of the Pacific Coast League, in 1932 at age nineteen.

Life's Work

Almada had a .311 batting average his rookie season and was called up by the Boston Red Sox in September, 1933. He played fourteen games with the Red Sox that season, batting .341 with three runs batted in. He was the first Mexican-born player in Major League Baseball. On October 1, 1933, the New York Yankees played the Boston Red Sox. It was the last game that Babe Ruth pitched. He gave up twelve hits, three of them to Almada.

During the offseason, Almada returned to California to stay with his parents. While there, he played a number of exhibition games with various all-star and local teams. Almada's batting average dropped to .233 in 1934 with the Red Sox. However, he played much of the season with the Kansas City Blues, part of the American Association. The following year, the Red Sox made Almada their starting center fielder. He continued to play in Boston until the 1937 season, when he was traded to the Washington Senators. While with the Senators, he reportedly played in a string band with teammates Rick and Wes Ferrell. Almada was a media star with both the English-language and Spanish-language press. The Spanish press called him a Mexican national hero. In the English media, Almada was initially and commonly described as being of Italian decent, because he was fairer-complected, taller, and broader than most Mexicans. On July 25, the Washington Senators and St. Louis Browns played a double-header. Almada scored five runs in the first game, tying a league record. In the second game, he scored four runs, setting the record for most runs scored in a double-header by a single player.

Early in the 1938 season, Almada was traded to the St. Louis Browns. He improved during the season, setting career highs for batting average, runs, hits, and doubles. He slumped again at the beginning of the 1939 season, and his contract was sold to the Brooklyn Dodgers. The Dodgers used Almada as a backup outfielder and pinch hitter. He played his last major league game October 1, 1939, then returned to the Pacific Coast League and, in 1941, was a player-manager for a Mexican League team. In 1944, Almada joined the United States Army. After completing basic training in Texas, he was assigned to the medical corps at Fort Sam Houston for the duration of World War II. While in the Army, Almada played baseball in the San Antonio Service League. During the 1950's, he managed a Mexican League team. In 1972, he was inducted into the Mexican Baseball Hall of Fame.

Almada had four children: Miguel, Eduardo, Lydia, and Cecilia. He died in Caborca, Mexico, on August 13, 1988, of heart problems.

Significance

Unlike Jackie Robinson, who became a civil rights icon when he broke baseball's color barrier in 1947, Almada is not well-known to the average American. Nonetheless, he was an important figure in baseball history as the major leagues' first Mexican-born player. Almada retired from playing professional ball in 1939, but continued to be involved with the game until late in his life. In an interview in the early 1980's, Almada said he never faced discrimination in baseball. Mexico's Pacific League still honors its rookie of the year with a Baldomero Melo Almada trophy.

Jennifer L. Campbell

Further Reading

Alamillo, José M. "*Peloteros* in Paradise: Mexican American Baseball and Oppositional Politics in Southern California, 1930 to 1950." In *Mexican Americans and Sports: A Reader on Athletics and Barrio Life*, edited by Jorge Iber and Samuel Regalado. College Station: Texas A&M University Press, 2007. Describes the political climate in which Almada spent his baseball career.

Alexander, Charles. *Breaking the Slump: Baseball in the Depression Era.* New York: Columbia University Press, 2004. Extensively researched and detailed, this history includes discussion of Almada's career.

Burgos, Adrian Jr. *Playing America's Game: Baseball, Latinos, and the Color Line.* Berkeley: University of California Press, 2007. A history of Latinos in baseball from 1880 through the present. Including the players' struggles against discrimination in both the major leagues and Negro Leagues.

See also: Bobby Ávila; Tom Flores; José Méndez; Minnie Minoso.

Roberto Alomar

Puerto Rican-born baseball player

Alomar was a switch-hitting second baseman who played in Major League Baseball (MLB) from 1988 to 2004. He was known for his acrobatic defensive play and offensive production. During his career, Alomar won ten Gold Gloves, four Silver Slugger awards, and two World Series rings with the Toronto Blue Jays.

Latino heritage: Puerto Rican

Born: February 5, 1968; Ponce, Puerto Rico

Also known as: Roberto Alomar Velázquez; Robbie Alomar

Area of achievement: Baseball

Early Life

Roberto Alomar Velázquez (AL-loh-mar veh-LAHS-kehz) was born in Ponce, Puerto Rico, on February 5, 1968, to Santos "Sandy" Alomar, Sr., and Maria Angelita Velázquez Alomar. He attended Luis Muñoz Rivera High School in Salinza, Puerto Rico. Alomar grew up around baseball, as his father and his older brother, Sandy, Jr., both played Major League Baseball (MLB). Sandy, Sr., played second base for six different MLB teams from 1964 to 1978 and coached teams such as the San Diego Padres, Chicago Cubs, and Colorado Rockies. Sandy, Jr., played catcher for seven different MLB teams from 1988 to 2004 and has served as a coach in the New York Mets and Cleveland Indians organizations.

At the age of seventeen, Alomar signed with the San Diego Padres. While playing for a minor league team in Wichita, Alomar hit for a .319 batting average with 41 doubles and 12 home runs. These were impressive numbers for second basemen of his era. The Padres were impressed and, just after the start of the 1988 season, called up Alomar and gave him the role

Roberto Alomar. (Getty Images)

as starting second baseman on April 22, 1988. Alomar stole 42 bases in his second season in the major leagues and hit for a .294 average during his three seasons with the Padres.

Prior to the beginning of the 1991 season, Alomar and outfielder Joe Carter were traded to the Toronto Blue Jays in exchange for Fred McGriff and Tony Fernandez.

Life's Work

Over his five-year career with the Blue Jays, Alomar improved his batting average and elevated his defensive play to new heights; he won the Gold Glove and was voted to the All-Star team in each season. Alomar became an integral part of the team that won two World Series (1992 and 1993). His series-changing home run off of Oakland Athletics relief pitcher Dennis Eckersley in the 1992 American League Championship Series, after which he pointed to the sky with both index fingers, became an iconic image for Blue Jay fans. This image also became the basis for Alomar's line of athletic clothing, Second 2 None. Alomar was especially productive offensively for Toronto, where he hit above .300 four out of five seasons and stole more than forty-five bases in three seasons.

By the end of the 1996 season, Alomar was a free agent and signed with the Baltimore Orioles as part of the team's transformation into a play-off contender. However, in his first season with the Orioles, Alomar's reputation was tarnished by his behavior toward MLB officials. Toward the end of the 1996 season, amid a play-off run by the Orioles, Alomar spit in the face of umpire John Hirschbeck after a called third strike. Alomar then compounded the controversial act by later implying that the death of the Hirschbeck's son had changed the umpire's personality and made him bitter. Alomar did not serve his five-game suspension for the spitting incident until the following season, which drew criticism of MLB officials for mishandling the situation. Because Alomar was not suspended during the 1996 season, he was able to help the Orioles win a wild card spot in the play-offs and surpass the Cleveland Indians in the American League Divisional Series. Alomar and Hirschbeck later reconciled.

After three seasons with the Orioles, Alomar signed a $32 million contract with the Cleveland Indians and rejoined his brother Sandy for two seasons. Alomar's 2001 season with the Indians proved to be his last productive season; he averaged .336, hit 20 home runs, and stole 30 bases.

Toward the end of his career, Alomar switched teams four times in three years and spent time with the New York Mets (2002 and 2003), Chicago White Sox (2003 and 2004), and Arizona Diamondbacks (2004). In 2002, Alomar fell apart defensively and had only a .266 average, with fifty-three runs batted in and seventy-three runs scored. Many, including the Mets organization, attributed his lack of productivity to the uncomfortable scrutiny of the New York fans and media. Alomar hit poorly in his final two seasons and was hampered by a broken hand for two months while with the Chicago White Sox, where he rejoined his brother.

On March 19, 2005, Alomar announced his retirement from Major League Baseball while a part of the Tampa Bay Devil Rays. Tampa Bay general manager Chuck LaMar stated, "For seventeen years, he has been one of the greatest, if not the greatest, second basemen ever to play the game." Throughout his career, Alomar played with the San Juan Senadores during the MLB offseason, winning the adoration of many fans in Latin America, especially Puerto Rico.

Significance

Alomar's career statistics, clutch play, and creative style made him one of baseball's top second basemen for most of the 1990's. In 2,379 games, Alomar hit for a career .300 average while hitting 210 home runs and amassing 2,724 hits. He also earned a .371 career on-base percentage and stole thirty or more bases in a season eight times throughout his career (1989, 1991-1993, 1995, 1999-2001). Alomar revolutionized how second basemen play their position—on the field and in the batter's box. Overall, his unique style of play and invention of new techniques to playing his position have left a lasting mark on baseball.

Kevin-Khristián Cosgriff-Hernández

Further Reading

Bjarkman, Peter C. *Baseball with a Latin Beat: A History of the Latin American Game*. Jefferson, N.C.: McFarland, 1994. This text provides a focused review of the experience of Latin American ballplayers and traces their contributions to the game up to the early 1990's.

Curry, Jack. "Baseball Analysis: Now It Is Alomar Who Should Be Looking Up to Soriano." *The New York Times*, June 28, 2003. Documents the woes of Alomar in his time as a New York Met.

Griffin, Richard. "Roberto Alomar Enters One Hall, Deserves Call from Another." *The Star*, June 20, 2010. Shows how Alomar was perceived by Canadians fans.

Miller, William J. "Roberto Alomar." In *Latino and African-American Athletes Today: A Biographical Dictionary*, edited by David L. Porter. Westport, Conn.: Greenwood Press, 2004. Good overall biography of Alomar. Bibliography provides the reader with more potential research material.

Namee, Matthew. "Roberto Alomar: A Forgotten Legend?" *Hardball Times*, June 28, 2004. Reminds baseball fans and others of the significance of Alomar's style of play and how it affected how subsequent second basemen master their craft.

Suttell, Scott. "All Eyes on Alomar." *Crain's Cleveland Business* 20, no.13 (March 3, 1999). Documents Alomar's arrival in Cleveland and his contribution to the Indians.

"Twelve-Time All-Star Retires; Has Back, Vision Problems." The Associated Press, March 19, 2005. Provides a summary of Alomar's career and describes his final moments as a major league ballplayer.

See also: Sandy Alomar, Jr.; Bobby Bonilla; José Canseco; Andrés Galarraga; Ozzie Guillén; Rafael Palmeiro; Manny Ramirez; Sammy Sosa.

Sandy Alomar, Jr.

Puerto Rican-born baseball player

Alomar played catcher and first base for a number of Major League baseball teams. Although his career numbers (.273 batting average, 112 home runs, .309 on-base percentage) were not stellar for a player of his position, his work ethic and defensive ability to manage pitching staffs made Alomar one of the more highly respected catchers of the 1990's.

Latino heritage: Puerto Rican

Born: June 18, 1966; Salinas, Puerto Rico

Also known as: Santos Alomar Velázquez

Area of achievement: Baseball

Early Life

Santos Velázquez Alomar, Jr. (veh-LAHS-kehz AL-loh-mar) was born on June 18, 1966, in Salinas, Puerto Rico, to Santos "Sandy" Alomar, Sr., and Maria Angelita Velázquez Alomar. Sandy, Sr., played Major League Basseball (MLB) from 1964 to 1978, as did Alomar's brother Roberto Alomar from 1988 to 2004. Sandy, Sr., and Roberto were second basemen and known for their athletic and acrobatic defensive play. Sandy, Jr., and Roberto played together three times in their MLB careers.

On October 21, 1983, Alomar signed with the San Diego Padres as an amateur free agent. Just over four years later, he broke into the major leagues at the age of twenty-two on September 30, 1988. While playing for the Padres, he was coached by his father and had Roberto as a teammate. However, Alomar only played in eight games over two seasons. On December 6, 1989, Alomar, Carlos Baerga, and Chris James were traded to the Cleveland Indians for Joe Carter. Things would change for Alomar and Baerga in Cleveland, as they both played pivotal roles in the resurgence of the Indians in the 1990's. During Alomar's tenure with the Indians, the team won five straight American League Central titles.

Life's Work

Alomar made a name for himself in Cleveland. In his first season with the Indians, Alomar hit for a .290

average and belted 9 home runs in 132 games as their starting catcher. Alomar's 1997 season with the Indians was a memorable one. That season he was named the most valuable player of the All-Star game, which was held in Cleveland, and hit a dramatic home run off of the New York Yankees' feared closer, Mariano Rivera, to propel his team to their second American League Championship Series in three years. In the 1997 season, Alomar hit a career-high .324 average, 21 home runs, and 83 runs batted in. In more than eleven seasons with the Indians, Alomar amassed a .277 average with 92 home runs, 416 runs, and 435 runs batted in.

At 6 feet, 5 inches and close to 230 pounds, Alomar was large for a catcher and was frequently hindered by injuries. From 1991 to 1995, Alomar was on the disabled list at some point in every year. He suffered from knee, leg, shoulder, back, and arm injuries that limited him to fewer than ninety games in seven of his prime seasons. On October 27, 2000, the Cleveland Indians granted him free agency, and that December, he signed with the Chicago White Sox for a career-high $2.9 million.

Toward the end of his career, Alomar played sparingly. On July 29, 2002, he was traded by the White Sox to the Colorado Rockies. In 2002, he returned to the White Sox as a free agent. He remained in Chicago until 2004 and again played with his brother Roberto. From 2004 to 2007, Alomar played with five different teams. Like most catchers, Alomar's career was cut short by knee injuries. In 2007, he retired from baseball and shifted his attention to coaching. After retiring from the New York Mets as a player, Alomar served as a catching instructor on the same staff as his father, Sandy, Sr., who was a bench coach. In 2009, Alomar was hired by the Cleveland Indians as their first-base coach and as part of their innovative catcher development program. Manny Acta, the Indians' manager, called Alomar "a guy who has the potential to do whatever he wants to do in this game." In the summer of 2009, Alomar was inducted into the Cleveland Indians Hall of Fame for his contributions to the club as a player and coach.

SIGNIFICANCE

Alomar played twenty seasons in the major leagues. This is a signifanct career for someone of his size and for a position that is so physically demanding. Part of his longevity has been attributed to the use of product known as "knee-savers." Alomar was the first to wear the large triangular pads, which attach to the straps of the catcher's shin-guards, and provide support when squatting behind the plate. Although his career statistics are not considered exceptional, Alomar was a fan favorite in Cleveland because of his hustle and positive attitude. During the Cleveland Indians' successful campaigns in the 1990's, Alomar was the "heart and soul and guts" of a perennial contender. His work ethic as a player and ability to coach has served as an example for many Latin American players, especially younger generations of Puerto Rican ballplayers.

Kevin-Khristián Cosgriff-Hernández

FURTHER READING

Bjarkman, Peter C. *Baseball with a Latin Beat: A History of the Latin American Game*. Jefferson, N.C.: McFarland, 1994. This text provides a focused review of the experience of Latin American ballplayers and traces their contributions to the game up to the early 1990's.

"Sandy Alomar Jr. Returns to Indians as First-Base Coach." The Associated Press, November 17, 2009. Provides an update on Alomar's career in Cleveland as a coach.

Shipgel, Ben. "Mets Are Packing Roster for the Early Bird Specials." *The New York Times*, February 20, 2007. Documents the signing of Alomar to the New York Mets toward the end of his career.

Sims, Damon. "Ex-Catcher Sandy Alomar Jr. Reflects on Joy, Heartache of Time Here as He Enters Team Hall of Fame" *The Cleveland Plain Dealer*, July 31, 2009. Alomar provides detail about his career as a Cleveland Indian and the significance that the organization has to him.

Smith, Claire. "Two Catchers Caught in Battle for Limelight." *The New York Times*, October 24, 1997. Reviews Alomar's accolades at the 1997 All-Star game amid the best season of his career.

Snyder, John. *Indians Journal: Year by Year and Day by Day with the Cleveland Indians Since 1901*. Cincinnati, Ohio: Clerisy Press, 2008. This text provides an in-depth discussion of the Cleveland Indians and in the process places Alomar's story into context in this organization with a rich baseball history.

See also: Roberto Alomar; Bobby Bonilla; José Canseco; Tony Fernandez; Andrés Galarraga; Ozzie Guillén; Rafael Palmeiro; Sammy Sosa.

María Conchita Alonso

Cuban-born actor and singer

A multitalented beauty from Cuba, Alonso first garnered attention in her teens as a pageant winner and model. Since the late 1970's, she has achieved fame as both a popular Latina singer and an actor in English-language and Spanish-language television and film productions.

Latino heritage: Cuban

Born: June 29, 1957; Cienfuegos, Cuba

Also known as: María Concepción Alonso Bustillo; Ambar

Areas of achievement: Music; acting; radio and television

Early Life

María Conchita Alonso (mah-REE-ah cohn-CHEE-tah ah-LOHN-so) was born María Concepción Alonso Bustillo in Cienfuegos, Cuba, the daughter of Ricardo Alonso and María Conchita Bustillo. Alonso grew up with her brothers Ricardo and Roberto. At the age of five, she moved with her family to Venezuela. Educated in Venezuela, Switzerland, and Spain, Alonso became fluent in Spanish, English, French, and Italian. An attractive and poised young woman, Alonso began competing in beauty pageants, and in 1971 she won the Miss Teenager of the World title. Four years later, she was crowned Miss Venezuela and placed sixth in the Miss World pageant. Soon afterward, she became a model.

In the late 1970's, Alonso debuted as both a singer and an actor. In 1978, she appeared in the Spanish-language film *Savana*. Performing under the stage name Ambar, she released her initial album, the disco-oriented, English-language *Love Maniac*, in 1979, and scored her first gold record. Throughout the late 1970's and early 1980's, Alonso became a familiar face on Latino television as a regular on nine different series, including lead roles in *Marielena* (1981), *Luz Marina* (1981), and *Claudia* (1982). Meanwhile, she continued racking up musical hits with two English-language albums, *The Witch* (1980) and *Dangerous Rhythm* (1982).

Alonso moved to the United States in 1982. She attracted immediate attention by singing the Georgio Moroder tune "Vamos a Bailar," for which she wrote the lyrics, on the soundtrack of the film *Scarface* (1983). Singing in Spanish under her own name, she achieved major successes with her next two albums, *Te Amo* (1983) and *María Conchita* (1984), with the latter garnering the singer a Grammy Award nomination as best Latin artist.

Life's Work

Alonso first appeared in an American film in 1984 in the critically acclaimed *Moscow on the Hudson*. Since then she has continued to forge a respectable, if not spectacular, career as both a singer and actor. On the musical front, Alonso released a dozen albums between 1985 and 2009, some produced through her own label, Ambar Entertainment. Virtually all of Alonso's albums feature popular songs sung in Spanish, many of which she has written, and are aimed at the Latin market, always her strongest audience. She has received three Grammy nominations for her efforts, and her songs have occasionally been selected for film soundtracks.

Alonso has expanded her repertoire as an actor, and she appears regularly in films, made-for-television films, and television series and miniseries in the United States and elsewhere. She also starred on Broadway in 1995, when she was the first Latin-born actor to perform as Aurora, one of the leading roles in *Kiss of the Spider Woman*. Alonso operates her own production company, Ambyth Productions, and has occasionally served as a film producer or coproducer. Equally adept at comedy or drama, she has appeared alongside some of Hollywood's biggest stars in more than forty films, playing supporting roles to Robin Williams, Nick Nolte, Arnold Schwarzenegger, Meryl Streep, Sean Penn, Robert Duvall, Ted Danson, Billy Dee Williams, Nicholas Cage, Jeremy Irons, Vanessa Redgrave, Glenn Close, Antonio Banderas, Edward James Olmos, and Anjelica Huston. Her highlight performances include *The Running Man* (1987), *Colors* (1988), *Predator 2* (1990), *The House of the Spirits* (1993), *Caught* (1996), *Material Girls* (2006), and *Spread* (2009). Alonso has also become a staple on American and Spanish-language television. She was a regular on *One of the Boys* (1989) and *Saints and Sinners* (2007); hosted and produced her own variety show, *Picante* (1992); voiced a character on the animated program *Big Bag* (1996-1998); and made guest appearances on numerous television series. In 2008, she hosted the VH1 reality television program *Viva Hollywood!*

Since becoming an American citizen in 2005, Alonso increased her visibility with a fashion line called Soy (I am). She has also been more politically outspoken.

María Conchita Alonso. (AP Photo)

Alonso publicly supported the 2008 presidential candidacy of John McCain and has appeared on a number of conservative talk shows to denounce Venezuelan president Hugo Chavéz.

SIGNIFICANCE

One of Latin America's best-selling recording artists, María Conchita Alonso achieved fame as a singer-songwriter throughout South and Central America and the Caribbean and among Latino listeners in the United States. In addition to three Grammy Award nominations, she has five certified gold albums and one certified platinum album to her credit between 1979 and 2009. During the same period, Alonso also earned a reputation as a dependable, versatile actor in lead and supporting roles in English-language and Spanish-language films and television programs, including several stints as a hostess of variety or reality shows. She has received Golden Globe, American Latino Media Arts (ALMA), and Independent Spirit awards for acting. For her contributions to the entertainment and Latino communities she was named the 1990 Hispanic Woman of the Year and the 1994 Hispanic Entertainer of the Year. As vice president of the Global Medical Relief Fund, a charitable organization, Alonso was the first Latin American woman to receive the key to the city of Las Vegas, Nevada.

Jack Ewing

FURTHER READING

Baynham, Angela. *Insight Guide Venezuela.* New York: Langenscheidt, 2002. Guide to Venezuela's history and culture, which includes details of Alonso's career as a singer and actor.

Bender, Steven. *Greasers and Gringos: Latinos, Law, and the American Imagination.* New York: New York University Press, 2005. A study focusing on Hispanics, including Alonso, who, through acting and other contributions, either reinforced or exploded cultural stereotypes.

Roman, James. *From Daytime to Primetime: The History of American Television Programs.* Santa Barbara, Calif.: Greenwood, 2008. This overview of more than fifty years of television, emphasizing how the medium changed American culture, includes information about Alonso's television appearances.

See also: Catherine Bach; Andy Garcia; Edward James Olmos; Elizabeth Peña; Jimmy Smits.

FELIPE ALOU

Dominican-born baseball player and manager

Alou was both a successful player and a manager, becoming the inaugural manager from the Dominican Republic in Major League baseball. Alou is also famous as a member of the Alou baseball family which consists, as of 2010, of Felipe and his two brothers and Felipe's son, Moises.

Latino heritage: Dominican

Born: May 12, 1935; Bajos de Haina, Dominican Republic

Also known as: Felipe Rojas Alou

Area of achievement: Sports

Early Life

Felipe Rojas Alou (feh-LEE-pay ROH-hahs ah-LEW) was born in the Dominican Republic on May 12, 1935. Born into poverty, he aspired to go to college. Alou was a track star early in his athletic career but shifted to baseball and this caused his talent to be noticed. As a member of the Dominican Republic's national baseball team, he won gold in the Pan-American Games of 1955.

Alou wanted to stay in college but was forced by family circumstances and his own lack of resources to sign a professional baseball contract soon after the games. He quickly rose through the minors and then made it into Major League baseball in 1958.

Life's Work

Alou's life in the major leagues can be divided up into two main parts: playing and managing. He made it to the majors with the San Francisco Giants shortly after they moved from New York. Alou did well in his early years and was joined by his brothers Matty and Jesus. In 1963, the three Alou brothers became the first (and, as of 2010, the only) all-brother outfield in history. Alou hit 25 home runs in 1962 and was named to the All-Star team. That season was his best in a Giants uniform. Alou was a respectable hitter who averaged .300 four times in his career, but he did not have a lot of power, nor did he drive in many runs, although the latter was a consequence of regularly batting first in the lineup.

After the 1963 season, San Francisco traded Alou in a multiplayer deal with the Milwaukee Braves. The Braves soon moved to Atlanta, and Alou moved with them. Soon after this move to Atlanta, Alou had the best season of his career. In 1966, he hit 31 home runs and led the league in several categories (but not in home runs, as his teammate Hank Aaron hit 44 that year). Alou also was named an All-Star and hit .327, a high average, but did not lead the league in that category either—in this case, he lost out to his brother Matty. Two years later, in 1968, Alou made the All-Star team for a third time and led the majors in hits with 210. The following year was his last with the Braves, and he was traded to the Oakland Athletics.

After leaving the Braves, Alou's career declined. His best year after 1968 was 1969, when he hit .280 with sixty-nine runs batted in. He stayed in the league until 1974, playing for five different teams. In his career, Alou collected more than 2,000 hits, a fairly significant milestone, but he never received much support for the Hall of Fame. His only year on the ballot was in 1980, when he got only 0.8 percent of the votes and so was not included on the next year's ballot.

Alou took a year off from baseball and then became a minor league manager for the Montreal Expos. Working his way up through the organization, he started at the Class-A West Palm Beach Expos, then moved to the Class-AA Memphis Chicks. After a year with the Denver Bears, another AA team, Alou became manager of the Wichita (Kansas) Aeros, the Expos' AAA team. After two years of managing the Aeros, he returned to the big leagues as a first-base coach. In 1992, Alou became the manager of the Montreal Expos. Even though other teams had offered him positions, he stayed with the Expos as they were the ones to first give him a managing opportunity. In his first two years, the Expos finished second in their division both times and thus missed the play-offs. In 1994, his team finished first, but the play-offs were canceled by a strike. After the strike ended, Alou's teams never did as well, and Montreal ownership did not want to spend the money to retain the team's young talent. However, Alou did have the chance to manage his son, Moises, who went to the All-Star game in 1994. That year, Alou also was named manager of the year. He had offers to coach other teams but stayed with the Expos, eventually becoming their all-time winningest

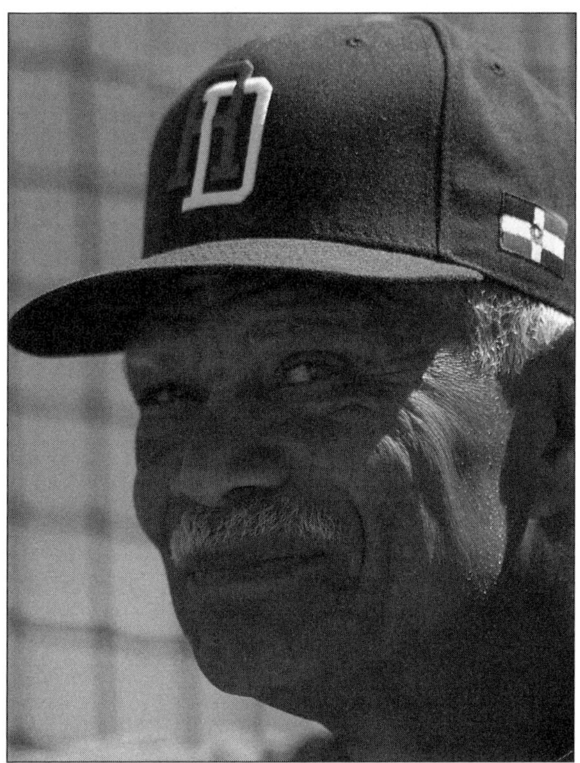

Felipe Alou. (Getty Images)

The Alou Family and the Major Leagues

The Alou family greatly helped Dominicans and Latinos in general enter Major League baseball. They demonstrated that Latinos could be successful, and the all-Alou outfield of Felipe, Jesus, and Matty drew great interest. Both Matty and Felipe appeared in at least two All-Star games. Felipe's son Moises later became a baseball player who spent seventeen seasons in the major leagues. Felipe Alou also became a manager well-respected for his dignity. Although he faced a difficult situation with the Montreal Expos, a team that struggled for recognition and failed to hold onto key players, he performed his duties with composure and took his firing with grace. He later was commended for his handling of a situation in which a San Francisco Giants radio host used ethnic slurs to critize Alou's team. In the 1960's and beyond, the Alou family greatly increased Latino interest in baseball.

manager. However, he was fired in the middle of the 2001 season.

Alou returned to baseball in 2001, serving as the bench coach for the Detroit Tigers. In 2003, he became the manager of the San Francisco Giants (who had tried to hire him previously). In his first year at the helm, the team made the play-offs but lost to the eventual champion Florida Marlins. Alou served for three more seasons as manager but never reached the postseason again. He became an assistant to the Giants' general manager and was still in that role in 2010, when the Giants won a long-awaited World Series championship.

Significance

Alou was one of the first Dominicans to play regularly in the major leagues and paved the way for generations of players that followed. He also was Major League baseball's first Dominican manager and took on that role only a few years after Frank Robinson became the sport's first African American manager. He is a member of one of baseball's great families, as he, his brother Matty, and his son Moises all played in All-Star games.

Scott A. Merriman

Further Reading

Burgos, Adrian. *Playing America's Game: Baseball, Latinos, and the Color Line*. Berkeley: University of California Press, 2007. Examines Latinos in baseball, going back before formal integration and discussing how Latinos maneuvered their way into the major leagues. Also examines post-integration issues and how integration did not necessarily lead to equality.

Gedda, George. *Dominican Connection: Talent from the Tropics Changes Face of National Pastime*. New York: Eloquent Books, 2009. Discusses the wave of players coming from the Dominican Republic. Includes a profile of Alou and an explanation of Alou's experiences in the minors and majors.

Nan, Chuck. *Fifty Years by the Bay: The San Francisco Giants 1958-2007*. Bloomington, Ind.: Author House, 2006. Examines the Giants from the year they moved to San Francisco. Includes chapters on the years Alou played there.

Regaldo, Samuel O. *Viva Baseball! Latin Major Leaguers and Their Special Hunger*. 2d ed. Urbana: University of Illinois Press, 1998. Discusses Latin American players' successes and the challenges they faced. Utilizes interviews with Alou and other Latin American players.

See also: Luis Aparicio; Bobby Ávila; Orlando Cepeda; Dave Concepción; Juan Marichal; Tony Oliva; Luis Tiant.

Ignacio Manuel Altamirano

Mexican-born writer, politician, and judge

Altamirano was a prominent Mexican politician and judge of Nahuatl descent who promoted the modernization agenda of the Liberal Party during the nineteenth century. His novels Clemencia *(1869),* Julia *(1870),* La Navidad en las montañas *(1871;* Christmas in the Mountains, *1961), and* El Zarco: Episodios de la vida Mexicana en 1861-1863 *(1901;* El Zarco: The Bandit, *1957) played an important role in shaping Mexican cultural identity.*

Latino heritage: Mexican

Born: November 13, 1834; Tixtla, Guerrero, Mexico

Died: February 13, 1893; San Remo, Italy
Also known as: Ignacio Manuel Altamirano Basilio
Areas of achievement: Government and politics; journalism; literature

Early Life

Ignacio Manuel Altamirano Basilio (eeg-NAH-see-oh mah-new-EHL AHL-tah-mee-RAH-noh bah-SEE-lee-oh) was born in the village of Tixtla in the state of Guerrero, Mexico, in 1834. Altamirano, the son of Nahuatl-speaking parents, did not learn Spanish until he turned twelve. The political influence of his father, the mayor of Tixtla, secured him a place in Tixtla's middle school, and his excellent academic skills allowed him to receive a scholarship to the Instituto Literario Toluca. He went on to become a lawyer.

Altamirano's early life was marked by the constant struggle for power that followed Mexico's declaration of independence in 1810. The ruling elites had split into two groups: conservatives and liberals. The conservatives supported the rule of the Creole (descendants of the Spanish colonizers) and resisted any attempt to integrate the indigenous populations into the government; the liberals promoted the modernization of the country and advocated for a rearticulation of Mexican culture in accordance with the dictates of the Enlightenment.

As a young man, Altamirano participated in the revolution of Ayutla that aimed to remove Antonio López de Santa Anna from power and draft a federal constitution. After the War of Reform, the Constitution of 1857 finally was approved. The next year, Benito Juárez, a Zapotec Indian and the first Mexican leader without a military background, was elected president of Mexico. Altamirano initially supported Juárez's presidency but soon became disillusioned with his conciliatory approach to nation-building. Altamirano favored a more radical reform of the country and opposed Juárez's decision to offer amnesty to all the conservatives who had fought against the liberals.

Life's Work

Although Altamirano retired from military life as a decorated colonel and went on to become attorney general and to win an election to Mexico's Supreme Court, he is best remembered for his tireless promotion of modern Mexican culture. Altamirano played a crucial role in developing the infrastructure that allowed Mexican national culture to flourish. He founded four newspapers—*El Federalista*, *La Tribuna*, *El Correo de México*, and *La República*—as well as a literary journal, *El Renacimiento*, that helped launch a generation of Mexican writers.

Early in his literary career, Altamirano wrote an essay titled "Elementos para una literatura nacional" (1868; "Elements of a National Literature") in which he describes how his political agenda is aided by his literary production. Altamirano, like many other Latin American writers of this period, chose the romance as the ideal genre to promote the articulation of a Mexican national identity. In his novels, the traditional plot of star-crossed lovers becomes an allegory for Mexicans' need to overcome personal differences and love their homeland.

Despite Altamirano's firm belief in the power of the novel to shape national conscience, he was painfully aware of the limitations that the high index of illiteracy in nineteenth century Mexico entailed for his modernizing project. In an essay titled "De la poesia epica y de la poesia lirica en 1870" (1872; "Of Epic Poetry and Lyric Poetry in 1870"), Altamirano complained that only a small cultural elite had access to his romances. His prolific literary production, his predilection for the sentimental romance, and his interest in publishing much of his work in serial form are examples of Altamirano's earnest efforts to overcome this obstacle.

Between 1869 and 1889, Altamirano wrote six novels, the last two of which were published posthumously: *Clemencia* (1869), published serially in *El Renacimiento*, *Julia* (1870), *La Navidad en las montañas* (1871; *Christmas in the Mountains*, 1961), *Idilios y elegías* (published in two volumes in 1872 and 1873; *Idylls and Elegies*), *El Zarco: Episodios de la vida Mexicana en 1861-1863* (1901; *El Zarco, the Bandit*, 1957) and *Atenea* (1935). Besides promoting national pride, Altamirano's sentimental prose often comments directly or indirectly on the political reality of his time. *El Zarco*, one of his most popular novels, is a thinly disguised critique of Mexican president Juárez's inability to control the conservative insurrection.

Significance

The quality of Altamirano's literary production often has been questioned, but as the literary critic Doris Sommer has explained, his novels—as well as the sentimental novels of his contemporaries throughout Latin America—constitute the foundational narrative on which the new nations built their identities. Although Latin American fiction would not achieve international recognition until the arrival of the writers of the Latin American Boom in the 1960's, the work of writers like Gabriel

García Márquez or Mario Vargas Llosa was deeply influenced by writers such as Altamirano. The nineteenth century sentimental romance was the tradition on which the writers of the Boom modeled their prose.

Altamirano's sentimental romances also have been criticized for their supposed complicity in liberal efforts to homogenize Mexican culture. It is certainly true that Altamirano had no patience with indigenous traditions that he interpreted as backward superstitions, but he was equally impatient with Creole provincialism. Altamirano was a pragmatic statesman. His critique of Mexican culture did not intend to replace it with an enlightened version of Spanish or French culture but to provide it with the coherence that a nation requires as his detailed analysis of indigenous culture in his collection of essays *Paisajes y Leyendas* (1884; *Landscapes and Legends*) suggests.

Adolfo Campoy-Cubillo

FURTHER READING

Altamirano, Ignacio M. *El Zarco, the Blue-Eyed Bandit: Episodes of Mexican Life Between 1861-1863*. Translated by Ronald J. Christ. Edited by Christ and Sheridan Phillips. Santa Fe, N. Mex.: Lumen Books, 2007. Altamirano's literary attempt to reconcile the interests of nineteenth century marginal bandits and mainstream Mexicans.

Sommer, Doris. *Foundational Fictions: The National Romances of Latin America*. Berkeley: University of California Press, 1991. A seminal exploration of the significance of Altamirano's work and that of other Latin American writers in developing national discourses.

Wright-Rios, Edward. "Indian Saints and Nation-States: Ignacio Manuel Altamirano's Landscapes and Legends." *Mexican Studies/estudios Mexicanos* 20, no. 1 (2004): 47-68. An analysis of the precarious balance of traditional, indigenous, and modern Mexican identities in Altamirano's work.

See also: Román Baldorioty de Castro; Eugenio María de Hostos; Cleofas Martinez Jaramillo.

ALURISTA

Mexican-born poet, educator, and activist

Known for politically charged verse that critiques the inequities of consumer capitalism and for dense, profoundly symbolic poems that invoke the spiritual and mythic traditions of his native Mexico, Alurista became a pioneering figure in contemporary Chicano literature by being the first to publish verse that blended Spanish and English.

Latino heritage: Mexican
Born: August 8, 1947; Mexico City, Mexico
Also known as: Alberto Baltazar Urista Heredia; Alberto H. Urista
Areas of achievement: Poetry; education; activism

EARLY LIFE

Alurista (AHL-yew-REE-stah) was born Alberto Baltazar Urista Heredia in Mexico City on August 8, 1947. He grew up south of the capital in the tiny state of Morelos, important to Mexican history as the birthplace of the revolutionary Emiliano Zapata, and that sense of Mexican identity played a significant part in the boy's upbringing. His childhood was comfortable; his father was a successful entrepreneur with significant contacts in the United States.

As a child, Alursita revealed a felicity for language and a precocious sense of the music of poetry. He was selected in elementary school to recite long epic verses at assemblies. By twelve, he was writing his own verse—love poems that he, in turn, would sell to affluent boys who would present them to girls as their own work.

When Alurista was thirteen, he was sent to live with an aunt in San Diego, just north of the American border. Having been raised in a household where both English and Spanish were spoken, Alurista adjusted to life in American schools easily and excelled in the classroom. In 1965, he matriculated at nearby Chapman University, a small Christian school, initially to study business management. However, his heart was not in it—he volunteered as a child-care worker and glimpsed the problems that many immigrants faced. Amid the political unrest of the Chicano movement centered in Southern California, particularly the bold political activism of César Chávez and his work with the United Farm Workers, Alurista transferred to the far more politically charged campus of San Diego State University, where over the next several years he explored a variety of his growing interests. After studying topics including philosophy and comparative religion, he graduated in 1970 with a B.A. in psychology.

While an undergraduate, Alurista helped establish the university's Chicano studies program, a first in the United States. He would remain as an adjunct professor in the department until 1974 (he returned from 1976 to 1979). In the process, Alurista studied the religious literature of Mexico, particularly the Aztecs. During his senior year, he helped form MEChA (Movimiento Estudiantil Chicano de Aztlán), a campus organization dedicated to Mexican American identity. During that time, he first published poems under the pen name Alurista.

Life's Work

In 1971, at the encouragement of colleagues who had published his verse in a scattering of small, prestigious literary journals, Alurista published his first collection of poetry, *Floricanto en Aztlán* (*Flower and Song* in Aztlán). The book, greeted with lavish national critical praise, broke new ground by mingling English, Spanish, and Mexican dialects, a polyglot approach that created stunning new rhythms and lush sounds. Drawing on his fascination with pre-Columbian religion, Alurista presented an evocative sense of a fabulous paradise he called Aztlán, where Mexican Americans could live in peace, their complex cultural identity intact. His follow-up collection, *Nationchild Plumaroja, 1969-1972*, published a year later, expanded that exploration of cultural identity and positioned Alurista at the forefront of the Chicano arts movement.

Alurista returned to school, completing his master's degree (1978) and his doctorate (1983) in literature at the University of California at San Diego. During his postgraduate work, he published three additional volumes of poetry, each successively more experimental in its use of language as Alurista drew on more obscure dialects to create often-impenetrable lines of dense sonic effects. Critics and readers alike found these collections inaccessible; however, with the publication of the appropriately titled *Return: Poems Collected and New* (1982), Alurista returned to his conceptual political verse in energetic free form. The poems were far more personal, complex, and witty investigations into the implications of his ethnic identity and mystical speculations on death, love, and family.

Over the next two decades, Alurista published several more collections of verse (most notably 1996's *Et tu . . . Raza*?), a body of work that established him among the foremost Chicano poets of his generation. During the 1990's, he participated in ambitious national reading tours in which he presented his verse with animation and charisma. The grueling schedule took its toll—in the mid 1990's, Alurista temporarily abandoned his hectic public life amid rumors that he was suffering from drug addiction. He spent more than two years reorienting his life; although he did not abandon his Catholicism, he embraced the serene and contemplative principles of Buddhism. Alurista relocated to San Jose, California, drawn to its thriving Chicano cultural community.

Apart from his poetry, Alurista established a national reputation for his promotion of the Chicano cultural identity, specifically the need for Mexican immigrants in America to explore and understand their ethnic roots. His work crafting the Chicano studies program at San Diego State became the template for dozens of similar academic programs throughout the Southwest. Alurista took the lead in founding the Centro Cultural de la Reza in San Diego, a center dedicated to preserving and celebrating the Mexican American heritage. He was not only a noted (and often incendiary) public speaker but also a tireless promoter of Chicano culture

Aztlán

Aztlán is the mythic home of the Nahua people, better known as the Aztecs. Aztlán is a rich part of the Mexican cultural mind, celebrated as a paradise—economic, cultural, and religious—before the encroachment of Europeans disrupted the Aztec empire. Although rumors of the actual existence of such a city often compelled European conquistadors searching for riches, it existed in the collective conscience of a people that, over the next several centuries, would be degraded by European invaders. In drawing on the rich cultural associations with the fabled land of Aztlán in his earliest poetry, Alurista tapped into the fierce pride of the peoples of northern and central Mexico, specifically the vast reaches of land acquired by the United States during the nineteenth century border wars. For many militant political activists, the term "Aztlán" became a call for radical action, specifically the return of much of the American Southwest to Mexico; however, Alurista, despite a fierce commitment to his native people, uses the fabulous city for its rich and bittersweet Edenic symbolism, a reminder of the pride he views as the right of Mexican Americans. For Alurista, Aztlán is part of Chicano identity, celebrating the often neglected historic achievements of an empire that predated Columbus by centuries.

in newspaper and magazine columns, essays, and longer nonfiction works.

In 2010, Alurista renounced his long commitment to the university system (he had held numerous appointments and writer-in-residence postings over twenty years), citing its abandonment of the liberal thinking of the 1970's and its embrace of conservatism, specifically its resistance to Chicano studies as a legitimate curriculum. Instead, he devoted his time to political and social community activism and to teaching Chicano literature part time at middle schools in the San Jose area, seeing in both commitments the opportunity to genuinely affect the evolution of Chicano culture.

Significance

In pioneering verse that brought together Spanish and English, Alurista was the first major post-war Chicano poet. In his signature works from the early 1970's, Alurista—like Irish poet William Butler Yeats, to whom he is frequently compared—mingled bold political idealism with rich religious symbols from his native culture, such as the sun, the eagle, the serpent. The poems celebrate the spiritual endurance of the Chicano people as part of a civilization that predates Christopher Columbus's arrival by centuries. Like Yeats's work, Alurista's poetry often is deeply ironic, juxtaposing the visionary possibility of his conception of a fabulous nation-state where the Chicano people can assert their identity with pride and dignity against the alienation and spiritual ennui of the contemporary Chicano oppressed by a capitalist system and lost in an English-speaking land.

Joseph Dewey

Further Reading

Bruce-Novoa, Juan. *Chicano Poetry: A Response to Chaos*. Austin: University of Texas Press, 1982. Scholarly look at Alurista's generation of Chicano poets. Includes a chapter on Alurista's first collection. Focuses on the struggle to assert identity against the elegiac sense of lostness.

Calderón, Héctor, and Ramón David Saldivar, eds. *Criticism in the Borderlands: Studies in Chicano Literature, Culture, and Ideology*. Durham, N.C.: Duke University Press, 1991. Although they do not treat Alurista directly, these essays create an important context for understanding Alurista's poetics as ideology specifically compelled by a Marxist critique of capitalist consumerism.

Garcia, Cristina. *Bordering Fires: The Vintage Book of Contemporary Mexican and Chicana and Chicano Literature*. New York: Vintage, 2006. Wide-ranging anthology of Alurista's generation and later writers who reflect his influence. Focuses particularly on the question of immigrant literature and the ethnic identities of Mexican Americans.

Keller, Gary D. "Alurista, *Poeta-Antropologo*, and the Recuperation of the Chicano Identity." Introduction to *Return: Poems Collected and New*, by Alurista. Tempe, Ariz.: Bilingual Review Press, 1982. Comprehensive introduction to Alurista's life and poetry that includes a helpful assessment of Alurista's use of pre-Columbian mythology.

McKenna, Teresa. *Migrant Song: Politics and Process in Contemporary Chicano Literature.* Austin: University of Texas Press, 1997. A groundbreaking cultural study of Alurista's generation with particular emphasis on how the poetry developed from the Mexican traditions of oral recitation. The study is an early call for including Chicano literature in the canon of American literature.

See also: Oscar Zeta Acosta; Rodolfo F. Acuña; Juan Bruce-Novoa; Norma Elia Cantú; Martha P. Cotera; Américo Paredes.

Juan Bautista Alvarado

American politician

Emerging as a political force in the contentious period when Mexico fought against expanding American interests to maintain control over Alta California, Alvarado staunchly advocated the short-lived dream of an independent California, serving twice as territorial governor before American annexation in 1848.

Latino heritage: Spanish

Born: February 14, 1809; Monterey, Alta California (now in California)

Died: July 13, 1882; Rancho San Pablo, California

Also known as: Juan Bautista Valentín Alvarado y Vallejo

Area of achievement: Government and politics

Early Life

Juan Bautista Valentín Alvarado y Vallejo, better known as Juan Bautista Alvarado (wahn bah-TEES-tah ahl-vah-RAH-doh), was born in Monterey, the most important Pacific coast port in a vast tract of land known as Alta California, at the time a territory belonging to Spain that included parts of present-day California, Nevada, New Mexico, Arizona, Colorado, Wyoming, and Utah. Both Alvarado's father and grandfather had served with distinction in the Spanish military. His father died when Alvarado was only ten days old and left his family no financial security. His mother remarried three years later and Alvarado was raised by his grandparents, the Vallejos. Fitting to his station, Alvarado received the best education during a tense era marked by insurgencies from forces challenging Spain's interests.

Mexico's independence from Spanish control in 1821 significantly changed the political operations of Alta California. For Mexico, maintaining military and economic control over such a great expanse of open territory was especially taxing; the area consisted primarily of ranches and farms, with a relatively small population. Recognizing the necessity of granting limited autonomy, Mexico instructed Alta California to establish its own legislature and empowered this legislature to name a governor approved by the Mexican government. These decisions set off nearly three decades of contentious military and political maneuvering pitting the Mexican government against the rising tide of Californios, California-born residents of different ethnicities, among them Alvarado, who conceived of Alta California as independent.

Life's Work

At age eighteen, Alvarado was elected secretary to the legislature, and then within a year was the territory's treasurer, controlling the distribution of Alta California's financial holdings. As part of the Mexican government's strategy to disenfranchise the Catholic Church by seizing its missions throughout Alta California and parceling out these considerable landholdings to private owners, Alvarado was given the charge to secularize the mission at San Miguel, one of the oldest and largest of the Church's outposts. Alvarado was subsequently appointed in 1834 to the powerful position of collector for the Custom House at Monterey, which, as the only seaport on the Pacific coast, was the gateway for all materials heading into the continent. He was only twenty-four years old.

Beginning in 1835, Alta California reeled under a succession of unpopular governors that only encouraged the movement toward an independent California. However, even as each governor alienated his office from the people and reduced his position to a puppet figure in the control of the Mexican government, whose presence was becoming more oppressive, Californios began to contend with the growing presence of American interests, military and economic. American interests sought to annex Alta California, part of a land grab conducted under the proclamation of Manifest Destiny. Indeed, Alvarado, who at the time served as the political head of the territory's legislature, rejected the growing American presence and argued that Alta California should remain aligned with Mexico but should demand political, military, and economic autonomy.

The tension climaxed in 1835, when the governor threatened to arrest Alvarado on trumped-up charges of mismanagement at the Custom House. Alvarado departed Monterey but returned with a jerry-rigged army of fervent Californios, who lay siege to the governor's fortress. A single cannon shot convinced the governor to surrender. Alvarado became the de facto governor of California. Facing the prospect of a bloody civil war or a protracted war against Mexico, Alvarado wisely followed the protocol of the territory's constitution and placed his name, along with two others, in nomination for governor. Mexico agreed and approved Alvarado as governor in 1836, an office he would hold, save for a brief stint in 1838, until 1842, when southern Californios, unhappy with Alvarado, requested Mexican intervention. The Mexican president obliged. Confronted by an expeditionary force, Alvarado surrendered and went into exile outside the city.

However, the new governor sent by Mexico was disastrous, and California was again rocked by insurgencies. Alvarado was returned as the collector of customs in 1845. He was elected to represent California in the Mexican congress in 1846, and as he prepared to head south, war was declared between Mexico and the United States. The American forces invaded Monterey and quickly took the capital, but even as other California officials fled to Mexico, Alvarado stayed and was granted protective custody. Repeatedly offered positions within the new American government, Alvarado refused, preferring to remain in a palatial ranch north of Monterey in San Pablo with his wife and nine children. Although in the thick of the California gold rush in 1849, Alvarado never prospered from mineral strikes. Instead he dabbled in several unsuccessful businesses, most notably running a hotel, and he wrote a much-respected history of California before American annexation. He died in 1882.

Significance

Given the tangled alliances that defined California's political environment between Mexican independence and the American annexation, it is easy to lose sight of Juan Bautista Alvarado's significance. Given that both the Mexican and American governments considered California largely as a commodity, Alvarado pledged his allegiance to the fortunes of his people, those born in California, and sought to preserve their self-determination and self-government. Though he lacked the army to make this vision a reality, his staunch support of these basic rights and his unswerving integrity at a time when politicians were routinely corrupt, as well as his heroic one-shot revolutionary victory, secured him a place in California history and folk culture.

Joseph Dewey

Further Reading

Beebe, Rose Marie, and Robert M. Senkewicz. *Lands of Promise and Despair: Chronicles of Early California, 1535-1846*. Berkeley, Calif.: Heyday Books, 2001. Original historic documents create a vivid, compelling picture of the era leading up to California's annexation. Discusses the political impact of Alvarado. Illustrated.

Hackel, Steven W. *Alta California: Peoples in Motion, Identities in Formation*. San Marino, Calif.: Huntington Library Press, 2010. Fascinating account of the politics, economics, and cultural diversity of colonial life in independent California.

Henderson, Timothy J. *A Glorious Defeat: Mexico and Its War with the United States*. New York: Hill and Wang, 2008. Reexamination of the pivotal conflict in Alvarado's political career. Describes how the Mexican government engaged in a war it was sure to lose.

See also: Tomás Estrada Palma; José Antonio Navarro; Miguel Antonio Otero; Pío Pico; Juan Seguin.

Linda Alvarado

American business executive and baseball team owner

The chief executive officer of Alvarado Construction Incorporated and Palo Alto Incorporated, Alvarado also was the first Latino to own a share of a Major League baseball franchise.

Latino heritage: Spanish

Born: June 15, 1951; Albuquerque, New Mexico

Also known as: Linda G. Alvarado; Linda G. Martinez

Areas of achievement: Business; baseball

Early Life

Linda G. Alvarado (AHL-vah-RAH-do) was born on June 15, 1951, in Albuquerque, New Mexico, and grew up the only daughter among six siblings. She and her five brothers were treated equally by their parents, who encouraged all of their children to pursue challenging careers.

Alvarado ran track and played softball, volleyball, and basketball in high school and college. She graduated from Pomona College, a small liberal arts college in Claremont, California. This achievement was notable in the community, as it was rare for a young Hispanic women at that time to attend college, much less graduate. While at Pomona, Alvarado chose to work as a laborer on the grounds of the college. She did so against the advice of college administrators, who advised her that women were not usually assigned jobs outdoors. This experience led to Alvarado's goal of making a career in construction management.

The path to a management job was challenging. Alvarado faced opposition from male colleagues who believed that construction management was not a woman's job, but she wanted to be her own boss. It was an uphill climb, but eventually she landed a position as a construction manager. Her parents took out a mortgage on their modest home to finance Alvarado's dream of starting her own construction company.

Life's Work

After graduating from Pomona College, Alvarado remained on campus and briefly worked in the botany laboratory as an assistant. Next, she went to work for a development company in California, where she learned the construction business in its totality. She learned how to prepare bids and write contracts for construction projects. This experience afforded Alvarado the opportunity to learn the construction business from the bottom up.

Alvarado started the Martinez Alvarado Construction Management Corporation in Denver, Colorado,

Linda Alvarado. (AP Photo)

in 1974 along with a business partner. She bought out her partner in 1976 and became chief executive officer (CEO) of Alvarado Construction Incorporated. Alvarado's first construction projects as CEO of her own company consisted of building shelters and sidewalks at bus stops in Colorado. Later, she progressed to management of bigger projects.

By 2010, Alvarado Construction employed more than six thousand workers and had a net worth of more than $30 million. The company has built many industrial and commercial buildings, including Invesco Field (the Denver Broncos' football stadium) and the Denver Convention Center. Alvarado Construction also took part in the construction of the Denver International Airport.

In 1991, Alvarado was a member of an ownership group that was awarded a Major League Baseball (MLB) expansion team, the Colorado Rockies, which began playing in 1993. She was the first Latino to become a part owner of an MLB franchise and the first woman to become an owner through entrepreneurship rather than inheritance. Alvarado, an avid sports fan, often uses baseball as a metaphor for business, particularly for teaching lessons on management. Because Latinos are numerous in Major League baseball, she also recognized the historical significance and importance to the Hispanic community of her ownership of a baseball team.

Alvarado also is CEO of Palo Alto Incorporated, which owns and operates more than one hundred YUM! Brand restaurants such as Taco Bell. She has served on the boards of directors of Pitney Bowes, 3M, Pepsi Bottling Group, Qwest Communications International, and Lennox International.

Significance

Alvarado defied cultural and gender stereotypes to make major strides in the business and professional-sports worlds. She has been the recipient of numerous honors, including the U.S. Hispanic Chambers of Commerce Business Woman of the Year Award, the Revlon Business Woman of the Year Award, and the Sara Lee Frontrunner Award. She also was a member of President Bill Clinton's Advisory Commission on Educational Excellence for Hispanic Americans.

Sandra W. Leconte

Further Reading

Barreto, Hector V. *The Engine of America: The Secrets to Small Business Success from Entrepreneurs Who Have Made It!* Hoboken, N.J.: John Wiley & Sons, 2007. Discusses Alvarado's career in construction management and her decision to buy the Colorado Rockies franchise.

Martin, Renee, and Don Martin. "Linda Alvarado, Alvarado Construction." In *The Risk Takers: Sixteen Women and Men Share Their Entrepreneurial Strategies for Success*. New York: Vanguard Press, 2010. Offers an overview of Alvarado's career and describes her parents' influence and her ambition to succeed in the male-dominated construction industry.

Packard, Mary. *Linda Alvarado: Breaking New Ground.* Parsippany, N.J.: Pearson Learning Group, 2008. Biography of Alvarado written for younger readers.

See also: Ralph Alvarez; Laura Contreras-Rowe; Arte Moreno; Samuel A. Ramirez, Sr.; Nina Tassler.

ANNE MAINO ALVAREZ

American scientist and educator

Alvarez advanced pathology research to prevent and control plant diseases impacting agricultural and floral industries, especially those operating in tropical environments. She developed a laboratory in which she mentored researchers and pursued scientific efforts to impede bioterrorism. Alvarez contributed funds to professional organizations to help scientists conduct investigations and assist agriculturists.

Latino heritage: Mexican

Born: April 14, 1941; Rochester, Minnesota

Also known as: Anne Lucia Maino Alvarez; Anne Lucia Maino

Areas of achievement: Science and technology; education

EARLY LIFE

Anne Lucia Maino Alvarez (MAY-noh AHL-vah-rehz) was born on April 14, 1941, at Rochester, Minnesota, to Dr. Charles Runston Maino and Jeannette (Gould) Maino. Her father, a physician, was affiliated with the Mayo Clinic as a surgery resident at the time of her birth. During World War II, Alvarez lived in Modesto, California, while her father served with the U.S. Navy, providing medical services. Her maternal grandfather, Dr. Ned B. Gould, had been a physician in that community since 1913. After the war, Alvarez, her parents, and two brothers, settled in Modesto, where, in 1948, her father and four associates, including a female physician, established the Gould Medical Group.

Alvarez's parents encouraged her scientific curiosity and adventurous nature. She flew in her family's airplane to vacation sites, such as their cottage at Carmel. *The Modesto Bee* reported some of Alvarez's scholastic and community activities, including her serving as president of her 4-H club. She qualified for a California Scholarship Federation life membership pin because of her academic performance.

After graduating from Downey High School in June, 1958, Alvarez studied during that summer at the Universidad de Guadalajara in Mexico. A biology major, she enrolled at Stanford University, her parents' alma mater. As an exchange student, she studied German in the summer of 1961 at the Goethe-Institut in Kochel, Germany, before beginning classes at Universität Tübingen in November. She returned to California and received a bachelor's degree in June, 1963.

LIFE'S WORK

Studying plant pathology, Alvarez completed a master's of science degree at the University of California at Berkeley in 1966. She was awarded a research fellowship at the agricultural science school, Ciências Agrárias, in Costa Rica that year. Continuing her studies at Berkeley, Alvarez conducted experiments on bacteria and diseases that affect agricultural crops. Starting in 1969, she researched in Argentina while teaching at the University of Neuquén, examining tropical plants indigenous to the Amazon region. Alvarez received her Ph.D. in 1972.

The next year, Alvarez moved to Kaneohe, Hawaii, where Windward Community College employed her as a botany instructor. She started working as an extension specialist for the University of Hawaii. Initiating her careerlong affiliation with the College of Tropical Agriculture and Human Resources (CTAHR), Alvarez accepted a plant pathologist position at the University of Hawaii in 1975. *Phytopathology News* noted that she was the first female plant pathologist on that school's faculty. She married soil scientist Robustiano Alvarez.

Alvarez focused her phytopathological investigations of pathogens on crops commonly grown in Hawaii, especially papaya, pineapple, macadamia nuts, cabbage, and tomatoes, all of which were crucial to that state's agricultural industries. The United States Department of Agriculture provided Alvarez grants. She utilized antibodies to develop tests for pathogens that could be conducted directly in fields and orchards.

Starting in 1985, Alvarez was an associate editor of the journal *Plant Disease*. She also held that position for *Phytopathology*. Alvarez served on the American Phytopathological Society (APS) Press's editorial board and as senior editor of *Plant Health Progress*. She wrote many scientific articles discussing her research. Alvarez was the lead author of the August, 1987, bulletin "Black Rot of Cabbage in Hawaii." She researched methods to protect anthurium, a decorative plant grown by Hawaiian nurseries, from blight; the plant is a valuable crop to the Hawaiian economy. As chair of the proceedings committee, Alvarez edited several volumes of papers presented at Hawaii Anthurium Industry Conferences.

In the early twenty-first century, Alvarez incorporated scientific advances—including genetic methodology using deoxyribonucleic acid (DNA) and biosensors to identify pathogens in seeds—into her research. Because of terrorism threats involving biological agents, she applied her research to agrosecurity, helping Hawaiians guard agricultural products from being maliciously contaminated or used to transmit toxins. Her monetary donations to the APS Foundation supported her peers' research. She was an editor for the educational compact disc *Plant Diseases Caused by Bacteria: An Image Database and educational Resource* (2010).

Significance

Alvarez enhanced agricultural industries, including production of seeds, foods, and decorative plants, in Hawaii and other places where people have applied her strategies to determine potential biological hazards to plants and how to diagnose and treat diseases. Her epidemiological insights reinforced agriculturists' capabilities to prevent crop losses by controlling pathogens that threatened consistent production of high yields of crops worth millions, helping farmers thrive economically. She alerted officials how to keep vulnerable plants from becoming weapons to spread disease to human populations or deplete food resources necessary to sustain life. Alvarez shared her expertise to create new generations of plant pathologists.

Elizabeth D. Schafer

Further Reading

Alvarez, Anne. "Differentiation of Bacterial Populations in Seed Extracts by Flow Cytometry." In *Plant Pathogenic Bacteria*, edited by Solke H. De Boer. Dordrecht, Netherlands: Kluwer Academic Publishers, 2001. Emphasizes benefits of using electronic sensor technology to identify antibodies associated with *Clavibacter* and *Xanthomonas* bacteria to isolate contaminated seeds efficiently.

________. "Sleuthing in the Alvarez Laboratory." *CTAHR Research News* 3, no. 1 (January, 2007): 3-6. Alvarez summarizes investigations she and students conduct at the University of Hawaii.

O'Neill, Lois Decker. *The Women's Book of World Records and Achievements*. Garden City, N.Y.: Anchor Press/Doubleday, 1979. Discusses Alvarez's pioneering role as a female plant pathologist in a section devoted to agricultural accomplishments by women.

See also: Walter Alvarez; Margarita Colmenares; Arturo Gómez-Pompa; Eugenia Kalnay; Michael A. Mares.

Julia Alvarez

American novelist, poet, and educator

Best known for her evocative novels, Alvarez has enjoyed a successful career as an educator and award-winning writer. Drawing upon her own experience as an exile from the Dominican Republic, she captures the hybrid Latino immigrant perspective of straddling two cultures, two languages, and two worlds.

Latino heritage: Dominican

Born: March 27, 1950; New York, New York

Also known as: Julia Altagracia Maria Teresa Alvarez

Areas of achievement: Literature; poetry; education

Early Life

Julia Altagracia Maria Teresa Alvarez (hewl-YAH AHL-vah-rehz) was born in New York City to Dominican immigrants Eduardo Alvarez and Julia Tavares de Alvarez. Within a few months, her parents moved the family (Alvarez and her older sister) back to the Dominican Republic. During this time, Alvarez's two younger sisters were born, and the four girls spent their days encircled by a large extended family within a compound owned by their wealthy grandfather. Alvarez and her sisters attended the Carol Morgan School to acquire an American English-language education. At the school, Alvarez was reprimanded for using Spanish and began to understand the struggles of a bilingual child who used one language at home and another at school.

The girls often were surrounded by female-dominated households where women managed everything from diapers and laundry to dinners. It was in this world that Alvarez learned about gender inequality in Latin American culture. Later she would attribute this time period as having a significant influence on her early feminist writings.

Alvarez and her family lived their life of privilege for ten years until they were forced back to the United States in 1960 to seek asylum from Dominican dictator Rafael Trujillo. The move was traumatic for the girls,

Julia Alvarez. (AP Photo)

who were forced into a new culture with a language they were not comfortable using. Alvarez recalls the difficulties of this transition as a theme in many of her writings.

The move also served as the impetus that led to Alvarez's love of words and writing. While in the Dominican Republic, she was not exposed to books outside the basal readers at her school. Alvarez did not see Dominicans reading often, and books represented a language and culture that she found foreign and largely uninteresting. After her family moved to the United States, Alvarez spent her days in fear of classmates who taunted her for speaking accented English. During this time, she turned to books for comfort, seeking a homeland—a place to escape. Books sheltered her from the turmoil about her in the classroom and on the far-off island she had left. When she was in sixth grade, Alvarez was inspired by an English teacher who had students write stories. Through these stories, Alvarez could capture her homesickness as well as elements of her culture that had been left behind.

Alvarez moved to Abbot Academy (now part of Phillips Academy in Andover, Massachusetts), a private boarding school, to finish her education. Upon graduation, she attended Connecticut College in New London, where she received prizes for her poetry and was invited to attend the Bread Loaf School of English Writers' Conference held in the summer of 1969. Alvarez's experience at the conference was transformative; for the first time, she was treated as an equal by her classmates and completely surrounded by passionate writers. She transferred to Middlebury College in Vermont, the college affiliated with the Bread Loaf School of English, to finish her studies.

In 1971, Alvarez graduated summa cum laude with a bachelor of arts. She later attended Syracuse University's master of fine arts program in creative writing, where she taught and continued to develop her skills. In 1974, she won the university's Academy of American poetry Prize and graduated with her master's degree in 1975.

Life's Work

Between 1975 and 1978, Alvarez held writer-in-residence positions in Kentucky, Delaware, and North Carolina. From 1979 to 1981, she taught English at Phillips Academy, her former high school. Immediately afterward, she transitioned to teaching in higher education with faculty positions in several universities between 1981 and 1988.

Alvarez returned in 1988 to join the English Department faculty at Middlebury College, where she was a professor for ten years and then became a writer-in-residence in the department. In 1989, Alvarez married Bill Eichner, a doctor from Nebraska with whom she would later purchase the Alta Garcia farm in the Dominican Republic, a 60-acre coffee farm practicing sustainable farming and offering literacy education. Alvarez's writing is rooted in her experiences as an immigrant and bicultural, bilingual American. Latino culture, strong familial ties, and self-exploration play major roles in her work, which includes essays, poems, and fiction and nonfiction for children and adults.

Alvarez's first published collection of poetry was *Homecoming* (1984). In this volume of poems, she vividly describes her search for identity and the significant role that Latinas played in her life. In 1991, Alvarez secured her foothold in the literary world with the publication of her first novel, *How the García Girls Lost Their Accents*. Originally intended as a way to guarantee Alvarez's tenure, this largely autobiographical work about four Dominican American sisters struggling to acclimate to life in the United States garnered positive attention from both readers and critics. The novel was selected as a *New York Times* Notable Book in 1991, named one of the American Library Association's Notable

How the García Girls Lost Their Accents and Secured an Author's Future

In the early 1990's, Julia Alvarez made a decision that would forever change her literary career. She hired Susan Bergholz, an influential literary agent who represented the work of Latina writers such as Sandra Cisneros, to place her first novel, *How the García Girls Lost Their Accents* (1991), with Algonquin Books of Chapel Hill, North Carolina.

How the García Girls Lost Their Accents was a success, garnering several literary awards. Readers and critics alike responded to the colorfully drawn García sisters, Sandi, Carla, Yolanda, and Sofia. Written in reverse chronological order from 1989 to 1956, the fifteen interrelated stories describe the childhood, adolescence, and adulthood of four sisters with Dominican roots trying to adapt and survive in a world where being bicultural and bilingual makes them outsiders.

Often called semiautobiographical, *How the García Girls Lost Their Accents* represents Alvarez's own immigrant experience as well as that of her three sisters. She explores her experiences not as a Dominican but as a Dominican American trying to navigate the choppy waters of America. The book also reflects the lives of Latinos across the United States—those juggling two cultures and two languages, living as hyphenated Americans, not fully belonging.

Books in 1992, and awarded the 1991 Pen Oakland/Josephine Miles Award for writing depicting a multicultural experience.

Just three years later, Alvarez published *In the Time of Butterflies* (1994), a historical novel detailing the assassination of political activists and sisters Minerva, Maria Teresa, and Patricia Mirabel (Las Mariposas) by Trujillo in 1960. Critics have touted this moving novel as one of Alvarez's finest works, and in 2001, it was made into a film starring Salma Hayek.

Alvarez later published another book of poetry, *The Other Side/El Otro Lado* (1995), exploring her life as a hyphenated "Dominican-American"—neither fully American nor Dominican. This collection was followed by several more works for adults such as: *¡Yo!* (1997), a companion to *García Girls* written from the viewpoint of characters describing Yolanda, Alvarez's literary alter ego; *Something to Declare* (1998), an autobiography exploring topics such as assimilation, acculturation, and ethnic identity; and *In the Name of Salomé* (2000), a novel about the life of Dominican poet and activist Salomé Ureña de Henríquez.

In 2000, Alvarez published *The Secret Footprints*, a children's picture book recounting the Dominican folktale of the Ciguapas tribe of women who live underwater. It was followed by *How Tía Lola Came to (Visit) Stay* (2001), the first novel in a series for middle elementary school-aged children which describes a colorfully outlandish Dominican aunt who comes to visit her nephew and niece in the United States. Alvarez wrote several more novels for young adults, such as *Before We Were Free* (2002), which received the 2002 Américas Award for Children's and Young Adult literature administered by the Consortium of Latin American Studies Programs (CLASP) and the 2004 Pura Belpré Author Award given by the American Library Association and REFORMA (the National Association to Promote Library and Information Services to Latinos and the Spanish Speaking); and *Return to Sender* (2009), which received the 2010 Américas Award and the 2010 Pura Belpré Author Award. She also created more picture books celebrating the folklore of the Dominican Republic, such as *The Best Gift of All: The Legend of La Vieja Belén* (2009).

Significance

In a time when Latinos were struggling to gain equal recognition for their literary contributions in U.S. publishing, Alvarez emerged as a strong, eloquent voice recounting the prejudice, acculturation, and assimilation struggles experienced by thousands of immigrants. Her work, along with that of other Latina writers throughout the twentieth century such as Nicholasa Mohr, Sandra Cisneros, Cherríe Moraga, and Ana Castillo, planted the seeds for the fertile fields that characterize U.S. Latin American literature. Alvarez consistently has challenged social and political structures in both the United States and the Dominican Republic, branding her as one of the most influential writers throughout Latin America.

Jamie Campbell Naidoo

Further Reading

Alvarez, Julia. *Something to Declare*. Chapel Hill, N.C.: Algonquin Books of Chapel Hill, 1998. Collection of twenty-four autobiographical essays intended to answer queries that readers have about the author's life and work.

Aykroyd, Clarissa. *Julia Alvarez: Novelist and Poet*. Detroit: Lucent Books, 2008. An accessible biography highlighting Alvarez's childhood, writing, accomplishments, and Latino identity. Includes color photos, time line, and suggested readings.

Johnson, Kelli Lyon. *Julia Alvarez: Writing a New Place on the Map*. Albuquerque: University of New Mexico Press, 2005. One of the first volumes to critically examine the ideals and themes in a substantive body of Alvarez's works.

Suárez, Lucía M. "Julia Alvarez and the Anxiety of Latina Representation."*Meridians: Feminism, Race, Transnationalism* 5 (October, 2004): 117-145. Suárez suggests that Alvarez's search for identity reinforces her ability to effectively invent herself through her writing.

See also: Alma Flor Ada; Giannina Braschi; Monica Brown; Ana Castillo; Sandra Cisneros; Judith Ortiz Cofer.

Luis W. Alvarez

American scientist, inventor, and educator

Called one of the twentieth century's greatest experimental physicists, Alvarez made significant contributions in World War II to the development of radar and the atomic bomb. In the postwar period, he improved the hydrogen bubble chamber and helped build the first proton linear accelerator; these inventions led to the pivotal discoveries in elementary particles for which he received the 1968 Nobel Prize in Physics.

Latino heritage: Spanish

Born: June 13, 1911; San Francisco, California

Died: September 1, 1988; Berkeley, California

Also known as: Luis Walter Alvarez; Luie Alvarez

Areas of achievement: Science and technology; education; military

Early Life

Luis Walter Alvarez (LEW-ees AHL-vah-rehz) was born on June 13, 1911, in San Francisco. His father, Walter Clement Alvarez, was a doctor of Spanish descent, and his mother was Harriet (Smythe) Alvarez. Alvarez was educated at a San Francisco elementary school and began attending the Polytechnic High School there, but he finished his secondary school education in Rochester, Minnesota, where his father went to work for the Mayo Clinic. In later life Luis attributed his love of experimental research to his father, who brought his son into his laboratory and explained various pieces of apparatus to him. His father even got a summer job for Luis at a scientific instrument-maker's shop in the Mayo Clinic.

Alvarez's initial passion was for chemistry, and he entered the University of Chicago to study to become a chemist. Because he was only able to get B's in the seven chemistry courses he took in his early years, he decided to switch to physics, principally because of a course in optics, which allowed him to work with such instruments as spectrometers and interferometers. Under the guidance of Dean Gale, who was in charge of the optical shop, Alvarez ground a 10-inch mirror for a telescope; Gale, serving as an informal patron, helped Alvarez obtain some financial aid with scholarships and assistantships. Alvarez's formal superior was Professor J. Barton Hoag, who encouraged him to build the University of Chicago's first Geiger counter. Dr. George Monk's course in experimental spectroscopy convinced Alvarez to attend graduate school in

Luis W. Alvarez. (The Nobel Foundation)

physics, which he did after he received his bachelor of science degree in 1932.

While Alvarez was working for his master's and doctoral degrees at the University of Chicago, major discoveries were being made about elementary particles in Europe (the neutron) and the United States (the positron). Alvarez observed some of the experiments confirming the neutron's existence in various laboratories, but he was unable to study nuclear physics at Chicago because it was not being taught. His adviser was Arthur Holly Compton, who had discovered that X-rays, when scattered by an electron, increased in wavelength (an effect named in his honor). Compton had become interested in cosmic rays, believing that they consisted of charged particles. Alvarez constructed a cosmic ray telescope through which the east-west (or latitude) effect of these rays was discovered (a disproportionate amount of cosmic radiation came in from the west). Alvarez helped establish that primary cosmic rays were positively charged. For this and other accomplishments, he received his Ph.D. in 1936. In the same year, he married Geraldine Smithwick, with whom he would have a son and a daughter.

LIFE'S WORK

In California, Alvarez's sister Gladys served as secretary to Ernest Orlando Lawrence, the inventor of the cyclotron. Lawrence had met Alvarez on a visit to Chicago and offered him a position at the University of California, Berkeley, which led to Alvarez's more-than-fifty-year career at this institution. Alvarez and his wife arrived in Berkeley in May, 1936, and for the next year at the Radiation Laboratory he remedied his deficiency in nuclear physics by studying everything he could find on the subject. He was particularly assiduous in mastering the publications of the German physicist Hans Bethe and in learning how to operate and repair the cyclotron. Compared to Chicago's researchers, Alvarez found Berkeley's more enthusiastic and collaborative. For example, he borrowed a quartz fiber electroscope built by Edwin McMillan (who later would win a Nobel Prize for discovering neptunium, the first transuranic element) and used it to discover how electrons in the lowest (or K-) level of radioactive elements could be captured by the nucleus. Alvarez's discovery of K-capture was published in 1938.

During the years before World War II, Alvarez made two other significant discoveries. Using the 60-inch cyclotron he produced tritium, a radioactive isotope of hydrogen that would later play an essential part in the research leading to the hydrogen bomb. He also used the cyclotron in his work with the Swiss American physicist Felix Bloch in studying beams of neutrons. They published an accurate value for the magnetic moment of the neutron in 1940 (this work also laid the foundation of Bloch's later research on nuclear magnetic resonance, for which he would receive the Nobel Prize).

In World War II, Alvarez worked at the Massachusetts Institute of Technology (MIT) Radiation Laboratory on radar systems and at Los Alamos, New Mexico, where he worked on the atomic bomb project. At the MIT Radiation Laboratory, he helped develop an improved radar system for aircraft that facilitated the detection and destruction of surfaced enemy submarines. He also collaborated with a group that researched, developed, and fielded the Ground-Controlled Approach (GCA) radar system to guide piloted aircraft to safe landings at night, in fog, and in poor weather conditions. In the postwar period, this GCA system played a pivotal role in civilian aircraft control. His contributions to pioneering research on the Microwave Early

The Theory of Dinosaur Extinction by Luis W. and Walter Alvarez

The history of paleontology has been populated with numerous theories of what caused the extinction of dinosaurs about 65 million years ago, from diseases and epidemics to climate change to extraterrestrial events. In the early 1980's, Luis W. Alvarez and his son, Walter, proposed a theory that the dinosaurs' demise was caused by an asteroid impact that generated massive amounts of dust and debris that blocked sunlight for months, destroying ecosystems on which dinosaurs had grown dependent. They also asserted that experimental evidence existed to support this theory. In particular, they predicted that a layer between the Cretaceous and Tertiary geological formations (the so-called "K-T boundary") should have large amounts of iridium (a chemical characteristic of asteroids). When this "iridium anomaly" was found in K-T boundaries all over the world, many scientists became convinced of the validity of the Alvarez theory. Furthermore, when the asteroid impact site was discovered near Chicxulub on the Yucatan Peninsula of Mexico, more scientists became converts to this theory. In 2010, an international group of scientists who had reviewed decades of research concluded that the Alvarez asteroid theory provided the most likely scenario for dinosaur extinction.

Warning System were helpful, but in the middle of the war, he left radar research to participate in the Manhattan Project, first at the University of Chicago with Enrico Fermi, the Italian American physicist who had led the effort to build the first nuclear reactor, and then at Los Alamos with J. Robert Oppenheimer, the "father of the atomic bomb." Alvarez participated in the design and development of the plutonium weapon, especially its sophisticated "implosion" technique for efficiently bringing subcritical masses of the fissionable isotope plutonium-239 together rapidly and uniformly. This was the bomb that was successfully tested at Alamogordo, New Mexico (code-named "Trinity") and used to devastating effect on Nagasaki, Japan. Alvarez was a trained eyewitness at the Trinity test and, in an observation plane, at Hiroshima, where the world's first wartime use of a nuclear weapon occurred.

After World War II, Alvarez returned to the University of California, Berkeley, as a full professor and concentrated his research on creating and developing new and improved particle accelerators. For example, working in a group under the leadership of Ernest Lawrence, he helped construct the world's largest proton accelerator. Alvarez also became fascinated with the bubble chamber, a device that allowed physicists to see the tracks of elementary particles. He championed the use of liquid hydrogen in bubble chambers and constructed one nearly 2 meters (7 feet) long. This device helped Alvarez and other physicists discover several new nuclear particles that were created from high-energy collisions in accelerators, such as short-lived mesons and baryon resonance particles. These discoveries led to Alvarez's induction into the Inventors Hall of Fame and to his 1968 Nobel Prize in Physics.

In his later career, Alvarez brought his expertise and inventive mind to a variety of projects, including an investigation of elementary particles and radiation in the universe's early history, a study of the ascertainable scientific facts involved in the assassination of President John F. Kennedy, an X-ray examination of the Egyptian pyramids, and, most famously, a new theory to explain dinosaur extinction. The recipient of many awards, Alvarez remained actively engaged in originating new ideas and novel inventions almost to the time of his death in 1988.

SIGNIFICANCE

Alvarez's career is distinctive not only for the number and variety of his original ideas and inventions within physics but also for his application of the scientific method to such diverse fields as the military, paleontology, cosmology, and history. His more than forty patents ranged from linear accelerators to X-ray spectroscopic systems to nitrogen detectors. Colleagues characterized him as the "consummate engineer" and a prolific founder of new research fields. His ideas and inventions also helped to transform civil and military aviation (he himself was a pilot). He had a deep belief in the necessity of both collaboration and competition for the progress of science and technology.

Robert J. Paradowski

FURTHER READING

Alvarez, Luis W. *Alvarez: Adventures of a Physicist.* New York: Basic Books, 1987. Intended for both fellow physicists and the general public, this scientific autobiography is revelatory of how physicists live their lives while discovering new ideas and inventions.

Buderi, Robert. *The Invention that Changed the World: How a Small Group of Radar Pioneers Won the Second World War and Launched a Technological Revolution.* New York: Simon & Schuster, 1996. Alvarez played an important part in the evolution of radar, and his contributions are analyzed in this ably-told story of radar's history. Illustrated with photographs. Extensive bibliography along with an index.

Heilbron, J. L., and Robert W. Seidel. *Lawrence and His Laboratory: A History of the Lawrence Berkeley Laboratory.* Vol. 1. Berkeley: University of California Press, 1989. Some of Alvarez's most important early work was done in Lawrence's laboratory, and it is insightfully covered in this book. Illustrated with photographs and diagrams. Extensive bibliography along with a detailed index.

"Luis W. Alvarez." In *The One Hundred Most Influential Scientists of All Time*, edited by Kara Rogers. New York: Brittanica, 2010. Brief biography and summary of Alvarez's career.

Trower, Peter, ed. *Discovering Alvarez: Selected Works of Luis W. Alvarez with Commentary by His Students and Colleagues.* Chicago: University of Chicago Press, 1987. The editor has collected several of Alvarez's most remarkable articles, which are accompanied by illuminating comments by his students, collaborators, colleagues, and friends.

See also: Walter Alvarez; Albert V. Baez; Manuel Cardona; José D. García; Vicente José Llamas; Ramon E. Lopez; Severo Ochoa.

Mabel Alvarez

American artist

In a career defined as much by its longevity as by its productivity, painter Alvarez pioneered the use of revolutionary avant-garde theories about the harmonic relationship between color and form to pursue a restless metaphysical inquiry into the spiritual dimension of the material world.

Latino heritage: Spanish
Born: November 28, 1891; Oahu, Hawaii
Died: March 13, 1985; Los Angeles, California
Area of achievement: Art

Early Life

Mabel Alvarez (MAY-buhl AHL-vah-rehs) was born to privilege. Her father, Luis Alvarez, was a respected Spanish-born California physician who had come to the Hawaiian Islands to assist in the groundbreaking research work at the world-renowned leper colony started in 1866 on the island of Molokai by Catholic missionary Saint Damien. In addition, he pursued lucrative real estate opportunities on the islands to accrue a significant fortune. The family returned to California in 1906, eventually settling in the Los Angeles area. By then Mabel, the youngest of their five children, had already evidenced remarkable proficiency in both drawing and painting. Her high school art teacher, James Edwin McBurney, mentored her to develop her understanding of design and color, line and shape. Early on, Alvarez thought of pursuing a career as a fashion illustrator, a conventional career for a woman with artistic gifts. Through McBurney, however, Alvarez received her first recognition as an artist: She helped McBurney design and execute a lavish Art Nouveau-styled mural depicting springtime in California for the 1915 Panama-California Exhibition in San Diego commemorating the opening of the Panama Canal. The mural, which was awarded a Gold Medal, was heavily allegorical, using springtime to suggest San Diego's new prominence as an international port.

Alvarez was intrigued by the bold theories and vivid canvasses of the new movement dubbed California Impressionism, founded by Los Angeles painter William Vincent Cahill. His internationally respected School for Illustrating and Painting was quickly becoming the epicenter for new artists, including Alvarez, who was engaged by the audacious bright colors and revolutionary rough brushwork of the new school and its interest in capturing the natural landscapes of Southern California. She quickly emerged as one of the school's most promising artists.

Life's Work

However, Alvarez became restless. Her free-spirited intellectual curiosity led her in the late 1910's to become involved in a neospiritual retreat founded outside Hollywood by Will Levington Comfort, who, before pioneering a philosophical movement that stressed interior exploration in the pursuit of transcendent harmony, had made his name as the author of pulp Westerns. Alvarez relished the mystical elements of the colony experience and its sense that the physical world was a manifestation of spiritual emanations. Her paintings during this period reflected her embrace of vivid colors and playful technique, as clear lines and set forms began to blur into swirls of hue and shade.

However, it was her 1919 encounter with avant-garde painter and art theorist Stanton Macdonald-Wright that set Alvarez into a bold new direction. For the next decade, under Macdonald-Wright's tutelage, Alvarez produced some of her most accomplished and revolutionary canvasses. Macdonald-Wright, and later his protégé Morgan Russell, had begun to push art away from the long tradition of representation by suggesting that colors maintain the same kind of integrity and interpretative value as notes in the musical scale, and that painters, like composers, could create harmonic canvasses, or composition, by manipulating colors with and even against each other in subtle and complex arrangements rather than by imitating recognizable objects; such paintings would in theory by "heard" by the perceptive, receptive visual imagination. Painting became more about feeling than about composition and aesthetic design. The movement, which came to be known as synchromism, intrigued Alvarez, who matriculated in Macdonald-Wright's studio in 1924. His uncompromising vision of the radical possibility of art appealed to her mystical investigations into reality.

During the next decade, her paintings renegotiated real-world representation and became increasingly dreamlike, even allegorical, drawing on archetypal figures, such as the Child or Innocence or the Earth Spirit, using such abstract concepts to experiment with visual harmony. In these paintings,

Themes and Motifs in Alvarez's Paintings

It is, of course, difficult to define a painter who so deliberately defied definition, who set out early in her career to embrace change and to explore new aesthetic ideas, whose intellectual curiosity pushed her own perceptions of artistic expression into progressively broader and more experimental forms. However, if there is a central theme that threads seven decades of Mabel Alvarez's work it undoubtedly begins with her early fascination with the theosophy of Will Levington Comfort. Although the tenets of Comfort's philosophy can seem arcane and obscure to contemporary audiences, what is key is his perception that each mind must probe with rigorous intellectual audacity the spiritual dimension of the physical universe; for Comfort, the material universe is a richly layered symbol of cosmic energy and harmony that unites all humanity.

For more than seventy years, Alvarez pursued this sort of metaphysical harmony, seeing in color and shape the implication of a universal spiritual resonance. Despite her career-long fidelity to capturing elements of the world around her—portraits, still lives, landscapes, seascapes, and even her symbol-rich allegorical studies—she pushed the reach of simple representational realism by suffusing her subjects with ethereal, at time eerily haunting, light and a feeling of spirituality, an effect achieved through the application of hard, deliberate brush strokes, a process she first embraced in her initial discovery of the Impressionists.

If a career of such longevity and productivity can be said to have a signature work, it would be Alvarez's 1925 masterpiece *In the Garden*, which juxtaposes the delicate ivory-hued face of a beautiful young girl, itself a study in Oriental calm, against a tangled florescent background bursting in barely restrained swirls of vivid blues, oranges, and reds. This bold yoking of rich oppositions—stasis and kinesis, white and colors, sterility and fecundity, distance and immediacy, reality and metaphor—embodies Alvarez's broad fascination with the yin-yang complexity of the material world.

vivid arrangements of broad, flat applications of colors were expressive of potent emotion, including green as newness, red as passion, and blue as nature's power. Alvarez's work became prominent in the Los Angeles area, where she emerged as one of the most accomplished and prolific of the regional avant-garde painters known collectively as the Group of Eight.

Alvarez, however, never entirely abandoned her fascination with the objects in the real world even as the more extreme of her colleagues did. By the 1930's, Alvarez had returned to her interest in the human form and the natural world, with her investigation inevitably informed by her long study of the emotional impact of color and the harmony of shapes. Although Alvarez was never a social activist, despite a decade in which the work of most artists of her generation became increasingly political, with the advent of World War II she virtually set aside her career to assist in a variety of home front volunteer organizations, perhaps most notably giving painting lessons as therapy to the wounded soldiers in Los Angeles area veterans hospitals.

After the war, when she was approaching sixty, Alvarez with typical vigor moved in a new direction. She returned her attention to recording the vivid images of the real world, specifically the primitive cultures she observed during extensive travels in the Caribbean Basin and Mexico. Her paintings from the 1950's captured lively scenes of the tropics—churches decorated for the high holy days, town squares alive at festival time, cafés crowded with locals, fruit stands animated by vendors—in a bold style of uncharacteristically layered colors applied with lush sweeping strokes. These canvasses are among the most vivid—and personal—of Alvarez's long career.

Although interest in her work flagged during the heyday of trendy postmodern experimentation in the 1960's and 1970's, Alvarez continued to paint well into her eighties, her canvasses regularly showcased in regional shows. In the early 1980's, she became increasingly dependent on assisted care and died in a convalescent home in Los Angeles in 1985. She was ninety-three years old.

SIGNIFICANCE

Across nearly seven decades of rich productivity, the only constant in the work of Mabel Alvarez was her restless dedication to the principle of artistic change and her remarkable evolution, specifically, her achievement in three of the dominant genres that defined twentieth century art: impressionism, modernism, and realism. Given the widely differing artistic visions of each of the genres, few artists of her generation managed to work successfully in each. That she achieved international reputation in each genre testifies both to her intellectual vigor and to her evolution as an artist.

Apart from such an academic distinction is Alvarez's work itself, a stunning legacy of hundreds of canvasses that, whatever their subject, delight the eye by invigorating her representations of the real world, from bowls of fruit to the human form itself, with her transcendent mysticism and her exuberant, intuitive sense of color and the play of forms.

Joseph Dewey

Further Reading

Gerdts, William H., and Will South. *California Impressionism.* New York: Abbeville, 1998. Handsomely illustrated period study of the genre most associated with Alvarez. Explains the context of European Impressionism and its adaptation to the California school.

South, Will. *Color, Myth, and Music: Stanton Macdonald-Wright and Synchromism.* Raleigh: North Carolina Museum of Art, 2001. Seminal study by an authoritative figure in the genre, with helpful explication of Macdonald-Wright's complex religious vision. Includes a generous account of Alvarez.

Trenton, Patricia. *Independent Spirits: Women Painters of the American West, 1890-1945.* Berkeley: University of California Press, 1995. Still considered the definitive study of the generation of women painters that includes Alvarez. Sees the influence of the cultural diversity and rugged geography of the West as critical in defining the era.

See also: José Aceves; Francisco Oller.

Ralph Alvarez

Cuban-born business executive

Alvarez is best known for his astute leadership of some of the world's best-known companies. His illustrious career—which includes stints as president and chief operating officer of McDonald's Corporation, president of Burger King Canada, corporate and divisional vice president of Wendy's, and directorships of companies including Eli Lilly and Lowe's—has made him one of the highest-ranking and most influential Hispanic executives of his era.

Latino heritage: Cuban

Born: 1955; Havana, Cuba

Also known as: Raul Alvarez

Area of achievement: Business

Early Life

Ralph Alvarez (AHL-vah-rehz) was born in Havana, Cuba, in 1955 to parents who were socially and financially well-positioned in their native land. His mother was a marine biologist and his father was the president of Cuban Airways. However, when Fidel Castro took over Cuba in 1959, Alvarez's family decided to immigrate to the United States, where his mother accepted a position as professor at the University of Miami. His father was incapacitated by a severe stroke, rendering him unable to work. Alvarez was reluctant to take on debt and put a financial burden on his family, so he chose to get his undergraduate education at the University of Miami, where he received free tuition because of his mother's position.

Alvarez's motivation, drive, and commitment to hard work were evident early in his life. He graduated cum laude from University of Miami's School of

Ralph Alvarez. (AP Photo)

Business Administration and nurtured his association with the school, which eventually culminated in his appointment as member of the President's Council and the International Advisory Board. After graduation, he used his first job at a highly regarded accounting firm as a stepping-stone into the food services industry.

LIFE'S WORK

Alvarez's first position after college was with Deloitte & Touche, a prestigious accounting firm. His exemplary work for Burger King, a company client, provided Alvarez an opportunity for a career in the fast-food industry, which was to become his legacy. The global food services retailer appointed Alvarez as managing director of operations in Spain. This appointment was helped in no small part by Alvarez's fluency in Spanish. He worked for Burger King from 1977 to 1989, during which time he went on to serve in a leadership capacity in the company's operations in the United Kingdom and Canada. He served as president of the Canadian operations from 1986 to 1988. In 1990, Alvarez left Burger King to join Wendy's, another well-known food services entity. At Wendy's, he primarily managed acquisitions, serving as division vice president for Florida and then as corporate vice president. In both of these jobs, he continued to develop his industry skill set while building a solid reputation among his peers and subordinates.

In 1994, Alvarez left Wendy's to join McDonald's, one of the world's most recognizable food service retailers. He started as vice president for the Sacramento region before being appointed regional director for Chipotle Mexican Grill, an affiliate chain. In 2000, Alvarez was appointed president of McDonald's Mexico, and the next year, he was appointed president of the company's U.S. Central division. After serving in this position for two years, he was appointed chief operations officer of McDonald's United States in 2003, and by 2004, he had been named president of the business unit.

After a year, Alvarez was promoted to president of the North American region. Finally, in 2006, he ascended to the coveted job of president and chief operations officer of McDonald's, responsible for global operations. He was seen as a potential successor to the company's chief executive officer. At the time, McDonald's had more than thirty-one thousand restaurants in more than one hundred countries. In 2008, he was appointed to the board of McDonald's. During his tenure at McDonald's, Alvarez was a firm supporter of the company's initiatives to support children and children's charities.

Alvarez also has served on the boards of directors of other companies, including KeyCorp, Eli Lilly and Company, and Lowe's. He retired from McDonald's in December, 2009, citing chronic knee pain. He and his wife have two children.

SIGNIFICANCE

Alvarez's rise from young immigrant to high-ranking business leader at major global corporations made him one of the most esteemed Hispanic entrepreneurs of his generation. A role model to the Latino community as well as to immigrants in general, Alvarez has shown that success is attainable through hard work and determination.

Jeff Naidoo

FURTHER READING

Bingham, Tony and Galagan, Pat. "Training: They're Lovin' It." *T+D*, 60, 11. (November, 2006): 28-32. Highlights Alvarez's interest in the training and development of employees as a way to add value to any organization.

Cendón, Sara. "In Good Company." *Hispanic* 21, no. 1 (February, 2008): 31-41. Describes Alvarez's commitment to children and children's charities as a McDonald's executive.

Galagan, Pat. "Old School Gets New Role." *T+D* 60, no. 11. (November, 2006): 36-39. This article speaks to Alvarez's commitment to training and empowering new leaders.

Phillips, Bruce. "The Most Important Hispanics in Technology and Business." *Hispanic Engineer and Information Technology* 20, no. 1 (June/July, 2005): 20-42. The article, which features Alvarez, recognizes Hispanic executives, managers, and researchers in industry, government, and academia.

See also: Linda Alvarado; Laura Contreras-Rowe; Arte Moreno; Samuel A. Ramirez, Sr.; Nina Tassler.

Walter Alvarez

American geologist and writer

Best known for his discovery, along with his father, Luis W. Alvarez, of an iridium-enriched clay layer marking the geological boundary between the Cretaceous and Tertiary periods. Walter and Luis W. Alvarez hypothesized that the layer may have been created by a major asteroid impact, causing the extinction of the dinosaurs.

Latino heritage: Spanish

Born: October 3, 1940; Berkeley, California

Areas of achievement: Science and technology; education

Early Life

Walter Alvarez (AHL-vah-rehz) was born in Berkeley, California, to Nobel Prize-winning physicist Luis W. Alvarez and his first wife, Geraldine Smithwick. Alvarez's paternal great-grandfather, Luis Fernández Álvarez, was a Spanish-born doctor who practiced in California and Hawaii. Alvarez had one full sibling, Jean, and two half-siblings by his father's second wife.

In 1962, Alvarez earned a B.A. in geology from Carleton College in Northfield, Minnesota, followed by a Ph.D. from Princeton University in 1967. His thesis focused on the geology of the Simarua and Carpintero areas in the Guajira Peninsula, Colombia.

Following completion of his dissertation, Alvarez worked as a petroleum geologist in the Netherlands from 1967 to 1968 and Libya from 1968 to 1970. After developing an interest in archaeological geology, Alvarez moved to Italy, where he held a postdoctoral fellowship from 1970 to 1971 and studied how Roman volcanic rocks influenced ancient settlement patterns.

Alvarez's academic career was established during his time as a research associate at the Lamont-Doherty Geological Observatory of Columbia University. At the time, the theory of plate tectonics was still new, and fundamental changes to geologists' understanding of the Earth were taking place. Alvarez studied tectonic paleomagnetism, demonstrating the movement of very small plates in the Earth's oceanic crust. He also was involved with research into Earth's paleomagnetic reversals, which led to a new technique for dating sequences of sedimentary rocks.

Life's Work

The majority of Alvarez's academic career took place at the University of California, Berkeley, where he became an assistant professor in the Department of Geology and Geophysics (now the Department of Earth and Planetary Sciences) in 1977.

At UC Berkeley, Alvarez began the work for which he became famous. While studying Italian limestones around the boundary between the Cretaceous and Tertiary periods of geologic time (commonly called the K-T boundary), Alvarez identified a clay-rich layer about 65 million years old, contemporaneous with the exinction of the dinosaurs. He gave a sample of the clay layer and surrounding limestone to his father, Luis W. Alvarez, who had retired from Berkeley in 1978. Luis and nuclear chemists Frank Asaro and Helen Michel found the clay layer to be extremely rich in iridium, while the limestones were not.

The Alvarezes suspected that the clay layer might be extraterrestrial in nature. They considered a number of explanations but finally agreed with astronomer Chris McKee that a 10-kilometer asteroid striking the Earth could have produced the layer, with catastrophic environmental impacts. The Alvarezes attributed the K-T mass extinction, in which all land animals heavier than fifty pounds disappeared from the fossil record, to the effects of this asteroid.

In 1980, the Alvarezes, Asaro, and Michel published a paper about their findings, putting forth the impact hypothesis for extinction. The paper was met with strong debate in the scientific community, but over the following decades, Walter Alvarez and others published numerous papers about the K-T boundary and iridium-enriched layers. Evidence of the iridium-enriched K-T layer showed up in more and more locations around the world, and Alvarez also found evidence of iridium-enriched layers at some other extinction boundaries, such as the terminal Eocene boundary. In 1990, geologists looking for an impact site that would be a candidate for the K-T extinction confirmed the presence of a 10-kilometer-wide impact crater under the Yucatan, Chicxulub, greatly strengthening the evidence for Walter and Luis W. Alvarez's hypothesis.

During this time, Alvarez maintained a range of research interests—particularly involving the geology of Italy—taught at UC Berkeley, and advised doctoral students. He published two books: *T. Rex and the Crater of Doom* in 1997 and *The Mountains of Saint Francis: The Geologic Events that Shaped Our Earth* in 2009.

Through the 2000's, Alvarez was a professor of earth and planetary sciences at Berkeley, where he lived with his wife, Milly. Alvarez's research interests included the development of "Big History," a synthesis of Earth history, the history of life, and human history. He received numerous awards and honors, including the Geological Society of America's Penrose Medal in 2002.

Significance

The impact theory of mass extinction originated by Walter and Luis W. Alvarez changed the field of paleontology dramatically. While it was initially met with skepticism, most geologists today accept that extraterrestrial impact played a role in at least some mass extinction events. Today, research focuses primarily on the Permian-Triassic extinction event 251.4 million years ago, in which 96 percent of marine species and 70 percent of terrestrial species are estimated to have become extinct. Alvarez's extensive and groundbreaking scientific work also contributed greatly to the field of geology. His popular science books and work on big-picture, integrated science and history also contributed to public understanding of science.

Melissa A. Barton

Further Reading

Alvarez, Walter. *The Mountains of Saint Francis: The Geologic Events that Shaped Our Earth.* New York: W. W. Norton, 2009. A look into some of the geological processes that shape Earth's history, using examples from Italy.

_______. *T. Rex and the Crater of Doom.* Princeton, N.J.: Princeton University Press, 1997. An informal, personal account by Alvarez of how he and his father developed their impact-extinction theory.

Alvarez, Walter, P. Claeys, and A. Montanari. "Time-Scale Construction and Periodizing in Big History: From the Eocene-Oligocene Boundary to All of the Past." *Geological Society of America Special Paper* 452 (2009): 1-15. A paper outlining some of the key concepts of "Big History."

Powell, James Lawrence. *Night Comes to the Cretaceous: Comets, Craters, Controversy, and the Last Days of the Dinosaurs.* San Diego, Calif.: Harvest Books, 1998. A third-party version of the story of the impact extinction theory and the controversy it caused, written at a more advanced reading level than *T. Rex and the Crater of Doom.*

See also: Luis W. Alvarez; Franklin Ramón Chang-Díaz; Margarita Colmenares; Arturo Gómez-Pompa; Michael A. Mares; Mario Molina; Adriana C. Ocampo.

Ralph Amado

American physicist

Amado is an outstanding researcher in the complex field of theoretical nuclear physics. He has completed a number of challenging projects and was instrumental is providing a foundation to allow the University of Pennsylvania to enhance its already strong reputation of a leading research institution.

Latino heritage: Spanish

Born: November 23, 1932; Los Angeles, California

Also known as: Ralph David Amado

Areas of achievement: Science and technology; education

Early Life

Ralph David Amado (ah-MAH-doh) was born in Los Angeles to an attorney father and a housewife mother. He did not consider himself Latino. His ancestors lived in Spain until 1492, when all Jews in the country were forced to convert to Christianity or leave. They moved to Turkey, where they stayed until early in the twentieth century, then moved to the United States and finally settled in Los Angeles. Amado's parents spoke Judeo-Spanish, based on fifteenth century Spanish. Amado has served on the board of the Maurice Amado Foundation, which provides grants to keep the Sephardic heritage alive.

Amado attended public school in Los Angeles. He earned his bachelor of science degree in physics from Stanford University in 1954 and his doctorate in theoretical nuclear physics from Oxford University in 1957 as a Rhodes scholar. Amado attended the University of Pennsylvania (Penn) as a postdoctoral student to work with Professor Keith Bruecker. When

Bruecker left Penn to help found the University of California at San Diego, he invited Amado to join him as an assistant professor. Penn also offered Amado an assistant professorship, which he accepted partly because of his relationship with a young woman from New York, Carol Stein. They were married in 1961. Amado and Carol had two boys, Richard and David. Carol was a talented violinist and had a successful career in chamber music in the Philadelphia area. She died in 1997 of leukemia.

Life's Work

Amado progressed through the academic ranks to become a full professor in 1965. His work in theoretical nuclear physics involved scattering theory, and particle physics. Nuclear physicists work to understand how the nucleus of a cell is held together, how the forces within the nucleus affect particles outside the nucleus, what particles are involved, and how they act. The field today relies heavily on computers, but even with the limited computer abilities at the time, Amado's early work was successful. Amado was the first physicist to produce a correct theory for the neutron-deuteron scattering problem.

Particle physics is a very difficult field. Particles sometimes can be detected by the trail they leave in a cloud chamber or other special atmosphere. Some particles leave no trail and can only be inferred by the trails of other particles. Amado was able to produce quality research in the field of theoretical nuclear physics for nearly forty years. He continued publishing articles in top journals when he became vice provost of research. He was a member of the Institute for Advanced Study at Princeton and a visiting staff member at Los Alamos Scientific Laboratory and the Swiss Institute for Nuclear Physics.

In addition to teaching classes and mentoring graduate students, Amado was director of the general honors program and the university scholars program, as well as being faculty adviser to the Arts House. He was chair of the Physics Department from 1983 to 1987 and again in 1994. He also was associate dean and chair of the faculty senate. He served on several national committees, including for the National Science Foundation. He began serving as vice provost for research in 1995 and retired in 2001. He is married to Anne Rodig.

Significance

Amado has made significant advances in the study of theoretical nuclear physics. These advances have enabled other physicists to further the understanding of the field. He also has supplied leadership for the outstanding research accomplished at Penn while he was vice provost for research. He developed infrastructure for research in all areas of the university, and during his tenure as vice provost, the research capability and reputation of Penn was greatly enhanced. His work attracted donations that provided stability necessary for future development.

C. Alton Hassell

Further Reading

"Ralph D. Amado." University of Pennsylvania. http://www.physics.upenn.edu/people/r.d.amado.html. Provides an overview of Amado's research and selected publications.

Veltman, Martinus, *Facts and Mysteries in Elementary Particle Physics.* River Edge, N.J.: World Scientific, 2003. Offers a basic overview of particles and particle physics.

"Vice Provost for Research: Dr. Amado." *University of Pennsylvania Almanac* 43 no. 1 (July 16, 1996). Offers information on Amado's career at Penn.

See also: Luis W. Alvarez; Albert V. Baez; Manuel Cardona; Vicente José Llamas; Ramon E. Lopez.

Rudolfo Anaya

American writer and educator

An acclaimed writer, Anaya is a leading figure in U.S. Latino literature who is admired for his innovative style and his ability to write stories capturing the essence of New Mexico and the Latino experience. His best-known work is his novel Bless Me, Ultima *(1972).*

Latino heritage: Mexican

Born: October 30, 1937; Pastura, New Mexico

Also known as: Rudolfo Alfonso Anaya; Rudolfo A. Anaya

Area of achievement: Literature

Early Life

Rudolfo Alfonso Anaya (roo-DOLF-oh al-FON-soh ah-NAH-yah) was born October 30, 1937, in Pastura, New Mexico. He was the fifth of seven children born to Martin and Rafaelita Anaya. His father, Martin, was a cattle herder and horseman who was employed on the ranches around Pastura. His mother, Rafaelita, came from a family of poor hardworking farmers, who lived traditional lives tied to their land. Soon after he was born, the family moved to Santa Rosa, New Mexico, which was the social hub of the surrounding communities at that time.

Anaya was raised in the Roman Catholic faith and spent his early childhood roaming the countryside, swimming and fishing in the Pecos River and learning catechism. His family spoke Spanish, and Anaya did not learn English until he went to school. His mother encouraged his education and motivated him to do well in his studies. The frequent visits from extended family members, and the oral tradition of recounting family tales and anecdotes, formed Anaya's natural instinct for storytelling.

The time he spent as a child in Santa Rosa had a significant influence on his writing, and many of his novels feature references and images from his early experiences in New Mexico. Folklore and superstitions are blended together in his later fiction to create rich stories of culture, tradition, and history.

In 1952, Anaya's family moved to Albuquerque, New Mexico. The city brought new challenges for Anaya, and he was introduced to ethnic diversity, racism, and prejudice against Hispanics, something he had never experienced. Despite the culture shock of moving from a small rural town and a close-knit community to a large urban environment, Anya continued to thrive in his studies.

One of the turning points in his life occurred when he was sixteen years old. Anaya was swimming with his friends in a shallow irrigation ditch. He dove into the water and hit the bottom, resulting in a severe spinal injury. Anaya was instantly paralyzed and barely escaped drowning. He spent the entire summer in the hospital, but he was determined to recover from his injuries. Although the recovery was slow, this experience fueled Anaya's love of life and made him appreciate the power of adversity.

Anaya graduated from Albuquerque High School in 1956 and went to business school to become an accountant. This career choice, however, did not inspire him, and he later enrolled in the University of New Mexico. Although he found university life to be isolating and culturally challenging, Anaya channeled his angst and uncertainty through writing. He valued the material in his freshman English class, enthralled by literature and poetry. However, the literature he was exposed to in his class was devoid of any meaningful cultural connection or relevance to his Latino experiences. Around this time, Anaya discovered El Movimiento, the Chicano civil rights movement of the 1960's, which spurred his interest in writing books that would convey the importance of his cultural heritage.

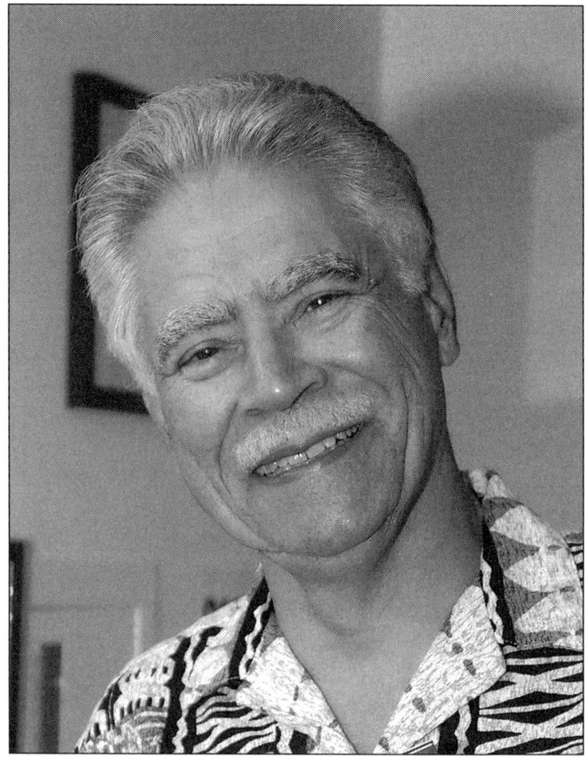

Rudolfo Anaya. (Getty Images)

Anaya graduated with a bachelor's degree in English from the University of New Mexico in 1963. He took a job in the Albuquerque public schools as a junior high and high school teacher, still finding time every day to work on his writing. He struggled to tie his own voice and experiences into his writing, to make his words fit his understanding of the world. He worked to develop his own unique Mexican American style that would convey his upbringing, beliefs, and cultural heritage. In 1966, he married Patricia Lawless, who shared her husband's love of books and storytelling and encouraged his writing.

In 1968, Anaya earned a master's degree in English from the University of New Mexico, and he took a job as the director of counseling at the university in 1971. In 1974, after the success of his first novel, he was offered a position as an associate professor at this university, and he taught in the English department for the next nineteen years.

Life's Work

After being visited by a vision of an old woman dressed in black, he was inspired to begin writing *Bless Me, Ultima* (1972). This novel tells the story of a little boy growing up in rural New Mexico. He is befriended by a healer, who comes to stay with his family. The story juxtaposes Anaya's Catholic upbringing and the mystic folklore of the Mexican culture.

Anaya had difficulty finding a publisher for the novel because of its incorporation of both English and Spanish words. Finally, seven years after starting the book, it was published by Quinto Sol Publications, a small press in Berkeley, California, in 1972. Critics responded enthusiastically to the work and it received the Premio Quinto Sol Award for the best Chicano novel of 1972. *Heart of Aztlan*, his second novel, was published in 1976, and his third novel, *Tortuga,* in 1979. By the time he retired from the University of New Mexico as a full professor in 1993, Anaya had published numerous novels, short stories, poems, and children's books.

Following his retirement from teaching, Anaya spent his time writing and traveling. He traveled extensively throughout South and Central America and continued to write books infused with New Mexican and Latino culture and identity.

Significance

Anaya has received several literary awards during the course of his career, including the Before Columbus Book Award, (1980), the New Mexico Governor's Award for Excellence and Achievement in Literature (1980), the Award for Achievement in Chicano Literature (1983), the Mexican Medal of Friendship from the Mexican Consulate (1986), the PEN-West Fiction Award (1992), and the National Medal of Arts (2002). An advocate of multiculturalism and bilingual authors, Anaya has translated, edited, and contributed to various works of Latino literature. Because of his literary acclaim, he is often referred to as the "father of Chicano literature."

Alison S. Burke

Anaya's New Mexico Trilogy

Bless Me, Ultima (1972), *Heart of Aztlan* (1976), and *Totruga* (1979), three novels by Rudolfo Anaya, are loosely tied around the Chicano experience over several generations. *Bless Me, Ultima* is a story of rural folkways, myths, and ethnic culture. It is a coming-of-age story about a young boy who learns about life, religion, superstitions, and his own destiny. Since its publication in 1972, the novel has become an essential part of high school English and university Chicano literature curricula.

Heart of Aztlan is a political story of a displaced Hispanic family that is forced to move from a rural community to the barrios of Albuquerque, New Mexico. In the novel *Tortuga,* the protagonist is a young boy who is partially paralyzed and unable to move because he is in a body cast. The story takes place in a hospital for crippled children, and while Tortuga contemplates suicide, he is befriended by a terminally ill boy, who helps Tortuga appreciate his life. This novel is both a spiritual and medical tale of suffering and recovery. Together, these novels form a trilogy focusing on Mexican-American life in the years after World War II.

Further Reading

Anaya, Rudolfo. *Bless Me, Ultima*. Berkeley, Calif.: Tonatiuh-Quinto Sol, 1972. Anaya's first novel is a coming-of-age story about a young boy in New Mexico in the 1940's. The book deals with theconflicts of good and evil and of Hispanic culture versus American culture. Many of the themes are influenced by Anaya's own childhood.

Authors and Artists for Young Adults. Detroit: Gale Research, 1992-1999. A literary source for teens, where they can learn interesting and entertaining facts about the writers, artists, film directors, and other creative individuals that they find most fascinating.

Fernandez Olmoz, Margarite. *Rudolfo A. Anaya: A Critical Companion*. Westport, Conn.: Greenwood Press, 1999. A guide to Anaya's literature. Each chapter analyzes a different work and offers explanations for understanding the symbolism and complexities that are present in his writing.

Kanoza, Theresa M. " The Golden Carp and Moby Dick: Rudolfo Anaya's Multi-Culturalism." *MELUS* 24 (February, 1999). Examines the themes, characters, and influences present in *Bless Me, Ultima.*

Klein, Dianne. "Coming of Age in Novels by Rudolfo Anaya and Sandra Cisneros." *English Journal* 81, no. 5 (September, 1992): 21-26. Examines the commonalities in the coming-of-age novels written by Anaya and Cisneros and the importance of these ethnic works in literature classes.

Lamadrid, Enrique R. "Myth as the Cognitive Process of Popular Culture in Rudolfo Anaya's *Bless Me, Ultima*: The Dialectics of Knowledge." *Hispania* 68, no. 3 (September, 1985): 496-501. Explores the central themes and cultural expressions within the book.

See also: Oscar Zeta Acosta; Alma Flor Ada; Lourdes Casal; Sandra Cisneros; Arturo Islas; Mary Helen Ponce; Estela Portillo Trambley; John Rechy; Tomás Rivera; Luis Rafael Sánchez.

TONEY ANAYA

American politician

One of the first Latino politicians to win statewide office in New Mexico, Anaya was a notably progressive governor in the mid-1980's. In 2009-2010, he coordinated New Mexico's distribution of federal stimulus money.

Latino heritage: Mexican

Born: April 29, 1941; Moriarty, New Mexico

Area of achievement: Government and politics

EARLY LIFE

Toney Anaya (TOH-nee ah-NAH-yah) was born into a poor family in Moriarty, New Mexico, and grew up in an adobe house with no plumbing, no electricity, and a dirt floor. He attended New Mexico Highlands University in Las Vegas before transferring to Georgetown University in Washington, D.C., where he earned a bachelor's degree while working for Democratic New Mexico senator Dennis Chavez. Anaya remained in Washington and received a law degree in 1967 from American University. During law school, he worked for another New Mexico senator, Joseph M. Montoya. Like many politicians of his generation (such as future president Bill Clinton), Anaya chose to return to his home state, forsaking a high legal salary to pursue greater political opportunity. In 1974, Anaya was elected state attorney general.

LIFE'S WORK

Anaya's positions throughout his career have been reformist in tenor, liberal in political stance, optimistic about the capacity of government to change lives, and not averse to using his personal charm as an asset in political life. Anaya's early career also coincided with the rise of Latino cultural awareness in New Mexico and the assertion of Chicano pride in cultural and political spheres. Although Anaya was far less radical than the figures associated with such activist Latino movements as La Raza or Aztlán, he recognized the opportunities for constructive change in the wake of the Civil Rights movement.

Anaya's service as attorney general brought him wide visibility and cemented two of his most enduring passions: his advocacy of immigrants' rights and his adamant stand against capital punishment. In 1978, Anaya ran for U.S. Senate against Republican incumbent Pete Domenici, who was then completing his first term. Anaya lost (and Domenici became a perennial New Mexico political powerhouse) but remained in the public eye. At that time, New Mexico governors were barred from

Toney Anaya. (AP Photo)

serving consecutive terms in office; the frequent turnover in the state's top office created an opening for Anaya to run in 1982. Two years earlier, in February, 1980, a riot in the maximum-security New Mexico State Prison had inflamed concerns about racial discrimination and social divides in the state. This worry, in addition to the early 1980's recession that wounded the popularity of Republican president Ronald Reagan, led to an easy victory for Anaya in November, 1982.

Many of the Democratic governors elected in the 1980's were, like Clinton, fiscal moderates who adapted their policies to the era's dominant conservative orientation. Anaya, however, challenged this consensus, calling for liberal immigration laws and challenging the death penalty, which went against both his Roman Catholic faith and his personal convictions. Anaya also tried to rally Latinos nationwide for liberal causes. Often, though, his efforts were polarizing and had little national impact.

Anaya did not fade into the political background after the end of his gubernatorial term; indeed, he had one of the longest and most productive careers of any ex-governor in New Mexico history. In 2009, Governor Bill Richardson appointed Anaya to distribute money allotted to the state from the federal stimulus package. These funds, furnished to each state by Congress as requested by President Barack Obama, were intended to help revive a national economy crippled by recession. Although Anaya was praised for the transparency and low overhead with which his office was run, the process of doling out the funds was slow and drew criticism from opponents for lacking real economic impact. The election of Republican Susana Martinez as governor of New Mexico in November, 2010, spelled an end to Anaya's role in distributing the funds. However, Martinez's ascent also was a reminder of Anaya's role in making a Latino governor of New Mexico a routine event, whatever the candidate's party affiliation

Significance

New Mexico's large Latino population has made the election of Latino polical figures a more common occurrence there than even in neighboring Arizona. Anaya was not the first Latino governor of his state; however, his impact was considerable because of the unapologetic liberalism of his policies, which sharply contrasted with the moderation generally espoused by Democrats of his era. Although his views were controversial at times, Anaya was a political figure who had the courage of his convictions.

Nicholas Birns

Further Reading

Morris, Roger. *The Devil's Butcher Shop: The New Mexico Prison Uprising*. Albuquerque: University of New Mexico Press, 1992. Portrays Anaya as a political opportunist who benefited from the riot.

Sarat, Austin. *Mercy on Trial: What It Means to Stop an Execution*. Princeton, N.J.: Princeton University Press, 2006. One of America's leading legal thinkers considers Anaya's role in the anti-capital-punishment movement.

Szasz, Ferenc Morton. *Larger than Life: New Mexico in the Twentieth Century*. Albuquerque: University of New Mexico Press, 2006. Puts Anaya's career in the context of the changes that have occurred in New Mexico during his lifetime.

Vigil, Maurilio. *Hispanics in American Politics: The Search for Political Power*. Lanham, Md.: University Press of America, 1987. Chronicles Anaya's ambitions and disappointments as he sought an influential role in 1980's national politics.

See also: Jerry Apodaca; Dennis Chavez; Joseph M. Montoya; Bill Richardson.

Joaquín Andújar

Dominican-born baseball player

During his twelve seasons in the major leagues, Andújar enjoyed several outstanding years as a pitcher for the Houston Astros, the St. Louis Cardinals, and the Oakland Athletics. He helped the Cardinals win two National League championships and the 1982 World Series.

Latino heritage: Dominican

Born: December 21, 1952; San Pedro de Macoris, Dominican Republic

Also known as: One Tough Dominican

Area of achievement: Baseball

Early Life

Joaquín Andújar (wah-KEEN ahn-DEW-har) was born on December 21, 1952, in San Pedro de Macoris, Dominican Republic. He was an only child, and his parents were so poor that they turned to his paternal grandparents to raise him. Despite its small population, San Pedro de Macoris has produced an inordinately large number of baseball players. Andújar's first love was basketball, but at age ten he began playing baseball. Like many Dominican youngsters, he played baseball in the streets with a rag ball and a broomstick. His big break came in 1969 when he signed a contract with the Cincinnati Reds. He played for the local team Estrellas under manager Hubert "Hub" Kittle. His pitching talent was obvious, but he lacked control and had a quick temper. He languished in the minor leagues until he was traded to the Houston Astros organization on the advice of Kittle, who was then Houston's pitching coach.

Life's Work

Andújar was called up to the major leagues by the Astros in 1976, and compiled a pitching record of 9 wins and 10 losses. The 1977 season began well for Andújar, who was selected to the National League All-Star team for his 10 early wins. He faltered in the second half of the season, however, winning only one more game. His inconsistent pitching continued into 1978, leading to his demotion to a relief role for part of the season. He rebounded in 1979 with a terrific first half, recording 11 wins and only 5 losses and another All-Star team selection. Once again, though, his performance slipped in the remainder of the season, and he finished with a12-12 record.

Andújar quickly gained a reputation for a volatile temper and eccentric personality. He ran the bases with his jacket on his left arm (he pitched righthanded) and showered with his uniform on. He also took a liking to cowboy culture and the television Western series *Bonanza*. He began wearing cowboy hats and listening to country music. This affinity led Andújar to adopt a controversial pitching trademark: After striking our a batter, he would point his index finger and blow on it, as though blowing away the smoke after firing a gun.

After another uneven year with the Astros, Andújar was traded to the St. Louis Cardinals in June, 1981. Manager Whitey Herzog recognized Andújar's potential and was willing to take a chance on the mercurial pitcher. Andújar was reunited with his former mentor, Kittle, who was Herzog's pitching coach, and with their support, Andújar regained his confidence. He became the ace of the pitching staff in 1982, winning 15 games

Joaquín Andújar. (AP Photo)

and helping the team win the National League championship. His earned run average (ERA) of 2.47 was the second lowest among National League pitchers. Andújar won game three in the National League Championship Series against the Atlanta Braves, and also won games three and seven in the World Series, as St. Louis defeated the Milwaukee Brewers. His ERA in the two World Series games was a remarkable 1.35.

Andújar rebounded from a poor 1983 season with 20 wins and a 3.34 ERA, earning him the *Sporting News* Comeback Player of the Year award for 1984. The 1985 regular season was again spectacular for Andújar, who recorded 21 victories and a 3.40 ERA. However, his postseason pitching was a disappointment. Although the Cardinals bested the Los Angeles Dodgers for the National League pennant, Andújar lost the one game he pitched in the series. In the World Series against the Minnesota Twins, he started and lost game three. He appeared in relief in game seven, became irate over calls by umpire Don Denkinger, and was ejected when he bumped the umpire. St. Louis lost that deciding game and the World Series.

Cardinals owner August Busch, angered by Andújar's antics, ordered that he be traded. He was sent to the Oakland Athletics in the offseason. In his first year with the Athletics, he recorded a respectable 12 wins and 7 losses. His last two seasons in the majors were marred by injuries and ineffectiveness, with only 3 wins with Oakland in 1987 and, after a trade back to Houston, a 2-5 record in 1988. After his pitching career ended, Andújar became a scout for the California Angels before returning to the Dominican Republic. He eventually settled into a less active retirement spent relaxing, fishing, and working with youths in sports, especially baseball.

Significance

Andújar was one of the premier pitchers in baseball in the 1980's. Darrell Porter, the Cardinals' catcher during Andújar's best seasons, regarded him as the best pitcher Porter ever caught. Andújar's eccentric personality made him well-liked by teammates and fans. In an interview with *Sports Illustrated*, he said that his favorite English word was "youneverknow." Proud of his origins, he wanted to be known as "one tough Dominican."

Mario Morelli

Further Reading

Golenbock, Peter. *The Spirit of St. Louis: A History of the St. Louis Cardinals and Browns.* New York: Avon Books, 2000. Brief but interesting discussion of Andújar's role on the successful Cardinals' teams in the 1980's.

Hummel, Rick. "Andújar Gets Big Ovation on His Return to St. Louis." *St. Louis Post-Dispatch*, April 2, 2007, p. 9. Reminiscences of high points of Andújar's playing days and update on his post-retirement activities.

Wulf, Steve. "Here's a Hot Dog You've Got to Relish." *Sports Illustrated* 58, no. 3 (January 24, 1983): 28-31. Informative account of Andújar's early life and career.

See also: César Cedeño; Pedro Guerrero; Willie Hernández; Dennis Martínez; Luis Tiant; Fernando Valenzuela.

Gloria Anzaldúa

American writer and scholar

Anzaldúa is best known as the founder of border theory, which explores the geographical, bodily, and emotional conflicts inherent in Chicano identity. Her works connect notions of indigenous mythology, the implications of language use among Spanish speakers in an English-dominant society, Chicana lesbian sexuality, and spiritual activism.

Latino heritage: Mexican

Born: September 26, 1942; Jesus María of the Valley, Texas

Died: May 15, 2004; Santa Cruz, California

Also known as: Gloria Evangelina Anzaldúa; Gloria E. Anzaldúa

Areas of achievement: Scholarship; literature; social issues; gay and lesbian issues

Early Life

Gloria Evangelina Anzaldúa (AHN-zahl-DOO-uh) was born in the Rio Grande Valley of south Texas to Urbano and Amalia Anzaldúa. The eldest of four children, Anzaldúa and her family spent time working on various ranches and farms as migrant workers throughout her adolescence. When Anzaldúa was eleven years old, her parents made the decision to relocate the family to Hargill, Texas, so the children would have the opportunity to attend school. In *Borderlands/La Frontera: The New Mestiza* (1987), Anzaldúa described the punishment inflicted by white teachers upon her and other Chicano students for speaking Spanish. The pain of those experiences resonated throughout her life.

In 1962, Anzaldúa graduated from Edinburgh High School and began taking courses at Texas Women's University. Tuition proved to be too expensive, and she was forced to withdraw from school. Anzaldúa later earned her bachelor's degree from the University of Texas-Pan American in 1969 and began teaching in primary and secondary schools. She had been a writer throughout high school and resumed her dedication to writing during this period. She earned a master's degree in English and education from the University of Texas at Austin in 1972.

Anzaldúa later returned to the University of Texas in 1974 to work toward a doctoral degree in literature. She was involved as an activist in several groups while in Austin, but she ultimately felt unsupported by her doctoral department and made the decision to relocate to the San Francisco area to pursue her writing.

Life's Work

Anzaldúa's firsthand experiences with racism, sexism, classism, and heterosexism in south Texas influenced

This Bridge Called My Back

Coedited by Gloria Anzaldúa and Cherríe Moraga, *This Bridge Called My Back: Writings by Radical Women of Color* (1981) is a text that defies simple categorization because it not only contains autobiographies, poems, essays, stories, manifestos, and theories, but also voices the oppressions and experiences of women of color based on race, gender, sexuality, and class. The text was revolutionary on numerous levels considering its publication history, content, and authorship. The anthology initially was published by Persephone Press, primarily a publisher of work by white women. The second publication came in 1983 after Persephone shut down; this edition was released by Kitchen Table: Women of Color Press, which counted Moraga among its founders and had the express purpose of publishing the works produced by women of color. When Kitchen Table ceased operations, Third Woman Press, founded by Norma Alarcón, published the third edition of *This Bridge Called My Back.*

The content of the text was groundbreaking for its attention to issues relating specifically to women of color because the essays, poems, and stories come directly from these women. The Combahee River Collective's "A Black Feminist Statement" is a manifesto describing the goals and beliefs of a group of African American women, many of whom were lesbians, in response to movements that ignore their identities. In "Chicana's Feminist literature: A Re-Vision Through Malintzín/or Malintzín: Putting Flesh Back on the Object," Alarcón explores the uses and abuses of the figure of Malintzín Tenepal in Chicano culture and the ways Chicana authors respond to and write about this historical figure. Also present are poems such as Donna Kate Rushin's "The Bridge Poem," mary hope lee's "on not bein," and Chrystos's " I Walk in the History of My People." The women within *This Bridge* were, through the writing and publication of their works, bringing their marginalized status in U.S. society to the center and interrogating it, therefore defying the notion of the center and redefining the margin.

her autobiographical writings, poetry, and essays. While attending a writing retreat with other women and experiencing the elitisim and racism of other individuals present, Anzaldúa had the idea for the collection *This Bridge Called My Back: Writings by Radical Women of Color* (1981), which she coedited with Cherríe Moraga. This foundational feminist text offered a space for women of color to share their experiences and frustrations in the forms of poetry, essays, and theories.

After the publication of *This Bridge Called My Back*, Anzaldúa continued to write and eventually published her essays and poetry in *Borderlands/La Frontera.* This text is considered the basis for border theory. Within the text, Anzaldúa rejects a stable notion of identity for Chicanas because borders of space, mind, language, and body are constantly in flux. Chicanas, according to Anzaldúa, must constantly negotiate these shifting borders and address what it means to be mestiza, or individuals of mixed identity. This mestiza consciousness requires Chicanas to embrace all aspects of their identity, including the indigenous. *Borderlands/La Frontera* both critiques and examines Chicano culture on the grounds of sexism, heterosexism, and elitism related to language. Anzaldúa reclaims and reimagines the histories of various female figures relevant to Chicana mestiza identity because they have previously been subject to the accounts of patriarchal historians and storytellers. Indigenous Nahua female figures are important in Anzaldúa's theory, so the forced mistress and translator to Hernán Cortés, Malintzín Tenepal, is no longer a traitor to the indigenous people; rather, she is the forgotten and abandoned mother of all mestizas. Mythological deities such as Coatlicue and Coyolxauhqui also are redeemed in Anzaldúa's work. She reimagines the histories of La Llorona and La Virgen de Guadalupe. In Anzaldua's text, these women are no longer subject to virgin/whore dichotomies or the monstrous historical interpretations previously offered by religious and historical patriarchs. *Borderlands/La Frontera* defies categorization because it contains elements of history, mythology, prose, poetry, and linguistics.

Anzaldúa began the Ph.D. program in literature at the University of California at Santa Cruz and in 1990 published the anthology *Making Face, Making Soul/ Haciendo Caras: Creative and Critical Perspectives by Feminists of Color.* She also published two children's books, *Friends from the Other Side: Amigos del otro lado* (1993) and *Prietita and the Ghost Woman/Prietita y la llorona* (1995). Along with AnaLouise Keating, Anzaldúa published *Interviews/Entrevistas* (2000), a collection of interviews with Anzaldúa conducted over the course of nearly twenty years. In a subsequent collaboration, Anzaldúa and Keating edited and published *This Bridge We Call Home: Radical Visions for Transformation* (2002). This anthology, released more than twenty years after the publication of *This Bridge Called My Back*, expands the earlier conversation to include the voices of men and women, as well as people of color and whites. The text expressed Anzaldúa's growing concept of feminism that included transformation and activism grounded in work on public and individual levels.

While working on numerous projects, Anzaldúa continued to teach and work toward her doctoral degree; however, she did not live to receive it. She died on May 15, 2004, of complications from diabetes. The University of California at Santa Cruz posthumously awarded Anzaldúa her doctorate.

Significance

In *Borderlands/La Frontera,* Anzaldúa urges Chicanas to reject a singular approach to identity and instead work to interrogate and understand the various aspects inherent in a new mestiza consciousness: race, gender, sexuality, class, location, language, and history. Her work is the foundation for Border Theory and has fundamentally impacted queer, Chicana/o, and feminist studies. Her commitment to writing, collaborating, teaching, and public speaking, as well as her emphasis on spiritual activism, identity, and creativity are Anzaldúa's legacy.

Erin Ranft

Further Reading

Anzaldúa, Gloria. *The Gloria Anzaldúa Reader*, edited by AnaLouise Keating. Durham, N.C.: Duke University Press, 2009. Released posthumously, Analouise Keating compiled and edited several works by Anzaldúa that were previously unpublished.

_______. "Now Let Us Shift." In *This Bridge We Call Home: Radical Visions of Transformation*, edited by AnaLouise Keating and Gloria Anzaldúa. New York: Routeldge, 2002. One of the last works published by Anzaldúa before her death, this essay details her theory on the path to *conocimiento*, or deep knowledge. Individual work, according to Anzaldúa, will lead to transformation and spiritual activism.

Anzaldúa, Gloria, and AnaLouise Keating. *Interviews/Entrevistas*. New York: Routledge, 2000. A collection of interviews with Anzaldúa, each containing an introductory retrospective interview with Keating.

Pérez, Emma. "Gloria Anzaldúa: La Gran Nueva Mestiza Theorist, Writer, Activist, Scholar." *NWSA Journal* 17, no. 2 (Summer, 2005): 1-10. Pérez analyzes the theories within Anzaldúa's work.

Yarbro-Bejarano, Yvonne. "Gloria Anzaldúa's *Borderlands/La Frontera*: Cultural Studies, 'Difference,' and the Non-Unitary Subject." *Cultural Critique* 28 (1994): 5-28. In this article, Yarbro-Bejarano examines Anzaldúa's theory of mestiza consciousness, as well as the positive and negative responses to this work.

See also: Mercedes de Acosta; Alurista; Rigoberto González; Arturo Islas; Cherríe Moraga; John Rechy; Helena María Viramontes.

Luis Aparicio

Venezuelan-born baseball player

The dominant defensive shortstop of his era, Aparicio was even more impressive as a base stealer and helped to return the running game to prominence in Major League baseball. He also inspired a generation of young Venezuelans to embrace baseball.

Latino heritage: Venezuelan

Born: April 29, 1934; Maracaibo, Venezuela

Also known as: Luis Ernesto Aparicio Montiel; Little Looie

Area of achievement: Baseball

Early Life

Luis Ernesto Aparicio Montiel (LOO-ees AP-a-REE-see-oh) was born in Maracaibo, Venezuela, where his father was a tractor driver for an oil company. Luis Aparicio, Sr., was the first Venezuelan to be offered a contract to play Major League baseball, but he stayed at home to play in the Venezuelan League until he was forty-one. Because of the younger Aparicio's small stature—5 feet, 9 inches and 155 pounds by the time he reached high school—and the legacy left by his father, he was called "Little Looie," a nickname that stuck with him throughout his baseball career.

Following his father's teachings, Aparicio became a shortstop and left high school after two years to play with an amateur team in Caracas, helping his team to the Latin American World Series. After playing briefly with the Barquisimeto Cardinales, Aparicio replaced his father as the shortstop of the Maracaibo Gavilanes in

1953. That same season he was signed to a minor-league contract by the Chicago White Sox. Aparicio played for White Sox minor-league teams in Iowa, and Tennessee in 1954 and 1955. He had difficulty adjusting to life in the United States, struggling to learn English while enduring the constant travel of minor-league baseball, but he persevered.

Life's Work

In 1956, Aparicio replaced fellow Venezuelan Chico Carrasquel as the White Sox's starting shortstop. Carrasquel had recommended the White Sox send a scout to look at his countryman. Aparicio led the American League in stolen bases for the first of nine consecutive seasons and was named rookie of the year, receiving twenty-two of twenty-four votes. That same year, Aparicio married Sonia Llorente; the couple went on to have six children.

With Aparicio and second baseman Nellie Fox anchoring the defense and leading off the batting order, the White Sox quickly improved their fortunes after decades of futility; the team had not reached the World Series since the Black Sox gambling scandal of 1919. In 1959, Fox was named the league's most valuable player and Aparicio placed second in the voting as the team known as the "Go-Go White Sox" won the American League pennant but lost to the Los Angeles Dodgers in the World Series.

Luis Aparicio. (AP Photo)

Aparicio was traded to the Baltimore Orioles in 1963 and helped lead that team to a four-game sweep of the Dodgers in the 1966 World Series. He returned to the White Sox in 1968 and had his best offensive season in 1970, hitting .313. Aparicio played his final three seasons with the Boston Red Sox before retiring after the 1973 season. Returning to his homeland, Aparicio stayed active in baseball as a co-owner and manager of Venezuelan teams.

Aparicio played 2,599 games, during which he accumulated 2,677 hits and 506 stolen bases. In 1961, he became the first player since Ty Cobb in 1917 to steal more than fifty bases in three consecutive seasons. Aparicio was equally adept as a fielder, winning nine Gold Gloves as the American League's best shortstop between 1958 and 1970 and leading the league's shortstops in fielding percentage for eight consecutive years. He retired as the all-time leader among shortstops in games played, assists, putouts, and double plays. Aparicio was chosen for the American League All-Star team ten times.

Significance

In addition to being one of the best-fielding shortstops of all time, Aparicio helped restore base-stealing to popularity, paving the way for the success of Maury Wills of the Dodgers and Lou Brock of the St. Louis Cardinals. In an era dominated by home-run hitters, Aparicio and the White Sox proved that a team could succeed through outstanding defense and smart base running. The White Sox had a winning record each season from 1951 through 1967, primarily because of the leadership of Aparicio and his close friend Fox. Statues of Fox and Aparacio were unveiled outside the White Sox's stadium in 2006.

Aparicio was the sixth Venezuelan to play in the major leagues, and his example encouraged teams to examine the Latin American talent pool more closely. While only four natives of Venezuela began their major-league careers during the 1950's, by the 1980's that number had grown to twenty-eight. In 1984, Aparicio became the first Venezuelan and third Latino player elected to the baseball Hall of Fame. In 1999, he was named his country's athlete of the century. Since 2004, the Luis Aparicio Award, selected by journalists in Venezuela, has been given yearly to an outstanding Venezuelan player in the major leagues.

Michael Adams

Further Reading

Bjarkman, Peter C. *Baseball with a Latin Beat: A History of the Latin American Game*. Jefferson, N.C.: McFarland, 1994. A leading baseball historian traces the development of baseball in Latin America,

Regalado, Samuel O. *Viva Baseball!: Latin Major Leaguers and Their Special Hunger*. Urbana: University of Illinois Press, 1998. Examines how Latino players adjusted to life in the United States. Covers highlights of Aparicio's career.

Segura, Melissa. "Catching Up with Luis Aparicio, Hall of Famer." *Sports Illustrated* 103, no. 12 (September 26, 2005): 16. Briefly recaps Aparicio's career and discusses his life after retirement.

Wendel, Tim. *The New Face of Baseball: The One-Hundred-Year Rise and Triumph of Latinos in America's Favorite Sport*. New York: Rayo, 2003. Includes an account of Aparicio's early career.

See also: Felipe Alou; Orlando Cepeda; Dave Concepción; Ozzie Guillén; Tony Oliva; Luis Tiant.

Jerry Apodaca

American politician

Apodaca served eight years in New Mexico's state senate before winning the governorship in 1974. Able to accomplish large goals while remaining focused on the needs of the state's Hispanic population, Apodaca remained a visible presence long after his term in office ended.

Latino heritage: Mexican

Born: October 3, 1934; Las Cruces, New Mexico

Also known as: Raymond S. Apodaca

Area of achievement: Government and politics

Early Life

Raymond S. Apodaca (AP-oh-DA-kuh) was born in Las Cruces, New Mexico, on October 3, 1934, the son of a family that had lived in the area for more than a century. Although his parents were bilingual, he struggled with English in his childhood and had to repeat first grade. At Las Cruces High School, Apodaca excelled on the football team, achieving all-state honors and receiving a scholarship to attend the University of New Mexico.

Apodaca earned his bachelor's degree in education in 1957 and, shortly after graduating, married Clara Melendres, whom he had dated since high school. Over the next six years, the couple had five children. Apodaca taught history and coached football at a high school in Albuquerque for three years before entering the insurance business. He opened his own agency, with help from his wife; when that business proved successful, he built on his momentum, opening shoe stores and selling real estate. Now a successful Las Cruces businessman with a widely recognized name, Apodaca decided to enter politics.

Stating that "being rich wasn't exciting enough," Apodaca helped a friend with his unsuccessful 1964 campaign for mayor of Las Cruces, then decided to run for office himself. Later that year he ran for state senator but was defeated, in part because he was not an effective public speaker. Apodaca took speech lessons and tried his luck again, this time winning the Twenty-seventh District state senate seat in 1966.

Life's Work

After taking office, Apodaca served for eight years as a state senator before seeing in 1974 an opportunity not only to succeed Democratic governor Bruce King, who could not run because of term limits, but also to become one of the first Latino governors in the United States since New Mexico's Octaviano A. Larrazolo left the governorship in 1920. In the New Mexico gubernatorial race, Apodaca narrowly defeated Republican Joseph R. Skeen by fewer than four thousand votes.

Once in office, Apodaca shed light on problems specific to New Mexico's large and well-established Hispanic population. He called for unity among the state's Latinos but paid a political price among non-Latinos for his activism. His efforts to replace state engineer Steve Reynolds, who essentially ran the arid state's water systems, were rebuffed, as Reynolds was able to get many of New Mexico's most powerful businessmen and bankers to come to his defense.

Apodaca found success in reorganizing the state's government. Calling the state's bloated bureaucracy a "700-pound marshmallow," he first made dramatic cuts in the number of state employees, then implemented a massive restructuring during his first year in office. By 1977, he had pushed through the Executive Reorganization Act, which made permanent his cabinet-style system, with twelve government departments headed by secretaries that reported to the governor. By allowing individual departments to concentrate on specific, specialized areas, the government was able to function more efficiently. Seeking greater efficiency, Apodaca also consolidated many agencies and eliminated a number of state commissions and boards.

After Apodaca left office in 1978, he was appointed by President Jimmy Carter to chair the President's Council on Physical Fitness. In 1982, he launched an unsuccessful campaign for a U.S. Senate seat, losing to Republican Jeff Bingaman. He later returned to the business world, starting a company to publish periodicals, such as *VISTA* and *Hispanic*, aimed at Latino readers. He has served in the Marine Corps Reserves and on the University of New Mexico Board of Regents.

SIGNIFICANCE

Apodaca's governorship demonstrated his political acumen and ability to accomplish major goals. He was the first Latino elected governor of any state in more than fifty years; however, his election is most significant for what it portended: the rise in Hispanic political influence in the Western states.

Steven L. Danver

FURTHER READING

Demaret, Kent. "New Mexico Gov. Jerry Apodaca Survives the Agony of the Boston Marathon—but Barely." *People* (May 1, 1978). Although this article focuses on the Boston Marathon, it presents a good amount of information on Apodaca's background, including his childhood and early political career.

Lavash, Donald. *A Journey Through New Mexico History*. Santa Fe, N. Mex.: Sunstone Press, 2006. A general history of New Mexico, this work presents a very good overview of the cabinet system that Apodaca implemented in his reorganization of the state government.

Roybal, David. *Taking on Giants: Fabián Chávez, Jr., and New Mexico Politics*. Albuquerque: University of New Mexico Press, 2008. This profile of another high-profile Hispanic politician in New Mexico presents some interesting anecdotes about Apodaca.

Vigil, Maurilio. "Jerry Apodaca and the 1974 Gubernatorial Election in New Mexico: An Analysis," *Aztlán* 9 (Spring/Fall, 1978): 133-149. Examines Apodaca's victory, noting that the power of Hispanic voters in New Mexico was exercised for the first time, allowing Apodaca to win despite losing many important parts of the state.

See also: Toney Anaya; Dennis Chavez; Robert Martinez; Joseph M. Montoya; Bill Richardson.

ART ARAGON

American boxer and actor

Aragon was a popular West Coast boxer of the late 1940's and 1950's. In addition to his boxing career, he was also known for his out-of-the ring celebrity that included friendships with many popular Hollywood figures of the day as well as his own appearances in films and television.

Latino heritage: Mexican

Born: November 13, 1927; Belen, New Mexico

Died: March 25, 2008; Northridge, California

Also known as: Arthur Benjamin Aragon; Arthur Anthony Aragon; Golden Boy

Areas of achievement: Boxing; acting

EARLY LIFE

Arthur Benjamin Aragon (EHR-ah-gahn) was born in Belen, New Mexico, on November 13, 1927. He was one of ten children born to Blasita and Desi Aragon. As a result of his family's extreme poverty he was sent at an early age to live with an aunt and uncle who moved frequently during his formative years, residing for various periods in Albuquerque, New Mexico; Cincinnati, Ohio; and Newport, Kentucky. By his midteens, he had arrived in Los Angeles, where he worked in a machine shop and at various other jobs and managed to complete a high school diploma. It was around that time also that he became interested in boxing.

Following a brief amateur boxing career, Aragon engaged in his first professional fight on May 23, 1944, lying about his age to obtain a boxing license. He won his first eleven bouts before losing to Bert White in five rounds in Ocean Park in October, 1944. He continued fighting at a somewhat reduced rate during the year that followed and then in January, 1946, shortly after his eighteenth birthday, enlisted in the U.S. Coast Guard.

While stationed in Boston, Aragon fought on several fight cards there during the year and a half that followed, winning the majority of his fights, frequently by knockout. After his discharge from the Coast Guard in June, 1947, he returned to the Los Angeles area and resumed his boxing career there. By 1949, under the guidance of manager Jimmy Roche, Aragon was well on his way to establishing himself as a local favorite and box-office draw.

Life's Work

During the 1950's, continuing to fight primarily on the West Coast, Aragon fought many of the best fighters in the lightweight and welterweight divisions. In August, 1951, he defeated then-lightweight champion Jimmy Carter in a nontitle bout but lost to the champion in a match for the title in November. In March, 1952, he won a ten-round decision over future lightweight champion Lauro Salas and in 1955 twice defeated future welterweight champion Don Jordan. Among the other boxing greats of the era that Aragon fought were welterweight contenders Billy Graham, Chuck Davey, Vince Martinez, and Joe Miceli. Perhaps his highest-profile bout was against former welterweight and middleweight champion Carmen Basilio in September, 1958, a bout in which Aragon was stopped in the eighth round (one of his few knockout losses).

Despite Aragon's success in the ring—he ended his career in 1960 with a total of 89 victories in 115 fights, including 61 wins by knockout—he was known as much for his ring persona as he was for his boxing skills. Wearing a gold-colored robe and using the nickname "the Golden Boy," he frequently was booed by fight audiences who turned out in large numbers in hopes of seeing him lose. (The custom, especially strong among individuals of Mexican descent, began in 1950 when Aragon twice defeated a popular Mexican-born fighter of the period.) Playing the villain, however, never seemed to bother Aragon as long as the seats were full. He was also well known for his dislike of training and was involved in at least two high-profile boxing-related scandals during the course of his career.

In addition to his boxing fame, Aragon also achieved a fair amount of celebrity outside of the ring. He played golf with Mickey Rooney and Bob Hope and had friendships with a number of other film stars of the era, including a romantic relationship with actor Mamie Van Doren. Beginning in 1952, he appeared in several Hollywood films, among them *To Hell and Back* with Audie Murphy in 1955 and *Fat City*, directed by John Huston, in 1972, and made appearances in several popular television series. He was married four times and died in Northridge, California, in 2008 at the age of eighty.

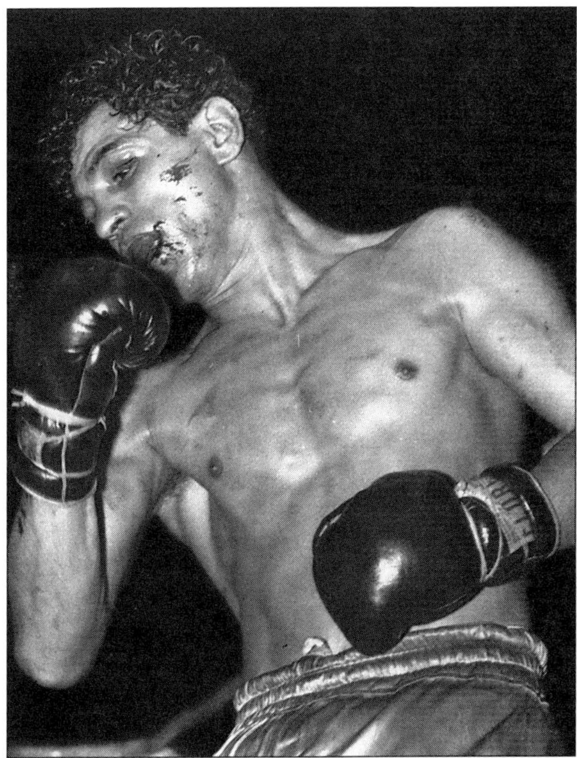

Art Aragon. (AP Photo)

Significance

Aragon parlayed his skills as a professional boxer and his flamboyant lifestyle outside of the ring into a successful and lucrative career during the 1950's. While he never won a world title, he fought many of the best boxers of the era in his weight class. His good looks and gold-colored boxing robe gained him the nickname the Golden Boy, and his bouts, most of which took place on the West Coast, drew large audiences, even if many came to root against him. He also followed earlier boxers such as Max Baer and Max ("Slapsy Maxie") Rosenbloom into a brief career in film and television. Never particularly fond of boxing, he nevertheless used it as a stepping-stone to success in a pattern followed by members of numerous other ethnic groups throughout U.S. history.

Scott Wright

FURTHER READING

Goldstein, Richard. "Art Aragon Dies at 80; Was One of the Ring's Golden Boys." *The New York Times*, March 28, 2008, p. B7. Provides a good basic summary of Aragon's life and career.

Maynard, John. "They Came to See Him Clobbered." *Saturday Evening Post* 227, no. 23 (December 4, 1954): 25, 115-119. Offers a colorful account of Aragon midcareer as well as providing good information on his early life not available in other sources.

Murray, James. "Exit Art, Laughing." *Sports Illustrated* 9, no. 11 (September 15, 1958): 56-58. Interesting popular account of Aragon's loss to Carmen Basilio and his outside-the-ring life at the time.

See also: Wilfred Benitez; Oscar de La Hoya; Aurelio Herrera; Félix Trinidad.

MARIE ARANA

Peruvian-born editor, journalist, and writer

As a voice for Hispanic literature, an influential editor, and a commentator on cultural issues, Arana has brought her unique Peruvian American perspective into the world of books.

Latino heritage: Peruvian

Born: September 15, 1949; Lima, Peru

Areas of achievement: Journalism; literature

EARLY LIFE

Marie Arana (ah-RAHN-ah) was the third of three children born to Jorge Enrique Arana, a Peruvian engineer, and Marie Elverine Clapp, an American musician. The couple met in Boston, where Jorge was attending graduate school at Massachusetts Institute of Technology. After World War II, they moved to Peru, where they lived until 1959. For much of Arana's childhood, her father managed a sugar mill in Cartavia, Peru, where the smell of sugar filled the air. Her mother at first home-schooled the three children; later, Arana attended the American-sponsored Roosevelt School in Lima.

In 1959 the family moved to Summit, New Jersey. Arana's father had renewed his previous connection with the W. R. Grace Company and commuted to their corporate offices in New York City. Nine-year-old Arana was bilingual, but the English she spoke, practiced in Wyoming, sounded strange to New Jerseyites. Nevertheless, she adapted. At twelve, she was taking the bus alone into Manhattan for ballet and voice lessons.

After high school, Arana attended Northwestern University, graduating in 1971 with a degree in Russian language and literature. Subsequently she studied Mandarin Chinese. By 1972, she was married to a banker, Wendell B. Ward, Jr., and living in Malaysia.

LIFE'S WORK

Arana lived in the Far East for the next decade. She earned a master's degree in linguistics from the British University of Hong Kong. She then edited *Studies in Bilingualism* and was a lecturer in linguistics at the university in 1978-1979. When she returned to the United States in 1980, she had spent one-third of her life in each of three continents: South America, North America, and Asia.

From that point on, Arana's work was primarily with the printed word. She took a senior editor position with the powerhouse publisher Harcourt Brace Jovanovich. Working as an editor, she concentrated mostly on nonfiction, editing books by such public figures as Patrick Moynihan and Eugene McCarthy. In 1989, she left Harcourt to become vice president and senior editor at Simon & Schuster, another major publisher. By working in these editorial positions, she became known to many major American literary figures. However, at the time, she did not especially identify herself as part of a broader Hispanic American minority,

This changed in 1989.On her first day on her next job, as a deputy book editor at *The Washington Post,* a colleague asked if she was a "minority hire," a jarring experience for a woman who had worked at the highest levels of mainstream publishing. She took it as an opportunity, joining Hispanic literary groups and promoting diversity by reviewing works of minority authors.

In 1998, Arana spent a month at Stanford University on a fellowship project about Peruvian women in poverty. As she delved into the library's rich holdings on Latin America, she solved some mysteries about her paternal relatives, especially Julio Cesar Arana, a jungle robber baron whom the Arana family refused to recognize as kin. This research drew her into studying her own family's background. The result, several years later, was her first book. She credits the self-awareness she gained while writing the book, *American Chica* (2001), as a factor in both the breakup of her marriage and her subsequent remarriage to a colleague, Jonathan Yardley.

In 1999, Arana was promoted to editor-in-chief of the paper's prestigious *Book World.* In this position, she was on the forefront of the literary scene and had the chance to write several books, such as *The Writing Life* (2002) and *Through the Eyes of the Condor* (2007). Her memoir *American Chica* was published in 2001.

Despite Arana's long association with literature, she did not write her first novel until 2006. *Cellophane*, a saga centered on a paper factory in the Peruvian Amazon region, was published that year. Next came a very different novel, *Lima Nights* (2009), the unsentimental story of an intense May-September affair and its aftermath. In late 2008, she retired from the *Washington Post* position to pursue her own writing projects.

Significance

Arana often has said that her dual-cultural and bilingual upbringing means she has two different selves, and never feels wholly at home as either one. The experience of being outside a majority consciousness is a common one, making her work resonate with readers from many backgrounds. As an influential figure in the world of books, Arana often has been a voice for Latinos, offering interesting and unusual perspectives on issues and events.

Emily Alward

Further Reading

Arana, Marie. *American Chica.* New York: Dial Press, 2001. Gracefully written memoir explores Arana's childhood, her parents' rocky but rock-solid bicultural marriage, and Peruvian history.

_______. "Uniting Worlds Through Language." Interview by Joseph Barbato and Michael Coffey. *Publishers Weekly* 248 (June 4, 2001): 23. Wide-ranging interview covering Arana's approach to writing and thoughts on the status of American publishing.

McIntyre, Loren. "Puzzles of Life and History." *Americas* 65 (September-October, 2002): 5. A Hispanic magazine reviews Arana's memoir, offering another view of the history she describes in the book.

See also: Fernando Alegría; Julia Alvarez; Lourdes Casal.

Julio Arce

Mexican-born journalist

As a columnist for his own highly successful newspaper, which served the Hispanic community of San Francisco, Arce became the most influential Latino journalist of his day. His satiric pieces on the everyday culture of the city's teeming Mexican neighborhoods are considered an invaluable record of the era.

Latino heritage: Mexican

Born: January 9, 1870; Guadalajara, Jalisco, Mexico

Died: November 15, 1926; San Francisco, California

Also known as: Julio G. Arce; Jorge Ulica

Area of achievement: Journalism

Early Life

Julio G. Arce (HEW-lee-oh AHR-say) was born in Guadalajara along the Pacific coast of west central Mexico. He was born into privilege and education—his father was a respected surgeon. Although his father wanted him to study medicine, Arce lacked the commitment to the sciences and opted to study pharmacy. His first love, however, was journalism; unlike popular novels, which romanticized life in flowery prose, journalism was committed to depicting the real-life world and in turn could affect real social and political change. Such power intrigued Arce. While completing his pharmacy studies, Arce started his own student newspaper, *El amigo del pueblo* (*Friend of the People*).

After finishing his degree, Arce went north to Mazatlán in the state of Sinaloa, where he, along with a friend, opened a pharmacy. He remained a frequent contributor to local newspapers and even started his own limited-circulation paper that published original fiction and poetry as well as literary reviews. Now in his mid-twenties, Arce decided he needed the challenge of a large city and moved to Culiacán. His writings there caught the eye of the local newspaper, *El occidental*, run by long-entrenched political powers. Seen as their friend, Arce enjoyed the respect such government support brought—his career was set.

Life's Work

Arce soon grew restless. His observations of life in the city, particularly the impoverished neighborhoods of the working class, led him to increasingly more strident objections to the political status quo. In 1909, as the editor of the newspaper *El diario del pacifico* (*The Pacific Diary*), Arce came under fire more frequently from the government. As a precaution, he returned to his hometown, where he immediately began another antigovernment newspaper, *El diario de occident* (*Occidental Diary*). He also agitated publicly on behalf of journalists who had been jailed. In late 1915, after being jailed himself for two months, Arce and his family went into exile to the United States, determined, unlike other political refugees, never to return.

Arce headed to San Francisco, which had a large Mexican American community, many of them exiles sympathetic to Arce's politics. He acquired a small-run neighborhood newspaper and within three years built it into *Hispano-America*, which quickly became the most influential and respected newspaper covering San Francisco's Hispanic population.

In 1916, in addition to his work as managing editor of the newspaper, Arce began writing a short weekly column (a genre known as a *crónica*) that recorded the everyday life of the Mexican working-class community in the Bay Area, specifically the struggle to adjust to the cultural, social, religious, and economic life of their adopted country. To distance himself from the often caustic observations offered in the columns, which were written in the first person, Arce used the pseudonym Jorge Ulica.

Over the next decade, Arce's *Crónicas diabólicas* (*Diabolical Chronicles*) became a staple of the Mexican community in San Francisco; within five years, it was syndicated throughout the Southwest. Each column, usually less than one thousand words, told a story drawn from Arce's own familiarity with the Latino community, a story that was intended to teach, often with little subtlety, how immigrants should deal with the challenges of adjusting to their adopted country. With often biting (if ferociously funny) satire, the columns encouraged immigrants not to be too quickly mesmerized by the American way of life (broadly seen as amoral and mercenary) and not to lose too quickly their cultural, religious, and familial ties to the homeland. Arce was particularly harsh with immigrants who sought to adopt the English language, mocking their fractured Spanglish, and those who would abandon the Catholicism of their homeland for American Protestantism. He also directed criticism to Mexican women, whom he felt were far more susceptible to the fetching glitter of American influences and in turn made Mexican men Americanized—that is, effeminate and domesticated. The columns made Jorge Ulica the most widely read Hispanic writer in the American Southwest of his time, and Arce's untimely death in his mid-fifties robbed the community of one of its most vital and engaged observers. His work lapsed into neglect until, as part of the Chicano studies movement, a collection of his best pieces was published in 1982.

Significance

Like Samuel Clemens (better known as Mark Twain), Arce was both an elitist and a satirist who used a persona to deliver his most acerbic pieces. That makes placing Arce within a broad Chicano literary tradition problematic as he (or his persona) appears to be looking down with disdain on the very culture he is seeking to define and maintain, although the satire is so blunt and so heavy-handed that it may be ironic. However Arce's success as a newspaper publisher and his unswerving and passionate defense of the working-class Mexican culture, its lifestyle, and its customs in the face of the pressures of immigration mark his journalistic pieces as critical, even seminal texts in the study of assimilation in America as an immigrant culture.

Joseph Dewey

Further Reading

Barrera, Magdalena. "Of *Chicharrones* and Clam Chowder: Gender and Consumption in Jorge Ulica's *Crónicas Diabólicas*." *Bilingual Review* 29, no. 1 (January-April, 2008): 49-65. Scholarly analysis of Arce's columns. Emphasizes Arce's concerns over the loss of the ideal of the strong, working-class Mexican male.

Kanellos, Nicholas. "Recovering and Re-Constructing Early Twentieth-Century Hispanic Immigrant Print Culture in the U.S." *American Literary History* 19, no. 2 (Summer, 2007): 438-455. Helpful context for Arce's career that argues the importance of newspapers (and journalists such as Arce) in establishing and maintaining the immigrant community and in providing a voice for that community in their new land.

Tatum, Charles M. *Chicano and Chicana literature: The Mexican American Experience*. Tucson: University of Arizona Press, 2006. Comprehensive survey of nearly four centuries that includes a detailed look at journalism in the first generations of immigrants with particular emphasis on the *crónistas*, among them Jesús Colón, Alberto O'Farril, Ignacio G. Vásquez, and Arce.

See also: Jesús Colón; Ernesto Galarza; Cleofas Martinez Jaramillo; José Martí; Sara Estela Ramírez.

Reinaldo Arenas

Cuban-born writer

One of Cuba's most controversial and potent writers of the twentieth century, Arenas wrote novels, poetry, short stories, essays, and plays. Although he initially was a supporter of the Cuban Revolution of 1959, he became a dissident after Fidel's Castro's regime started persecuting him because of his homosexuality.

Latino heritage: Cuban

Born: July 16, 1943; Aguas Claras, Holguín, Oriente, Cuba

Died: December 7, 1990; New York, New York

Areas of achievement: Literature; poetry; gay and lesbian issues

Early Life

Reinaldo Arenas (ray-NAHL-doh ah-RAY-nahs) was born to a very poor, rural family on July 16, 1943, in Aguas Claras, Holguín, Oriente, Cuba. In search of a better life, his family moved to the town of Holguin. Arenas was the only boy among many women: several sisters, his mother, and grandmother. His father left home when he was a baby.

When Arenas was a teenager, he supported Fidel Castro's dissident communist group against Cuban dictator Fulgencio Batista. In order to give his total support to the communist regime, he moved to Havana in 1959, the year Castro finally took power. There, he attended the Escuela de Planificación (School of Planification), where he was indoctrinated in communism. Later, he attended the Universidad de Habana. After graduating with a degree in philosophy and literature in 1964, he started working at the José Martí National Library. Arenas had been a great reader as a youngster, and his new job provided a wider contact with books, which enhanced his love for literature.

Life's Work

During this period, Arenas wrote "Alucinaciones" ("Hallucinations"), his first short story. This work won a nomination in the Cuban Cirilo Villaverde literary contest and received honorary mention. Nevertheless, and in spite of the fact that Castro's regime called itself socially vanguard, Arenas still was writing in a very conservative environment. His open homosexuality and the contents of some of his works exasperated Castro, who began persecuting Arenas.

Arenas was working as a reporter for *La gaceta de Cuba* (*The Gazette of Cuba*) in 1967 when *Celestino antes del alba* (*Singing from the Well*, 1987) was published. This was his only publication in Cuba, but it was enough for the regime to intensify its hounding and to

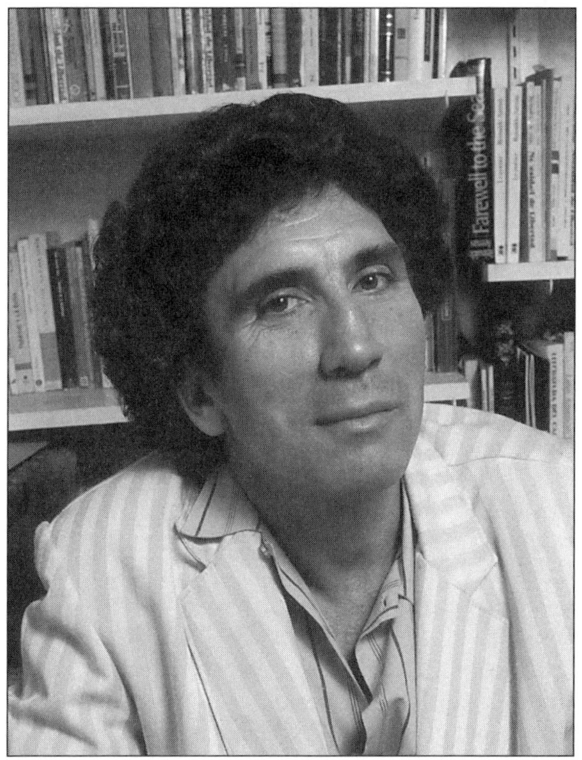

Reinaldo Arenas. (Getty Images)

hinder any opportunities for Arenas to develop a career as an intellectual. He suffered harassment not only because of his homosexuality but also because he clearly defied the government in his book.

Eventually, he was imprisoned, brutally tortured, and forced to reject his sexuality. It was at this time that he began the manuscript for his autobiography, *Antes que anochezca* (1992; *Before Night Falls*, 1993). He also wrote a number of unpublished short stories in this period.

In the early 1970's, Arenas was freed. He decided to escape from Cuba and made two attempts, but he was caught both times. The first time, he tried to paddle away in a tire from the shore. The second time, he almost was killed by a burst of machine-gun fire at the Bay of Pigs. Because of a clever ruse, Arenas finally managed to leave in 1980. Castro had established the Mariel Exodus, which permitted all dissidents and undesirable individuals to leave the island, but Arenas was not allowed to go. However, he falsified his passport, changing his last name to Arinas, and succeeded. He traveled to several countries, finally establishing his home in New York in 1987.

While still in Cuba, Arenas had found a way to continue writing and publishing his works. He had two French friends who could come and go freely and who took Arena's manuscripts to Europe, where they were published. Among the books that they smuggled are *El mundo alucinante* (1969; *Hallucinations: Being an Account of the Life and Adventures of Friar Servando Teresa de Mier*, 1971; also translated as *The Ill-Fated Peregrinations of Fray Servando*, 1987) based on the life of Fray Servando Teresa de Mier, a friar who wrote about philosophy in relation to Mexico's independence; *El palacio de las blanquísima mofetas* (1975; *The Palace of the White Skunks*, 1990); and *La vieja Rosa* (1980; *Old Rosa*, 1989). As a result, when he finally left Cuba, Arenas already had the recognition of the European literary world.

Once in New York, Arenas was free to conduct a normal life, writing and publishing extensively. His most praised works are from this period include *Otra vez el mar* (1982; *Farewell to the Sea*, 1986), *La loma del ángel* (1987; *Graveyard of the Angels*, 1987), and *El asalto* (1991; *The Assault*, 1994). Also, he was able to diversify his writings and produced quality dramaturgy, essays, and poetry. In New York, he also was finally able to live with his longtime partner, Lazaro Gomez.

In 1987, Arenas was diagnosed with acquired immune deficiency syndrome (AIDS). This prompted him to complete his autobiography, *Antes que anochezca*, which was adapted into a film in 2000. According to his friends, Arenas was a sensitive man who could not stand to watch himself decay. On December 7, 1990, he committed suicide with an overdose of pills. He left letters for all his friends and the media, explaining that the person to blame for his death was Fidel Castro. According to Arenas, he had to leave the island in order to escape persecution, and because of that, he suffered the pains of exile. These pains led him down path that he would not have followed if he was living in his home country. In the letters, he also urged his friends to continue fighting for freedom. His letters end with the sentence, "Cuba will be free. I already am."

Significance

Arenas is considered a major literary figure of what some call the post-boom literary production of Latin America, which began in the mid-1970's. His works engage the subjects of exile and hopelessness, always inserted in a narrative of historical discourse. He is recognized today as an advocate for his country's freedom through literature.

Maria Eugenia Silva

Further Reading

Canaparo, Claudio. *The Manufacture of an Author: Reinaldo Arenas' Literary World, His Readers and Other Contemporaries.* London: King's College Press, 2000. Examines the many political, personal, and social factors that influenced Arenas's writing.

Soto, Francisco. *Reinaldo Arenas: Tradition and Singularity.* New York: New York University Press, 1988. Discusses Arenas's writing in the context of Latin American literature and the period in which he wrote.

Zendegui, Ileana C. *The Postmodern Poetic Narrative of Cuban Writer Reinaldo Arenas.* Lewiston, New York: Edwin Mellen Press, 2004. Scholarly discussion of Arenas's work and its political and literary implications.

See also: Gloria Anzaldúa; Lourdes Casal; Maria Irene Fornes; Rigoberto González; Oscar Hijuelos; Arturo Islas; Eduardo Machado; John Rechy.

Ron Arias

American journalist and fiction writer

A journalist who received the Los Angeles Press Club Award for his 2004 People magazine coverage of the Laci Peterson murder, Arias is celebrated in literary circles for his 1975 novel, The Road to Tamazunchale*, which won top prize in the University of California at Irvine's annual Chicano/Latino literary competition.*

Latino heritage: Mexican

Born: November 30, 1941; Los Angeles, California

Also known as: Ronald Francis Arias

Areas of achievement: Literature; journalism

Early Life

Born in Los Angeles on November 30, 1941, Ronald Francis Arias (AH-ree-ahs) had an itinerant childhood because of his stepfather's U.S.Army career. His mother was born in El Paso, Texas, his biological father in Juárez, Mexico, and his stepfather in Nogales, Arizona. Arias has said that he identified with both fathers and with his maternal grandmother, with whom he practiced speaking Spanish. Arias graduated in 1959 from the American High School in Stuttgart, Germany. Soon after, he began traveling on his own, hitchhiking around Argentina, Peru, Spain, and the United States.

Arias's mother inspired him to pursue writing when he was nine years old and recovering from a tonsillectomy. To keep him occupied, she gave him writing materials and encouraged him to write down his observations and feelings in his journal every day. Arias continued to write daily and began his journalistic career by writing for high school and college newspapers. He studied at Oceanside-Carlsbad Community College in California, Universidad de Barcelona in Spain, Universidad de Buenos Aires in Argentina, and the University of California at Berkeley before completing his bachelor's degree in Spanish and master's degree in journalism from the University of California at Los Angeles.

Life's Work

After beginning his career as a reporter for several newspapers, Arias joined the staff of the Associated Press (AP) wire service. He covered earthquakes, bombings, and other disasters as an AP correspondent. In his 2002 memoir, *Moving Target: A Memoir of Pursuit*, Arias describes being caught in combat crossfire while on assignment in Latin America and characterizes his early AP years as focused on "death and destruction." His travels also brought him into contact with international celebrities, including writers Ernest Hemingway and Jorge Luis Borges, and political leaders such as Indira Gandhi. He went on to write for *People* magazine for more than twenty years.

Arias's life experiences echo in the themes and techniques of his fiction. In one of his first published stories, "El mago" ("The Shaman"), which appeared in the journal *El Grito* in 1970, he captures the struggle between imagination and rationality in a constantly shifting world. Arias's literary prominence rests on his debut novel, *The Road to Tamazunchale* (1975), which received widespread acclaim and was nominated for a National Book Award. The novel chronicles the last week in the life of an old man, Fausto Tejada, living in a Los Angeles barrio. In the story, which draws on Magical Realist themes, the retired encyclopedia salesman and widower embarks on a fairytale-esque journey as he fights to stay alive. He guides the reader through his memories and drops in and out of consciousness rather than succumb to death. Fausto's wanderings are no less real because the action occurs within his mind; he visits his ancestors and dead wife, rescues immigrants crossing the desert, and tours a Hollywood film set where he is mistaken for an extra. Employing a reporter's vivid description and minute-by-minute action, Arias fills the story with poignant feeling and raucous humor.

After *The Road to Tamazunchale*, Arias published short fiction while continuing his work as a reporter. His story "The Castle" (1976) chronicles the relationship between Sam, a homeless derelict residing in an abandoned structure, with a quiet, introverted boy named Carlos, who is preoccupied with thoughts of his father, a prisoner of war who has been gone for more than three years. A story of loneliness, friendship, and love, "The Castle" expresses the same longing for family connections amid upheaval sketched in *The Road to Tamazunchale*.

Another successful story from the same period, "El señor del chivo" (1976), presents the life of a sidewalk taco vendor in Michoacán, Mexico. By showing how the vender juggles the making of his goat-meat tacos with his lively, nonstop banter with his customers, Arias reveals the urban vendor's life as a metaphor for his own views on the intersections of art, life, and society. Revisiting many of these themes, the story "Chinches" (1977) depicts a female protagonist, Gabriela, a young teacher who already is fatigued with life. The action depicts her imagination's attempts to escape from the known to the excitement of the unknown.

Significance

From his prize-winning 1975 novel to his acclaimed 2002 memoir, Arias's career has fulfilled the destiny he began as a nine-year-old keeping a notebook of his thoughts. The complex characters and major themes of his fiction resonate with the same vibrant urgency of his *People* magazine reporting on breaking news and famous lives.

Cordelia Chávez Candelaria

Further Reading

Amparano García, Julie. "Ron Arias." In *Encyclopedia of Latino Popular Culture,* Vol. 1. Westport, Conn.: Greenwood Press, 2004. Biographical profile that summarizes Arias's career and significance.

Arias, Ron. *Moving Target: A Memoir*. Tempe, Ariz.: Bilingual Review Press, 2002. Arias's memoir covers his extensive travels and career as a journalist and fiction writer.

Saldívar, Ramón. "Romance, the Fantastic, and the Representation of History in Rudolfo A. Anaya and Ron Arias." In *Chicano Narrative: The Dialectics of Difference*. Madison: University of Wisconsin Press, 1990. Scholarly analysis of Arias's and Anaya's writing.

See also: Rudolfo Anaya; Jimmy Santiago Baca; Raymond Barrio; Cristina García; Arturo Islas.

Desi Arnaz

Cuban-born musician, actor, and business executive

Immortalized as "Ricky Ricardo" in the 1950's television sitcom I Love Lucy, *Arnaz began his entertainment career as a musician and film actor before becoming the first major Latino television star. However, he made his most significant contributions to the entertainment industry as an innovative producer.*

Latino heritage: Cuban

Born: March 2, 1917; Santiago de Cuba, Cuba

Died: December 2, 1986; Del Mar, California

Also known as: Desiderio Alberto Arnaz y de Acha III; Ricky Ricardo

Areas of achievement: Music; radio and television; acting; business

Early Life

Desiderio Alberto Arnaz y Acha III, better known as Desi Arnaz (DEH-zee ahr-NAZ), was born in 1917 in Santiago de Cuba, near the eastern end of Cuba. His father, Desiderio Alberto Arnaz, then the mayor of the town of Santiago, was a popular local politician who also served in the Cuban legislature. His mother, Dolores de Acha, was the daughter of a founder of the Bacardi rum company. Arnaz grew up as an only child, enjoying the privileges of membership in a wealthy and elite family, but all that ended abruptly in 1933, when Fulgencio Batista y Zaldívar overthrew Gerardo Machado y Morales's government. In the tumultuous revolution following Batista's coup, the Arnazes lost all their property, and Arnaz's father was imprisoned. After his father was released six months later, the family fled to Miami, Florida. Meanwhile, Batista built a dictatorial regime in Cuba that would last nearly three decades. Although Arnaz's father eventually reached an accommodation with Batista's regime, Arnaz seems never to have considered returning to Cuba permanently.

Arnaz had begun studying English at his Cuban high school, but mastering that language came slowly to him, impeded his employment opportunities in the United States, and left him with a distinctive and permanent accent. He wanted to go to college, but his formal education ended in 1936, when he graduated from a Roman Catholic school in Miami, where the gangster Al Capone's son was his best friend. Meanwhile, he struggled to find remunerative work, taking on such odd jobs as cleaning bird cages in stores. During the winter of 1936 he began playing guitar and singing in a small

Desi Arnaz. (AP Photo)

rumba band. While performing in Miami, Arnaz caught the attention of the big-time Latin bandleader Xavier Cugat, who invited him to join his traveling band in New York after he finished school a few months later.

Life's Work

Through working with Cugat, Arnaz learned how to run a band and launched his professional career. By the following winter, he was leading his own Cuban band in Miami. Becoming known for popularizing Cuban conga-line dancing, Arnaz got another major break in 1939 when he was cast in the Broadway production of Lorenz Hart and Richard Rodgers's new musical *Too Many Girls* as a Latin American boy who comes to an American college to play football. Afterward, he reprised that role in a film version of *Too Many Girls* (1940) that starred Lucille Ball. He and Ball quickly hit if off and eloped to Connecticut in November, 1940. By the accounts of both partners and other observers, the twenty-year marriage that ensued was both passionate and stormy and was not helped by Arnaz's persistent womanizing. Only a few years later, Ball filed for divorce, but the couple quickly reconciled. Meanwhile, they lived on a small ranch in Los Angeles's San Fernando Valley, not far from the Hollywood film industry and Los Angeles music clubs. Ball continued to work in films, but Arnaz's film roles were limited because of his heavy accent, so he concentrated on working with his Cuban band.

After the United States and Cuba entered World War II at the end of 1941, Arnaz was given a commission in the Cuban navy but decided instead to enlist in the U.S. Navy. Because he was not a citizen, he was not allowed to volunteer. Nevertheless, in May, 1943, he was drafted into the U.S. Army. A recent knee injury kept him from combat duty, so he did his service out of a military hospital near his home, directing United Services Organizations' (USO) programs for wounded soldiers.

After the war, Arnaz organized another Latin orchestra. In 1948, Ball was cast as a dizzy housewife on the CBS radio series *My Favorite Husband*. A few years later, CBS invited Ball to adapt the series for television. Ball agreed—on the condition that she could play opposite her real-life husband, Arnaz. The network was reluctant to air a television series featuring a Latino married to a white woman but eventually relented, allowing Arnaz and Ball's new Desilu Productions to produce the show. This development transformed Arnaz's life. Not only did it allow him to work regularly with his wife for the first time since they were married, but it also allowed him to develop what may have been his greatest talent—that of a television producer.

The original concept for the new television show was to pair Arnaz and Ball as show-business stars whose busy careers left them little time together, as had been the couple's real-life experience. Eventually, however, it was decided to make Arnaz a moderately successful Cuban bandleader named Ricky Ricardo and Ball a zany housewife who ceaselessly connives to get into show business. This formula worked perfectly. The resulting *I Love Lucy* program topped television ratings throughout its long run (1951-1960) and continued in syndication into the twenty-first century. More importantly, however, the show revolutionized television. Arnaz and Ball were nominally coproducers, but Arnaz made most of the business decisions. He began by persuading CBS to let Desilu produce the show in Los Angeles, instead of New York. Back then, most shows were broadcast live in the East, and viewers in the West later watched low-quality kinescope pictures filmed off studio television monitors. To make West Coast production acceptable, Arnaz had *I Love Lucy* shot directly on film, ensuring that all regions would see high-quality pictures. Using film also ensured that every episode would be permanently preserved for future reruns.

Arnaz as a Cuban in *I Love Lucy*

When *I Love Lucy* was conceived, the Columbia Broadcasting System (CBS) feared that American audiences would not accept a Cuban leading man. However, because Desi Arnaz and Lucille Ball insisted on appearing together, Arnaz was cast as Ricky Ricardo, a Cuban bandleader working in New York's Tropicana nightclub. Ball played Lucy Ricardo, an ordinary American housewife obsessed with getting into show business. Ricky's Cuban ethnicity was rarely forgotten throughout the series, but references to it were mostly subtle. Besides the obvious fact that Ricky led a Latin band, he typically switched from English to rapid-fire Spanish when exasperated with Lucy's antics. Explicit jokes about his Latin ethnicity were rare, however, and only Lucy was allowed to mock his flawed English. Nevertheless, his Cuban accent became iconic, and Arnaz himself became indelibly associated with the catch-phrase, "Lucy, you got some 'splainin' to do!"

The first *I Love Lucy* episode focusing on Ricky's Cuban background, "Cuban Pals" (April 21, 1952), played on Latin lover stereotypes by making Lucy jealous when she discovers the Cuban dancer performing with Ricky is a sexy fireball. (The making of this episode was later reenacted in the 1992 film *The Mambo Kings*.) In "The Ricardos Visit Cuba" (December 3, 1956), Ricky returns to Cuba for the first time since he married Lucy fifteen years earlier. Filmed entirely in a California studio, the episode revolves around Lucy's anxiety about meeting Ricky's extended Cuban family and lets Ricky tease Lucy about her fractured Spanish. Perhaps ironically, the episode aired on the day that Fidel Castro landed on Cuba with the revolutionary band that would eventually overthrow Fulgencio Batista y Zaldívar's government. Two years later, on January 1, 1959, Castro would proclaim victory from the balcony of the Santiago city hall in which Arnaz's father had once been mayor.

At the same time, Arnaz persuaded CBS to grant Desilu full ownership of all *I Love Lucy* episodes. Because kinescoped programs had never been used for reruns, CBS appeared to be giving up nothing of value. However, filmed episodes later proved to be enormously valuable, and Desilu's ownership of all the television programs it would go on to produce enabled the company to expand its studio space as it grew under Arnaz's guidance. Eventually, Desilu took over the studios of RKO Pictures.

Despite Arnaz and Ball's busy producing and performing schedules, they made several feature films together during the 1950's. They also had two children, Lucie Arnaz (born in 1951) and Desi Arnaz, Jr. (born in 1953), both of whom would later go into show business. Arnaz oversaw the production of other Desilu television programs. The strains in Arnaz and Ball's marriage became mutually intolerable, and the couple divorced in 1960. By this time, their show business careers were going in different directions. As they divested their interests in Desilu Productions, Ball continued to star in television situation comedies, and Arnaz gradually withdrew from producing. In 1963, Arnaz married Edith Mack Hirsch, remaining with her until she died in 1985. Ball also remarried, but she and Arnaz remained friends through the remainder of Arnaz's life.

Throughout the 1970's, Arnaz appeared frequently on daytime television shows and made occasional guest appearances in primetime shows. In 1976, he published his autobiography, *A Book,* a candid and lively account of his life up to 1960. He and his second wife spent their remaining years in semiretirement in Del Mar, California. Arnaz was planning a second volume of his autobiography when he succumbed to lung cancer on December 2, 1986.

Significance

The public will long remember Arnaz as "Ricky Ricardo," but to people in the entertainment industry he will be remembered as a producer who pioneered modern production techniques, helped shift television production from New York to California, and set a precedent for rich syndication deals. He will also be remembered as the first Latino to star in an American television series. Indeed, during the 1950's, he was probably the best-known Cuban in America until the rise of the revolutionary leader Fidel Castro.

R. Kent Rasmussen

Further Reading

Arnaz, Desi. *A Book.* Reprint. Cutchogue, N.Y.: Buccaneer Books, 1994. First published in 1976, this frank and revealing autobiography covers Arnaz's life through 1960.

Fidelman, Geoffrey Mark. *The Lucy Book: A Complete Guide to Her Five Decades on Television.* Los Angeles: Renaissance Books, 1999. Year-by-year guide to every television program in which Lucille Ball appeared. Provides useful details on Cuban themes in episodes of *I Love Lucy*.

Gordon, John Steele. "What Desi Wrought." *American Heritage* (December, 1998): 20. Appreciation of the contribution that Arnaz made to the television industry by obtaining the syndication rights to *I Love Lucy.*

Sanders, Coyne Steven, and Tom Gilbert. *Desilu: The Story of Lucille Ball and Desi Arnaz.* Reprint. New York: It Books, 2011. Dual biography with detailed attention to the financial history of the Desilu studio and its impact on the entertainment industry.

See also: Dolores del Río; José Ferrer; Mel Ferrer; Rita Hayworth; Fernando Lamas; Ricardo Montalbán; María Montez; Anthony Quinn; Gilbert Roland; César Romero.

Claudio Arrau

Chilean-born pianist

Widely recognized as one of the greatest pianists of the twentieth century, Arrau had a legendary international career that spanned eight decades. He was praised by critics and audiences worldwide for his exceptional virtuosity and artistry and was celebrated as a profound interpreter of nineteenth century Romantic music.

Latino heritage: Chilean

Born: February 6, 1903; Chillán, Chile

Died: June 9, 1991; Mürzzuschlag, Austria

Also known as: Claudio Arrau León

Area of achievement: Music

Early Life

Claudio Arrau León (KLOW-dee-oh ah-ROW leh-OHN) was born in Chillán, Chile, to Lucrecia León Bravo de Villalba, a piano teacher, and Carlos Arrau Ojeda, an oculist who died when Arrau was only one year old. A child prodigy, Arrau received his early training from his mother and gave his first public performance in Chillán at the age of five. After studying with Bindo Paoli in Santiago for two years, at the age of eight, he was sent on a scholarship from the Chilean government to study at the Stern Conservatory in Berlin, where he worked with Martin Krause, a former pupil of Franz Liszt.

Arrau made his Berlin debut recital in 1914 and his first European tour in 1918. He was the winner of several competitions, including the Rudolph Ibach Competition in 1915, the Franz Liszt Prize in 1919 and 1920, and the Grand Prix International des Pianistes in Geneva in 1927. Throughout the 1920's and 1930's, he toured extensively in Europe, South America, and the United States. His international reputation was solidified by his series of highly acclaimed recitals in Berlin between 1935 and 1937, performing the complete solo keyboard works of Johann Sebastian Bach, Wolfgang Amadeus Mozart, Ludwig van Beethoven, Franz Schubert, and Carl Maria von Weber. From 1924 to 1940, he was on the faculty at the Stern Conservatory. With the outbreak of World War II, Arrau returned to his native Chile in 1940, where he founded a piano school in Santiago. In 1941, he and his family moved to the United States, settling in New York.

Claudio Arrau. (Hulton Archive/Getty Images)

Life's Work

In subsequent years, Arrau's countless concert and recital tours took him to Europe, North America, Latin America, Australia, South Africa, India, Israel, Japan, and South Korea. In the United States, he appeared with all the major orchestras. Not only was he recognized as an authoritative interpreter of Beethoven, whose complete sonata and concerto cycles he performed in several prestigious venues, but he also achieved a special reputation for his interpretations of Liszt, Johannes Brahms, Robert Schumann, Frédéric Chopin, and Claude Debussy. Arrau also supervised an Urtext edition of the complete Beethoven piano sonatas, published by C. F. Peter Verlag in Frankfurt in the 1970's. His extensive discography, mostly on the Philips label, includes the thirty-two complete Beethoven piano sonatas, the five complete Beethoven piano concertos, the complete piano music of Schumann, the two Brahms piano concertos, the complete works for piano and orchestra by Chopin, and numerous solo works of Chopin, Brahms, Debussy, and Liszt, among others.

Arrau received numerous honors and awards throughout his long career, including the International UNESCO music Prize (1983), the Beethoven Medal of New York (1983), the Highest Distinction Award from the Inter-American Music Council and the Organization of American States (1984), and the Gold Medal of the Royal Philharmonic Society of London (1990). He was decorated as La Orden del Águila Azteca (Mexico, 1982), a chevalier de l'Ordre des Arts et des Lettres (France, 1965), a commandeur de la Légion d'Honneur (France, 1983), and a commandatore of the Accademia Nazionale di Santa Cecilia (Italy, 1984). He received honorary doctorates from the Universidad de Chile (1949), Oxford University (1983), and the Universidad de Concepción of Chile (1984) and was an honorary member of the Robert Schumann Society and the Royal Philharmonic Society of London. Arrau died at the age of eighty-eight in Austria while preparing for a recital at the newly renovated Brahms Museum in Mürzzuschlag.

Significance

In protest against the military government of Augusto Pinochet, Arrau did not visit Chile for seventeen years, from 1967 to 1984. He gave up his Chilean citizenship in 1978 and became a naturalized American citizen in 1979. Nevertheless, he remained an influential figure in his homeland. His return tour to Chile in 1984 was highly acclaimed by the media and the public. During the same year, he received the Premio Nacional de Arte—Mención Música, presented by the Chilean Ministry of Education, and was appointed permanent professor honoris causa by the Universidad del Bío-Bío. In 2005, the Museo Interactivo Claudio Arrau León was inaugurated in his hometown of Chillán, in memory of the prolific musician.

Sonia Lee

Further Reading

Arrau, Claudio. "Claudio Arrau." Interview by David Dubal. In *Reflections from the Keyboard: The World of the Concert Pianist.* 2d ed. New York: Schirmer Books, 1997. An interview with Arrau, who talks about his early musical influences and the performance of the music of Beethoven, Chopin, Liszt, Schumann, and Debussy.

Dubal, David. "Claudio Arrau." In *The Art of the Piano: Its Performers, Literature, and Recordings.* 3d ed. Pompton Plains, N.J.: Amadeus Press, 2004. Profiles the life and career of Arrau. Discusses his repertoire, playing style, and recordings.

Horowitz, Joseph. *Conversations with Arrau.* 2nd ed. New York, N.Y.: Limelight Editions, 1992. Centering on interviews the author conducted with the pianist between May 1980 and July 1981, this is a major book in English on the career and music of Arrau. Includes reprints of a 1909 article, "The Chilean Mozart," by Antonio Orrego Barros, and a 1967 article, "A Performer Looks at Psychoanalysis," by Arrau himself. Also contains a comprehensive discography.

Selmon, Diane. "Remembering Claudio Arrau." *Clavier* 33, no. 2 (February, 1994): 24-26. Australian pianist Selmon, a former student of Arrau, reminisces about her teacher's teaching style, precise technical system, and approach to interpretation.

See also: Jorge Bolet; Justino Díaz; Eduardo Mata; Jesús María Sanromá; Claudio Spies.

Alfredo M. Arreguín

Mexican-born artist

Arreguín is a highly regarded painter whose work reflects the influence of his Mexican heritage and life in the Pacific Northwest. He originated the "Pattern and Decoration" style, in which intricately designed, brilliantly colored images overlay complex background designs.

Latino heritage: Mexican

Born: January, 20, 1935; Morelia, Mexico

Also known as: Alfredo Mendoza Arreguín

Area of achievement: Art

Early Life

Born in Morelia, Mexico in 1935, Alfredo Mendoza Arreguín (AH-reh-GEEN) moved to Mexico City at the age of thirteen. As a youth, Arreguín lived with his mother in his grandparents' household. After his grandparents' deaths, the Dam family (whom he had met when they had visited Mexico) offered him a home in Seattle. At age twenty-one, Arreguín moved to Seattle, where he earned a bachelor's degree (in 1967) and a master of fine arts degree (in 1969) at the University of Washington. He then became a major player in the growing Latino artistic presence in the Pacific Northwest. Arreguín was naturalized as a U.S. citizen in 1984.

Life's Work

In 1979, Arreguín represented the United States and won the Palm of the People Award at the eleventh International Festival of Painting in Cagnes-sur-Mer, France. He received a fellowship from the National Endowment for the Arts in 1980. Nine years later, competing against more than two hundred other artists, he won a commission to design a poster for the Centennial Celebration of Washington State. In 1988, Arreguín designed the official White House Easter egg. In 1994, the Smithsonian Institution's National Museum of American Art acquired his triptych *Sueño (Dream: Eve Before Adam)* (1992). A year later, in 1995, Arreguín was honored by the Mexican government with an Ohtli Award, its most distinguished accolade for expatriates who contribute to Mexican culture.

Arreguín also exhibited at the Smithsonian National Portrait Gallery's show "Framing Memory: Portraiture Now." One of his paintings, *The Return to Aztlán* (2006), was added to the gallery's permanent collection. His work also is part of the permanent collection of the National Academy of Sciences, Washington, D.C., as well as many other local and regional archives.

In *Patterns of Dreams and Nature* (2007), Lauro Flores, chair and professor of American ethnic studies at the University of Washington, described Arreguín as an American painter in a truly hemispheric sense, an artist of magic, mystery, and revelation whose place in the history of North American art is secure. Flores's anthology *The Floating Borderlands: Twenty-five Years of U.S. Hispanic Literature*, received an American Book Award in 1999.

According to Flores, Arreguín draws inspiration from designs on Mexican ceramics, textiles, and wood handicrafts, as well as the art of the Olmec, Aztec, and Maya, while tapping his North American environment as well. From the Northwest, he has borrowed snow-capped mountains, seascapes, rushing streams, salmon runs, birds, and rainforests. His 1981 painting *La Push* evokes a sunset on Washington's Pacific coast. The effect of the sunset, like many of Arreguin's works, is nearly hypnotic.

Like that of many accomplished artists, Arreguín's work is a cultural mosaic, even incorporating Japanese and Korean themes on occasion. He became acquainted with these Asian styles while serving in the U.S. military during the Korean War. Tess Gallagher, a poet, short story writer, and essayist in Port Angeles, Washington, who has known Arreguín more than thirty years, and Raymond Carver, Gallagher's late husband, professed admiration of Arreguín's work, finding it rich in imagination, and open to multiple interpretations. The complexity of his work demands attention. As Gallagher describes it, his paintings burst with "butterflies, parrots and red berries, baboons and iguana, tendrils and primordial eyes emerging from indigo leaves."

As of 2011, Arreguín continues to live in Seattle. His wife and daughter also are artists.

Significance

An originator of the "Pattern and Decoration" style of art, Arreguín produces works composed of intricate designs in brilliant colors overlaying complex backgrounds with deep, rich, multilayered landscapes and other imagery drawn from Mexican rainforests and Pacific Northwest terrain, among other themes. He paints these intricate works with a very small brush. His twentieth anniversary poster for El Centro de la Raza uses the image of a horse that appears to gallop over an undulating background pattern of reds and blues. He also has used Japanese printmaking techniques in creating portraits of Latino historical figures, such as artists Frida Kahlo and Diego Rivera and activist César Chávez.

Political and environmental activism are evident in Arreguín's *Sacrificio na Amazonia* (1989), with its homage to Chico Mendes, a Brazilian rubber worker and organizer who was killed in 1988 in Brazil's Amazon jungle. Mendes appears in Arreguin's work defiant of death. In *Siete Leguas* (1991), Arreguín brings to life a legendary horse ridden by Emiliano Zapata when he was killed in an ambush during the Mexican Revolution of 1910. The riderless horse escaped to the mountains and became a mythical symbol of Zapata's irrepressible spirit.

Bruce E. Johansen

Further Reading

Flores, Lauro. *Alfredo Arreguin: Patterns of Dreams and Nature/Diseños, Sueños y Naturaleza.* Seattle: University of Washington Press, 2007. 2d ed. A major biography of Arreguín, containing many color reproductions of his work.

Goldman, Shifra M., and Tomas Ybarra-Frausto. *Arte Chicano: A Comprehensive Annotated Bibliography of Chicano Art, 1965-1981.* Berkeley: Chicano Studies Library Publications Unit, University of California, 1985. Includes descriptions of Arreguín's early works.

Kangas, Matthew. "Arreguín Throws Open Windows to Sumptuous Worlds of Imagination." *The Seattle Times*, April 5, 2002, p. 40-H. A locally oriented review of the artist's work in the Pacific Northwest.

See also: Juan Boza; José Antonio Burciaga; Gaspar Enríquez; Carmen Lomas Garza; Yolanda M. López; Leo Tanguma; Jesse Treviño.

Gus Arriola

American cartoonist and animator

Arriola was a largely self-taught cartoonist and animator. His highly acclaimed comic strip Gordo *ran for more than forty years in dozens of newspapers, humorously and artistically introducing American readers to the rich Latino culture and its diverse traditions.*

Latino heritage: Mexican
Born: July 17, 1917; Florence, Arizona
Died: February 2, 2008; Carmel, California
Also known as: Gustavo Montaño Arriola
Area of achievement: Art

Early Life

Gustavo Montaño Arriola (goo-STAH-voh mon-TAHN-yoh ar-ee-OH-lah), the son of Mexican-born Aquiles Arriola, was the youngest of nine children. His mother died when he was an infant, and an older sister brought him up. As a child, Arriola spoke only Spanish. He learned to read English and gained an early interest in sequential art from colorful Sunday comic strips, such as *The Katzenjammer Kids*, *Krazy Kat*, and *Little Orphan Annie*.

In 1925 the Arriola family moved from Arizona to Los Angeles, California. Gustavo, known as Gus, attended Manual Arts High School, where he first took classes in art, design, and life drawing. He graduated from high school in 1935 and because of the Depression was unable to afford further education.

In 1936, Arriola was hired at Mintz Columbia-Screen Gems studios, where he worked on in-between animation for *Krazy Kat*, *Scrappy*, and other cartoons. The following year, he moved to Metro-Goldwyn-Mayer (MGM) studios, where he did in-between work before joining the Screen Cartoonists Guild, after which he became an assistant animator and eventually contributed original stories to animated short subjects. At MGM, Arriola worked on Tom and Jerry cartoons and was part of the team that produced such other titles as *The First Swallow* and *The Dance of the Weed*. It was while designing Mexican characters for the film short *The Lonesome Stranger* that he first conceived of an idea for his own comic strip. MGM was also where Arriola met his future wife, Mary Frances Servier, who worked as an inker and painter; they married in 1942 and later became parents of a son, Carlin.

Life's Work

In 1941, Arriola sold the concept of his comic strip *Gordo* to United Features, a New York syndicate. He

Themes in *Gordo*

Gordo (Spanish for "Fatso") concerns the cartoon exploits of the unflatteringly nicknamed central character Perfecto Salazar Lopez, a chubby Mexican bean farmer who later becomes a tour guide. Gordo, modeled on comic actor Leo Carrillo, interacts with a human cast that includes nephew Pepito, best friend Paris Keats Garcia ("The Poet"), romantic widow Artemesia Gonzalez, and housekeeper Tehuana Mama. The strip also features a group of animals that make incisive comments to one another but whom humans cannot understand. These include Senior Dog, a Chihuahua; cats, such as Poosy Gato; six-legged hipster spider Bug Rogers; and miscellaneous talking owls, worms, pigs, and chickens.

A major thrust of the well-drawn, beautifully designed strip was the universality of experience: Although humans throughout the world may look and sound different from one another, they have the same hopes and fears and the identical range of emotions. Humor, too, is a common bond. Arriola gave readers plenty of opportunities to smile through funny situations, wisecracking dialogue (particularly in the mouths of his animals), and his use of outrageous puns in the pen names he employed for his Sunday strips, like Bob N. Frapples or Overa Cheever, that elicited laughter when spoken aloud.

A second primary theme of *Gordo* was pride of heritage. Once the central character became a tour guide in the 1950's, he took American visitors to places of interest that extolled the accomplishments of the highly advanced Maya and Aztec civilizations. Arriola, especially in his more experimental Sunday strips, wove ancient Mexican designs into the comic's headers and borders to emphasize the artistry of his ancestors. Throughout *Gordo*'s run, Arriola incorporated threads from folktales, showcased native culture, and illustrated examples from local traditions that collectively encouraged readers to discover and explore the uniqueness of Mexico for themselves.

left MGM to produce the strip just before the American entrance into World War II. Susceptible to the draft, Arriola enlisted in the U.S. Army Air Force. Thanks to the Hollywood grapevine, he learned that a new group was being formed to produce military training materials, and he secured an assignment with the First Motion Picture Unit. Stationed in Culver City, California, Arriola spent the war working with a cadre of writers, directors, artists, and cartoonists who made animated films about how to use top-secret equipment, like the Norden bombsight, and created three-dimensional models and realistic landscapes for practice bombing runs. While in military service, Arriola received special dispensation to continue his fledgling comic strip. For more than forty consecutive months, he did a series of single gags on Sundays, which was enough to keep *Gordo* going through the war years.

After the war, Arriola and his wife moved to La Jolla, California. To get into the flow of producing six daily strips and a Sunday page for *Gordo*, Arriola for eighteen months hired a former Warner Brothers animator to handle lettering and background inking, the only time in the strip's forty-four-year run that he used an assistant. (In the mid-1950's, *Playboy* cartoonist Eldon Dedini and *Dennis the Menace* creator Hank Ketcham completed the strip for a few weeks while Arriola was ill.) During its peak, *Gordo* ran in more than 250 newspapers across the country and was featured in the comic pages of English-language dailies in Mexico and Finland. Popular with fans and peers alike, *Gordo* was nominated four times as the National Cartoonists Society's best humor strip, winning the awards in 1957 and 1965. Arriola also won an award in 1957 from the San Francisco Artist's Club for his use of color and design and received an Inkpot Award in 1981 for his work.

Arriola lived for a time in Phoenix, Arizona, before moving permanently to Carmel, California, where for two years in the early 1960's he operated a Mexican crafts shop. Arriola ended *Gordo* in 1985, partly because his son, the inspiration for one of the characters in the strip, died. Another reason was that he had developed a slight tremor, the precursor of Parkinson's disease, complications from which eventually took his life.

He and his wife remained on the Monterey Peninsula, where they lived off the proceeds from sales of the original artwork from *Gordo* strips, which were sold through the Carmel Art Association gallery. Arriola also contributed artwork to benefit more than a dozen community causes, including the Alliance on Aging, Carmel Public Library Foundation, Guide Dogs for the Blind, Hospice of the Central Coast, Monterey Jazz Festival, Pacific Grove Museum of National History, Salvation Army, Red Cross, and Society for the Prevention of Cruelty to Animals. The Arts Council of Monterey bestowed on Arriola a lifetime achievement award shortly before his death in 2008 at age ninety.

Significance

From 1941 to 1985, Gus Arriola authored *Gordo*, the first syndicated, widely circulated comic strip to focus on Latino culture and traditions, and one of the few ethnically based cartoons of its era. The only other comparable effort was William de la Torre's *Pedrito,* or Little Pedro, a minimalist strip which appeared in *The New Yorker* magazine between 1948 and 1953 and was distributed in the United States and Canada by the small Mirror Enterprise Syndicate. Though in its early years *Gordo* perpetuated stereotypes of Mexicans, complete with fractured dialogue, for most of its lengthy run the strip presented positive aspects of Latino culture. For example, in 1948, Arriola included a recipe for refried beans and cheese, anticipating by many years the popularity of Mexican food. He also inserted many Spanish words and phrases, such as "amigo," "compadre," and "hasta la vista," that have since become commonplace in American speech. Beginning in the 1960's, when Arriola took frequent jaunts south of the border to gather information, he also incorporated aspects of Mexican history and folklore into the strip.

Arriola was also one of the first cartoonists to address environmental concerns; his tribute to author Rachel Carson won recognition from the Smithsonian Institution. He received a Citizen of the Year award from Parade of Nations for promoting education and positive attitudes, and California honored him by designating a Gus Arriola Day. Perhaps his most lasting contribution, however, was in paving the way for future Hispanic-themed cartoons, such as *Baldo* and *La Cucaracha,* that celebrate the Latino experience.

Jack Ewing

Further Reading

Aldama, Frederick Luis. *Your Brain on Latino Comics: From Gus Arriola to Los Bros Hernandez.* Austin: University of Texas Press, 2009. An overview of the development of Latino-themed comic strips and comic books that includes interviews with more than twenty contemporary comic artists and writers.

Arriola, Gus. *Gordo's Critters: The Collected Cartoons.* Berkeley, Calif.: Celestial Arts, 1989. A compendium of Sunday strips from *Gordo*, featuring the animal characters who often contributed pithy and revealing remarks illustrating aspects of Latino culture.

Harvey, Robert C. *Accidental Ambassador Gordo: The Comic Strip Art of Gus Arriola.* Jackson: University Press of Mississippi, 2000. A biography of Arriola and a profusely illustrated examination of his work.

Whyte, Malcom. *Great Comic Cats.* Rohnert Park, Calif.: Pomegranate Communications, 2001. Includes a section on one of Arriola's characters, Poosy Gato.

See also: Lalo Alcaraz; Lorenzo Homar; Bill Melendez

Carlos Arroyo

Puerto Rican-born basketball player

Arroyo is one of the growing number of Latino players in the National Basketball Association (NBA). His basketball accomplishments include playing in the 2006 NBA Finals and leading the Puerto Rican national team in its historic upset of the star-studded U.S. team during the 2004 Olympics.

Latino heritage: Puerto Rican

Born: July 30, 1979; Fajardo, Puerto Rico

Also known as: Carlos Alberto Arroyo Bermudez

Area of achievement: Basketball

Early Life

Carlos Alberto Arroyo Bermudez (ah-ROY-yoh behr-MYEW-dehz) was born in Fajardo, Puerto Rico, on July 30, 1979. He developed his basketball skills as a youth and later joined the local professional club, Los Cariduros de Fajardo. He won the rookie of the year award for the 1997 season. At 6 feet, 2 inches tall, he was considered among the best young guards in the league.

After the Cariduros club began to collapse amid financial problems, Arroyo joined Los Cangrejeros de Santurce, a club that was backed financially by music mogul Angelo Medina. One of his teammates at the club was José "Piculín" Ortiz, a legendary Puerto Rican basketball figure. With Ortiz and Arroyo on their roster, the Cangrejeros won five Puerto Rican Professional Basketball League championships (1998-2001, 2003). This winning streak cemented Arroyo's star status among Puerto Rican basketball aficionados.

At the time, the National Collegiate Athletics Association (NCAA) did not consider the Puerto Rican league professional, so Arroyo also was eligible to play college basketball in the United States. From 1998 to 2001, he played for Florida International University, where he became the second-leading scorer in school history.

Life's Work

After his success at the Puerto Rican Professional Basketball League and the NCAA, Arroyo began to gain international fame as part of the Puerto Rican national team. He also achieved success in some international professional leagues, including the NBA. These achievements have led him to evolve from a specifically Puerto Rican star to one followed by the pan-Hispanic community in the United States. In the 2000's, Arroyo participated in most of the international basketball tournaments as Puerto Rico's starting point guard. At that time, Puerto Rico was a regional powerhouse, winning several tournaments and qualifying for the 2004 Olympic Games in Athens, Greece. Arroyo was the flag bearer for Puerto Rico at the Olympics, and he and his countrymen stunned the world in the first round by beating the highly favored American team, which included NBA stars such as LeBron James, Carmelo Anthony, and Tim Duncan by a score of 92-73. This was the first Olympic defeat of an American basketball team that included professionals. Arroyo led the Puerto Rican team to victory with 25 points, 7 assists, and 4 steals. The historic win spurred a wave of nationalism that took the island by storm.

Carlos Arroyo. (AP Photo)

Arroyo's international professional career had its ups and downs. It included a short European stint in the 2001-2002 season with the Liga ACB club TAU Cerámica as well as a successful championship run in 2008 with the powerhouse Israeli team Maccabi Tel Aviv. In the NBA, he signed with the Toronto Raptors in 2001 and then with the Denver Nuggets after being waived. He then played with the Utah Jazz, where he had two solid seasons (2002-2004) and became the first Puerto Rican player to score 30 points in an NBA game.

After a few public disputes with his Utah coach Jerry Sloan, Arroyo was traded to the reigning NBA champions, the Detroit Pistons, and came very close to winning a championship with his new team. However, in the 2005 play-offs, the Pistons lost in the NBA Finals to the San Antonio Spurs, and Arroyo missed the opportunity to be the second Puerto Rican player to win an NBA championship (the first was Alfred "Butch" Lee in 1980). He eventually traded to the Orlando Magic in 2006, and in 2009, he signed with the Miami Heat. In March, 2011, he was picked up by the Boston Celtics as a backup point guard.

Significance

Arroyo's career is important on several levels. Arroyo's perseverance has helped other Puerto Rican players, such as José Juan "J. J." Barea, to be considered for and accepted in the NBA. His success has fueled the ambitions of many Puerto Ricans to aspire to play professional sports. In addition, Puerto Rico's defeat of the American basketball team at the 2004 Olympics was an important triumph for a minority group and underdog over the mainstream powerhouse team of the United States, which is why this triumph had major nationalistic connotations for Puerto Rican society.

Enrique García

Further Reading

Iber, Jorge, et al. *Latinos in U.S. Sport: A History of Isolation, Cultural Identity, and Acceptance*. Chicago:

Human Kinetics, 2011. Discusses the growing number of Latinos in the NBA and the particular importance of Arroyo, one of the few Puerto Ricans to play in the league.

NBA.com. "Carlos Arroyo." http://www.nba.com/playerfile/carlos_arroyo. Contains Arroyo's full NBA statistics by season and a brief biography.

Paese, Gabrielle. "Carlos Arroyo, Puerto Rico Show USA How It's Done." *Puerto Rico Herald*, August 20, 2004. Long article describing the national pride evoked by the Puerto Rican team's Olympic victory over the U.S.

See also: Manu Ginóbili; Rebecca Lobo; Eduardo Nájera; Diana Taurasi.

Elizabeth Avellán

Venezuelan-born film producer

Avellán has produced numerous films, most of which feature Latino casts and themes. She has a longstanding artistic partnership with writer-director Robert Rodriguez, with whom she cofounded Troublemaker Studios.

Latino heritage: Venezuelan

Born: November 8, 1960; Caracas, Venezuela

Also known as: Elizabeth Avellán-Veloz

Area of achievement: Filmmaking

Early Life

Elizabeth Avellán (AH-veh-YAHN) was born in Caracas, Venezuela, in 1960, one of seven children in a family of media pioneers. Her maternal grandfather was Gonzalo Veloz Mancera, a radio broadcaster, early television innovator, and creator of Televisa (now Venevision), the first privately owned television station in Venezuela. In 1973, Avellán's father moved the family to the United States to pursue graduate studies at Rice University in Houston, Texas. Avellán spent her teenage years there, returning to Venezuela for frequent visits. In 1978, she enrolled as an architecture major at Rice, where involvement with student theater and film groups shifted Avellán's focus to film. In 1988, she met Robert Rodriguez, an aspiring screenwriter and film director, at the University of Texas at Austin, where they both worked in the office of the provost. They married in 1990.

In 1991, Rodriguez and Avellán cofounded Los Hooligans Productions, an Austin-based film production company that they renamed Troublemaker Studios in 2000. The early years of their marriage were consumed with the making of Rodriguez's first films, including the short *Bedhead* (1991), on which Avellán worked as an animator, and *El Mariachi* (1992), her first project as producer. The pattern of their artistic partnership was established early in their relationship, with Avellán working behind the scenes while Rodriguez acted as the public face of their company. Initially conceived as a product for the direct-to-video Mexican market, *El Mariachi* went on to win the Audience Award at the 1993 Sundance Film Festival, making Rodriguez a star of the emerging independent American cinema movement.

Life's Work

The success of *El Mariachi* proved to be life-changing for Avellán and Rodriguez, who relocated to Los Angeles and began work on a sequel, *Desperado* (1995), the project that established them as major figures in the mainstream film industry. The film, which stars Antonio Banderas and Salma Hayek, features many hallmarks of Rodriguez and Avellán's work: a multicultural cast with Latino stars, dialogue in Spanish and English, and a plot that addresses social justice for Latinos with humor and kinetic action. After the completion of *Desperado*, Rodriguez and Avellán began work on Rodriguez's first collaboration with Quentin Tarantino, the horror film *From Dusk Till Dawn* (1996). Shortly after production ended, Rodriguez and Avellán's first child was born, and they returned to Austin.

Operating outside the Hollywood film industry, Avellán and Rodriguez have pioneered a new type of filmmaking that emphasizes independence and reflects their engagement with the Latino community. Avellán and Rodriguez's Troublemaker Studios has become known for the efficient and inexpensive film production generated by its Austin-based creative team. This reputation can be largely attributed to Avellán, who has produced all of Rodriguez's films since *El Mariachi,* notably the Spy Kids series, and *Once Upon a Time in Mexico* (2003), the sequel to *Desperado.* The content of these films often has emulated the tropes of mainstream action cinema, but the fruits of Avellán and Rodriguez's collaboration never departed from their outsider sensibility and commitment to representing diverse perspectives onscreen.

In 2005, Avellán executive produced *Secuestro Express,* a Venezuelan film about the kidnapping epidemic in Latin America. Directed by Avellán's protégé Jonathan Jakubowicz, the film was her first project independent from Rodriguez and became the top-grossing film in Venezuelan box office history. During the same year, she produced two high-profile Rodriguez projects, *Sin City* and *The Adventures of Sharkboy and Lavagirl in 3-D.* The latter film was cowritten by Avellán and Rodriguez's son Racer Max Rodriguez, then eight years old, and reflected Troublemaker Studios' increasing engagement with children's entertainment.

In 2006, Rodriguez and Avellán announced their plans to separate; their divorce became final in 2008. Both have affirmed their commitment to remaining artistic partners, and Avellán has continued to produce Troublemaker films, including *Grindhouse* (2007), a Rodriguez-Tarantino collaboration that paid tribute to 1970's exploitation cinema, and *Machete* (2010), a revenge film that addressed anti-Latino immigrant sentiment in the United States. Other independent projects have included *The Truth in Terms of Beauty* (2007), a documentary about the photographer Herman Leonard, and the long-in-development *Queen of the South*, a drug-trafficking drama with Jakubowicz attached to direct. The mother of six children, Avellán was inducted into the Texas Film Hall of Fame in 2007 and honored with the first Ann Richards Award.

Significance

As one of the few prominent Latinas in the film industry, Avellán has blazed a path for aspring filmmakers from all walks of life, especially women, immigrants, and working mothers. Her work with Troublemaker Studios has economically stimulated Austin's burgeoning film industry and brought new attention to the role of film producers. Her films have had substantial impact on media depictions of Latino characters. Avellán is a prominent example of an emergent class of independent Latino businesspeople engaged in the arts and a champion of young filmmakers whose philanthropy and vision has enriched American cultural discourse.

Lisa Locascio

Further Reading

Avellán, Elizabeth. "The Marriage Is Over, but the Show Goes On." Interview by Whitney Joiner. *The New York Times*, September 30, 2007. An interview with Avellán in the wake of her separation from Rodriguez.

King, Michael. "'Secuestro Express': Jonathan Jakubowicz and Elizabeth Avellán on Venezuela's Surprise Hit." *Austin Chronicle*, October 28, 2005. This profile highlights Avellán's commitment to bringing new Latino voices to a broader audience and includes insight into her creative process.

Patoski, Joe Nick. "The Power Couple: Robert Rodriguez and Elizabeth Avellán." *Texas Monthly* 26, no. 5 (May, 1998): 108-109. Examines the details of Rodriguez and Avellán's personal and artistic relationship at the height of its success.

Rodriguez, Robert. *Rebel Without a Crew, or, How a 23-year-old Filmmaker with $7,000 Became a Hollywood Player*. New York: Penguin, 1996. Rodriguez's how-to book on guerilla filmmaking techniques describes the creative process that informs his and Avellán's work at Troublemaker Studios.

See also: Miriam Colón; Sylvia Morales; Robert Rodriguez; Nina Tassler; Danny Trejo.

Bobby Ávila

Mexican-born baseball player

Ávila, known as "Beto" in his native Mexico, was a gifted, right-handed second baseman who was the first player signed out of the Liga Mexicana de Béisbol (Mexican League) by an American Major League baseball team, the Cleveland Indians.

Latino heritage: Mexican

Born: April 2, 1924; Veracruz, Mexico

Died: October 26, 2004; Veracruz, Mexico

Also known as: Roberto Francisco Ávila González; Roberto Ávila; Beto

Area of achievement: Baseball

Early Life

Growing up, Roberto Francisco Ávila González, better known as Bobby Ávila (AH-vee-lah), played soccer. By

Bobby Ávila. (Getty Images)

the time he was fourteen, he was a professional soccer player. His father, a wealthy lawyer, discouraged Roberto from playing sports and tried to steer him into more intellectual pursuits.

Devoting more time to baseball in high school against his father's wishes, Ávila was heavily influenced by *Baseball: Individual Play and Team Strategy*, written by former major league pitcher Jack Coombs. Ávila then set his sights on a professional baseball career. He began his career by playing for Cordoba in the Veracruz State League. By the age of nineteen, he was the regular second baseman for the Pericos de Puebla (Puebla Parrots) of the Liga Mexicana de Béisbol (Mexican League).

By the late 1930's and 1940's, the Mexican League was attracting some of the best players from the American Negro Leagues, including Satchel Paige and James "Cool Papa" Bell. As a result, by 1940 Mexican ballplayers had practically been run out of the league, and three of the former Negro League players led the league in batting averages, home runs, and runs batted in during a four-year period.

In 1946, Jorge Pasqual, a wealthy Mexican team owner, began offering lucrative contracts to encourage American major league baseball players, like Max Lanier and Sal Maglie, to come to Mexico; Pasqual also offered blank contracts to Ted Williams, Joe DiMaggio, and Stan Musial. While the American players added prestige to the Mexican League, they generally were of lesser talent. In addition, by the mid-1940's, Mexican players were more prevalent in the league and were more productive than they had been in the earlier part of the decade.

LIFE'S WORK

Ávila, who joined the Mexican League in 1943, benefited from Pasqual's efforts. Pasqual's work raised the quality of the league and increased the visibility of young players, like Ávila. Ávila also realized he had the talent to compete in the American major leagues. In 1946, Ávila hit .359, finishing third in the league in batting. His winter play in Cuba attracted the attention of Leo Durocher of the Brooklyn Dodgers, who offered Ávila an annual salary of ten thousand dollars to sign on to the team. When Ávila demanded a bonus, Branch Rickey, the Dodgers' general manager, acquired another promising second baseman: Jackie Robinson.

Undaunted, Ávila in 1947 won the Mexican League batting title, hitting .346 with 11 triples and 18 stolen bases. His secret for successful batting was to concentrate only on the pitcher's chest and not on his arms. As a result, he was not distracted by the moves and quirks of the pitcher's delivery.

Before the 1948 season, the Cleveland Indians offered Ávila a tax-free bonus of twenty thousand dollars. He took it, debuting with the team on April 30, 1949. Initially, Ávila played backup to aging star Joe Gordon, but it was not an easy transition. Ávila spoke no English. It was not until the Indians roomed Ávila with pitcher Mike Garcia, whose parents were Mexican, that Ávila could communicate with the rest of the team.

In 1951, he replaced Joe Gordon full time at second base. In an effort to "Americanize" Latin players, the Indians told Ávila to use the name "Bobby" instead of "Roberto." The year 1951 was a breakout year for Ávila. He hit .304, stole 18 bases, and played a sparkling second base. He also was an aggressive base runner. Ávila perfected the scissors-kick slide; he would slide into base with his right leg tucked against his body and then spring his right leg to kick the ball and glove away from the fielder.

Ávila had his best season in 1954. Led by one of the greatest pitching staffs in baseball history, the

Indians won a then American League record of 111 games. The team's players included Hall of Famers Bob Feller, Early Wynn, Bob Lemon, and American League home run champion Larry Doby. That year, Ávila was the American League batting champion. He edged out Minnie Minoso with a .341 batting average while playing with a broken thumb for almost the entire season. In an interview for *Splendor on the Diamond*, Ávila recalled how his thumb injury could not stop him: "I started to hit well early, and once you're hitting well you build confidence. . . . I felt like I could hit anybody."

The Indians faced the New York Giants in the 1954 World Series, in which the two leagues' batting champions, Ávila and Willie Mays, competed with each other. Although the Indians were favored, the Giants swept the series in four games, with Ávila struggling against Giants' pitching. After 1954, injuries and stomach ulcers began to plague Ávila, and his playing began to suffer.

He remained with the Indians until the end of the 1958 season, and the next year he played for brief stints with the Baltimore Orioles, Boston Red Sox, and Milwaukee Braves. Wanting to retire only after he played one more season in Mexico, Ávila returned in 1960 to play for the Tigres del México (Mexico City Tigers). That year, he hit .333, with 125 runs scored on the way to leading the Tigers to the league title.

After retiring from baseball, the charismatic Ávila became an owner in the Mexican League and was the president of the Veracruz Eagles. Later in the 1980's he became president of the Mexican League. He went into politics following retirement from baseball and was elected mayor of Veracruz. Ávila died on October 26, 2004, because of complications from diabetes. He was eighty years old.

Significance

Bobby Ávila was the first Latin American player to win the American League batting title. Ávila was an excellent contact hitter and defensive second baseman. More than any other player, he helped develop Mexican baseball, and as the first Mexican League player to join the major leagues, he led the recruitment of Latin American players into Major League Baseball.

Michael J. Bennett

Further Reading

Knight, Jonathan. *Summer of Shadows: A Murder, a Pennant Race, and the Twilight of the Best Location in the Nation.* Covington, Ohio: Clerisy Press, 2010. Interweaves the story of the 1954 Cleveland Indians with details of the murder that year of the wife of physician Sam Sheppard in the couple's home on Lake Erie. Includes information on Ávila's background, history with the Indians, and achievements during the 1954 season.

Lebovitz, Hal. "Cleveland's Bobby Ávila: A Real Good Hitter." *Baseball Digest* 14, no. 5 (June, 1955): 5-13. Reports on Ávila's hitting prowess, which led him to be the American League batting champion in 1954. Ávila discusses his secrets of successful batting.

Westcott, Rich. "Bobby Ávila: First Hispanic Batting Champ." In *Splendor on the Diamond: Interviews with 35 Stars of Baseball's Past.* Gainesville: University of Florida Press, 2000. Ávila recalls important moments in his baseball career.

See also: Mel Almada; Minnie Minoso.

Joaquín G. Avila

American lawyer and professor

As president and general counsel for the Mexican American Legal Defense and Educational Fund (MALDEF), Avila translated his passion for equal rights into concrete action on behalf of the Latino community. An authority on voting rights, he has written, lectured, and argued cases focused on increasing Latinos' political access and participation.

Latino heritage: Mexican

Born: June 23, 1948; Compton, California

Also known as: Joaquín Guadalupe Avila

Areas of achievement: Law; activism; scholarship

Early Life

Joaquín Guadalupe Avila (wah-KEEN gwah-dah-LOO-pay ah-VEE-lah) was born and raised in Compton, a notoriously violent and gang-ridden city in Southern California. Despite the pressures associated with growing up in an economically depressed inner city, he graduated as the valedictorian of Centennial High School. In 1970, Avila received his bachelor of arts in political science from Yale University. Three years later, Avila earned his juris doctorate from Harvard Law School, where he served as the *Harvard Civil Rights-Civil Liberties law Review*'s case and comments editor. After graduating in 1973, Avila clerked for Justice James Fitzgerald of the Alaska Supreme Court.

LIFE'S WORK

Avila's first position after his clerkship was as staff attorney in the San Francisco office of the Mexican American Legal Defense and Educational Fund (MALDEF), a Latino civil rights organization, from 1974 to 1976. He then served for six years as the organization's associate counsel, concurrently acting as director of MALDEF's Political Access and Voting Rights Project in Texas. Ultimately, Avila served as president and general counsel of MALDEF from 1982 to 1985. During his eleven years with the organization, Avila testified before Congress and various legislative committees about discrimination against Latino voters, challenged discriminatory voting and election practices such as gerrymandering, and helped amend the 1982 reauthorization of the federal Voting Rights Act.

In 1985, Avila established a private practice focused on the voting rights of minority groups. During this time, Avila addressed numerous instances of voting discrimination and helped dismantle inequitable election practices in the Southwest. He spearheaded efforts at the California legislature to increase access for Latinos to the electoral process and helped pass the first state voting rights act in the country (California State Voting Rights Act of 2001). While in private practice Avila also argued two successful appeals before the United States Supreme Court involving enforcement of Section 5 of the 1965 Voting Rights Act (*Lopez v. Monterey County*, 1996 and 1999).

Avila also taught law courses at University of California at Berkeley and the University of Texas. From 2003 to 2004, Avila was a law lecturer at the University of California at Los Angeles in the School of law and the Chicano Studies Research Center. Next, he served as a visiting professor at Seattle University's School of Law (2004) and transitioned to assistant professor in 2005. Avila successfully coached students for the National Black Law Students Association's Frederick Douglass Moot Court Competition and trained government officials and law professors from Mexico to initiate a similar national moot court competition in that country. Avila's efforts to mentor students were honored with the Faculty Award from the Black Law Students Association. January, 2009, marked the release of *Everyday Law for Latinos*, a textbook that Avila cowrote with Steven W. Bender, Raquel Aldana, and Gilbert Paul Carrasco. The text examines major factors that affect the Latino experience in the legal arena, namely immigration, ethnic bias and racism, and linguistic regulation.

In August, 2009, Avila was named executive director of the National Voting Rights Advocacy Initiative, housed in the Fred T. Korematsu Center for Law and Equality at Seattle University's School of Law. Under Avila's leadership, the initiative's goal is to challenge voting rights abuses and positively influence redistricting at community, state, and national levels.

Numerous organizations have acknowledged Avila for his efforts to ensure political access for marginalized communities. In 1986, the Hispanic National Bar Association bestowed upon him the Benito Juarez/Abraham Lincoln Award for his dedication to the Latino community. Avila became a MacArthur Foundation Fellow in 1996, receiving a John D. and Catherine T. MacArthur Foundation Fellowship or "genius grant" for his work on protecting minority voting rights. Also in 1996, he was the recipient of the Social Justice Sabbatical from the Vanguard Public Foundation. Avila was honored with the 2001 Loren Miller Legal Services Award—the California State Bar's highest honor—for his long-term advocacy of the disenfranchised.

SIGNIFICANCE

Avila blazed a trail out of the inner city and into two Ivy League schools. Beginning with his work at MALDEF and throughout his successful litigation of dozens of prominent case, Avila has guided individuals, communities, and organizations to confront discrimination and systemic inequities. He is recognized as one of the leading authorities on voting rights, and his commitment to Latino civil rights is felt at all levels of society. Evidence of Avila's influence especially can be seen in Texas and California, where Latino political figures have greatly increased their prominence on city, county, and state councils.

Karie Mize

FURTHER READING

"Above the Bar: Faculty Achievements." *Lawyer: Seattle University School of Law* (Summer, 2010):

10. Brief article covering Avila's election into the American law Institute, along with other presentations and achievements.

Avila, Joaquín G. "Equal Educational Opportunities for Language Minority Children." In *Latinos in the United States: History, Law and Perspective*, edited by Antoinette Sedillo López. New York: Garland, 1995. A chapter exploring MALDEF's contributions toward establishing bilingual educational programs for Spanish-speaking students.

_______. "Political Apartheid in California: Consequences of Excluding a Growing Noncitizen Population." *Latino Policy and Issues Brief* 9 (December, 2003). Avila outlines the impact of excluding noncitizens from the electoral process in California, where 28 percent of the population is unable to vote.

"Joaquín Avila: School of Law." *Seattle University Magazine* (Spring/Summer, 2008): 28. Biography covering Avila's journey from his youth in Compton, California, to become a leading expert on Latino voting rights at Seattle University's Law School.

See also: Norma V. Cantú; José Ángel Gutiérrez; Antonia Hernández; Vilma Socorro Martínez.

Francisco Ayala

Spanish-born scientist, educator, and philosopher

One of the leading evolutionary biologists of the twentieth century, Ayala has made fundamental contributions to the fields of genetics, molecular biology, evolution, philosophy of biology, and the dialogue on science and religion.

Latino heritage: Spanish
Born: March 12, 1934; Madrid, Spain
Also known as: Francisco José Ayala; Francisco J. Ayala
Areas of achievement: Science and technology; education; religion and theology

Early Life

Francisco José Ayala (ah-YAH-lah) was born on March 12, 1934 in Madrid, Spain, to Francisco Ayala and Soledad Pereda Ayala. He was the fourth of six children. Ayala grew up during the Francisco Franco dictatorship and attended Catholic primary and secondary schools. His interest in science was stimulated by a priest in lower secondary school who passionately taught about scientific discoveries.

Ayala elected to study physics at the University of Madrid, receiving his bachelor of science degree in 1955. While an undergraduate, he encountered the work of the Jesuit priest and paleontologist Pierre Teilhard de Chardin. This sparked his interest in pursuing the priesthood. Ayala entered the Pontifical Faculty of San Esteban in Salamanca. While there, he studied under Antonio de Zulueta, the leading Spanish geneticist.

Upon his ordination as a Dominican priest in 1960, Ayala left for Columbia University to study genetics under the famous Ukranian-born Eastern Orthodox geneticist Theodosius Dobzhansky. He received his Ph.D. in 1964 with a thesis on fruit flies. He left the priesthood the same year. Dobzhansky moved to Rockefeller University that same year and brought Ayala with him as a

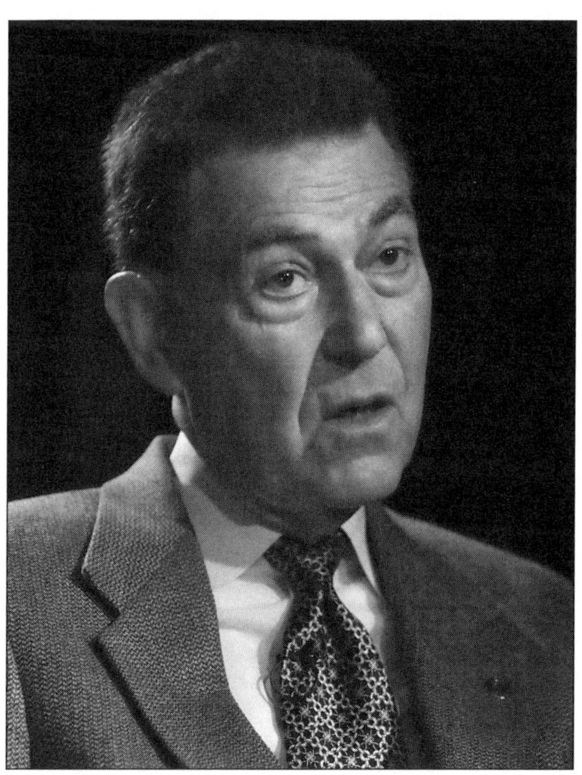

Francisco Ayala. (AP Photo)

research assistant. From. 1965 to 1967, he taught at Providence College and then returned to Rockefeller University as an assistant professor of biology, working with Dobzhansky until 1971 on measuring the rate of evolutionary change at the genetic level. Dobzhansky served as best man at Ayala's wedding in 1968 to Mary Henderson. Two sons, Francisco José and Carlos Alberto, issued from this marriage, which ended in divorce in 1985. Ayaka married the Czech ecologist Dr. Hana Lostakova that same year.

In 1971, Ayala accepted a post as assistant professor at the University of California at Davis (UC Davis) and also became a U.S. citizen. He advanced to full professor in 1974. Dobzhansky joined Ayala at UC Davis and served there until his death in 1975, and the two colleagues produced an impressive body of genetics work that altered scientific understanding of the processes of evolutionary change.

Life's Work

Throughout the 1970's, Ayala's laboratory pioneered new techniques for the study of proteins and deoxyribonucleic acid (DNA) at the molecular level. It became possible to compare the genetic diversity of species in various environments and measure with far greater precision the process of evolutionary change, which was conclusively shown to vary in light of different factors, including the stability of the environments in which the subjects lived. The range of papers produced addressed fundamental questions in paleontology, evolutionary biology, genetics, and molecular biology.

By the time of Ayala's election as a member of the American Academy of Arts and Sciences (1977) and the Medal of the College de France (1979), he was an influential evolutionary biologist. He became interested in Chagas disease while leading some expeditions to Latin America in the early 1980's and, working with colleague Michel Tibayrenc, produced a series of breakthrough studies that showed how asexual reproduction of the parasitic protozoa that caused the disease occurred. This led to the development of vaccines and drugs that targeted key elements of this process, interrupting the spread of this disease as well as a number of others.

Ayala continued to make fundamental contributions to the genetic study of disease by reporting in 2009 that a form of deadly malaria in humans originated from a parasite carried to humans from chimpanzees, possibly via a single mosquito. In 2010, he reported that the disease also had been transmitted to gorillas, meaning that eradicating it from humans alone would not stop its spread. Work of this nature led to many awards, including the 2001 National Medal of Science from President George W. Bush, election to the National Academy of Sciences (1980) and many other national and international scientific bodies, and serving as president of Sigma Xi (2004) and the American Association for the Advancement of Science (1994-1995). In 2003, he began serving as a distinguished university professor within the University of California system (its highest honor) and held joint appointments at UC Davis in an endowed chair as a full professor in biological sciences, ecology, evolutionary biology, logic, philosophy, and philosophy of science; he has contributed fundamental research and insights to all of these fields.

Ayala is a staunch opponent of creationism and intelligent design and served as a key witness in *McLean v. Arkansas* (1981), which challenged an Arkansas law that required the teaching of creationism alongside evolution in public schools. The law was ruled unconstitutional, as the judge deemed creationism to be a religious belief, not science. Ayala also led the panels at the National Academy of Sciences that produced three editions of *Science, Evolution, and Creationism*, and has published numerous books, articles, and lectures for the general public on evolution and religion. In 2010, he received the Templeton Prize in recognition of building understanding among religious communities about evolutionary science and explaining why it is no threat to religion but rather a bulwark for it, especially as it relates to the age-old theological problem of evil.

Significance

Ayala has made some of the most important discoveries of the twentieth century about the process of evolution and has contributed substantially to human understanding of issues at the intersections of biology, philosophy, logic, ecology, theology, and religion. He is a passionate professional scientist who has made significant contributions to improve scientific literacy on the part of nonscientists and helped ensure that evolutionary science holds its rightful place in school curricula and the wider culture.

Dennis W. Cheek

Further Reading

Ayala, Francisco. "Genetics Researcher Francisco Ayala Discusses His Life, His Work, and Creationism." Interview by Rachel Saslow. *The Washington Post*, April 27, 2010, p. HE03. A wide-ranging interview covering Ayala's life and work.

Heffern, Rich. "Biologist, Former Dominican, Wins Templeton Prize." *National Catholic Reporter* 46, no. 13 (April, 2010): 17. A brief overview of Ayala's career and contributions that led to this prestigious award for work in science and religion.

Newton, David E. "Francisco Ayala." In *Latinos in Science, Math, and Professions*. New York: Facts On File, 2007. Describes Ayala's life and scientific achievements.

See also: Baruj Benacerraf; Francisco Dallmeier; Jose Alberto Fernandez-Pol; Elma González; Michael A. Mares; Severo Ochoa; Marian Lucy Rivas; David Domingo Sabatini.

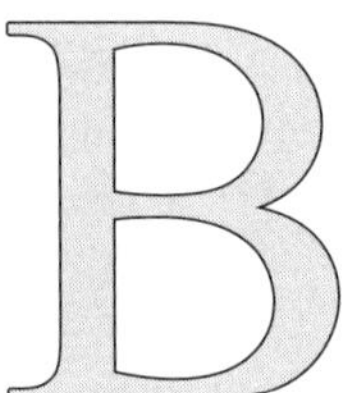

Elfego Baca

American lawman and lawyer

Baca was a law-enforcement official, lawyer, and politician in New Mexico Territory beginning in the mid-1880's. He was most noted for his willingness to defend the Hispanic minority in the region against prejudice from the white majority.

Latino heritage: Mexican
Born: February 10, 1865; Socorro, New Mexico Territory (now in New Mexico)
Died: August 27, 1945; Albuquerque, New Mexico
Areas of achievement: Law; social issues

Early Life

Elfego Baca was born in Socorro in what then was New Mexico Territory, the youngest of Francisco and Juana Maria Baca's six children. According to the (likely apocryphal) story he wrote in his autobiography, Baca was born when his pregnant mother jumped while playing ball, came down hard, and proceeded to give birth. In order to provide an education for his children, Francisco moved his family east to Topeka, Kansas, where he worked as a contractor. When Juana Maria died in 1880, Baca and his brother Abdenago returned to Socorro. Their father rejoined them in New Mexico a year later and became marshal in the town of Belen.

While serving as marshal, Francisco killed two local cowboys. He was arrested and jailed in Los Lunas and sentenced to a term in the state penitentiary. Baca and a friend walked to Los Lunas and proceeded to break his father out of jail. Francisco fled to Texas, where he remained some seven years before safely returning.

Baca received only a minimal education, hardly unusual for the period, and although he would later become well respected by the Hispanic community, he never learned to speak Spanish well. Hoping to follow his father into law enforcement, he purchased a sheriff's badge, obtained some guns, and became a self-appointed law officer in Socorro County. Baca claimed he learned to shoot from Western outlaw Billy the Kid; the "Kid" was killed in 1881, and while Baca's and Billy's paths might have crossed, the story is probably one of many that was embellished over time.

Life's Work

The Baca legend is centered primarily on an October, 1884, gunfight he survived in Lower San Francisco Plaza (Frisco), a town now known as Reserve and located near the Arizona border. While serving as a self-appointed law officer, Baca had arrested a local cowboy, Charlie McCarthy, who was harassing local Hispanics. McCarthy was freed by a judge, and his friends decided to teach Baca a lesson. Baca fled to a nearby *jacal*, a small hut or cabin, where he held off some forty to eighty gunmen for thirty-six hours. As many as four thousand shots might have been fired at Baca's hiding place, none of which managed to hit him. Baca became a local legend. His story later inspired a 1958 television series, Walt Disney's *The Nine Lives of Elfego Baca*, which served to introduce Baca to a larger audience.

Baca was acquitted of any charges in the shootout and shortly afterward became the official sheriff of the county. He was noted for his tough approach to the law, including sending letters to lawbreakers giving them the choice of turning themselves in or being shot for "resisting arrest." The ploy apparently was successful.

After several years as a United States marshal, Baca began to study law. He passed the bar in 1894 and practiced law in Socorro and then in El Paso, Texas. Over the following decade, he served in a number of positions, including county clerk and law clerk, then was mayor of Socorro from 1896 to 1898.

Baca earned a reputation for willingness to defend the needs of the poor during his career. Once he recovered the stolen inventory of a store from a group of inebriated miners. When the store owners did not return, Baca allowed the local (Hispanic) poor to help themselves to the stock.

Beginning in 1913, Baca served for several years as representative in New Mexico for the Mexican government, although the story of a "price on his head" because he stole a gun from Pancho Villa was likely apocryphal as well. Baca spent his last decades supporting Spanish causes in the state. He was unsuccessful in running for public office, in part the result of criminal accusations during his years practicing law and a problem with alcohol abuse.

Significance

Baca was willing to represent both as a law officer and then as a lawyer the Hispanics of New Mexico, most of whom lived in poverty, at a time in which discrimination against them was commonplace. That he was controversial in his personal life—a lawyer and politician not above some underhanded dealings—is a portion of the Baca biography; however, he also was a role model for Hispanics in New Mexico. Although he was born in poverty, he used courage and education to become a successful lawyer and politician with a life story appropriate enough to later warrant a television series.

Richard Adler

Further Reading

Ball, Larry. *Elfego Baca in Life and Legend.* El Paso: Texas Western Press, 1992. This popular biography is short on details but provides a concise and easily readable life story of Baca.

Crichton, Kyle Samuel. *Law and Order, Ltd.: The Rousing Life of Elfego Baca of New Mexico.* 1928. Rev. ed. Santa Fe, N.M.: Sunstone Press, 2008. Addresses the legends associated with Baca, often using first-person accounts.

Sager, Stan. *Viva Elfego!: The Case for Elfego Baca, Hispanic Hero.* Santa Fe, N.M.: Sunstone Press, 2008. Detailed biography of Baca. The author also provides a detailed analysis of the 1884 gunfight that became the basis for the Baca legend.

See also: Gregorio Cortez; Juan Cortina; Joaquín Murieta; Tiburcio Vásquez.

Jimmy Santiago Baca

American writer and activist

Baca's writing explores the complex connections among poverty, race, addiction, and incarceration in the United States. He aims to empower oppressed people, especially Chicanos, to find hope and strength through an appreciation of their cultural heritage and self-worth.

Latino heritage: Mexican

Born: January 2, 1952; Santa Fe, New Mexico

Also known as: José Santiago Baca; Cyclone

Areas of achievement: Literature; poetry; activism

Early Life

Jimmy Santiago Baca (SAHN-tee-AH-go BAH-kah) was born in 1952 in Santa Fe, New Mexico. For the first six years of his life, he lived with his biological parents and older brother and sister. His father, an itinerant worker and alcoholic, was in and out of jail for drunkenness, and his mother eventually ran off with an Anglo American man to assimilate into his culture, denying her Latino heritage.

More or less orphaned, the three children then lived with their paternal grandparents in Estancia, New

Jimmy Santiago Baca. (AP Photo)

Mexico. Baca recalls this time fondly, although it ended abruptly with the death of his grandfather and the subsequent inability of his aged, blind grandmother to care for the three children on her own. Consequently, the boys were delivered to a parochial orphanage, from which they ran away after a parish priest molested Baca's brother.

Living on the streets as a young teenager, Baca hustled to survive, often coming into contact with law enforcement and eventually landing in a correctional center for boys. Back on the streets in his late teens, he fell into drug dealing, for which he ultimately served approximately six years in an Arizona federal prison.

In prison, Baca learned to read and write, and he fell in love with poetry. He shared his work with fellow inmates, who encouraged him to send it to readers beyond the prison's walls. With that aim, he mailed three poems to Denise Levertov, poetry editor of the magazine *Mother Jones*. Recognizing Baca's talent, she published the poems in her magazine and helped him to secure the publication of his first collection, launching his literary career.

Life's Work

An award-winning writer with an international reputation, Baca published his first book, *Immigrants in Our Own Land*, in 1979. A book of profound compassion, courage, and resilience, it celebrates Chicano heritage and illuminates the status of the indigent and incarcerated in the United States. It also posits Chicanos as among the most abused, disempowered, and exploited peoples in the United States, and the book therefore marks the emergence of an important literary voice, one with the eloquence and experience to captivate the public and influence its discourse about race, justice, poverty, and addiction.

Baca's subsequent books of poetry further engage the richness of Chicano heritage in relation to poverty and violence in the United States. They also illuminate the disfiguring impact of racism and the horrors of incarceration. Those books include *Martín & Meditations on the South Valley* (1987), which won the American Book Award for poetry; *Black Mesa Poems* (1989); *C-Train (Dream Boy's Story) and Thirteen Mexicans* (2002); *Winter Poems Along the Rio Grande* (2004); *Spring Poems Along the Rio Grande* (2007); and the fully bilingual *Selected Poems/Poemas selectos* (2009).

Baca's unflinching memoir, *A Place to Stand: The Making of a Poet* (2001), earned the International Award for deftly chronicling the first twenty-five years of his troubled life. With similar grit and vigor, Baca also chronicles his experiences with gangs, poverty, and violence in *Working in the Dark: Reflections of a Poet of the Barrio* (2008).

Baca's fiction includes the collection of short stories *The Importance of a Piece of Paper* (2004) and the novel *A Glass of Water* (2009). These books exemplify his lucid, flowing prose style, through which he dignifies some of the most dejected and disempowered members of U.S. society. Similar concerns permeate his play *Los tres hijos de Julia* (1991) and his critically acclaimed screenplay *Bound by Honor* (1992).

Baca also created a nonprofit foundation, Cedar Tree, in 2005. It aims to combat poverty through education, and in addition to working directly with disadvantaged people, it helps inmates improve their lives through literacy. Cedar Tree has produced documentaries for the Department of Education.

Significance

For his fierce and nuanced depictions of the intricate interconnectedness of the problems of poverty, racism, and incarceration in the United States, Baca has earned many awards, including the Pushcart Prize, the American Book Award for poetry, a literary fellowship from the National Endowment for the Arts, the International Hispanic Heritage Award, and the International Award, among others. He also is a sought-after guest speaker at universities, penitentiaries, and community centers, where he elucidates the stories, hopes, and sufferings of the exploited and oppressed. In doing so, he powerfully challenges institutionalized violence, racism, legal injustice, and official histories in the United States. He aspires for his work to imbue the dispossessed and oppressed with a new sense of self-worth, which he often links to the richness of Chicano heritage.

Seth Michelson

Further Reading

Baca, Jimmy Santiago. *A Place to Stand: The Making of a Poet.* New York: Grove Press, 2001. This memoir chronicles Baca's life from his childhood through imprisonment, thereby contextualizing his poetry, fiction, and drama.

_______. *Selected Poems/Poemas selectos.* New York: New Directions Books, 2009. This book samples Baca's poetry from twenty years of his publications.

Gilmore, Ruth Wilson. *Golden Gulag: Prisons, Surplus, Crisis, and Opposition in Globalizing California.* Berkeley: University of California Press, 2007. This is an accessible, informative entrance to critical investigations of the prison-industrial system.

James, Joy, ed. *Imprisoned Intellectuals: America's Political Prisoners Write on Life, Liberation, and Rebellion.* Lanham, Md.: Rowan & Littlefield, 2003. This book samples the writing of imprisoned intellectuals from various ethnic, racial, geographical, and religious backgrounds.

See also: Oscar Zeta Acosta; Miguel Algarín; Alurista; Reyes Cárdenas; Miguel Piñero; Luis Alberto Urrea.

Judith F. Baca

American muralist

Baca brings together diverse communities through her participatory approach to mural production. An artist whose work has been exhibited worldwide, Baca also is a university professor, community activist, and founder of a nonprofit public art resource center.

Latino heritage: Mexican

Born: September 20, 1946; Los Angeles, California

Also known as: Judith Francisca Baca; Judy Baca

Areas of achievement: Art; social issues; education

Early Life

Judith Francisca Baca (BAH-kah) was born in Los Angeles, California, to Ortensia Baca. As a child, Baca and her mother moved to Watts, California, where they lived with Baca's grandmother and two aunts. Baca's biological father was absent from her youth. Ortensia never told Baca's father, who had been deployed by the Navy, about her pregnancy, and the two were never married. Baca later investigated and learned the identity and whereabouts of her biological father, Valentino Marcel.

Baca began painting as a kindergartener. A fluent Spanish-speaker, she had yet to learn English and could not participate fully in class lessons. In 1952, Baca's mother married an Italian American named Clarence Ferrari. The family moved to Pacoima, California, where Baca's stepsiblings Gary and Diane were born.

Baca was enrolled in public schools through junior high, then attended Bishop Alemany High School in Mission Hills. Compared with the public schools she previously had attended, the Catholic school had limited art resources. Baca practiced art informally, entertaining her high school peers by drawing on blackboards. She won popularity with her creative sketches and whimsical cartoons of nuns.

Although neither her mother, who worked at a tire factory, nor her stepfather, an upholsterer at Lockheed Martin, had completed college, Baca enrolled at California State University, Northridge (CSUN) after high school. She enjoyed taking courses in art, philosophy, and history. She earned a bachelor's degree in art in 1969 and ten years later received a master's in art education, both from CSUN. Baca married at age nineteen but was divorced six years later.

LIFE'S WORK

Baca's earliest jobs included working as a production illustrator at Lockheed Martin and teaching at her former high school. Baca's pivotal employment opportunity, however, arose in the early 1970's when she was hired to teach art classes at community centers in East Los Angeles. Here she befriended young local residents, primarily teenage boys, who would pass time at the parks. They chatted about tattoos and about their mutual artistic interests; a collaborative energy began to blossom. When Baca proposed that she and the youths paint together, her boss resisted, chiding her naïveté; partnership implied that the youth might be crossing rival gang territories. Undeterred, Baca began her grassroots efforts in muralism. In 1970, she and the teenagers collaboratively painted *La Abuelita* as a backdrop to the local open-air theater. The mural depicts a loving, dark-skinned grandmother with outstretched arms. Soon, local newspapers published articles applauding her transformative work organizing peace treaties among rival gangs. Shortly thereafter, Baca was promoted to director of Eastside murals. She initiated a citywide mural project that ultimately produced more than four hundred urban murals and employed more than one thousand residents.

During the summers of 1974 through 1984, Baca created one of her most famous murals, *The Great Wall of Los Angeles*. Located in the Tujunga Wash drainage channel in the San Fernando Valley, *The Great Wall of Los Angeles* is 2,754 feet long, making it one of the longest murals in the world. With powerful imagery grounded in a visual history of Los Angeles, the piece is most famous for its comparative representations of the city's ethnic history. The impact of Baca's work generated tremendous interest and sponsorship from various community agencies, leading her to cofound the Social and Public Arts Resource Center (SPARC) in 1976 in Venice, California, with artist Christina Schlesinger and filmmaker Donna Deitch. Baca's leadership style solidified her democratic and innovative approach to art production. Former Los Angeles mayor Tom Bradley commissioned her to work on a series of public art displays in 1988 for the Great Walls Unlimited: Neighborhood Pride program, which put hundreds of young artists to work on more than eighty murals.

The magnitude, scope, and tremendous collaborative efforts involved in *The Great Wall of Los Angeles* earned Baca critical acclaim and set the tone for her increasingly ambitious future cultural projects. Baca's dramatic use of color juxtaposed with tranquil imagery is exemplified in *World Wall: A Vision of the Future Without Fear* (1990). This portable mural addressing world peace, spirituality, and social justice consists of numerous 10-foot-by-30-foot panels arranged in a semicircle. The exhibit has traveled around the globe, adding new panels by local artists in many of the countries it has visited. Baca's more recent work uses computer technology to draft initial concepts, create and arrange visual images, and prepare pieces for transfer to public spaces.

Baca's academic career kept pace with her artistic prominence, flourishing after she took a professorship in Visual Arts at the University of California, Irvine in 1981. Baca later served as vice chair at the University of California at Los Angeles (UCLA) César Chávez Center for Interdisciplinary Studies in 1996 and was appointed as full professor in UCLA's World Arts and Cultures department. Beyond teaching and painting, Baca forged new academic territory by establishing the visual and

Beyond Mexican Muralism: Baca's Innovative Style

Judith F. Baca's murals are most heavily influenced by the work of Mexican muralist David Alfaro Siqueiros. Siqueiros is one of Mexico's three most famous muralists, along with Diego Rivera and José Clemente Orozco, who are known as "Los Tres Grandes" (the three great ones). Baca's artistic education in college did not, however, include their work. Rather, Baca learned about the Mexican muralists by chance. In the early 1970's, she received a book on Mexican muralism while she was working with inner-city youths in East Los Angeles. Inspired to learn more, Baca traveled to Mexico to see their murals. In 1977, she was one of twenty-five artists to participate in a muralism workshop hosted at Taller Siquieros (Siquieros's studio) in Cuernavaca, Mexico. There she mastered Siquieros's artistic techniques, which incorporate musical ratios, creative spatial divisions, and visual connectivity. Baca departs from the style of Mexican muralists, however, in her participatory style of mural-making. Her murals are produced through intense collaboration with community affiliates. The historiography of her murals is intimately intertwined with the method in which they are produced. Unlike Los Tres Grandes, who produced art for the public, Baca produces art with the public, thereby empowering local communities to reclaim and take pride in their communal open spaces.

public art program at California State University, Monterey Bay, when she served as one of thirteen founding campus faculty members in 1995-1998. As of 2010, she continues teaching visual art at UCLA.

Significance

A renowned artist and scholar, Baca remains grounded in community activism. Her cultural and artistic identity is infused with her Mexican American heritage. Her approach to art and the substance of her work exemplify a participatory-action approach to social awareness through murals. Baca's legacy is reflected in the art she produces and the young artists she trains. Her art depicts generational diversity and conveys respect for the elderly; the empowerment of women; familial bonds and unity; the value of education; and most importantly honor and respect for community practices and history. One of the persistent challenges faced by Baca is the lack of funding and political leverage to protect established murals in public spaces, which is why SPARC created Save L.A. Murals, an organization that raises awareness and preserves Los Angeles murals.

Michelle Madsen Camacho

Further Reading

Baca, Judith F. "The Human Story at the Intersection of Ethics, Aesthetics and Social Justice." *Journal of Moral Education* 34, no. 2 (June, 2005):153-169. A transcript of Baca's speech at the Association for Moral Education Conference in which she reflects on art and its relation to broader socio-political issues in the United States.

_______. Official Web site. http://www.judybaca.com. Baca's professional Web site includes a biography, photos and video of her work, and many other useful resources.

_______. "Oral History Interviews with Judith Baca." Interview by Amalia Mesa-Bains. *Archives of American Art, Smithsonian Institution* (August, 1986). Baca tells her life story to historian Amalia Mesa-Bains in 1986, at the beginning of Baca's academic career.

_______. "*World Wall: A Vision of the Future Without Fear*." *Frontiers: A Journal of Women Studies* 14, no. 2 (1994): 81-85. This scholarly article provides Baca's own subjective analysis of her mobile mural *World Wall*.

_______. "*World Wall: A Vision of the Future Without Fear*—An Interview with Judith F. Baca." Interview by Frances K. Pohl. *Frontiers: A Journal of Women Studies* 11, no. 1 (1990): 33-43. An interview by art historian Frances Pohl providing contextual background and analysis of Baca's mural *World Wall*.

Olmstead, Mary. *Judy Baca*. Chicago: Raintree, 2005. Written for a younger audience, this monograph provides an accessible biography of Baca.

Social and Public Art Resource Center. http://www.sparcmurals.org. Official Web site for Baca's nonprofit organization, which produces, preserves, and educates the public on murals.

See also: José Antonio Burciaga; Barbara Carrasco; Amalia Mesa-Bains; Leo Tanguma; Jesse Treviño.

Catherine Bach

American actor

While best known for her role as the scintillating Daisy Duke on the hugely popular 1979-1985 television series The Dukes of Hazzard, Bach also achieved success as a singer and fashion innovator. In the years after her breakthrough role, Bach emerged as an advocate for a variety of national and women's issues.

Latino heritage: Mexican
Born: March 1, 1954; Warren, Ohio
Also known as: Catherine Bachman
Areas of achievement: Radio and television; acting; fashion

Early Life

Catherine Bach (bahk) was born Catherine Bachman in Warren, Ohio, to Bernard Bachman, an Air Force officer of German heritage, and Norma Kucera, an acupuncturist of Mexican decent. The family soon moved to western South Dakota, where Bach was raised on a ranch near the small town of Faith in Meade County. As a young child, she made her professional stage debut in a production of the musical *The Sound of Music*.

From 1976 to 1982, Bach was married to David Shaw, son of legendary actor Angela Lansbury. She wed again in 1991, this time to Peter Lopez, an entertainment attorney who at one time represented singers Michael Jackson, Andrea Bocelli, Michael Bublé, and the Eagles. Bach and Lopez had two children together: Sophia Isabelle, born in 1996, and Laura, born in 1998. Lopez died in 2010.

LIFE'S WORK

As a performer, Bach is best known for her portrayal of Daisy Duke on CBS's *The Dukes of Hazzard.* From 1979 to 1985, she costarred as the scantily clad yet endlessly capable tomboy cousin of the protagonists, greatly influencing fashion trends with her revealing cutoff denim shorts, which came to be known as "Daisy Dukes." More than just a sexpot, Daisy was a waitress-cum-action heroine who often helped the male adventurers save the day.

The character's iconic style was developed by Bach herself. An experienced designer, she put herself through the University of California at Los Angeles by creating costumes for local theater groups and making clothing for individual clients. The producers of *The Dukes of Hazzard* had intended for Daisy to be a Dolly Parton-type character, dressed in a gingham poodle skirt, high-heeled boots, and a tight white turtleneck. Recognizing that few women would identify with that style, Bach persuaded the producers to allow her to design the now-famous costume that catapulted her to sex-symbol status and made an indelible mark on 1980's fashion: a homemade T-shirt, high-heeled pumps, and the signature suggestive shorts. During the height of the show's popularity, Bach's legs were insured for $1 million. Bach also took creative control of a Daisy Duke poster marketed by the show's producers; it went on to sell more than five million copies. Her fans reportedly included First Lady Nancy Reagan. A resurgence of the shorts' popularity occurred in the early 1990's, highlighted by a double-platinum hip-hop song, "Dazzey Duks" by Duice.

Bach recreated the role of Daisy Duke for the short-lived animated version of the series, *The Dukes*, which ran during the 1983 season on CBS. From 1991 to 1994, she starred alongside Robert Mitchum on the Fox Family Channel series *African Skies*, a drama that chronicled life in post-apartheid South Africa. Over the course of her acting career, which began in the early 1970's, she appeared in more than a dozen films, including *Thunderbolt and Lightfoot* (1974) and *Cannonball Run II* (1984), performed onstage in William Mastrosimone's *Extremities* (1982), found success as a singer on the nightclub circuit, and toured internationally with the United Service Organizations. In 1995, she was selected to host the fifteenth annual Tejano Music Awards.

Catherine Bach. (AP Images)

Citing her Mexican ancestry and descent from one of California's oldest families, Bach was chosen in 1985 to serve as the model for the figurehead of the state's official schooner, *Californian.* San Diego artist Frank Morgan sculpted her likeness as Califia, the mythical queen of the Amazons for whom the state is named.

Resuming her design career, Bach launched a jewelry line through Debenhams, the British department store chain, in 2002. She also designed a line of denim pants and shorts modeled after her famous costumes from *The Dukes of Hazzard.* The end of the decade saw Bach as an outspoken opponent of outsourcing in manufacturing and a supporter of positive images of women in the media.

SIGNIFICANCE

Bach's performance as Daisy Duke made her a style icon of the late 1970's and early 1980's. Particularly impressive was Bach's ability to create a character who was at once vivacious and sexy without being exploited. Her behind-the-scenes contributions also were notable.

Bach met the producers' mandate for a sensuous character on her terms, styling herself in a manner she saw as both appealing to and respectful of women.

Leon James Bynum

Further Reading

Bates, Billie Rae. *Them Dukes! Them Dukes!: A Guide to TV's "The Dukes of Hazzard."* Seattle: BookSurge, 2006. Bates's cast guide offers a thorough narrative of Bach's professional accomplishments.

Hofstede, David. *The Dukes of Hazzard: The Unofficial Companion*. New York: Macmillan, 1998. Bach's foreword and anecdotes provide extensive details on her contributions to *The Dukes of Hazzard* and 1980's fashion.

Jensen, Richard. *Trespass in Hazzard County: My Life as an Insider on "The Dukes of Hazzard."* Bloomington, Ind.: iUniverse, 2003. Behind-the-scenes information from those involved with *The Dukes of Hazzard* provides a foundation for understanding how Bach shaped Daisy Duke's image.

Levine, Elana. *Wallowing in Sex: The New Sexual Culture of 1970's American Television*. Durham, N.C.: Duke University Press, 2007. The career of Bach and other sex symbols of the 1970's are told against the backdrop of the nation's changing sexual mores.

See also: María Conchita Alonso; Lynda Carter; Elizabeth Peña; Raquel Welch.

Herman Badillo

Puerto Rican-born politician

Badillo is a prominent New York City politician who has held several important offices including Bronx borough president, congressman, and other positions at the state and city level. He also has been a candidate for mayor several times.

Latino heritage: Puerto Rican

Born: August 21, 1929; Caguas, Puerto Rico

Area of achievement: Government and politics

Early Life

Herman Badillo (bah-DEE-yoh) was born in Puerto Rico in August 1929. His parents, Francisco and Carmen, both died of tuberculosis by the time he was about five years old. At the age of eleven, and not then proficient in English, he went to live with an aunt in New York City. At the time he entered high school, Puerto Ricans generally were not expected to go to college, and Badillo was enrolled in a vocational curriculum; however he defied the odds and went on to obtain a bachelor's degree in business administration from the City College of New York and a bachelor of laws degree from the Brooklyn Law School. He was admitted to the New York State Bar in 1955 and about a year later also became a certified public accountant. He worked at that profession while attending law school, where he became a member of the *Law Review* and was the valedictorian of his graduating class.

Life's Work

In the late 1950's, Badillo became active in New York Democratic Party circles and was appointed commissioner of the New York City Department of Relocation. He began a political career that included serving as borough president of the Bronx from 1966 to 1970. He next was elected to Congress representing a district that included portions of the Bronx, Queens, and Manhattan. Badillo thus was the first person of Puerto Rican nationality ever elected to Congress. He was easily reelected for three more terms and was one of the founders of the Congressional Hispanic Caucus. He served on several committees, one of his primary interests being employment discrimination. Badillo also initially was a strong proponent of bilingual education but would eventually reverse his position and became a strong opponent of it.

Badillo next ran for New York City mayor, becoming a perennial candidate. He had resigned from Congress at the end of 1977 to become deputy mayor in the administration of voluble Democrat Ed Koch, but after a disagreement with the mayor, Badillo resigned his post. By 2010, he had run for (or professed interest in) the mayor's office six times, the last time in 2001 against billionaire Michael Bloomberg. He also has run unsuccessfully for comptroller positions at the city and state level. Badillo served in the state government for two years as chairman of the board of directors of the

Herman Badillo. (AP Photo)

State of New York Mortgage Agency. He also was a delegate to the state's constitutional convention in the 1960's.

Over the years, Badillo has become more conservative, eventually turning to the Republican Party in the 1990's. When Rudolph Giuliani became New York's mayor, Badillo was named his special counsel on education policy and he served as chairman of the board of the City University of New York. Badillo also was the mayor's liaison to the city's board of education; he advocated more control of the perennially troubled system by the city administration. After abandoning his quest for higher office, he joined a law firm and a conservative think tank. Badillo has been married three times (once widowed) and has a son and two stepsons; his third wife was a New York City school teacher.

Significance

Badillo has the distinction of being the first Puerto Rican elected to Congress; before that, he was the first to be elected or appointed to various major offices in New York. While in Congress, his advocacy of bilingual education did much to encourage its implementation in numerous school systems. He stated, "If we fail in education, we fail everywhere. It has to be our most urgent priority." However, Badillo later rejected bilingual education as it was implemented and came to believe that it impeded immigrants' assimilation into American society.

As his political views have become more conservative, he has generated considerable controversy among Latinos by implying that, despite their numbers, they are too disorganized and disinterested to wield proportionate influence. While chairman of the City University of New York, he was instrumental in abolishing its thirty-year-old open enrollment policy, another controversial action.

Roy Liebman

Further Reading

Badillo, Herman. *A Bill of No Rights: Attica and the American Prison System*. New York: Outerbridge & Lazard, 1972. An attack on the response of New York state authorities to the violent Attica prison riot.

_______. *One Nation, One Standard: An Ex-Liberal on How Hispanics Can Succeed Just Like Other Immigrant Groups*. New York: Sentinel, 2006. Badillo offers a plan by which Latinos can increase their influence in American society. He is especially critical of the bilingual education system that he once supported.

Fried, Joseph P. "Following Up." *The New York Times*, January 18, 2004. Brief article noting Badillo's announcement that he would not run for office again. Offers an overview of his political career.

Neidle, Cecyle S. *Great Immigrants*. New York: Twayne, 1973. A book about prominent immigrants to America that contains an entry about Badillo.

See also: Joe J. Bernal; Irma Rangel; Edward R. Roybal.

Albert V. Baez

Mexican-born physicist and educator

Baez was a physicist who coinvented the first X-ray microscope and helped launch the science of X-ray imaging optics. A pacifist, he refused to use his physics background to develop nuclear arms during the Cold War; instead, he turned his focus to education and pioneered the discipline of science education worldwide.

Latino heritage: Mexican

Born: November 15, 1912; Puebla, Mexico

Died: March 20, 2007; Redwood City, California

Also known as: Albert Vinicio Baez

Areas of achievement: Science and technology; education; social issues

Early Life

Albert Vinicio Baez (vee-NEE-see-oh BI-ehz) was born November 15, 1912, in Puebla, Mexico, to Alberto Baez, Methodist minister, and his wife, Thalia. Although Baez moved with his family to the United States when he was two years old, he did not become a naturalized citizen until 1938. The family settled in Brooklyn, New York, where his mother was a social worker for the Young Women's Christian Association. When Baez was seven, the family returned to Puebla for a year, which strengthened connections to his Mexican heritage and identity. He also was greatly influenced by his grandfather, who had established the Instituto Metodista Mexicano (an institute to train and educate Methodist ministers).

Baez attended Drew University, receiving a bachelor's degree in mathematics and physics in 1933. After attending Syracuse University, where he earned a master's degree in mathematics in 1935, he taught physics and mathematics in colleges in New York. In 1936, he married Joan C. Bridge, whom he had met in high school. They had three daughters: Pauline and folk singers Mimi Fariña and Joan Baez.

During World War II, Baez moved his family to California, where he had been hired to teach a physics course for the Army at Stanford University. At the end of the war, he joined the faculty and continued teaching while working on his doctorate in mathematics and physics, which he earned in 1950. While conducting graduate research, Baez and his adviser, Paul Kirkpatrick, built an X-ray microscope that used angled mirrors to focus the X-rays. This tactic became known as Kirkpatrick-Baez geometry. In his dissertation, Baez referred to the ability to use X-rays for imaging as "X-ray optics."

Life's Work

Baez remained a physics professor in California until 1956. Although colleagues were recruited to use their expertise in the arms race during the Cold War, Baez objected to using his research for destruction. Because science and mathematics were becoming increasingly important, he turned his attention to improving high school science programs in the United States and eventually establishing science and mathematics curriculum in other countries. From 1951 to 1952, he took a leave from teaching at the University of Redlands in California. He took his family to Iraq, where he taught physics and set up a laboratory and program of study at the University of Baghdad. He and his wife later wrote a memoir of the family's experiences abroad, which included drawings by their daughter Joan.

Throughout his life, Baez continued to improve on the technology of X-ray optics. Although attempts to create a hologram image using X-rays failed (because the X-rays could not be focused narrowly enough), he did eventually modify the X-ray microscope to use an array of curved mirrors to focus the rays. This modification later was used in creating the X-ray telescope.

By the end of the 1950's, Baez had become increasingly interested in effective science education. He advocated for fundamental scientific literacy and the need for an investigative and experimental approach in order to develop skills in observation and interpretation. From 1958 to 1960, Baez was studio physicist for the Physical Science Study Committee. He appeared in training films created to improve the teaching of high school physics. Between 1961 and 1967, he served as the first director of science education for the United Nations Educational, Scientific, and Cultural Organization (UNESCO). He developed and oversaw programs to improve the teaching of science and mathematics worldwide and helped developing nations adapt curricula to their cultures. In 1967, he published a physics textbook.

Baez was a lifelong pacifist (he and his wife became Quakers after marriage) who opposed the Vietnam War, and during that time he became increasingly involved in activism and humanitarian programs. He also became concerned about the environment and the impact of science and technology on our planet. After his retirement, Baez continued to promote science education through speeches and lectures. He became involved in and served as president of Vivamos Mejor/USA, an organization that works to improve health, housing, nutrition, and environmental technology in Latin America.

In 1991, Baez and Kirkpatrick received the Dennis Gabor Award for their pioneering work in development of X-ray optics in both microscopes and telescopes. To honor his contributions to both science and humanity, the Hispanic Engineer National Achievements Awards Corporation (HENAAC) established the Albert V. Baez Award in 1995. It is awarded to engineers and scientists for outstanding technological achievement and humanitarian service. Baez died of natural causes on March 20, 2007, in Redwood City, California. He was ninety-four years old.

Significance

Baez was a major figure in the field of physics and in science and technology education. His pioneering work in the physics of light during World War II led to the development of a discipline, X-ray imaging optics, that had important applications in the technologies used for space exploration into the 1990's. He also had a significant impact on the methods used to teach science and mathematics internationally. Baez worked to establish science laboratories as part of curriculum in high schools as well as colleges and universities and advocated for science education that was practical and relevant.

Lisa A. Wroble

Further Reading

Baez, Albert V. *Innovation in Science Education World-Wide*. New York: UNESCO Press, 1976. Baez draws on twenty-five years of experience in the field of science education, describing his philosophy for and reasoning in improving how science is taught.

Baez, Albert V., and Joan Baez. *A Year in Baghdad.* Santa Barbara, Calif: John Daniel, 1988. Describes couple's experiences trying to settle their family into life in Baghdad in 1951 while Baez taught physics at the university. Offers insight into the family's values, which were clarified through their trials and travails.

Reimers, Fernando. "Albert Vinicio Baez and the Promotion of Science Education in the Developing World 1912-2007," *Prospects* 37 (September, 2007): p. 369-381. Provides a brief biography of the scientist and describes the impact he had on physics and education. Discusses Baez's approach toward and contributions to science education.

See also: Fernando Alegría; Luis W. Alvarez; Ralph Amado; Joan Baez; José D. García; Vicente José Llamas.

Joan Baez

American folk singer and activist

A pioneer in the American folk music revival of the late 1950's and 1960's, Baez blended pacifist and progressive views with her talent as a singer and guitarist to become one of the best-known social, political, and human rights activists of the era. Her protest songs galvanized a generation fighting for civil rights and against the Vietnam War.

Latino heritage: Mexican

Born: January 9, 1941; Staten Island, New York

Also known as: Joan Chandos Baez

Areas of achievement: Music; activism; social issues

Early Life

Joan Chandos Baez (BI-ehz) was born on Staten Island, New York, to physicist Albert V. Baez, a native of Puebla, Mexico, and Joan Bridge Baez, who was born in Edinburgh, Scotland. Albert and the elder Joan had three daughters, Pauline, Joan, and Mimi, who married American writer and folk singer Richard Fariña. Because Albert worked as a university professor, the family moved frequently and lived in various locations nationally and internationally, including Redlands, California; Baghdad, Iraq; and Belmont, Massachusetts, near Boston.

Baez's parents held progressive social and political views and raised their children as Quakers. When she was a junior high school student in Redlands, Baez was ostracized by her white classmates because of her dark skin and Mexican surname. Her first act of civil disobedience occurred when she was a student at Palo Alto High School. She refused to leave her desk during an air

Joan Baez. (Library of Congress)

raid drill because she was opposed to the arms buildup during the Cold War. School officials punished her, and her fellow students shunned her because of her pacifist beliefs. Feeling isolated, Baez took refuge in music and began to develop her distinctive soprano voice. Her interest in traditional folk music was awakened when she was exposed to Pete Seeger's work. Other influences included Harry Belafonte and Odetta.

After Baez finished high school in 1958, her father accepted a teaching position at the Massachusetts Institute of Technology and moved his family to the Boston area. Baez briefly attended Boston University but dropped out when she discovered the vibrant folk music community flourishing in the Harvard Square coffee houses. Her career as a folk singer began when she became a regular at Club Mt. Auburn 47 (also known as Club 47) in Cambridge. She became more widely known when folk artist Bob Gibson invited her to perform at the Newport Folk Festival in 1959. A record contract with Vanguard followed in 1960.

Life's Work

By 1961, Baez was the reigning queen of folk music, but she had not yet engaged in the high-profile activism that would mark her later career. When she met Bob Dylan at Gerde's Folk City in New York City, she was primarily known as a traditional folk singer. The two were part of a larger folk revival that included Carolyn Hester, Eric Von Schmidt, Jim Kweskin, Dave Van Ronk, Maria and Geoff Muldaur, Bob Neuwirth, Mimi and Richard Fariña, and other musicians who lived in New York and Boston.

Baez and Dylan's meeting and subsequent love affair led to one of the most fruitful professional partnerships of the 1960's. At the time he first met Baez, Dylan was establishing his reputation as a writer of popular protest songs. Deeply impressed by his socially conscious lyrics, especially those in "With God on Our Side," Baez began to include such songs in her own repertoire. One of the highlights of their collaboration occurred when they appeared together during the March on Washington for Jobs and Freedom held on August 28, 1963. Organized by Martin Luther King, Jr., among others, the rally for civil and economic rights for African Americans drew more than 250,000 people. The two ardent young artists singing "We Shall Overcome" inspired other young activists of the 1960's.

Although Dylan and Baez ended their relationship in 1965, their partnership left its mark on Baez's personal and professional life. In 1965, she recorded *Farewell Angelina*, which included several of Dylan's songs. In 1968, she released an album of Dylan covers titled *Any Day Now*. In 1975, she recorded her acclaimed album *Diamonds and Rust*. The title song was a reflection on her star-crossed affair with Dylan.

Baez continued her work for social justice throughout the turbulent 1960's. In 1965, she joined King on his civil rights marches, most notably the journey from Selma to Montgomery, Alabama. In 1966, she supported César Chávez in his efforts to secure fair wages and safe working conditions for migrant farmworkers in California. A passionate opponent of the Vietnam War, she founded the Institute for the Study of Nonviolence in 1964 and participated in numerous antiwar protests. In 1967, Baez was arrested in Oakland, California, for obstructing the doorway of the Armed Forces Induction Center. While serving a monthlong sentence in the Santa Rita Jail, she met David Harris, a fellow antiwar protester, whom she married in March, 1968.

Shortly after their marriage, Harris refused to be drafted and was arrested in July, 1969. Pregnant with their son, Gabriel, Baez continued to perform. She wrote a number of songs in honor of Harris, including "A Song for David" and "Fifteen Months," which was

Hispanic Influences in Baez's Music

Joan Baez has featured some Spanish songs on her English-language albums, including "El Preso Numero Nueve" ("Prisoner Number Nine") on *Joan Baez* (1960) and "Dida" on *Diamonds and Rust* (1975). Both songs appear on *Gracias a la vida: Joan Baez canta en español* (*Here's to Life: Joan Baez Sings in Spanish*, 1974), a work she has called "my gift to the Spanish people." Offering selections from Mexico, Cuba, Spain, and other Hispanic countries, the song list for the 1974 release was suggested by a group of exiled Chileans who had suffered under the repressive government of Augusto Pinochet, the successor of the murdered Salvador Allende. The title track was contributed by Chilean Violetta Parra, and "Te recuerdo Amanda" ("I Remember You, Amanda") was written by her countryman, Victor Jarra, who was killed during the 1973 coup d'état. Other selections include the protest song "No nos moveran" ("We Shall Not Be Moved") and Catalan folk song "El rossinyol" ("The Nightingale"). Latin rhythms prevail, and two songs are performed by a traditional mariachi band. The album sold moderately well in the United States but was a best seller in Spain and Latin America.

the term of Harris's imprisonment. She also released a tribute recording titled *David's Album* in 1969. Harris's imprisonment took a toll on their relationship, however, and they divorced in 1973.

Although the folk music revival waned in the late 1960's, Baez continued to record and perform. She regularly released albums and toured nationally and internationally. In December, 1972, she traveled to North Vietnam with a peace delegation. She experienced the horrors of war firsthand when the United States engaged in eleven days of carpet bombing over Hanoi. She also witnessed human rights violations on the part of the North Vietnamese. Her experiences led her to found her own human rights organization, Humanitas International, and launch an American branch of Amnesty International. In addition to Vietnam, she has spread her message of peace and justice to many countries throughout Europe and Latin America.

For many years, Baez refused to sing in Spain because she disagreed with the oppressive policies of dictator Francisco Franco. After his death in 1977, as she toured the country, she paid tribute to those who were murdered under his regime. Although she does not speak fluent Spanish, during her concerts she sang some songs in Spanish, including "No nos moveran" ("We Shall Not Be Moved"), an anthem of resistance that had not been sung publicly in Spain during Franco's rule. Her willingness to sing in the native language of the country demonstrated her solidarity with the Spanish people.

Baez also fought for human rights on behalf of the residents of several Latin American countries, including Brazil, Venezuela, Argentina, and, in particular, Chile. Disturbed about alleged Central Intelligence Agency involvement in the assassination of Salvador Allende on September 11, 1973, Baez gave a series of concerts sponsored by Amnesty International in support of Chileans who were repressed by the new regime. Her work gave birth to Baez's only Spanish-language album, *Gracias a la vida: Joan Baez canta en español* (*Here's to Life: Joan Baez Sings in Spanish*), released in 1974.

Significance

An artist whose work is inextricably linked to her philosophical and political beliefs, Baez was an icon of the 1960's and 1970's counterculture and protest movements. Although her vocal opposition to war and violence and support of various human-rights causes made her a controversial figure at times, she remained steadfast in her dedication to activism. Baez's music was part of a rich tapestry of protest music that defined a generation and continues to speak to the antiwar fervor of new generations of activists.

Pegge Bochynski

Further Reading

Baez, Joan. *Daybreak.* New York: Avon, 1970. Baez's first autobiography offers an inside look at her family life and Quaker upbringing.

_______. *And a Voice to Sing With: A Memoir.* New York: Simon & Schuster, 2009. Baez's second memoir presents an honest, no-holds-barred account of her life, from her childhood in a progressive household through her long career as a singer, songwriter, and activist.

Fuss, Charles, J. *Joan Baez: A Bio-Bibliography.* Westport, Conn.: Greenwood Press, 1996. A concise biography, plus detailed entries that include release dates, songs, songwriters, musicians, production credits, review excerpts, and critical commentary offer a comprehensive look at Baez's life, career, and activism.

Hajdu, David. *Positively 4th Street: The Lives and Times of Joan Baez, Bob Dylan, Mimi Baez Fariña, and Richard Fariña.* New York: Farrar, Straus and

Giroux, 2001. An illuminating account of the key roles Baez, Dylan, and the Fariñas played in the rise of the folk era in the mid-1960's.

See also: Albert V. Baez; César Chávez; Helen Fabela Chávez; Mimi Fariña; Jerry Garcia; Linda Ronstadt.

Lourdes G. Baird

Ecuadorian-born lawyer and judge

Baird has served as an assistant U.S. attorney, U.S. attorney, and U.S. district court judge in the largest federal district in the nation, California's Central District. She was the first Latina to serve as a judge in the district. She also was the lead prosecutor in the federal trial of four police officers involved in the beating of African American motorist Rodney King in 1992.

Latino heritage: Ecuadorian
Born: May 12, 1935; Quito, Ecuador
Also known as: Lourdes Gillespie Baird; Lourdes Gillespie
Area of achievement: Law

Early Life

Lourdes Gillespie Baird (LOHR-dehs behrd) was born on May 12, 1935, in Quito, Ecuador; she was one of seven children born to James C. Gillespie and Josefina Delgado. When she was one year old, her family moved to Los Angeles, California. Growing up, Baird attended Roman Catholic parochial schools, including the all-girls Immaculate Heart high school, which was run by a group of very independent, progressive nuns. Baird found this to be an especially encouraging environment.

After graduating high school, Baird attended secretarial school briefly before marrying businessman William T. Baird in 1956. The couple had three children and divorced in 1975. Baird was a stay-at-home mother for eleven years before returning to school part-time at Los Angeles City College, where she earned an associate of arts degree in 1972. She then transferred to the University of California at Los Angeles (UCLA), where she earned a bachelor's degree in sociology in 1973 and her J.D. from the UCLA School of Law in 1976. She took and passed the California bar exam soon after graduation at the age of forty-one.

Life's Work

After completing her education, Baird became an assistant United States attorney, working under William Keller. She left the U.S. Attorney's Office to become a partner in the all-female firm Baird, Munger, and Myers in 1983. Three years later, she was appointed a judge in the East Los Angeles Municipal Court, and in 1988, she was appointed to the juvenile court division of the Los Angeles Superior Court.

In November, 1989, California Senator Pete Wilson, a Republican, nominated the Democrat Baird to the post of U.S. Attorney for California's Central District—the nation's largest federal district and the office in which she started her career. She was officially nominated for the post in May, 1990, by President George H. W. Bush and confirmed by the Senate in July of that year.

The district held numerous challenges for Baird. Besides the drug-related crimes that were a particular concern for her, Baird was faced with the task of

Lourdes G. Baird. (AFP/Getty Images)

investigating Los Angeles's mayor, Tom Bradley, who was accused of benefitting from insider stock information. Shortly after she assumed office, the Los Angeles Sheriff's Department was the focus of a grand jury investigation for allegedly mishandling jailhouse informants. Her office, along with the other U.S. Attorney's offices, was also responsible for investigating and prosecuting the fraud cases resulting from the savings and loan crisis of the late 1980's and early 1990's.

In 1992, Baird became involved in the prosecution of four Los Angeles police officers accused of violating the civil rights of Rodney King, an African American motorist whom the officers had beaten in a videotaped incident. This case followed the officers' acquittal on criminal charges, which sparked the Los Angeles riots.

Baird left the U.S. Attorney's Office in 1992 to accept an appointment to the bench of the U.S. District Court for the same district. She presided over the 1996 lawsuit filed against the U.S. Immigration and Naturalization Service by Jorge Guzman, a senior supervisor and one of the highest ranking Hispanics in the bureau's Los Angeles district. The suit alleged that Guzman was being harassed because of his heritage, citing two dozen internal investigations with no reprimands or blocked promotions and a raid on his home by armed officers. The suit was settled out of court. In 1998, Baird refused to block the implementation of California's Proposition 227 which ended bilingual education programs in California public schools. In 1999, she heard arguments in a case brought by the U.S. Customs Service against three Mexican banks suspected of laundering money and, in a separate case, ruled that a restraint chair used by the Ventura County Sheriff's Department violated the constitutional rights of detainees.

In 2000, Baird overturned a $143 million judgment against the pharmaceutical company Pfizer over its antibiotic Trovan when it was determined that the plaintiff had falsified evidence. Her last high-profile ruling came in a 2003 case involving a group of Mexican migrant workers invited to Ventura County under the H-2A federal guest-worker program. Baird ruled the workers were protected under state labor laws under the program and transferred the case back to the state court system. She retired from the court in 2005 and went to work in the field of alternative dispute resolution in affiliation with Judicial Arbitration and Mediation Services.

Baird received numerous awards and honors over the course of her career. In 1991, she was named UCLA School of Law Alumnus of the Year and a Woman of Promise by the Hispanic Women's Council. In 1993, she was given the UCLA Professional Achievement Award, and she received the Young Women's Christian Association's Silver Achievement Award for the Professions the following year. In 2001, Baird was named Outstanding Jurist of the Year by the Los Angeles County Bar Association. She also was recognized as one of the top arbiters in California in 2007, 2009, and 2010, and she was selected as a Southern California Super Lawyer in the field of alternative dispute resolution for 2010.

Baird has been a member of the California Women Lawyers since 1984; a member of the Rule of Law delegations in Latin America, Africa, Asia, Europe, and the Middle East since 1988; and a member of the Hispanic National Bar Association since 1992.

Baird's Role in Rodney King's Federal Trial

Lourdes G. Baird served as the United States Attorney for the Central District of California from 1990 to 1992. During her tenure, in March, 1991, four Los Angeles police officers were charged in the beating of African American motorist Rodney King. The officers involved in the incident were tried on state criminal charges but were acquitted of all but one count in April, 1992. After their acquittal was announced, several days of violent riots and protests erupted in Los Angeles, resulting in the deaths of more than fifty people and some $800 million in damages. The federal courthouse that housed Baird's office also was targeted during these riots.

A federal investigation by Baird's office began immediately after the initial incident but was suspended while the state pursued its charges against the officers. After the officers' acquittal, Baird reopened the federal investigation and filed civil charges against the officers, accusing them of violating King's civil rights. Two of the officers ultimately were convicted, and Baird is credited with leading the prosecution in the case. By the time the case was concluded, however, she had taken a seat as a judge in the United States District Court for the Central District of California, where she served until 2005.

Significance

Baird is a significant figure in California legal history. At the time that she became the U.S. Attorney for the nation's largest judicial district, she was one of only five women to hold that post in the nation and the only Latina. She also was the first Hispanic woman ever to serve as a district court judge for California's Central District.

While the bulk of her career focused on the courtroom, her post-judicial career has been dedicated to alternative forms of conflict resolution, for which she been highly decorated.

Tammy L. Reedy-Strother

Further Reading

Cannon, Lou. *Official Negligence: How Rodney King and the Riots Changed Los Angeles and the LAPD.* Boulder, Colo.: Westview Press, 1999. This detailed examination of the King case includes discussion of Baird's role.

Garcia-Johnson, Ronie-Richele. "Lourdes G. Baird." In *Latinas!: Women of Achievement*, edited by Diane Telgen and Jim Kamp. Detroit, Mich.: Visible Ink Press, 1996. Overview of Baird's career and achievements in the context of race and gender.

Mendoza, Sylvia. *The Book of Latina Women: 150 Vidas of Passion, Strength, and Success.* Avon, Mass.: Adams Media, 2004. Contains a brief overview of Baird's life and career.

Newton, Jim, and Leslie Berger. "U.S. Files Civil Rights Charges Against Four Officers in King Case." *The Los Angeles Times*, August 6, 1992. Newspaper article focusing on Baird's comments regarding the federal indictments against the Los Angeles police officers involved in the Rodney King case.

See also: Joaquín G. Avila; Norma V. Cantú; José Ángel Gutiérrez; Antonia Hernández; Vilma Socorro Martínez.

Román Baldorioty de Castro

Puerto Rican-born educator, politician, journalist, and abolitionist

One of the most important political figures of his day, Baldorioty de Castro fought for Puerto Rican self-rule throughout his life and labored to abolish slavery and obtain civil rights for all. He was a founder of the Autonomist Party, which was dedicated to Puerto Rican political self-determination, and wrote extensively on political and historical topics. Baldorioty de Castro also was a professor of the natural sciences and maritime studies.

Latino heritage: Puerto Rican

Born: February 28, 1822; Guaynabo, Puerto Rico

Died: September 30, 1889; Ponce, Puerto Rico

Areas of achievement: Government and politics; activism; education; science and technology

Early Life

The illegitimate son of Juan de Castro (who later recognized him) and a woman whose family name was Baldorioty, but whose given name is unknown, Román Baldorioty de Castro (roh-MAHN BAHL-doh-ree-OH-tee deh KAHS-troh) was born and raised in Guaynabo, Puerto Rico. He chose to use his mother's family name first and his father's family name second, a reversal of Spanish custom, making a clear public statement that it was his mother, rather than his father, who was the great inspiration of his life.

Although his family was poor, Baldorioty de Castro obtained an outstanding primary education at the school of the celebrated black teacher Rafael Cordero. He next enrolled at the Jesuit minor seminary in San Juan, where he performed outstandingly. Baldorioty de Castro gained the admiration of Father Rufo Manuel Fernández, who obtained a scholarship from the Royal Under-Secretariat for Pharmacy for the boy to continue his studies at the University of Madrid, with the understanding that he would return to Puerto Rico to teach for at least six years after his graduation. In Madrid, Baldorioty de Castro joined the Society for the Gathering of Historical Documents of the Island of Saint John the Baptist. He was awarded his bachelor's degree in physical sciences and mathematics in 1851.

Life's Work

True to his promise, Baldorioty de Castro returned to San Juan, Puerto Rico, in 1853 to teach botany and nautical sciences at the School of Commerce, Agriculture, and Nautical Sciences and physics and chemistry at his alma mater, the Jesuit Seminario Conciliar. Seeking to instill both scientific knowledge and enlightened political concepts in the minds of his students, Baldorioty de Castro soon found himself being watched by government officials. After the Grito de Lares (the Shout of Lares), the failed attempt to overthrow the Spanish government on the island, Baldorioty de Castro felt that he had to leave his post. In 1860 and 1865, he was named to the Secretariat for Fairs and Expositions, a position that required him to write programs and pamphlets for cultural events, among them the Universal Exposition held in Paris in 1867.

Baldorioty de Castro began his political career in 1870, when he was elected as a Puerto Rican delegate to the Spanish Cortes, the empire's highest governing body. He distinguished himself as an impassioned orator and defender of civil rights, as well as a tireless opponent of slavery. As a means of propounding his ideas, Baldorioty de Castro founded two publications, *Puerto Rican Affairs* and *Spanish Mail*. Upon his return to Puerto Rico in 1873, he learned that his teaching appointments had been rescinded because of his opposition to the monarchy and to slavery. He lived in poverty in Río Piedras but then moved to Ponce, where he became the editor of an autonomist newspaper, *The Right*. Thanks to his efforts, slavery was outlawed in Puerto Rico on March 22, 1873. Soon after, Baldorioty de Castro was forced to seek political asylum in the Dominican Republic but founded the Antillean High School while he was there.

Returning to Puerto Rico in 1878, Baldorioty de Castro advocated for political rights, such as direct taxation, decentralization of government functions, freedom of commerce, and the right to prepare local government budgets. In order to spread his doctrine of political autonomy, he joined the staff of the newpaper *The Chronicle* in 1878, galvanizing those who longed for self-determination. In 1887, Baldorioty de Castro and José de Diego cofounded the Autonomist Party of Puerto Rico, with Baldorioty de Castro assuming the presidency. Because of the perceived threat to his rule, the governor briefly imprisoned Baldorioty de Castro and several other prominent autonomists in El Morro Castle for sedition. Unfortunately, this brief time in the harsh conditions of El Morro destroyed Baldorioty de Castro's health, and he died shortly thereafter on September 30, 1889, in Ponce.

SIGNIFICANCE

Baldorioty de Castro was one of the towering figures of late nineteenth-century Puerto Rican society. Not only did he bring vast and profound scientific knowledge to the island from Spain, he also dedicated his life to spreading enlightened ideas of self-government and proclaiming the equality of all men and women. His years of teaching gave him a forum in which to influence some of the greatest young minds of the next generation of Puerto Rican thinkers. Perhaps more important was the role that Baldorioty de Castro played in winning the good will and support of many Spaniards and Puerto Ricans in his quest for Puerto Rican autonomy. Baldorioty de Castro's greatest achievement was the abolition of slavery, which he achieved through his tireless opposition in his speeches and writings. Baldorioty de Castro's organization of the Autonomist Party and his work with other Puerto Rican intellectuals and political figures prepared the way for the transition from Spanish to American rule.

Mark T. DeStephano

FURTHER READING

Ayala, César J., and Rafael Bernabé. *Puerto Rico in the American Century: A History Since 1898*. Chapel Hill: University of North Carolina Press, 2009. A brief but good description of the important role that Baldorioty de Castro played in the quest for Puerto Rican autonomy under Spanish rule.

Schmidt-Nowara, Christopher. *Empire and Antislavery: Spain, Cuba, and Puerto Rico, 1833-1874*. Pittsburgh, Pa.: University of Pittsburgh Press, 1999.

Wagenheim, Kal, and Olga Jiménez de Wagenheim. *The Puerto Ricans: A Documentary History*. Princeton, N.J.: Marcus Wiener, 2008. Baldorioty de Castro's influence in the political process appears here in primary documents from the period.

See also: José Celso Barbosa; Luis Muñoz Rivera.

JOSÉ CELSO BARBOSA

Puerto Rican-born physician and politician

Throughout his life, Barbosa worked in the area of public medicine but also dedicated himself to political reform. First an active member of the Autonomist Party under Spanish rule, Barbosa founded the Republican Party of Puerto Rico, which advocated acceptance of American rule and eventual American statehood.

Latino heritage: Puerto Rican

Born: July 27, 1857; Bayamón, Puerto Rico

Died: September 21, 1921; San Juan, Puerto Rico

Areas of achievement: Medicine; government and politics

Early Life

Born in Bayamón, Puerto Rico, to Hermógenes Barbosa Tirado and Carmela Alcalá, José Celso Barbosa (SEHL-soh bahr-BOH-sah) was raised mostly by his maternal aunt, Lucía Alcalá. He first attended the local school of Olegario Núñez and then the public elementary school of Gabriel Ferrer Hernández, both in Bayamón. Barbosa then became the first mulatto to be enrolled in the Jesuit minor seminary, which was located in San Juan. He excelled as a student and was awarded his diploma in 1875.

Being from a poor family, Barbosa next tutored younger students, such as the children of José Escolástico Berríos, the owner of the San Antonio Sugar Mill, in order to earn enough money to go to the United States to attend college. At that time, Puerto Rico did not yet have a university. In 1876, he went to New York City to study English, which he learned fairly well in one year's time, and to pursue studies in law or engineering. He briefly enrolled in the School of Engineering at Fort Edwards, New York, but soon contracted pneumonia. At the urging of his physician, he investigated the possibility of a career in medicine. In 1877, he began his studies in general medicine and surgery at the University of Michigan, Ann Arbor. He completed these studies in 1880 and was honored as the valedictorian of his class.

After taking several months to tour a number of American clinics and hospitals, Barbosa returned to Puerto Rico in October, 1880. There, he encountered difficulties in establishing his medical practice, as the Spanish government would not accept a degree from an American institution. At the request of the American consulate, Spanish officials relented and accepted Barbosa's medical degree as valid. He began to practice medicine in San Juan just as a smallpox epidemic broke out.

Life's Work

Barbosa quickly earned the reputation of being an excellent physician and distinguished himself through his use of innovative techniques in treating the smallpox. He was named a staff physician at the Society for Mutual Aid, which put him in contact with poor and often desperately ill patients, whom he treated with respect, kindness, and competence. In 1882, he joined the Liberal Reformist Party, beginning a lifelong involvement in politics.

Barbosa married Belén Sánchez Jiménez in 1886 and was elected as a member of the Liberal Reformist Committee. His increasing interest in the civil affairs of the island led Barbosa to participate in the organizational meeting of the Autonomist Party of Puerto Rico in Ponce in 1887. In 1890, Barbosa was appointed professor of natural history at the Institute of Higher Learning, which was organized under the auspices of the Puerto Rican Athenaeum, where he offered courses in zoology, botany, and mineralogy. Two years later, he was named professor of anatomy and physiology and taught classes in various aspects of anatomy and obstetrics. Seeking greater Puerto Rican political liberties, Barbosa founded the Orthodox (or Pure) Autonomist Party in 1897 and served as undersecretary for public instruction.

With the arrival of American rule, Barbosa was energized to work for a new and more stable system of government and a higher standard of living for all of Puerto Rico's citizens. He actively supported closer cooperation with American attempts to modernize the island's health and educational systems and encouraged his fellow Puerto Ricans to embrace the ideals of democracy.

In 1899, Barbosa founded the Republican Party of Puerto Rico, which was dedicated to strengthening the island's ties to the United States and to obtaining acceptance of Puerto Rico as a state. President William McKinley appointed him a member of the executive cabinet of Governor Charles H. Allen, a position he would hold from 1900 to 1917. Recognizing the need for linguistic and cultural integration, Barbosa founded Puerto Rico's first bilingual newspaper, *El tiempo*, in 1907. He deepened his governmental commitments by serving as a member of the senate of Puerto Rico from 1917 until his death in 1921. Barbosa succumbed to cancer in San Juan at the age of sixty-four.

Significance

Not only was Barbosa a powerful supporter of a strong public health system, he also was a dedicated professor who brought advanced scientific learning and medical techniques to Puerto Rico from the United States. Today, he is best remembered as the father of the Puerto Rican statehood movement and as the founder of the Republican Party of Puerto Rico, which worked for American statehood for the island. Puerto Rico's political status always has been the central issue in the search for Puerto Rican identity; Barbosa's was one of the most important voices in that debate, under both Spanish and American rule.

Mark T. DeStephano

FURTHER READING

Ayala, César J., and Rafael Bernabé. *Puerto Rico in the American Century: A History since 1898*. Chapel Hill: University of North Carolina Press, 2009. Barbosa's role in the new American system of government is highlighted here, with special attention being given to his efforts to gain U.S. citizenship and statehood for Puerto Ricans.

Cabán, Pedro A. *Constructing a Colonial People: Puerto Rico and the United States, 1898-1932*. Boulder, Colo.: Westview Press, 1999. Describes Barbosa's political views and activism on behalf of Puerto Rican statehood.

Malavet, Pedro A. *America's Colony: The Political and Cultural Conflict Between the United States and Puerto Rico*. New York: New York University Press, 2004. Malavet makes brief mention of Barbosa as a member of the Autonomist movement under Spain and his activities in the pro-statehood movement.

See also: José de Diego; Luis A. Ferré; Luis Muñoz Marín; Luis Muñoz Rivera.

GERTRUDIS BARCELÓ

Mexican-born entrepreneur

Barceló was one of the best-known women involved in the Santa Fe trade starting in 1821, after Mexico declared itself independent from Spain. Her interactions with American traders and soldiers are credited with giving birth to the myth that women in the borderlands were money-hungry and sexually liberated.

Latino heritage: Mexican
Born: c. 1800; Sonora, Mexico
Died: January 17, 1852; Santa Fe, New Mexico Territory (now New Mexico)
Also known as: María Gertrudis Barceló; Dona Tules; La Tules; Gertrude Barcelo
Area of achievement: Business

EARLY LIFE

María Gertrudis Barceló (bahr-seh-LOH) was born to Juan Ignacio Barceló and Dolores Herrero y Barceló de Pino in Sonora, Mexico, around 1800. She had an older brother, Jose Trinidad, and a younger sister, Maria de la Luz. In 1815, Juan moved his family north from Sonora to what is now the state of New Mexico. They settled in the village of Valencia, south of Albuquerque, where they were in position to benefit from the emerging business and trade associated with the Santa Fe Trail.

In June, 1823, Barceló married Don Manuel Antonio Sisneros. After their marriage, Barceló moved with Sisneros to a mining camp near Santa Fe, New Mexico. Within the first two years of marriage, Barceló lost two sons in infancy; despite these losses, Barceló reached out to individuals throughout her life and was considered a mother to many. In 1826, Barceló and her husband adopted a daughter, Maria del Refugio. In 1825 and 1826, Barceló embarked on her career as a professional gambler. She settled in Oso Springs, which would eventually become Oro Springs in the Ortiz Mountains, about twenty-six miles from Santa Fe.

LIFE'S WORK

Within five years of Barceló's move to Oro Springs, the settlement was renamed El Real de Dolores. With the emergence of gold mining and influx of miners to the settlement, Barceló's career as an expert dealer of monte, a simple gambling card game, flourished. By June, 1833, Barceló's skills at dealing cards had brought her enough money to move her mother, adopted daughter, and husband to Santa Fe. Santa Fe traders such as Josiah Gregg felt that Barceló—who smoked, drank, and gambled—reflected Mexican women's bad behavior. Despite such Anglo opinions, however, Barceló often was asked to be a godmother to children. She adopted a second daughter, Petra Gutierres; both adopted daughters married men heavily involved in the Santa Fe trade.

Through her success as a monte dealer and an entrepreneur, Barceló was able to purchase a saloon and gambling hall by 1846. At this time, American soldiers started entering New Mexico during the Mexican-American War, and Barceló adapted to a new clientele. American soldiers saw Barceló as one of the elite in Santa Fe. Their general, Stephen Kearny, soon realized that the U.S. government had not provided him with enough funds to pay all of his soldiers, and he found himself turning to Barceló for financial support.

When Barceló died on January 17, 1852, she included in her will monies for those whom she had adopted or taken responsibility, as well as funds for the Catholic Church. She request an elaborate funeral presided over by Jean-Baptiste Lamy, an incoming French bishop, who arrived in Santa Fe just in time to perform the rites. He received a great deal of criticism from the Catholic community, who felt that Barceló's lifestyle should have precluded her from the attentions of a bishop. At the time of her death, her wealth was valued at more than ten thousand dollars, more than twice what the most wealthy men of her area had acquired in their lifetimes.

Significance

Barceló was notable for her remarkable success in business and her philanthropy. Owning a saloon and gambling hall brought her into contact with American businessmen and soldiers at a time when Mexican-American relations were in their infancy. While she provided her Anglo clients with entertainment and loans, they returned home believing that all Mexican American women gambled, drank, smoked, and were shrewd in their business dealings. These accounts of Barceló shaped early perceptions of Mexican women as clever and capable but less feminine or pious than American women.

Fawn-Amber Montoya

Further Reading

Cook, Mary Straw. *Doña Tules: Santa Fe's Courtesan and Gambler*. Albuquerque: University of New Mexico Press, 2007. This biography focuses on the life of Barceló and emphasizes how the Santa Fe Trade and the Mexican-American War expanded her wealth. It references historical sources to show Barceló as more than just the myth of La Tules but a hard working individual who took advantage of the growing New Mexican economy.

Gonzalez, Deena. *Refusing the Favor: The Spanish Mexican Women of Santa Fe*. New York: Oxford University Press, 2001. This text address the changing roles of women in New Mexico as they encountered the complexities of living under Spanish, Mexican, and U.S. authority. Gonzalez uses Barceló as one of her case studies and reveals the complicated nature of what it meant to be a businesswoman living in New Mexico in the 1800's.

Winter, Jonah. "Doña María Gertrudis `La Tules' Barceló." In *Wild Women of the Wild West*. New York: Holiday House, 2011. Succinct, illustrated biography of Barceló for young readers.

See also: Esteban Ochoa; Loreta Janeta Velázquez; Vicente Martinez Ybor.

Ray Barretto

American Latin jazz musician

Known as the godfather of Latin jazz, drummer and bandleader Barretto is music's most important and influential Latin jazz percussionist. He integrated the African conga drum into American jazz music and, because of his prowess as conga player or conguero, he came to be known as the "King of the Hard Hands" (rey de las manos duras).

Latino heritage: Puerto Rican
Born: April 29, 1929; Brooklyn, New York
Died: February 17, 2006; Hackensack, New Jersey
Also known as: Raymond Barretto Pagán
Area of achievement: Music

Early Life

Raymond Barretto Pagán (bah-REHT-oh) was born in Brooklyn, New York, to parents who had immigrated from Puerto Rico. Raised by his mother in the South Bronx, Barretto stayed at home listening to the radio while his mother worked or attended school; as a result, he was highly influenced by the music of the popular big bands of the day, such as those led by Duke Ellington, Count Basie, Benny Goodman, and Tommy Dorsey.

At age seventeen, Barretto joined the Army to escape the restrictions of school and the racial tensions of his neighborhood. While stationed in Germany, his life changed when he heard a recording of "Manteca" by bebop trumpeter Dizzy Gillespie. It was conguero Chano Pozo's drum work on that record that inspired Barretto to enter the music world as a conga player. Discharged from the Army in 1949, Barretto returned to New York and joined jam sessions in Harlem with jazz greats such as Charlie Parker. Through the 1950's and into the 1960's, he began his lifelong practice of moving in both jazz and Latin music circles. In 1978, Barretto married Annette "Brandy" Rivera, with whom he had a son; an earlier marriage had produced three other children.

LIFE'S WORK

Barretto began his musical career as a jazz musician in the style of swing and bebop, but soon also made his mark in the world of Latin music. His greatest commercial hit came early in his career with 1963's "El Watusi." One of the first Latin songs to be successful in the United States, "El Watusi" combined charanga music's flutes and violins with the new, catchy fusion of African American soul music and Latin rhythms known as boogaloo and featured an ebullient "Spanglish" rap. An early crossover hit, "El Watusi" demonstrated Barretto's musical range, which enabled him to join Afro-Carribbean and Cuban rhythms with various forms of American music, including blues, rock, disco, and jazz.

A major phase in Barretto's career began in 1967 when he joined Fania Records, the legendary New York record company known for its blend of traditional Latin dance music and American jazz called salsa. In 1968, he became a member of the Fania All-Stars, an orchestra composed of the leading Latin jazz artists of the day. Barretto was a part of this group for the rest of his life and was crucial to the formulation of the group's musical identity as well as the unique identity of the Fania label itself. The move to Fania Records also allowed Barretto to develop his jazz-oriented percussive style and to continue his interest in fusing Latin sounds with American musical currents. His musical compositions became more sophisticated, including experimentation with electronic music and novel instrumental combinations. These musical explorations led to his 1968 album *Acid*, one of his most influential works. An inventive hybrid of soul, Latin, and jazz music that Baretto himself saw as a major reinvention of his musical identity, *Acid* is widely regarded as a landmark in Latin jazz. From 1968 to 1975, Barretto made eight more bold and diverse albums for Fania, establishing the label as the center of Latin jazz in America and worldwide.

Barretto recorded with many different musicians but is especially associated with major jazz figures such as Sonny Stitt, Wes Montgomery, Kenny Burrell, Art Blakey, Cal Tjader, Cannonball Adderley, and Dizzy Gillespie. He became the jazz world's most recorded conga player but, considering himself at heart a jazz musician, he turned away from salsa music to form the jazz sextet New World Spirit in 1992. This later period produced such admired albums as 1993's *Ancestral Messages* and 1994's *Taboo*, which fused Latin soul, salsa, and Afro-Cuban sounds with hard bop and bebop. Barretto died in 2006 in Hackensack, New Jersey.

Ray Barretto. (AP Photo)

SIGNIFICANCE

Barretto's intense, innovative drumming style pioneered the role of the conga in jazz, establishing its validity as a jazz instrument. His sustained significance in the world of mainstream jazz was such that he won the *DownBeat* magazine's critics poll for percussion as late in his career as 2003 and 2005. Barretto's significance in the world of Latin music led to his induction into the International Latin Music Hall of Fame in 1999.

One of the industry's most influential Latin musicians, Barretto was vital to all of the developments in Latin music in the last half of the twentieth century. He also was a major force in the cross-cultural blending of Latin music with such American idioms as bebop, rock, soul, and rhythm and blues. Barretto was awarded many honors, including a Grammy for an album with vocals by Cuban salsa legend Celia Cruz, and a Jazz Masters lifetime achievement award from the National Endowment for the Arts in 2006.

Margaret Boe Birns

Further Reading

Alava, Silvio H. *Spanish Harlem's Musical Legacy: 1930-1980*. New York: Arcadia, 2007. Includes consideration of Barretto's contribution to Spanish Harlem's influential music scene from the 1930's to the 1980's.

Flores, Juan. *From Bomba to Hip-Hop*. New York: Columbia University Press, 2000. Barretto is examined in the context of the development of Puerto Rican culture in the United States over the second half of the twentieth century.

Morales, Ed. *The Latin Beat: The Rhythms and Roots of Latin Music, from Bossa Nova to Salsa and Beyond*. New York: Da Capo Press, 2003. Barretto is placed in the context of the history of Latin music.

Rondón, César Miguel. *The Book of Salsa: A Chronicle of Urban Music from the Caribbean to New York City*: Chapel Hill: University of North Carolina Press, 2008. This thorough examination of salsa music from the 1950's to the 1970's includes detailed coverage of Barretto and a discography.

Waxer, Lise. *Situating Salsa: Global Markets and Local Meanings in Latin Popular Music*. New York: Routledge, 2002. Includes Barretto in a comprehensive examination of salsa music, including its global impact.

See also: Rubén Blades; Celia Cruz; Paquito D'Rivera; Flaco Jiménez; Trini López; Tito Puente; Poncho Sánchez.

Raymond Barrio

American artist and writer

Barrio was an able artist and exponent of modern art as well as a talented writer and teacher. He wrote not only about art but also about the exploitation of the Hispanic laborers by California agribusiness in the 1960's and 1970's.

Latino heritage: Spanish

Born: August 27, 1921; West Orange, New Jersey

Died: January 22, 1996; Escondido, California

Areas of achievement: Art; literature

Early Life

Raymond Barrio (BAHR-ee-oh) was born to Spanish immigrant parents in New Jersey, the elder of two boys. His parents, Saturnino and Angelita Barrio, had arrived in the United States in 1920. Saturnino died in an industrial accident when the two boys were still young. Angelita made a living as a dancer, while the boys were raised by foster parents, receiving a Protestant rather than a Catholic upbringing.

In 1936, Barrio moved to California. He entered the University of Southern California in 1941 before enlisting in the U.S. military in 1943. During the next three years, he saw active service in Europe but managed further academic study at Yale and the University of California at Berkeley. He received his B.A. from Berkeley in 1947, then went to the Art Center College of Los Angeles to study for a bachelor of fine arts degree, which he earned in 1952.

For the rest of his life, Barrio painted, taught art, and wrote. His teaching included courses on modern art, creative writing, and Chicano studies, mostly at colleges and universities in the San Francisco Bay area. In 1957, he visited Mexico and met Yolanda Sánchez, whom he married. The couple had five children.

Life's Work

Barrio's first writing dates back to 1967. It was published by a Ventura, California, company as *The Big Picture: How to Experiment with Modern Techniques in Art*. A year later, he published *Experiments in Modern Art*, a revision of the previous work that enjoyed a New York publisher. The same year, he released *Art: Seen*, a much more informal, even whimsical and personal publication, consisting mainly of graphics with some commentary.

Further works on art followed. *The Prism* (1968) was a series of essays on art. A focus on Mexican art produced *Mexico's Art and Chicano Artists* in 1975. He combined art and text in *Walden: A Selection* (1968), a small booklet, followed by *The Fisherman's Dwarf*, a book for children, the same year. He never ceased to be active in the art world; by the end of his life, his work had appeared in eighty national exhibitions.

In 1969, Barrio made a significant change of direction. Having moved to Guerneville, California, he became aware of the plight of the fruit and vegetable pickers in Santa Clara County, a plight not dissimilar to that portrayed thirty years earlier in John Steinbeck's *The Grapes of Wrath* (1939). Steinbeck described the exploitation of the "Okies," migrants from Oklahoma. This time, the exploited were either Chicanos, American Latinos, or temporary farmworkers from Mexico. They had been depicted a little earlier in José Villareal's novel *Pocho* (1959).

Barrio's response was the novel *The Plum Plum Pickers* (1969). At first, he could find no publisher. The story's style was ironic, fragmentray, and the subject matter politically incendiary, with contemporary attempts to unionize the migrant laborers often resulting in violent clashes. In the end, Barrio formed his own publishing house. Once the novel had sold ten thousand copies, a national publisher—Harper—offered to buy the manuscript. Later, Barrio bought it back in 1976, when the book had sold twenty-two thousand copies. Selections from the novel are now widely anthologized, especially in textbooks.

Barrio's second description of the migrant laborer situation appeared as the play *The Devil's Apple Corps: A Trauma in Four Acts,* in 1976. Meanwhile, expanding on his political career as writer, he ran a weekly column, "Barrio's Political Estuary," in a number of local and national periodicals. The best of these pieces were published as *Barrio's Estuary* in 1981. A further collection of political writing came out in 1985 as *Political Portfolio.* A further long-planned novel, *Carib Blue*, appeared in 1990. Barrio died in Escondido, California, in 1996.

Significance

Although he was not a Mexican American himself, Barrio identified himself politically with Chicanos, both in his art and in his writing. His lasting influence will be felt through his first novel, *The Plum Plum Pickers*. It is significant as an early piece of Chicano literature, a significant social statement, and also as a historical text in an ongoing social and political situation.

David Barratt

Further Reading

Lattin, Vernon E. "Paradise and Plums: Appearance and Reality in Barrio's *The Plum Plum Pickers*." *Selected Proceedings of the Third Annual Conference on Minority Studies* 2 (April, 1975). A definitive essay on Barrio's most famous work.

Lomelí, Francisco A. "Depraved New World Revisited: Dreams and Dystopia in *The Plum Plum Pickers.*" Introduction to *The Plum Plum Pickers*, by Raymond Barrio. Tempe, Ariz.: Bilingual Press, 1984. A good introductory essay to Barrio's novel, setting out the main themes and characters to study.

Preslar, Andrew B. "Latino Long Fiction." In *Critical Survey of Long Fiction*, edited by Carl Rollyson. 4th ed. Pasadena, Calif.: Salem Press, 2010. Places Barrio's work in the context of other Latino writings and the social movements of his era.

See also: Rudolfo Anaya; Martha P. Cotera; Rolando Hinojosa; Rafael López; Yolanda M. López; Américo Paredes; Pedro Juan Soto.

Gregg Barrios

American playwright, poet, and journalist

Barrios's plays, musicals, and poetry reflected the political concerns about racial, sexual, and economic injustice that characterized the Chicano rights movement of the 1960's and 1970's. A nationally recognized journalist, he also was part of artist Andy Warhol's circle in New York City.

Latino heritage: Mexican

Born: October 31, 1945; Victoria, Texas

Areas of achievement: Theater; poetry; journalism

Early Life

Gregg Barrios (grehg BAH-ree-ohs) was born in Victoria, Texas, in 1945. Barrios has credited his father, Gregorio Barrios, Sr., a Mexican-born photographer and part-time film projectionist, for his early exposure to the arts. Barrios became interested in film through the frequent free showings at the theater for which his father worked. Barrios has also attributed his work to the racial, economic, and social diversity of urban Texas.

As a teenager, Barrios began writing novels and poetry, as well as book reviews for school newspapers. His first professional position was as a book reviewer for the local *Victoria Advocate*, a job offer that was a striking vote of confidence in the young writer's skills during a time when workplace discrimination against Texan Chicanos was rampant.

In 1962, seeking affordable higher education through the G.I. Bill, Barrios enlisted in the Air Force. Although the war in Vietnam was becoming an increasingly pressing concern, Barrios served for three years as a medic at a base in Austin, Texas, where he became a part-time student, majoring in English, at the local campus of the state university. During this time, he regularly wrote political and literary articles for area newspapers and magazines. In addition, his childhood love of films led him to an association with artist Andy Warhol and the New York experimental film scene. Under Warhol's mentorship, Barrios produced his own film, *BONY* (Boys of New York). Later in his career, *BONY* would be recognized as an important Chicano work, and several of Barrios's films would receive screenings across the country.

Life's Work

Upon graduation from the University of Texas in 1968, Barrios became active in El Movimiento, the emerging Chicano movement that espoused political, cultural, and artistic goals. In 1970, he became a teacher in Crystal City, Texas, which he identified as the environment that gave birth to his mature creative work.

In the late 1970's and early 1980's, Barrios expanded his writing oeuvre to poetry and drama. Many of his poems, beginning in 1982 with *Puro Rollo* and spread over four collections, address politics and El Movimiento issues. Subsequently, his work in the theater, as both a producer and a playwright, began to attract public notice. His early plays are frequently political, like *Dale Gas Cristal!*, a response to the decadelong gas cutoff in Crystal City. Often his plays subversively reinterpret earlier works, as with his "Chicano rock operas" drawing on Georges Bizet's *Carmen* and Andrew Lloyd Webber's *Evita*.

After spending most of the 1980's teaching drama and journalism, first in Texas and then in Los Angeles, Barrios retired to San Antonio to dedicate his energies to writing. By 2011, his journalism had appeared in *The New York Times, Newsday*, the *San Francisco Chronicle*, the *Los Angeles Times,* and many other publications.

Notable plays from Barrios's later period include the controversial *Dark House/Pale Rider*, which deals with writer Katherine Anne Porter's relationships with black men; *Hard Candy*, the story of Latina burlesque performer Candy Barr, also known as Juanita Dale Slusher; and *¡Carrasco!*, a reworking of an earlier Barrios play about Mexican outlaw and folk hero Juan Carrasco. One of his most popular plays is *Rancho Pancho*, about the fraught relationship between playwright Tennessee Williams and his Mexican American lover Pancho Rodriguez. In 2008, San Antonio's Our Lady of the Lake University staged a single performance of Barrios's *I-DJ Mofomixmaster*, which also explores the perceived conflict between Chicano identity and homosexual identity.

As of 2011, Barrios had received grants from the Ford Foundation and the Macondo Foundation, as well as fellowships from the Mark Taper Forum and the National Endowment for the Humanities. Officially retired from teaching, he remained a writer and critic for the *San Antonio Current,* served on the board of the National Book Critics Circle, and worked his "dream job" as a bookseller.

Significance

Barrios was a major force, both politically and artistically, in the forging of twentieth-century Chicano identity. Perhaps even more important, he tended to complicate any monolithic notion of that identity, emphasizing the intersections and contradictions among various communities that were historically marginalized by American society, particularly poor and working-class (especially urban), homosexual, and Latino people. Many of his writings provide a window into the world of Southwestern barrios, a setting often ignored in the art of mainstream Anglo America. Additionally, Barrios's career is itself a success story of Chicano culture triumphing over privation and prejudice, beginning with his unlikely hire as a young Latino by a southern Texas newspaper.

Leigh Barkley

Further Reading

Barrios, Gregg. *La Causa.* East Brunswick, N.J.: Hansen , 2010. A collection of poetry providing an insider's view of the development of El Movimiento in the latter half of the twentieth century.

_______. *Puro Rollo (A Colores).* Los Angeles: Quetzalcóatl, 1982. This first collection of Barrios's poetry attracted some of his earliest public attention.

_______. *Rancho Pancho.* East Brunswick, N.J.: Hansen, 2010. Showcasing one year in the life of Tennessee Williams and his lover Pancho Rodriguez, this play drew attention to the subject of homosexuality and masculinity in Latino culture.

Navarro, Armando. *The Cristal Experiment: A Chicano Struggle for Community Control.* Madison: University of Wisconsin Press, 1998. An account of how

Crystal City, Texas, the city that first inspired Barrios as a fiction writer, became an epicenter of El Movimiento in the 1960's and 1970's, during the period when Barrios lived and worked there.

Rosales, Francisco Arturo. *Chicano! The Story of the Mexican American Civil Rights Movement.* Houston: Arte Publico Press, 1997. A comprehensive history of Chicano identity in America and its flowering into a civil rights movement. Provides a useful contextual frame.

See also: Gloria Anzaldúa; Norma Elia Cantú; Denise Chávez; Cherríe Moraga; John Rechy; Luis Miguel Valdez; Alma Villanueva.

Ruth Behar

Cuban-born cultural anthropologist and writer

Behar, a cultural anthropologist, has made a career of exploring "the meaning of home in an age of travel and homesickness." A prominent scholar and professor of anthropology at the University of Michigan, she is a passionate ethnographer, artistically retelling stories of home and belonging in the diaspora.

Latino heritage: Cuban and Spanish

Born: 1956; Havana, Cuba

Areas of achievement: Anthropology; literature

Early Life

A few years before the start of the Cuban Revolution, Ruth Behar (rooth BAY-hahr) was born in Havana, Cuba, the daughter of the recently married Rebeca and Alberto Behar. Rebeca was an Ashkenazic Jew of Polish descent, and Alberto was a Sephardic Jew with Ladino heritage from Turkey via Spain. Though her parents were both born in Cuba, their union was considered a mixed marriage. They conceived their first and only child, Ruth,on their honeymoon in Varadero. Four years later, in 1961, they left Cuba along with thousands of others in the Jewish exodus at the start of the Cuban Revolution. Behar's family immigrated to Israel, where they lived for a year in a kibbutz outside of Tel Aviv. In 1962, the family moved to Queens, New York, where Behar's maternal grandparents had settled and where she was to grow up.

In Cuba, Behar attended a Spanish-Yiddish day school, and she also spoke Yiddish in Israel. However, at her school in Queens she faced the sink-or-swim approach to the English-only instruction. She struggled for a year before she learned English, the language that would be the foundation for her future scholarly work.

Behar suffered a sort of amnesia regarding her early years in Cuba. She has no memory of life there and laments that her earliest recollection is of arriving in Queens. This inability to recall her early years, or to have any memory of Cuba, haunts Behar and has been the impetus for her continual search for home and memory on the island of her birth. Another formative experience involving trauma and recollection was the debilitating car crash she suffered at age nine, which left her bedridden with a badly broken leg for almost a year. Forgetting or suppressing the fear of learning to walk again resurfaced for Behar as an adult in a series of panic attacks that left her bedridden for two weeks just before her first trip back to Cuba.

Ruth Behar. (courtesy of Ruth Behar)

Behar studied at Wesleyan University, from which she received a B.A. in 1977. At Wesleyan she met her future husband, David Frye, who also received his B.A. from this university. The couple continued their studies at Princeton University, each receiving a master's degree and Ph.D. in anthropology, with Ruth completing her M.A. at Princeton in 1980 and her Ph.D. in 1983. She began her graduate school fieldwork in the Spanish village of Santa María del Monte in 1978. This was to be the site of fourteen years of study and travel and formative experiences that informed Behar's future work. David and Ruth were married in the early 1980's, and Ruth gave birth to their only child, Gabriel, in 1986. The death of Ruth's maternal grandfather in 1987 while she was on an extended stay in Spain, studying the eroding Catholic death rituals of Santa María's residents, led her to question her own abandoned Jewish faith and was another personally formative moment that would influence her future work.

Life's Work

Behar has written prolifically in numerous genres, including ethnography, poetry, memoirs, essays, and fiction. Her anthropological and personal essays can be found in a number of anthologies and numerous scholarly journals, including *Anthropology and Humanism, The Chronicle of Higher Education,* and *American Studies.* The topics of her writings range far afield from studying the rituals of death and memory in a Spanish village to sex and witchcraft in Mexico and, most important, exploring the Latin-Jewish identity in the Diaspora. She has also published several opinion pieces in *The New York Times* and the *Los Angeles Times*. In addition, Behar has published poetry and short stories, including a series of esoteric limited-edition prints published by Ediciones Vigia in Cuba , with illustrations by the artist Rolando Estévez.

Work from Behar's doctoral dissertation was published by Princeton University Press as a book entitled *The Presence of the Past in a Spanish Village: Santa María del Monte* (1986). Another of Behar's books, *Translated Woman: Crossing the Border with Esperanza's Story* (1993), was "untranslated" and published in Spanish as *Cuentame algo aunque sea mentira: Las historias de la comadre Esperanza* (2009). Behar garnered much attention and attracted some criticism for her book *The Vulneral Observer: Anthropology That Breaks Your Heart* (1996), in which she challenges the traditional maxim requiring anthropologists to remain detached from the subjects of their study. Instead, Behar argues that the role of the anthropologist is to observe others through a lens that includes the self. Her other books include *An Island Called Home: Returning to Jewish Cuba* (2007), with photographs by Humberto Mayol, and she has edited three anthologies: *Bridges to Cuba (Puentes a Cuba,* 1995), *Women Writing Culture* (1995), and *The Portable Island: Cubans at Home in the World* (2008).

Adding the credit "filmmaker" to her résumé, Behar wrote, produced, and directed the documentary *Adio Kerida* (*Goodbye Dear Love: A Cuban Sephardic Journey*). This film is about recovering both lost identity and the history that has been left behind. It is a very personal journey that weaves her family's experiences with Cuba and the island's loss among the histories of other Latino Jews in America and Cuba. Behar's son, Gabriel, assisted with filming and camera work.

Behar has the distinction of being the first Latina to receive the John T. and Katherine D. MacArthur Foundation's "genius grant" fellowship in 1988, and she has since been affiliated with the MacArturos, a group of other Latino MacArthur fellows who assist each other in reaching and helping a larger community. This group was founded by her friend, writer Sandra Cisneros. Other notable awards that Behar has received for research, teaching, and writing include a John Simon Guggenheim Foundation fellowship in 1995, two Harry Frank Guggenheim Foundation grants in 1985 and 1989, and a Fulbright fellowship in 2007. She was also named one of fifty Latinas who made history in the twentieth century by *Latina Magazine* in 1999.

In 2011, Behar was a tenured professor of anthropology at the University of Michigan, where she also was involved in the women's studies, Latino studies, and Latin American and Caribbean studies programs. She has been the recipient of numerous awards for excellence in education, including the D'Arms Faculty Award for Distinguished Graduate Mentoring in the Humanities and an Institute for the Humanities Faculty fellowship. In addition, she was a visiting distinguished professor at the University of Miami from January through May, 2008, and January through May, 2009.

Significance

Behar's innovations in the research and writing of ethnography have influenced the way anthropology is taught in universities. Her insistence that to observe others is also to observe the self has taken her own anthropological inquiries to a very personal level. By acknowledging how her longing for identity influenced her decision to become an anthropologist, she has turned the scholar's lens on her life and unearthed feelings of longing, displacement, and home among Latino Jews living in the diaspora within a Diaspora. Exploring her family and personal history, she has artfully related the stories of a few to the reality of many, elevating both art and history.

Erika C. Noguera

FURTHER READING

Behar, Ruth. "El Beso." In *Telling to Live: Latina Feminist Testimonios*, edited by the Latina Feminist Group. Durham, N.C.: Duke University Press, 2001. Behar is one of the members of the Latina Feminist Group, an organization of Latina educators who, in this book, relate the discrimination and marginalization they experienced in their attempt to become an accepted part of academia.

_______. "Death and Memory: From Santa María del Monte to Miami Beach." *Cultural Anthropology* 6, no. 3 (Summer, 1991): 346-384. Behar's account of her visits to Santa María del Monte challenges traditional ethnographic reports by focusing on herself as well as on her subjects.

_______. "Learning English with Shotaro." In *How I Learned English: Fifty-five Accomplished Latinos Recall Lessons in Language and Life*, edited by Tom Miller. Washington, D.C.: National Geographic, 2007. Behar is one of the Latinos who recounts her experience of learning English when her family moved to the United States.

_______. "My Habana." *The Chronicle of Higher Education* 56, no. 3 (September 11, 2009): B6-B10. Behar's personal narrative examines her experience of being raised in Havana by her parents.

_______. "The Story of Ruth, the Anthropologist." In *People of the Book: Thirty Scholars Reflect on Their Jewish Identity*, edited by Shelley Fisher Fishkin and Jeffrey Rubin-Dorsky. Madison: University of Wisconsin Press, 1996. Behar and other educators examine how their Jewish identity interacts with their experiences in academia.

See also: Lydia Cabrera; Carlos Castaneda; Margarita Bradford Melville.

PURA BELPRÉ

American librarian, storyteller, and writer

The first Puerto Rican librarian in the New York Public Library system and an ardent advocate for social justice for Spanish-speaking communities, Belpré enjoyed a successful career as a librarian, storyteller, and children's writer, publishing the first Puerto Rican folktale for children in the United States.

Latino heritage: Puerto Rican

Born: February 2, 1903; Cidra, Puerto Rico
Died: July 1, 1982; New York, New York
Also known as: Pura Teresa Belpré Nogueras; Pura Belpré-White; Pura Belpré White
Areas of achievement: Literature; education; activism

EARLY LIFE

Pura Teresa Belpré Nogueras, better known as Pura Belpré (POOR-ah BEHL-pray), was born in Cidra, Puerto Rico, to Felipe Belpré Bernabe and Carlota Nogueras. She and her five siblings were surrounded by a family of storytellers who instilled a love for the rich stories and folktales handed down from generation to generation. Belpré's family was quite nomadic, as her father was a contractor whose work took him to various parts of the island. Belpré attended primary and secondary schools in Cayey, Arroyo, Guayama, and Santurce. Often, she would spend hours exploring the natural world around her, amassing a vast storehouse of images and feelings that would later play an important role in her folktales for children

In 1919, Belpré enrolled in the University of Puerto Rico at Rio Piedras with the intent to follow her sister's footsteps and become a teacher. However, her plans were cut short when she immigrated to New York City in August, 1920, amid the flood of Puerto Ricans entering the continental United States. She planned to attend her older sister's wedding and return to Rio Piedras. Not long after her arrival, Belpré met the African American librarian Catherine Allen Latimer at the Countée Cullen Library, a branch of the New York Public Library. Belpré was fascinated by Latimer's demeanor and skill as she interacted with numerous teenagers, and Belpré would later recall this encounter as the pivotal moment when she began considering librarianship as a career path.

Life's Work

In May, 1921, Belpré was asked by librarian Ernestine Rose to become the Spanish-speaking assistant at the 135th Street branch of the New York Public Library. She eagerly accepted the position, establishing herself as the first Puerto Rican librarian in the system. Immediately, she began training and eventually enrolled in the library school of the New York Public Library around 1925. Years later, Belpré would cite Rose and Latimer, along with librarians Ann Carroll Moore and Maria Cimino, as major influences in her professional life.

As a librarian, she began to notice that Puerto Rican literature, particularly folktales, were absent from the library shelves. While taking a storytelling class under librarian Mary Gould Davis, Belpré was encouraged to write her first folktale—a love story from her native Puerto Rico about Pérez the mouse and Martina the cockroach. This particular story was one that she performed with handmade puppets for children during her story programs. A few years later, she was persuaded by a classmate to submit this folktale to a publisher for review. In 1932, *Pérez and Martina: A Portorican Folk Tale* was published by Frederick Warne, becoming the first Puerto Rican folktale to be published in the United States.

Throughout the late 1920's and 1930's, Belpré transferred to various branches of the New York Public Library, conducting Spanish and bilingual storytelling programs, planning community outreach efforts to Puerto Ricans, and welcoming Jewish, black, Latino, and various immigrant populations into the library. At the 115th Street branch, she hosted the first El día de reyes (epiphany) program, firmly establishing the library within the heart of the Puerto Rican and Latino community.

In 1942, Belpré traveled to Cincinnati, Ohio, to present a paper at an American Library Association conference. While there she met the famous African American composer, concert violinist, and Harlem musician Clarence Cameron White. They were married in 1943, and two years later Belpré resigned from the library to travel around the country with her husband.

Belpré's initial experiences in the library working with Spanish-speaking and Puerto Rican children and their families strongly influenced her writing and her career. She had the opportunity to work one-on-one with newly arrived immigrants and poverty-stricken Americans who were trying to find their piece of the proverbial American pie. She had firsthand experience of the daily problems faced by Spanish-speaking children struggling to succeed in an English-dominant society. Belpré also understood the disappointment of not finding familiar cultural stories at the library.

From 1945 to 1960, Belpré wrote and told stories, presented lectures, and traveled with her husband. She penned many of the folktales told during her programs at the various branches of the New York Public Library. In 1946, Belpré published some of these stories as *The Tiger and the Rabbit, and Other Tales,* the first collection of Puerto Rican folktales in English published in the United States.

In June, 1960, Belpré's husband died from cancer, and shortly thereafter she returned to the New York Public Library to work as the Spanish children's specialist. For the next seven years, she traveled around

The Pura Belpré Awards: A Literary *Celebracíon* of Latino Cultures in Children's Literature

Established through the grassroots efforts of Mexican American librarians Oralia Garza de Cortés and Sandra Rios Balderrama, the Pura Belpré Awards are presented to a Latino author and a Latino illustrator who create an outstanding work of children's literature that positively represents the experiences of Latinos in the United States. From 1996 to 2008, the awards were presented biennially by their cosponsors, the American Library Association's Association for Library Service to Children and REFORMA (The National Association to Promote Library and Information Services to Latinos and the Spanish Speaking). Beginning in 2009, the award was presented annually to honor the best Latino children's books published during the previous year by a Latino author and Latino illustrator. Additional awards can be presented each year to honor other titles that are deemed worthy of recognition.

The intent of the awards is to encourage Latino artists to record their cultural experiences for children and to persuade publishers to make these works available to families across the United States. The goal of honoring positive representations of Latinos furthers Belpré's mission of preserving the cultural heritage of Latino children and providing a window into Latino culture for non-Latino children. Incidentally, one of the 2009 Pura Belpré honor books, *The Storyteller's Candle = La velita de los cuentos,* by Lucia González and Lulu Delecre, is the first picture book to highlight the outreach work of Belpré. Additional information about the awards can be found in *The Pura Belpré Awards: Celebrating Latino Authors and Illustrators* (2006), edited by Rose Zertuche Treviño.

New York City, assisting in the development of library programs for Puerto Rican children, conducting bilingual storytelling programs for both Puerto Rican and non-Puerto Rican populations, selecting Spanish-language children's books for library collections, and advocating for equal library services for impoverished communities.

In 1962, she began a translating career with the publication of her Spanish version of Munro Leaf's *The Story of Ferdinand.* That same year she published the picture book *Juan Bobo and the Queen's Necklace: A Puerto Rican Folk Tale.* She continued to publish original stories and translate Spanish versions of children's classics throughout the 1960's and 1970's.

In March, 1968, Belpré was forced to retire from the library because of age restrictions, but she was contracted later that year by Augusta Baker to work on a per diem basis on the South Bronx Library Project, an outreach-based program dedicated to establishing library services and collections for low-income, Spanish-speaking neighborhoods in New York City. While working on the project, Belpré traveled to branch libraries, day care centers, school libraries, and youth centers conducting puppet shows and sharing bilingual stories with children from various cultural backgrounds. In 1971, she and Mary Conwell published the professional resource *Libros en Español: An Annotated List of Children's Books in Spanish.*

Throughout her life, Belpré received notable and lifetime achievement awards for her work as a librarian, storyteller, puppeteer, advocate, and author. In May, 1982, she received the New York City Mayor's Award of Honor for Arts and Culture, and on June 30, 1982, Belpré was honored by the coordinator's council of the New York Public Library. The following day, she died in her sleep. In 1996, as a way to honor the librarian and her work in children's literature, the Pura Belpré Awards were established by the American Library Association and REFORMA (The National Association to Promote Library and Information Services to Latinos and the Spanish Speaking).

SIGNIFICANCE

A quiet but passionate advocate for library services and programs for immigrant, low-income, and Spanish-speaking families, Belpré left a lasting legacy as the first Latino librarian in the New York Public Library System, the first Puerto Rican librarian in the United States, and the author of the first English editions of Puerto Rican folktales for children. Her grassroots efforts in New York City have become a shining example to future generations of librarians serving Spanish-speaking, Latino, and culturally diverse populations. At a time when race relations were tense, Belpré showcased the importance of intercultural understanding and social justice not only in her career as a librarian but also in her children's books that immortalize her passion to preserve her cultural heritage.

Jamie Campbell Naidoo

FURTHER READING

Centro de Estudios Puertorriqueños. Puerto Rican Writers and Migration: Folklore, Autobiography, and History. http://www.centropr.org/prwriters/belpre.html. This Web page, created by the Hunter College-based Centro de Estudios Puertorriqueños, provides a biographical essay about Belpré and links to numerous primary documents about her, including photographs, papers, speeches, and letters.

Hernández-Delgado, Julio. "Pura Teresa Belpré, Storyteller and Pioneer Puerto Rican Librarian." *Library Quarterly* 62, no. 4 (October, 1992): 425-440. Covers Belpré's life in Puerto Rico, her career as a librarian and storyteller, and her persistent drive to connect children from all cultures to Puerto Rican literature.

Núñez, Victoria. "Remembering Pura Belpré's Early Career at the 135th Street New York Public Library: Interracial Cooperation and Puerto Rican Settlement During the Harlem Renaissance." *Centro Journal* 21, no. 1 (Spring 2009): 53-77. Thoughtful examination of Belpré's early library work with black, Purerto Rican, and immigrant populations during the Harlem Renaissance. Highlights various archival pieces from Belpré's papers.

Sánchez González, Lisa. "Pura Belpré: The Children's Ambassador." In *Latina Legacies: Identity, Biography, and Community,* edited by Vicki Ruiz and Virginia Sánchez Korrol. New York: Oxford University Press, 2005. Overview of Belpre's work as a children's author, librarian, and storyteller, with particular emphasis on her books for children.

See also: Alma Flor Ada; Monica Brown; Nicholasa Mohr; Arturo Alfonso Schomburg.

Baruj Benacerraf

Venezuelan-born Nobel Prize-winning immunologist

While studying the ability of inbred strains of animals to respond to certain foreign proteins or antigens, Benacerraf discovered a series of genes that regulated the interactions of immune cells. Benacerraf termed these the immune response (Ir) genes, and the discovery earned him a Nobel Prize.

Latino heritage: Spanish

Born: October 29, 1920; Caracas, Venezuela

Area of achievement: Science and technology

Early Life

Baruj Benacerraf (bah-ROOK beh-NAH-seh-rahf) was born in Caracas, Venezuela, to parents of Spanish-Jewish (Sephardic) ancestry. His father, Abraham Benacerraf, was born in Tetuán in Spanish Morocco, while his mother, Henrietta Lasry, had been born and raised in French Algeria. His father was a prosperous textile merchant, and Benacerraf was raised in a (French) cultured, relatively wealthy household. When he was five years old, the family moved to Paris, where he spent most of his youth and received his early schooling. Benacerraf attended the Lycée Janson de Sailly, a prestigious high school, where he became fluent in French and was immersed in French culture.

Recognizing the threat to France posed by the expansion of Nazi Germany, Abraham returned with his family in 1939 to Venezuela, where he continued his success in the textile import business. The following year, the family moved to New York, where Benacerraf continued his education at the college level. He first enrolled in a textile engineering school in Philadelphia but left after two weeks. Benacerraf then enrolled in the School of General Studies at Columbia University, from which, in 1942, he graduated with a bachelor of science degree. His father had expected Benacerraf to join the family textile business, but having also completed the general science requirements for admission to medical school, Benacerraf decided upon a career in medicine.

While his academic credentials were more than sufficient for admission to medical schools, Benacerraf's religious and ethnic backgrounds resulted in rejection of his application by some two dozen schools, including Harvard, Yale, and Columbia. However, the father of a friend happened to be an assistant to the president of the Medical College of Virginia in Richmond, and he arranged an interview for Benacerraf. Benacerraf was accepted into the program in the summer of 1942. He became a naturalized American citizen the following year, and as a result of the wartime training program, he completed his medical training in three years and was drafted by the Army. In 1943, he also married Annette Dreyfus, a French refugee and relative of both Captain Alfred Dreyfus, who was convicted of treason in 1894 in the notorious "Dreyfus Affair" in France, and future Nobel laureate Jacques Monod. Benacerraf and Annette would have one child, a daughter, Beryl.

After a two-year internship at Queens General Hospital, Benacerraf received a commission as first lieutenant in the Army Medical Corps and was assigned to a position as head of a medical unit in Paris, where he served for two years.

Life's Work

After his discharge from the Army in 1947, Benacerraf decided to continue his medical career. Because he had suffered from bronchial asthma in his youth, he decided to pursue research in the field of immunology with emphasis on hypersensitivity. In February, 1948,

Baruj Benacerraf. (AP Photo)

Discovering Immune Response Genes

The immune response (Ir) genes discovered by Baruj Benacerraf were only the first of several dozen closely linked genes determined to be within the major histocompatibility complex (MHC) of animals, including humans. Unlike other genes located within the MHC that were first described because of their role in transplant rejection, the Ir genes regulate the ability of immune cells to interact with each other, determining the body's ability to respond to foreign proteins and also governing the level of that response. Products of the response genes, referred to as Ia antigens, are displayed on the surface of immune cells such as macrophages; the presence of receptors for these surface molecules on other classes of white blood cells such as the T lymphocytes determines whether such cells are activated, resulting in the immune response. While Benacerraf and others made their discoveries using inbred animals such as guinea pigs, nearly identical mechanisms regulate the immune response in humans.

Benacerraf joined the laboratory of Elvin Kabat in the Neurological Institute at Columbia University, where he became adept at research in immunochemistry and experimental research methods in immunology. Benacerraf worked with Kabat for more than a year; however, because his father—who had returned to Paris—was incapacitated by a stroke, and Annette's family lived there as well, Benacerraf decided to return to France in 1949. He spent six years there working with Bernard Halpern at the Broussais Hospital in Paris studying cellular immunology. Benacerraf came to realize, however, that as a naturalized American he stood little chance of becoming an independent researcher in France. He returned to the United States in 1956, accepting a position as assistant professor of pathology at New York University School of Medicine.

The research atmosphere at NYU was particularly productive during the years Benacerraf was on the faculty. The field of immunology was evolving from one that was primarily observational to one in which molecular mechanisms underlying the immune response were becoming clearer. Benacerraf had the opportunity to work with future Nobel laureate Gerald Edelman in his studies of antibody structure. Among the experimental results Benacerraf observed in his own study of antibodies was that when guinea pigs were immunized with small molecules (antigens), some animals responded well ("responders"), while others produced little or no antibody ("nonresponders"). Attempting to understand the genetic basis for the difference, Benacerraf mated responders and nonresponders and discovered the difference was related to genes that he termed the immune response (Ir) genes. He had now entered the field of immunogenetics, in which he would spend much of his later scientific career.

By 1968, Benacerraf had been promoted to professor of pathology; however, an opportunity for further professional advancement appeared when he was offered the position of director of the laboratory of immunology at the National Institute of Allergy and Infectious Diseases in Bethesda, Maryland. The NIAID laboratory also provided him with a wide selection of strains of guinea pigs, allowing further analysis of the role played by Ir and other genes in regulating the immune response. For example, Benacerraf determined that these genes are found within the larger major histocompatibility complex, a region containing several hundred genes that regulate most aspects of immunity.

In 1970, Benacerraf was named chair of pathology at Harvard Medical School, where he had greater opportunity not only to direct his research but also to interact with students in the field. Among his discoveries was that in order for antibodies to be produced, antigens not only must be "presented" to lymphocytes by a class of cells known as "antigen-presenting cells," but also that these cells all must share identical Ir molecules. In 1980, Benacerraf was awarded the Nobel Prize in Physiology or Medicine, primarily for his research on Ir genes. That year, he also was appointed to the presidency of the Sidney Farber Cancer Institute, which is affiliated with Harvard Medical School. Among Benacerraf's other awards are the T. Duckett Jones Memorial Award of the Helen Hay Whitney Foundation (1976), the Waterford Biomedical Science Award (1980), and the Charles A. Dana Award (1996). Benacerraf also has received numerous honorary doctorates.

SIGNIFICANCE

Prior to Benacerraf's research, scientists knew that three classes of white blood cells were somehow involved in the immune response: macrophages, subsequently termed antigen-presenting cells, and B and T lymphocytes; however, they had little knowledge of the discrete functions of these cells. Benacerraf's work led to an understanding of specific immune response genes that regulated immune processes. The Ir genes subsequently were mapped to the region of the major histocompatibility complex, a region in which gene products determine whether, and to what extent, white cells can interact with each other. The understanding that these gene products play a significant role in organ transplant rejection later was used to help improve the process of organ transplantation.

Richard Adler

Further Reading

Benacerraf, Baruj. *From Caracas to Stockholm: A Life in Medical Science*. Amherst, N.Y.: Prometheus Books, 1998. In this autobiography, Benacerraf describes his early privileged life and the challenges he faced in developing his scientific career.

Coico, Richard, and Geoffrey Sunshine. *Immunology: A Short Course*. Hoboken, N.J.: John Wiley & Sons, 2009. A concise review of immunology, including the molecular basis for white blood cell interactions.

Kurian, George Thomas. *The Nobel Scientists: A Biographical Encyclopedia*. Amherst, N.Y.: Prometheus Books, 2002. Contains a brief biography of Benacerraf and a summary of his historic work with Ir genes.

Scientific American Presents Nobel Prize Winners on Medicine. New York: Kaplan, 2009. A collection of writings by Nobel laureates in physiology or medicine. While Benacerraf is not among the authors, the application of his work is noted in several articles by immunologists.

See also: Daniel Acosta; Richard Henry Carmona; Jose Alberto Fernandez-Pol; David Domingo Sabatini.

Santos Benavides

Military leader, entrepreneur, and politician

As a colonel, Benavides was the highest ranking Tejano soldier in the Confederacy during the American Civil War. He also is known for facilitating the shipment of Texas cotton along the Rio Grande and into Matamoros, Mexico. During Reconstruction, he was a successful merchant, rancher, and politician.

Latino heritage: Mexican

Born: November 1, 1823; Laredo, Texas

Died: November 9, 1891; Laredo, Texas

Areas of achievement: Military; business; government and politics

Early Life

Santos Benavides (behn-ah-VEE-dehs) was born in the border city of Laredo, Texas, to a prominent family. The family's wealth and influence is mainly attributed to Basilio Benavides, a wealthy uncle who was elected three times as the alcalde (local administrator or magistrate) under Mexican rule, then mayor and state representative after the annexation of Texas.

Benavides's father, José Jesús Benavides, was a captain in the Mexican army and moved to Laredo to command his company of military men. There he met Margarita Ramón, a granddaughter of Tomas Sanchez, the founder of Laredo. José Jesús and Margarita had two sons, Refugio and Santos. After Margarita died, José Jesús married Tomasa Cameras. Together they had four children, Eulalio, Cristóbal, Juliana, and Francisca.

On March 2, 1836, Texas declared independence from Mexico. Texas became known as the Republic of Texas after the Battle of San Jacinto in April of that year. As a young man in 1838 to 1840, Benavides fought in the Mexican Federalist-Centralist wars. He supported the Federalists, who wrested control from the Centralists of Mexico.

In 1842, Benavides married Augustina Villareal, and eventually they adopted four children.The ensuing years were tumultuous in Texas with the annexation of the state, its secession, and the Civil War.

Life's Work

Mexico did not recognize the annexation of Texas, which occurred in December, 1845, for three years. Benavides and his brothers likewise rejected the annexation, fearing that the character of the northern region of Mexico would be compromised. In 1856 and 1857, Benavides was elected mayor of Laredo. In 1859, he was elected chief justice of Webb County. After the election of President Abraham Lincoln in 1860, South Carolina seceded from the Union, followed by Texas. Benavides and his brothers Refugio and Cristóbal supported the Confederacy at that time because of their belief in states' rights.

Benavides rejected an offer to be general in the Union army. In the spring of 1861, he was made a captain in the Thirty-third Texas Cavalry (also known as Benavides's Regiment) and assigned to the Rio Grande military district, where he gained much of his fame as a military leader. Landowners and merchants supported the Confederacy but the poor supported Juan Cortina, a kind of Robin Hood figure in the area. In May, 1861, in the famed Battle of Carrizo, Benavides successfully drove Cortina into Mexico. The Thirty-third Regiment was ill-equipped and often lacked provisions. Even so, they were undefeated in battle under Benavides, who in 1863 was promoted to the rank of colonel. In 1864, Benavides led two dozen men against the Union First Texas Cavalry and Colonel Edmund J. Davis, the man who had offered Benavides a place in the Union army as general.

During Reconstruction, Benavides remained active as a civic leader. Even with the Union occupation of Brownsville in 1864, he helped facilitate the passage of Texas cotton into Matamoros, Mexico. He returned to ranching and politics with his brother Cristóbal. His interest in maintaining states' rights and regional independence never wavered.

After the Civil War, Benavides served as an alderman in Laredo in the sixteenth, seventeenth, and eighteenth state Legislatures. He was the Texas delegate to the World Cotton Exposition in 1884. Benavides died on November 9, 1891, at his home in Laredo.

Significance

Known for a gentle nature but also a restless spirit, Benavides was a charismatic and effective leader who did much to maintain the character of the South Texas region. He was respected by friends and foes alike. A legend in his own time, he earned a record of unqualified success in defending the border region. As the highest-ranking Mexican American in the Confederacy during the Civil War, he lived under five flags: the Republic of Mexico, Republic of the Rio Grande, Republic of Texas, the United States, and the Confederacy. Even under such disparate rule for his entire life, his belief in regional independence helped shape the region for generations to come.

Yvette D. Benavides

Further Reading

Adams, John A. *Conflict and Commerce on the Rio Grande: Laredo, 1755-1955*. College Station: Texas A&M University Press, 2008. Discusses Benavides's influence on the politics and economy of the Laredo area.

Thompson, Jerry Don. *Cortina: Defending the Mexican Name in Texas*. College Station: Texas A&M University Press, 2007. Thompson is arguably the foremost expert on the Civil War soldiers of South Texas.

_______. *Vaqueros in Blue and Gray*. Austin, Tex.: State House Press, 2000. An important work offering a clear and thorough explanation of the saga of South Texas during 1800's.

See also: Juan Cortina; David G. Farragut; Joseph Marion Hernández; Pío Pico; Juan Seguin; Loreta Janeta Velázquez.

Roy Benavidez

American soldier

Raised in poverty in Texas, Benavidez dropped out of school and eventually joined the U.S. Army, in which, as a member of Special Forces, he displayed such heroism in battle against North Vietnamese soldiers on May 2, 1968, that, years later, he received the Medal of Honor.

Latino heritage: Mexican

Born: August 5, 1935; Lindenau, near Cuero, Texas

Died: November 29, 1998; San Antonio, Texas

Also known as: Raul Perez Benavidez; Tango Mike Mike; That Mean Mexican; Roy P. Benavidez

Area of achievement: Military

Early Life

On August 5, 1935, Raul Perez Benavidez (rah-EWL PEH-rehz beh-nah-VEE-dehz) was born in Lindenau, near Cuero, Texas.

His father, Salvador Benavidez, Jr., was a sharecropper descended from a Hispanic supporter of Texas in its war for independence from Mexico. Teresa Perez, Raul's mother, was a Yaqui Indian born in Mexico, and older members of the Benavidez family objected to her because they considered Yaquis barbarians.

When her husband died in 1937, Teresa moved with Raul and his younger brother to nearby Cuero, where she worked as a housemaid but died when Raul was seven. Upon her death, he and his brother went to El Campo, Texas, to live with their paternal grandfather, their uncle Nicholas Benavidez, and other relatives. In El Campo, where persons who looked Mexican were subject to discrimination, Raul retained his habit of fighting at almost any provocation, but he also heard from his uncle that his behavior should honor the Benavidez name, and he learned to work hard to help support the family. His work included harvesting sugar beets in northern Colorado and cotton in western Texas, and his work-related absences from school put him so far behind that he dropped out in 1950. He returned to El Campo, where he worked at a tire store under the Reverend Art Haddock's benevolent supervision, and at the age of seventeen he joined the Texas National Guard.

Life's Work

Benavidez began his full-time military career by volunteering for the U.S. Army in 1955, and he soon changed his first name to Roy. In the fall of that year, he shipped out to South Korea and later served in Germany. Back in El Campo, he married Hilaria Coy in 1959. The devoted couple eventually had three children.

Later in 1959, Benavidez entered airborne training and, completing the course despite his short stature, served in the United States until he went overseas in December, 1965, as an adviser to the South Vietnamese army. In Vietnam, an exploding landmine traumatized his spinal cord. The prognosis was that he would never walk again, but, putting himself through painful rehabilitation, Benavidez not only avoided discharge from the Army but also eventually entered Special Forces.

As a Green Beret, Staff Sergeant Benavidez returned to Vietnam in January, 1968. On this tour, his Army comrades gave him the radio code name in which he took pride—Tango Mike Mike, or That Mean Mexican. On May 2, 1968, Benavidez was at Loc Ninh when three of his Special Forces friends, along with nine anticommunist Vietnamese guerillas, encountered hundreds of North Vietnamese across the nearby Cambodian border and found themselves trapped. When Benavidez heard of the situation, he volunteered to helicopter to the scene, where for six hours he fought off the enemy, tended to the wounded, retrieved classified documents, and suffered so many wounds that, upon rescue, he seemed dead. However, after a long recuperation, Benavidez continued his military service until disability led to his retirement, at the rank of master sergeant, in 1976.

Before his retirement, he heard that he had been recommended for the Medal of Honor, a higher award than the Distinguished Service Cross, which he had received in September, 1968. Three obstacles, however, blocked him from receiving the Medal of Honor: There did not seem to be enough surviving eyewitnesses of his actions in Cambodia; the recommendation had not been submitted in time; and the battle had taken place in a country where U.S. troops were not supposed to be fighting. However, Benavidez and his supporters eventually overcame those obstacles, and he received the Medal of Honor from President Ronald Reagan on February 24, 1981.

A popular speaker during his retirement, Benavidez won a figurative battle in 1983 against the Social Security Administration, which he believed had treated him unjustly by questioning whether he was truly disabled. Inevitably, however, Benavidez lost his battle against declining health. Afflicted by diabetes, which had cost him a leg, he died in San Antonio on November 29, 1998, with shrapnel still near his heart.

Significance

Benavidez was proud to be an Army veteran and proud of the Green Berets who had fought with him, including those who had died on May 2, 1968. Knowing that a lack of formal education had hampered him, he encouraged youths to take school seriously, stay out of gangs, and fight only for just causes. Through the upgrading of his Distinguished Service Cross to the Medal of Honor, Congress and the Department of Defense cleared the way for other U.S. servicemen, living or dead, who should have received the highest military decoration in America for their valor in the Vietnam War. It was to America that Roy Benavidez, of Mexican and Yaqui ancestry, gave his allegiance.

Victor Lindsey

Further Reading

Benavidez, Roy, with John R. Craig. *Medal of Honor: A Vietnam Warrior's Story*. Washington, D.C.: Brassey's, 1995. Autobiography in which Benavidez initially describes his ancestry and subsequently gives details of his youth, military career, and retirement.

Benavidez, Roy, and Oscar Griffin. *The Three Wars of Roy Benavidez*. New York: Pocket Books, 1988.

Dramatic stories of events from Benavidez's Army and retirement years, with references to other biographical events.

Bohrer, David. *America's Special Forces*. St. Paul, Minn.: Zenith Press, 2002. Richly illustrated account of Army Special Forces, along with the Army Rangers, Navy Seals, Marine Force Reconnaissance, and Air Force Special Operations.

Farinacci, Donald J. *Last Full Measure of Devotion: A Tribute to America's Heroes of the Vietnam War*. Bloomington, Ind.: AuthorHouse, 2007. Brief history of the war as a frame for narratives of extraordinary heroism, including the battle for which Benavidez won the Medal of Honor.

McCain, John, with Mark Salter. *Why Courage Matters: The Way to a Braver Life*. New York: Random House, 2004. Collection of inspirational stories, including an account of Benavidez's actions on May 2, 1968, with a meditation on his courage.

See also: Richard E. Cavazos; Guy Gabaldon; Horacio Rivero, Jr.

Wilfred Benitez

American boxer

Benitez was a defensive specialist and effective counterpuncher who earned the nickname "the boxing Brain." At 5 feet, 10 inches, he also was exceptionally tall for his weight class. He was the youngest fighter to win a world championship and became only the fifth fighter to win world titles in three different weight classes—junior welterweight, welterweight, and junior middleweight.

Latino heritage: Puerto Rican

Born: September 12, 1958; Bronx, New York

Also known as: The Boxing Brain; El Radar; the Bible of Boxing

Area of achievement: Boxing

Early Life

Wilfred Benitez (beh-NEE-tehz) was born on September 12, 1958, in the Bronx, New York, and raised in Puerto Rico. His father trained him to be a boxer and served as his manager. At only fifteen years of age in November, 1973, Benitez had his first professional fight; he knocked out Hiram Santiago in the first round in San Juan.

Fighting in Puerto Rico, the Antilles, and New York City, Benitez would win his next twenty-four fights before fighting World Boxing Association (WBA) light welterweight champion Antonio Cervantes in San Juan on March 6, 1976. At seventeen years and five months old, Benitez became the youngest fighter to win a world title with a split-decision victory. In May and October, Benitez defended his title against Emiliano Villa and Tony Petronelli, respectively, before moving up to the welterweight division, where he obtained the first blemish on his record with a draw against Harold Weston in February, 1977.

After winning his next three fights but being stripped of his WBA title, Benitez fought Ray Chavez Guerrero on August 3, 1977, and won recognition from the New York State Athletic Commission as the lineal light welterweight champion. After two close decision wins against future World Boxing Council (WBC) light welterweight champion Bruce Curry, he fought for the

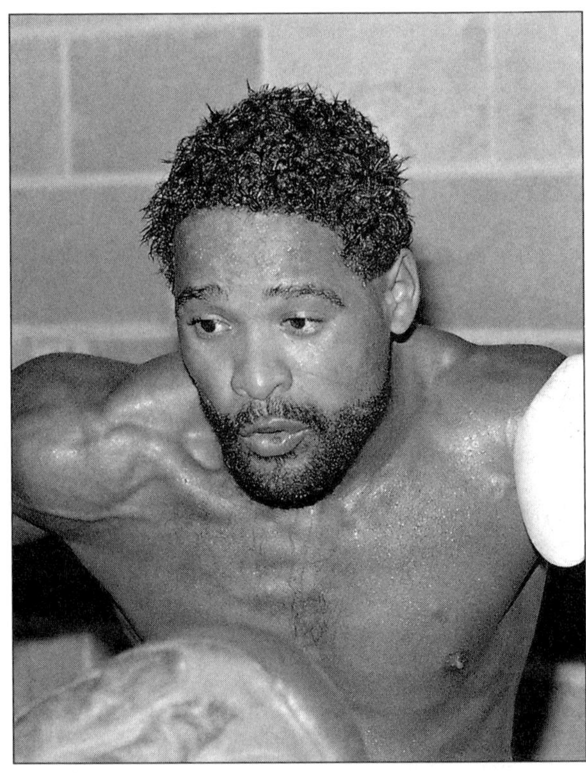

Wilfred Benitez. (AP Photo)

WBC welterweight title. On January 14, 1979, Benitez out-pointed Carlos Palomino in Puerto Rico for a split decision win. After avenging his draw with Weston, he defended his title in a fifteen-round fight against 1976 Olympic gold medalist Sugar Ray Leonard in November, 1979. Benitez was only twenty-one years old and the undefeated Leonard twenty-three; this was a fight between the two best young boxers in the world. Enduring a knockdown in the third round and a cut forehead in the sixth, Benitez was stopped with just six seconds to go in the final round.

Life's Work

Benitez came back in 1980 with three wins, two by knockout, before challenging Maurice Hope for the WBC light middleweight title. He stopped Hope in the twelfth round. With this win, he became only the third fighter to win titles in three divisions. He successfully defended the title twice: once against undefeated Carlos Santos in November, 1981, and once against the legend Roberto Duran, considered by many one of the best fighters of all time, in January, 1982. Benitez won a close unanimous decision over Duran. Almost a year later, in December, he faced Thomas Hearns and lost a majority decision.

Benitez continued to fight through the 1980's but was never the same. After fighting Hearns, his record was 9 wins against 6 losses—3 of which were by knockout. He often was brought in to fight young fighters to build up their résumés. This included a loss to future junior middleweight champion Matthew Hilton in Montreal in 1986. Benitez suffered a final indignity in 1986 when, after a knockout loss in Argentina, the promoter stole his money and his passport, leaving him stranded in the country for more than a year. That was Benitez's last fight before his final comeback attempt in 1990.

After retiring from boxing, it became apparent that Benitez had suffered brain damage in his years in the ring. Because he has a brother who boxed and who suffered from the same condition, many believe Benitez had a predisposition to it. He soon was living in a care facility, supported by a pension from the Puerto Rican government. Despite having earned millions of dollars during his boxing career, including $1.2 million for his fight with Leonard, Benitez ended up destitute and damaged.

In 1996, Benitez was inducted into the International Boxing Hall of Fame. *Ring* magazine named Benitez the fourth greatest junior middleweight of all time in 1994 and the thirtieth best fighter of the previous fifty years in 1996. In 2006, boxing historian Bert Sugar ranked him the ninety-sixth best fighter of all time. Benitez finished his career with a record of 53 wins, 8 losses, and 31 knockouts.

Significance

Benitez is remembered as the youngest champion in boxing history and as one of the first to win titles in three weight divisions. Although Leonard, Hagler, Hearns, and Duran are remembered as the best of Benitez's era, Benitez deserves to be included in that group. He also is a symbol for the damage boxing can do to a fighter. A great defensive fighter, he still suffered severe brain damage in the ring, which ended his career as a top fighter before he was twenty-five years old.

Brett Conway

Further Reading

Ashe, Arthur R., Jr. *A Hard Road to Glory—Boxing: The African-American Athlete in Boxing*. New York: Amistad, 1988. This overview of African American fighters includes discussion of Benitez in connection with some of his major bouts.

Haksins, James. *Sugar Ray Leonard*. London: Robson, 1989. This biography of Leonard covers his fifteen-round title win over Benitez.

Kimball, George. *Four Kings: Leonard, Hagler, Hearns, Duran, and the Last Great Era of Boxing*. Ithaca, N.Y.: McBooks, 2008. Well-researched examination of the major fighters of Benitez's era.

Nieves, Evelyn. "Too Many Beatings: The Boxer's Disease Haunts Wilfred Benitez and His Family." *The New York Times*, November 12, 1997. Discusses Benitez's poor health after the end of his boxing career.

Sugar, Bert Randolph. *Boxing's Greatest Fighters*. Guilford, Conn.: Lyons Press, 2006. Sugar ranks Benitez ninety-sixth among the best boxers of all time. Includes useful analysis of his boxing style and career highlights.

See also: Art Aragon; Oscar De la Hoya; Sixto Escobar; Aurelio Herrera; Félix Trinidad.

JOE J. BERNAL

American politician and educator

A coach and educator, Bernal served in the Texas legislature in the 1960's, where he championed legislation to provide bilingual education in this state and served his constituents in San Antonio. His service on the Texas Board of Education later in his career enabled him to advance education in the state.

Latino heritage: Mexican

Born: March 1, 1927; San Antonio, Texas

Also known as: Joseph Juarez Bernal; José María Bernal, Jr.

Areas of achievement: Government and politics; education

EARLY LIFE

Joseph Juarez Bernal (JOH-zehf WAH-rehz bur-NAHL) was born José María Bernal, Jr., in San Antonio, Texas, to José and Antonio Juarez Bernal. His father died when Bernal was eleven, and his single mother raised her nine children without accepting government housing or food stamps. Bernal attended Lanier High School in San Antonio, where he served on the student council. The student council participated in a program in which students were given ribbons reading, "I'm an American, I speak English." Council members who heard students speaking Spanish would take away these students' ribbons for failing to speak English.

Joe J. Bernal. (AP Photo)

Bernal graduated from high school in 1944 and was drafted into the U.S. Army. He trained at Fort Hood in Texas and received additional training at Fort Ord in California before being sent across the Pacific to the Philippines. By the time he arrived, World War II had ended, and he worked as a clerk for the American occupation forces in Tokyo. He was discharged on December 9, 1946, and Sergeant Bernal returned to San Antonio. Taking advantage of the G.I. Bill, he enrolled in Trinity University to study physical education. His goal was to become a high school teacher and coach. He graduated from Trinity in 1950 and earned a master of education degree from Our Lady of the Lake College in 1956. Bernal married Mary Esther Martinez in 1956.

LIFE'S WORK

Bernal's teaching career started in the Edgewood Independent School District, and he soon moved to the San Antonio Independent School District. In 1950, he was elected Democratic precinct chairman. From 1950 until 1964, Bernal worked with a number of community organizations as his stature in local Democratic Party politics grew. He was recruited by the Westside Good Government League, a slating organization primarily composed of conservative white Anglos who nominated most of the candidates for city offices, to run against Rudy Esquivel in the 1964 Democratic primary for state representative. Bernal was successful and entered the Texas House of Representatives in 1965. One of his first committee assignments was as a member of the redistricting committee; the U.S. Supreme Court had ordered states to redraw district lines on the basis of one voter, one vote.

In 1966, he ran for a seat in the state senate. He was elected, becoming the first Hispanic member of the Texas senate. The new senator began to work with striking Rio Grande Valley farmworkers, who were being harassed by the Texas Rangers. In 1968, Bernal requested that the senate investigate the Texas Rangers' tactics, a recommendation that was denied by the senate leadership. Working with state Representative Carlos Truan, a

Bilingual Education

Until the 1960's, schools commonly punished children for speaking Spanish. The first bilingual program in the state of Texas was created in 1964 by Superintendent Harold Brantley of the Laredo United Consolidated School District. He modeled the program on the first program in the nation, which was started at the Coral Way Elementary School in Dade County, Florida.

Prior to 1964, it had been illegal to speak any language other than English in Texas public schools. The bilingual programs worked to transition Spanish-speaking children from instruction in Spanish to English-only teaching and learning. By May, 1969, Texas had sixteen schools with bilingual programs. Officially, the Texas Education Agency could not recognize these programs because of the state's English-only law. In 1969, state Representative Carlos Truan and state Senator Joe J. Bernal carried a bill through the Texas legislature to permit school districts to offer non-English-speaking children an instructional program using two languages. The Texas legislature further advanced bilingual education in 1973 when it approved, and the governor signed, the Bilingual Education and Training Act. This legislation required that all Texas public elementary schools enrolling twenty or more children of limited English ability in a given grade level must provide bilingual instruction.

By 1998, opposition to bilingual education grew, resulting in the passage that year of Proposition 227, which prohibited bilingual education in California. Members of the Texas Board of Education regularly debated the issue into the twenty-first century. In February, 2006, board members engaged in a lively debate over the value of bilingual education compared with the alternative, structured English immersion.

Democrat from Corpus Christi, Bernal introduced a law permitting local school districts to offer non-English-speaking children an instructional program using two languages. The bill was enacted in 1969.

Bernal was reelected to the senate in 1970. In 1971, the legislature redistricted the state and required that all senators stand for reelection in 1972. Bernal's opponent in 1972 was Nelson Wolff, a moderate Democrat. Wolff defeated Bernal, although there is controversy about the role of the La Raza Unida Party in Bernal's defeat. Some Bernal supporters claim that the party's activities in the district kept some potential voters from casting ballots in the Democratic primary, because voters could not vote in the primary if they had signed La Raza Unida's petition for a state convention.

After leaving the senate, Bernal returned to teaching. He was a principal in the Edgewood Independent School District for five years and subsequently moved to the Harlandale Independent School District to become an assistant superintendent. In 1978, he completed his Ph.D. degree at the University of Texas at Austin, writing his dissertation on "A Study of Bilingual Education: Contrasting Influences on Texas Legislators with Results of an Attitudinal Survey of the Members of the 64th Legislature." He also taught as an adjunct professor at the University of Texas at San Antonio, Trinity University, and Our Lady of the Lake University.

In 1996, Bernal decided to run for the state Board of Education, representing most of Bexar County and several other counties in south Texas. He defeated José de Lara, the Republican candidate, with 70 percent of the vote. He was easily reelected twice. He worked hard to maintain bilingual education as a member of the Board of Education, and he also tried to extend educational opportunities for elementary and secondary school students in Texas. Bernal retired from the board in 2006.

Significance

Bernal devoted his career to education as an educator, school administrator, college professor, state legislator, and member of the Texas Board of Education. As a legislator, he introduced bills to provide elementary school teachers a forty-five-minute planning period, created free statewide kindergarten for some five-year-old children, and established the University of Texas at San Antonio. His primary contribution, however, was in the area of bilingual education. As a senator, he worked to repeal a state statute that prohibited the speaking of Spanish in public schools. As a member of the state Board of Education, he protected bilingual education from the conservative members of the board who wished to end the program in favor of English-immersion education. Even in retirement from public office, Bernal continued to participate in social action by marching for immigration reform.

John David Rausch, Jr.

Further Reading

Rosales, Rodolfo. *The Illusion of Inclusion: The Untold Political Story of San Antonio*. Austin: University of Texas Press, 2000. An examination of politics in San Antonio from 1951 through 1991, reviewing the growth of the Chicano community's participation in politics. Includes a discussion of Bernal's short career in the Texas legislature.

Samora, Julian, Joe Bernal, and Albert Pena. *Gunpowder Justice: A Reassessment of the Texas Rangers*. Notre Dame, Ind.: University of Notre Dame Press, 1979. Reviews the history of the iconic Texas Rangers, showing how the force had a history of racism. Details Senator Bernal's call for an investigation of the Rangers' tactics during the farmworkers' strike in the 1960's.

San Miguel, Guadalupe. *Contested Policy: The Rise and Fall of Federal Bilingual Education in the United States, 1960-2001*. Denton: University of North Texas Press, 2004. Considers the history of bilingual education in the United States. San Miguel finds that bilingual education is controversial because it is misunderstood.

_______. *"Let All of Them Take Heed": Mexican Americans and the Campaign for Educational Equality in Texas, 1910-1981*. College Station: Texas A&M University Press, 1987. In addition to documenting the history of Mexican American education in Texas, this book also briefly considers Bernal's role in expanding bilingual education with House Bill 103 in 1969.

Zehr, Mary Ann. "Bilingual Education Debated in Texas." *Education Week* 25, no. 24 (February 22, 2006): 26. Briefly reviews one debate of the Texas Board of Education over the value of bilingual education. Clearly shows the ethnic and partisan cleavages present in the controversy.

See also: Joaquín Castro; Julián Castro; Irma Rangel; Raul Yzaguirre.

Martha Bernal

American psychologist and educator

Bernal was the first woman of Mexican heritage to receive a doctorate in clinical psychology from an American university. She became a leading researcher on methods of correcting behavioral problems in children and an expert in the training of psychologists on minority and multicultural issues.

Latino heritage: Mexican

Born: April 13, 1931; San Antonio, Texas

Died: September 28, 2001; Black Canyon City, Arizona

Also known as: Martha E. Bernal

Areas of achievement: Psychology; social issues; education

Early Life

Martha Bernal (behr-NAHL) was born in San Antonio, Texas, and raised in El Paso by her parents, Alicia and Enrique de Bernal, who emigrated from Mexico during the Mexican Revolution. Her parents instilled in her traditional Mexican values, including an emphasis on the importance of family. The family spoke Spanish at home. When Bernal enrolled in elementary school unable to speak English, she began learning about discrimination toward Mexican culture. She experienced difficulties growing up in a bicultural community from this young age because interaction among children of different races was discouraged.

Bernal graduated from El Paso High School and desired more formal education, a choice that was not typical for Mexican women, who generally were encouraged to then marry and raise families. Although resistant, her parents eventually agreed to Bernal's wishes and financially supported her while she attended Texas Western College, now known as the University of Texas at El Paso.

After graduating from college with a bachelor's degree in psychology, Bernal continued her education by earning a master of arts degree from Syracuse University in New York (1955). She subsequently obtained a doctoral degree in clinical psychology from Indiana University in 1962. As a woman, Bernal was not allowed to participate in research projects with her psychology professors and often considered dropping out because of this gender discrimination. By persevering, Bernal became the first Mexican American woman to earn a doctorate in clinical psychology.

Life's Work

Bernal had great difficulty obtaining her first academic job because institutions only wanted to hire male psychologists. Instead, she completed a two-year postdoctoral fellowship in human psychophysiology through the U.S. Public Health Service at the University of California at Los Angeles (UCLA). With this added

Bernal's Work on Negative Stereotypes of Mexican Americans

Martha Bernal focused much effort on cultural education to overcome stereotypes that persons of Mexican heritage are criminals, violent, and drug users. Her research attempted to provide a greater understanding and respect of the Mexican culture and to discourage the exploitation of its people. While at Arizona State University, Bernal created a method of measuring ethnic identity called the Ethnic Identity Questionnaire. Bernal used this tool to interview Mexican and Mexican American children and families. The research brought to light common feelings and thoughts, including how Mexican identity is influenced and formed and how American society can better appreciate Mexican culture. She published the findings of these studies in a book titled *Ethnic Identity: Formation and Transmission Among Hispanics and Other Minorities* (1993), as well as in several peer-reviewed scientific journals. Bernal frequently lectured about her research findings in order to raise multicultural awareness. For three years, she also coordinated an annual Ethnic Identity Symposium to address these issues.

experience, Bernal eventually obtained her first academic position in 1969 as assistant professor at the University of Arizona at Tucson.

Bernal returned to UCLA's Neuropsychiatric Institute to begin her scientific research. She was awarded a grant by the National Institute of Mental Health (NIMH) to study learning theory and classical conditioning in children with behavior problems, most notably autism. Her research concentrated on altering the parents' behavior by teaching them skills and lessons to help change their children's behavior. Bernal believed that children with autism did not have an innate cause for their disorder but rather had learned their behaviors. For this work, Bernal was bestowed several National Research Service Awards from the NIMH and is cited as one of the first psychologists to study this subject in an empirical manner.

After several years at UCLA, Bernal relocated to the University of Denver to continue her work. There she evaluated the efficacy and validity of her previous studies. In addition to her professional research, Bernal became more involved in minority issues regarding race and gender discrimination after attending the influential Conference on Chicano Psychology (1973). Bernal refocused her scientific research in order to make it more applicable to minority issues. She also acted as an advocate for minorities and professionally sought the help of the American Psychological Association to bring attention to minority issues in the profession. In 1979, the NIMH gave Bernal another National Research Science Award to educate psychologists about multicultural issues.

Bernal's initial findings regarding diversity in the psychology field were not encouraging: training programs lacked appropriately sensitive multicultural lectures and curricula, had little to no minority students enrolled, and did not employ minority professors. She completed a second postdoctoral fellowship through the Ford Foundation in which she studied ways to eliminate these disparities. In 1986, Bernal moved to Arizona State University, where she focused on marriage counseling of minority couples when mental illness was diagnosed in the wife. Additionally, it was at Arizona State University that she performed much of her groundbreaking work on how identities are established in Mexican American children and families. The research has been hailed as pioneering because of the creative and new interview approaches used in an attempt to understand how ethnicity is created and transmitted from influences such as parents, families, other adults, and peers.

Bernal raised awareness of multicultural issues by speaking at many professional conferences. She spoke at the 1972 Vail Conference on Training in Psychology and the Lake Arrowhead National Conference of Hispanic Psychologists (1979). She was influential with drafting the bylaws of the Board of Ethnic Minority Affairs (1979) and helped establish the National Hispanic Psychological Association (1979), now known as the National Latino/a Psychological Association, of which she eventually became president. Bernal was appointed to the Commission on Ethnic Minority Recruitment, Retention and Training (1994) and served on the board for the Advancement of Psychology in the Public Interest (1996-1998).

Among the noteworthy awards that Bernal received are the Distinguished Life Achievement Award from Division 45 of the Society for the Psychological Study of Ethnic Minority Issues (1979), the Hispanic Research Center Lifetime Award (1979), the Pioneer Senior Women of Color Honor (1999), the Carolyn Attneave Diversity Award for lifelong contributions to ethnic minorities psychology (1999), and the Award for Distinguished Contributions to the Public Interest from the American Psychological Association (2001).

After three separate occurrences of cancer over two decades, Bernal died of lung cancer at seventy years of age. The Martha E. Bernal Memorial Award at Arizona State University was established in her honor.

Significance

Bernal overcame cultural and gender discrimination in her youth and throughout her career. She convinced not only her family but also her colleagues that Mexican women could become productive and successful in the professional and academic worlds. Although Bernal's early career path was not focused on ethnicity or minority issues, she realized the importance of these issues and fought for more than twenty years in order to incorporate them into the field of psychology. Bernal's groundbreaking research on minority populations serves as a basis for the now-common multicultural studies classes in undergraduate and graduate psychology and counseling programs.

Janet Ober Berman

Further Reading

Bernal, Martha E. "Behavioral Feedback in the Modification of Brat Behaviors." *The Journal of Nervous and Mental Disease* 148, no. 4. (April, 1969): 375-385. Bernal's initial clinical research findings on how to modify children's behavior problems using classical conditioning.

Bernal, Martha E., and George P. Knight. *Ethnic Identity: Formation and Transmission Among Hispanics and Other Minorities*. Albany: State University of New York Press, 1993. Details Bernal's research findings on multicultural awareness and the development of ethnic identification.

Bernal Martha E., et al, eds. "Mexican American Identity." Mountain View, Calif.: Floricanto Press, 2005. Edited by Bernal and colleagues, this book focuses on how society, politics, and public policy influence views of Mexican Americans and how Mexican identity is established.

Vasquez, Melba J. T. "The Life and Death of a Multicultural Feminist Pioneer: Martha Bernal (1931-2001)." *The Feminist Psychologist Newsletter* 30, no. 1 (Winter, 2003). A tribute to Bernal's life and work, chronicling the struggles Bernal faced both professionally and personally as a Mexican American woman in the field of clinical psychology.

See also: Daniel Acosta; Teresa Bernardez; Jane L. Delgado.

Teresa Bernardez

Argentine-born psychiatrist and feminist

As a pioneering female psychiatrist, Bernardez challenged society's attitudes regarding women professionals in academia and medicine. She advocated for female and minority patients who were unjustly labeled as having psychological problems because of sexism, racism, and other unaddressed socioeconomic issues.

Latino heritage: Argentinean and Spanish

Born: June 11, 1931; Buenos Aires, Argentina

Died: July 12, 2010; East Lansing, Michigan

Also known as: Teresa Bernardez-Bonesatti

Areas of achievement: Medicine; women's rights; scholarship

Early Life

Teresa Bernardez (teh-REH-sah behr-NAHR-dehz) was born to Spanish parents, Francisco Bernardez and Dolores Novoa, who named her after the saint reformer Santa Teresa de Avila. She was the youngest of seven children, five of whom were paternal half siblings. Bernardez later cited her mother's Catholicism and feminist beliefs as significant influences in her life; she also credited both parents for instilling the notion that she could achieve any goal.

Until her teenage years, Bernardez aspired to a career in religion. When she discovered female sexuality and women's rights, Bernardez abandoned this path and left the Catholic Church at age sixteen. She attended the Liceo No. 1 de Senoritas, where she received her bachelor of arts degree in 1948. She matriculated to University of Buenos Aires Medical School and was awarded her doctorate of medicine in 1956. Bernardez interned at the Hospital de Clinicas in Argentina. Because of the lack of freedom under the nation's dictatorship, Bernardez left Argentina for Paris, France, on a one-year academic scholarship as an intern at the Hospital Vaugirard.

Life's Work

Bernardez moved to the United States to complete her psychiatry residency in Topeka, Kansas, at the Menninger Clinic, one of only two women in her program. Although initially she was culturally isolated as the only Latina, Bernardez found a few influential female psychiatrists, slowly adjusted to life in the United States, and began studying psychoanalysis as the only female in her specialty. Bernardez became interested in studying the developmental period of female adolescence with respect to sexuality. She focused on issues such as pursuing education and a career rather than immediate motherhood, which at the time was considered a pathological decision for a teenage American girl. Bernardez served as a staff psychiatrist at the Menninger Memorial Hospital from 1960 to1965, and she assumed the same position with the department of psychiatry at the Menninger Foundation from 1965 to 1971.

Through her work at the Menninger Clinic, Bernardez volunteered to be a member of the first team to integrate healthcare efforts in Topeka's African American community. She culturally related to the needs of the African American minority in this Caucasian-dominated city. She established the first therapy groups for mothers and adolescent females in which participants could discuss medical concerns and become empowered to break racial and socioeconomic barriers. As a result of these groups, the mental health of the community significantly improved. Bernardez later published her groundbreaking work on the connection between racism, sexism, poverty, and mental illness. She hypothesized that women were incorrectly diagnosed as mentally ill because psychoanalysts did not appropriately account for the social disadvantages of minority populations.

Because psychoanalysts were unwilling to accept Bernardez's feminist views, she left psychoanalysis and relocated to the Department of Psychiatry at Michigan State University, in which she was a professor from 1971 to 1989. At Michigan she led research groups on gender and women's issues for more than fifteen years and created the first group for women medical students. Her research focused on the way social restrictions fueled women's anger. She sat on the first admissions committee that ensured that women and minorities were accepted into the university's medical school, and she chaired the medical school's first affirmative action committee, which recruited female and minority faculty members. Bernardez also taught courses on psychotherapy for women, trained male and female psychiatric medical residents to better understand gender issues, and created an obstetric consultation and liaison program in order to empower women during pregnancy and childbirth.

On a national level, Bernardez taught an annual course at the American Psychiatric Association's (APA) annual meeting. She was a founding member of the Association for Women Psychiatrists and the Michigan Psychoanalytic Council. She also chaired the APA's committee on women, and in this capacity she and her colleagues fought to have inappropriate diagnoses of women removed from the 1985 edition of the Diagnostic and Statistical Manual of Mental Disorders (DSM).

Awards for Bernardez include the Pawlowski Foundation's Peace Award (1974), the American Medical Women's Association First Leadership Workshop Award (1977), and Michigan State University's Distinguished Faculty Award (1982).

Bernardez was married to Jorge Bonesatti and had one son, Diego Bonesatti. She divorced after twenty-two years of marriage because of her feminist ideals. Bernardez's hobbies included poetry and world travel. She had a private psychiatric practice in Michigan at the time of her death on July 12, 2010, at the age of seventy-nine.

Significance

Bernardez's determination to overcome racism and sexism throughout her career laid the foundation for women and minorities to advance in the academic and professional worlds. Her work on affirmative action resulted in pivotal documentation that helps afford all individuals equal opportunity in school admittance and the workplace. Bernardez continued her involvement in the field of psychiatry even after she retired into private practice. In her seventies, she remained outspoken about the diagnoses included in the DSM, displaying a continual commitment to the mental health of women and minorities.

Janet Ober Berman

Further Reading

Bernardez, Teresa. "By My Sisters Reborn." *Feminist Foremothers in Women's Studies, Psychology and Mental Health* 1(1995): 55-70. Bernardez's autobiographical account of her influential family upbringing and the professional obstacles she overcame to become a psychiatrist and feminist.

_______. "Studies in Countertransference and Gender: Female Analyst/Male Patient in Two Cases of Childhood Trauma." *Journal of the American Academy of Psychoanalysis and Dynamic Psychiatry* 32, no 1 (2004): 231-254. An example of Bernardez's continued research on gender issues as part of her work with the Michigan Psychoanalytic Council.

Rankman, Angie. "Have We Got PMS All Wrong?" *Aprhodite Women's Health,* June, 2006, 1. Discusses the diagnosis of premenstrual syndrome (PMS) and the controversy regarding its inclusion in the DSM, an issue which Bernardez fought over for many years.

See also: Martha Bernal; Jane L. Delgado.

Rubén Berríos

President of the Puerto Rican Independence Party

Berríos is a longtime activist for the Puerto Rican Independence Party (PIP) who has served almost continuously as the organization's president since 1970. Berríos, a self-proclaimed social democrat, has run unsuccessfully for the governorship of Puerto Rico on several occasions. In addition to serving four terms in the Puerto Rican Senate, he was a leader of protests in Culebra (1971) and Vieques (1999) against the presence of U.S. military bases on the islands.

Latino heritage: Puerto Rican

Born: June 21, 1939; Aibonito, Puerto Rico

Also known as: Rubén Ángel Berríos Martínez

Areas of achievement: Government and politics; social issues; law

Early Life

Rubén Ángel Berríos Martínez (behr-EE-ohs) was born in Aibonito, Puerto Rico, to Cándida Martínez and Rubén Berríos. He completed his secondary education at the Colegio San Ignacio de Loyola in San Juan in 1957. Berríos earned his undergraduate degree in business administration from Georgetown University in 1961. He subsequently earned his M.A. and J.D. in law from Yale University and his Ph.D. in international rights from Oxford University before returning to Puerto Rico. Berríos obtained a position as a professor of law at the University of Puerto Rico's Law School in 1967.

During the 1960's, Berríos, who favored Puerto Rican independence as a panacea for the island's economic and social woes, became involved in the Puerto Rican Independence Party (PIP). Founded on October 20, 1946, by Gilberto Concepción de Gracia after Luis Muñoz Marín's Popular Democratic Party (PPD) abandoned the idea of independence, the PIP is the largest pro-independence party in Puerto Rico and the only pro-independence party listed on ballots during elections. Concepción de Gracia led the PIP until his death in 1968. Berríos was elected president of the party in 1970.

Life's Work

Since assuming leadership of the PIP, Berríos has pursued a nonviolent, democratic socialist agenda. Although the PIP receives support from various academic, journalistic, and intellectual sectors of Puerto Rican society,

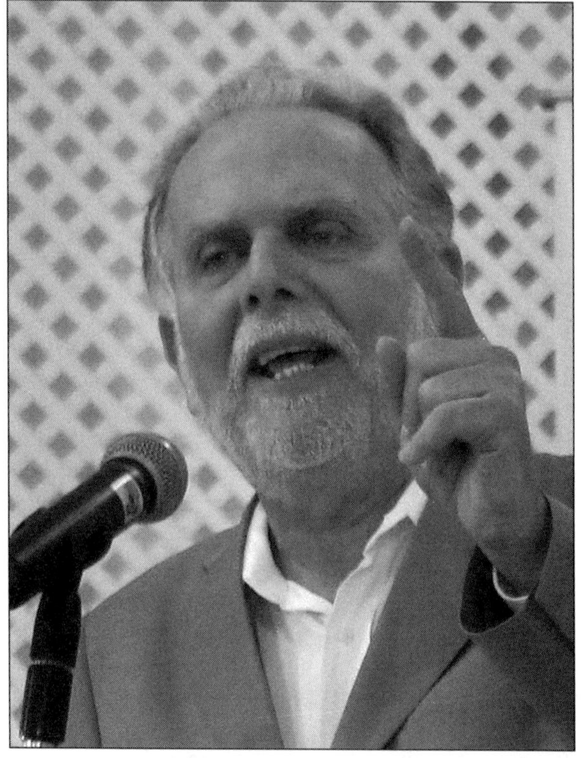

Rubén Berríos. (AP Photo)

Berríos and the PIP have not been able to match the success of the pro-commonwealth and pro-statehood parties in Puerto Rican elections. Berríos ran unsuccessfully for governor in 1976, 1980, 1988, 2000, and 2004, never winning more than 5.69 percent of the vote. However, he was elected to the Puerto Rican Senate in 1972, 1984, 1992, and 1996. In all four Senate elections, Berríos won one of eleven at-large seats, receiving more votes than any other at-large candidate. The Senate, the upper house of the Legislative Assembly of Puerto Rico, comprises two senators representing each of the eight senatorial districts and eleven at-large senators elected by the general population. In addition to voting for senators in their districts, Puerto Ricans can vote for one at-large candidate. The eleven candidates with the most island-wide votes join the Senate.

Utilizing nonviolent tactics, Berríos organized protests against the U.S. Navy's use of the islands of Culebra and Vieques for military exercises in 1971 and 1999, respectively. During the 1960's, weapons training by the U.S. Navy on Culebra intensified. In February, 1971, after an unscheduled discharge of mortar fire that landed on a beach occupied by children, Berríos squatted on the U.S. government-owned beach for three days before being arrested and sentenced to three months in prison along with thirteen other protesters. In 1975, the Navy terminated all weapons training activities on Culebra. The victory, however, was fleeting, as the Navy relocated its weapon training exercises to nearby Vieques.

In May, 1999, Berríos began a yearlong squatting protest on U.S. bombing grounds on Vieques. The catalyst that triggered this act of civil disobedience was the April 19, 1999, death of David Sanes, a bystander who died when two bombs veered away from their designated target. Berríos and others established the Gilberto Concepción de Gracia encampment, named in honor of the PIP's founder. Because of his lengthy stay on the island, Berríos resigned his Senate seat in December, 1999. In May, 2000, federal marshals disbanded the encampment and Berríos was sentenced to prison. He was released in August, 2001. Berríos's actions were praised by his supporters and vilified by his detractors. The U.S. Navy terminated its occupation of Vieques in 2003.

Significance

Berríos, who remains hopeful about the future of the Puerto Rican independence movement, was elected an honorary president of the Socialist International, a worldwide organization of socialist parties, in 2000. In 2006, Panamanian president Martín Torrijos hosted the Latin American and Caribbean Congress in Solidarity with the Independence of Puerto Rico, an international summit that supported Berríos's efforts to achieve Puerto Rican independence. In the 2008 elections, which were a landslide victory for the pro-statehood New Progressive Party, the PIP lost official recognition because it obtained only 2.04 percent of the gubernatorial vote, short of the minimum 3 percent. Undeterred, Berríos organized an island-wide petition with 100,000 signatures to regain the party's official status in 2009. Regardless, as of 2011, the majority of Puerto Ricans continued to favor statehood or a modification of commonwealth status.

Michael R. Hall

Further Reading

Barreto, Amílcar Antonio. *The Politics of Language in Puerto Rico*. Gainesville: University of Florida Press, 2001. The first major study to examine the connections between language, cultural identity, and politics in Puerto Rico.

Ferández, Ronald. *The Disenchanted Island: Puerto Rico and the United States in the Twentieth Century*. New York: Praeger, 1996. The author contends that the United States has made Puerto Rico dependent on the United States.

McCaffrey, Katherine T. *Military Power and Popular Protest: The U.S. Navy in Vieques, Puerto Rico*. New Brunswick, N.J.: Rutgers University Press, 2002. Excellent study that also examines the role Berríos played in Culebra and Vieques.

Rivera Ramos, Efrén, *The Legal Construction of Identity: The Judicial and Social Legacy of American Colonialism in Puerto Rico*. Washington, D.C.: American Psychological Association, 2001. Rivera Ramos contends that American colonialism in Puerto Rico has transformed Puerto Rico's national identity and weakened the appeal of independence.

See also: Pedro Albizu Campos; José de Diego; Lolita Lebrón; Luis Muñoz Marín; Felisa Rincón de Gautier.

ROLANDO BLACKMAN

Panamanian-born basketball player

A professional basketball player in the United States and abroad from 1979 to 1996, Blackman excelled at both the collegiate and professional levels of the game.

Latino heritage: Panamanian

Born: February 26, 1959; Panama City, Panama

Also known as: Rolando Antonio Blackman; Ro

Area of achievement: Basketball

EARLY LIFE

Rolando Antonio Blackman (roh-LAHN-doh ahn-TOH-nee-oh BLAHK-mahn) was born in Panama City, Panama, on February 26, 1959. After graduation from the William E. Grady Career and Technical High School in Brooklyn, New York, he played collegiate basketball at Kansas State University from 1977 to 1981. During his years with the Kansas State Wildcats basketball team, Blackman made almost 52 percent of his field goals and almost 72 percent of his free throws, and the team won two-thirds of its games. The highlight of this period came in 1980, when the team won the Big Eight Conference championship, and Blackman was named both the Big Eight Conference Player of the Year (one of only three players in the Kansas State's history to receive this award) and All-American; the latter honor he garnered twice in consecutive seasons. Blackman also was Defensive Player of the Year in the Big Eight Conference for three consecutive years beginning in 1978, as well as a three-time selection to the Big Eight's team of outstanding players. While at Kansas State, he wore the number twenty-five; the Wildcats retired that number in 2007. In 2011, his 1,844 career points ranked him second in Kansas State basketball history.

During the summer before his senior year at Kansas State, Blackman was a starting member of the U.S. Olympic basketball team. However, this team never got a chance to play, as the United States boycotted the 1980 games in Moscow because of America's political conflict with the Soviet Union.

LIFE'S WORK

On June 9, 1981, in the second year of its existence as a franchise, the Dallas Mavericks of the National Basketball Association (NBA) made Blackman their first draft choice; he was the ninth player selected overall. Blackman played eleven seasons with the Mavericks. His impact was immediate, as in his first season he helped the team almost double its win total by playing in all eighty-two games and scoring more than thirteen points per game, the team's third-highest point count. Blackman remained a model of consistency over the next ten years, playing in at least 71 games each year and averaging between 17.7 and 22.4 points per game every year. In 2011, he remained the Mavericks' second all-time leading scorer with 16,643 points. Blackman made the NBA All-Star team four times (1985, 1986, 1987, 1990), and the Mavericks made the play-offs six times during his stint with them. Seven years before Kansas State retired Blackman's number, the Mavericks retired his jersey number of twenty-two.

Despite leading the Mavericks in scoring during the 1991-1992 season, on June 24, 1992, Blackman was traded to the New York Knicks for a first-round draft choice in 1995, with which pick the Mavericks took player Loren Meyer, who averaged just five points per game during the 1995-1996 season. Blackman spent the last two years of his NBA career with the Knicks. Although Blackman had been a starter throughout his time

Rolando Blackman. (AP Photo)

with the Mavericks, and although the Knicks were paying him the highest salary ($1.995 million in 1993-1994) of his career, he started in only 34 of his 115 games with the Knicks and averaged 9.7 and 7.3 points per game, respectively, in the final two seasons of his NBA career. The Knicks waived Blackman on July 6, 1994.

After his NBA career ended, Blackman spent two years playing professionally in Europe. During the latter half of the 1994-1995 season he played with AEK Athens B.C., a Greek professional basketball club. In 1995-1996, Blackman led the Olympia Milano team to win an Italian National Championship and the Italian Cup, and he was named the most valuable player.

After his playing career was over, Blackman continued to serve a number of basketball teams in various capacities. In 2002, he was an assistant coach for Germany's national team, which won a bronze medal in the 2002 World Basketball Championship. In 2010, Blackman was an assistant for the Turkish national team, which took a silver medal in Istanbul at the 2010 FIBA World Basketball Championship.

Since 2000, Blackman has worked for the Mavericks as either a coach of player development, director of basketball development (during the 2010-2011 season), television analyst, or assistant coach. During the 2005-2006 season, Blackman assisted head coach Avery Johnson in piloting the Mavericks to its only NBA Finals appearance thus far (the team lost to the Miami Heat).

Significance

Rolando Blackman gained a reputation for being a model basketball player, coach, and representative of both collegiate and professional basketball. In an age in which many professional athletes are notorious for their selfishness or controversy, Blackman has always been known for consistency, intelligence, and good sportsmanship.

John E. Thorburn, Jr.

Further Reading

Aron, Jaime. *Tales from the Dallas Mavericks*. Champion, Ill.: Sports Publishing, 2003. Story of the team told through various anecdotes and stories.

Basketball Reference.com. Rolando Blackman.http://www.basketball-reference.com/players/b/blackro01.html. Contains statistics from Blackman's NBA career.

Berendt, Johannes. "Euro Clash." www.nba.com/features/europeancup_030826.html. Discusses Blackman's coaching experience in Germany.

D'Agostino, Dennis, ed. *Knicks 1992-1993 Media Guide*. New York: New York Knickerbockers, 1992. The complete guide to the New York Knicks basketball team during one of the seasons in which Blackman played for the team.

Friedman, Ian C. *Latino Athletes*. New York: Facts On File, 2007. Includes an article providing an overview of Blackman's life and career.

Macmahon, Tim. "Blackman Moves to Mavs' Front Office." *Dallas Morning News*, July 25, 2006. Reports on Blackman's promotion to director of basketball development for the Dallas Mavericks.

Melton, Sarah, Scott Tomlin, and Alan Rakowski, eds. *Dallas Mavericks Media Guide 2010-2011*. Dallas: Dallas Mavericks, 2010. The complete guide to the basketball team.

See also: Carlos Arroyo; Manu Ginóbili; Rebecca Lobo; Eduardo Nájera; Diana Taurasi.

Rubén Blades

Panamanian-born salsa musician, actor, and activist

Blades is an internationally known singer, songwriter, bandleader, actor, and political activist. Although he is primarily viewed as a salsero, Blades also includes elements of jazz, reggae, rock and roll, Afro-Cuban rhythms, and other types of Latin American music in his works.

Latino heritage: Panamanian and Cuban

Born: July 16, 1948; Panama City, Panama

Also known as: Rubén Blades Bellido de Luna

Areas of achievement: Music; social issues; acting

Early Life

Rubén Blades Bellido de Luna (blaydz or BLAH-dehs) was the second of five children born to Anoland Belida, a Cuban-born pianist, singer, and actor, and Rubén Blades, Sr., a Panamanian police detective of West Indian descent. In his youth, Blades spent numerous hours listening to the radio and learned to sing to the music of the Beatles, the Platters, and other rock-and-roll groups. He preferred rock-and-roll to other types of music and was inspired by one of his favorite bands, Frankie Lymon and the Teenagers, which was composed of African American and Latino youths. Blades believed that if these teenagers could succeed in the music industry, he, too, could be a singer. At the age of fifteen, Blades began singing American songs with his older brother's rock band, the Saints. After the 1964 Panama Canal Riots that left more than twenty students dead and hundreds wounded, he stopped singing in English. This incident left Blades more socially conscious and politically aware.

While studying law at the University of Panama, Blades found that his studies were too rigorous to allow him to pursue music professionally. Only after a 1968 military coup that triggered a confrontation between student protesters and the army and consequently closed the university for a year did Blades return to music. In 1969, Blades left Panama for New York City and released his first album, *De Panamá a Nueva York: Pete Rodríguez presenta a Rubén Blades* (1970). When the university reopened, he returned to finish his law degree and became the first person in his family to graduate from college. Blades worked as an attorney at the Banco Nacional de Panamá for two years before moving to New York to pursue his music career in 1974.

Rubén Blades. (AP Photo)

LIFE'S WORK

In New York, Blades initially found an entry-level job working in the mailroom at Fania Records, a major Latin-music recording company, and visited salsa nightclubs after work. Blades's big break came when he replaced Tito Allen as a backup singer in Ray Barretto's band; he debuted with the band at Madison Square Garden in 1974. In 1975, Blades was hired as a vocalist on Willie Colón's *El bueno, el malo, y el feo* (*The Good, the Bad, and the Ugly*), and just a year later, he was hired to write songs and sing with Colón and his band. The partnership lasted five years and produced the bestselling album *Siembra* (1978), which sold more than three million copies. Other collaborative albums include *Metiendo mano* (1977), *Maestra vida* (1980), *Canciones del solar de los aburridos* (1981), and *The Last Fight* (1982). The latter was released in conjunction with the film *The Last Fight*, which starred Blades and Colón.

In 1982, Blades formed his own six-man band, Seis del Solar (Six from the Tenements), and infused elements of jazz, rock, soul, reggae, doo-wop, Cuban, and other musical styles into the salsa that had made him famous. Social and political commentary were everpresent in his lyrics. Inspired by the Argentinian singer Piero, whose music tackled social issues in his homeland, Blades sought to create music relevant to people's lives. Some of Blades's popular albums from the period include *Buscando America* (1984), which contained songs lamenting the murder of Oscar Romero of El Salvador and the "disappeared ones," victims of military dictatorships in Chile and Argentina; Grammy Award-winning albums *Escenas* (1985), *Antecedente* (1988) , and *La rosa de las vientos* (1996), and *Tiempos* (1999), which contained many songs related to the conquest of Central America and hope for its future.

Blades briefly put his music career on hold while he pursued a graduate degree. After participating in the 1984 Montreux Jazz Festival in France and touring Latin America with Seis del Solar, Blades enrolled in Harvard Law School to obtain a master's degree in international law. He finished his degree in 1985 and returned to music, playing Carnegie Hall that same year. In 1990, Blades released the album *Calminando*, and his collaboration with Colón titled *Tras la tormenta* (*After the Storm*) was released in 1995.

In 1994, Blades's interests shifted to politics. He ran for president of Panama, campaigning for the independent, nationalist, pan-Caribbean party Papa Egoró (Mother Earth in the Embará language) and finished third out of seven candidates. In 2004, he was appointed to a five-year term as Panama's minister of tourism. After this foray into public service, Blades resumed touring, and in August, 2009, he dedicated the album *Cantares del subdesarrollo* to Puerto Rico and Cuba. Soon after that album's release, he toured U.S. and Latin American cities to mark the twenty-fifth anniversary of *Buscando America*.

Blades also has engaged in a successful film career. He acted in and helped write the script and music for *Crossover Dreams* (1985) and can be seen in films such as *Critical Condition* (1987), *The Milagro Beanfield War* (1988), *Predator II* (1990), *Color of Night* (1994), *The Devil's Own* (1997), *Cradle Will Rock* (1999), *All the Pretty Horses* (2000), and *Once Upon a Time in Mexico* (2003). Television appearances include *Dead Man Out* (1990), *The Josephine Baker Story* (1991), *One Man's War* (1991), *Crazy from the Heart* (1991), *Miracle on Interstate 880* (1993) and *Gideon's Crossing* (2000-2001). In addition, Blades starred in Paul Simon's Broadway musical *The Capeman* (1998).

Blades's Latin American Jazz

Latin influences in jazz have been evident since the early twentieth century. Examples include Jelly Roll Morton's habanera-based compositions, tango and rumba influences in the 1920's and 1930's, 1950's big band mambo, jazz-bossa nova in the 1960's, and Latin-jazz-funk in the 1970's and 1980's. Although these influences resulted in widely different sounds, they all fall under the heading "Latin jazz." Latin jazz is a term used to describe jazz that includes Latin American rhythms and percussion such as conga, timbale, guiro, or claves. Most Latin American musicians have produced music that might be considered Latin jazz, and Rubén Blades is no exception.

With his band Seis del Solar, Blades created a smooth sound, incorporating elements of rock and roll and jazz, in order to focus on his lyrics. Whereas a traditional salsa band includes one or two lead singers, two to five brass players, a piano, bass, congas, timbales, bongos, and other Latin percussion instruments, Seis del Solar replaced the horns with synthesizers and added vibraphones and a trap set. The band has performed at jazz festivals such as the Montreux Jazz Festival and the 2000 Playboy Jazz Festival, but their music is best described as a fusion of different styles—not only jazz but also rock, soul, reggae, and Latin American sounds and rhythms.

SIGNIFICANCE

Blades is one of the most influential Latin American musicians of the late twentieth century and beyond. His music has brought political and social commentary to the salsa scene. His blend of jazz, reggae, rock and roll, salsa, and other musical styles also made him a trendsetter. With multiple Grammy Awards and two Emmy nominations for his roles in *The Josephine Baker Story* and *Crazy from the Heart*, Blades has been rewarded for his musical originality and dedication to the arts.

Sandra J. Fallon-Ludwig

FURTHER READING

Blades, Rubén. "Rubén Blades." In *Noise of the World: Non-Western musicians in Their Own Words*, edited by Hank Bordowitz. Brooklyn, N.Y.: Soft Skull Press, 2004. In this short essay, Blades explains the different pronunciations of his name, discusses his exposure to different types of music in Panama and the need for similar exposure in other countries, and talks about Seis del Solar and the meanings behind many of his songs.

Cruz, Barbara C. *Rubén Blades: Salsa Singer and Social Activist*. Springfield, N.J.: Enslow, 1997. A biography of Blades with chapters dedicated to his early life, music and film career, and his political interests. The book also includes a useful chronology and a selected list of films, television appearances, and sound recordings.

Rodríguez, Ana Patricia. "Encrucijadas: Rubén Blades at the Transnational Crossroads." In *Latino/a Popular Culture*, edited by Michelle Habell-Pallán and Mary Romero. New York: New York University Press, 2002. A scholarly look at Blades's songs and the meaning in his lyrics, particularly "La rosa de los vientos." The article includes some history of emigration from Central America and situates his music within a Central American narrative.

Wald, Elijah. "New York: Rubén Blades." In *Global Minstrels: Voices of the World*. New York: Routledge, 2007. Provides information on Blades's music, lyrics, and the way he views himself as an artist.

See also: Ray Barretto; Willie Colón; Paquito D'Rivera; José Feliciano; Julio Iglesias; Tito Puente; Poncho Sánchez; Carlos Santana.

Jorge Bolet

Cuban-born concert pianist

One of the great exponents of the grand romantic style, Bolet was a brilliant but thoughtful virtuoso whose mainstays were the works of Franz Liszt, Frédéric Chopin, Sergei Rachmaninoff, and Leopold Godowsky. He taught throughout his life at the Curtis Institute of Music and Indiana University and was the first to conduct W. S. Gilbert and Arthur Sullivan's The Mikado: Or, The Town of Titipu (1885) in Japan.

Latino heritage: Cuban

Born: November 15, 1914; Havana, Cuba

Died: October 16, 1990; San Mateo, California

Also known as: Jorge Leopoldo Bolet Tremoleda

Areas of achievement: Music; education

Early Life

Jorge Leopoldo Bolet Tremoleda (boh-LEHT), was born in Havana, Cuba, to Antonio Bolet and Adelina Tremoleda. Bolet's family was upper-class (his father was a lieutenant in the Cuban army) and neither parent had any musical background. Despite this, three out of six of their children seriously pursued music: the second oldest, Alberto, was a professional conductor and violinist who spent much of his life devoted to the promotion of Spanish and Latin American music, and Maria, eleven years Bolet's senior, studied piano with a graduate of the Conservatoire de Paris. Maria was Bolet's first teacher when he was seven years old.

With funding help from an important Cuban musical society, the Pro Arte Musical, Bolet was sent to study at the newly formed Curtis Institute of Music in Philadelphia in 1927. While there, he studied with famous pianists Leopold Godowsky and Josef Hofmann (then director of the Curtis Institute) but his main teacher was David Saperton (Godowsky's son-in-law), who was a strict disciplinarian and instructed Bolet in a European nineteenth century repertoire. Upon graduating in 1935, Bolet's program included the work of Johannes Brahms, Frédéric Chopin, and a Godowsky paraphrase. Bolet also took lessons in Europe with Abram Chasins, and upon returning to the United States, he studied conducting at the Curtis Institute with Fritz Reiner.

Life's Work

In 1937, Bolet won the Naumburg International Piano Competition and his debut recital, later that year in New York, included transcriptions by Godowsky and Liszt as well as works by Chopin, Franz Schubert, and Sergei Rachmaninoff, who actually attended the concert along with Horowitz and other music luminaries. Despite rave reviews from *The New York Times*, however, Bolet's career was slow to evolve. In 1939, he became Rudolf Serkin's teaching assistant at Curtis, a post he held until 1942, when he began serving in the U.S. Army.

After the fall of Cuban president Fulgencio Batista, Bolet joined the U.S. Army as a military attaché, and in 1945, he became an American citizen. The following year, while travelling with the Army, Bolet premiered W. S. Gilbert and Arthur Sullivan's *The Mikado: Or, The Town of Titipu* (1885) in Japan as conductor. During the 1950's and 1960's, Bolet began recording with a number of minor labels, including Boston and Remington. In 1960, he recorded the sound track to a film about Liszt titled *Song Without End.*

Bolet continued to perform in Europe, the United States, and Latin America, but his concert schedule was relatively sparse. After the Fidel Castro-led Cuban Revolution in 1959, Bolet never returned to his home country (his brother Alberto escaped to the United Kingdom and his sister Maria was already living in Spain). From 1968 to 1977, he served on the piano faculty at Indiana University.

In the 1970's, Bolet began receiving greater recognition, beginning with a series of concerts in New York that culminated with a performance of Liszt's *Totentanz* (1849) with the New York Philharmonic. In 1974, he performed a legendary concert at Carnegie Hall that received rave reviews and was recorded and released by RCA. This led to a similarly successful recital in London two years later and an exclusive contract with Decca. In 1977, Bolet was appointed head of piano studies at the Curtis Institute. He remained at Curtis until 1986.

The 1980's were very busy for Bolet, who played ninety to ninety-five concerts a year, featuring many of the world's major orchestras. In 1983, he recorded a four-part series for BBC television (*Bolet Meets Rachmaninoff*) of a master class of several students performing Rachmaninoff's Third Concerto, followed by a recording of Bolet playing the work himself. By 1988, Bolet's health began to decline, and in 1989, he underwent a brain operation. He died of heart failure in his home in San Mateo, California, in 1990.

Significance

Bolet did not achieve international success until he was in his sixties, when there was a revival of the interest of the romantic style of playing. His legacy lies primarily with the works of Liszt, Chopin, and often remarkably difficult nineteenth-century transcriptions, especially Godowsky. Bolet's repertoire, however, was surprisingly wide and included works by Joseph Marx and Giovanni Sgambati. Interpretively, he treated the piano as a human voice rather than as a percussion instrument, and consequently his sound was never harsh but often glittering, intimate, and nuanced in its detail. He chose to use a Baldwin piano over the more popular Steinway, because he felt that the Baldwin's "soft" pedal gave a more even tone change.

Sonya Mason

Further Reading

Bolet, Jorge. "Jorge Bolet." Interview by Elyse Mach. In *Great Contemporary Pianists Speak for Themselves*, edited by Elsye Mach. Vol. 2. New York: Dover, 1988. A frank discussion with the artist (this is the largest published interview) about the ups and downs of his career and his opinions of other pianists.

_______. "Jorge Bolet." Interview by Linda J. Noyle. In *Pianists on Playing: Interviews with Twelve Concert Pianists*, edited by Linda J. Noyle. Metuchen, N.J.: Scarecrow Press, 1987. An interesting interview on the process of learning the piano.

Hill, Brad. "Jorge Bolet." In *Classical*. New York: Facts On File, 2006. Entry in a reference book offering useful details on Bolet's repertoire and recordings.

See also: Claudio Arrau; Justino Díaz; Eduardo Mata; Jesús María Sanromá.

Bobby Bonilla

American baseball player

An athlete from the Puerto Rican community of the South Bronx, Bonilla played professional baseball for almost twenty years, and in his prime was among the most highly compensated players.

Latino heritage: Puerto Rican

Born: February 23, 1963; Bronx, New York

Also known as: Roberto Martin Antonio Bonilla; Bobby Bo

Area of achievement: Baseball

Early Life

Roberto Martin Antonio Bonilla (roh-BEHR-toh mahr-TEEN ahn-TOH-nee-oh boh-NEE-ah) was born in Bronx, New York, in 1963 to Roberto Bonilla, Sr., and Regina Bonilla. Although his parents separated when he was eight, Bonilla remained close to his father and relied on his father to financially support his participation in sports. By his late teen years, Bonilla was more than six feet tall, a powerful switch-hitter, and eager to put his South Bronx neighborhood far behind him.

When his first effort to leave New York City—a hoped-for scholarship to Arizona State University—was unsuccessful, Bonilla's father and friends scraped together one thousand dollars to send him on a tour of Europe as part of a high school all-star baseball team. One of Bonilla's teammates was a relative of Syd Thrift, a longtime scout for Major League Baseball's Pittsburgh Pirates. Recognizing talent when he saw it, Thrift quickly signed the young man to a minor league contract in mid-1981. While playing minor league baseball in the Pirates organization, Bonilla also played winter ball in Puerto Rico. Over the course of five years in the mid-1980's, he played for teams in San Juan and Mayagüez, Puerto Rico, helping the latter team win several championships.

Life's Work

For most of his almost twenty years in professional baseball, Bonilla developed a reputation as an effective batter. His overall batting average was about .280, with almost 290 home runs and almost 1,200 runs batted in (RBI). During his prime years, from 1988 to 1993, Bonilla averaged more than 25 home runs and 93 RBI per season. In 1991, his final year with the Pirates, Bonilla was clearly one of the best young players in the league.

In early December, 1991, after negotiating with several teams, Bonilla signed a five-year contract with the New York Mets for $29 million, at the time the most lucrative contract in Major League Baseball. For Bonilla, the years in New York were a mixed blessing.

Bobby Bonilla. (AP Photo)

His father attended many of his games, and he had the vocal support of the city's large Puerto Rican community. However, the amount of his compensation inevitably generated unrealistic expectations from fans and bad press from the sports media. Because he was the highest-paid player, he was a natural target for criticism. In fact, he was booed so consistently that at one point he tried wearing earplugs at the plate to improve his concentration. Bonilla's performance as a Met was inconsistent. Frustrated, Bonilla reacted poorly, snarling at reporters and generally conveying the impression of a petulant, overpaid prima donna.

After three and a half unsuccessful seasons with the Mets, Bonilla spent two seasons with the Baltimore Orioles. In 1996, he signed a free-agent contract with the Florida Marlins. At this time, the Marlins were signing as many high-ticket veteran players as possible, both to compete for a pennant and to attract fans to the ballpark. At the time, baseball writers remarked that the team's owner was trying to buy success; if so, these plans came to fruition with a World Series championship in 1997. It was Bonilla's only World Series.

As a small-market team with a bloated payroll, the Marlins could not afford to keep their championship team together, and in 1998, most of the high-priced veterans were traded away or released. After a brief stint with the Los Angeles Dodgers, Bonilla was re-signed by the Mets.

If his previous tenure with the Mets was disappointing, Bonilla's 1999 season was disastrous. In the sixty games he played, Bonilla's batting average was only .160, with just 4 home runs. Clearly unhappy and with eroding physical skills, Bonilla traded words with the team's manager in both the clubhouse and the press. After the season, Bonilla was allowed to pursue opportunities with other teams. The Mets, in fact, were so eager to let him go that his agents convinced the team to make an unusual financial arrangement: The final year of his contract, worth about $5.9 million, was deferred until 2011, when the Mets would pay Bonilla approximately $1.2 million each year for the next twenty-five years.

Significance

Although the end to his career was unfortunate, in his prime Bonilla was among the best players in baseball. Although he lacked the home run hitting power of some of his contemporaries, Bonilla accumulated enough home runs to place himself in the top five among switch-hitters, behind such figures as Mickey Mantle and Eddie Murray. Besides his accomplishments on the field, Bonilla was able to take advantage of the rapid increase in the number of contracts for baseball players during the 1990's. Unlike many athletes, Bonilla was able to parlay his athletic ability into long-term financial stability with a savvy contract buyout.

Michael R. Meyers

Further Reading

Finoli, David, and Bill Ranier. *The Pittsburgh Pirates Encyclopedia*. Champion, Ill.: Sports Publishing, 2003. Includes an article providing a short overview of Bonilla's career, both during and after his time with the Pirates.

Friedman, Ian C. *Latino Athletes*. New York: Facts On File, 2007. Includes an article providing an overview of Bonilla's life and career.

Gregory, Sean. "The Top-Salary Curse." *Time*, March 1, 2004, 20. A brief article arguing that free agents who have been signed to lucrative contracts rarely bring a team success.

Shouler, Kenneth. "Swinging for the Fences." *Cigar Aficionado*, August 1, 1998. A fan-friendly overview of Bonilla's life and career.

Sielski, Mike. "There's No Accounting for This." *The Wall Street Journal*, July 1, 2010, p. A27. Describes the antecedents and terms of Bonilla's deferred contract with the Mets.

Van Hyning, Thomas. *Puerto Rico's Winter League*. Jefferson, N.C.: McFarland, 1995. Provides a short account of Bonilla's time in Puerto Rican baseball.

See also: Roberto Alomar; Sandy Alomar, Jr.; José Canseco; Tony Fernandez; Julio Franco; Andrés Galarraga; Rafael Palmeiro; Sammy Sosa; Fernando Valenzuela.

JUAN BOZA

Cuban-born artist

Boza's Afro-Cuban heritage and Santería faith provided the backdrop of his art, including prints, drawings, altars, paintings, and photographs of his installations. He infused his strong religious beliefs into his works, which are pre-Columbian depictions of images related to his faith.

Latino heritage: Cuban

Born: May 6, 1941; Camagüey, Cuba

Died: March 5, 1991; Brooklyn, New York

Also known as: Juan Boza Sánchez

Areas of achievement: Art; gay and lesbian issues

EARLY LIFE

Juan Boza Sánchez (BOH-zah) was born on May 6, 1941, in Camagüey, Cuba. By the age of ten, he had decided he wanted to be an artist. He also was a participant in Yoruba/Lucumí religious ceremonies.

After winning a local art competition in his hometown with his Santería-inspired painting *La Lucumiguera* in 1959, Boza received a scholarship to attend the prestigious La Escuela Nacional de Bellas Artes (National School of Fine Arts), also known as San Alejandro, where he studied art from 1960 to 1962. Afterward, he received a scholarship to study at the newly established Escuela Nacional de Arte. He studied there for two years before being expelled in the wake of a student riot. After his dismissal from the school in 1964, Boza became a professional artist and studied lithography. That same year, he was invited to join La Unión de Escritores y Artistas (Artists' and Writers' Union).

Boza had his first solo exhibition at the Havana Gallery in 1967, a watershed year in his career. That year, he also began work as a designer at the Coliseo Nacional de Cultura and won the Casa de las Américas Award, a major Cuban cultural prize. In 1971, he was censored and forbidden by the government to work as a professional artist. Before being exiled nine years later, he was sent to a reeducation camp because he was homosexual.

LIFE'S WORK

Boza left Cuba via the Mariel boatlift in 1980 and settled in New York City, where he felt he had to reinvent himself. It was there that he also reconnected with his Afro-Cuban roots and strengthened his Yoruba/Lucumí religious beliefs, which inspired most of his artworks. He recommitted to his faith, an Afro-Cuban Santería religious system in which he was also a priest.

As a young man, Boza was influenced by the works of Roberto Matta and Wilfredo Lam, a prominent Afro-Cuban artist. As his career progressed, however, he offered his distinctive interpretations of traditional iconography in both two- and three-dimensional works.

Although Boza was a talented artist and produced innumerable drawings and paintings, he was best known for his altar installations, many of which were offerings to or representations of Yoruba/Lucumí deities. He used an extensive assortment of organic and manmade materials for the altars, or *tronos*. Some of the materials included sequined fabric, cellophane, garbage bags, metal, and handicrafts such as bowls and utensils. Boza exhibited his artwork in galleries and museums in New York, Chicago, Miami, Berlin, Barcelona, Mexico City, Milan, Krakow, and San Juan among others. In addition to being hailed as a trailblazer, he received numerous awards for his artwork. He received a Cintas Foundation Fellowship and the Jerome Foundation Fellowship to the Robert Blackburn Printmaking Workshop. His work also was featured in the 1985 documentary *Cuba-USA: Three Cuban Artists and New York City*.

In 1991, Boza died from an illness related to acquired immunodeficiency syndrome (AIDS) at the height of his professional career. He did not have a will at the time of his death, and as a result, the city of New York claimed temporary ownership of his artwork and other personal belongings. They were held in storage for years while their legal ownership was debated. In addition, Boza was denied a traditional Santería funeral because his friends did not have access to his personal altar in his apartment.

SIGNIFICANCE

Boza was a versatile artist who produced paintings, drawings, designs, and installations using a wide variety of manmade and natural materials. He is considered one of the most prominent altar makers, one whose works have influenced countless Afro-Cuban artists. By focusing on themes related to his Yoruba/Lucumí religious beliefs, he defined art in primitive and non-European standards while breaking ground in Afro-Cuban religious iconography.

Alyson F. Lerma

FURTHER READING

Conner, Randy P., and David Hatfield Sparks. *Queering Creole Spiritual Traditions: Lesbian, Gay, Bisexual, and Transgender Participation in African-Inspired Traditions in the Americas*. New York: Harrington Park Press, 2004. Discusses artistic interpretations of the African diaspora religions, which are tolerant of homosexuality and gender deviation. Information on Boza, his artistic representations related to Santería, and their relationship to his homosexuality is essential.

Morris, Randall. "Juan Boza: Travails of an Artist-Priest." In *Santería Aesthetics in Contemporary Latin American Art*, edited by Arturo Lindsay. Washington, D.C.: Smithsonian Institution Press, 1996. Chapter focusing on details of Boza's life and work. One of the most informative works on the artist.

Rice, Robin. "The Art of Religion: Reading Between the Lines in the Work of a Cuban Artist." *The Philadelphia City Paper*, June 17, 1999. Reviews several of Boza's works on display at the Painted Bride Art Center and discusses their religious basis and significance.

Viera, Ricardo. "Juan Boza: Reinventing Himself." In *Santería Aesthetics in Contemporary Latin American Art*, edited by Arturo Lindsay. Washington, D.C.: Smithsonian Institution Press, 1996. Viera discusses Boza's exile to New York and artistic success there.

See also: Olga Albizu; Tony Labat; Ana Mendieta.

GIANNINA BRASCHI

Puerto Rican-born poet, novelist, and essayist

Known for her literary works, which examine Hispanic experiences in the United States, Braschi is especially renowned for her novel Yo-Yo Boing! *The publication of this celebrated half-English, half-Spanish book generated a new genre of novels called "Spanglish."*

Latino heritage: Puerto Rican

Born: February 5, 1953; San Juan, Puerto Rico

Areas of achievement: Poetry; literature; sports

EARLY LIFE

Giannina Braschi (jee-ah-NEEN-ah BRAHS-chee) was born in San Juan, Puerto Rico, the daughter of Euripides "Pilo" and Edmee Firpi Braschi. The Braschis were a well-to-do family. Euripides was a champion tennis player, and his wife Edmee worked as a realtor. Giannina's grandparents were also accomplished and affluent. Her maternal grandfather, Miguel Firpi, imported many of the first automobiles onto the island, while her maternal grandmother, Juanita Firpi Miranda, taught English at the University of Puerto Rico.

Following in her father's footsteps, Braschi became a champion tennis player while still an adolescent. In 1966, at the age of thirteen, she became the youngest female tennis player to win in the women's division of the U.S. Tennis Association's national tournament. After her athletic accomplishments, Braschi focused on her collegiate education and pursued opportunities abroad. Moving between Rome, Madrid, London, and Paris throughout the early 1970's, Braschi studied comparative literature at universities throughout Europe.

Enrolling in the State University of New York at Stony Brook's graduate literature program in 1974, Braschi specialized in the Golden Age of Spanish literature. This era, known as El Siglo de Oro in Spanish, refers to a literary and artistic movement within and outside of Spain, which began with Christopher Columbus's arrival in the Americas and coincided with the political ascent and subsequent fall of the Spanish Habsburg dynasty. (Though the era has no official end date, many scholars believe that Pedro Calderón de la Barca, who died in 1681, is the last writer associated with the Golden Age.) Braschi, focusing on several of the notable authors and artists of this period, completed her doctoral degree in literature in 1980.

Life's Work

Braschi's early written works were scholastic essays and books in which she discussed Spanish Golden Age writers, such as Miguel de Cervantes and Garcilaso de la Vega. Indeed, her first book examined the life and work of the Romantic poet Gustavo Adolfo Bécquer. In addition to her writing, Braschi has taught at several universities throughout the northeastern United States, including Rutgers University, the City University of New York, and Colgate University. At Colgate, she was appointed the distinguished chair of creative writing in 1997.

Braschi began writing fiction and poetry in the early 1980's, and her works were heavily influenced by the Nuyorican culture. "Nuyorican" is a combination of the words "New York" and "Puerto Rican" and refers to the Puerto Rican diaspora in, and around, New York City, which has the world's second-largest Puerto Rican population, outside of the island. The literary movement inspired by the diaspora experience examines issues of imperialism, immigration, and intergenerational conflicts within families.

Braschi published her first collection of poetry, *Asalto al tiempo*, in 1980. As much performance art as poetry, Braschi wrote, recited, and published her work entirely in Spanish, which limited her audience to Nuyoricans and literary bilingualists. A second collection of poetry, *La comedia profana*, appeared in 1985, while *El imperio de los sueños* was published in 1988. These works were noted for their use of rhythm and humor and an anti-imperialist ethos.

In 1994, Braschi's collected works were translated and published by Yale University Press in *Empire of Dreams*. Translated into English by Tess O'Dwyer, *Empire of Dreams* served as the inaugural volume for the Yale Library of Literature in Translation, an endeavor by the university to enhance access to literature written in languages other than English. This translated volume of poetry introduced Braschi to a wider audience and sparked further interest in her work.

Braschi won a National Endowment for the arts fellowship in 1997. This award undoubtedly supported her while she worked on what would become her most prominent and well-known novel, *Yo-Yo Boing!* When this novel was published in1998, Braschi described it as a literary experiement. *Yo-Yo Boing!* is a nonlinear narrative that discards traditional concepts of literary chronology. The novel is written half in Spanish and half in English in order to capture the authenticity and emotional intensity of contemporary Nuyorican speakers. With diverse characters from different backgrounds, each speaker conveys his or her feelings and thoughts about experiences and events specific to the cultural clash between Anglo-American colonial culture and the many Latin American cultures.

Yo-Yo Boing! won critical acclaim and ushered in a new genre: the Spanglish novel. Noted primarily for a combination of English and Spanish language called "code-switching," the Spanglish novel often examines the cultural legacies of Hispanic cultures in

The Spanglish Novel

Giannina Braschi's novel *Yo-Yo Boing!* won critical acclaim upon publication in 1998 and ushered in a new genre: the Spanglish novel. "Spanglish" is an informal term that refers to a lingual phenomenon where a speaker combines two languages in a technique called "code-switching." It is important to note that there is no one form of Spanglish. Indeed, different Latin American cultures speak different Spanglish dialects. While Puerto Rican Americans in New York speak Nuyorican Spanglish, Cuban Americans speak Cubonics, or Cuban-influenced Spanglish. In another example, Junot Díaz's acclaimed novel *The Brief and Wondrous Life of Oscar Wao* (2007) makes use of Dominican Spanglish.

The following statement is one example of Nuyorican Spanglish, taken from *Yo-Yo Boing!*:

> *Spanglish:* ¿Por qué yo? Tú tienes las keys. Yo te las entregué. Además, I left mine adentro.
>
> *English:* Why me? You've got the keys. I gave them to you. Besides, I left mine inside.

The lingual differences of the Spanglish novel are immediately apparent. However, the thematic content and the socioethnic identities of the fictional narrators can vary greatly. Often the Spanglish novel examines the cultural legacies of Hispanic cultures in contrast to, and in relationship with, Anglo-American colonial imperialism. Whatever the literary content, the Spanglish novel provides a public venue in which to examine the experiences of historically underrepresented and marginalized populations in the United States.

contrast to, and in relationship with, Anglo-American colonial imperialism. In 1999, Braschi won the PEN American Center's Open Book Award for *Yo-Yo Boing!*, and in 2000, she received the New York Foundation for the Arts Fellowship in Fiction. After a stint as writer-in-residence at the Baltic Center for Writers and Translators, Braschi was selected as a judge of Latin American literature for the PEN American Center, the U.S. branch of a worldwide literary and human rights organization.

Significance

Giannina Braschi's poetry and novels have shed light on the narratives within Nuyorican culture, and her other literary works have examined Hispanic experiences in the United States, particularly in New York City. Braschi is especially renowned for her novel *Yo-Yo Boing!*, which created the Spanglish literary genre. Her work is well-recognized, and she has received numerous honors, including the Danforth scholarship and fellowships from the Ford Foundation and the New York Foundation for the Arts; she was also named one of *El Diario La Prensa*'s Outstanding Women of 1998.

Rebecca M. Marrall

Further Reading

Barnstone, Willis. *Literatures of Latin America: From Antiquity to the Present.* Upper Saddle River, N.J.: Prentice Hall, 2003. Provides an overview of Latin American literature and the significance of individual writers.

Carrion, Maria M. "Geographies, Mother Tongues, and the Role of Translation in Giannina Braschi's *El imperio de los sueños*." *Studies in Twentieth Century literature* 20, no. 1 (1996): 167-191. Examines Braschi's use of language and geography in her third collection of poetry.

Fuentes, Yvonne, and Margaret Parker. *Leading Ladies: Mujeres en la Literatura Hispana y en las Artes*. Baton Rouge: Louisiana State University Press, 2006. Explores female-centric contributions to Hispanic literature and their sociocultural impact.

Goldstein, David S., and Audrey B. Thacker. *Complicating Constructions: Race, Ethnicity, and Hybridity in American Texts*. Seattle: University of Washington Press, 2007. Collection of essays examining the construction of ethnic identity and associated experiences within literature about the United States.

See also: Miguel Algarín; Victor Hernández Cruz; Junot Díaz; Esmeralda Santiago.

Benjamin Bratt

American actor and activist

Bratt is best known for his role on the television series Law and Order, *in which he played Detective Rey Curtis from 1995 to 1999. Bratt also has appeared in* E-Ring *and* The Cleaner *and several films, including* La Mission *(2010), a film written and produced by his brother Peter.*

Latino heritage: Peruvian

Born: December 16, 1963; San Francisco, California

Also known as: Benjamin G. Bratt

Areas of achievement: Radio and television; acting; activism

Early Life

Benjamin G. Bratt was born on December 16, 1963, in San Francisco, California. His parents divorced when he was young, and he was raised by his mother, a member of a Peruvian Indian tribe. She was active in American Indian causes and took young Bratt along when she joined the occupation of Alcatraz by Native Americans, which ran from November, 1969, to June, 1971. She instilled in him her passion for such activism.

Bratt was raised in San Francisco and attended Lowell High School, whose alumni include Bill Bixby (star of *The Incredible Hulk* television series) and Supreme Court Justice Stephen Breyer. Bratt participated in the Lowell Forensic Society there and then attended the University of California at Santa Barbara (UCSB). He earned a bachelor's degree in fine arts at UCSB and took graduate courses at the American Conservatory Theatre in San Francisco; however, opportunities in the film industry came before he had a chance to finish his master's degree.

Life's Work

Bratt won his first film roles in the early 1990's, in *One Good Cop* (1990) and *Bright Angel* (1991). He went on to play significant supporting roles in several films and television shows in the mid-1990's, including the

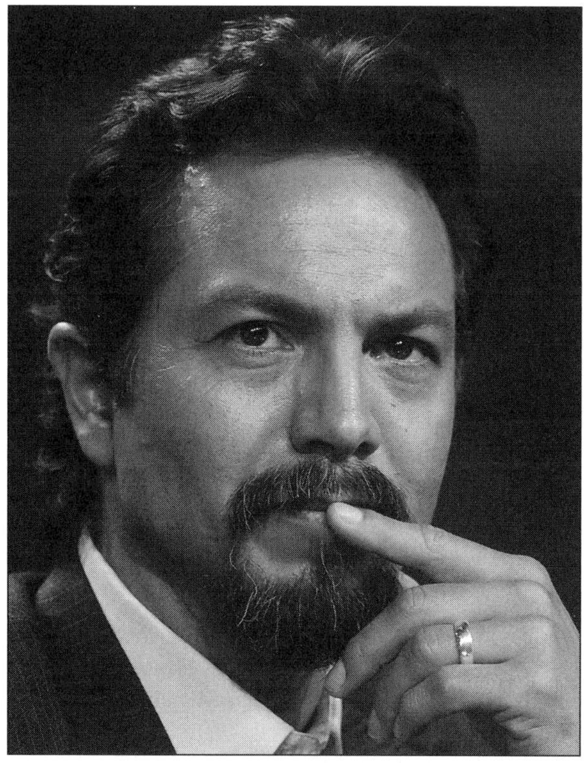

Benjamin Bratt. (AP Photo)

military thriller *Clear and Present Danger* (1994), based on the novel by Tom Clancy.

Bratt achieved major mainstream success in 1995 when he joined the cast of the established television drama *Law and Order* as police detective Rey Curtis. The long-running show had a large and faithful audience eager to debate the merits of new characters and actors. Bratt, as one of the male leads, was noted for his handsome looks and for playing a straight-laced and pious character. The series was in its heyday at the time and consistently performed well in the ratings. Bratt also received an Emmy Award nomination in 1999, his last season on the show before he left to focus on his film career.

In 2000, Bratt had a busy year with five films, including *Miss Congeniality*, in which he played the male lead opposite Sandra Bullock. He also appeared in the ensemble drug drama *Traffic*. After that run, Bratt turned his attention to smaller, less mainstream projects, including *Piñero* (2001), which chronicled the life of Miguel Piñero. That film resulted in Bratt being nominated for an ALMA (American Latino Media Arts) Award.

In 2001, Bratt and actor Julia Roberts ended their three-year relationship. Soon afterward, he met Talisa Soto on the set of *Piñero* and they married in 2002. They have two children, a boy and a girl.

In the years that followed, Bratt has mixed success in Hollywood. He costarred with Halle Berry in the widely panned *Catwoman* (2004), but did better in the television series *E-Ring* and *The Cleaner*; for his role in the latter, he was nominated for a 2009 ALMA Award. He also appeared in the 2010 film *La mission*, which was directed by his brother Peter.

Bratt also is active in Native American causes. He narrated episodes of PBS's *American Experience* documentary series that dealt with Native American history and appeared in *The People Speak*, a series based on the work of historian Howard Zinn.

Significance

Bratt is a successful actor in television and film who has used his fame to advance understanding of Native Americans and their history. He is an example of an actor of Latino and American Indian descent who has found popularity and acclaim in mainstream entertainment.

Scott A. Merriman

Further Reading

Bratt, Benjamin. "Benjamin Bratt." Interview by Brendan Lemon. *Interview* 30 (May, 2000): 122-125. In this interview, given soon after Bratt left *Law and Order*, the actor discusses his heritage, facing discrimination, and his film projects.

Duralde, Alonso. "Unspoiled Bratt." *The Advocate* (March 5, 2002): 40-46. Discusses Bratt's portrayal of a bisexual writer in *Piñero* as well as his acting in *The Next Best Thing* (2000) and on *Law and Order*.

Green, Susan, and Kevin Courrier. *Law and Order: The Unofficial Companion—Updated and Expanded.* Rev. ed. Los Angeles: Renaissance Books, 1999. Provides a summary of the first nine seasons of *Law and Order*, including those in which Bratt starred.

Peretz, Evgenia. "The Bratt Pact." *Vanity Fair* 504 (August, 2002):112-119. Covers Bratt's activities after leaving *Law and Order*, his relationship with Julia Roberts, and his interactions with the media.

Spada, James. *Julia: Her Life*. New York: St. Martin's Press, 2004. This biography of Roberts includes a treatment of Bratt, who dated her for three years.

See also: Jessica Alba; Luis Alfaro; Hector Elizondo; Andy Garcia; Eva Longoria; Esai Morales; Charlie Sheen; Jimmy Smits; Cameron Diaz.

MONICA BROWN

American writer

A college professor, children's author, and outspoken advocate for social justice, Brown has been a strong voice in contemporary U.S. Latino children's literature. Her works have made the accomplishments of famous Latin Americans, such as Celia Cruz and Gabriel García Márquez, accessible to young audiences.

Latino heritage: Peruvian

Born: October 24, 1969; Mountain View, California

Also known as: Monica Alexandria Brown

Areas of achievement: Literature; education; social issues

EARLY LIFE

Monica Alexandria Brown (MOH-nee-kah ahl-ehks-AHN-dree-ah brown) was born in Mountain View, California, to Peruvian American artist Isabel Maria Vexler Valdivieso Brown and Daniel Doronda Brown, who was of Hungarian Jewish and Scot-Italian heritage. Brown, her sister Carolyn, and her brother Daniel spent their childhoods growing up in upper-middle-class neighborhoods where most Latinos were the hired help. Throughout her public education, Brown never encountered positive representations of Latinos or the works of great Latin American writers. However, she understood the transformative power of books and often used literature as a way to escape her surroundings.

When she began her undergraduate degree in English at the University of California at Santa Barbara, Brown had the opportunity to learn about the great works of Chicano and other Latino authors. During this time she became very involved in political theater and various social justice groups. Brown's interests in social equality and Latin American literature were further fueled by salvation theology and egalitarian efforts in Central America. In her senior year, she was greatly influenced by her first Chicano literature professor, Carl Guitérrez-Jones, who encouraged her to pursue a graduate degree in literature.

After graduating in 1991 with a B.A. in English, Brown spent a year in Guadalajara, Mexico, as a journalist writing for the American-owned newspaper the *Guadalajara Colony Reporter*. Almost immediately, she realized that journalism was not for her, and she soon enrolled in Boston College, where she studied Latino and multiethnic literature before graduating in 1994 with a M.A. in English. Brown then moved to Columbus, Ohio, to begin a doctoral program with a focus in Latino literature at Ohio State University. While at the university, she received numerous awards for her writing, including the Helen Earhart Harley Creative Writing Fellowship Award in 1995 and the Common Difference Award from the university's Center for Women's Studies for her work about the contributions of women of color.

Brown received her doctorate in 1998, the same year that her first daughter, Isabella, was born. In 1999, Brown and her family moved to Flagstaff, Arizona, where she began her academic career as a professor in Northern Arizona University's Department of English. Her second daughter, Juliana, was born a few years later. While teaching at the university Brown published numerous articles about the marginalization of Latino youth in the American education system and society. In 2002, she published an academic book, *Gang Nation: Delinquent Citizens in Puerto Rican, Chicano, and Chicana Narratives*, which examines how society's understanding of Latino gang members is shaped by representations in literature and popular youth culture.

LIFE'S WORK

Although she has received critical acclaim for her academic writing, Brown is best known for her bilingual Spanish/English children's biographies that celebrate the lives of important Latinos throughout the Americas. Her first book, *My Name is Celia: The Life of Celia Cruz* (*Me llamo Celia: La vida de Celia Cruz*), was a picture-book biography about salsa singer Celia Cruz, illustrated by Latino artist Rafael López and published in 2004 by Luna Rising, an imprint of Northland Publishing. This book was a huge success and received the prestigious Américas Award for Children's and Young Adult Literature, which honored both López and Brown as distinguished contributors in the area of Latino children's literature.

In 2005, Brown published *My Name is Gabriela: The Life of Gabriela Mistral* (*Me llamo Gabriela: La vida de Gabriela Mistral*), another picture-book biography that describes the life of Chilean poet Gabriela Mistral. Illustrated by Latino artist John Parra, this book also garnered literary praise in the field of children's literature and received the 2006 International Latino Book Award.

Brown continued writing children's books and released her first work of fiction in 2007, *Butterflies on Carmen Street* (*Mariposas en la calle Carmen*), published by Piñata Books, an imprint of Arte Público Press. In this picture book, Brown depicts a young, self-confident Latina child who fits comfortably into modern society. Unlike many depictions of Latinos in children's literature published in previous decades, the main character is not dealing with a problem related to her family's immigration status or cultural heritage.

In 2007, Brown also published her third picture-book biography, *My Name Is Gabito: The Life of Gabriel García Márquez* (*Mi llamo Gabito: La vida de Gabriel García Márquez*), which firmly established her as the only Latina author writing bilingual children's biographies about famous Latin Americans. This biography also received literary acclaim and was followed in the next four years by several other picture-book biographies featuring notable figures, such as Pelé (Edson Arantes do Nascimento), the King of Soccer; union leaders César Chávez and Dolores Huerta; Chilean poet Pablo Neruda; Colombian teacher and librarian Luis Soriano; and musician Tito Puente.

Significance

Inspired by her mother's artistic passion for her Latino cultural heritage, Brown has dedicated her career to creating positive representations of Latinos in children's literature, thereby providing role models for contemporary Latino children and diffusing preconceived stereotypes held by non-Latino children and educators. Her biographies are some of the only pieces of literature for young children that celebrate the accomplishments of Latin Americans and encourage contemporary youth to explore the achievements that Latinos throughout the Americas have made to society. While encouraging future generations of aspiring Latino writers, Brown's body of work exemplifies the best in contemporary Latin children's literature.

Jamie Campbell Naidoo

Further Reading

Brown, Monica. Monica Brown: Children's Book Author. http://www.monicabrown.net. Brown's official Web site includes biographical information, as well as suggestions on how teachers can use her books and other resources in their lessons.

_______. "From a Writer's Perspective: Recreating Images of Community in Multicultural Children's Books." *Language Arts* 85, no. 4 (March, 2008): 316-321. An informative article describing Brown's childhood, the influences of Latino culture on her writing, and the inspiration behind her scholarly book and several of her children's picture books.

_______. *Gang Nation: Delinquent Citizens in Puerto Rican, Chicano, and Chicana Narratives.* Minneapolis: University of Minnesota Press, 2002. Examines the influence of gang literature and narratives on the lives of young Latino gang members and provides an underlying foundation for understanding the power struggles in some of Brown's children's books.

See also: Alma Flor Ada; César Chávez; Celia Cruz; Dolores Huerta; Nicholasa Mohr.

Juan Bruce-Novoa

Costa Rican-born scholar, educator, and writer

Bruce-Novoa was a pioneering Chicano scholar and prolific writer who argued for an eclectic approach to Chicano studies that some labeled neoformalist. His numerous essays and books sought to introduce, explicate, or recover the work of Chicano authors, painters, photographers, and filmmakers and to expand the international canon.

Latino heritage: Mexican

Born: June 20, 1944; San José, Costa Rica

Died: June 11, 2010; Newport Beach, California

Also known as: Juan David Bruce-Novoa; John David Bruce-Novoa

Areas of achievement: Scholarship; education; literature

Early Life

Juan David Bruce-Novoa (brews-noh-VOH-ah) was born in San José, Costa Rica, where his father, James H. Bruce, worked as an accountant for Otis McAllister coffee importers. His mother, Dolores "Lola" Novoa; older sisters, Patsy and Lillian; older brother, Jim; and his father returned to the United States in 1945, after James was drafted into the United States Army near the end of World War II. Three years later, the family reunited when they moved from San Antonio, Texas, to Denver, Colorado.

Bruce-Novoa attended Holy Family High School, where he was especially influenced by Sister Agnes Regina, who asked him to substitute teach history and Spanish while he was still a student. While attending Regis College in Denver, he was particularly influenced by a Jesuit priest, Father Edward L. Maginnis, who encouraged an interdisciplinary approach to study. Bruce-Novoa majored in European history and minored in psychology, graduating cum laude in 1966. He earned his master's degree in twentieth-century Spanish literature in 1968 and his Ph.D. in Latin American literature in 1974 at the University of Colorado at Boulder.

Growing up, Bruce-Novoa was athletic and musical: a high school All-American as a football player, catcher on his high school baseball team, and bass player in a band called the Star Tones (later called Dr. Who and the Daleks). An avid reader from an early age, he was unhindered by dyslexia, which was discovered when he was in the fifth grade. Mexico also factored heavily in his youth, as he visited his uncle, a director of the Bank of Mexico, in Mexico City during the summers. Later, he would take intensive Spanish classes there so that he could become fluent in Spanish and qualify for the master's program at the University of Colorado. All his life, Bruce-Novoa was a renowned fabulist, telling audiences that he could read a book while riding his bicycle or while playing bass at live concerts, that he was descended from Robert the Bruce of Scotland, and that he could count Rasputin (whom he called "Uncle Raspy") as a member of his family tree.

LIFE'S WORK

Bruce-Novoa's professional career was notable for its energy, breadth, and impact on literary, cultural, interdisciplinary, and Chicano studies. He especially is known for his articulation of what he called a "topological space" of Chicano and other Latino literatures—the term, borrowed from mathematics, refers to the study of texts' and events' relationships to one another and how these relationships form and affect meaning. In his book *RetroSpace: Collected Essays on Chicano Literature* (1990), he wrote that art "functions as a spiritual, moral force in the world, far beyond its prosaic, informational function."

Bruce-Novoa served as an instructor of Spanish and Mexican American studies at the University of Colorado at Boulder from 1967 to 1974. His first position after earning his doctorate was at Yale University as associate professor of Spanish and Portuguese and Latin American studies; he broke ground as a pioneer in Chicano studies. During this time, he wrote his seminal essay, "The Space of Chicano Literature," which was published in 1975.

Bruce-Novoa was a Fulbright Scholar in Germany at the University Mainz, then was named a full professor in the Foreign Languages Department at Trinity University in 1985. After two more Fulbright appointments (both at the University of Erlangen-Nürnberg) and visiting professorships in English at Harvard University and in Berlin and Dusseldorf, Germany, he finished his career at the University of California at Irvine as a full professor in the Department of Spanish and Portuguese, critical theory, film studies, screenwriting, and Chicano-Latino studies.

Bruce-Novoa was prolific in his scholarly and creative output. He published six books, including *Inocencia perversa/Perverse Innocence* (1977), a collection of largely autobiographical poetry; *Chicano Authors: Inquiry by Interview* (1980), the first book-length study of Chicano criticism, which includes extensive interviews with fourteen important Chicano writers; *Chicano Poetry: A Response to Chaos* (1982), the first book-length critical study of Chicano poetry; an experimental novel, *Only the Good Times* (1995); and *Manuscrito de origen* (1995), a collection of short stories. He also edited three anthologies and wrote more than one hundred articles and interviews.

Bruce-Novoa won numerous awards during his lifetime, including the National Chicano Council for Higher Education Fellowship (1977); Rockefeller Foundation Grant (1979-1980); José Fuentes Mares National Prize for Literature (Mexico, 1989); and the Critica Nueva Award for distinguished writing in literary theory (University of New Mexico, 1997). He married Mary Ann Giroux in 1969, and they had a son, Juan Carlos. Bruce-Novoa died on June 11, 2010, in Newport Beach, California.

SIGNIFICANCE

In addition to his influence on academia, particularly in the field of Chicano studies, Bruce-Novoa founded the Conference on Mexican Literature and Art at the University of California at Irvine; Biennial European Conference on Latinos of North America; the literary magazine, *Cambios phideo*; and the Chicano library, poster art collection, and Chicano theater group at Yale. He also contributed to and consulted on many scholarly journals. He helped introduce Chicano authors and artists such as Cecile Pineda, Kathy Vargas, John Rechy,

Sheila Ortiz Taylor, and Tino Villanueva to larger audiences. Ultimately, he defined and reshaped cultural studies, and, in contrast to dialectical-historical and poststructural approaches to literary theory, constantly challenged the reader to let the "text itself, and not the critic's interpretation, remain the central point of the reading encounter."

Moumin M. Quazi

Further Reading

Bruce-Novoa, Juan. Juan Bruce-Novoa Papers. Nettie Lee Benson Latin American Collection, University of Texas Libraries, the University of Texas at Austin. An eight-box collection of original manuscripts, including an unpublished scathing poem aimed at Yale University and a published short story called "Autobiowishfulography," in which the protagonist introduces a live grenade to a group of lackadaisical students at the end of their final exam.

_______. *RetroSpace: Collected Essays on Chicano Literature*. Houston, Tex.: Arte Público Press, 1990. Important work in which Bruce-Novoa explains his approach to art and literature.

Lawhn, Juanita Luna. "Juan Bruce-Novoa." In *Chicano Writers: First Series*. Vol. 82 in *Dictionary of Literary Biography*, edited by Francisco A. Lomelí and Carl R. Shirley. Detroit, Mich.: Gale, 1989. Written by one of Bruce-Novoa's colleagues, this brief biography details his career and gives special attention to the reception of his most important works.

Wood, Jamie Martinez. *Latino Writers and Journalists*. New York: Facts On File, 2007. An anthology of entries about important Latino writers, with a detailed entry on Bruce-Novoa.

See also: Edna Acosta-Belén; Rodolfo F. Acuña; María Herrera-Sobek; Margarita Bradford Melville; Mary Helen Ponce.

Tedy Bruschi

American football player

Bruschi played thirteen seasons for the New England Patriots, becoming a face of the franchise for his all-out playing style, unassuming demeanor, emotional intensity, and knack for making the big play. While he was beloved by the fans for his play, the stroke he suffered, and from which he recovered, is a more endearing memory of a revered athlete and man.

Latino heritage: Mexican
Born: June 9, 1973; San Francisco, California
Also known as: Tedy Lacap Bruschi; Brew
Area of achievement: Football

Early Life

Tedy Lacap Bruschi (BREW-skee) was born in San Francisco, California, on June 9, 1973 to Juanita and Anthony Bruschi, Sr. His parents divorced when he was three, and Tedy and his brothers moved to Roseville, California, with their mother, who remarried two years later. Tedy saw his father on weekends. His family had little money, and Tedy grew up interested in music, specifically alto saxophone. He started playing football during his freshman year at Roseville High School, playing on the defensive line, even though some considered him too short for this position. Bruschi was a two-year team captain, lettering twice and earning all-conference, all-Northern California, and all-metro honors. He also lettered in wrestling and track and field while maintaining good grades. The *Sacramento Bee* ranked Bruschi number one in their list of the top area high school football players ever.

Life's Work

Bruschi earned an athletic scholarship to the University of Arizona, and although he was undersized and little known, he emerged as the leader of the "Desert Swarm" defense. He tied the National College Athletic Association (NCAA) Division I-A record with fifty-two career quarterback sacks, was a two-time consensus All-American, won the Morris Trophy as the best conference defensive lineman, and received team Most Valuable Player awards. He also earned his bachelor's degree in communications and met his future wife Heidi while at the university.

The New England Patriots selected Bruschi in the third round of the 1996 National Football League (NFL) draft with the eighty-sixth overall pick. The Patriots assigned the undersized defensive end the more natural position of linebacker. Bruschi played every game during his rookie season, helping the Patriots reach the

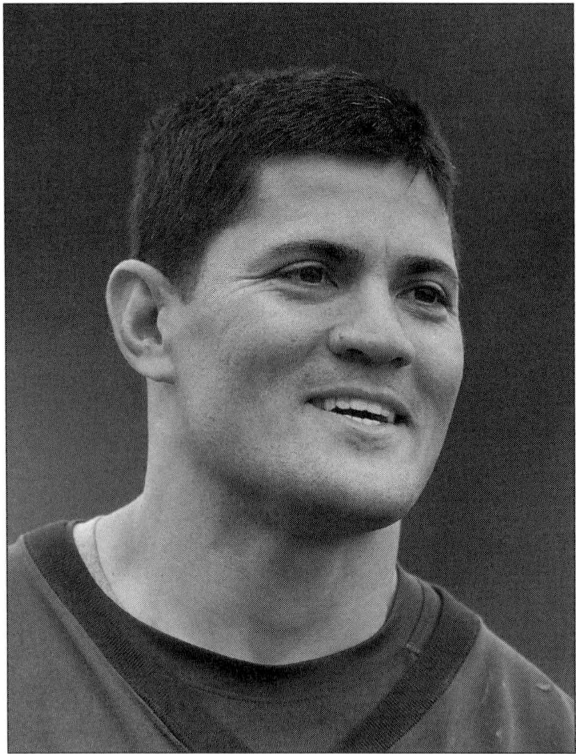

Tedy Bruschi. (AP Photo)

Super Bowl. He improved every year and developed a knack for making key plays at the most critical times, including intercepting four passes and returning them for touchdowns and forcing two fumbles that were returned for touchdowns.

Bruschi and his Patriot teammates helped change professional football, as the team began to value intelligence, heart, and versatility over mere athleticism. The Patriots' priorities enabled the team to win the Super Bowl in 2002, 2004, and 2005.

When the Patriots played in Super Bowl XXXIX on February 6, 2005, Bruschi's wife, Heidi, had just given birth to their third son, and Tedy was selected to play in his first NFL Pro Bowl, the league's all-star game. Just ten days later, Bruschi, now thirty-one, awoke in pain with blurry vision, but he dismissed these problems because he was a tough football player who constantly dealt with injuries. However, a computerized axial tomography (CAT) scan later revealed that Bruschi had suffered a stroke when a blood clot passed through a small hole in the upper chamber of his heart and lodged in his brain. The entire country took notice, and Bruschi's health received media coverage far beyond the sports world.

After the stroke, Bruschi established Tedy's Team, a foundation and platform to increase awareness of and education about strokes, and he became a spokesman for the American Heart Association. His book detailing his recovery and return to football, *Never Give Up: My Stroke, My Recovery, and My Return to the NFL*, serves as an inspiration to stroke survivors, and he has worked tirelessly to raise stroke awareness.

During the summer of 2005, Bruschi announced he would sit out the season, but he kept training. He had the hole in his heart repaired and worked to win the support of doctors, the Patriots, and his wife Heidi in order to return to the game. He was medically cleared to resume playing on October 16, and he rejoined the Patriots two weeks later in a game against the Buffalo Bills. At the end of the season he was named the 2005 Comeback Player of the Year.

Bruschi played three additional seasons but was slowed, not from the stroke but from age and the wear and tear of the game. After a preseason game in 2009, Bruschi realized it was time to retire. Legendary Patriots coach Bill Belichick, a man of few compliments, called Brushi the "perfect player." In his retirement Bruschi contributed to numerous charities, remained connected to the Patriots, and worked as an on-air NFL analyst for ESPN.

SIGNIFICANCE

Tedy Bruschi spent his entire thirteen-year professional career with the New England Patriots, winning three Super Bowls and playing on five of the six Patriots' teams to reach the Super Bowl. While his achievements as a football player were cheered by millions, his recovery from a stroke and subsequent return to the game, as well as his tireless dedication to stroke research, funding, and awareness, are the more remarkable achievements.

Bruschi came from a poor, broken home; he was an undersized athlete and remained an overlooked and unassuming player during his time in the NFL. However, he had intelligence, determination, and heart, which helped him excel as a football player and battle back from his debilitating stroke. While a good number of stroke victims can regain functional independence or even achieve a full recovery, only No. 54 of the New England Patriots returned to play for nearly four more seasons as a professional football player.

Jonathan E. Dinneen

FURTHER READING

Bruschi, Tedy. *Never Give Up: My Stroke, My Recovery, and My Return to the NFL.* Hoboken: John Wiley

& Sons, 2007. A terrific memoir detailing Bruschi's personal life, football career, stroke, and journey back to the football field.

Friedman, Ian C. *Latino Athletes*. New York: Facts On File, 2007. Includes an article providing an overview of Bruschi's life and career.

Holley, Michael. *Patriot Reign*. New York: HarperCollins, 2004. An all-access pass was given to this Boston sports columnist who chronicled the New England Patriots, covering team ownership, management, player acquisition, and results on the field.

MacMullan, Jackie. "Bruschi Has Battled on, off Field." *Boston Globe*, January 15, 2005, p. C1. Details Bruschi's struggles while growing up and how he later tried to balance his playing intensity with being a "normal guy" off the field.

See also: Jeff Garcia; Tony Gonzalez; Tony Romo.

Fernando Bujones

American ballet dancer

Bujones's precise, classical execution of ballet performances in the Romantic tradition brought distinction to the American Ballet Theater, burnishing its reputation in the United States and around the world. He was the first male ballet star primarily trained in the United States and led the way for a generation of Latino dancers in the country.

Latino heritage: Cuban

Born: March 9, 1955; Miami, Florida

Died: November 10, 2005; Miami, Florida

Area of achievement: Dance

Early Life

Although he was born in Miami, Florida, Fernando Bujones (boo-HOH-nehs) spent his early childhood in Cuba. Because he was sickly as a child, doctors recommended physical exercise. His mother, a dancer, tutored him in ballet, supported by the noted Cuban choreographer Alicia Alonso and a cousin who was a ballet professional. His family returned to live in Miami, where Bujones made his stage debut at ten years of age in a production of *The Nutcracker*.

On a visit to Florida, the New York City ballet star Jacques d'Amboise, saw the twelve-year-old Bujones dance and recommended that he enter the School of American Ballet in New York. Bujones financed his studies with scholarships and grants, training with leading dancers such as Stanley Williams and André Eglevsky. He debuted in Carnegie Hall at age fifteen.

Life's Work

The noted choreographer and dancer George Balanchine invited Bujones to dance with the New York City Ballet. While that company had the widest repertoire in the country, Bujones opted instead to join the American Ballet Theater (ABT). The ABT allowed him to pursue a wider classical repertoire, dancing romantic lead roles in works such as *La Sylphide*, *Giselle*, and *La Bayadère*. Among the most competitive and prestigious events in ballet is the International Ballet Competition in Varna, Bulgaria. In 1974, Bujones not only won the contest's gold medal, the first such win by an American, but also

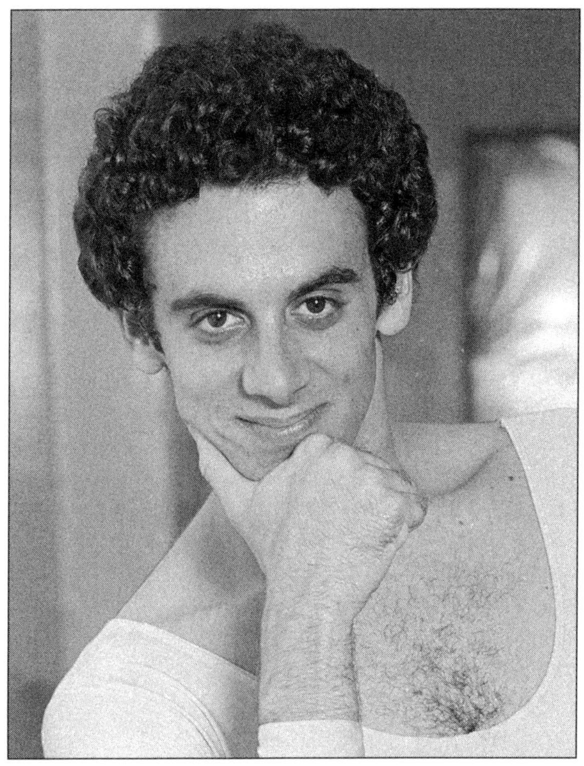

Fernando Bujones. (AP Photo)

received a citation from the head of Moscow's Bolshoi Ballet commending his extraordinary technical achievement. Slight of build, Bujones possessed a suppleness of movement based on precise physical control. He appeared as himself in the 1978 Golden Globe Award-winning ballet drama *The Turning Point*.

In the same year as Bujones's triumph in Varma, Mikhail Baryshnikov, the Russian ballet star, fled the Soviet Union and settled in New York. Bujones considered the Russian to have an inferior technique to his own and lamented the exaggerated publicity the defector received. However, in 1980, Baryshnikov became artistic director of the American ballet Theater; Bujones left the company five years later and began a series of freelance engagements. During the 1980's, Bujones performed roles in Twyla Tharp's *Bach Partita* and Maurice Béjart's *Trois études pour Alexandre*. In 1989, new management at the American Ballet Theater requested he return as a guest artist. Bujones gave his farewell performance with the company in 1995. A number of Latino dancers followed Bujones into the American Ballet Theater, including Carlos Acosta, Julio Bocca, Herman Cornejo, Angel Corella, and Xiomara Reyes, supplanting an earlier vogue of Russian dancers.

Bujones married Márcia Kubitschek (1943-2000), the daughter of the former president of Brazil, Juscelino Kubitschek, in 1980. They had one child, Alejandra; Márcia had two daughters from a previous marriage. The couple divorced in 1988. Bujones's second marriage was to the Peruvian-born dancer Maria Arnillas. He met her at the Boston Ballet, where he was a leading guest artist from 1987 to 1993 after a short stint with the Joffrey Ballet. Throughout his career, Bujones danced with more than sixty companies in more than thirty countries. Among his leading ballerina partners were Margot Fonteyn, Cynthia Gregory, Gelsey Kirkland, and Natalia Makarova.

The great challenge in the life of a ballet dancer is to make the transition from performer to director. In 1998, Bujones received the A Life for the Dance Award from the International Ballet Festival of Miami; two years later, he became head of the Orlando Ballet (then known as the Southern Ballet Theatre). The appointment followed brief, frustrating periods with companies in Tampa, Florida, and Jackson, Mississippi. Bujones significantly improved the technical quality, training, and range of offerings of the Orlando Ballet. While still heading the company, he died of lung cancer and melanoma in 2005.

Significance

Bujones excelled as a dancer because of his precisely executed body movement, limpid buoyancy, and dramatic sensitivity. His bravura performances burnished the reputation of the American Ballet Theater and enhanced the roles of the numerous star ballerinas with whom he was partnered. Although his life was relatively short, Bujones established the reputation and precedent of Latino distinction in male ballet. His discipline and commanding technique allowed him to perform brilliantly in a multitude of venues around the world.

Edward A. Riedinger

Further Reading

Barnes, Clive. "Attitudes." *Dance Magazine* (April, 2006). In this obituary, the noted dance and theater critic Barnes cites Bujones as among the first major Latino dancers to contribute to the development of American ballet.

Bujones, Fernando, and Zeida Cecilia-Mendez. *Fernando Bujones: An Autobiography with Memories by Family and Friends*. Doral, Fla.: Higher Education and Technology Consultants, 2009. A posthumously published "autobiography" of Bujones by his cousin and longtime collaborator that emphasizes his life as a trajectory to success and superstardom. Supported amply with photographs.

Eichenbaum, Rose, and Aron Hirt-Manheimer. "Fernando Bujones" in *The Dancer Within: Intimate Conversations with Great Dancers*. Middletown, Conn.: Wesleyan University Press, 2008. Interview given in 2004 in which Bujones, then head of the Orlando Ballet, traces the main points in the development of his personal and professional life.

Torres, Neri, et al. "Latins: A Moving Force." *Dance Magazine*, June, 2005. Delineates the role of Latino performers in the development of modern American dance and ballet.

See also: Evelyn Cisneros; Royes Fernández; José Arcadio Limón.

José Antonio Burciaga

American artist, writer, and activist

A Chicano activist, Burciaga is known for his art, poetry, and prose. He made important contributions to affirming Chicano cultural identity by producing murals, poetry, and essays that document the Chicano experience, and he did so with humor and irony.

Latino heritage: Mexican

Born: August 23, 1940; El Paso, Texas

Died: October 7, 1996; Carmel Highlands, California

Also known as: Tony Burciaga

Areas of achievement: Activism; art; literature

Early Life

José Antonio Burciaga (BOOR-see-AH-gah) was born in El Paso, Texas, to José Cruz Burciaga and Maria Guadalupe Burciaga. Both his parents hailed from Mexico. His mother was a deeply religious woman who taught elementary school in Mexico before she was married. Shortly after Burciaga's birth, his father worked as the janitor and Shabbos goy (a worker who performs tasks that Jews may not on the Sabbath) in a Jewish synagogue. His family lived in the basement of the synagogue for most of his childhood, creating a unique cultural experience for the Roman Catholic Mexican family.

Burciaga attended Catholic schools in El Paso and frequently visited family and friends in Juarez, Mexico. After graduating from Cathedral High School, Burciaga joined the U.S. Air Force in 1960. The first time he lived outside El Paso was when he was stationed in Iceland and Spain. After completing active duty, Burciaga returned to his hometown. With the financial assistance of the G.I. Bill, he enrolled at the University of Texas at El Paso and obtained a Bachelor's degree in fine arts. Burciaga also studied at the San Francisco Art Institute in California.

In 1968, Burciaga returned to Texas to work as a civil service illustrator in Mineral Wells, eight hours from El Paso. He encountered severe racial discrimination there, making it difficult to secure housing. After searching for several days, an elderly woman rented Burciaga a small apartment. Unable to find other work, Burciaga left shortly thereafter, moving to Washington, D.C., for employment as an illustrator with the National Photographic Interpretation Center, a unit under the Central Intelligence Agency.

Burciaga's time in Washington, D.C., was a turning point in his life. In the early 1970's, he began creating artwork that was critical of U.S. domestic and foreign policy. This marked the beginning of a lifelong pursuit of activism. He also met Cecilia Preciado during this period and, in 1972, they married. In 1974, Cecilia was hired as an administrator at Stanford University, and the couple moved to California. While there, they had two children, Rebeca and José Antonio, Jr.

Life's Work

Burciaga's working-class, multicultural upbringing and experiences with racism informed his artistic production. While in California, he wrote for local newspapers and the national Hispanic Link news service. Burciaga's journalism addressed assimilation and the attacks on bilingualism occurring in California during the 1980's. He defended the importance of preserving Chicano culture against the pro-assimilation ideology of that time.

From 1985 to 1994, Burciaga and Cecilia were resident fellows at Stanford's Casa Zapata, a Chicano-themed dormitory. It was there that he produced one of his best-known murals, *The Last Supper of Chicano Heroes* (1989). He incorporated community views by surveying students and activists to determine which Chicano heroes to include. The result was a mural depicting César Chávez, Dolores Huerta, Martin Luther King, Jr., and Che Guevara, among many others. The spirit of the mural was communal and inclusive. This was only one of several murals Burciaga painted at Casa Zapata and around the San Francisco Bay Area.

Aside from journalism and murals, Burciaga also was known for his creative writing. His first book, *Restless Serpents* (1976), was self published and followed by several other collections of essays and poetry. These collections included *Weedee Peepo: A Collection of Essays* (1988), *Undocumented Love: A Personal Anthology of Poetry* (1992), *Drink Cultura: Chicanismo* (1993), *Spilling the Beans: Loteria Chicano* (1995), and *In Few Words/En pocas palabras* (1996). Burciaga created the cover art for some of these anthologies, most notably for *Drink Cultura*, the cover of which parodied the Coca-Cola logo. Burciaga's writings intermixed Spanish and English and drew from his experiences, focusing on topics such as food, language, and religion.

Burciaga also was a performing artist. He was a founding member of Culture Clash, a Chicano comedy troupe that performed political skits and monologues. Burciaga's performances highlighted his comedic talent, which was evident in writing but had a different flavor in live contexts. The traveling and lifestyle negatively impacted his family life, however, and he left the group after several years.

Burciaga received many awards. In 1986, he received the Journalism Award from the World Affairs Council. He also received the American Book Award in 1992 for *Undocumented Love*. He was also given the National Hispanic Heritage Award for literature in 1995 and posthumously declared a Texas Treasure in 1997. Burciaga died on October 7, 1996, after a two-year battle with stomach cancer.

Significance

An artist, poet, journalist, writer, and comedian, Burciaga was a versatile and highly skilled activist. He referred to himself as a "multi-undisciplinary" artist. His talents, tireless work, and public recognition in multiple arenas illustrate that he was a true "Renaissance man." Further, his life and work were dedicated to bettering his community. Burciaga was able to communicate complex messages about culture and identity in highly accessible ways. These messages conveyed "inside jokes" and cultural affirmation for Latinos and taught lessons using language, religion, and food, aspects of daily living common to people of all cultural backgrounds. Teaching through art, Burciaga was able to speak to the culturally specific and universal dimensions of human existence simultaneously.

Mrinal Sinha and Aída Hurtado

Further Reading

Burciaga, José. *Drink Cultura: Chicanismo*. Santa Barbara, Calif.: Joshua Odell Editions, 1993. Collection of essays describing Burciaga's views on culture. Probably his most widely read work.

_______. *The Last Supper of Chicano Heroes: Selected Works of José Antonio Burciaga*. Edited by Mimi R. Gladstein and Daniel Chacón. Tucson: University of Arizona Press, 2008. Collection of Burciaga's essays and poetry published posthumously. This anthology includes previously unpublished materials.

Wood, Jamie Martinez. "José Antonio Burciaga." In *Latino Writers and Journalists*. New York: Facts On File, 2007. Biography and career overview focusing on Burciaga's literary output and journalism.

See also: Miguel Algarín; Alurista; Judith F. Baca; Barbara Carrasco; Gaspar Enríquez; Tony Labat; Gary Soto; Leo Tanguma; Jesse Treviño.

Julia de Burgos

Puerto Rican poet

One of the most important figures in Caribbean literature, Burgos overcame poverty and discrimination as a Puerto Rican woman of African descent to win critical acclaim as a poet and writer. Burgos's work often explores such issues as anti-imperialism, feminism, African heritage, and social justice.

Latino heritage: Puerto Rican

Born: February 17, 1914; Carolina, Puerto Rico

Died: July 6, 1953; Harlem, New York

Also known as: Julia Constanza Burgos García

Areas of achievement: Poetry; literature

Early Life

Julia Constanza Burgos García (HOO-lee-uh) was born in Carolina, Puerto Rico, on February 17, 1914, to Francisco Burgos Hans and Paula García de Burgos. The eldest of thirteen children, six of whom died of malnutrition, Burgos confronted poverty throughout her life.

Burgos started school at the age of five in Carolina. Neighbors contributed money so that Burgos could pursue her education. In high school, which she completed in three years at the Escuela Superior de la Universidad de Puerto Rico, Burgos's favorite subjects were math and science, but she already was receiving recognition for her literary talent.

Burgos attended the University of Puerto Rico in Río Piedras, graduating in 1933 with a general diploma in education. She worked as a teacher in rural Cedro Arriba, Naranjito, where she enjoyed the natural beauty of the countryside that would appear in much of her poetry. In 1934, Burgos married the Puerto Rican journalist Rubén Rodríguez Beauchamp. The couple divorced in 1937.

Life's Work

In the 1930's, Burgos participated in nationalist demonstrations and also gave public speeches defending Puerto Rican culture. The poems Burgos wrote during this time also reflect her engagement with Puerto Rican nationalism. *Poemas exactas a mí misma* (*Poems Exactly Like Me*), Burgos's first collection of poetry, was completed in 1937 but was never formally published. Her 1938 collection, *Poemas en viente surcos* (*Poems in Five Furrows*), reflects Burgos's concern with the issues of nationalism, feminism, and racial discrimination. The 1939 *Canción de la verdad sencilla* (*Song of the Simple Truth: The Complete Poems*, 1997) evokes the themes of eroticism and love from a female perspective and won first prize for poetry from the Institute of Puerto Rican Literature. Published posthumously in 1954, the collection *El mar y tú: Otros poemas* (*The Sea and You: Other Poems*) contains Burgos's later poems, which are characterized by a preoccupation with such themes as interpersonal relationships, love, and death.

In 1940, Burgos moved to New York City and became actively involved in the Puerto Rican community there. Later that year, Burgos went to Cuba, where she enrolled in the Universidad de La Habana and came into contact with other politically engaged Latin American writers, including Pablo Neruda. In Cuba, Burgos joined the Dominican Dr. Juan Isidro Jiménez Grullón, whom she hoped to marry; rejected by his family because of her African heritage, she returned to New York in 1942.

Burgos became a reporter for the New York weekly publication *Pueblos Hispanos*. In 1943, she married Armando Marín and moved with him to Washington, D.C. She returned to New York in 1945 and, for the next several years, was hospitalized for a variety of illnesses, including alcoholism. On July 6, 1953, Burgos was found unconscious on a street in East Harlem. She died as an unknown in Harlem Hospital and was buried in Potter's Field in New York. Burgos was identified a month after her death, at which time her family arranged for the return of her body to her birthplace in Carolina, Puerto Rico.

Significance

Literary criticism has emphasized the literary and political value of Burgos's poetry, recognizing its engagement with issues of sexism and racism as well as workers' rights and Puerto Rican nationalism. Burgos is seen as a precursor to such Puerto Rican women writers as Rosario Ferré and, by the 1970's, had become an important Puerto Rican cultural icon: musical versions of her poetry have been produced since the 1970's; in 1984, the San Juan Ballet presented Ramón Molina's "A Julia de Burgos" (*To Julia de Burgos*). Her name graces parks, streets, schools, and many other public spaces in Puerto Rico.

Erin Redmond

Further Reading

Adams, Clementina R. *Common Threads: Themes in Afro-Hispanic Women's Literature*. Miami, Fla.: Ediciones Universal, 1998. This study contains an introduction that discusses the themes of nature and humanism in writings by Afro-Hispanic women and an essay about Burgos, including biographical information, literary analysis of her poetry, examples of her poetry, and a bibliography.

Burgos, Julia de. *Song of the Simple Truth: The Complete Poems*. Compiled and translated by Jack Agüeros. Willimantic, Conn.: Curbstone Press, 1997. This anthology of the poetry of Burgos contains English translations of a comprehensive selection of her poems and includes fifty poems published in newspapers and magazines but not included in collections published by the author.

Gelpí, Juan G. "The Nomadic Subject in the Poetry of Julia de Burgos." In *The Cultures of the Hispanic Caribbean*, edited by Conrad James and John Perivolaris. Gainesville: University Press of Florida, 2000. This analysis of the poetry of Burgos focuses on its multiple political preoccupations, including feminism and the valorization of African heritage and racial mixture.

Torres-Padilla, José L., and Carmen Haydée Rivera. "Introduction: The Literature of the Puerto Rican Diaspora and Its Critical Practice." In *Writing Off the Hyphen: New Critical Perspectives on the Literature of the Puerto Rican Diaspora*, edited by José L. Torres-Padilla and Carmen Haydée Rivera. Seattle: University of Washington Press, 2008. This chapter provides historical background on Puerto Rican migration to the United States and the development of literature of the Puerto Rican diaspora.

See also: Victor Hernández Cruz; Rosario Ferré; Judith Ortiz Cofer; Lola Rodríguez de Tió.

CRUZ BUSTAMANTE

American politician

In the 1990's and 2000's, Bustamante was one of the highest-profile Latino politicians in California. After serving in the California State Assembly for five years, including two years as speaker, Bustamante was elected lieutenant governor of California in 1998. He became the first Hispanic American to hold statewide office in the state in more than one hundred years.

Latino heritage: Mexican

Born: January 4, 1953; Dinuba, California

Also known as: Cruz Miguel Bustamante

Area of achievement: Government and politics

EARLY LIFE

Cruz Miguel Bustamante (BOOS-tah-MAHN-tay) was born in the small town of Dinuba, California, in the San Joaquin Valley, the state's richest agricultural region, on January 4, 1953. The oldest of six children of second-generation Mexican Americans Cruz and Dominga Bustamante, he grew up in a close-knit extended family where Spanish was the main language spoken.

Cruz Bustamante. (AP Photo)

Bustamante's paternal grandparents emigrated from Chihuahua, Mexico, to New Mexico, and then to Dinuba, California, settling there because of the availability of agricultural jobs.

Bustamante's father began the family's interest in politics. A barber by trade who often worked three jobs to support his family, the elder Cruz was elected to the San Joaquin City Council, served as mayor pro tem, and sat on many community service and educational boards. Bustamante's mother also was heavily involved in community groups, helping to shape her son's values regarding public service. Bustamante graduated from Tranquility High School in San Joaquin before attending Fresno City College to pursue a degree in butchery. When not in school, he worked as an agricultural laborer, just as many members of his family had before him. These experiences strongly influenced his views and priorities during his political career.

Bustamante's course into politics was set in the summer of 1972, when he left school to serve as an intern in the office of Congressman B. F. Sisk, the chairman of the House Rules Committee. Through this internship, Bustamante discovered the power of government to help people. Afterward, he returned to California to pursue a degree in public administration at Fresno State College (later California State University, Fresno), intent on a career in politics. Bustamante became involved with the Chicano rights group MEChA (Movimiento Estudiantil Chicano de Aztlán), an association that provided him an opportunity to get involved with student government but that would haunt him later in his career.

LIFE'S WORK

In 1977, Bustamante married Arcelia De La Pena and started a family, once more postponing his education. He was offered a part-time position by California state assemblyman Rick Lehman but needed full-time employment to support his family, so he took a job as director of the Fresno Summer Youth Employment Program. In 1983, Lehman, by then a U.S. congressman, offered Bustamante a position as a district representative. In 1988, Bustamante took the same position in the office of California state assemblyman Bruce Broznan and won his seat in a special election in 1993 after Broznan decided to abandon his run for reelection.

During the first three years of his tenure in the California State Assembly, Bustamante became known as a moderate and reconciler. Bustamante did not take many controversial stands but was not shy about speaking out on issues he considered important, such as the agriculture industry, immigrant rights, education, public safety, and employment. Although he is a Democrat, Bustamante also has espoused positions that are less traditionally Democratic, such as support for the death penalty and backing agribusiness against environmental groups in some lawsuits. One issue that was especially important to him was opposition to California's Proposition 187 in 1994. The ballot initiative, which voters passed with a 60 percent majority, effectively cut off undocumented immigrants from the state's social services. It was later declared unconstitutional and never enacted. Although Bustamante had strongly opposed the proposition, he was easily reelected to his Assembly seat in that same election, and, shortly thereafter, began actively campaigning among his colleagues to become speaker of the Assembly when Democrats took control of the chamber in 1996.

Bustamante's election and speakership owed as much to non-Hispanics as it did to Hispanic voters, which may help to explain his centrism and moderation. However, this also disappointed some supporters, who expected Bustamante to take a more revolutionary approach. In 1998, Bustamante decided to run for lieutenant governor of California, alongside gubernatorial candidate Gray Davis. Both Democrats won their seats, although it quickly became clear that they did not get along well. Although both were reelected in 2002, their relationship grew even more strained the following year, when opponents launched an effort to recall Davis through a special election. Bustamante tried to balance support for his party's standard-bearer in the state and his own political ambition, urging voters to reject the recall but vote for Bustamante as Davis's replacement just in case the bid was successful.

Bustamante's Republican opponent in the recall election, film star Arnold Schwarzenegger, enjoyed several advantages, including wealth, name recognition, and charisma. Bustamante also weathered controversy over his college affiliation with MEChA, an organization whose radical roots unnerved conservatives. The recall succeeded, Schwarzenegger won the governorship handily, and Bustamante went back to work as lieutenant governor until the end of his term in 2006. After the end of his second and final term as lieutenant governor (term limits kept him from pursuing reelection again), Bustamante won the Democratic nomination for state insurance commissioner but was defeated by Republican Steve Poizner.

Hispanics and Statewide Offices in California

When Cruz Bustamante became lieutenant governor of California in 1998, he was the first Hispanic to hold statewide office in more than 120 years. Although the history of Hispanic politicians in the state is distinguished, very few have held statewide office. During the first decades after California became part of the United States, Romualdo Pacheco was state treasurer from 1863 until 1867, then lieutenant governor from 1871 until 1875, finally ascending to the top office when Governor Newton Booth was elected to the United States Senate. Pacheco served out the final nine months of Booth's term. Thereafter, few Hispanics even ran for statewide office, the highest-profile being Edward R. Roybal, who ran unsuccessfully for the Democratic nomination for lieutenant governor in 1954 before becoming the first Hispanic elected to Congress in more than eighty years in 1963. However, things began to change during the 2000's. Even while Bustamante served as lieutenant governor, Peter Camejo ran for governor on the Green Party ticket. Latinos also are increasingly better-represented at the city, county, and congressional district level, a reflection of the growing political clout of Hispanic voters in the state.

Significance

When he won California's lieutenant governorship, Bustamante became the first Hispanic to be elected to statewide office in the California since 1878. When he ran for governor, he sought to become California's first Hispanic governor since Romualdo Pacheco served briefly in 1875. Although he was unsuccessful in his bid to become California's chief executive, his achievements paved the way for many other Latinos to pursue state and federal office. He demonstrated that, although he was proud of his Hispanic roots, his politics could embrace a wider agenda that transcended racial issues.

Steven L. Danver

Further Reading

Bustamante, Cruz. "Humble Roots: Mastering the Art of Making the Impossible Possible." Interview by Lizelda Lopez. *Harvard Journal of Hispanic Policy* 15 (2002-2003), 11-17. This is a relatively extensive interview with Bustamante, conducted as he was beginning his gubernatorial campaign, in which he discusses his background, the obstacles encountered by

Hispanics in politics, and ways to increase Hispanic participation in American political life.

LaVelle, Phillip J. "Bustamante's MEChA Past Fuel for Conservative Critics." *The San Diego Union-Tribune*, August 30, 2003. Examines Bustamente's ties with MEChA in the 1970's, during his years at Fresno State College, including Bustamente's comments regarding the group.

Maass, Peter. "'Built moderate' and rising fast in California." *U.S. News and World Report*, March 17, 1997, 28. Profile of Bustamante written when he became speaker of the California Assembly.

Murphy, Dean E. "Chance has Looked Kindly on California's No. 2 Official." *The New York Times*, August 22, 2003. A detailed biographical piece produced in the run-up to California's 2003 gubernatorial recall election.

See also: Gloria Molina; Edward R. Roybal; Loretta Sánchez; Hilda L. Solis; Antonio Villaraigosa.

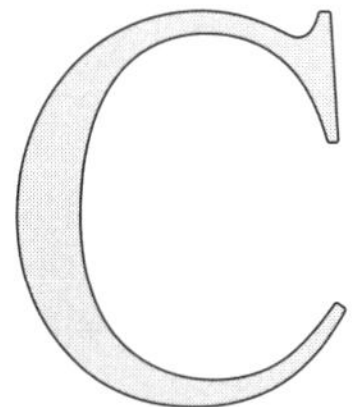

Lydia Cabrera

Cuban-born anthropologist and writer

Cabrera, a pioneering ethnologist, focused on the assimilation of African traditions into Cuban culture, producing many written works combining anthropology and literature, and she continued her studies after moving to the United States.

Latino heritage: Cuban

Born: May 20, 1899; Havana, Cuba

Died: September 19, 1991; Miami, Florida

Areas of achievement: Literature; anthropology; gay and lesbian issues

Early Life

Lydia Cabrera (LIHD-ee-yah cah-BREHR-ah) was the youngest of eight children. Her father was Raimundo Cabrera y Bosch, a wealthy intellectual, lawyer, writer, publisher, and advocate for Cuban independence. Her mother was socialite Elisa Bilbao Marcaida y Casanova. Cabrera briefly attended a private girl's school and spent six months at the Academy of San Alejandro, but she was primarily tutored at home because at this time young Cuban women were not allowed to receive public secondary education. As a girl Cabrera was raised under the care of servants and nannies of African heritage, the descendants of slaves, who entertained their young charge with folktales. Bright, well read, and insatiably curious, Cabrera as a teenager began writing an anonymous gossip column, "Young Women in Society," for her father's journal, *Cuba and America*.

Cabrera was initially interested in an artistic career. Her paintings were successfully exhibited in a 1922 show in Havana. Soon afterward, she opened a store that sold imported artworks, antiques, and handcrafted objects. She also cofounded the Association of Retrospective Arts, which instituted a festival, "Old Havana," to celebrate Cuba's diverse artistic traditions. In 1923, she became associated with the Society of Cuban Folklore, for which her brother-in-law, anthropologist Fernando Ortíz, served as president. That same year, her father died. Seeking financial independence, Cabrera saved the money earned from her various enterprises with the intention of moving abroad to continue her education.

In 1927, Cabrera traveled to France. She studied painting at L'Ecole du Louvre, earning a degree in 1930. During a decade when she lived primarily in the Montmartre section of Paris, Cabrera enthusiastically embraced a bohemian lifestyle. Enamored of American jazz, she associated freely with a multitude of intellectuals from a variety of social and artistic movements, including negritude, avant-garde, cubism, and surrealism, and her early interest in Afro-Cuban folklore, inspired by her childhood caregivers and Ortíz, was reawakened. She began a romantic relationship with German-born Venezuelan novelist Teresa de la Parra. The two women often traveled together throughout Europe and back and forth to Cuba as Cabrera began collecting information on the Afro-Cuban community. When Parra fell ill with tuberculosis, Cabrera entertained her sick friend by writing and reciting new versions of African stories she had heard as a young child. A collection of these stories was published as *Cuentos Negros de Cuba* (*Black Cuban Tales*) in Paris in 1936, the year Parra died in a Swiss sanitarium.

El Monte

El Monte was Lydia Cabrera's first important nonfictional study of African themes in Cuban culture, and is fully titled *El Monte: Igbo-Finda, Ewe Orish, Vititi Nfinda—Notes on Religions, Magic, Superstitions, and Folklore of the Creole Blacks and the Cuban People* (1954). The words "el monte" can be variously translated as "the mountain," "the wild," or "the woods." Regardless of the particular interpretation, the place is understood to be sacred, replete with supernatural elements. This profusely illustrated publication, the result of the author's recorded interviews with poor working blacks, established the trend for all of Cabrera's ethnographic studies to follow.

El Monte is an important study of the finer points of the Santería religion. Also known as Lucumí, Santería is a system of multideity worship that originated among the Yorubas of Africa and was blended into Catholicism in Cuba. Unlike other anthropologists, Cabrera was not merely an impartial observer in her examinations of the progeny of slaves but was a subjective participant. She used memories and her own fertile imagination to enhance or emphasize the poetry and rhythm of the rituals. She incorporated African words to underscore the exoticism of the religion and used fictionalized accounts to give storytellers clear, distinctive voices.

The first part of *El Monte* is a narration about the qualities of Yoruba gods, a recounting of legends, and a description of ceremonies, all of which reveal much about African character. The second part is a listing of plants used in native medicine. Both subjects would provide Cabrera considerable material to focus on in subsequent writings, which collectively illuminate the ideas, attitudes, and beliefs of the Africans who have made powerful contributions to Cuban society.

Life's Work

Cabrera returned to Cuba in the late 1930's to immerse herself in the study of her native country's African heritage. She found a new companion, María Teresa de Rojas, nicknamed "Titina," who would remain with Cabrera for the rest of her life. The two women resided in a refurbished mansion called La Quinta San José in Marianao, a hilly suburb of Havana alongside the working-class Barrio Pogolotti, where Cabrera undertook much of her research. She also explored the province of Matanzas, an hour away, where there was a strong concentration of Afro-Cubans. In venturing into the barrios, Cabrera broke local taboos of gender, class, and race; an upper-class white woman, she freely mingled with poor blacks of both sexes in tracing the African origins of language, religion, traditions, and rituals that permeated Cuban society.

As Cabrera gained the trust of her subjects through her interest, enthusiasm, and nonjudgmental acceptance of their culture, they opened up to her, providing a rich source of material she drew upon for half a century. Alternating between fiction and nonfiction, Cabrera regularly published books on various aspects of the Afro-Cuban community that might otherwise have vanished over time. In 1948, she released a second collection of folktales entitled *Why? Black Stories from Cuba*. After years of firsthand research, she released her best-known work, *El Monte*, a study of the secret Santería religion, in 1954. Other books soon followed, demonstrating the full range of Cabrera's scholarship. *Sayings from Old Blacks* (1955) was a collection of pithy and philosophical remarks. *Amagó, Lucumí Vocabulary: The Yoruba Spoken in Cuba* (1957) was a remarkable study of words transposed from Africa centuries before and still in use on the island. *The Abakuá Secret Society: Narrated by Old Followers* (1959) was, like her earlier *El Monte*, an intimate look at another African-based religion that had survived transplantation to Cuba.

In 1960, soon after Fidel Castro ousted Fulgencio Batista and intellectuals were no longer welcome in Cuba, Cabrera and Rojas were among the first to voluntarily become exiles from their homeland. The two women moved briefly to Spain before relocating permanently in Miami, Florida, where there was a large Cuban community. After a decadelong hiatus from writing, Cabrera again took up the Afro-Cuban cause. For the last thirty years of her life she released new works on an almost annual basis, capturing and preserving facets of traditions originating on the African continent that had survived and evolved in the New World. These publications included new short-story collections, *Ayapá: Turtle Stories* (1971) and *Stories for the Adult Child and the Mentally Retarded* (1983); religious studies, *Anaforuana: Ritual and Symbols of Initiation to the Abakuá Secret Society* (1975) and *The Kimbisa Cult of the Holy Christ of Good Travels* (1977); and a lexicon, *Congo Vocabulary: The Bantú Spoken in Cuba* (1984). Cabrera's last of more than twenty books, published the year after Rojas's death, was *The Animals in the*

Folklore and Magic of Cuba (1988). Cabrera died in 1991, at the age of ninety-two.

Significance

With little formal training in the discipline, Lydia Cabrera became a respected anthropologist and ethnologist, specializing in the Afro-Cuban community from the late 1920's until the end of her long life. She refused to be influenced by the writings of other social scientists, instead working directly with people who were the descendants of slaves to document long oral traditions that were on the point of disappearing. By preserving folktales, religious rituals, natural medicinal cures, superstitions, and native wisdom handed down over generations, she demonstrated how African themes had merged with the dominant Spanish presence for self-preservation. The combination of cultures produced a vibrant hybrid society that has contributed in a multitude of ways—in art, music, dance, literature, beliefs, and language—to the unique national character of Cuba.

Jack Ewing

Further Reading

Arnedo-Gómez, Miguel. *Writing Rumba: The Afrocubanista Movement in Poetry*. Charlottesville: University of Virginia Press, 2006. An annotated study showing how Cabrera and other intellectuals worked to incorporate black themes and rhythms into the national literature of Cuba.

Betancourt, Madeleine Cámara. *Cuban Women Writers: Imagining a Matria*. Translated by David Frye. New York: Palgrave Macmillan, 2008. This scholarly work studies the writings of four women, including Cabrera, who contributed to an understanding of the importance of race, gender, and language in modern Cuba.

Quiroga, José. *Tropics of Desire: Interventions from Queer Latino America*. New York: NYU Press, 2000. An examination of how gay Latinos and lesbian Latinas, like Cabrera, influenced Hispanic literature, art, music, and film.

Rodríguez-Mangual, Edna M. *Lydia Cabrera and the Construction of an Afro-Cuban Cultural Identity*. Chapel Hill: University of North Carolina Press, 2004. A well-researched study of Cabrera's life and work that demonstrates how her approach to information gathering differed from, and improved upon, traditional academic methods.

See also: Ruth Behar; Carlos Castaneda; Margarita Bradford Melville.

Miguel Cabrera

Venezuelan-born baseball player

From the beginning of his Major League Baseball career, Cabrera was one of the best all-around hitters in the sport.

Latino heritage: Venezuelan

Born: April 18, 1983; Maracay, Venezuela

Also known as: José Miguel Torres Cabrera

Area of achievement: Baseball

Early Life

José Miguel Torres Cabrera (kah-BREH-rah), better known as Miguel Cabrera, was born on April 18, 1983, in Maracay, Venezuela, an industrial center fifty miles west of Caracas. His mother, Gregoria Torres Cabrera, was formerly the starting shortstop for Venezuela's national women's softball team. His father, also named Miguel Cabrera, played on amateur baseball teams with Dave Concepción, future shortstop for the Cincinnati Reds. Several of Cabrera's uncles also played baseball, including David Torres, who played in the St. Louis Cardinals' minor-league system and managed a baseball academy in Venezuela.

Cabrera began accompanying his mother to softball practice when he was three. When he was five he climbed over his backyard fence to watch games at adjacent Maracay Stadium, later renamed for his uncle. He began training at David Torres's baseball academy around the same time and was playing in a national youth league by the age of ten.

Young Cabrera attracted attention from scouts for several teams before signing with the Florida Marlins in 1999 for $1.8 million, a record for a Venezuelan player. Around the same time, Cabrera married Rosangel, his high school sweetheart. He spent the summer of 1999 with the Aragua Tigers of the Liga Venezolana de Béisbol Profesional (Venezuelan Professional Baseball

Miguel Cabrera. (AP Photo)

League) and began playing in the Marlins' minor league system in 2000.

Life's Work

Because Cabrera grew from 6 feet, 2 inches and 180 pounds at the beginning of his minor league career to 6 feet, 4 inches and as much as 255 pounds, he was shifted from shortstop to third base. He improved steadily as a batter, hitting .365 in sixty-nine games for the Carolina Mudcats of the Southern League in 2003 before being promoted to the Marlins that June. After going hitless in his first four plate appearances in his debut against the Tampa Bay Devil Rays, Cabrera hit a game-winning three-run home run in the eleventh inning, becoming the third-youngest player to record a walk-off homer in his first major league game. Alternating between third base and left field, he hit 12 home runs, drove in 62 runs, and batted .268 in eighty-nine games, finishing fifth in the rookie-of-the-year voting. More important, he helped lead the Marlins to a World Series victory over the New York Yankees, hitting four home runs and driving in a dozen runs in seventeen postseason games.

Playing right and left field, Cabrera lived up to his considerable potential in 2004, with 33 home runs, 101 runs scored, 112 runs batted in, and a .294 batting average. In 2005, he won a Silver Slugger Award as the best offensive player at his position, left field, in the National League. This success, however, was clouded by concerns about Cabrera's attitude. He arrived late for one game and clashed with some teammates, who held a closed-door meeting to discuss his behavior. Cabrera fanned the flames of this uneasy situation by telling a reporter he had nothing to learn from the Marlins' veterans.

Cabrera moved to third base in 2006, set a team record with a .339 batting average, and won another Silver Slugger Award. He continued, however, to behave immaturely and had a fistfight in the dugout with pitcher Scott Olsen, who had criticized his lackadaisical play. Cabrera had another outstanding season at the plate in 2007, becoming the third-youngest player to accumulate five hundred runs batted in during his career. Thanks to arbitration, his salary had increased from $472,000 to $7.4 million, and the Marlins, desperate to reduce their payroll, traded Cabrera to the Detroit Tigers after the season.

Cabrera was moved to first base by the Tigers and had an outstanding first season in Detroit, leading the American League with thirty-seven home runs. He was just as good in 2009, becoming the fifth Venezuelan to hit two hundred home runs in the major leagues. The Tigers had hoped that Cabrera would lead the team to the play-offs, but the team lost fifteen of its final twenty-six games to tumble from first place in the American League Central Division.

During the final weekend of the 2009 season, Cabrera returned to his Birmingham, Michigan, home at six o'clock in the morning after a night of drinking at a nearby hotel and got into an argument with his wife. Police took him in for questioning and discovered his blood alcohol level was three times the legal limit. Cabrera later spent three months in an alcohol-abuse treatment center.

Recovering from his addiction and in better physical shape than in previous years, Cabrera returned to the Tigers with a new attitude in 2010. He was less introverted and became a mentor to younger players. Cabrera led the American League with 126 runs batted in and a .420 on-base percentage, while hitting a career-high 38 home runs and batting .328. He finished second to Josh Hamilton of the Texas Rangers in the voting for the league's most valuable player.

Significance

In the first decade of the twentieth-first century, Cabrera was Major League Baseball's most consistent offensive threat after Albert Pujols of the St. Louis Cardinals. He hit between 26 and 38 home runs a season from 2004 through 2010, drove in between 103 and 127 runs, scored more than 100 runs four times, and batted more than .300 five times, with a career average of .313.

Few players in Major League Baseball history have been so productive from the beginning of their careers. His Tiger teammate Johnny Damon, who had played with such stars as Manny Ramirez and Alex Rodriguez, called Cabrera the best hitter he had ever played with.

Michael Adams

Further Reading

Chen, Albert. "The Natural." *Sports Illustrated,* April 26, 2004, 166, 168. Assesses Cabrera's superstar potential.

Nightengale, Bob. "Cabrera Changes Stripes, Life." *USA Today*, July 2, 2010, p. 1C. Cabrera talks about dealing with the consequences of his actions and learning from his mistakes.

Verducci, Tom. "The Wake-up Call." *Sports Illustrated,* July 19, 2010, 54-56, 58. Describes how recovery from alcohol abuse revitalized Cabrera's career.

See also: Dave Concepción; Ozzie Guillén; Albert Pujols; Manny Ramirez; Alex Rodriguez.

José Canseco

Cuban-born baseball player

One of the biggest baseball stars of the late 1980's and early 1990's, Canseco was the first player to hit 40 home runs and steal 40 bases in the same season. With his teammate Mark McGwire, he led the Oakland Athletics to three straight American League pennants. After the end of his playing career, Canseco released a tell-all book describing the rampant use of performance-enhancing drugs in Major League Baseball.

Latino heritage: Cuban

Born: July 2, 1964; Havana, Cuba

Also known as: José Canseco y Capas, Jr.; Parkway Joe; the Chemist

Area of achievement: Baseball

Early Life

José Canseco y Capas, Jr. (kahn-SAY-koh) was born on July 2, 1964 in Havana, Cuba. He left Cuba with his family when he and his twin brother, Ozzie, were infants. They relocated to Miami, Florida, where José and Ozzie grew up and attended Coral Park High School.

After high school, Canseco was selected in the fifteenth round of the Major League Baseball (MLB) draft by the Oakland Athletics in 1982. In 1983, while playing at the Class-A level in Madison, Wisconsin, the scrawny 6-foot-3, 185-pound Canseco did not impress. He was demoted to Medford, Oregon, where, after 34 games, he was hitting a mere .159 with 3 home runs, 10 runs batted in (RBI), 2 stolen bases, and 36 strikeouts It was then that Canseco first turned to steroids. Embarking on a rigorous strength-training program, he bulked up to 230 pounds. He added an inch to his height and became a different player. Home run blasts of 500 feet became common. In Double-A, Canseco hit .318 with 25 home runs and 80 RBI in 58 games. Promoted to Triple-A, he hit .348. By the end of the 1985 season, the already renowned slugger was deemed ready to crack Oakland's formidable lineup. He recorded a .302 batting average in 29 games.

Although Canseco was physically imposing, however, he was insecure and defensive about his skills and intellect. He told teammates and staff that, even when he was in Little League, his father had denied him encouragement.

Life's Work

The Oakland Athletics (A's) teams of the late 1980's were built around power hitters. Three dominated—left fielder Rickey Henderson, right fielder Dave Parker, and first baseman Mark McGwire. Henderson, a Hall of Famer, was arguably the best leadoff hitter and base stealer of all time. Canseco, who dwarfed Henderson, soon showed that he, too, was a threat on the basepaths.

In 1986, Canseco won the American League rookie of the year award. To many sports observers, he seemed to be the future of baseball—a consummate athlete with the ideal mix of power, speed, and agility. In 1988, at age twenty-four, he led the league in home runs (42), RBI (124), and slugging percentage (.569). He also stole 40 bases and was named the American League most valuable player. He was the first player in baseball history to record 40 home runs and 40 stolen bases in the same season.

Canseco's success made him a strong believer in the power of steroids to improve athletic performance. Because Major League Baseball did not mandate testing for steroids before 2004, his use of the drugs went undetected, although he did not hide it from teammates or team officials. Rather, his feats made him a celebrity, and Canseco and fellow power hitter McGwire were dubbed the "Bash Brothers." The A's won three straight American League pennants from 1988 to 1990 and won the World Series in 1989.

Despite his success, Canseco often found trouble off the field. He was arrested twice in 1989, once for driving over 125 miles per hour and once for carrying a loaded handgun onto a college campus. His first wife, Esther, accused him of domestic violence after he reportedly rammed her car with his own. In the late 1990's, Canseco was sentenced to probation and counseling after another domestic incident, this time with his second wife. He also attracted tabloid attention for a reported tryst with pop singer Madonna. He remained productive as a hitter but was frequently hampered by injuries.

In August, 1992, Canseco was pulled from a game and subsequently traded to the Texas Rangers for two pitchers and All-Star outfielder Ruben Sierra. He never regained the awe-inspiring prowess of his early seasons, and after two years in Texas, Canseco spent the rest of his career shuttling among a variety of teams. Injuries limited his effectiveness and quickly reduced him to the role of designated hitter. He retired in 2002, attempted a comeback in 2004, but did not make the Los Angeles Dodgers' roster after a spring tryout. Canseco finished his career with a total of 462 home runs.

José Canseco. (AP Photo)

After his playing days ended, Canseco appeared eager to remain in the spotlight. He took part in celebrity boxing matches and reality television shows. He also began to speak out about steroid use in baseball, including his own. He released a tell-all book in 2005, *Juiced: Wild Times, Rampant 'Roids, Smash Hits, and How Baseball Got Big*. In it, Canseco described the effects of steroids on his own body and career and accused many other players of using drugs. There was an immediate backlash in which Canseco was portrayed as a scandal monger desperate for attention and money. Players he named as steroid users were quick to deny his charges. However, over time, many of Canseco's claims gained credibility as drug test results implicated scores of players, including Alex Rodriguez, Miguel Tejada, and Rafael Palmeiro. Former A's sluggers McGwire and Jason Giambi eventually admitted to using steroids and apologized to fans. Against all odds, Canseco emerged as a whistleblower whose revelations helped push the MLB toward stricter drug policies and enforcement. His follow-up book was titled *Vindicated: Big Names, Big Liars, and the Battle to Save Baseball* (2009).

SIGNIFICANCE

Although his early years were filled with remarkable feats, Canseco never achieved the kind of historic career for which he seemed destined as injury and scandal took their toll. However, in the late 2000's, he returned to the spotlight as an unlikely hero amid Major League Baseball's steroid scandal. His legacy is inextricably linked to steroids, both because of how they influenced his career and for his role in revealing the extent of their use in professional baseball.

Richard Hauer Costa

FURTHER READING

Bryant, Howard. *Juicing the Game: Drugs, Power, and the Fight for the Soul of Major League Baseball.*

New York: Viking, 2005. Sportswriter Bryant examines the history of performance-enhancing drugs in baseball.

Canseco, José: *Juiced: Wild Times, Rampant 'Roids, Smash Hits, and How Baseball Got Big.* New York: HarperCollins, 2005. Canseco's autobiography describes his extensive steroid use and names names of other players he claims to have introduced to the drugs.

_______. *Vindicated: Big Names, Big Liars, and the Battle to Save Baseball.* New York: Simon & Schuster, 2009. Chronicles the fallout from *Juiced* and contains more accusations of drug use by current players.

Chabon, Michael. "José Canseco, Hero." *The New York Times*, March 18, 2005. The best-selling writer presents a novelistic portrait of Canseco as a rare breed, the rogue hero.

See also: Roberto Alomar; David Ortiz; Rafael Palmeiro; Manny Ramirez; Alex Rodriguez; Sammy Sosa; Miguel Tejada.

Mario Cantú

American activist and restauranteur

Cantú was an activist and restauranteur who offered a more Latin-American-centric perspective on the Chicano civil rights movement than most other activists and who worked to establish closer ties between Chicanos and dissident groups in Mexico and other parts of Latin America

Latino heritage: Mexican
Born: April 2, 1937; San Antonio, Texas
Died: November 9, 2000; San Antonio, Texas
Also known as: Mauro Casiano Cantú, Jr.
Areas of achievement: Activism; business

Early Life

Mario Cantú (kahn-TEW) was born Mauro Casiano Cantú, Jr., in San Antonio, Texas, on April 2, 1937. He became known as Mario in elementary school, when his teachers found it difficult to remember "Mauro" and nicknamed him "Mario," a name he subsequently used throughout his life. His parents were Mauro Cantú and Lucrecia Casiano Cantú, owners and operators of the M. Cantú Super Mercado in San Antonio, where Mario and his brothers and sisters worked as children.

After graduating from high school, Cantú married his first wife and went to work in the family grocery store full time. He soon realized that the encroachment of larger grocery chains and the move of much of the store's clientele from the city's center to the suburbs threatened the long-term viability of the store, and he persuaded his father to turn the grocery into a restaurant. Mario's Restaurant was a great success, becoming the favorite gathering place of Chicano and Mexican politicians and celebrities, and it was one of a very few restaurants in San Antonio that served blacks, as well as Latinos and whites.

While the restaurant thrived, Cantú did not. He began to sell drugs and, after a heroin bust and conviction in 1962, he was sentenced to federal prison. There is some disagreement among his biographers as to precisely where he was incarcerated; some say it was the correctional facility at Leavenworth, Kansas, while others maintain it was a facility at Terre Haute, Indiana. What is certain is that the prison stint would prove to be his making, as it was there that Cantú first met and was befriended by Puerto Rican *independentistas*, activists agitating for the independence of Puerto Rico from the United States. The relationships Cantú built with these fellow prisoners and the discussions they had, both in prison and in Cantú's postrelease correspondence, were to greatly influence his future thinking and activism for Chicano civil rights.

Life's Work

Upon his release from prison in 1969, Cantú returned to San Antonio with a new sense of purpose. He began his career as an activist by organizing Semana de la Raza celebrations to take place around September 16, Mexican Independence Day. He also founded Tu-Casa, an organization that helped Mexican citizens living illegally in the United States to gain legal status. In addition, Cantú worked with La Raza Unida Party, an American political party founded with the objective of improving the lives and increasing the economic and political opportunities of Mexican Americans. After his release he also met and married his second wife, Irma Medellín, and he took over Mario's Restaurant upon the death of his father. The restaurant subsequently became the favored gathering place for Chicano activists and politicians.

Mario's Restaurant was raided by the Immigration and Naturalization Service in 1976. The restaurant employed a number of illegal aliens, and Cantú was arrested and charged with harboring these workers. Despite organizing a Mario Cantú Defense Committee and rallying support from prominent Chicano activists, politicians, and religious leaders, Cantú was convicted and sentenced to five years probation, becoming the first U.S. citizen to be convicted of harboring illegal aliens.

After his conviction, a newly radicalized Cantú turned to Mexico for both inspiration and new allies in his civil rights work. He led a protest in San Antonio against visiting Mexican president Luis Echeverría in 1976, calling him an assassin and a tool of the Central Intelligence Agency (CIA). He became involved with the Partido Proletário Unido de América (PPUA), a guerrilla resistance organization that sought to arm Mexican *campesinos* (farmers) so they could seize land appropriated by the Mexican federal government. Cantú befriended PPUA's leader, Florencio Medrano,and made a number of trips from Texas to Mexico to deliver weapons to PPUA. Such activities were in violation of his parole, and after Cantú appeared on television in 1978 in news footage of a PPUA-led uprising, he was summoned to appear before the court to explain his involvement. Rather than appear, Cantú fled with his wife to Paris, where he spent several years touring and speaking about the injustices perpetrated by the Mexican government against the nation's indigenous peoples. He finally returned to the United States in 1979, at which time his parole was revoked and he served the rest of his sentence in a halfway house.

After completing his probation, Cantú's activism took a back seat to his restaurant business. He returned to Paris briefly to open a restaurant, Mario's Papa Maya, with his third wife. The restaurant was well received and a critical success, but Cantú came back to the United States. He established and ran a series of restaurants in different locations, but none were as successful as the original Mario's Restaurant in San Antonio, and by 2011, none but the San Antonio restaurant survived. Continued drug use began to take a toll on his mental and physical health, and Cantú died in 2000 at the age of sixty-three.

SIGNIFICANCE

Cantú's primary importance as a Chicano activist came not only from his work for Mexican Americans in the United States but also from his internationalist views of the civil rights struggle, which led him to advocate closer ties to dissenting groups in Latin America. He believed that Chicanos needed to develop a greater sense of solidarity with oppressed indigenous peoples of Mexico and Latin America, as well as a sense of themselves as Mexicans living on land that was once a part of Mexico. In this, he offered a much-needed alternative viewpoint to the better-known, more United States-oriented thinking of Chicano activists like César Chávez and José Ángel Gutiérrez, whom Cantú felt had been co-opted by Anglo politicians.

Unlike other Chicano activists, and notwithstanding his own efforts to shield the illegal aliens working in Mario's Restaurant, Cantúe was opposed to amnesty for illegal immigrants, as he believed such programs failed to address the root problems of oppression of indigenous peoples and capitalist abuses in Mexico. Throughout his activist career, Cantú remained a forceful critic of American foreign policy in Mexico and Latin America and of the Mexican government's internal struggles with indigenous separatists.

Olivia Olivares

FURTHER READING

Cervantes, Leo. *More than a Century of the Chicano Movement.* Phoenix, Ariz.: Editorial Orbis Press, 2004. A good overview of the major movers and shakers of the Chicano civil rights movement, including Cantú and those who worked closely with him.

Gomez, Alan Eladio. "'Nuestras Vidas Corren Casi Paralelas': Chicanos, Independentistas, and the Prison Rebellions in Leavenworth, 1969-1972." *Latino Studies* 6 (Spring, 2008): 64-96. Examines the influence of the Puerto Rican *independentistas* on Cantú and other Mexican American prisoners in the Leavenworth penitentiary, as well as the origins of Cantú's internationalist philosophy.

Reavis, Dick J. "Rebel With a Cause." *Texas Monthly*, February 1979. 130-133.

_______. "Taste for Trouble." *Texas Monthly*, January 2001. 64-68. Reavis, a reporter for the National Broadcasting Company (NBC) who covered Cantú's activities with PPUA in Mexico, was also Cantú's friend, and he writes in both articles about Cantú's philosophy and thinking, as well as his activities in Mexico.

See also: César Chávez; José Ángel Gutiérrez; Dolores Huerta.

Norma Elia Cantú

Mexican-born writer and educator

Cantú is a postmodernist writer and a professor. Her published poetry, essays, short stories, and novels focus on Latino and Chicano studies, as well as border studies and folklore.

Latino heritage: Mexican

Born: January 3, 1947; Nuevo Laredo, Mexico

Areas of achievement: Literature; poetry; education

Early Life

Norma Elia Cantú (cahn-TEW) was born in Nuevo Laredo, Mexico, in 1947, the oldest of eleven children born to Florentino Cantú Vargas and Virginia Ramón Becerra Cantú, She was raised in Laredo, Texas, where she attended public schools. She began writing poetry when she was seven, and since the age of thirteen she has included her stories and other written works in a journal. After graduating high school, eighteen-year-old Cantú enrolled at Laredo Junior College, from which she graduated with her associate's degree in 1970. She received a Rotary International Scholarship that paid for her community college tuition. Cantú continued her education at Laredo State University (now Texas A&M International University at Laredo), from which she graduated cum laude with a bachelor's degree in English and political science in 1973. She then transferred to Texas A&M University at Kingsville, where she worked as a teaching assistant for two years before she graduated with honors and received her master's degree in English, with a minor in political science, in 1976.

Cantú then enrolled in the doctoral program at the University of Nebraska at Lincoln. During this time, she was awarded a Ford Foundation Graduate Fellowship (1977-1979), a Fulbright-Hays Research Fellowship that enabled her to travel to Spain (1979-1980), and a Ford Foundation Chicano Dissertation Completion Grant (1982). Cantú received her Ph.D. in English in 1982. While she was in school, Cantú focused on a variety of research interests, including Chicano literature, border studies, folklore, women's studies, and U.S. Latino studies. Cantú's dissertation was on *The Offering and the Offerers: A Generic Illocation of a Laredo Pastorela in the Tradition of the Shepherds' Plays.*

Life's Work

In 1980, Cantú became an assistant professor at Laredo State University, teaching courses on Chicano literature, creative writing, and women's studies. In 1985, she received a second Fulbright-Hays fellowship that enabled her to return to Spain for postdoctoral research. Two years later, she was promoted to associate professor at Laredo State/Texas A&M International University, a position she held until 1993, when she became a full professor . In addition to teaching, she was chair of the university's division of arts and sciences from 1987 to 1991 and interim dean of the school of education and arts and sciences from 1991 to 1992.

In 1993, Cantú served as a senior arts specialist at the National Endowment for the Arts' (NEA) Folk and Traditional Arts Program. In this position, she reviewed and advised on grant applications. During the 1998-1999 academic year, Cantú was the acting director for the Center for Chicano Studies at the University of California at Santa Barbara.

In 2000, Cantú accepted a position as a full professor in the English department at the University of Texas at San Antonio, where she directed the English doctoral program. Her teaching interests included cultural studies, contemporary literary theory, border studies, Chicano and Latino literature and film, folklore, and women's studies.

At the same time she was teaching, Cantú pursued her literary interests, publishing poems, short stories, and excerpts from her novel. Her first significant fiction publication was her novel *Canícula: Snapshots of a Girlhood en la Frontera* (1995), which by 2011 was in its fifth printing. *Canícula*, the Spanish word for "dog days," is a fictionalized memoir about a Mexican American family living in the border city of Laredo from the 1940's until the early 1960's. This novel won the 1995 Premio Aztlán Award, and the Spanish version, *Canícula: Imágenes de una niñez fronteriza*, was published in 2000. By 2011, Cantú had finished her second novel, *Cabañuelas*, and she was working on another novel, *Champú: Or, Hair Matters*. She is also the author of numerous journal articles, essays, and book chapters.

In addition, Cantú has edited *Flor y Ciencia: Chicanas in Science, Mathematics, and Engineering* (2006), *Paths to Discovery: Autobiographies from Chicanas with Careers in Science, Mathematics, and Engineering* (2008), and *Moctezuma's Table: Rolando Briseño's Mexican and Chicano Tablescapes* (2010). In 2001, she was a coeditor with the Latina Feminist Group of the anthology *Telling to Live: Latina Feminist Testimonies*, which included two of her poems and two of her essays. The following year, she and Olga Nájera Ramírez coedited *Chicana Traditions: Continuity and Change*; and the two women, along with Brenda M. Romero, coedited *Dancing Across Borders: Danzas y Bailes Mexicanos* (2009). In 2010, she and Marie E. Fránquiz coedited *Inside the Latin Experience: A Latin Studies Reader.*

Cantú has been an active member of many organizations and committees, including the Texas Committee on Higher Education (1987), Modern Language Association (MLA) Commission on the Languages and Literatures of America (1987-1989), Texas Committee for the Humanities (1987-1993), American Association of University Women (1990-1992), and Council for Women in Higher Education (1991). She was the faculty representative on the Formula Funding Committee of the Texas Higher Education Coordinating Board (1992-1993), and she served on the editorial board of the MLA Commission on the Literatures and Languages of America (1992-1994). She also chaired the National Association of Chicana and Chicano Studies (2003-2004), was a member of the board of Humanities Texas (2004-2007), and was an NEA panel review member (2005-2008).

Significance

Norma Elia Cantú is the recipient of numerous honors, including induction into the Laredo Women's Hall of Fame (1995), Outstanding Alumni Award, Laredo Community College (2001), American Folklore Society Distinguished Scholar Award from the Division on Chicana and Chicano Literature (2003), and the National Association of Chicana and Chicano Studies Scholar of the Year (2008). Her work as a professor, writer, and folklorist has done much to advance the understanding of Latino life, literature, and culture, particularly the border culture of south Texas.

Macey M. Freudensprung

Further Reading

Cantú, Norma Elia. *Canícula: Snapshots of a Girlhood en la Frontera.* Albuquerque: University of New Mexico Press, 1995. A novel in which Cantú addresses her family on both sides of the border in a recollection of memories from her upbringing.

_______. "Mexican Citizen." In *Art at Our Doorstep: San Antonio Writers and Artists*, edited by Nan Cuba and Riley Robinson. San Antonio, Tex.: Trinity University Press, 2008. A compilation of works by various authors and artists that includes one of Cantú's essays, as well as a brief biography.

_______, ed. *Paths to Discovery: Autobiographies from Chicanas with Careers in Science, Mathematics, and Engineering.* Los Angeles: UCLA Chicano Studies Research Center, 2008. Includes a preface written by Cantú that provides an understanding of her thinking.

See also: Alurista; Gloria Anzaldúa; Marie Arana; Lorna Dee Cervantes; Denise Chávez; Lucha Corpi; Alma Villanueva; Victor Villaseñor.

Norma V. Cantú

American lawyer, educator, and activist

As an attorney for the Mexican American Legal Defense and Educational Fund (MALDEF) and the U.S. Department of Education, Cantú worked to ensure equal educational opportunities for Latino students.

Latino heritage: Mexican

Born: November 2, 1954; Brownsville, Texas

Areas of achievement: Law; education; activism

Early Life

Norma V. Cantú (kahn-TEW) was the oldest of six children raised in a bilingual Mexican American family in Brownsville, Texas. Cantú's mother was a homemaker who went back to school and became a public school teacher and then an assistant principal. Her father Federico drove a milk truck and then became a postal carrier. Cantú's grandfather, who had little formal education, instilled in her the importance of acquiring an education, and Cantú was an excellent student. In 1971, after attending high school for just three years, she graduated with honors from Brownsville High School. Cantú majored in English and education at Pan American University (now the University of Texas-Pan American), from which she received a B.A. degree, summa cum laude, in December, 1973. The following year she taught English in Brownsville. In 1977, at the age of twenty-two, Cantú became the second Hispanic woman to graduate from Harvard University when she earned her degree from the Harvard

Norma V. Cantú. (AP Photo)

Law School. She began her legal career in the office of the Texas attorney general, where she worked on the nursing home task force from 1977 through 1978. She then taught English in San Antonio, Texas, in 1979.

Life's Work

Also in 1979, Cantú took a job as a trial and appellate lawyer for the Mexican American Legal Defense and Educational Fund (MALDEF). Four years later, she became the national director for MALDEF's Education Litigation and Advocacy Project, and she was the organization's regional counsel and education director from 1985 to 1993. At MALDEF, Cantú was the lead council for many education-centered lawsuits, including litigation supporting equal educational funding for Latino students, mandatory school busing, and equal educational opportunities for disabled students, minorities, and English-language learners. An aggressive litigator, Cantú took legal action against the state of Texas for alleged discrimination in its public school funding formula and in higher education. As an advocate for policies supporting affirmative action, Cantú was challenged by those who did not share her belief in the need for these policies.

On March 5, 1993, President Bill Clinton nominated Cantú to be the U.S. Department of Education's assistant secretary for civil rights. After being sworn in on May 24, 1993, Cantú worked to run an efficient administration. Her goals included streamlining the department, supporting bilingual education, promoting race-based scholarships, improving equal educational opportunities, and promoting greater opportunities for female athletes. She created and enforced federal policies and guidelines and advised the secretary of education on civil rights issues. She had the right to withhold funding from educational institutions that violated federal civil rights statues. She also investigated and resolved more complaints than previous administrations had handled and hired more bilingual staff.

From 1998 to 2001, Cantú was a representative of the U.S. State Department for the International Commission on the Child. After she retired from government work, she was a visiting professor of law and education at the University of Texas, where she taught graduate writing seminars in education and courses about politics and policies in education, school reform, and disability law. She was a frequent guest lecturer at other universities, a speaker at several national conferences, and a member of the editorial board of the *Texas Hispanic Journal on Law and Policy*, published by the University of Texas's law school.

As she progressed in her profession, Cantú maintained her connections with the Hispanic community, often taking a proactive stance and lecturing on social equality, particularly equal opportunity in education, health issues, and the value of affirmative action. In 2002, she cofounded the Mexican American Legislative Leadership Foundation, which provided opportunities for students to work with the Texas legislature.

Cantú is the author of "Emerging Legal Issues: A Proposed Agenda for Advocacy for Hispanics," one of the essays in *Latino Empowerment: Progress, Problems, and Prospects* (1988). Her awards include the University of Texas-Pan American Distinguished Alumnus Award (1996), the National Association of Collegiate Women Athletic Administration Honor Award (1996), and the 2004 Spirit of Excellence Award from the American Bar Association's Commission on Racial and Ethnic Diversity in the Profession.

Significance

As an aggressive litigator, civil rights advocate, and educator, Cantú has demonstrated a hard drive and a keen interest in providing opportunity to the disadvantaged. The first Latina assistant secretary for the U.S. Department of Education's Office of Civil Rights did not forget her heritage. Her efforts created more student scholarships and experiential opportunities, provided better prospects for female athletes, reduced harassment of minority students, and fostered equality in education. She shared her experiences and knowledge in her publications and in her university classes.

Cynthia J. W. Svoboda

Further Reading

Glaze, Melissa. "Latino Focus: Norma Cantú; In Recognition of Norma Cantú." *Texas Hispanic Journal of Law and Policy* 9, no. 1 (Fall, 2003): 2-5. An overview of Cantú's background, her work with MALDEF and the Office of Civil Rights, and her teaching career.

Healy, Patrick. "A Lightning Rod on Civil Rights." *Chronicle of Higher Education* 46, no. 4 (September 17, 1999): A42-A44. Scrutinizes Cantú's strategies and the controversial issues involving her political and legal career.

Hoff, David J. "In the Line of Fire." *Education Week* 17, no. 15 (December 3, 1997): 30-36. Provides an overview of the impact of affirmative action on Cantú's education, her major career accomplishments, and her position in the Office of Civil Rights. Includes comments from her critics.

Pell, Terence J. "A More Subtle Activism at the Office of Civil Rights. *Academic Questions* 10, no. 3 (Summer1997): 82-89. Covers Cantú's appointment with the Office of Civil Rights, the office's function, and her work for the office.

See also: Joaquín G. Avila; José Ángel Gutiérrez; Antonia Hernández; Vilma Socorro Martínez.

José Raúl Capablanca

Cuban chess grandmaster

Capablanca helped modernize the game of chess both in playing tactics and in the organization of its world championships. His book on chess fundamentals brought clarity to the game's tactics and strategies for the ordinary chess player. Moreover, his international victories brought diversity to high-level chess, which was dominated at the time by European players.

Latino heritage: Cuban and Spanish

Born: November 19, 1888; Havana, Cuba

Died: March 8, 1942; New York, New York

Also known as: José Raúl Capablanca y Graupera

Area of achievement: Sports

Early Life

José Raúl Capablanca y Graupera (kah-pah-BLAHN-kah) was born on November 19, 1888, in Cuba, which was then a Spanish colony. His father was attached to the Spanish military, and Capablanca was his second surviving son. Capablanca learned to play chess at four years old by watching his father, a rather poor player, and was able to pick up the moves of the game very quickly without any formal instruction. He was taken to the Havana Chess Club, where he became something of a child prodigy. However, on the advice of his doctor, Capablanca's father kept him from becoming too absorbed in the game.

The political situation in Cuba became precarious, and the family had to move several times before settling in Matanzas, where he attended school for two years. From the ages of eleven to thirteen, Capablanca apparently had little formal education and devoted himself to chess, although he was also a keen baseball player.

On returning to Havana, he played the leading Cuban chess player of the time, Juan Corzo, often beating him, but was unable to win the Cuban championship in 1902. A rich sponsor, who wanted Capablanca to enter his sugar business, sponsored him to travel to the United States to prepare himself for study at Colombia University, New York. Capablanca went to a school in New Jersey and made contact with the Manhattan Chess Club, one of the leading American clubs. His genius soon was recognized, and he became one of the club's best players. Capablanca did enroll at Columbia, but did not complete his studies, deciding to devote himself to chess, a decision that put an end to his sponsorship. From then on, Capablanca had to make much of his living as a professional chess player.

José Raúl Capablanca.
(Gamma-Keystone via Getty Images)

Life's Work

In order to launch Capablanca's professional career, *The American Chess Bulletin* arranged a tour for him throughout the United States, in which he would play a number of simultaneous chess matches with the leading local amateurs. Already, Capablanca was noted for his quickness of play, a skill required for simultaneous exhibitions. This quickness was based on an intuitive understanding of position and an exceptional knowledge of endgame tactics. The 1909 tour became the first of many such tours. As a result of his astounding triumph, winning more than 96 percent of his games, a match was set up against the longstanding U.S. champion, F. J. Marshall. Capablanca beat Marshall convincingly, 8-1, with fourteen matches drawn.

On the strength of this victory, Marshall insisted that Capablanca be invited to play at a major international tournament to be held in San Sebastian, Spain, in 1911, even though he did not stricly qualify. Most of the European masters present had little regard for the Latino chess player and so were shocked when Capablanca convincingly won the tournament, beating such grandmasters as Ossip Bernstein and Aron Nimzowitsch. Capablanca suddenly was considered a possible challenger for Dr. Emanuel Lasker, the world champion since 1894. However, Lasker demanded large purses and difficult conditions unacceptable to Capablanca.

Capablanca, meanwhile, consolidated his position as the leading chess player in the Americas, playing tournaments in New York, Havana, and Buenos Aires, Argentina; however, he needed more European victories to stake his claim as Lasker's challenger. The most significant of these matches came at the St.Petersburg, Russia, tournament of 1914. For the first time, Capablanca had the opportunity to play Lasker. It was a long, drawn-out tournament, with a preliminary round and a final round. Capablanca led after the preliminary round but tired rapidly, and Lasker was able to overtake him to win the tournament by half a point. The leading Russian, Alexander Alekhine, was third.

European chess came to an abrupt halt with the outbreak of World War I, and Capablanca had to confine himself to competing in the Americas for the next five years. At the close of the war, the longstanding Hastings Chess Tournament in England was revived in 1919. Capablanca won, dropping only one-half point. This triumph enabled him to sign an agreement with Lasker in 1920 for a world championship match. Cuban sponsors arranged for the match to take place in Havana. Lasker surprisingly resigned the world championship before the tournament, acknowledging Capablanca as world champion, and thus entered the tournament as the challenger. The match was played in the spring of 1921, and Lasker resigned after failing to win in fourteen straight games.

Capablanca remained world champion until 1927, enjoying a successful international playing career throughout this period. In 1927, he accepted a challenge by Alekhine. Capablanca was widely expected to win. The match was played in Buenos Aires, and Alekhine finally won by a score of 6-3 with twenty-five draws, one of the longest-ever world championships. A return challenge never took place as Alekhine demanded too large a purse.

In 1931, Capablanca, perhaps disheartened by his inability to challenge Alekhine again, withdrew somewhat from top-class international events for a few years. He returned to play significant tournaments at Hastings, Moscow, and Nottingham, England. His health began to decline, and in a 1938 tournament in Holland, he finished nearly last. However, representing Cuba in the eighth Chess Olympiad held in Buenos

Capablanca as a Celebrity

José Raúl Capablanca always was a modest and serious player, although he did not hesitate to make favorable commentaries on his own good games. His status as a child prodigy was never exploited. However, his natural brilliance at simultaneous chess, in which one player takes on a large number of opponents at once, occasioned many demonstrations and exhibitions all over the United States and wherever he traveled in Europe and South America. He was rarely beaten on such occasions. To make things more difficult for himself, he sometimes played blindfolded, or with major opponents working in consultation against him. Such occasions were usually widely publicized.

Just before his first trip to St. Petersburg, Capablanca was given a position with the Cuban Foreign Affairs Office as a sort of roving diplomat. This status gave him additional income, as well as official status and entree into diplomatic circles. He sometimes lectured and wrote several books on chess tactics and strategy. In his own home country of Cuba, he was a hero, and as a Latino representative in the traditionally European stronghold of chess, he was held in high esteem throughout Latin America.

Aires a few months later, he won the prize for best top board. The start of World War II broke off international tournaments again, and Capablanca died of heart failure in New York in 1942.

SIGNIFICANCE

Despite great interest in chess in many Latin American countries at the beginning of the twentieth century, particularly in Cuba, Argentina, and Mexico, there was no great international recognition of standards of chess there. Occasional visits of European masters and small torunaments were all that existed to encourage Latino chess players. There was not even a Spanish-language chess magazine. Capablanca's success changed this considerably. High-class tournaments were held in Havana and Buenos Aires; Capablanca himself started a Spanish-language chess magazine. Europeans' near monopoly on the world championship was broken. Capablanca himself helped to reform the world championship rules to what are recognized today as standard procedures. His understanding of middle-game combinations and endgames entered chess wisdom, paving the way for modern chess geniuses such as Mikhail Botvinnik, Bobby Fischer, and Anatoly Karpov.

David Barratt

FURTHER READING

Capablanca, José Raúl. *José Raúl Capablanca: World's Championship Matches, 1921 and 1927.* New York: Dover, 1977. Capablanca recounts his championship matches against Lasker and Alekhine.

_______. *My Chess Career.* 1920. Reprint. New York: Dover, 1966. Capablanca's autobiography, written before he became world champion, covers his early career and offers commentaries on many of his best early games.

Linder, Isaak, and Vladimir Linder. *José Raúl Capablanca: Third World Chess Champion.* Milford, Conn.: Russell, 2010. One of the Chesscafe World Chess Champions Series. It is the most up-to-date account of Capablanca's life and acgievements.

Reinfeld, Fred. *The Immortal Games of Capablanca.* New York: Dover, 1990. Probably the best collection of Capablanca's most famous games, with commentaries on each one.

Winter, Edward. *Capablanca: A Compendium of Games, Notes, Articles, Correspondence, Illustrations, and Other Rare Archival Materials on the Cuban Chess Genius José Raúl Capablanca, 1888-1942.* Jefferson, N.C.: McFarland, 1989. A very full collection of previously unpublished notes, letters, and memoirs. Winter also has collected a number of newspaper and magazine articles.

See also: Sixto Escobar; Pancho Gonzales; Aurelio Herrera; Chi Chi Rodriguez.

Luisa Capetillo

Puerto Rican activist and writer

Best known as a labor leader and champion of the working class, Capetillo also was a pioneer feminist in Puerto Rico. As a writer, Capetillo denounced religion, capitalism, the exploitation of workers by political parties, and the patriarchal system that kept women from full economic and social independence.

Latino heritage: Puerto Rican
Born: October 28, 1879; Arecibo, Puerto Rico
Died: April 10, 1922; Río Piedras, Puerto Rico
Also known as: Luisa Capetillo Perone; Louisa Capetillo
Areas of achievement: Activism; women's rights; social issues; literature

Early Life

Luisa Capetillo Perone (kah-peh-TEE-yoh) was born to Luisa Margarita Perone, a domestic worker, and Luis Capetillo Echevarria, an unskilled laborer, on October 28, 1879, in Arecibo, Puerto Rico. Although they were members of the working class, Capetillo's parents ensured that she had an education and exposed her to many forms of literature. In addition to her education, Capetillo assisted her mother in domestic service to wealthy families in Arecibo. Capetillo's mother's passion for literature and experience as a domestic worker no doubt influenced Capetillo's later work.

In 1898, having fallen in love with and been courted by Manuel Ledesma, Capetillo gave birth to her first child, Manuela. Ledesma was the son of a wealthy dignitary, and his family never approved of the relationship. Shortly after the birth of their second child, Gregorio, Ledesma and Capetillo separated.

While working as a reader in a cigar factory, Capetillo became deeply involved with the Free Federation of Workers (Federacion Libre de Trabajadores, or FLT). Her position as a reader exposed Capetillo to important political and philosophical works as well as news from around the world. At this time, her activism flourished as she traveled throughout Puerto Rico to participate in strikes and speak at rallies. Her knowledge and eloquence allowed Capetillo to emerge as a leader in the male-dominated labor movement.

In 1904, Capetillo began writing for newspapers and magazines, which eventually led to the publication of her first book, *Ensayos libertarios* (*Libertarian Essays,* 1907), which employs socialist and anarchist rhetoric to advocate for an equal society free from exploitation of laborers and women.

Life's Work

By the early 1900's, Capetillo's articulate perspectives and skilled organizing had made her the best-known woman labor leader in Puerto Rico. As an active member of the FLT, Capetillo used her prominence to reach female workers by publishing a magazine called *La mujer*. In an effort to raise money to sustain the magazine, Capetillo published her second book, *La humanidad del futuro* (*Humanity's Future,* 1910). *La humanidad del futuro* depicts Capetillo's vision of a utopian society and advocates for a reform of social services including health and education, as well as free love, vegetarianism, and communal responsibility.

In 1911, Capetillo gave birth to Luis, her third child, who was the result of a brief relationship with a married pharmacist. The same year, she published her most renowned book, *Mi opinión sobre las libertades derechos y deberes de la mujer* (*My Opinion About the Freedom, Rights, and Duties of Women*), which is considered the first feminist treatise in Puerto Rico and possibly Latin America. In a collection of essays, the book provides a comprehensive feminist analysis of issues such as sexual exploitation, domestic and other women's work, education, politics, motherhood, and religion. Capetillo's work concludes that education is the key to women's emancipation.

In 1912, Capetillo began working as an international labor organizer. Her work brought her to New York, where she wrote for a Hispanic labor newspaper and other labor publications. Her labor work eventually took her to Ybor City, a section of Tampa, Florida. While in Florida, Capetillo collaborated with a variety of cigar workers to organize for better working conditions, higher wages, and the right to unionize.

Three years later, Capetillo moved to Havana, Cuba, to participate in labor rallies and strikes. In 1915, she was arrested in Havana for wearing pants in public. This incident and her anarchist activities led to her deportation to Puerto Rico in 1916.

While in Puerto Rico, Capetillo published her final book *Influencias de las ideas modernas*

(*Influences of Modern Ideas,* 1916).The work reiterates many of the same subjects in *Mi opinión sobre las libertades, derechos, y deberes de la mujer* in a compilation of letters, a three-part play, and a number of personal reflections. After the publication of *Influencias de las ideas modernas*, Capetillo continued to write for labor publications and promote her books. From 1919 to 1920, Capetillo lived in New York City, where she worked as a reader in a cigar factory, ran a hostel, and wrote.

In 1920, Capetillo returned to Puerto Rico to start an education project called Escuela Granja Agricola (Agricultural Farm School). The project would teach children agricultural and leadership skills in addition to a traditional education. However, before that dream could come to fruition, Capetillo died on April 10, 1922, from tuberculosis.

Significance

Capetillo's work as a labor organizer and feminist activist not only brought together the working class of Puerto Rico but also revealed gender disparities within progressive movements and political revolutions. As the first feminist treatise in Puerto Rico, her *Mi opinión sobre las libertades, derechos, y deberes de la mujer* captured the social history and experiences of Puerto Rican women in the early twentieth century. Furthermore, her prominence as an international labor leader revealed a commonality among working women throughout North America. Capetillo's legacy has given generations of labor and feminist activists a historical context in which to base their work.

Erin E. Parrish

Further Reading

Capetillo, Luisa. *A Nation of Women: An Early Feminist Speaks Out—Mi opinión sobre las libertades, derechos, y deberes de la mujer*. Edited with an introduction by Félix V. Matos Rodríguez. Houston, Tex.: Arte Público Press, 2004. Matos Rodríguez provides a short biography of Capetillo and a historiography of her works. This text also includes a translation of Capetillo's landmark feminist treatise.

Hewitt, Nancy A. "Luisa Capetillo: Feminist of the Working Class." In *Latina Legacies: Identity, Biography, and Community*, edited by Vicki L. Ruia and Virginia Sanchez Korral. New York: Oxford University Press, 2005. Includes a brief biography, historical context, and an analysis of Capetillo's significance.

Valle Ferrer, Norma. *Luisa Capetillo, Pioneer Puerto Rican Feminist.* New York: Peter Lang, 2006. Valle Ferrer provides an in-depth biography and study of Capetillo's life. Appendix includes selections from Capetillo's final book, *Influencias de las ideas modernas*

See also: César Chávez; Helen Fabela Chávez; Dolores Huerta; Antonio Orendain; Felisa Rincón de Gautier.

José A. Cárdenas

American educator and activist

While best known as the founder and executive director of Intercultural Development Research Association, a nonprofit organization supporting children's right to education, Cárdenas was also the first Mexican American superintendent of San Antonio's Edgewood Independent School District. Cárdenas played a major role in a Texas court case involving equality in school finance.

Latino heritage: Mexican

Born: October 16, 1930; Laredo, Texas

Also known as: José Angel Cárdenas

Areas of achievement: Education; social issues

Early Life

José Angel Cárdenas (hoh-ZAY ahn-HEHL KAHR-day-nahs) was the fourth of five children born to Justo Cárdenas, Jr., and Matilde Ochoa de Cárdenas. His Mexican American family was raised near a border crossing point in Laredo, Texas. A bright child, fluent in both English and Spanish, Cárdenas graduated from high school when he was only fifteen years old, and he then earned his B.A. from the University of Texas at Austin in 1950. From 1950 to1951 Cárdenas taught science at the Christian Junior High School in Laredo. He was then drafted to serve two years in the Army.

After completing his military service, Cárdenas went to work for the Edgewood Independent School

District (ISD) in San Antonio, first teaching at the Coronado Elementary School and then transferring to the high school, where he taught biology. In 1955, Cárdenas earned his master's degree at Our Lady of the Lake University and became vice principal of Edgewood High School. He left the high school in 1958, when he became principal of Stafford Elementary School, another school in the district. While working on his doctorate degree, Cárdenas took a position in the Department of Education at St. Mary's University and became chairman of the department. He earned his doctorate from the University of Texas in 1966, and he then spent two years at Southwest Educational Development Laboratory in Austin. Cárdenas accepted the position of superintendent of Edgewood Independent School District, a poor district with a large number of Mexican American students, in 1969.

Life's Work

As superintendent, Cárdenas was an especially strong advocate of bilingual education and a sponsor of early childhood education programs. In 1968, a group of parents filed a lawsuit against the school district, arguing that its funding formula, which was based on property taxes, was unfair. A three-judge district court found in favor of the parents. However, the U.S. Supreme Court in *San Antonio School District v. Rodriguez* 411 U.S. 1 (1973) overturned the lower court decision and ruled that a school-financing system based on local property taxes did not violate the Fourteenth Amendment's equal protection clause. Cárdenas, who supported the parents, resigned from the Edgewood ISD after the Supreme Court decision.

In 1973, Cárdenas founded Texans for Educational Excellence in order to carry on the fight for equitable school funding. A year later the organization was renamed the Intercultural Development Research Association (IDRA). Cárdenas created a database of information and statistics on school funding. Over the years, Cárdenas personally worked with legislators and organizations to support multicultural and bilingual education. His database and the addition of other staff and resources were used to support the Mexican American Legal Defense and Educational Fund (MALDEF) in later legal challenges.

Cárdenas also occupied himself with several court cases involving the Texas Education Agency. IDRA has worked on many school-related issues, including finance, salaries, curriculum, and student dropout problems. In 1984, the organization founded the Coca-Cola Valued Youth Program, which helps at-risk junior and senior high school students gain self-esteem and confidence by tutoring younger at-risk children.

As part of his mission to improve teaching and learning, Cárdenas has authored several articles and books. His books include *All Pianos Have Keys, and Other Stories* (1994), *Multicultural Education: A Generation of Advocacy* (1995), *Texas School Finance Reform: An IDRA Perspective* (1997), and *My Spanish-Speaking Left Foot* (1997). In 1998, Cárdenas donated his papers to the Nettie Lee Benson Latin American Collection at the University of Texas at Austin. His publications, papers, and IDRA records document many important events in the history of education in Texas.

On September 9, 1972, Cárdenas married Laura D. Tobin. The couple had five children: Jose, Jr., Mary, Michael, Christine, and Laura.

Significance

Cárdenas has won several awards, including the St. Mary's University's Public Justice Award, the Ford Motor Company's Hispanic Salute to Education Award, the League of United Latin American Citizens' Education Award, and the Austin Equity Center's Champion of Equity Award. He has devoted his life to improving education and making it more equitable for all students. After twenty-five years, his nonprofit organization continued to provide support not only for south Texas school districts but also for other school systems that have multicultural and bilingual education programs. On September 5, 1997, the Ex-Students' Association, the alumni organization of the University of Texas (UT), honored Cárdenas with the UT Distinguished Alumnus Award for his significant contributions to public education in Texas. Cárdenas taught at the elementary and secondary levels, as well as at the University of Texas at San Antonio, Our Lady of the Lake University, San Diego State University, University of Chicago, and Chicago State University. His determination, persistence, and strength continue to influence education, particularly in San Antonio, where the José Cárdenas Early Childhood Center prepares future generations of Americans.

Cynthia J. W. Svoboda

Further Reading

Cárdenas, José A. "The Role of Native-Language Instruction in Bilingual Education." *Ph Delta Kappan* 67, no 2 (January 1986): 359-363. Cárdenas outlines the evolution of and rationale for bilingual education, including the value of native language, and addresses criticism of bilingual education.

_______. *Texas School Finance Reform: An IDRA Perspective.* San Antonio, Tex.: IDRA, 1997. A history of Texas school finance reform from 1968 to 1995.

Gutiérrez, José Angel. *Oral History Interview with José Cárdenas.* Arlington: University of Texas at Arlington, 2002. Provides information on Cárdenas's life, work, educational philosophy, and involvement in founding the Intercultural Development Research Association.

Salina, Cinthia. "A Generation of Defiance and Change: An Oral History of Texas Educator and Activist Blandina 'Bambi' Cárdenas." In *Explorations in Curriculum History Research*, edited by Lynn M. Burlbaw and Sherry L. Field. Greenwich, Conn.: Information Age, 2005. Blandina Cárdenas discusses the articles she cowrote with José A. Cárdenas, mentions his book *Multicultural Education*, and highlights some of his work at Edgewood ISD.

See also: Rodolfo F. Acuña; Lauro Cavazos; Jaime Escalante; Julian Nava.

Reyes Cárdenas

American poet

Cárdenas advanced the genre of Chicano literature by writing poems that gave voice to many Mexican Americans growing up in Mexican border towns, especially in the Southwest, where Mexican Americans were simultaneously valued for their cheap and willing labor and discriminated against by the Anglo community for their Mexican identity.

Latino heritage: Mexican

Born: January 6, 1948; Seguin, Texas

Area of achievement: Poetry

Early Life

Reyes Cárdenas (RAY-ehs KAHR-day-nahs), a fourth-generation Tejano (Texan of Mexican descent), was born to Mexican parents in the southwest Texas border town of Sequin. Seguin, like many places along the border, drew heavily on Mexican and Mexican American labor for farm work, especially for picking cotton. Cárdenas, his parents, two brothers, and sister lived in the barrio (Mexican neighborhood) of Seguin in a modest dwelling, a house that used kerosene for lighting and drew water from a well. The family meal time staples were the inexpensive and nutritious tortillas and beans.

Cárdenas's parents did the back-breaking, dusty work of picking cotton during the hot Texas summers. Cárdenas worked with them until he was enrolled in school at age ten. When he started school, he was laughed at for his dusty bare feet. On the second day of school, his teacher provided him with a pair of sneakers. When he was twelve years old, his mother was taken to the doctor's office to deliver a child. She died there, as did the baby, because of the inadequacy of the medical facilities. His father, overcome with grief and despair, left the children with his parents, became a mechanic, and moved to California. For Cárdenas, his *abuela* (grandmother), a strong matriarchal presence who lived to be one hundred, became the most important person in his life.

Life's Work

Cárdenas's vocation began at age thirteen when he discovered the public library, a place that was open to Mexicans, as well as Anglos. He rode his bicycle there to read poetry; his favorite poet was Delmore Schwartz. Inspired by Schwartz and others, he soon began writing his own poetry, admitting that, ironically, his first poem, published in his junior high school's newspaper, was a celebration of Christopher Columbus. Throughout the 1950's, Cárdenas, like other Mexican Americans, felt himself a second-class citizen, for that is how Chicanos were treated in Sequin.

At age sixteen, Cárdenas was diagnosed with tuberculosis. He spent more than a year in a San Antonio hospital, where a part of one lung was removed. After leaving the hospital, Cárdenas took heart in the new spirit of pride arising in Mexican American communities. Motivated by the work of César Chávez, who was mobilizing support for migrant workers, Chicano activists and writers began to assert themselves and reject discrimination. They recognized the value and beauty of their traditions and culture. An important voice at this time was a poet from Laredo, Texas, Cecilio García-Camarillo, who wrote poems describing the experiences of the barrio, as well as the Mexican and Spanish folklore that the barrio had inherited. His language mixed words from the three cultures. The result of his work came to be recognized as a new identity— the Chicano identity—and a new genre—Chicano literature.

Cárdenas became one of the early writers and supporters of this literary movement, contributing to and helping publish the small but influential San Antonio-based literary journal *Caracol*, published between 1974 and 1977 and reaching more than sixty thousand readers. Cárdenas also began regularly publishing his work. In 1975, he published a collection of poems, *Chicano Territory*, followed by *Anti-Bicicleta Haiku* (1976). Cárdenas, García-Camarillo, and Carmen Tafolla co-authored *Get Your Tortillas Together* (1976). In 1981, Cárdenas published *Survivors of the Chicano Titanic*, followed by *I Was Never a Militant Chicano* (1986), for which he received the Austin Book Award. Creating poems for publication and his Internet blog, Cárdenas has described the Chicano experience, as well as his personal reflections, including discussions of the influence of the many poets he admires, from William Shakespeare to Wallace Stevens.

Significance

In capturing and promoting the voice and experience of the many Mexican Americans who lived and worked along the border or traveled to more northern states, often doing the work other Americans rejected, Cardenas has described a particular culture that evolved in the United States. This Chicano culture celebrates Mexican Americans and reflects the language, traditions, icons, folklore, and myths drawn from Mexican indigenous people, as well as Spaniards and Americans. The Chicano literary culture developed a flexible language, using variations of English and Spanish to mix and adapt words and to describe generationally shared experiences. The people who identify with Chicano literature needed and valued the voice of Cárdenas, who, in describing this culture within a culture explored its roots and its evolution with pride, accuracy, and articulate poetic expression.

Bernadette Flynn Low

Further Reading

Bruce-Novoa, Juan. "Chicano Poetry." In *A Gift of Tongues: Critical Challenges in Contemporary American Poetry*, edited by Marie Harris and Kathleen Aguero. Athens: University of Georgia Press. 1987. Traces the roots of Chicano poetry, demonstrating the ways poets draw from American and Mexican cultures.

Lamadrid, Enrique. Introduction to *Selected Poems of Cecilio García-Camarillo*. Houston, Tex.: Arte Público Press of the University of Houston, 2000. Discusses the Chicano poetic movement initiated by García-Camarillo through *Caracol* (1974-1977), a magazine providing a forum for Chicano writers. Cárdenas contributed to and helped publish this magazine.

Tafallo, Carmen. "Chicano Literature." In *A Gift of Tongues: Critical Challenges in Contemporary American Poetry*, edited by Marie Harris and Kathleen Aguero. Athens: University of Georgia Press, 1987. Describes the emergence of Chicano literature as a new and progressive genre that mixes languages—English and Spanish and sometimes Mayan and Aztec.

_______. "Reyes Cárdenas." In *Chicano Writers. Second Series*, edited by Francisco A. Lomeli and Carl R. Shirley. Detroit: Gale Research, 1992. Provides an overview of Cárdenas's life and works.

See also: Rudolfo Anaya; Gloria Anzaldúa; Jimmy Santiago Baca; Norma Elia Cantú; Lorna Dee Cervantes; Sandra Cisneros; Tomás Rivera; Gary Soto; Carmen Tafolla; Alma Villanueva; Bernice Zamora.

Manuel Cardona

Spanish-born physicist and educator

One of the leading solid-state physicists in the world, Cardona made fundamental discoveries across a range of areas, particularly those related to semiconductors and superconductors. He was for twenty-eight years an able founding administrator of the Max Planck Institute for Solid State Research.

Latino heritage: Spanish

Born: July 9, 1934; Barcelona, Spain

Also known as: Manuel Cardona Castro

Areas of achievement: Science and technology; education

Early Life

Manuel Cardona Castro (mahn-WEHL KAHR-doh-nuh KAHS-troh), the son of Juan Cardona and Angela Castro, was born in Barcelona, Spain. From an early age he demonstrated excellent mathematical aptitude and skill in tinkering with materials he obtained from old radios. Because some of the physics teachers in his high school stoked his enthusiasm for physics, Cardona elected to pursue a physics degree at the University of Barcelona. He graduated in 1955, winning an award as the best university science student in the nation. Knowing that American physicists were doing the best work, in 1956 he entered Harvard University, where he obtained an M.S. in 1958. That same year, he successfully defended a doctoral thesis at the University of Madrid. He wrote a second doctoral thesis at Harvard and received his Ph.D. in 1959.

For the next two years he worked in Switzerland at RCA Laboratories in Zurich, where he met and married Inge Hecht, with whom he would have three children: Michael, Angela, and Steven. He returned to the United States to work at RCA Laboratories in Princeton, New Jersey, from 1961 to1964. In 1963, he also was a visiting professor at the University of Pennsylvania. He became an associate professor of physics at Brown University in Providence, Rhode Island, in 1964, and he served as a professor of physics there from 1966 to1971.

Life's Work

Cardona's exemplary research in solid-state physics, especially as it applied to semiconductors, established him as a world-class authority. Brown University granted him a sabbatical beginning in the fall of 1971, which he intended to use to study at the Hamburg Synchrotron Radiation Laboratory in Germany. However, the Max Planck Institute for Solid State Research had recently been established in Stuttgart, Germany, and Cardona was named a scientific member and the inaugural director of the institute in 1971. The institute quickly became a world leader in solid-state physics under his able leadership. His own interests centered on optical spectroscopy of semiconductors and superconductors and electron-phonon interaction, which affects both types of devices. The institute's international program of research involved sites at Hamburg (where Cardona was originally going to study); Berlin, Germany; Grenoble, France; and Brookhaven, Texas. It resulted in the creation of new techniques, new theoretical and practical understandings, and advanced computational applications. Additional collaborations with the University of California at Berkeley, Kurchatov Institute in Moscow, and Simon Fraser University in Vancouver, British Columbia, resulted in the creation and study of new crystals with interesting and useful physical properties.

Cardona wrote many advanced textbooks, book chapters, and more than 1,800 technical articles, establishing himself as perhaps the leading solid-state physicist in the world. ISI Web of Knowledge has consistently rated him as a physicist of the highest reputation and status. His impact across Latin America was recognized by the 1997 John Wheatley Award from the American Physical Society for his mentoring and guidance to a "whole generation of Latin American physicists." He has received honorary doctorates from eleven universities on four continents.

Cardona also was elected a fellow of the National Academy of Sciences in the United States, the Royal Society of Canada, the European Physical Society, Academia Europea, the Mexican Academy of Sciences, the Royal Academy of Sciences in Spain, the Japanese Society for the Promotion of Sciences, the Institute of Physics in London, the World Innovation Foundation in England, and the German Physical Society. He has been a visiting or honorary professor at the University of California at Berkeley, University of Konstanz in Germany, University of Stuttgart, and the University of Buenos Aires. Cardona is a member of many professional societies, was the editor in chief of *Solid State Communications* (1992-2005), and served on the editorial boards of *Physical Review Letters* (1989-1992), *Journal of Physics, Condensed Matter* (1988-1992), *Journal of Physics C* (1974-1978), and *Physical Status Solidi* (1972-2011). In addition, Cardona was honorary chairman of the 27th International Conference on Physics of Semiconductors (2004). He was awarded the Gold Medal of the University of Pavia (Italy), the Blaise Pascal Medal of the European Academy of Sciences, the Matteucci Medal of the Italian National Academy of Sciences, the Sir Nevill Mott Medal and the Mott Prize from the Institute of Physics (London), the Ernst Mach Honorary Medal for Merit in the Physical Sciences from the Academy of Sciences of the Czech Republic, the Max Planck Research Prize from the Max Planck Society and von Humboldt Foundation, and numerous other medals and awards.

Significance

Considered to be the greatest living Spanish scientist, Cardona is one of the world's top solid-state physicists and a well-known mentor of young scientists, especially those whose first language is Spanish. His contributions across several areas of modern experimental physics are without parallel and his abilities as an administrator of a scientific research institution enabled the Max Planck Institute for Solid State Research to attain and maintain world-class status.

Dennis W. Cheek

Further Reading

Maresma, Assumpció. "Manuel Cardona." *Catalónia Cultura*, 23 (1991): 36-41. A candid interview with Cardona at the peak of his career, in which he discusses his scientific work and the changing world of science in the 1990's.

Romero, A. H., R. K. Kremer, and W. Marx. "The Scientific Road of Manuel Cardona: A Bibliometric Analysis. *Annalen der Physik*, 523, nos. 1/2 (January, 2011): 179-190. Uses the prolific writings of Cardona to investigate how to chart a scientist's career based on his or her publications and how to measure his or her impact on the field of solid-state physics and science more generally.

See also: Luis W. Alvarez; Ralph Amado; Albert V. Baez; Franklin Ramón Chang-Díaz; José D. García; Vicente José Llamas.

David Cardús

Spanish-born physician

Trained in cardiology, Cardús combined his medical expertise with knowledge of computers and mathematics in order to advance the field of sports medicine by studying the effects of physical exercise on the body. He was one of the physicians who monitored astronauts in the first U.S. space mission.

Latino heritage: Spanish
Born: August 6, 1922; Barcelona, Spain
Died: June 2, 2003; Houston, Texas
Also known as: David Cardús y Pascual
Areas of achievement: Medicine; science and technology

Early Life

David Cardús y Pascual (DAY-vihd kahr-DUHS ee pahs-KUHL) was born to Jaume and Ferranda Pascual Cardús. His mother died when he was only eleven years old. Cardús went to secondary school at the Institut-Escola de la Generalitat de Catalunya in Barcelona, Spain, in 1938. Because of the Spanish Civil War, he had to travel back and forth from Spain to France in order to complete his higher education. He earned both B.A. and B.S. degrees from the University of Montpellier in France in 1942.

Cardús returned to Spain to serve in the army for four years and then to attend medical school at the University of Barcelona. He completed his internship through the University of Barcelona's Hospital Clinico and performed his respiratory disease residency at the Barcelona Sanatorio del Puig d'Olena. Following this training, Cardús received funding from the French government for a two-year cardiology fellowship in Paris. At the end of the fellowship, Cardús once again returned to Spain, where in 1956 he earned a postgraduate cardiology degree at the University of Barcelona's School of Cardiology. He received a second fellowship at the Royal Infirmary at the University of Manchester, England.

Life's Work

Cardús moved to the United States after completion of his fellowships. From 1957 to 1960, he was a research associate at the Lovelace Foundation, an organization based in Albuquerque, New Mexico, that assessed astronauts' physical preparedness for flight. Cardús began working with the National Aeronautics and Space Administration (NASA) in 1958. Through both NASA and Lovelace, Cardús helped select the first astronauts for the space program by providing medical evaluations. He additionally assisted in the health monitoring of the first seven astronauts in space during Project Mercury.

After leaving the Lovelace Foundation, Cardús accepted a teaching position at Baylor College of Medicine's Institute for Rehabilitation and Research in Houston, Texas. He began as a lecturer for the Physiology and Rehabilitation Departments and would eventually become professor of physical medicine and rehabilitation, remaining at the college from 1960 to 1999. He also was appointed head of the Department of Biomathematics, a field that applies mathematical principles to the understanding of biological functions, and he ran the exercise and cardiopulmonary laboratories. While at Baylor College, Cardús's research focused on advances in computer technology and mathematical programs in physical rehabilitation. He recorded respiratory data through digitalized computer programs rather than through hand calculations.

Cardús earned a doctorate in mathematics for life scientists from the University of Michigan at Ann Arbor in 1966. He lectured at Rice University in Houston, Texas, through the Department of Statistics and Mathematical Science and as an adjunct professor of physiology from 1970 to1988. Cardús also served as a planning consultant for the United States Public Health Service, and in this position he helped to design and construct health facilities.

In the 1990's, he was involved in a joint effort with NASA and the Texas Medical Center at Baylor College, in which his team developed a spinning centrifuge to simulate gravity. Although the spinning centrifuge was originally created to test the effects of space on an astronaut's muscles, such as the heart, Cardús used this invention to study other patient populations, such as those with spinal cord or cardiovascular injuries. He found that this centrifuge improved the sitting and standing tolerance of these patients.

Cardús's awards and honors include a gold medal from the United States International Congress of Physical Medicine and Rehabilitation (1972), the Elizabeth and Sidney Licht Award for Excellence in Scientific Writing (1981), the Narcis Monturiol Medal for scientific and technical merit (1984), and an honorary doctorate from the University of Barcelona (1993). He published numerous peer-reviewed scientific journal articles, edited the book *Rehabilitation in Ischemic Heart Disease* (1983), and wrote the introduction to *A Hispanic Look at the Bicentennial* (1976). Cardús was an active member of professional and cultural societies in both the United States and Spain, serving as vice chair of the Gordon Conference on Biomathematics (1970), president of the International Society for Gravitational Physiology (1993), president of Spanish Professionals in America, and chairman of the board of the Institute of Hispanic Culture. In 1970, he founded the American Institute for Catalan Studies (1979).

Cardús married Francesca Ribas in 1951, and the couple had four children. Cardús became an American citizen in 1969. He died of a stroke on June 2, 2003, at the age of eighty, and his ashes were scattered in the Mediterranean Sea after an official Catalonian ceremony.

SIGNIFICANCE

Cardús had the foresight to integrate computer technology and mathematical programs into medical care decades before the field of telemedicine gained popularity. His groundbreaking work with NASA laid the foundation for an understanding of the physical effects of space on the human body. Although he became an American citizen, Cardús continued to advocate for the Catalonian community both from a cultural and educational perspective. His research was based in the United States, but he was involved with the Spanish community by using computer technology to collect and share data for experiments between Spain and America. Likewise, he created the American Institute for Catalan Studies aimed at educating American citizens about the importance of Catalan culture.

Janet Ober Berman

FURTHER READING

Cardús, David, and Lawrence Newton. "Development of a Computer Technique for the On-Line Processing of Respiratory Variables." *Computers in Biology and Medicine* 1, no. 2 (December, 1970): 125-131. Study comparing the older techniques of collecting patient respiration information with a new computer program that allowed patient data to be digitalized by the computer.

Guerrero, Richard. "A Man of Science." *Catalonia Today* (November, 2003): 21-24. Article detailing Cardús's professional research and achievements, as well as his devotion to Catalonian culture.

Wendler, Rhonda. "Out of This World Research Seeks to Improve Health on Earth." *Texas Medical Center News* 23, no. 19. (October, 2001). Retrieved January 12, 2011 from http://www.tmc.edu/tmc-news/10_15_01/page_02.html. Article lists joint research studies, including Cardús's work with the Texas Medical Center and NASA.

See also: Francisco Ayala; Baruj Benacerraf; Teresa Bernardez.

Rod Carew

Panamanian-born baseball player

Carew enjoyed a Hall of Fame career in Major League Baseball. He played both first base and second base for the Minnesota Twins and ended his career with the California Angels. After his playing career, he served as a coach with the Milwaukee Brewers. Carew will long be remembered as one of baseball's greatest hitters.

Latino heritage: Panamanian

Born: October 1, 1945; Gatun, Panama Canal Zone (now Panama)

Also known as: Rodney Cline Carew; Cline Carew; Sir Rodney

Areas of achievement: Baseball; activism

Early Life

Rodney Cline Carew (cah-ROO) was born on a train in Gatun, Panama Canal Zone, the second son of Eric and Olga Carew. Three sisters completed the family. Olga was traveling by train to a Panama City clinic to give birth to Carew when she went into labor. She was riding in one of the back cars of the train, those reserved for people of color. A white physician, Dr. Rodney Cline, delivered the baby, and the grateful Olga gave her son his name. Although he would achieve athletic fame as Rod Carew, his family always called him Cline.

The Carews were poor. Eric worked as a painter on the Panama Canal, and Olga was a domestic worker. Eric's drinking and abusive behavior made Carew's home life miserable, as he was never able to meet his father's demands and was the child most likely to bear the brunt of his father's rage. Carew's mother was the most important influence in his life. An uncle, Joseph French, who was also his Little League coach, served as a father figure and took up for Carew on the rare occasions when his mother had to discipline him. From his early childhood, Carew loved baseball; he joined the local Little League as soon as he was old enough. Prior to that, he sometimes had to play with balls made from balled up paper tightly wrapped with tape. He hit the balls with a broom handle and used a paper bag as a glove.

Olga eventually left Eric and emigrated with her children to New York when Carew was fourteen years old. Instead of playing on his high school team, he was able to play semiprofessional baseball with the Bronx Cavaliers and was spotted by a Minnesota talent scout. Carew signed with the Minnesota Twins the day after his high school graduation in 1964. He played three seasons in the minor leagues and was called up to the major league team in 1967.

Life's Work

In his early years in Major League Baseball, Carew faced racial discrimination but learned to ignore it and concentrate on his game. That discrimination turned to death threats when he and his Jewish fiancée, Marilynn Levy, announced their engagement. He and Levy married in 1970 and had three daughters: Charryse, Stephanie, and Michelle. Although they raised their daughters in the Jewish faith, Carew has remained true to his Protestant roots and attends the Camelback Baptist Church near his California home.

As a baseball player, Carew is best known for his batting. Over the course of his career, he came close to batting .400 and consistently had an average in the high .300's. When he retired, his lifetime batting average

Rod Carew. (Getty Images Sport/Getty Images)

was .328. Interestingly, Carew threw right-handed while batting left-handed.

In an illustrious career spanning nearly two decades, Carew spent twelve years with the Minnesota Twins and his final six with California Angels. Among his many awards, he was named rookie of the year in 1967, an achievement he followed by being selected as an All-Star eighteen times. He also received the 1977 American League most valuable player award after batting .388 for the season. Carew recorded the 3,000th base hit of his career in 1985 in a game against the Twins. Carew was also an accomplished base runner and base stealer who successfully stole home seventeen times. He remains one of the all-time leaders in All-Star votes.

A Baseball Hall of Fame inductee in 1991, Carew's first year of eligibility, he was only the twenty-second player to be inducted on his first ballot. Because Carew served six years in the military as a Marine Reserve combat engineer, he also was inducted into the United States Marine Corps Sports Hall of Fame.

When the Angels retired his number, 29, in 1991, Carew became one of only three major league players to have his number retired by two teams. The Minnesota Twins had retired his number (also 29) four years earlier, in 1987. Both professionally and personally, Carew is held in high regard. Former Twins manager Gene Mauch said, "As impressed as I am with Rod Carew the hitter, Rod Carew the baseball player, I am more impressed with Rod Carew the man." After he retired as a player, Carew remained involved in baseball, becoming part of the Twins' executive management team. In addition, he is an adviser to the Office of the Commissioner of Baseball.

In mid-1990's, Carew was spurred to activism by his daughter Michelle's battle with leukemia. Michelle's mixed Russian, Jewish, and Panamanian/West Indian heritage made it extremely difficult to find a matching bone-marrow donor. After her death in 1996, Carew became a board member and spokesman for the Marrow Foundation and has encouraged people—particularly African Americans and Latinos—to register as donors.

Carew also runs the Rod Carew Baseball School in Placentia, California, which he founded in 1986. While the venture originally was intended for children, it has emerged as a popular resource for baseball professionals in search of hitting instruction. Carew's marriage to Marilynn Levy ended in divorce in 2000. A year later, he married his second wife, Rhonda.

Great Players Who Never Reached the World Series

Many great players have spent their entire careers trying in vain to reach the World Series. Rod Carew is considered one of the the best of these players and certainly the best hitter to never play in baseball's championship series. He is in good company: Ernie Banks, Joe Torre, Sammy Sosa, Lee Smith, Frank Thomas, Rafael Palmeiro, Andre Dawson, Edgar Martínez, and Ken Griffey, Jr., are among the retired greats whose teams always fell short of the World Series. Carew leads the pack in All-Star Game appearances; his nearest competitor, Griffey, had thirteen. Most of these players also won most valuable player (MVP) honors—Banks and Thomas received the award twice. Carew was named American League MVP in 1977. Carew and Dawson are the only members of this group who were named rookie of the year.

Significance

Carew's legacy encompasses both his successful baseball career and his tireless work in support of pediatric cancer research and treatment. He was profoundly affected by his daughter's struggle with acute nonlymphocytic leukemia. His public appeal for a bone marrow donor, a cause taken up by the United States Postal Service, led more than seventy thousand people to register as potential donors, but no match was found for Michelle. Her death spurred him to action. After he addressed Congress in 1996, $50 million was appropriated for research into pediatric cancer; his annual Rod Carew Children's Cancer Golf Classic continues to raise funds for the cause as well.

Norma Lewis

Further Reading

Brackin, Dennis, and Patrick Reusse. *Minnesota Twins: The Complete Illustrated History*. St. Paul, Minn.: MBI, 2010. This exhaustive resource includes information on Carew and many more stars from the team's history.

Carew, Rod, and Ira Berkow. *Carew*. 1979. Rev. ed. Minneapolis: University of Minnesota Press, 2010. A straightforward account of Carew's early life of poverty, racial discrimination, and ultimate success.

Carew, Rod, Armen Keteyian, and Frank Pace. *Rod Carew's Art and Science of Hitting*. New York: Penguin, 1986. This is an excellent how-to on what is arguably baseball's hardest skill to master.

Wallace, Joseph E. *Grand Old Game: 365 Days of Baseball*. Foreword by Rod Carew. New York: Harry N. Abrams, 2004. An ambitious book of baseball images from the National Baseball Hall of Fame, covering more than a century.

Wendell, Tim, and José Luis Villegas. *Far From Home: Latino Baseball Players in America*. Washington, D.C.: National Geographic Society, 2008. Examines the careers of major league players from Latin America.

See also: Felipe Alou; Luis Aparicio; César Cedeño; Dave Concepción; Tony Oliva; Rafael Palmeiro; Sammy Sosa; Luis Tiant.

Mariah Carey

American singer and actor

Best known for her extraordinary vocal range and her record-setting record sales, Carey has had a successful, multifaceted career as a singer, songwriter, actor, and entrepreneur. She also has been recognized for her philanthropic work.

Latino heritage: Venezuelan
Born: March 27, 1970; Huntington, Long Island, New York
Also known as: Mariah Angela Carey
Areas of achievement: Music; acting

Early Life

Mariah Angela Carey was born on March 27, 1970, in Huntington, New York, to Patricia Carey (née Hickey) and Alfred Roy Carey and was named after the song "They Call the Wind Mariah," from the Broadway musical *Paint Your Wagon* (1951). Patricia, an opera singer and vocal coach, is Irish American; Alfred, an aeronautical engineer, was of African and Venezuelan ancestry, and his father changed his surname from Nuñez to Carey upon arriving in the United States. The Carey family was subjected to racial prejudice and occasional violence that caused them to move several times; the stress eventually led to Patricia and Alfred's divorce when Carey was three years old. Carey's sister Alison moved in with their father, while Carey and her brother Morgan remained with their mother.

Carey demonstrated an early interest in music: When she was only three years old, Patricia discovered her daughter attempting to imitate her as she sang from Giuseppe Verdi's opera *Rigoletto* (1851). As a result, Patricia began teaching Carey how to develop her vocal talent, and at the age of six, Carey gave her first public performance. She quickly became involved in the New York music scene, missing so many days as a student at Harborfields High School that she was nicknamed "Mirage" by her peers. After graduating from high school, Carey moved to New York, working several part-time jobs and completing five hundred hours of cosmetology school while trying to forge her music career. Carey eventually found work as a backup singer for Brenda K. Starr, and it was Starr who gave Columbia Records executive Tommy Mottola a copy of Carey's demo tape. Mottola offered Carey a record deal within the week.

Mariah Carey. (AP Photo)

Her eponymous debut album was released in 1990 to enormous commercial success.

Life's Work

Carey's debut album spawned four hit singles and garnered her two Grammy Awards. It was the best-selling album in the United States in 1991. The title track from her second album, *Emotions* (1991), became Carey's record-setting fifth consecutive number-one single. Her next album, *MTV Unplugged* (1992), was recorded during an appearance on MTV's acoustic-music show and featured a cover of the Jackson Five single "I'll Be There" that quickly became another number-one hit.

Carey and Mottola started dating while she worked on her debut album and were married in a lavish ceremony—modeled on the wedding of Princess Diana and Prince Charles—at St. Thomas Episcopal Church in Manhattan on June 5, 1993. That same year, Carey released her third album, *Music Box*, which produced the hit singles "Dreamlover" and "Hero," and began her first U.S. tour.

"All I Want for Christmas Is You," from Carey's 1994 album, *Merry Christmas*, became one of her best-selling singles to date. Her fourth studio album, *Daydream* (1995), deviated from her previous pop sound and contained more hip-hop and rhythm-and-blues influences, including a remix of her single "Fantasy" with rapper Ol' Dirty Bastard from Wu Tang Clan. The then-controversial collaboration proved successful, and many credit Carey for influencing the now-common practice of combining the musical styles. Other successful singles from the record include "One Sweet Day," a collaboration with Boyz II Men, which spent sixteen weeks at the top of the *Billboard* charts, and "Always Be My Baby," which became Carey's eleventh number-one single in the United States and was nominated for a Grammy Award for Best Female R&B Performance.

In 1997, Carey and Mottola separated, and a year later, they divorced. Carey's next album, *Butterfly* (1997), continued her successful run. Its first single, "Honey," featured a more provocative Carey in both fashion and musical style. Carey also began composing songs for film sound tracks and released an album of number-one hits alongside some new music (*#1's*, 1998). "When You Believe," a duet with Whitney Houston, was featured on the sound track for the animated film *The Prince of Egypt* (1998).

Carey's sixth studio album, 1999's *Rainbow*, was her final recording with Columbia Records and her lowest-selling album to date. She began taking acting lessons and auditioning for roles, eventually making her film debut with a small role in *The Bachelor* (1999). Carey was honored with *Billboard*'s Artist of the Decade award in 1999, and received a World Music Award for best-selling female artist of the millennium before signing a new contract with EMI's Virgin Records.

By 2001, Carey's grueling schedule had taken a toll on her health. She checked into a hospital to treat what her publicist described as "an emotional and physical breakdown." Carey next starred in the film *Glitter* (2001), which was widely panned, and the soundtrack failed to match Carey's previous success, prompting EMI/Virgin to buy out the remainder of her contract in 2002. Later that year, Carey signed a new deal with Island Records, and her father died of cancer; *Charmbracelet* (2002), her first album on the Island label, received mixed reviews and included a song dedicated to him.

In 2005, Carey's tenth studio album, *The Emancipation of Mimi*, became a critical and commercial success. It was the year's best-selling album in the United States and garnered Carey three more Grammy wins. "Touch My Body," the lead single from Carey's next album, *E = MC²* (2008), catapulted Carey past Elvis Presley as the artist with the most number-one singles; however, it did not sell as well as her previous album. On April 30, 2008, Carey married actor and rapper Nick Cannon at her Bahamian estate; the following year, she released her twelfth studio album, *Memoirs of an Imperfect Angel*, and began her seventh concert tour. In 2010, Carey released a second Christmas album, *Merry*

Sales of Carey's Recordings

Mariah Carey was the best-selling female performer of the 1990's in the United States, and by 2011, she had sold more than 200 million singles, albums, and music videos worldwide. Carey was recognized as the best-selling pop female artist of the millennium at the 2000 World Music Awards. Carey also was the first female artist in the United States to have eight albums go platinum five times or more. Her album *Merry Christmas* (1994) has sold more than12 million copies to date, making it one of the top-selling holiday albums of all time. Carey surpassed Elvis Presley's record in 2008 when "Touch My Body" became her eighteenth *Billboard* Top 100 hit; by 2011, Carey had the most number one Hot 100's of any female artist, and *Billboard* dubbed her single "We Belong Together" the top song of the first decade of the twenty-first century.

Christmas II You, and announced that she was pregnant with twins. The twins, Moroccan and Monroe, were born in April, 2011.

Significance

Carey's vocals have influenced numerous other singers both in the United States and abroad, and she often is credited for bringing hip-hop and rhythm-and-blues styles into mainstream pop music. Carey also is recognized for her songwriting—a skill that set her apart from some of her musical contemporaries—and her significant record of album sales. Despite an inauspicious beginning, Carey's acting skills also have garnered her attention, and she won critical acclaim for her supporting role in the film *Precious: Based on the Novel "Push" by Sapphire* (2009). Carey's philanthropic activity includes work with organizations such as the Fresh Air Fund and the Make-a-Wish Foundation.

Anastasia Pike

Further Reading

Nickson, Chris. *Mariah Carey Revisited: Her Story*. New York: St. Martin's Press, 1998. This unauthorized biography provides a good starting point for learning about Carey's life and early career.

Norment, Lynn. "Mariah Carey: Singer Talks About Storybook Marriage, Interracial Heritage and Sudden Fame." *Ebony* (April, 1994). A wide-ranging profile covering Carey's life through mid-career.

Sapet, Kerrily. *Mariah Carey: Singer, Songwriter, Record Pruducer, and Actress*. Broomall, Pa.: Mason Crest, 2010. This biography for younger readers offers an overview of Carey's career and life.

Shapiro, Marc. *Mariah Carey: The Unauthorized Biography*. Toronto: ECW Press, 2001. An easy-to-read biography accompanied by color photographs.

See also: Jennifer Lopez; Ricky Martin; Jon Secada; Selena; Jaci Velasquez.

Richard Henry Carmona

American physician and United States surgeon general (2002-2006)

Carmona became only the second person of Hispanic ancestry to hold the title of United States Surgeon General. Through this position, he fought to reduce healthcare disparities and issued a groundbreaking report concerning the harmful health effects of secondhand smoke.

Latino heritage: Puerto Rican

Born: November 22, 1949; New York, New York

Areas of achievement: Medicine; government and politics; military

Early Life

Richard Henry Carmona (kahr-MOH-nah) was the oldest of four children born to Puerto Rican parents Raoul and Lucy Carmona. The family lived in a small home in Harlem, New York. Although his home life was unstable, Carmona's parents were hard-working and caring people, and his grandmother was a positive force in his life. He attended DeWitt Clinton High School but dropped out at the age of sixteen.

Carmona earned a general equivalency diploma while serving in the United States Army (1967-1970). He advanced through the Army by joining the Special Forces, where he became a medic. Carmona fought in the Vietnam War as a Green Beret, earning a Bronze Star, two Purple Hearts, the Combat Medical Badge, and a Vietnam Service Medal.

After completion of his military service, Carmona attempted to enroll in college but was not immediately accepted. Instead, he earned his associate of arts degree in nursing from Bronx Community College. He paid for school by working as a registered nurse and paramedic and credits this training with educating him about disparities in health care.

Carmona matriculated to the University of California at San Francisco (UCSF), where he was awarded his bachelor of science degree in biology and chemistry in 1976. Carmona's achievement made him the first individual in his family to graduate college. Three years later he earned his medical degree from the same institution, the only person in the class to graduate one year early. Carmona was the top graduate in his class.

Upon completion of medical school, Carmona was accepted for a residency in general and vascular surgery at UCSF. He also obtained a fellowship from the National Institutes of Health concentrating on burns, trauma, and critical care.

Richard Henry Carmona. (Getty Images)

LIFE'S WORK

Carmona relocated to Arizona to create the area's first regional trauma center. He became director of trauma services for Tucson Medical Center in 1985. Carmona also accepted positions as physician for the Pima County Sheriff's Department and leader of their special weapons and tactics (SWAT) team and served as chairman of the state's Southern Regional Emergency Medical System. Carmona was named professor of surgery, public health, and family and community medicine at the University of Arizona in 1985 as well. While working, he received his master's degree in public health from the university in 1998. Carmona served as chief executive officer of the Pima County health care system from 1997 to 1999.

Carmona's wide range of experience in medicine, public health, and the military led President George W. Bush to appoint him the seventeenth surgeon general of the United States in 2002. Carmona was only the second Latino to hold this title. His goals were to promote cultural understanding and to increase international sharing of health care knowledge. He addressed issues such as increasing health literacy, decreasing obesity, and better publicizing the importance of prenatal care and childhood development. As surgeon general, Carmona issued several reports, the most notable of which regarded the harmful health effects of secondhand smoking. Although it met with resistance from the Bush administration, this report led to the banning of indoor smoking at public locations such as restaurants and bars. Carmona desired to publish many more reports on topics such as stem-cell research and emergency contraception, but he later testified in Congress that the Bush administration interfered with his ability to speak publicly about these controversial issues.

After serving his term as surgeon general, Carmona accepted a position as vice chairman of the Canyon Ranch resort and spa company in Tucson, Arizona. He became president of the Canyon Ranch Institute, a nonprofit organization that focuses on preventive health care.

Carmona's numerous awards and honors include being named Top Cop by the National Association of Police Organizations, SWAT Officer of the Year, and Pima County (Arizona) Physician of the Year. Carmona is a fellow of the American College of Surgeons. He sits on the board of trustees for Ross University School of Medicine and Clorox. He also is chairman of the Partnership to Fight Chronic Disease and Strategies to Overcome and Prevent (STOP) Obesity.

Carmona and met his wife, Diana Sanchez, in high school. The couple has two daughters and two sons.

SIGNIFICANCE

A high school dropout, Carmona persevered to earn his medical degree and become one of the top public health officials in the country. His training and experience in the military, emergency medicine, bioterrorism, and law enforcement provided him with the depth and breadth of knowledge necessary for the creation of effective public health policies. He continues to advocate for the reduction of health disparities in the medical field.

Janet Ober Berman

FURTHER READING

Carmona, Richard Henry. "Been There, Done That." Interview by James Mattson. *Reflections on Nursing Leadership*, First Quarter, 2005, 10-36. A candid interview with Carmona regarding his family upbringing, educational challenges, and why he continues to support nurses as leaders in the medical field.

Dusenberry, Mary Branham. "Butts Out." *State News*, August, 2007, 16-19. Article detailing the impact of Carmona's report on the effects of secondhand smoke.

Harris, Gardiner. "Surgeon General Sees Four-Year Term as Compromised." *The New York Times*, July 11, 2007. Describes the tension between Carmona and the Bush administration regarding off-limits health topics during Carmona's term.

See also: John F. Alderete; Norma Martinez-Rogers; Antonia Novello.

Vikki Carr

American singer

Carr has had a successful singing career in both English and her Spanish. She took American popular music by storm in 1967 with her hit "It Must Be Him," the first of her many recordings to be certified gold. Also a stage actor, Carr has appeared in theater productions around the country.

Latino heritage: Mexican

Born: July 19, 1941; El Paso, Texas

Also known as: Florencia Bisenta de Casillas Martínez Cardona

Areas of achievement: Music; philanthropy

Early Life

Vikki Carr was born Florencia Bisenta de Casillas Martínez Cardona in El Paso, Texas, on July 19, 1941. She was the first of seven children born to Mexican immigrants Carlos Cardona and Florencia Martínez. Her father was a self-taught construction engineer, her mother a homemaker. When funds were low, Florencia would harvest wild berries and edible cacti to help feed her large family. The Cardona family moved to California, in the San Gabriel Valley region, where Carr grew up. Carlos was a strict but loving father, and his children nicknamed him "the priest" because of his tendency to preach to them about their behavior and his expectations for them. It was a tight-knit, devoutly Catholic family.

Carr's musical talent became evident at age five when she sang Christmas carols in Latin in a school pageant. Always a good student, she took college-preparatory classes in high school but abandoned her dream of attending college. Feeling duty-bound, she went to work in a local bank after high school to help support the family.

Carr gradually began to consider music as a potential career. Since childhood, she had performed in various school and church choirs. She began her vocal career in nightclubs in and around Los Angeles. After gaining both confidence and experience, she joined Pepe Callahan's Mexican American band, choosing Carlita—the feminine version of her father's name, Carlos—as her stage name. Eventually she left the band and performed solo in Las Vegas, Reno, and other Nevada venues. Her rich, smooth voice, at once sweet and sensual, made her popular wherever she performed. Carr received her first recording contract in 1961. Her first major recording, 1966's "He's a Rebel," became a hit in Australia before she was discovered by American audiences.

Life's Work

The recording that launched Carr to stardom in the United States was her 1967 song "It Must Be Him." The

Vikki Carr. (AP Photo)

single climbed the charts and soon went gold. "It Must Be Him" remains the song audiences most closely associate with Carr. She won Grammy Awards that year in three categories: Best Contemporary Female Solo Vocalist, Album of the Year, and Best Female Vocal Performance. Carr also was chosen to give a royal command performance for Queen Elizabeth II. It would be her first of two performances for the British monarch.

The early years of Carr's career coincided with the Vietnam War, and the patriotic singer took great pride in traveling to that country to entertain U.S. troops with actor Danny Kaye. The two spent fourteen grueling days giving multiple performances for as many as ten thousand soldiers at a time.

Carr hosted musical television shows, including her own Christmas special, and was the first woman to guest host *The Tonight Show Starring Johnny Carson*. During the heyday of the television variety show, she made guest appearances on many series, including *The Carol Burnett Show*, *The Jackie Gleason Show*, and *The Dean Martin Show*.

In an international career that has spanned five decades, Carr has performed for five presidents: Richard Nixon, Gerald Ford, Ronald Reagan, George H. W. Bush, and Bill Clinton. President Ford, when asked to name his favorite Mexican dish, laughingly answered, "Vikki Carr."

Carr has performed for standing-room-only audiences in Japan, Australia, France, Britain, Germany, the Netherlands, and Mexico. She has recorded in both English and Spanish.

Throughout her music career, Carr has acted in community theater productions around the country, mostly doing musicals. She was critically acclaimed for her performance as Nellie Forbush in *South Pacific* at the Starlight Theater in Kansas City in 1966. Other shows in which she has appeared include *The Unsinkable Molly Brown* and *I'm Getting My Act Together and Taking It on the Road*. She also appeared in Carnegie Hall as part of a Judy Garland tribute. Carr has guest-starred in a number of popular television series, including *Baywatch*, *Fantasy Island*, and *The Mod Squad*, as well as HBO's made-for-television film *Mrs. Harris*.

Carr was honored with a star on the Hollywood Walk of Fame in 1981. Her personal life includes three marriages, two of which ended in divorce.

Significance

Carr has had a prolific career spanning five decades; stage and screen; and musical styles including pop, country, Latin, and mariachi. She has performed for heads of state in the United States, Mexico, and Europe. She also is an active philanthropist. In 1971, she established the Vikki Carr Scholarship Foundation, a nonprofit organization that awards financial assistance to deserving Latino students in California and Texas. Carr also is involved in causes including the American Lung Foundation and St. Jude's Children's Hospital.

Norma Lewis

Pressure to Change Hispanic Names in the Entertainment Industry

Florencia Bisenta de Casillas Martínez Cardona became Vikki Carr because of a form of discrimination practiced in the 1960's when she began her career in the American music industry. Because Carr was blue-eyed, blonde, and fair-skinned, record-label executives gave her a name that would obscure her Mexican American roots. Latino musicians and actors were routinely pressured to Anglicize their names or else settle for limiting their opportunities. Conventional wisdom had it that American audiences would not appreciate "foreign" talent, and if she used some variation of her birth name, Carr would have been considered foreign despite her El Paso, Texas, birth. Latinos in entertainment at that time also were required to shed their accents. Despite her name change, Carr remained proud of her heritage and, in most performances, shared her birth name with her audience.

Further Reading

Munson, Sammye. *Today's Tejano Heroes*. Austin, Tex.: Eakin Press, 1999. A short, easy-to-read look at the accomplishments of fifteen Texas-connected Latinos, including Carr.

Otfinoski, Steven. "Vikki Carr." In *Latinos in the Arts*. New York: Facts On File, 2007. Contains a brief overview of Carr's life, career, and significance to the music and entertainment industries.

Tawa, Nicholas E. *Supremely American: Popular Song in the Twentieth Century—Styles, Singers, and Milieus, and How They Reflected American Society*. Lanham, Md.: Scarecrow Press, 2005. A look at the popular music scene in which Carr was hugely successful.

See also: Gloria Estefan; Julio Iglesias; Trini López; Linda Ronstadt; Ritchie Valens.

Barbara Carrasco

American artist and educator

Carrasco is an award-winning artist and muralist whose works have been exhibited in museums and at conventions worldwide. Carrasco's work is particularly displayed in the Unites States, Europe, and Latin America. Aside from creating artwork, Carrasco has also taught at multiple American universities.

Latino heritage: Mexican

Born: 1955; El Paso, Texas

Areas of achievement: Art; education; social issues

Early Life

Barbara Carrasco (kah-RAHS-koh) was born in 1955 in El Paso, Texas. As a child, she was raised in the predominantly Mexican American, African American, and immigrant housing projects of Culver City, California. From first grade through eighth grade, she attended a Catholic school, where she felt the nuns treated white students better than Latino students. At this young age, Carrasco became aware of the difficulties she would face in life because of her skin color, ethnicity, and gender.

After graduating high school, Carrasco began attending West Los Angeles College. During this time, it was rare for Chicanas to receive any education beyond high school and even more rare for Chicanos to study art. Much of the art produced by Chicanos was considered primitive; however, many well-known Latino and Chicano artists now hold advanced degrees in the arts.

In 1976, Carrasco graduated from West Los Angeles College with her associate of arts degree. She immediately enrolled at the University of California at Los Angeles, from which she earned her bachelor of fine arts degree in 1978. After graduating, Carrasco traveled to Mexico, where she was able to meet many of renowned artist Frida Kahlo's students and read Kahlo's biography. This trip made a huge impact on Carrasco's life and served as a major source of inspiration for the young artist. She was heavily influenced by Kahlo's self-portraits and began drawing pictures of her own face. Carrasco sees this as a way to explore her autobiography while simultaneously repossessing her Chicana heritage. Her self-portraits also often examine her Catholic upbringing with satire and humor.

Life's Work

Although she took a break from school after receiving her bachelor's degree, Carrasco soon resumed her education. In 1991, she graduated from the California Institute of the Arts with a master of fine arts degree. From 1976 to 1991, Carrasco created banners for the United Farm Workers. She later produced a well-known portrait of UFW leader Dolores Huerta (*Dolores*, 1999). Carrasco also has painted murals in Leningrad and Armenia for the Union of Soviet Socialist Republics (1985 and 1987) and created the computer-animated piece *PESTICIDES!* for the Spectacolor light board in Times Square (1989). Since her graduation in 1991, Carrasco has exhibited her work not only in the United States but also in Europe and parts of Latin America.

Carrasco's style of work includes painting and murals that display and represent Chicano art, U.S. contemporary political art, U.S. public art, and women's cultural production. Carrasco often emphasizes skin color in her paintings to depict her experiences as a light-skinned Chicana stuck in a racial limbo. One piece in particular, *Self-Portrait* (1994), addresses Carrasco's feelings about her light skin.

Carrasco has received a number of awards, honors, and grants, including a fellowship from the J. Paul Getty Fund for the Visual Arts (1988); a Window Grant for Literature from the Los Angeles Cultural Affairs Department (1990); a Rockefeller Foundation artist grant (1992); an Andy Warhol Foundation artist grant (1992); and the Los Angeles Cultural Affairs Department's City of Los Angeles award (2000).

In 1993, Carrasco married writer, photographer, and video artist Harry Gamboa, with whom she had a daughter in 1994. One year later, Carrasco received a diagnosis of lymphoma; she underwent a bone-marrow transplant in 1996. Her illness briefly put a halt to her work, but in 1999, Carrasco returned to active participation in the art world. She also has worked as an art professor at the University of California, Riverside; University of California, Santa Barbara; and Loyola Marymount University.

Significance

Carrasco has exhibited her work around the world. After battling cancer, she reflected on her illness and mortality in a survey exhibition at the Vincent Price Art Museum at East Los Angeles College titled "Barbara Carrasco: A Brush with Life" (2008). Through her work, Carrasco examines issues of race, gender, identity, politics, class, sexuality, and social injustices. Known for her ballpoint-pen drawings as well as her large-scale murals and paintings, Carrasco is an activist and contributor to the iconography representing Chicana feminists.

Macey M. Freudensprung

FURTHER READING

Brown, Betty Ann. "Autobiographical Imagery in the Art of Los Angeles Women." In *Yesterday and Tomorrow: California Women Artists*, edited by Sylvia Moore. New York: Midmarch Arts Press. 1989. Describes Carrasco's youth and how it influenced her art career.

Shorris, Earl. *Latinos: A Biography of the People*. New York: W. W. Norton, 1992. Notes the origins and history of Latino culture from the first arrivals in America through the close of the twentieth century; includes information on Carrasco's role and significance.

Venegas, Sybil. "Brush with Life: Barbara Carrasco Powerfully Mixes Art with Race, Class, and Gender Politics." *Ms.*, Spring, 2008. This account of Carrasco's life and work includes many images of her artwork.

See also: Judith F. Baca; José Antonio Burciaga; Daniel DeSiga; Carmen Lomas Garza; Yolanda M. López; Amalia Mesa-Bains; Leo Tanguma; Jesse Treviño.

LEO CARRILLO

American actor and conservationist

Carrillo appeared in nearly all branches of show business and his career as an actor in motion pictures is celebrated with a star on the Hollywood Boulevard Walk of Fame. But equally, if not more, important was his dedication to the preservation of California's natural beauty and historic places so that everyone would have the opportunity to enjoy them. For his services to the state then-governor Edmund G. "Pat" Brown dubbed him "Mr. California."

Latino heritage: Spanish

Born: August 6, 1880; Los Angeles, California

Died: September 10, 1961; Santa Monica, California

Also known as: Leopoldo Antonio Carrillo; Mr. California

Areas of achievement: Acting; theater; social issues; philanthropy

EARLY LIFE

The scion of an old, distinguished California family, Leopold Antonio Carrillo (cah-REE-oh) was born in Los Angeles in 1880. His great-great-grandfather had emigrated from Spain to San Diego, California, where Carrillo spent many of his formative years. His great-grandfather was the provisional governor of California, a great-uncle was three times mayor of Los Angeles, and his father, Juan José Carrillo, served as the police chief and then mayor of Santa Monica, California. Carrillo's family wanted him to consider the priesthood, but he opted to attend college and earn a degree in engineering. He worked on a railroad construction crew to finance his education.

Leo Carrillo. (Getty Images)

LIFE'S WORK

Carrillo was destined to find his fulfillment in various creative endeavors. A talented caricaturist, he pursued a career as a newspaper political cartoonist and was hired by *The San Francisco Examiner*. While employed there, he became friendly with its publisher, William Randolph Hearst, and much later was involved with the fate of Hearst's home in San Simeon. Carrillo soon became interested in show business and performed in vaudeville shows for several years, utilizing his talent for mimicry and dialects. His cousin William Gaxton (born Arturo Gaxiola) became an important Broadway musical star and sometime film actor. Carrillo also went on the legitimate stage in the mid-1910's and appeared in some fifteen productions by 1927. Among the plays in which he appeared were *Lombardi, Ltd.* and *Twin Beds*.

With the advent of sound in film, Broadway actors were sought after for their presumed ability to speak well into microphones. Carrillo entered films in 1927 in an early Vitaphone sound short, made a few other short films, and then went on to appear as a character actor in about ninety feature films by 1950. His first full-length feature was 1929's *Mister Antonio*, based on a play in which he had appeared. In most of his roles, he played Mexican, Italian, and other Latin-type characters in the overly broad, comedic manner that came to be considered stereotypical and crude. It was how Hollywood had, for decades, portrayed people of "ethnic" backgrounds. Carrillo usually played excitable men with exaggerated accents who liberally mangled the English language.

Most of Carrillo's numerous motion pictures were B-films, but there were a few that could be called A-films. In these he generally played small supporting roles. They included *Manhattan Melodrama* (1934), *In Caliente* (1935), *History Is Made at Night* (1937), *Lillian Russell* (1940), and the 1943 version of *The Phantom of the Opera*. One important film in which he played a Latin character—but without the fractured accent—was John Ford's *The Fugitive* (1947). In his final role, in 1950, he portrayed the titular character in *Pancho Villa Returns*, one of his very few leading roles. Carrillo had previously appeared in *Viva Villa!* (1934) but not as the main character. Carrillo retired from acting in the late 1950's. For much of that decade, he had appeared as Pancho in the long-running western series *The Cisco Kid.*

A noted conservationist and preservationist with a great interest in the history of California, Carrillo purchased a large parcel of more than twenty-five hundred acres in Carlsbad, California, near San Diego, in 1937. It was known as the Rancho de los Kiotes, and he maintained it as a working ranch in the style of a Mexican hacienda. In the 1970's, after much of it had been sold off to developers, a small portion became the Leo Carrillo Ranch Historic Park.

Carrillo's marriage to Edith Haeselbarth, which lasted until 1953, produced a daughter named Antoinette. Carrillo died on September 10, 1961, in Santa Monica.

Role of Pancho in *The Cisco Kid* Series

Following other actors who had played the character in earlier films, Leo Carrillo assumed the role of the stereotypical sidekick Pancho in *The Cisco Kid* film series when it moved from Monogram Pictures to United Artists. It is now the role for which he is best known. The first picture of the series in which he appeared was *The Valiant Hombre* in 1948. The others were *The Gay Amigo* (1949), *The Daring Caballero* (1949), *Satan's Cradle* (1949), and *The Girl from San Lorenzo* (1950). In 1950, *The Cisco Kid* began a six-year run as a television series, with Carrillo continuing to play the part of Pancho. The series ultimately aired 156 episodes, some of which were shot in color. The show's star was Duncan Renaldo, who had essayed the title role in some of the films. As his sidekick, Pancho rode a horse named Loco and was handy with a bullwhip. He spoke in an exaggerated Latino accent, two of his oft-repeated lines being "Oh, Ceesco" and "Ceesco, let's went." Reportedly, in order for the television production company to obtain insurance, Carrillo claimed to be in his mid-fifties. By the time the series ended, he actually was in his mid-seventies. Although the character of the Cisco Kid first was depicted in an early twentieth century short story called *The Caballero's Way*, the character Pancho was loosely based on the comic character of Sancho Panza in Miguel de Cervantes's classic novel *Don Quixote de la Mancha* (1605, 1615). The characters also have appeared on a radio series, in comic books, and in several graphic novels.

SIGNIFICANCE

Carrillo's greatest significance probably was as a conservationist. His eighteen-year tenure on the California Beaches and Parks Commission was a distinguished one. He apparently was instrumental in California's acquisition of William Randolph Hearst's fabulous San Simeon estate, popularly known as Hearst Castle, and its preservation as a state park. He also had a hand in the establishment of the Los Angeles County Arboretum and the Anza-Borrego Desert State Park, as well as the preservation of Los Angeles's Olvera Street, an early landmark. In honor of his service, the governor appointed him as a goodwill ambassador, and he toured widely at home and abroad. Among the honors bestowed upon him was the 1959 designation of a beach area near Malibu as Leo Carrillo State Park. In addition, a school in Westminster, California, is named after him, as is the Leo Carrillo Ranch Historic Park in Carlsbad. For many years, he also supervised the production of the famed annual Fiesta de Santa Barbara. A wealthy man, Carrillo gave generously to various charities and to the restoration of California's Catholic missions.

Roy Liebman

FURTHER READING

Aaker, Everett. *Television Western Players of the Fifties: A Biographical Encyclopedia of All Regular Cast Members in Western Series, 1949-1959*. Jefferson, N.C.: McFarland, 1997. A reference book that contains an entry on Carrillo.

Carrillo, Leo. *The California I Love*. Englewood Cliffs, N.J.: Prentice-Hall, 1961. Less an autobiography than an account of the pioneering Californios, whose roots were in Mexico and who once ruled California.

Halliwell, Leslie. *Halliwell's Filmgoer's Companion*. 9th ed. New York: Charles Scribner's Sons, 1988. A well-regarded, long-running reference work that contains an entry on Carrillo.

Kindle, Alan K. *An Introduction to Carrillo Ranch: What, Where, When, Who*. Carlsbad, Calif.: City of Carlsbad Parks and Recreation Department, 1992. A history of the twenty-seven-acre Leo Carrillo Ranch Historic Park in Southern California, originally known as the Rancho de los Kiotes.

McKowen, Ken, and Dahlynn McKowen. "Leo Carrillo Ranch Historic Park: A Hollywood Star's Working Ranch." In *Best of California's Missions, Mansions, and Museums*. Berkeley, Calif.: Wilderness Press, 2006. This guidebook covers the ranch's history and significance.

Meyer, Nicholas E. *Biographical Dictionary of Hispanic Americans*. 2nd ed. New York: Facts on File, 2001. A reference book containing an article about Leo Carrillo.

See also: Dolores del Río; José Ferrer; Mel Ferrer; Fernando Lamas; Beatriz Noloesca; Ramón Novarro; Anthony Quinn; Gilbert Roland; César Romero.

LYNDA CARTER

American actor and singer

Best known as the title character from the television series Wonder Woman, *Carter became a role model for girls and women through her portrayal of a strong, proactive female character. She also has received recognition for her singing, appearing in a number of television variety specials in the 1980's and releasing a critically acclaimed jazz and blues album in 2009.*

Latino heritage: Mexican and Spanish
Born: July 24, 1951; Phoenix, Arizona
Also known as: Lynda Jean Córdova Carter
Areas of achievement: Radio and television; music

EARLY LIFE

Lynda Jean Córdova Carter was born in Phoenix, Arizona, to Juana Córdova and Colby Carter. She was the youngest of three children. Carter's mother was of Mexican and Spanish ancestry, while her father was Irish American. Carter realized at a young age that she enjoyed performing, and she began participating in talent shows and taking ballet lessons while still in elementary school.

Carter's parents divorced when she was ten years old, which had a negative financial impact on the family. Carter began working as a waitress in her early teens, but at age fourteen she found that she could make more money singing and joined a band called the Relatives that played at local restaurants. After a single semester in college, she joined another band, the Garfin Gathering, and began performing in Las Vegas and touring the United States. Carter took a break from touring to compete in a local beauty pageant in 1972, then went on to win the Miss World USA title. She reached the semifinals in the Miss World pageant. After she fulfilled her beauty pageant obligations, Carter moved to Los Angeles, California, to try her luck at acting.

Lynda Carter. (Albert L. Ortega/ PictureGroup.com via AP Images)

Life's Work

During her first few years in Los Angeles, Carter landed only a handful of guest roles on minor television shows such as *Starsky and Hutch*. She auditioned for but did not win the lead role as Wonder Woman in a 1974 television film that ultimately starred Cathy Lee Crosby. Just as Carter was about to move back to Arizona because of a lack of money, however, ABC decided to shoot a new version of the *Wonder Woman* series pilot in 1975, and producers chose Carter from among hundreds of actors to take over the role. The new pilot was a ratings success, and Carter won strong reviews for her portrayal of the strong yet vulnerable female action hero. Although it lasted for only three seasons before being canceled in 1979, the series—and Carter herself—gained something of a cult following over the subsequent decades.

In 1977, Carter married her agent, Ron Samuels, who encouraged her to market her career more aggressively. This strategy eventually led to starring appearances on several successful variety shows that allowed Carter to showcase her singing talent. In 1983, Carter starred in a television film biography of legendary actor Rita Hayworth, with whom Carter felt a great deal of kinship due in part to their shared Hispanic roots. Carter and Samuels divorced in 1982, and Carter met and married an attorney, Robert Altman, in 1984. The couple moved to the Washington, D.C., area for the sake of his work. During the following years, Carter and Altman had two children, and Carter pursued a variety of projects, making several made-for-television films and becoming a commercial spokesperson for companies such as Maybelline and Lens Express.

In 1991, Altman was accused of banking and securities fraud, resulting in a lengthy and highly publicized trial, but he ultimately was found not guilty. Carter also publicly acknowledged that she was alcoholic and underwent rehabilitation. Nonetheless, Carter continued to work. In 2002, she appeared in the comedy film *Super Troopers*, following it with small comedic roles in the 2005 films *The Dukes of Hazzard* and *Sky High*. In 2008, she received a Lifetime Achievement Award from the National Museum of Women in the Arts, and in 2009, her jazz and blues album *At Last* reached number six on the *Billboard* Top Jazz Albums chart.

Significance

Although Lynda was not widely known as a Latina actor during the height of *Wonder Woman*'s popularity, several Latinas in the entertainment industry have cited Carter as a role model. In addition to singing and acting, Carter has been active throughout her career in charitable causes such as the Susan G. Komen Foundation for breast cancer research.

Amy Sisson

Further Reading

Jarvis, Jeff. "Lynda Carter Plays Rita." *People* 20, no. 19 (November, 1983). Discusses Carter's starring role in the television film *Rita Hayworth: The Love Goddess*, highlighting the many parallels between the two women's careers, including their Latino heritage.

Marquez, Sandra. "Still Flying High." *Hispanic* 18, nos. 6/7 (June/July, 2005): 22. Retrospective interview that discusses Carter's Hispanic heritage and her significance as a role model to other Latino actors as well as to young women in general.

Wallace, David. "Lynda Carter: The Real Thing." *The Saturday Evening Post* 255, no. 4 (May/June, 1983): 42-45. Discusses Carter's early life, her success in the role of Wonder Woman, her marriage to and divorce from Ron Samuels, and her religious views.

See also: María Conchita Alonso; Coco Fusco; Rita Hayworth; Sonia Manzano; Lupe Ontiveros; Elizabeth Peña; Raquel Welch.

Lourdes Casal

Cuban-born writer, scholar, and activist

As a public intellectual, Casal contributed scholarly research and literary production in the form of poetry, essays, and fiction. Widely anthologized, Casal's work grappled with continuously evolving views on the tensions among gender, race, class, and nationality, expressing for many readers their own struggles.

Latino heritage: Cuban and Spanish

Born: April 5, 1938; Havana, Cuba

Died: February 1, 1981; Havana, Cuba

Also known as: Lourdes Emilia Irene de la Caridad Casal y Valdés

Areas of achievement: Scholarship; literature; poetry; activism

Early Life

Lourdes Emilia Irene de la Caridad Casal y Valdés (LOHR-dehs kah-SAHL) was born into a middle-class family to a physician-dentist father and an elementary schoolteacher mother. As a *china mulata* of African, Chinese, and Spanish descent, Casal experienced firsthand the class and race tensions in Cuba under Fulgencio Batista.

An ardent and accomplished student at the Universidad Católica de Santo Tomás de Villanueva, her wide-ranging interests led her from the school of engineering to psychology and on to literature and political science. While a student at university, Casal supported Fidel Castro and the anti-Batista group, but after Castro took power, she became disillusioned with the revolutionary movement. Casal belonged to the El Puente literary group and publishing house, and when it was closed for publishing "bourgeois" literature, she was among those arrested. Although she initially was in favor of the Cuban Revolution, by 1962 she had changed her mind and was opposed to Fidel Castro's government.

Casal traveled to Africa and ultimately moved to New York City, where she completed her clinical training, began teaching and writing, and became a naturalized citizen. She wrote Chinese Cuban history and anti-Castro essays and became politically active, arguing for open dialogue between the United States and Cuba. She wrote poems, stories, essays, and academic studies. She received a Ph.D. in psychology from New School for Social Research in 1975.

Life's Work

In 1972, Casal published *El caso Padilla*, a critical review of Cuba's imprisonment and censorship of dissident poet Heberto Padilla, in 1971. Many scholars assert that *El caso Padilla* signaled a change in Casal's political trajectory from opponent back to sympathizer with revolutionary Cuba. She reached out to the Cuban exile community, establishing an unprecedented rapport.

At the invitation of the Cuban government in May, 1973, Casal became the first exile to return to Cuba. Upon her return to the United States five months later, she was doubtful about the viability of democracy in Latin America, given Augusto Pinochet's coup in Chile and the problems inherent in the Cuban national process. In November and December, 1978, Casal gathered with other Cuban exiles to form the Group of Seventy-five in Havana. Castro and other Cuban officials met with the group for discussions in El Diálogo (The Dialogue), a discourse that led to the emancipation of thirty-six hundred political prisoners from Cuban jails.

Casal taught at Rutgers and the City University of New York, among other institutions. In 1972, she founded the Institute for Cuban Studies at Rutgers to promote free and open exchange between Cuba and the United States and serve as a clearinghouse for credible information on Cuba through publications, exchange programs, and art projects. Currently, the Center for Cuban Studies in New York documents Cuba's intellectual, social, historical, cultural, and political changes since the revolution. It includes the Lourdes Casal Library, which houses research materials on the visual arts, including books, periodicals, and ephemera.

Casal was in Cuba during the Mariel boatlift in the summer of 1980, at an Institute for Cuban Studies conference. While in Cuba, her health rapidly deteriorated, and she died on February 1, 1981.

Significance

Cubans on the island and those in the diaspora face an artificial but no less divisive separation, a political and cultural border, but Casal determined there should be dialogue between the two groups, worked to build bridges between them. She searched energetically for alternate ideas about Cuba's situation, believing that resuscitating communication among all Cubans, regardless of their location or politics, was paramount. To honor the memory of Casal, once a professor at Rutgers, the Department of Psychology faculty there each year select a graduating senior to receive the Lourdes Casal Memorial Award in recognition of both intellectual excellence and social commitment. It is a fitting tribute to a scholar, artist, and leader.

Jan Voogd

Further Reading

Casal, Lourdes. *Revolution and Race: Blacks in Contemporary Cuba. Latin American Program Working Paper Series* No. 39. Washington, D.C.: Woodrow Wilson International Center for Scholars, 1979. This working paper represents the distillation of Casal's scholarly reflection on the issues she also considered in her essays, poetry, and fiction.

"Lourdes Casal." In *Daughters of the Diaspora: Afra-Hispanic Writers*, edited by Miriam DeCosta-Willis. Miami, Fla.: Ian Randle, 2003. The section on Casal includes several examples of her work along with critical analysis and a brief biography.

"Lourdes Casal." In *The Norton Anthology of Latino Literature*, edited by Ilan Stavans and Edna Acosta-Belen. New York: W. W. Norton, 2011. Examines examples of Casal's poetry in the broader context of Latino literature.

Negron-Muntaner, Frances, and Yolanda Martinez-San Miguel. "In Search of Lourdes Casal's 'Ana Veldford.'" *Social Text* 25, no. 3 (2007): 57-84. Durham, N.C.: Duke University Press. This article reprints and explicates Casal's most often anthologized and enduring poem, "For Ana Veldford."

See also: Fernando Alegría; Reinaldo Arenas; Lydia Cabrera; Maria Irene Fornes; Oscar Hijuelos; Eduardo Machado.

Rosie Casals

American tennis player and women's rights activist

Best known for her aggressive style of play and diminutive size, Casals became a leader in advancing the status of female athletes through her role in the formation of the Women's Tennis Association; although she did not personally benefit from it, her efforts contributed to the equalization of prize money for women and men in 2006 in professional tennis.

Latino heritage: Salvadoran

Born: September 16, 1948; San Francisco, California

Also known as: Rosemary Casals; Rosebud

Areas of achievement: Sports; women's rights

Early Life

Rosemary Casals (kah-SAHLS) was born in San Francisco, California, to parents who had come to the United States from El Salvador. She was raised by her great uncle and aunt from an early age. It was through Manuel Casals, a former soccer player, that she was introduced to tennis on the public courts of Golden Gate State Park as a nine-year-old. Casals and her older sister, Victoria, quickly took to the game under Manuel's tutelage. However, Casals quickly surpassed her sister and spent hours improving her game through relentless practice and competitive matches against the men at the park. She was driven to become the best player in the world.

Casals was barely 5 feet tall and, unlike most other junior tennis players, did not come from a wealthy family. In response to these challenges, she developed an aggressive style of play and fiery temperament. She always sought out the best competition, even if meant playing older girls. In time, she channeled her energy into a fast, powerful, all-court game; the only weakness was her backhand, but she compensated by developing the ability to place shots.

An excellent student and an avid reader, Casals had set her academic sights on medicine. However, by age eighteen, she had become one of the best women's tennis players in the country and was mentored by the top American woman, Billie Jean Moffitt (King).

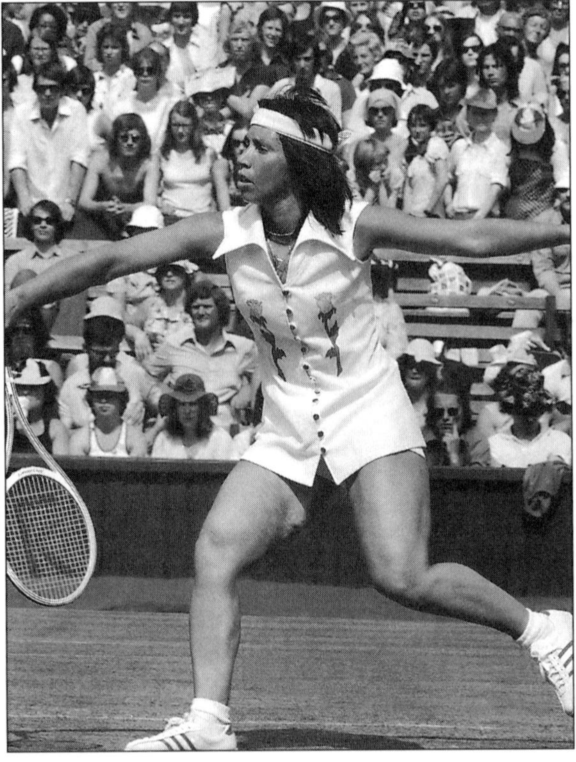

Rosie Casals. (AP Photo)

Life's Work

Casals's rise to the top of women's tennis coincided with the beginning of the Open era in professional tennis and the women's movement in society. Never fond of the tennis establishment, Casals was prominent in establishing the sport's professional presence and prestige. She was one of the first nine women to sign on with the Virginia Slims Tennis Tour (forerunner of the Women's Tennis Association) in 1970, the last year that cigarette advertising was allowed on television. Casals won the tour's inaugural tournament in Houston that year.

In addition to King, the best-known player and spokeswoman for the emerging movement, Casals became a noted figure who assisted her former mentor in assuring equality for women tennis players in opportunity and prize money. That struggle was not without other heroines, but King and Casals dominated on the tennis court as doubles partners as well, winning five Wimbledons and two U.S. National and Open doubles championships from 1967 to 1974. They also were seven-time runners-up in Grand Slam doubles events. Casals achieved a world number-three ranking in 1970 and spent twelve years in the top ten.

Ever-present on the court until a knee injury in 1978 limited her play, Casals's Grand Slam career included being a finalist in singles twice, in doubles twenty-one times, and in mixed doubles six times. She did return to win the U.S. Open doubles in 1982 and finish as runner-up at Wimbledon the next year.

Although Casals never achieved the fame as a singles player that she did in doubles, she left the game with titles in parts of three decades and a legacy of activism for women's causes. She won a title in each of the seven tournaments she entered. With a trademark headband and jet-black hair, Casals even challenged the customary "tennis whites" at the staid Wimbledon club, wearing colorful outfits that reflected her personality. At the height of her playing career, she was a co-commentator during the epic "Battle of the Sexes" tennis match between King and Bobby Riggs in 1973. Casals was inducted in the International Tennis Hall of Fame in 1996 and headed Sportswoman, Incorporated, a sports and charity event-planning company for corporations.

Significance

Casals was the second most notable pioneer of women's professional tennis, championing that cause with King during and after her playing career. Skilled and expressive, she captivated the tennis world as a 5-foot, 2-inch dynamo whose mastery of powerful shots and quick pace defined a style of play that influenced the women's game. Her legacy as a proponent of equal opportunity and prize money for women eventually allowed the women's game to parallel the men's in those respects.

P. Graham Hatcher

Further Reading

Altman, Linda J. *Rosemary Casals: The Rebel Rosebud.* St. Paul, Mo.: EMC, 1975. Discusses Casals's career and activism as a leader in challenging the tennis establishment and promoting equality in sports.

Amdur, Neil. "New Riches for Rosie Casals." *The New York Times*, December 17, 1982, p. A31. Casals reflects on the changes in the sport as well as her role of player, coach, social critic, and promoter.

Chapin, Kim. "A Bright Future for Little Miss Bombshell." *Sports Illustrated* 25, no. 17 (October 24, 1966): 68-70. Written about Casals at age eighteen, this profile chronicles her meteoric rise to capture the attention of the tennis world with her aggressive style of play.

Lichtenstein, Grace. *A Long Way, Baby: Behind the Scenes in women's Pro Tennis*. New York: William Morrow, 1974. Gives additional insight into Casals's devotion to being the best and her interaction with other pioneers of women's professional tennis.

Phillips, Dennis J. *Women Tennis Stars: Biographies and Records of Champions, 1800s to Today*. Jefferson, N.C.: McFarland, 2009. Reference work describing Casals's career and importance to the sport.

Thacher, Alida M. *Raising a Racket: Rosie Casals*. Milwaukee, Wis.: Raintree Editions, 1976. Written for a juvenile audience, this is a short biography of Casals's life and active playing career.

See also: Gigi Fernández; Pancho Gonzales.

Oscar Cásares

American writer and teacher

Best known for his short-story collection Brownsville *and his novel* Amigoland, *Cásares writes stories that offer insight into living in the border town of Brownsville, Texas, while also focusing on the lives of working-class Latinos. His novel explores the relationship between two brothers as they struggle to live on the Texas-Mexico border.*

Latino heritage: Mexican

Born: 1964; Brownsville, Texas

Areas of achievement: Literature; education

Early Life

Oscar Cásares (AHS-kahr KAH-suhr-ehs) was born in 1964 to Everardo Issasi and Severa Cásares in the border town of Brownsville, Texas. By the time Cásares was born, his father was sixty, his mother forty-two, and he was the youngest of four siblings, one of whom was in college and another a father of two. Cásares has said that, as a child, he did not have any interest in reading. Instead, he found that the stories his uncles often told him about his family were much more entertaining. For two years, Cásares attended the local community college and soon left Brownsville to attend the University of Texas at Austin, from which he graduated with a bachelor's degree in advertising in 1987.

His work in advertising took him to Minneapolis, Minnesota, for a decade, where he worked as a freelance copywriter. In addition to his advertising work, Cásares worked odd jobs at a movie theater and canoe store. After work he would often accompany his coworkers to a bar where he would tell stories about his hometown. In his early thirties, Cásares became an avid reader, beginning first with a recommendation to read *El llano en llamas, y otros cuentros* (1953, revised 1970 and 1980; *The Burning Plain*, 1967) by Mexican writer Juan Rulfo. Cásares initially did not feel that he had enough education or background in writing; however, he soon realized that his education in storytelling began long before with his uncle's stories. It was at this point that Cásares also recognized the unique role that oral storytelling plays in the lives of Latinos, especially those living on the border between Texas and Mexico. In 1996, Cásares wrote his first story and returned to Texas to work for GSD&M, a public relations company in Austin, eventually becoming an associate creative director.

Life's Work

While working in Minnesota, Cásares began to miss his hometown and the culture and people there. It was this nostalgia for his Latino culture that encouraged Cásares to move back to Texas and eventually pursue a writing career, specifically focusing on the area and the people with which he grew up. Cásares published his first story, "Yolanda," in *Threepenny Review* in 1998. In 2001, Cásares was offered a fellowship at the University of Iowa Writers' Workshop, from which he eventually earned a fine arts degree. For two years he worked on the short-story collection entitled *Brownsville* (2003), and he later published the novel *Amigoland* (2009). Cásares has also published short stories in the *Iowa Review*, the *Colorado Review*, and the *Northwest Review*. His collection of short stories was selected by the American Library Association for a Notable Book of the Year Award in 2004. He is also the recipient of a Dobie Paisano Fellowship, Texas Institute of Letters Fellowship (2002), a James Michener Award (2002), and Copernicus Society of America Fellowship (2002).

In 2004, Cásares became an associate professor in the Department of English at the University of Texas at Austin. His novel *Amigoland* was selected for the Austin Mayor's Book Club in December, 2009; as a result, Austin residents were encouraged to read the novel and to participate in related special events.

His short-story collection *Brownsville* is particularly significant because it provides an in-depth account of the border town of Brownsville, Texas. Through his descriptions of characters the reader is able to understand what it is like to live in a cross-cultural, international border town. *Amigoland* studies the relationship between two brothers and their ability to cope with the developments that accompany growing older. Of particular interest is Don Fidencio's obsession with telling a story as told to him by his grandfather about his capture by Indians and subsequent journey to the United States. Though most of the story becomes fiction as Don Fidencio tells it, Cásares reveals how fiction often becomes a way of telling and retelling family stories.

SIGNIFICANCE

In his writings, Cásares examines the conflict of national versus ethnic identity for people negotiating multiple cultures, as well as what it means to live on the boundary between Texas and Mexico. Though his stories are set at the border between Texas and Mexico, they could describe what life is like in any border town. These stories ultimately demonstrate how Latinos, specifically Mexican Americans, have transitioned from the margins to the mainstream of society without abandoning their origins. Though Cásares focuses on the lives of working-class Mexican Americans, he does not portray them as helpless or make them into heroes. Instead, his characters' stories are told in a manner that universalizes their experiences and enables readers to relate to them.

Margaret E. Cantú-Sánchez

FURTHER READING

Appelo, Tim. *The New York Times Book Review* (March 23, 2003): 20. In his review of *Brownsville*, Appelo says that the collection allows the reader to know and understand the city of Brownsville and the cross-cultural issues through which the city's inhabitants negotiate.

Balli, Cecilia. "Bard of the Border." *Texas Monthly* ([Curriculum]March, 2003): 100. Review of *Brownsville* states that Cásares's book examines the social differences of various characters in Brownsville without making them into stereotypes. .

Kirkus Reviews. "Review of *Brownsville.* " (December 15, 2002): 1785. Review of Cásares's debut short-story collection provides brief summaries of some of the stories.

Olszewski, Lawrence. "Review of *Brownsville*." *Library Journal* ([Curriculum]February 15, 2003): 171. Olszewski states that book contains universal themes that emphasize family, identities, and the problems that everyone encounters and to which everyone can relate..

Publishers Weekly. "Review of *Brownsville.*" (February 24, 2003): 52. Explains that *Brownsville* explores the lives of ordinary men, the drama that unfolds in their lives, and the neighborhood gossip they encounter.

See also: Norma Elia Cantú; Denise Chávez; Sandra Cisneros; Tomás Rivera; Victor Villaseñor; William Carlos Williams.

CARLOS CASTANEDA

Peruvian-born anthropologist and writer of popular books on shamanism

Castaneda is the author of a series of books that explore shamanism and sorcery and significantly influenced the New Age movement. The Teachings of Don Juan: A Yaqui Way of Knowledge *(1968) and its sequels became popular with readers throughout the world.*

Latino heritage: Peruvian

Born: December 25, 1925; Cajarmarca, Peru
Died: April 27, 1998; Los Angeles, California
Also known as: Carlos César Salvador Arana Castañeda; Godfather of the New Age Movement
Areas of achievement: Anthropology; religion and theology; literature

Early Life

Carlos César Salvador Arana Castañeda (KA-stah-NAY-dah) was born in Cajarmarca, Peru, on December 25, 1925. His parents were César Arana Burungaray, a goldsmith and watchmaker, and Susana Castaneda Navoa. Castaneda grew up in Cajamarca and Lima, Peru. He graduated from the Colegio Nacional Nuestra Señora de Guadalupe in Lima and studied painting and sculpture at the National Fine Arts School of Peru. In 1950, his mother died, and Castaneda locked himself in his room for three days; he refused to attend the funeral or to eat. In 1951, he immigrated to the United States. While immigration records support the above facts, Castaneda also told a number of contradictory stories about his early life. He claimed to have been born in São Paolo and reared by his grandparents; to have been born in Italy; to have lived with a foster family in the United States; and that his mother died when he was six years old.

From 1952 to the summer of 1955, Castaneda lived in Southern California, where he did odd jobs in order to save enough money to attend college. In the summer of 1955, he enrolled in Los Angeles Community College, where he took classes in literature, philosophy, creative writing, and journalism. On June 21, 1957, Castaneda became a naturalized citizen of the United States. Two years later, he received an associate of arts degree in psychology from Los Angeles Community College, and in September, 1959, he became a student at the University of California at Los Angeles (UCLA).

On January 27, 1960, Castaneda married Margaret Runyan, whom he had met in 1955. Castaneda and his wife separated less than a year after they were married, although their divorce was not finalized until 1973. Their marriage produced one child, Carlton Jeremy Castaneda, born August 12, 1961. Carlton's paternity has been called into question, however, as Castaneda reportedly asked a friend to father a child with his wife. During this time, Castaneda pursued studies at UCLA and developed an interest in shamanism and hallucinatory plants as a result of an anthropology class he took with Professor Clement Meighan.

Life's Work

In the spring of 1960, as part of his research for a term paper on the datura plant for Meighan's class, Castaneda began traveling into the Arizona desert to interview American Indians about plants and their medicinal uses. During the summer after the class ended, he continued his trips. On one of these research trips, he supposedly met a Yaqui Indian named Juan Matus. Although initially Castaneda simply wanted to interview Matus, whom he later referred to as Don Juan, the meeting resulted in an apprenticeship from 1961 to the fall of 1965. During this time, Don Juan introduced Castaneda to the use of plants such as peyote, datura, and psilocybe mexicana mushrooms as a means of experiencing a different reality and gaining knowledge.

Castaneda quickly found the process of becoming a sorcerer or shaman (man of knowledge) so stressful that he feared a mental breakdown. He abandoned his apprenticeship and returned to UCLA, where he received a B.A. in 1962. Castaneda then wrote a master's thesis based on his experiences with Don Juan. In 1968, he published his thesis as *The Teachings of Don Juan: A Yaqui Way of Knowledge*; the book was acclaimed by major scholars in the field of anthropology and also became a best seller within the counterculture movement of the 1960's and eventually with the general public. Castaneda returned to the desert to serve two more

The Teachings of Don Juan: A Yaqui Way of Knowledge

The Teachings of Don Juan: A Yaqui Way of Knowledge (1968) is the first in a series of books that brought Carlos Castaneda international fame. Written as the thesis for his master's degree in anthropology, the book recounts Castaneda's experiences as an apprentice to a Yaqui Indian sorcerer Don Juan Matus and analyzes the teachings from an anthropological viewpoint. Castaneda describes how he was introduced to peyote and other hallucinogens, which allowed hm to see Mescalito, a plant spirit that appears in many forms, including a dog. He also describes how he learned to perceive beings and objects as pure energy. The book was very successful both in the scholarly community and with general reading public, arriving at a time when mysticism and experimentation with psychedelic drugs were major elements of the counterculture. Castaneda published three more books detailing his continuing work with Don Juan before scholars and critics began accusing Castaneda of making up the story. The most serious criticism was based on the fact that no one but Castaneda had ever met Don Juan; indeed, the shaman's existence remains a mystery. However, by the time these questions were raised, *The Teachings of Don Juan* had become an influential and widely read work.

apprenticeships with Don Juan (1968 to 1971 and 1971 to 1973) and then wrote three more books based on his experiences. He was awarded a Ph.D. in anthropology from UCLA in 1973 for *Journey to Ixtlan: The Lessons of Don Juan* (1972).

That year, *Time* magazine published a cover story on Castaneda. Discrepancies between the facts known about Castaneda's life and his claims in the interview prompted questions about his credibility. Soon, critics and scholars began questioning the truth of the incredible nonreality experiences that Castaneda had recounted in his books. Psychologist Richard de Mille found chronological errors in the books. Various critics pointed out other problems, including the fact that Yaqui Indians did not use peyote, to which Don Juan introduced Castaneda; that Castaneda could not produce any field notes for his work; that no one else had ever seen Don Juan; and that most of what was contained in the books could be found in various sources in the UCLA library. Novelist Joyce Carol Oates, Jesus Ochoa of Mexico's National Museum of Anthropology, and others stated that the works revealed Castaneda's imaginative and storytelling skills and were good fiction rather than well-researched scholarly studies.

Castaneda defended the veracity of his work but became a recluse at his home in Westwood, California. He continued to publish books detailing his experiences as a sorcerer and surrounded himself with devoted followers including three women known as "brujas" (witches). In 1993, Castaneda began giving workshops in tensegrity, a program of activities leading to the perception of pure energy. In 1995, he founded Cleargreen Incorporated to promote tensegrity workshops and serve as a publishing house. His life remained shrouded in mystery. Castaneda died on April 27, 1998, of liver cancer. His death was not publicly announced for some two months; many of his followers disappeared.

Significance

Although Castaneda was dogged by controversy over his credibility, by 2011 his works had sold more than eight million copies and been translated into seventeen languages. For those who believe in shamanism and sorcery, they are a source of inspiration and guidance; for skeptics, they can be seen as well-written entertainment. Castaneda also is an important figure in the development of the New Age movement and its exploration of human consciousness and spirituality.

Shawncey Webb

Further Reading

Castaneda, Margaret Runyan. *A Magical Journey with Carlos Castaneda*. Victoria, B.C.: Millenia Press, 1996. This memoir by Castaneda's estranged wife concentrates on the 1960's and describes the couple's experiments with psychotropic mushrooms.

de Mille, Richard. *Castaneda's Journey: The Power and the Allegory*. Santa Barbara, Calif.: Capra Press, 1976. One of the first books to question the veracity of Castaneda's account of Don Juan.

Fikes, Jay Courtney. *Carlos Castaneda: Academic Opportunism and the Psychedelic Sixties*. Victoria, B.C.: Millenia Press, 1993. Questions the accuracy of Castaneda's accounts of his experiences with Don Juan. Points out possible errors and discrepancies.

Patterson, William Patrick. *The Life and Teachings of Carlos Castaneda*. Fairfax, Calif.: Arete, 2008. Well researched and documented. Excellent summary of Castaneda's teachings. Thorough investigation of his life and work, both negative and positive aspects.

Wallace, Amy. *Sorcerer's Apprentice: My Life with Carlos Castaneda*. Berkeley, Calif.: Frog Books, 2007. Details life with Castaneda at the Westwood compound, his relationship with his "witches" and followers, and his ways of controlling them.

Wolf, Felix. *The Art of Navigation: Travels with Carlos Castaneda*. San Francisco, Calif.: Council Oak Books, 2010. Written by a student of Castaneda, this resource describes and analyzes Castaneda's beliefs, methods, and goals.

See also: Fernando Alegría; Rudolfo Anaya; Raymond Barrio; Lydia Cabrera; Rolando Hinojosa.

Carlos E. Castañeda

Mexican-born historian and educator

Castañeda wrote many respected books and articles about the history and culture of Mexico and the U.S. Southwest. During World War II, his work with the Fair Employment Practices Committee made a significant contribution toward expanding employment opportunities for Latinos.

Latino heritage: Mexican

Born: November 11, 1896; Camargo, Tamaulipas, Mexico

Died: April 3, 1958; Austin, Texas

Also known as: Carlos Eduardo Castañeda

Areas of achievement: Literature; education; social issues

Early Life

Born in northeastern Mexico near the U.S. border, Carlos Eduardo Castañeda (KA-stah-NAY-dah) was the seventh child of Timoteo Castañeda, a politically active schoolteacher, and Elisa Leroux Castañeda, a U.S. citizen of French ancestry. When Castañeda was ten years old, the family moved to Brownsville, Texas. Both parents died four years later, requiring him to take a series of odd jobs in order to help support himself and his four sisters. He remained an excellent student, graduating as valedictorian of the class of 1916 at the Brownsville High School. He then taught for one year in a rural school before attending the University of Texas at Austin.

While studying for his bachelor's degree, Castañeda worked part time and lived in a small, unheated room in the Catholic chapel of the university. Initially enrolled as an engineering student, he soon discovered that he did not have the temperament to be an engineer. After experiencing "the sheer joy of reconstructing the past," Castañeda decided to major in history. His academic work was outstanding, and he earned membership in the prestigious Phi Beta Kappa honor society. In 1921, he graduated with a bachelor's degree and married Elisa Rios. He then taught high school Spanish in Beaumont and San Antonio. In 1923, Castañeda completed his master's degree in history, and during the next four years, he worked as an associate professor of Spanish and Spanish literature at the College of William and Mary in Virginia. During this period, he decided to specialize in the history of the Catholic Church in the Spanish borderlands, and he published his first scholarly article, "The Earliest Missionary Activities in Texas."

Life's Work

In 1927, Castañeda returned to the University of Texas to work as a librarian in the Latin American section. In addition to his duties in the library, he took courses for a doctorate and published his first book, *The Mexican Side of the Texas Revolution* (1928), which analyzed the positions of five Mexican leaders who opposed the revolution. Soon thereafter, while doing research in Mexico City, he accidentally came across a handwritten manuscript of a lost history by an early missionary, Father Juan Agustín Morfi's *History of Texas, 1673-1779*, and he prepared an annotated translation of the work as his Ph.D. dissertation, which he completed in 1932. His translation of Morfi's history was published in two attractive volumes and was widely recognized as a major contribution to the history of Texas.

Although Castañeda attempted to maintain an objective attitude and present factually accurate descriptions of the past, like all historians, he wrote his works with a particular point of view. A devout Catholic, he admired the missionary-priests who attempted to convert Native Americans to the Catholic religion, and he viewed conversion to Christianity as a step toward a higher morality and a superior culture. Although he appreciated U.S. political traditions and did not demonize Americans during the age of manifest destiny, he generally defended Mexican policies and recognized that President James K. Polk and other U.S. leaders had expansionist goals before the Mexican War. A realist, Castañeda understood the necessity of accepting the consequences of political and military power.

In 1933, Castañeda accepted a commission from the Knights of Columbus to write the history of Catholicism in Texas for the state's centennial. This commission resulted in his monumental achievement, *Our Catholic Heritage in Texas*, which was published in six volumes between 1936 and 1950. The title of the work is rather misleading, for it actually was a general history of Texas with an emphasis on the history of Catholicism in the state. In an autobiographical essay, Castañeda commented that the production of the books required "many hours of unrelenting toil and . . . many personal sacrifices." He became a member of the university's

Castañeda and the Fair Employment Practices Committee

In 1941, President Franklin D. Roosevelt, reacting to pressure from civil rights leaders, issued Executive Order 8802, establishing the Fair Employment Practices Committee (FEPC). The FEPC was tasked with monitoring discrimination against minority workers in businesses holding defense contracts with the federal government. In June, 1943, the chairman of the committee offered Carlos E. Castañeda the position of associate director of the Southwest regional office, located in Dallas. Castañeda accepted, and after obtaining a leave of absence from the University of Texas, he took the oath required of federal employees on August 23.

Castañeda served several months as the interim director of the Southwest region. In a press conference, he explained that the FEPC would "attempt to correct only economic discrimination and would take no action in social affairs." During the year and a half that Castañeda worked for the agency, he was extremely busy giving speeches and investigating complaints throughout the Southwestern states, and he suffered his first heart attack. Although able to resolve a number of complaints in the oil industry, he had less success in the mining sector. He was constantly frustrated at the bureaucratic limitations of the FEPC, but he nevertheless convinced a number of employers to expand employment opportunities for persons of Latino ancestry. In a report to a Congressional committee on September 8, 1944, he reported that over 70 percent of his investigations had not been resolved and encouraged the creation of a permanent Fair Employment Practices Commission.

history department in 1939 and seven years later was promoted to full professor, a position he held until his death in 1958. During World War II, he took a leave of absence to work with the federal Fair Employment Practices Committee.

A prolific writer, Castañeda published eighteen books, more than one hundred scholarly articles, and numerous book reviews. He also played an important role in development of the Nettie Lee Benson Latin American Collection at the University of Texas, a major repository of Latin American research materials. He was awarded numerous honors, including the presidency of the American Catholic Historical Association in 1939, knighthood in the Equestrian Order of the Holy Sepulchre of Jerusalem in 1941, and honorary doctorates from St. Edward's University and the Catholic University of America in 1951. At the University of Texas, the Perry-Castañeda Library, which opened in 1977, bears his name.

SIGNIFICANCE

Castañeda was one of the most distinguished historians and teachers of his day. His research and writings significantly advanced interest in and knowledge about Spanish-speaking persons in the Southwestern states, especially Texas. Also, his patient but persistent efforts to promote employment equality during World War II helped to establish the foundation for the later civil rights movement.

Thomas Tandy Lewis

FURTHER READING

Almaráz, Felix D., Jr. *Knight Without Armor: Carlos Eduardo Castañeda, 1896-1958*. College Station: Texas A&M University Press, 1999. Based on exhaustive research, this interesting and readable biography deals with all aspects of Castañeda's life and career.

_______. "The Making of a Boltonian: Carlos E. Castañeda of Texas—The Early Years." *Red River Valley Historical Review* 1 (Winter 1974): 329-350. Focuses on the influence of Herbert Bolton's thesis, which emphasized the historical similarities among the countries in the Western Hemisphere.

Castañeda, Carlos E. "Why I Chose History." *The Americas* 8 (April, 1952): 475-492. Interesting reflections on Castañeda's academic career and the study of history, followed by a bibliography of his numerous publications.

Del Castillo, Richard G. *World War II and Mexican American Civil Rights*. Austin: University of Texas, 2008. Includes much material about Castañeda's work at the Fair Employment Practices Committee; the appendix reprints his 1944 speech advocating a permanent Fair Employment Practices Commission.

Wunder, John R., ed. *Historians of the American Frontier: A Bio-Bibliographical Sourcebook*. New York: Greenwood Press, 1988. Includes an essay devoted to Castañeda and essays about most other historians relevant to his career.

See also: Edna Acosta-Belén; Rodolfo F. Acuña; Pura Belpré; Lauro Cavazos; Arturo Alfonso Schomburg.

Ana Castillo

American writer and feminist

A prolific and well-regarded writer, Castillo has produced poems, short stories, novels, and critical essays that call attention to the multiple challenges faced by contemporary Latinas. She is committed to feminism and to revealing the oppression of Latinas in U.S. society.

Latino heritage: Mexican

Born: June 15, 1953; Chicago, Illinois

Also known as: Ana Hernandez del Castillo

Area of achievement: Literature; poetry; women's rights

Early Life

Ana Hernandez del Castillo (kas-TEE-yoh) was born on June 15, 1953, to working-class parents, Ramon and Raquel Rocha Castillo. She grew up in a Mexican American inner-city neighborhood of Chicago. Castillo was nine years old when her paternal grandmother died, and she wrote her first poems about this event. Castillo shared these poems with her family and her classmates. At age twelve, she began to write longer stories she illustrated herself.

Castillo's parents selected for her a high school that trained its students for clerical careers. However, in the late 1960's, Castillo began to identify with the emerging Latino movement. She wrote her own small newspapers expressing her political beliefs and thought about a career in painting. After high school, Castillo attended Chicago City College for two years before transferring to Northeastern Illinois University, where she earned her bachelor of arts degree in art education in 1975.

Castillo found college stifling and felt that it quashed her aspirations as painter. Instead, she turned to writing poetry. In 1975, Castillo published her first poems. "The Vigil (and the Vow)" and "Untitled" appeared in the magazine *Revista Chicano-Riqueña*. "Mi maestro" was included in the anthology *Zero Makes Me Hungry* (1975).

Life's Work

After a year of teaching ethnic studies at Santa Rosa Junior College in California, Castillo enrolled at the University of Chicago in 1977. That year, she published her first collection of poetry, *Otro canto* (*Other Song,* 1977), adding Spanish to her primarily English verses. In 1979, Castillo earned her master of arts degree in Latin American and Caribbean studies. To support herself while writing, she worked as instructor or writer in residence at various U.S. colleges and universities. She gave birth to her son, Marcel Ramón Herrera, on September 21, 1983.

In 1984, Castillo published her second anthology of poetry, *Women Are Not Roses*, advocating a strong Latina identity. In 1986, she released her first novel, *The Mixquiahuala Letters*. Consisting of forty letters from Teresa, a Chicana, to her white friend Alicia, the letters explore female friendship and the pain inflicted by men. The novel won the American Book Award of the Before Columbus Foundation in 1986.

Castillo returned to California in 1986 and was invited on a reading tour of Europe by the German Association of Americanists. She was honored by the women's Foundation of California in 1987 and 1988. Her third collection of poetry, *My Father Was a Toltec* (1988), met with critical acclaim and contributed to Castillo winning a California Arts Council fellowship for fiction in 1989. In 1990, she published her second

Ana Castillo. (©Robert A. Molina)

novel, *Sapogonia*. Dedicated to Castillo's son, the novel chronicles the life and loves of the free-spirited Latina protagonist Pastora Velásquez Aké.

In 1991, Castillo earned her Ph.D. in American studies from the University of Bremen in Germany. Two years later, she released the novel *So Far from God*. It combines the tale of a strong Latina mother and her four different daughters with the genre of magical realism, concern for the environment, and feminist issues. The novel won the Carl Sandburg Literary Award in Fiction for 1993, and the 1994 Mountains and Plains Booksellers Award. It also contributed to Castillo's second National Endowment for the Arts fellowship.

In 1994, Castillo published her Ph.D. thesis, *Massacre of the Dreamers: Essays on Xicanisma*. By 1996, she had edited four scholarly anthologies. Her first collection of short stories, *Loverboys: Stories* (1996), features homosexual and heterosexual couples. Her next novel, *Peel My Love Like an Onion* (1999), depicts the world of a dancer struggling with the recurrence of childhood polio.

Castillo used Aztec and Nahuatl legends in her children's book *My Daughter, My Son, the Eagle, the Dove: An Aztec Chant* (2000). While holding the La Inés de la Cruz Endowed Chair at DePaul University from 2001 to 2006, and as visiting scholar at the Massachusetts Institute of Technology from 2007 to 2008, Castillo published four more books. Her fourth collection of poetry, *I Ask the Impossible* (2001), was followed by *Psst—I Have Something to Tell You, Mi Amor: Two Plays* (2005). Next was *Watercolor Women/Opaque Men* (2005), which won the Independent Publisher Outstanding Book of the Year Award in 2006. Castillo's novel *The Guardians* (2007) concerns itself with the effects of drug-trafficking violence on Latinos in the Southwestern United States.

Significance

Castillo's rich body of diverse writing is unified by the author's deep concern for the fate of Latina women in America. Her poetry, fiction, plays, and critical essays have won Castillo an impressive array of literary prizes and fellowships. Even readers and critics from different ethnic, political, and philosophical backgrounds have been impressed by the creative force of her texts.

R. C. Lutz

Further Reading

Bost, Suzanne. *Encarnación: Illness and Body Politics in Chicana Feminist Literature*. New York: Fordham University Press, 2010. Academic study on the meaning of illness in Chicana literary texts such as Castillo's *Peel My Love Like an Onion*.

Mujcinovic, Fatima. *Postmodern Cross-Culturalism and Politicization in U.S. Latina Literature: From Ana Castillo to Julia Alvarez*. New York: Peter Lang, 2004. Close literary analysis of Castillo's work that is placed in Latino cultural context.

Spurgeon, Sara. *Ana Castillo*. Boise, Idaho: Boise State University Western Writers Series, 2004. Compact biography that discusses the author and her work.

Torres, Hector Avalos. *Conversations with Contemporary Chicana and Chicano Writers*. Albuquerque: University of New Mexico Press, 2007. Contains two conversations with Castillo, who discusses her writing and creative drive.

See also: Julia Alvarez; Giannina Braschi; Norma Elia Cantú; Lorna Dee Cervantes; Denise Chávez; Martha P. Cotera; Cherríe Moraga; Judith Ortiz Cofer; Helena María Viramontes.

George Castro

American scientist and inventor

Castro was engaged in fundamental research about photoconductors which resulted in applications that greatly increased the memory capacity of organic materials now widely used in many data storage devices.

Latino heritage: Mexican

Born: March 23, 1939; Los Angeles, California

Areas of achievement: Science and technology

Early Life

George Castro (KAHS-troh) was born on March 23, 1939, the second of five children of Mexican American parents, Peter M. Castro and Carmen Chavez. He grew up in East Los Angeles, where he went to public schools that typically prepared working-class Mexican American children for vocations instead of higher education. As a boy, Castro liked taking things apart and

George Castro. (AP Photo)

trying to figure out how they worked. He also recalled dissecting neighborhood rats with friends to understand their physiology. After he was accidentally placed in an algebra class at Hollenbeck Junior High School, Castro successfully passed the course, and he found himself entering Roosevelt High School in the college-bound track rather than the vocational track of his Chicano peers. An average student, he graduated in 1956 with a modest Los Romanos scholarship from the local Hispanic community which enabled him to study physics at the University of California at Los Angeles (UCLA). He quickly switched to chemistry and carpooled to class with friends of various ethnic backgrounds from East Los Angeles.

A UCLA professor suggested Castro consider going on to graduate school in the new chemistry program at the University of California at Riverside (UCR). UCR provisionally offered a full scholarship and a research job if Castro would earn all "B" grades in his final semester at UCLA. Instead, he completed the semester with straight "A" grades and received his B.S. in 1960. Castro became an outstanding graduate school student, living on the Riverside campus, conducting research, and earning a 4.0 grade point average. He followed one of his UCR professors to Dartmouth College in 1962 as a research fellow and remained there until 1965. In 1963, he married a longtime acquaintance, Beatrice A. Melendez, with whom he would eventually have four children, Gerald, Sylvia, Valerie, and Cynthia. He obtained his Ph.D. in physical chemistry from UCR in 1965 with the important discovery that if the surface of organic materials was kept exceptionally clean, the material would conduct electricity in entirely predictable ways when exposed to light from a laser and could be used as a photoconductor.

Life's Work

Castro's doctoral work opened the door for him to work in the laboratory of Robin Hochstrasser at the University of Pennsylvania, where Castro went for a postdoctoral fellowship from 1965 to 1967. He picked up a second postdoctoral fellowship at the California Institute of Technology from 1967 to1968, during which he came to the attention of International Business Machines (IBM). IBM was just starting to conduct research into organic photoconductors for copy machines and offered him the princely sum of $18,000 a year to join their research staff at the IBM research laboratory in San Jose, California, where he would remain from 1968 to1986. After a few years of solid research effort that allowed IBM to offer the first consistent high-quality color copier, Castro was promoted in 1973 to manager of the company's organic solids department and again in 1975 to manager of the physical sciences function, a position he held until 1986. In 1977, he filed a patent, granted the following year, for a photochemical spectral hole-burning technique that could increase the memory capacity of organic materials. His early work on photogeneration also heavily influenced many developments in copying and printing technologies.

From 1987 to1992, Castro worked with IBM researchers and faculty at Stanford University to build a synchrotron x-ray facility at the Stanford Synchrotron Radiation Laboratory, having now been appointed manager of synchrotron studies at the IBM Almaden Research Center, a position he would retain until 1995. The next two years were spent on a joint IBM-University of Wisconsin at Madison effort to successfully build a Paraxial-Ray Imaging Spectromicroscope for IBM that allowed thin polymer films used on computer disks to be carefully examined because they were too sensitive for standard electron microscopy.

Throughout his distinguished career at IBM, Castro worked hard to advance the work of fellow Latinos. He cofounded the Society for the Advancement of Chicanos and Native Americans in Science (SACNAS), served as its president from 1991 to 1994, and twice received its Distinguished Service Award. He was awarded the 1986 Hispanics in Technology Award from the Society of Hispanic Professional Engineers and was a 2000 Great Minds in STEM (Science, Technology, Engineering, and Mathematics) Hall of Fame Inductee.

After twenty-seven years at IBM, Castro became an associate dean for the college of science at San Jose State University from 1995 until his retirement in 2004. In this position, he tirelessly advocated to enable Latinos and other disadvantaged populations to excel in science, technology, engineering, and mathematics. He also pioneered several new programs to reach out to area middle and high school students, as well as creating better support systems on campus for first-generation college students. The graduating classes of San Jose State University became prized recruiting grounds for technically oriented companies in the Silicon Valley and a path to upward mobility for many Latinos. Castro's outstanding efforts at mentoring underrepresented minorities were recognized by his 1999 receipt of a Presidential Award for Excellence in Science, Mathematics, and Engineering Mentoring from the National Science Foundation.

Significance

George Castro made fundamental and lasting contributions to a variety of technical fields related to printing, copying, and memory storage through the use of photochemical methods. His leadership and mentoring of minorities, including Latinos, had a significant impact on the next generation of scientists and engineers in northern California and across the nation.

Dennis W. Cheek

Further Reading

Mellado, Carmela. "Research Profile: Dr. George Castro, Research Scientist with IBM, San Jose." *Hispanic Engineer and Information Technology* (September 1987): 22-24, 44-45. A candid interview in which Castro discusses his challenges and opportunities as a young person and his scientific career at IBM.

Regua, Nannette, and Arturo Villarreal. *Images of America: Mexicans in San Jose*. Charleston, S.C.: Arcadia, 2009. A short profile of Castro set within the context of images, events, and profiles of other prominent Mexican Americans who helped make San Jose the vibrant scientific, technical, and cultural center of the Silicon Valley.

See also: Franklin Ramón Chang-Díaz; Margarita Colmenares; Severo Ochoa.

Joaquín Castro

American politician and lawyer

Castro has served in the Texas House of Representatives since 2002, representing District 125, a portion of Bexar County that includes the cities of San Antonio and Leon Valley.

Latino heritage: Mexican

Born: September 16, 1974; San Antonio, Texas

Areas of achievement: Government and politics; law

Early Life

Joaquín Castro (hwah-KEEN KAHS-troh) was born on September 16, 1974, in San Antonio, Texas. He was raised in the city's Westside neighborhood, where he attended Thomas Jefferson High School. He later graduated from Stanford University in 1996 and from Harvard Law School in 2000. He is closely tied to his identical twin brother Julián, who was elected mayor of San Antonio in 2009. Joaquín and Julián chose which schools to attend based upon which school would admit both brothers.

They continued this trend into their professional lives. The brothers joined Akin Gump Strauss Hauer & Feld, a large corporate law firm with offices worldwide, as associate attorneys. Both left this firm at the same time to form their own firm. In 2005, they opened the law Offices of Julián Castro, PLLC, a personal injury law firm. In one well-publicized case, they successfully represented the victims of a fatal drunken-driving accident, and this case earned them enough money to focus on political careers.

Sometimes the close association between the two brothers has been a detriment. For example, in April, 2005,

Julián, who was then a San Antonio city councilman and the frontrunner in the race for mayor, was accused of misleading the public when his brother Joaquín rode on the City Council float in the Texas Cavaliers River Parade. Julián attended a candidates' forum instead, and he sent his brother Joaquín to the parade. Joaquín was announced to the attendees as Julián Castro and waved to the throng from the float. The twins blamed the parade announcer for the mix-up and said that they had not intentionally tried to mislead voters. However, it was not the first time that the twins had been accused of impersonating one another. Julián has admitted that they used to trick teachers in school, and Julián was accused of impersonating Joaquín when Joaquín ran for state representative.

Life's Work

Castro is the son of Jessie Guzman, a retired teacher, and activist Maria "Rosie" Castro, a leader in the La Raza Unida movement in San Antonio in the 1970's . La Raza Unida was a third political party that focused solely on the racial and ethnic groups it called "Chicanos." Rosie, Joaquín's acknowledged political role model, has no love for San Antonio's past, including the history of the Alamo. She has said,

> When I grew up I learned that the 'heroes' of the Alamo were a bunch of drunks and crooks and slaveholding imperialists who conquered land that didn't belong to them. But as a little girl I got the message—we were losers. I can truly say that I hate that place and everything it stands for.

Joaquín has inherited his mother's leftist leanings, consistently opposing business interests, Christianity in the public sphere, and prolife legislation. Some people have called him and his brother the future of the Democratic Party, and he is closely identified with President Barack Obama. At the same time that Obama published *The Audacity of Hope* (2006), Castro drafted a message for his reelection campaign titled "Towards Tomorrow with Hope." In it, he set forth three priorities: educating future generations; helping people stay healthy by making healthcare affordable and accessible; and creating better jobs so families can live out the American Dream.

In 2007, Castro voted against a bill which allowed students to express their religious beliefs in classroom assignments, to organize prayer groups and religious clubs in the same way they are allowed to organize other extracurricular activities, and to discuss their opinions of religion at graduation ceremonies and other school events. In 2009, Castro, a practicing Roman Catholic, supported the interests of NARAL (National Abortion and Reproductive rights Action League) Pro-Choice Texas, an organization that opposes restrictions on abortions. In 2010, he voiced his opposition to Arizona's stringent immigration law, calling it a crude way of dealing with the issue: "It just has an ugly face on it."

In addition to his legislative career, Castro has been a visiting professor of law at St. Mary's University and an adjunct professor at Trinity University in San Antonio.

Significance

As a Texas state representative, Joaquín Castro has written and supported legislation on workforce development, highway safety, and education programs intended to reduce teenage pregnancy rates. He serves on the House of Representatives' Border and International Affairs Committee and the Juvenile Justice and Family Issues Committee. He and his brother Julián have been called the future leaders of the Democratic Party's Hispanic bloc.

Michael J. Bennett

Further Reading

Ball, Cecila. "Twins Peak." *Texas Monthly*, October, 2002, 100. A detailed biographical profile of the Castro twins, discussing the political activism and influence of their mother, Rosie; their upbringing and education; and their political ambitions.

Castillo, Jaime. "District 125 Contest Is Spirited: Bilingual Republican, Hometown Democrat Square Off." *San Antonio Express-News*, October 30, 2002, p. 1B. Provides an overview of Castro's first election for the state legislature.

Castro, Joaquín. Texas House Member Joaquín Castro. http://www.house.state.tx.us/members/member-page/?district=125. Representative Castro's official Web site, containing a biography, press releases, an analysis of the district he represents, and information about the legislation he has drafted and supported.

Jefferson, Greg. "Younger Castro Twin Has Future as Well as Brother." *San Antonio Express-News*, May 15, 2010, p. B3. Speculates on the future direction of Castro's career, including a possible run for Congress. Describes him as more "aggressive" and "partisan" than his twin brother Julián.

See also: Joe J. Bernal; Julián Castro; Eligio de la Garza II; Leticia Van de Putte.

Julián Castro

American politician and lawyer

Castro is the fifth Latino to be elected mayor of San Antonio, Texas. The twin brother of Texas legislator Joaquín Castro, Julián has been called the "post-Hispanic Hispanic politician."

Latino heritage: Mexican

Born: September 16, 1974; San Antonio, Texas

Areas of achievement: Government and politics; law

Early Life

Julián Castro (hoo-lee-AHN KAHS-troh) and his identical twin brother Joaquín were born on September 16, 1974, in San Antonio, Texas. Julián majored in political science and communications at Stanford University, from which he graduated in 1996; he has said that he began thinking about entering politics while at Stanford. Castro earned his law degree from Harvard University in 2000. His brother graduated from both schools at the same time; Julián told an interviewer that he and Joaquín chose to attend colleges that would admit them both.

They have continued this trend into their professional lives. Both brothers became associate attorneys at Akin Gump Strauss Hauer & Feld, a large corporate law firm with offices worldwide. Both left the firm at the same time to form their own firm. In 2005, they opened the law offices of Julián Castro, PLLC, a personal injury law firm. In one well-publicized case, they successfully represented the victims of a fatal drunken-driving accident, and this case earned them enough money to focus on political careers.

Life's Work

Castro is the son of Jessie Guzman, a retired teacher, and activist Maria "Rosie" Castro, a leader in the La Raza Unida movement in San Antonio in the 1970's. La Raza Unida was a third political party that focused solely on the racial and ethnic groups it called "Chicanos." Unlike most children, he has said that he "grew up with a real ideology." He has inherited his mother's leftist leanings, consistently opposing business interests, Christianity in the public sphere, and prolife legislation. Like a large number of his fellow San Antonians, Castro is a Roman Catholic. However, he was the first San Antonio mayor to be grand marshal in the city's annual gay rights parade. He also is pro-choice on the issue of abortion: "We disagree on this, the pope and I," he has said.

Castro served on the San Antonio City Council from 2001 to 2005, representing District 7. While on the council, he sought to become a leader in the areas of environmental protection, economic development, and education. Castro was considered the frontrunner in 2005, when he made his first bid to become mayor of San Antonio. His opponents in this election were Phil Hardberger, a retired judge, and Carroll Schubert, a conservative city councilman. Although Castro received a plurality of the vote in the May, 2005, election, he was narrowly defeated by Hardberger in the June, 2005, runoff.

His loss was no doubt affected by a controversy arising from the Texas Cavaliers River Parade in April, 2005. Julián was scheduled to ride on the City Council float, but he attended a candidates' forum, and he sent his twin brother Joaquín to participate in the parade. His brother, however, was announced to parade goers as Julián Castro. The brothers denied allegations that they intentionally misled the public and blamed the parade announcer for the mistake. However, Julián later

Julián Castro. (AP Photo)

admitted that the brothers had pulled similar pranks in the past.

Castro announced he would run for mayor in 2007 if Hardberger chose not to seek a second term. Hardberger sought reelection, so Castro did not run. Also in 2007, Castro married Erica Lira, and the couple had a daughter, Carina Victoria Castro, born March 14, 2009. Castro did enter the 2009 mayor's race, announcing his candidacy on November 5, 2008. He won the May 9, 2009, election with 56.23 percent of the vote.

He immediately became a favorite of the Barack Obama administration. In December, 2009, Castro visited the White House to attend President Obama's national forum on jobs and economic growth; he was one of five mayors to attend and, at age thirty-five, was the youngest. Castro returned to the White House in April, 2011, to participate in a strategy session aimed at reviving Obama's immigration policies.

Significance

Julián Castro has been hailed as an emerging national leader of the Latino bloc of the Democratic Party, in the tradition of politicians Henry G. Cisneros and Bill Richardson. The *Los Angeles Times* proclaimed him and his brother Joaquín as the "heirs to the Chicano movement."

Michael J. Bennett

Further Reading

Ball, Cecila. "Twins Peak." *Texas Monthly*, October, 2002, 100. A detailed biographical profile of the Castro twins, discussing the political activism and influence of their mother, Rosie; their upbringing and education; and their political ambitions.

Chafets, Zev. "The Post-Hispanic Hispanic Politician," *New York Times Magazine,* May 6, 2010. Provides an overview of Castro's life and career, speculating on his future in politics.

Russell, Jan Jarboe. "Alamo Heights." *Texas Monthly*, May, 2010, 82-100. Discusses Castro's accomplishments as mayor of San Antonio, including his plans to create twenty thousand new jobs in 2010, reduce the city's 50 percent high school drop-out rate, and invest in renewal energy sources.

Smith, Evan. "Julian Castro." *Texas Monthly*, July, 2009, 64-69. In this interview conducted after Castro was elected mayor, he discusses his plans for San Antonio, explains why he lost his bid for mayor in 2005, and describes how he sought support of the business community to win election in 2009.

See also: Joe J. Bernal; Joaquín Castro; Henry G. Cisneros; Eligio de la Garza II; Bill Richardson; Leticia Van de Putte; Antonio Villaraigosa.

Eduardo Catalano

Argentine-born architect

Catalano was an influential Argentine architect. He taught architecture at North Carolina State University and the Massachusetts Institute of Technology from the early 1950's until retirement in 1977. Catalano House, an innovative modernist design with glass walls and a large wooden hyperbolic paraboloid roof, was praised by architect Frank Lloyd Wright and named House of the Decade in the 1950's.

Latino heritage: Argentinean

Born: December 19, 1917; Buenos Aires, Argentina

Died: January 28, 2010; Cambridge, Massachusetts

Also known as: Eduardo Fernando Catalano

Area of achievement: Architecture

Early Life

Eduardo Fernando Catalano (ehd-WAHR-doh fehr-NAHN-doh kaht-ah-LAH-noh) was born December 19, 1917, in Buenos Aires, Argentina, the youngest child of a commercial artist. Little is known about his early life in Argentina. Catalano studied architecture at Buenos Aires University. He came to the United States after winning a scholarship to the University of Pennsylvania. Catalano continued his studies in architecture at Harvard University under architect Walter Gropius and architect and furniture designer Marcel Breuer; Gropius and Breuer are considered two of the pioneers of modernist architecture. Modernist architecture is characterized by simple, unembellished designs and buildings often constructed of glass, steel, and concrete.

In 1945, General Motors held a design competition; Catalano came in second out of more than nine hundred entries. Catalano's design featured a hyperbolic paraboloid, basically described as a double-ruled surface being shaped like a saddle. Following graduation from

Harvard with a master's degree in architecture, Catalano taught at the Architectural Association in London, England. He married fellow architect Gloria Lauersdorf, whom he had met in Argentina. The couple had two children, daughter Alex and son Adrian, before they divorced in 1960.

After teaching in London, Catalano accepted a position at North Carolina State University's School of Design in 1951. He was recruited by Henry Kamphoefner, dean of the design school and fellow modernist architect.

Life's Work

It was shortly after his move to North Carolina that Catalano designed one of his most famous structures: Raleigh House, later known as Catalano House. This three-bedroom home was built in 1954 on a wooded lot at the end of a quiet street in Raleigh, North Carolina. The 1,700-foot-square home had a modern, open floor plan and exterior walls made completely out of glass. The roof was a four-thousand-foot wooden hyperbolic paraboloid, two-and-a-half inches thick, and eighty-seven feet wide, with two opposing corners anchored to the ground, and the other two curving into the air. The roof was often compared to a saddle or described as shoehorn-shaped, and it even lead to the nickname the "potato chip house." The curvature of the roof provided privacy in some areas of the home and wide, unobstructed views of nature in others. Catalano's house was praised by famed architect Frank Lloyd Wright in the 1956 issue of *House and Home* magazine, which named it "House of the Decade." Catalano sold the home in 1957 after moving to Boston to teach at the Massachusetts Institute of Technology (MIT). The house was sold over the years, unoccupied beginning in 1996, and suffered from the elements and neglect. Attempts to save the home were made too late, and it was demolished in 2001.

Catalano worked at MIT until 1977, when he retired from teaching. Catalano designed his home in Cambridge, Massachusetts, in the 1980's; this house featured a three-story-high glass atrium, large enough for a mature ficus tree. He retired and closed his design offices in 1995. In 2002, Catalano came out of retirement to design the Floralis Generica, an eighteen-ton flower sculpture that he donated to the city of Buenos Aires. The petals of the flower open automatically each morning at eight o'clock and close in a reddish glow at sunset. The sculpture is 75 feet tall and 85 feet wide with the petals closed, 105 feet wide with the petals open.

In 2007, Catalano received an honorary doctorate from North Carolina State University. He wrote six books on architecture and was a member of Argentina's National Academy of Fine Arts and the Buenos Aires Academy of Science. After a brief illness, Catalano died in Cambridge on January 28, 2010, at the age of ninety-two. He was buried in Argentina.

Significance

Eduardo Catalano was an influential modernist architect, who had a long teaching career at North Carolina State University and MIT. His 1954 Raleigh House was revolutionary in modern architecture, and some consider it the most important home built in North Carolina during the twentieth century. Catalano designed the U.S. embassies in Buenos Aires and Pretoria , South Africa, the Guilford County Courthouse in North Carolina, MIT's Stratton Student Center in 1965, and the Juilliard School of Music in New York City in 1969. He also designed several office buildings in Boston, including the Charlestown branch of the Boston Public Library. While Raleigh House did not survive, Catalano's legacy will endure through students of architecture, the people who admire his work, and his Floralis Generica.

Jennifer L. Campbell

Further Reading

Catalano, Eduardo. *The Constant: Dialogues on Architecture in Black and White.* Cambridge, Mass.: Cambridge Architectural Press, 2000. A discussion between an architect and a mathematician about the history of architecture and the evolution of design. The two also discuss philosophy, aesthetics, and science. Aimed at students and educators of architecture but also interesting to the general reader.

Filler, Martin. *Makers of Modern Architecture.* New York: New York Review of Books, 2007. A series of essays on twentieth-century architecture and architects. An introductory work suitable for any reader interested in this subject. .

Lupfer, Gilbert. *Walter Gropius, 1883-1969.* Los Angeles: Taschen, 2005. Gropius was a father of modernism and one of Catalano's advisors and mentors while in graduate school at Harvard University. Includes a biography and summary of Gropius's work and more than 120 photographs and illustrations.

See also: Juan Estanislao Cotera; Cesar Pelli.

Lauro Cavazos

American first Hispanic cabinet member

Cavazos was sworn in as secretary of education in 1988. He served in the cabinets of Ronald Reagan and George H. W. Bush until his resignation amid controversy in December, 1990.

Latino heritage: Mexican

Born: January 4, 1927; Kingsville, Texas

Also known as: Lauro Fred Cavazos, Jr.

Areas of achievement: Education; government and politics; literature

Early Life

Lauro Fred Cavazos, Jr. (kah-VAH-zohs) is a sixth-generation Texan born to Mexican American parents Lauro, Sr., and Tomasa Quintanilla Cavazos. He grew up on the enormous King Ranch in Southern Texas, where his father worked as the foreman. Cavazos attended elementary school in a two-room, ranch-style schoolhouse. Later, he attended a secondary school in town; he was raised Roman Catholic.

Cavazos served in the United States Army from 1945 to 1946. After completing his service, he studied zoology at Texas Tech University, from which he earned a bachelor's degree in 1949 and a master's degree in 1952. He went on to receive a Ph.D. in physiology from Iowa State University in 1954. That December, Cavazos married Peggy Ann Murdock, a registered nurse. The marriage produced ten children.

Cavazos joined the faculty of the Medical College of Virginia as an instructor, then as an assistant professor from 1956 until 1960. He served as an associate professor of anatomy and physiology from 1960 to 1964. Next, he took a position as professor of anatomy and physiology at Tufts University's School of Medicine in Medford, Massachusetts, where he remained until 1980. Cavazos also served as chairman of the Anatomy and Physiology Department from 1964 to 1972 and as associate dean at the School of medicine from 1972 to 1973. He served as acting dean of the School of Medicine from 1972 until 1975, then was appointed as dean of the School of Medicine in 1975 and served in that capacity until 1980.

Life's Work

Cavazos left Tufts in 1980 and returned to his alma mater, Texas Tech, to serve as professor of anatomy and physiology, professor of biology, and head of the Health Sciences Division. He was soon appointed the tenth president of the university and served in that role until 1988, when he was appointed secretary of education. Cavazos became the first Hispanic member of a presidential cabinet, serving under Presidents Ronald Reagan and George H. W. Bush. As secretary of education, Cavazos emphasized the importance of reading in school curricula. He believed that reading should be the top priority during the first three years of a child's primary schooling.

In 1990, Cavazos was investigated in connection with his use of frequent-flyer miles, which he allegedly used to generate free travel for his wife on commercial flights. Cavazos also was criticized for apparently going out of his way to fly on Trans World Airlines, which employed one of his sons. Accused of ethics violations, Cavazos resigned his cabinet post in December, 1990.

Cavazos returned to Tufts University as a professor. He served on several boards of directors over the subsequent decades, including the Texas Medical

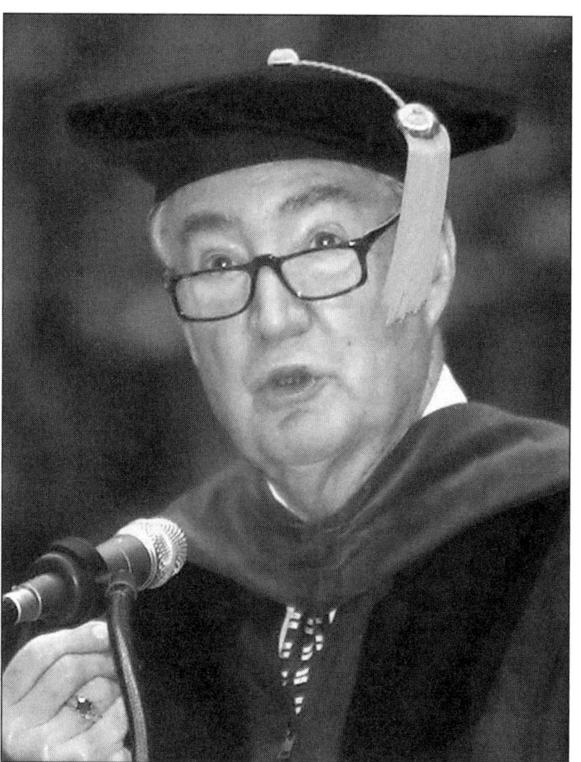

Lauro Cavazos. (AP Photo)

Association, the National Board of Medical Examiners, and the National Library of Medicine. He also has been a member of the Texas Governor's Task Force on Higher Education and received a number of honorary degrees. Cavazos has written numerous articles for professional journals and publications throughout his career.

Significance

Cavazos has achieved several historic "firsts" during his career. He was the first undergraduate alumnus of Texas Tech University to serve as its president; the first Hispanic to serve as the university's president; and the first Hispanic to serve in a cabinet position. In 2002, Texas Tech established the Lauro Cavazos and Ophelia Powell-Malone Mentoring Program, which aims to expand the quality of education for all minority students.

Sandra W. Leconte

Further Reading

Cavazos, Lauro. "Emphasizing Performance Goals and High-Quality Education for All Students." *Phi Delta Kappan* 83, no. 9 (2002): 690. In this peer-reviewed article, Cavazos offers his philosophies on how to improve education and discusses the goals he set during his tenure as secretary of education.

_______. *A Kineño Remembers: From the King Ranch to the White House*. College Station: Texas A&M University Press, 2006. Cavazos's memoir covers his early life in Texas, his family history, education, and career.

Crane, Edward H., et. al. "Bush and His Cabinet: A First-Year Report Card." *Policy Review* 51 (1990). A conservative examination of Bush's first year in office, including his decision to retain Cavazos as secretary of education

Elbow, Gary S. "Tenure at Texas Tech: A Step Backward." *Journal of the Texas Faculty Association* 1, no. 1 (Spring, 1985): 5-11. Describes a labor dispute between Texas Tech faculty and university president Cavazos.

Johnston, David. "Ex-education Secretary Under Inquiry on Travel." *The New York Times*, May 11, 1991. Reports on the investigation into Cavazos's use of frequent-flyer miles.

Controversy in Cavazos's Presidency of Texas Tech University

A tenure dispute erupted in 1984 on the campus of Texas Tech University during Lauro Cavazos's presidency. Cavazos proposed a weaker tenure policy that would decrease the bargaining power of the Faculty Senate. The Faculty Senate resisted the changes and issued a no-confidence vote against Cavazos. The parties consulted other labor organizations, including the American Association of University Professors and the Texas Tech University Faculty Legal Action Association, and ultimately negotiated tenure guidelines that were robust and satisfactory to faculty members. Cavazos remained as president and reestablished an effective working relationship with the Faculty Senate.

See also: Henry G. Cisneros; Alberto Gonzales; Edward Hidalgo; Manuel Luján, Jr.; Ken Salazar.

Richard E. Cavazos

American military leader

After distinguishing himself as a resourceful and courageous soldier during the Korean War, Cavazos went on to make military history twice: In 1976, he became the first Latino brigadier general in the United States Army, and in 1982, he was the first Latino to be promoted to the rank of four-star general.

Latino heritage: Mexican
Born: January 31, 1929; Kingsville, Texas
Also known as: Richard Edward Cavazos
Area of achievement: Military

Early Life

Richard Edward Cavazos (kah-VAH-zohs) was born to a farming and ranching couple, Lauro Cavazos, Sr., and Tomasa Quintanilla Cavazos. His older brother, Lauro, Jr., would later become secretary of education under Presidents Ronald Reagan and George H. W. Bush. The Cavazos family were what are called in South Texas *Kineños*, workers on the legendary King Ranch. At the time of the brothers' childhood, Latinos and Anglos often were segregated in South Texas society, and discrimination against people of Mexican descent was prevalent.

After high school, Cavazos participated in the Reserve Officers' Training Corps (ROTC) program at North Texas Agricultural College near Dallas, a school that later became the University of Texas at Arlington. Afterward, he attended Texas Technological College (later Texas Tech University) in Lubbock. At Texas Technological College, Cavazos again was active in ROTC and played football. He graduated in 1951 with a bachelor of science degree in geology.

By this time, Cavazos had chosen to pursue a career in the United States military. After his college graduation, his participation in ROTC earned him a commission as a second lieutenant in the U.S. Army. Later that year, he reported to Fort Benning in Georgia to undergo basic training, followed immediately by further training in the Army Airborne School. Upon completion of this training, he was assigned to the Sixty-fifth Infantry and was sent to fight in the Korean War.

Life's Work

The Sixty-fifth Infantry has become an important part of Latino history: It was composed almost entirely of Latinos, most of them of Puerto Rican descent, and the soldiers in the unit dubbed themselves "the Borinqueneers" in honor of an indigenous people in Puerto Rico. Cavazos quickly rose to positions of authority within the unit, first as platoon leader of Company E and then later as company commander. The valor and bravery of the Borinqueneers became legendary, and Cavazos became one of the unit's most illustrious members. Perhaps his most famous exploit during the Korean War took place in February, 1953: Leading a small band of fellow soldiers, he risked heavy enemy fire to take a wounded North Korean soldier prisoner. This act of bravery earned Cavazos a Silver Star. Before the war ended, he won another high military honor, the Distinguished Service Cross, in June, 1953.

When the Korean War ended, Cavazos embarked on a wide array of endeavors. He was an executive officer in the Army's First Armored Division and later went to West Germany to work in the European headquarters of the U.S. Army as an operations officer. In the late 1950's, he worked as a teacher and trainer in the ROTC program of his alma mater, Texas Technological College. Most of the first half of the 1960's saw Cavazos attending a number of prestigious officers' training schools, including the British Army Staff College and the United States Armed Forces Staff College. These experiences prepared him for the next armed conflict in which he would fight: the war in Vietnam.

Having attained the rank of lieutenant colonel, Cavazos was given command of the Eighteenth Infantry's First Battalion in early 1967. During his tour of duty in Vietnam, Cavazos's most notable encounter with the enemy came in the intense forty-eight-hour Battle of Loc Ninh in October, 1967. As his unit engaged the Viet Cong on an old rubber-tree plantation near the

Latinos in the United States Military

Latinos have served with distinction in practically every major American military endeavor, but perhaps the first conflict in which Latinos participated in large numbers was the War of 1812. The most famous Latino military man of the 1800's was Admiral David G. Farragut, who uttered the famous slogan, "Damn the torpedoes! Full speed ahead," while leading Union forces during the crucial Battle of Mobile in the Civil War. An early Latina soldier was Loreta Janeta Velázquez, who disguised herself as a man and fought for the Confederacy. In the Spanish-American War, at least ten Latinos served under Theodore Roosevelt in the "Rough Riders," most notably George W. Armijo, who later became a member of Congress.

In World War I, the most highly decorated Latino was Private Marcelino Serna, who took captive two dozen Germans while fighting in France and won two Purple Hearts. At the beginning of World War II, large numbers of Spanish-speaking recruits from the Southwest were sent to the Philippines. By the end of World War II, at least a dozen Latinos had been awarded Medals of Honor. In 1962, Horacio Rivero, Jr., received a promotion to four-star admiral, becoming the first Latino to attain that rank. During the Vietnam War, almost 100,000 Latinos fought, and about one-fifth that number took part in Operation Desert Shield/Desert Storm in the early 1990's in Iraq and Kuwait. In 1998, Luis Caldera became the first Latino to serve as secretary of the Army.

By the end of the first decade of the twenty-first century, there were more than one million Latino veterans and almost 125,000 Latinos serving actively, constituting roughly 12 percent of enlisted people and six percent of officers. Despite their growing demographics in the armed forces and the exemplary records of many Latino soldiers and sailors, however, Lieutenant General Ricardo Sanchez, who commanded the American forces in Iraq, spoke out in late 2010 about the inequities still facing Latinos, both as enlistees and as veterans.

Cambodian border, Cavazos led his men with such skill and diligence that the Viet Cong ended up fleeing not only the battlefield but also the fortified hillside trenches into which they had tried to escape. For this victory, he received his second Distinguished Service Cross.

After Vietnam, Cavazos continued his career. During the first half of the 1970's, he served as, among other things, a chief of the Offense Section of the Department of Division Operations at Fort Leavenworth in Kansas; a defense attaché to Mexico; and an assistant deputy director of operations in the Pentagon. In 1976, Cavazos became the first Latino to achieve the rank of brigadier general. He was quickly assigned thereafter a string of prestigious commands, ultimately becoming head of the Ninth Infantry Division. In 1982, Cavazos took on his final duty: head of the U.S. Army Forces Command (FORSCOM). He held this post until June 17, 1984, when he retired to San Antonio, Texas.

Significance

Cavazos's nearly thirty-five years of service in the U.S. Army are illustrious by any standard: He served in almost every conflict in which the U.S. became involved from the early 1950's to the mid 1980's—from the Korean War to the invasion of Grenada in the Caribbean. In addition to his two Distinguished Service Crosses and the Silver Star, Cavazos also garnered five Bronze Stars, two Legion of Merit awards, and the Purple Heart. Furthermore, he is a significant figure in Latino history as the first Latino four-star general.

Thomas Du Bose

Further Reading

Antal, John F. *Armor Attacks—the Tank Platoon: An Interactive Exercise in Small-Unit Tactics and Leadership*. Foreword by Richard Cavazos. New York: Presidio Press, 1991. Cavazos's foreword offers valuable insight into his approach to battle and leadership.

Cavazos, Lauro F. *A Kineño Remembers: From the King Ranch to the White House*. College Station: Texas A&M University Press, 2006. The best source for information on the childhoods of both of the Cavazos brothers.

Schwarzkopf, Norman. *It Doesn't Take a Hero: The Autobiography of General H. Norman Schwarzkopf.* New York: Bantam, 1992. Numerous references indicate Schwarzkopf's admiration and respect for his former superior, Cavazos, under whom he served in the Ninth Infantry Division.

Villahermosa, Gilberto N. *Honor and Fidelity: The Sixty-fifth Infantry in Korea, 1950-1953*. Washington, D.C.: Center of Military History, U.S. Army, 2009. Definitive group biography of the company of Latino warriors in which Cavazos experienced some of his early military successes.

See also: Roy Benavidez; Lauro Cavazos; Guy Gabaldon; Horacio Rivero, Jr.

César Cedeño

Dominican-born professional baseball player

Cedeño played Major League baseball (MLB) for seventeen seasons, from 1970 to 1986. Injuries and legal woes cast a shadow over much of his career, and Cedeño never achieved the level of superstardom expected from his early performance. Nevertheless, he is still remembered as one of the first great MLB players to emerge from the Dominican Republic.

Latino heritage: Dominican

Born: February 25, 1951; Santo Domingo, Dominican Republic

Also known as: César Cedeño Encarnación

Area of achievement: Baseball

Early Life

César Cedeño Encarnación, better known as César Cedeño (SAY-zahr seh-DEHN-yoh), was born on February 25, 1951, in Distrito Nacional in Santo Domingo, Dominican Republic. His father, Diogene, initially worked in a nail factory, but he eventually was able to purchase a small supermarket. Though his father did not support Cedeño's aspirations to become a professional baseball player, his mother nurtured his talent by buying his first baseball mitt. In order to help his impoverished six-person family, Cedeño dropped out of the school during the eighth grade to take a job at the same factory that employed his father.

César Cedeño. (AP Photo)

At only sixteen years old, Cedeño was discovered by Houston Astros recruiters Tony Pacheco and Pat Gillich in 1967. Upon realizing that the St. Louis Cardinals were scouting him simultaneously, Pacheco and Gillich rushed to sign Cedeño to a contract. After some persuading, Diogene Cedeño consented to his son joining the Astros. By his seventeenth birthday, Cedeño had moved to the United States to play baseball professionally.

Life's Work

In 1967, Cedeño was signed as an undrafted free agent by the Houston Astros. He played for four seasons on farm teams, including Covington, Cocoa, Peninsula, and Oklahoma City, before advancing to Houston's major-league branch on June 20, 1970, at age nineteen. Cedeño replaced Jimmy Wynn as the team's starting center fielder.

From the outset of his career, Cedeño drew constant comparisons to superstars Willie Mays, Hank Aaron, and Roberto Clemente. He batted .310 in his rookie year and .320 during the following two. Cedeño led the National League in doubles in 1971 and 1972. During each of the 1972, 1973, and 1974 seasons, he hit more than twenty home runs and stole more than fifty bases. Because of these successes, he was in serious contention for the 1972 National League Most Valuable Player (MVP) Award, finishing sixth. He continued his streak of stealing more than fifty bases per season in 1975, 1976, and 1977. During his first several years with the Astros, he was their highest-paid and most highly regarded player. During his eleven years with the Houston Astros, he was a league leader in bases stolen, runs batted in (RBI), doubles, and batting.

Cedeño remained with the Astros until December 18, 1981, at which time he was traded to the Cincinnati Reds for third baseman Ray Knight. He was again traded, this time to the St. Louis Cardinals, for outfielder Mark Jackson on August 29, 1985. In his time with the Cardinals, he batted .434 and scored six home runs, helping his team to secure a play-off berth. He was granted free agency the following November and was signed to and released from both the Toronto Blue Jays and the Los Angeles Dodgers during the 1986 season. The Cardinals signed him again as a free agent on July 19, 1986, before he decided to retire at age thirty-five at the end of that season.

After his retirement, Cedeño played briefly for a professional team in Mexico. By 2010, he had coached professional teams in his native Dominican Republic, as well as in Venezuela and in the United States.

His wattage was diminished somewhat by a number of separate criminal episodes, including convictions for assault, domestic violence, and drunken driving. Most significantly, at age twenty-two, he was convicted of involuntary manslaughter in the Dominican Republic for the murder of his nineteen-year-old girlfriend, Altagracia de la Cruz. After a two-day trial, Cedeño was ordered to pay one hundred pesos in restitution for the accidental shooting with a .38 caliber pistol that followed a particularly loud argument on December 11, 1973.

Significance

César Cedeño is regarded as one of the first great Dominican baseball players. Over the course of his seventeen year career, Cedeño batted a .285 average and achieved 199 home runs, 976 RBI, 550 stolen bases, and more than 2,000 hits. As of 2010, he ranks twenty-fifth on the list of most stolen bases in Major League Baseball and first on the same list for the Astros franchise. He was voted to the All-Star team four times, in 1972, 1973, 1974, and 1976. Additionally, he was a five-time recipient of the Golden Glove Award, claiming the prize every year between 1972 and 1976. Though plagued by injuries and somewhat stifled by the Astros' lack of major successes, Cedeño ranks high for batting average, RBI, doubles, and stolen bases.

Leon James Bynum

FURTHER READING

Briley, Ron. *Class at Bat, Gender on Deck and Race in the Hole: A Line-up of Essays on Twentieth Century Culture and America's Game.* Jefferson, N.C.: McFarland, 2003. Chapter 17 analyzes how views of Latinos shaped Cedeño's early career.

Klein, Dave. *Stars of the Major Leagues.* New York: Random House, 1974. The profile on Cedeño, written after the 1973 season, gives a contemporary analysis of his contribution and reputation.

Perry, Dayn. *Winners: How Good Baseball Teams Become Great Ones (And It's Not the Way You Think).* Hoboken, N.J.: John Wiley & Sons, 2006. Perry supplies extensive statistical information on both Cedeño and the teams for which he played.

Preston, Joseph G. *Major League Baseball in the 1970's: A Modern Game Emerges.* Jefferson, N.C.: McFarland, 2004. The era's changing demographics and how they affected Major League Baseball contextualize Cedeño's life and career.

See also: Joaquín Andújar; Roberto Clemente; Tony Fernandez; Pedro Guerrero; Albert Pujols.

ORLANDO CEPEDA

Puerto Rican-born baseball player

Cepeda, the National League's most valuable player in 1967, also was the unanimous choice for rookie of the year (1958), comeback player of the year (1967), and designated hitter of the year (1973). In seventeen seasons with six teams, most notably the San Francisco Giants and St. Louis Cardinals, Cepeda made six All-Star Game appearances and played in three World Series. However, after the end of his playing career, his reputation was tarnished by a drug conviction.

Latino heritage: Puerto Rican

Born: September 17, 1937; Ponce, Puerto Rico

Also known as: Orlando Manuel Cepeda y Penne; Baby Bull; Cha-Cha; Peruchin

Area of achievement: Baseball

EARLY LIFE

Orlando Manuel Cepeda y Penne (seh-PAY-dah) grew up poor in a Puerto Rican seaport town. His father Pedro "Perucho" Cepeda, was a legend in Caribbean baseball. Known as "The Bull" and "Babe Ruth of the Caribbean League," Perucho dreamed of his son playing Major League Baseball in America and taught him to hit, field, and throw at an early age.

At the age of seventeen, Cepeda was discovered by the New York Giants organization, given a $500 signing bonus, and sent to Salem, Virginia, to play Class D ball. As Cepeda was making his minor league debut, Perucho was dying from malaria in Puerto Rico. Cepeda used the money from his signing bonus to pay for his father's funeral. Perucho's death left his son depressed, and he considered not returning to America to play baseball.

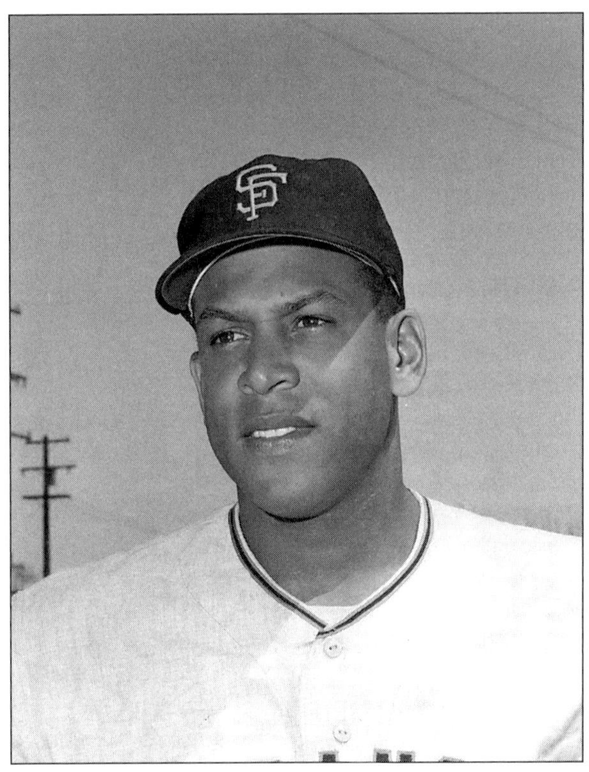

Orlando Cepeda. (AP Photo)

Cepeda's mother, however, told him to leave Puerto Rico because the family had no money and needed the $175 per month he was making. After two more seasons of playing minor league ball in Minneapolis, Cepeda was called up to the Giants in 1958, the team's first year in San Francisco. He became the first great Giants player to have never played with the New York Giants.

Life's Work

While many of his Giant teammates missed New York, Cepeda fell in love with San Francisco. He hit a home run in his first at-bat during the second game of the 1958 season. Two or three day games per week left plenty of time for nightlife, and Cepeda was a regular at the Copacabana, where he frequently went to dance and earned the nickname "Cha-Cha." A unanimous rookie of the year selection, Cepeda batted .312 with 25 home runs and 96 runs batted in.

In 1961, Cepeda led the major leagues with 46 home runs and 142 runs batted in. In 1962 the Giants won the National League pennant, but lost the World Series to the New York Yankees in seven games. After his rookie season, Cepeda was replaced at first base by rising star Willie McCovey. After a brief tryout at third base, Cepeda was moved to left field. Cepeda injured his knee playing in the outfield but kept his injury a secret. His manager at the time, Alvin Dark, was known for his prejudice against Latino players, and Cepeda wanted to prove his toughness. Injuries during the 1966 season led to a trade in the middle of his ninth season with the team.

After being traded to the St. Louis Cardinals, Cepeda led the team—whom he nicknamed "El Birdos"—to a World Series championship over the Boston Red Sox in 1967. His Cardinal teammates included Bob Gibson, Lou Brock, and Roger Maris. Although he did not play well in the World Series, Cepeda was the team's inspirational leader and the unanimous choice for his league's most valuable player award.

After two seasons with the Cardinals, Cepeda was traded to the Atlanta Braves. The team advanced to the 1969 National League Championship Series, where they lost to the New York Mets in three straight games. In 1970, although his career was on the wane, Cepeda continued to hit over .300 while driving in 111 runs. Injuries hampered his performance during the 1971-1972 season, however, and he was traded to the Oakland Athletics. In 1973, Oakland dealt Cepeda to the Boston Red Sox, where he was able to play in 142 games as a designated hitter. He responded by batting almost .290 and winning the designated hitter of the year award. Cepeda's final season, at the age of thirty-seven, came with the Kansas City Royals in 1974. Despite a drug conviction in 1975 that tarnished his reputation, in 1999, Cepeda was voted into the baseball Hall of Fame by the organization's Veterans Committee. He was only the second Puerto Rican player—after Roberto Clemente—to enter the Hall of Fame. The San Francisco Giants retired his number in 1999.

Drug Arrest and Rehabilitation

Upon returning from a baseball clinic in Colombia, Orlando Cepeda signed for two packages at Puerto Rico's San Juan International Airport on December 12, 1975. According to authorities, the packages contained a total of 170 pounds of marijuana. Cepeda was sentenced to five years in prison for possession with intent to distribute marijuana. He served ten months of his sentence in 1978 before being paroled. Cepeda's name once had been mentioned in the same breath as the great Roberto Clemente, the first Puerto Rican elected to the baseball Hall of Fame, who died in a plane crash while helping to deliver supplies to earthquake survivors in Nicaragua in 1972; now, Cepeda suddenly was an outcast. The arrest and conviction cost Cepeda everything: his reputation in Puerto Rico, his legacy in baseball, his family, his home, and his car.

After years of struggling to restore his reputation and redefine his identity, Cepeda was introduced to Buddhism in 1988. The Buddhist sect Nichiren Shosu taught him to deal with his anger and accept his mistakes. Cepeda's third wife, Mirian Ortiz, convinced him to return to San Francisco. Ashamed of his past errors, he assumed that the team had abandoned him. When he finally returned, Cepeda was surprised to receive a hero's welcome. He went to work for the Giants organization in community relations. In 1999, Cepeda was inducted into the baseball Hall of Fame. Upon returning to Puerto Rico, a parade honored the island's prodigal hero. In September, 2008, Cepeda was immortalized with a statue and a plaque at the Giants' AT&T Park.

Significance

Cepeda was a power hitter with a career 379 home runs and a batting average of .297. However, his is a cautionary tale about tremendous talent, early success, and loss of focus and direction. His sudden fall from stardom was fueled by poor personal choices.

Nevertheless, Cepeda's struggle to regain respect and rehabilitate his reputation among baseball fans remain worthy of recognition.

Randy L. Abbott

Further Reading

Cepeda, Orlando, and Charles Einstein. *My Ups and Downs in Baseball.* New York: Putnam, 1968. This autobiography, aimed at the young adult market, chronicles Cepeda's early struggles and challenges in baseball, including a nagging injury.

Cepeda, Orlando, and Herb Fagen. *Baby Bull: From Hardball to Hard Time and Back.* Dallas, Tex.: Taylor, 1998. Cepeda's third autobiography chronicles his rise as one of the first great Puerto Rican Major League Baseball players, his decline into drugs, and finally his rehabilitation through Buddhism and his return to the San Francisco Giants family.

Cepeda, Orlando, and Bob Markus. *High and Inside: Orlando Cepeda's Story.* South Bend, Ind.: Icarus Press, 1983. This book, written after Cepeda's release from prison, seeks to reestablish his reputation while explaining his mistakes.

Markusen, Bruce. *The Orlando Cepeda Story.* Houston, Tex.: Pinata Books, 2001. A biography for young adults that frames Cepeda as a man with immense natural talents whose greatest triumphs came after personal defeat.

See also: Felipe Alou; Luis Aparicio; Rod Carew; Roberto Clemente; Juan Marichal; Tony Oliva.

Lorna Dee Cervantes

American poet

Widely anthologized as a Chicana poet who speaks eloquently for women of her generation, Cervantes explores the struggles of working-class feminists in her introspective and reflective writings, finding strength through historical awareness and cross-generational bonding.

Latino heritage: Mexican and American Indian

Born: August 6, 1954; San Francisco, California

Area of achievement: Poetry; publishing

Early Life

Lorna Dee Cervantes (sur-VAHN-tayz) was born in the Mission District of San Francisco to Luis Cervantes, an artist, and his wife, Rose, a homemaker. When she was four years old, her parents divorced; Rose took Cervantes and her older brother, Esteban, to live with their maternal grandmother in the poverty-stricken Chicano barrio of Horseshoe located on the east side of San Jose. Cervantes's grandmother was of Chumash Indian descent and had been sold into servitude to a middle-class white family at the age of eleven. Cervantes helped her grandmother tend their garden and learned from her of their indigenous heritage and American Indian beliefs. Cervantes's mother was a chronic alcoholic who loved to listen to spoken-word poetry recordings but chided her daughter for her fascination with reading, regularly discouraging the girl's hopes for advancement through self-education. However, Esteban worked at a library, providing her access to literature, and Cervantes began her lifelong commitment to writing poetry at age eight.

Cervantes was discouraged from speaking Spanish at home as a strategy to better prepare her for overcoming ethnic discrimination in society. At age fifteen, she joined the National Organization for Women and soon became involved in the Chicano Moratorium, an antiwar political action movement. In her teens, Cervantes read many African American women poets, and she cites Phillis Wheatley, June Jordan, Sonia Sanchez, and Gwendolyn Brooks as influences on her crystallizing realization that poetry could and should speak politically to injustice and inequity based on gender, class, ethnicity, and race.

Life's Work

In her early adult years, Cervantes worked largely outside academia. She founded Mango Publications in 1974, introducing the literary magazine *Mango* in 1976 to help give voice to a rising generation of Chicanos and Chicanas. Her first book of poetry, *Emplumada*, was published to great acclaim in 1981 and won an American Book Award in 1982. It is in many ways a coming-of-age collection of poems and includes her highly autobiographical and celebrated work "In the Shadow of the Freeway." Also in 1982, her mother—

with whom she had a complicated and conflicted relationship as communicated in her poetry—was raped and killed by a stranger who burned down her home. After this tragedy, Cervantes chose to return to the classroom to keep honing her craft and studied under, among others, Robert Hass at San Jose State University. She cites him as a mentor and Pablo Neruda as another poet who strongly influenced her artistic development. After she earned her B.A. in creative arts from San Jose State in 1984, she enrolled in the history of consciousness doctoral program at the University of California at Santa Cruz, receiving a Ph.D. in philosophy and aesthetics in 1990.

From the Cables of Genocide: Poems of Love and Hunger, her second collection of poems, appeared in 1991. Working through the pain of grief and loss not only among individuals but also among subjugated peoples, these poems demonstrated a more complex style of progression and allusion, continuing her earlier themes of struggles against oppressive power while still conveying a sense of the redemptive power of love.

Cervantes joined the faculty of the Creative Writing Program at the University of Colorado at Boulder in 1989, eventually overseeing that program for a period as an associate professor. She remained on the faculty there until 2007. Her third collection of poems, *Drive: The First Quartet*, was published in 2006 and was nominated for a Pulitzer Prize. *Drive* offers collected unpublished works from 1980 through 2005 and contains five distinct sections that combine Cervantes's personal memories with a call to activism. It begins with a review of the horrible consequences of war, recalls her teenage years on Bird Avenue in San Jose, deals in depth with the death of a single man, and ultimately meditates upon both parental and sexual love.

In the fall of 2007, Cervantes returned to San Francisco, where she spent a semester teaching at San Francisco State University. She subsequently made San Francisco her base, from which she continued to write and offer a voice for multicultural perspectives.

Significance

Cervantes's Mango Publications first introduced the writings of later significant Chicano writers such as Luis Omar Salinas, Jimmy Santiago Baca, and Sandra Cisneros. She is one of the best-known Chicana poets of the twentieth century, and her poetry regularly conveys appreciation of ethnic and cultural heritages, a sensitivity to the struggles of people marginalized by issues of race, class, gender, and ethnicity.

Scot M. Guenter

Further Reading

Cervantes, Lorna Dee. "Lorna Dee Cervantes: Poet, Educator, Political and Feminist Writer." Interview by Karin Ikas. In *Chicana Ways: Conversations with Ten Chicana Writers.* Reno: University of Nevada Press, 2002. Cervantes shares her thoughts on Chicana identity, the evolution of her poetry, role models in Mexican and indigenous culture, and teaching and writing.

_______. "Poetry Saved My Life: An Interview with Lorna Dee Cervantes." Interview by Sonia V. Gonzalez. *MELUS* 32, no. 1(Spring, 2007): 163-180. A leading scholar on the poet's work asks her to reflect on autobiographical connections to her message and methodology.

Madsen, Deborah. *Understanding Contemporary Chicana Literature.* Columbia: University of South Carolina Press, 2001. The contributions of Cervantes and five other writers are explained as a creative "Chicana Renaissance" caught between mainstream feminism and male-dominated Chicano writing.

See also: Julia Alvarez; Marie Arana; Jimmy Santiago Baca; Giannina Braschi; Ana Castillo; Sandra Cisneros; Angela de Hoyos.

Willie Champion

American musician

The Champion family, known as the "First Family of Flamenco Music," spans four generations of dancers, singers, and musicians who were all born in San Antonio, Texas. The head of this gifted musical family is Willie "El Curro" Champion, a renowned flamenco guitarist, who is married to Teresa Champion, dubbed the "First Lady of Flamenco."

Latino heritage: Mexican

Born: June 21, 1933; San Antonio, Texas

Also known as: El Curro
Areas of achievement: Music; dance

Early Life

Willie Champion was born on June 21, 1933, in San Antonio, Texas. He graduated from Fox Tech High School in that city in 1954. Before and during the time he was in high school, he played guitar in a trio who called themselves El Cristales. Champion's wife, Teresa Martinez Champion, was born in San Antonio on October 15, 1938. She began dancing when she was six years old, performing in festivals at her church. The nuns at the church encouraged her to go to Mexico, where she could learn to become a professional dancer.

Teresa's father, Mexican immigrant Eusebyo Martinez, worked three jobs to earn the $300 needed to send Teresa to Mexico for dance lessons. Teresa's mother Maria accompanied her daughter to Mexico City, where Teresa studied at the Ballet Artes de Mexico in Mexico City.

Champion and Teresa married in 1957. Champion—whose nickname, "El Curro," means "the flashy one"—and Teresa appeared in actor John Wayne's 1960 epic film *The Alamo*. In the film, a beautiful Teresa is the featured flamenco dancer, performing on top of a table in a cantina, as the handsome Willie looks on and provides the musical sound track with his virtuoso flamenco guitar embellishments.

Life's Work

In their early years, Willie and Teresa performed in San Antonio and in many other places, with Teresa dancing the flamenco to Willie's guitar accompaniment. Teresa later recalled that she would receive a $5 paycheck and a basket of fried chicken as compensation for her performances. The couple had to work jobs outside of music in order to make a living, with Willie at one point earning $35 a week as a taxi driver.

The Champions also became the parents of two daughters. Chayito Champion, also known as "Chayo," became an internationally known flamenco singer. She has toured worldwide with José Greco and other flamenco artists, including Antonio Vargas, Teo Morca, and NaNa Lorca. In addition, Chayito has performed with DanzaActiva of Puerto Rico and has sung with Calo Flamenco, a twenty-member flamenco dance company. The Champions' younger daughter, Elsa Mari Champion Tere, also known as "La Chispita del Fuego," meaning "drop of fire," is a flamenco and folkloric dancer in San Antonio.

Champion and Teresa eventually were able to earn a living with their art. Champion has appeared on the television program *American Bandstand* and has performed with singers Tony Bennett and Marty Robbins and the Count Basie Orchestra. One of his greatest performances was delivered at Carnegie Hall, when he received a standing ovation for his appearance with renowned flamenco dancer José Greco and guitarist Andres Segovia.

In 1975, Champion began playing regularly at the Omni de La Mansion Hotel in San Antonio, and he continued to play at this venue into the twenty-first century. In a 2008 interview, Champion explained that, "I've surpassed every entertainer in San Antonio. Nobody has been in that hotel for thirty-three years. I'm part of the furniture now. When they sold La Mansion to Omni, I went along with the sell."

Throughout his career, Champion has served as a mentor to other guitarists. Teresa has similarly passed down the flamenco tradition. In 1970, she opened the Teresa Champion Dance Academy in San Antonio and has been its principal teacher and choreographer. Teresa was inducted into the San Antonio Women's Hall of Fame in 1987, and she has described this honor as one of her major accomplishments. Her dance academy celebrated its thirtieth anniversary in 2010, and Champion and Teresa performed at the celebration. That same year, Champion performed an encore rendition of his original performance in *The Alamo* at the Alamo Historical Society's celebration of the fiftieth anniversary of the film's release.

The Champions' grandchildren and great-grandchildren have followed in the couple's footsteps. Annette Champion Flores, the Champions' granddaughter and the daughter of Chayito Champion, is a dance instructor at San Antonio Community College and the artistic director of two dance groups, the Viva Dance Troupe and Soul Infusion. Grandsons Johnny Lopez and William Duran are musicians, with Lopez playing guitar and Duran playing electric and upright bass.

The fourth generation of performers is represented by Annette's oldest daughter, Janette Champion Flores, who has danced with Soul Infusion. Janette also has received scholarships to Ballet Hispanico de Nuevo York and the Broadway School of Dance. In addition, Duran's daughter Lilly is a dancer, while her brother, Christopher A. Duran, is a dancer and singer.

Significance

In 2007 Champion and Teresa celebrated fifty years of marriage. The couple has been a major influence in the

San Antonio music community, and they have helped uphold the tradition of flamenco music and dance in performances throughout the world.

Sandra W. Leconte

Further Reading

Adams, Ciarra. "San Antonio Flamenco Legends Still Sharing the Gift." *La Presna*, April 27, 2000, p. 7TV. An interview in which Willie and Teresa recall the hardships of their early career and discuss their current work.

Moore, Nicole. "Flamenco at El Calle's." August 24, 2009. *San Antonio Examiner.* Moore's review of the flamenco music scene in San Antonio offers candid insight into the world of flamenco music.

Nieto, Dustin Joe Thomas. Teresa Champion (née Martinez). http://www.alamo.edu/pac/faculty/InteractiveHistory/projects/people/categories/Women/Champion-Nieto/oralhstemplate.htm, Nieto interviewed Champion on February 24, 2007, for a course at Palo Alto College. His interview provides insight into Champion's professional and personal life history.

See also: Fernando Bujones; Evelyn Cisneros; Royes Fernández; Flaco Jiménez; José Arcadio Limón.

Franklin Ramón Chang-Díaz

Costa Rican-born astronaut, engineer, and scientist

One of the first Latin Americans to fly in space, Chang-Diaz developed technology for energy generation by nuclear fusion and applied those techniques to an advanced rocket engine.

Latino heritage: Costa Rican
Born: April 5, 1950; San José, Costa Rica
Area of achievement: Science and technology

Early Life

Franklin Ramón Chang-Díaz was born on April 5, 1950, in San José, Costa Rica. His father, Ramón Chang-Morales, was a construction foreman and son of a Chinese immigrant to Costa Rica. His mother, María Eugenia Díaz De Chang, was a housewife. Chang-Díaz spent much of his childhood in Venezuela, where he heard about the first artificial satellite, Sputnik, in 1957. The excited child climbed a tree to look for the satellite in the sky. That event sparked a lifelong interest in space exploration.

Chang-Díaz graduated from Colegio De La Salle in San José in November, 1967. He was determined to become an astronaut, but Costa Rica had no space program. His father took out a loan so Chang-Díaz could move to United States, where he lived with his cousins in Hartford, Connecticut. He knew very little English, so he enrolled in the Hartford High School to improve his language skills.

In 1969, Chang-Díaz entered the University of Connecticut, where he worked in the Physics Department, participating in high-energy physics experiments. He was awarded a bachelor of science degree in mechanical engineering in 1973.

He entered the graduate program at the Massachusetts Institute of Technology (MIT), where his research

Franklin Ramón Chang-Díaz.
(AP Photo/Houston Chronicle, Michael Paulsen)

Variable Specific Impulse Magnetoplasma Rocket (VASIMR)

A rocket functions by directing hot gas through a nozzle. The gas expelled in one direction accelerates the rocket in the opposite direction. Conventional rockets use chemical reactions to produce the hot gas; the chemical reactions burn only for a few minutes, accelerating a spacecraft until they run out of fuel. After the reaction ceases, the spacecraft "coasts" in space, subject to the gravitational pull of the sun and other bodies. This effect works to launch spacecraft into Earth orbit and even for relatively short missions to the moon; however, to go farther into space, the slow coasting phase results in a long flight time. An engine that accelerates the spacecraft continuously would significantly reduce flight time.

Plasma engines require relatively small amounts of fuel and operate for long periods of time. The exhaust of a plasma engine is a high-speed jet of ionized gas. The Variable Specific Impulse Magnetoplasma Rocket (VASIMR), being developed by Franklin Ramón Chang-Díaz's Ad Astra Rocket Company, draws on Chang-Díaz's earlier experience with fusion reactor technology. VASIMR uses electromagnetic waves to heat the gas, similar to the way a microwave oven heats a glass of water. Thew superheated plasma is confined by a strong magnetic field. By carefully designing the magnetic field so there is a small hole at one end, the plasma escapes in the same way that exhaust escapes through the nozzle on a conventional chemical rocket engine. Ad Astra successfully ground tested a prototype of the VASIMR engine, the VX-200, in September, 2009. The company plans to flight test a version of this plasma engine, the VF-200-1, in space in 2012.

focused on the behavior of "plasmas," gases in which the electrons have been stripped from the atoms. He worked on the design and operation of "fusion reactors," which generate energy by combining two light atoms into one heavier atom with the release of energy. Chang-Díaz was awarded a Ph.D. in applied plasma physics from MIT in 1977.

LIFE'S WORK

After graduating from MIT, Chang-Díaz was hired by the Charles Stark Draper laboratory in Massachusetts to work on designs and control systems for fusion reactors. While at the laboratory, Chang-Díaz assisted in the conceptual development of a new type of rocket engine based on magnetically confined high-temperature plasma.

In 1977, Chang-Díaz was one of about thirty-five hundred applicants for astronaut training. He was one of fifteen candidates selected by the National Aeronautics and Space Administration (NASA) in May, 1980. During training at NASA's Johnson Space Center in Houston, Texas, Chang-Díaz worked in the Shuttle Avionics Integration Laboratory, assisting in software checkout. He also participated in the early design studies for the Space Station. Upon completion of training in August, 1981, he became the first person of Costa Rican birth to become an astronaut.

In 1982, Chang-Díaz was selected as a support crewmember for the first Spacelab mission, in which a scientific laboratory was carried into orbit in the space shuttle's cargo bay. He served as a capsule communicator during the Spacelab flight. Later, he led the astronaut support team at the Kennedy Space Center in Florida, aiding in checkout of the space shuttles and providing flight crew support during the countdown.

Chang-Díaz's first opportunity to fly in space came in 1986, when he flew as a mission specialist, an astronaut who performs extravehicular activities, operates the remote manipulator arm, and is responsible for payloads and experiments, on the space shuttle *Columbia.* The six-day mission launched from the Kennedy Space Center on January 12, 1986. Chang-Díaz assisted in the deployment of a satellite, conducted astrophysics experiments, and operated the materials processing laboratory.

Chang-Díaz flew again as a mission specialist on the space shuttle *Atlantis*, which launched on October 18, 1989. On this five-day mission, he assisted in deploying the *Galileo* spacecraft, which explored Jupiter. Chang-Díaz's third spaceflight, again on *Atlantis*, was a eight-day mission that began on July 31, 1992. He assisted in the first test of the Tethered Satellite System, a joint project between NASA and the Italian Space Agency to extend a 20-kilometer space tether connected to a small satellite to monitor the electric current generated in the tether. The tether jammed after extending only 256 meters, compromising the results of the experiment.

Chang-Díaz next flew on the space shuttle *Discovery*'s eight-day mission, which launched on February 3, 1994. He carried out Earth observation and life science experiments in the Space Habitation Module-2. His longest spaceflight, fifteen days on the space shuttle *Columbia*, launched on February 22, 1996. A main objective was to repeat the Tethered Satellite System experiment. This time, the tether extended to a length of 19.6 kilometers before it broke and the satellite was lost. About five hours of scientific data on electrical currents and voltages in the tether and the plasma in space was obtained.

Chang-Díaz visited the Mir Space Station on his sixth flight, on the space shuttle *Discovery* in June, 1998. This ten-day mission resupplied Mir during four days the shuttle was docked there. Chang-Díaz assisted in operating the alpha magnetic spectrometer experiment, which investigated antimatter in space.

Chang-Díaz's last spaceflight, on the space shuttle *Endeavour*, launched on June 5, 2002. The thirteen-day mission delivered a new resident crew to the International Space Station (ISS). On this flight, Chang-Díaz performed three spacewalks, helping to install the Canadian Mobile Base System on the ISS's robotic arm.

During his years as an astronaut, Chang-Díaz remained interested in the development of advanced rocket propulsion technology. He served as a visiting scientist at the Plasma Fusion Center at MIT, where he headed the plasma propulsion program from October, 1983, to December, 1993. From December, 1993, until his retirement from NASA, he continued to work on plasma rocket engines as director of the Advanced Space Propulsion Laboratory at the Johnson Space Center.

Chang-Díaz retired from NASA in July, 2005, and founded the Ad Astra Rocket Company. The company, based in Webster, Texas, and Costa Rica, is developing an advanced plasma rocket engine, the Variable Specific Impulse Magnetoplasma Rocket (VASIMR).

Significance

Chang-Díaz was the first person born in Costa Rica to fly in space. He flew on seven missions, accumulating a total of 1,601 hours in space. He also worked to develop closer ties between astronauts and the scientific community, starting the Astronaut Science Colloquium Program.

Although he became a naturalized citizen of the United States, in April 1995, the government of Costa Rica conferred on him the title of "honorary citizen," the highest honor the country can give a foreign citizen. He received the Wyld Propulsion Award from the American Institute of Aeronautics and Astronautics for his research on the VASIMR engine, which could shorten the duration of a human flight to Mars from many months to about forty days.

George J. Flynn

Further Reading

D'Agnese, Joseph. "Space Explorer: Franklin Chang-Díaz." *Discover* (November, 2003): 36-38. An account of Chang-Díaz's life, discussing the challenges he faced in moving to the United States to follow his dreams of designing rockets and flying into space.

Evans, Ben. *Space Shuttle* Columbia*: Her Missions and Crews*. New York: Springer-Praxis Books, 2005. A detailed account of the flights of *Columbia*, including a description of Chang-Díaz's first and fifth spaceflights.

Sietzen, Frank, Jr. "A Hot Rod for the Solar System." *Aerospace America* (August, 2009): 38-42. A well-illustrated account of the design and testing of the VASIMR engine and its possible role in deep-space exploration.

See also: France Anne Córdova; Sidney M. Gutierrez; Ramon E. Lopez; Carlos Noriega; Ellen Ochoa.

César Chávez

American union leader and civil rights activist

Chávez was the most prominent Latino civil rights leader of the period, and as founder of the United Farm Workers (UFW), he helped to promote the conditions of migrant field workers, most of whom were of Mexican ancestry. Using aggressive but nonviolent tactics, he persuaded employers to recognize the UFW as the bargaining agent for some fifty thousand workers in Florida and California.

Latino heritage: Mexican

Born: March 31, 1927; North Gila Valley, Yuma, Arizona

Died: April 23, 1993; San Luis, near Yuma, Arizona

Also known as: César Estrada Chávez

Areas of achievement: Activism; social issues

Early Life

César Estrada Chávez (SAY-zahr CHAH-vehz) was raised in a hardworking, close-knit family that was deeply committed to the Catholic Church. His father, Librado Chávez, owned a small grocery store, pool room, and auto repair shop. After the Great Depression began in 1929, Librado lost his business, in part because

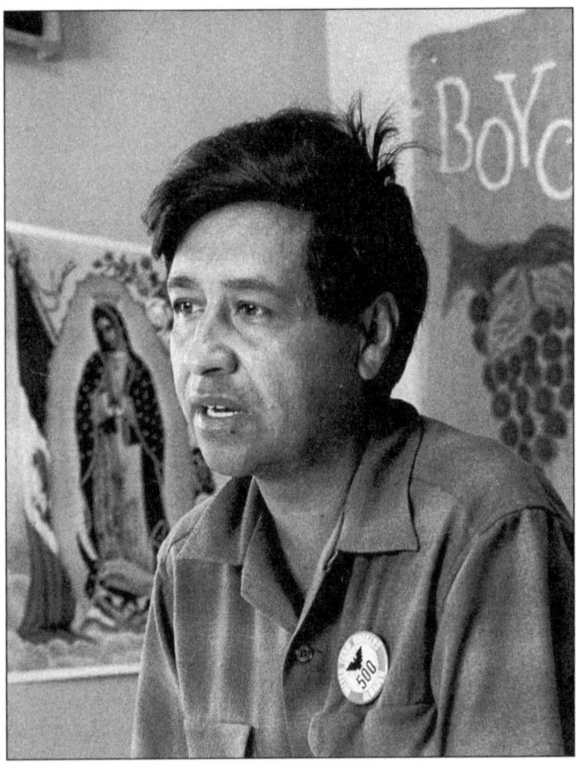

César Chávez. (AP Photo)

he trusted a dishonest neighbor in purchasing property, and the family was forced to move into an old adobe house on the small farm owned by Librado's widowed mother, Mama Tella. Chávez later described his life on the farm as happy and secure, and despite the poverty, he said that the family always had enough to eat.

The young Chávez did not do well in school, probably because his family spoke only Spanish at home. His teachers used corporal punishment whenever he spoke his native language, but he later said that the embarrassment of making mistakes in English was worse than the spankings. When white families from the South moved into the region in 1936, there were frequent fights between white and Chicano children. Chávez resented that the principal always seemed to blame the Chicanos. Because no Catholic Church was close to the family farm, Mama Tella gave Chávez most of his formal religious training. Never a skeptic, he would later write that her lessons in Christianity provided a foundation for the moral direction of his life.

In 1937, Chávez's father suffered a severe sunstroke, Mama Tella died, and the state took over the family farm because of unpaid taxes. Like thousands of others, the Chávezes moved to California, where they traveled from place to place in search of work picking fruits and vegetables. Wages were low, and housing conditions were miserable. Chávez attended some sixty-five different elementary schools, sometimes for only a few days. In 1942, the year that he graduated from the eighth grade, an accident left his father unable to work, forcing Chávez to leave school and work in the fields.

In 1944, Chávez joined the U.S. Navy so he would not be drafted into the Army. He disliked the regimentation and strongly resented the military's discrimination against minorities. He later described his two years of service as the worst in his life. Although he once sailed on a crew transport to the Mariana Islands, he never participated in combat. He observed that Latinos and other minorities rarely were in positions of leadership, and while on leave he was briefly arrested for refusing to sit in a segregated area in a theater. After completing his military service, Chávez returned to California to resume working in the fields. In 1948, he married Helen Fabela. The couple settled in Delano and would eventually have eight children.

Life's Work

In 1952, Chávez was introduced to the idea of collective organization by his parish priest, Father Donald McDonnell, who was strongly committed to the Catholic Church's doctrines on workers' rights. McDonnell provided Chávez with relevant papal encyclicals and books on labor history and social movements. Chávez was particularly impressed by Mahatma Gandhi's philosophy of using nonviolent protests in pursuit of social justice. Shortly thereafter, Chávez met Fred Ross, a militant leader in Saul Alinsky's Community Service Organization (CSO). Ross was urging Mexican Americans organize politically, emphasizing issues of voter registration, housing discrimination, police abuse, and public education. Chávez began working for the CSO, first as a volunteer and then as a full-time employee. By the late 1950's, he was a regional leader of the organization.

In 1962, Chávez resigned from the CSO because of its refusal to organize a union devoted to improving the conditions of farm laborers. He joined with Dolores Huerta to establish the National Farm Workers Association, which became the United Farm Workers (UFW) three years later. For the organization's logo, Chávez chose the colors red and black, and his brother Richard designed an Aztec eagle without wings, which was easy to draw on homemade flags. One of the major challenges of the union, which was primarily composed of poor

Chicano workers, was to collect enough dues to pay for its activities.

Chávez and the UFW captured national attention for the first time during a five-year grape strike in the region of Delano, California. Shortly after the strike began in 1965, Chávez led a twenty-one-day, 250-mile protest march from Delano to Sacramento. In December, Chávez called for a national boycott of grapes produced by the two largest grape-growing corporations in Delano. In 1968, when many strikers became impatient with Chávez's nonviolent tactics, he went on a twenty-five-day hunger strike in order to persuade his followers not to resort to violence. The widely publicized fast, which lasted from February 15 to March 11, was quite successful in gaining sympathy for the UFW. On the day that Chávez broke the fast, a rally of six thousand supporters, including Senator Robert F. Kennedy, assembled in Delano. The strike ended in 1970, when the UFW finally reached a collective bargaining agreement with the grape-growing corporations, covering more than ten thousand workers.

By the 1970's, the UFW was generally recognized as the nation's vanguard union of farmworkers, and it continued to organize strikes and boycotts. In 1972, Chávez undertook a twenty-four-day fast to protest an Arizona law that outlawed secondary boycotts. Although the fast failed to achieve its objectives, it succeeded in prompting the registration of thousands of Latino voters. The UFW's activities helped convince California's legislature to pass the Agricultural Labor Relations Act of 1975, which provided the right of collective bargaining to farmworkers in the state. Because growers often hired undocumented workers from Mexico as strikebreakers, the UFW supported stricter enforcement of the nation's immigration laws.

During the 1980's, Chávez changed his position on immigration and became an outspoken proponent of immigrants' rights. He also began to concentrate much of his attention on the health hazards posed by pesticides. To publicize the issue, he held a thirty-six-day fast, which was accompanied by nightly masses with thousands of sympathizers. Before he finally ended the fast, doctors warned that he had begun to burn muscle tissue and could experience kidney failure.

Chávez faced growing frustrations and challenges during the early 1990's. The UFW experienced internal dissent and was beset with serious financial difficulties, especially after two lawsuits that required it to pay more than $7 million. Chávez was forced to increase the number of fund-raising rallies. At the same time, he stepped up efforts to increase membership. On April 23, 1993, while in Arizona on UFW business, he began another fast but was convinced to call it off because of his deteriorating health. That night, he died in his sleep.

Chávez, Huerta, and the United Farm Workers

Dolores Huerta's efforts at organizing poor people predated those of César Chávez. In 1955, she cofounded the Stockton chapter of the Community Service Organization. A former schoolteacher who delivered impassioned speeches, Huerta became known as "La Pasionaria" (the Passionate One). Recognizing her dedication and communication skills, Chávez selected her to be the cofounder of the National Farm Workers Association in 1962. For more than three tumultuous decades, the two leaders had a symbiotic relationship. While Chávez was the face of the union, Huerta played a crucial role in formulating its goals and strategies. In 1965, she directed the union's national grape boycott, and the next year, she negotiated a landmark contract between the union and the Schenley Wine Company. Although she also was known for her radical socialist ideas, she served as an effective lobbyist in Washington and Sacramento. She was arrested at least twenty-two times for participating in demonstrations and other forms of nonviolent civil disobedience.

Significance

Although most farmworkers continued to receive low wages and live in poverty, Chávez's activities within the UFW promoted greater sympathy for their plight and achieved at least some amelioration for union members. After his death, he became a symbol of heroic personal sacrifice in pursuit of greater social justice. His birthday has been declared a state holiday in California and Texas and an optional holiday in Arizona and Colorado.

Thomas Tandy Lewis

Further Reading

Collins, David. *César Chávez*. Minneapolis, Minn.: Lerner, 2005. A good summary that is written primarily for young readers, presenting Chávez as an inspiration and positive role model.

Etulain, Richard W., ed. *César Chávez: A Brief Biography with Documents*. New York: Bedford/St.

Martin's, 2002. Primarily a supplementary text for college courses, this useful book includes a chronology, bibliographical essay, and collection of original documents.

Giswold del Castillo, Richard, and Richard A. Garcia. *César Chávez: A Triumph of Spirit*. Norman: University of Oklahoma Press, 1995. A relatively short biography that is well-written, balanced, and based on abundant research.

Jensen Richard, and John Hammerback. *The Words of César Chávez*. College Station: Texas A&M University Press, 2002. A collection of Chávez's speeches and correspondence organized into major periods, with chapter introductions emphasizing rhetorical analysis.

Levy, Jacques E. *César Chávez: Autobiography of La Causa*. New York: W. W. Norton, 1974. The author has taken selections from Chávez's taped interviews, producing an unsurpassed primary source of personal insights into the man and his life until the early 1970's.

Pawel, Miriam. *The Union of Their Dreams: Power, Hope, and Struggle in César Chávez's Farm Worker Movement*. New York: Bloomsbury, 2009. Written by a Pulitzer Prize-winning journalist, this book presents a poignant account of the movement and the people who made it, including both accomplishments and failures.

Stavans, Ilan, ed. *César Chávez*. Santa Barbara, Calif.: Greenwood, 2010. A collection of essays that captures the multiple aspects of a complex person and his career.

See also: Luisa Capetillo; Helen Fabela Chávez; Dolores Huerta; Antonio Orendain.

DENISE CHÁVEZ

American writer and actor

A writer, playwright, actor, educator, and activist, Chávez produces work that not only speaks specifically to women who share her culture and experiences but also educates and entertains other general readers through her exploration of universal themes.

Latino heritage: Mexican

Born: August 15, 1948; Las Cruces, New Mexico

Also known as: Denise Elia Chávez

Areas of achievement: Literature; theater; education; social issues

EARLY LIFE

Denise Elia Chávez (CHAH-vehz) was born in Las Cruces, New Mexico, to Ernesto, an attorney, and Delfina Rede Chávez, a schoolteacher. When she was ten years old, her parents divorced, and she subsequently lived in an all-female household with her mother, maternal grandmother, and two sisters, Faride and Margo. Education and bilingualism were valued; the family was engaged with literature, language, and storytelling. Chávez kept a diary and recorded the stories she heard at home. She also played school with her sisters.

At Madonna High School, a Catholic school for girls in Mesilla, New Mexico, Chávez discovered drama and theater and began to dream of becoming an actor. She performed in her school's theater productions and worked in a local hospital.

In 1970, Chávez received a scholarship to New Mexico State University to study drama. She won the school's best play award for her first written play, *The Wait*. She continued to write plays in the early 1970's, including, *Elevators* (1972) and *The Flying Tortilla Man* (1975). She completed a master of fine arts degree in drama from Trinity University, San Antonio, Texas, in 1974 with encouragement from her mentor, author Rudolfo Anaya (author of 1971's *Bless Me, Ultima*).

LIFE'S WORK

Chávez began teaching at Northern New Mexico Community College in Santa Fe in 1975, working hard to serve her community. She also worked as an artist in the schools and in the Dallas Theater Center from 1977 to 1983. Focusing on economic and social issues related to Chicano culture in her writings, she also uses humor and universal themes and draws on personal experiences. There are many similarities between Chávez's protagonists and the people and issues in her own life.

In 1986, *The Last of the Menu Girls*, a collection of short stories, was published. She also continued to write plays, including *The Mask of November* (1977), *The Adobe Rabbit* (1979), *Santa Fe Charm* (1980), *How Junior Got Throwed in the Joint* (1981), *Hecho en Mexico* (1982; *Made in Mexico*), *The Green Madonna* (1982), and *La morenita* (1983, *The Dark Virgin*). Chávez also

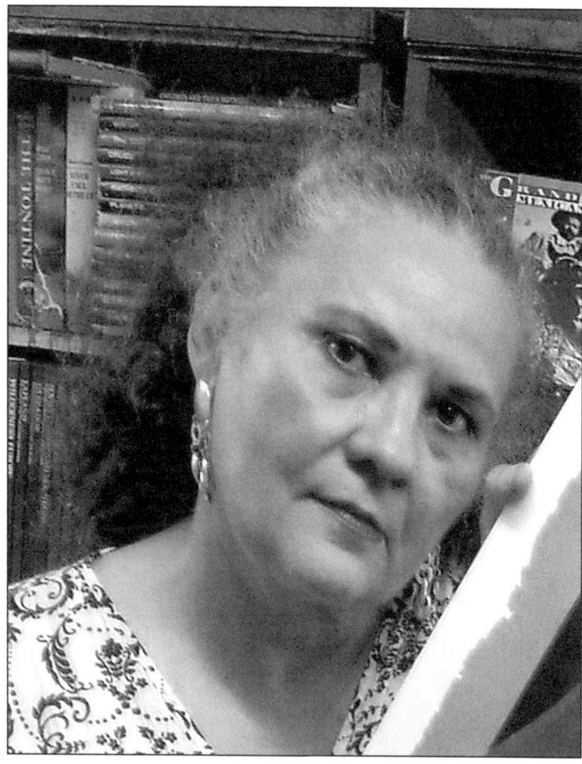

Denise Chávez. (AP Photo)

completed her master of arts degree in creative writing from the University of New Mexico in 1982.

Chávez moved back to Las Cruces in 1983 after her mother's death and began writing in the very room in her grandmother's house where she had been born. She wrote much poetry and many stories and plays in that room in the 1980's. She married photographer and sculptor Daniel Zolinsky in 1984. The plays she penned in the 1980's include *The Plaza* (1984), which was produced at the Edinburgh Festival in Scotland and at Joseph Papps's Festival Latino de Nueva York. Chávez also found success with the one-woman show *Women in the State of Grace* (1989), which she performed throughout the United States.

From 1988 to 1991, Chávez worked as a theater professor at the University of Houston in Texas. She stressed the importance of honesty and respect, encouraging her students to keep journals.

Chávez released her novel *Face of an Angel* in 1994; it was honored with an American Book Award, the Premio Aztlán Literary Prize, and the Mesilla Valley Author of the Year Award. She also won the New Mexico Governor's Award in literature and *The El Paso Herald-Post* Writers of the Pass distinction. Her work gives voice to subjects often considered taboo, such as incest, alcohol abuse, religion, and sexuality.

In 1994, Chávez founded the Border Book Festival in Las Cruces, New Mexico. The annual event features authors, storytellers, musicians, films, and art. It brings attention to issues and concerns of the communities of the border between Mexico and the United States with Chávez leading as a community activist. She also became the executive director of the Mesilla Cultural Center where she leads workshops, plans book and cultural events and works with volunteers of the Border Book Festival. Rare, out-of-print, first edition and bilingual books are featured at the Center. Chávez has received several awards for her literary and philanthropic work including: the New Mexico Community Luminaria Award, the Soroptomist International Woman of Distinction Award in education, and the New Mexico Governor's Award in literature.

In 2001, Chávez published *Loving Pedro Infante*, a passionate, engaging novel that examines friendship, love, and lust. In 2006, Chávez's memoir, *A Taco Testimony: Meditations on Family, Food, and Culture*, was published.

In addition to writing numerous books and plays, Chávez has had her work published in anthologies such as *An Anthology of Southwestern Literature* (1977), *Cuentos Chicanos: A Short Story Anthology* (1984), and *Chicana Creativity and Criticism: Charting New Frontiers in American Literature* (1996). She also has contributed her writings to periodicals including *Americas Review*, *New Mexico*, *Journal of Ethnic Studies*, and *Revista Chicano-Riqueña.*

Significance

Chávez has written poems, plays, stories, and novels that deal with difficult topics frankly and honestly, challenging the machismo status quo of many Latino communities. She draws on her own experiences in most of her works to confront issues of abuse, alcoholism, sexuality, and difficult relationships. Her books explore poignantly and humorously the topics families regard as taboo. In addition to writing, serving as the executive director of the Cultural Center of Mesilla, and organizing the Border Book Foundation and the annual Border Book Festival, Chávez lectures and leads workshops nationally and internationally. She teaches drama, monologue, performance writing, storytelling, and creative writing. She also wrote a children's book, *The Woman Who Knew the Language of Animals* (1992). Chávez's body of work speaks to

Chávez's Autobiographical Writings

In *A Taco Testimony: Meditations on Family, Food, and Culture* (2006), Denise Chávez shares her sometimes hilarious, often difficult experiences growing up on the border between Mexico and New Mexico. A mix of poetry, prose, history, and family recipes, the book highlights life along the Mexican-American border and focuses on the history of Chávez's family. Food and cooking—especially the preparation of tacos—plays a central role in her depiction of her family. She examines her identity and confesses that she feels more Mexican than anything else. She also recounts painful memories, such as her father's alcoholism and her parents' divorce, that profoundly affected her. In particular, the memoir describes how Chávez cared for her father until his death. In her sympathetic descriptions of these difficult events, Chávez appeals to readers regardless of ethnicity, class, or gender.

Latinas and non-Latinas who struggle with issues of identity, sexuality, and family. Through honesty, courage, and humor, she offers hope to all who read or perform her works.

Amada Irma Perez

Further Reading

Chávez, Denise. "Denise Chávez." In *This Is About Vision: Interviews with Southwestern Writers*, edited by William Balassi, John F. Crawford, and Annie O. Eysturoy. Albuquerque: University of New Mexico Press, 1990. Candid, personal interview in which Chávez discusses some of the themes in her writing.

_______. *A Taco Testimony: Meditations on Family, Food, and Culture*. Tucson, Ariz.: Rio Nuevo, 2006. Chávez's memoir is full of revealing and humorous details about her life and family.

"Denise Chávez." In *Feminist Writers*, edited by Pamela L. Shelton. Detroit, Mich.: St. James Press, 1996. This article on Chávez includes a brief biography and critical overview of her work from a feminist point of view.

Saldívar, José David, and Héctor Calderón, eds. *Criticism in the Borderlands: Studies in Chicano Literature, Culture, and Ideology*. Durham, N.C.: Duke University Press, 1991. This volume maps the literary contributions of Chicano writers; several of its essays reference Chávez's work.

Wood, Jamie Martinez. "Denise Chávez." In *Latino Writers and Journalists*. New York: Facts On File, 2007. Chronicles Chávez's extensive literary output and discusses recurring themes in her work.

See also: Gloria Anzaldúa; Norma Elia Cantú; Sandra Cisneros; Mary Helen Ponce; Estela Portillo Trambley; Esmeralda Santiago; Carmen Tafolla; Bernice Zamora.

Dennis Chavez

American politician

Following two terms in the U.S. House of Representatives, Chavez represented New Mexico in the U.S. Senate for twenty-seven years, from 1935 to 1962. He was without question the best-known and most successful Latino politician of his generation.

Latino heritage: Mexican

Born: April 8, 1888; Los Chaves, New Mexico

Died: November 18, 1962; Washington, D.C.

Also known as: Dionisio Chavez

Area of achievement: Government and politics

Early Life

Dennis Chavez (CHAH-vehs) was born Dioniso Chavez in Los Chaves, New Mexico Territory, on April 8, 1888. He was the third of eight children born to David and Paz (nee Sanchez) Chavez, both of whom were descendants of families that had long been established in the region.

In 1895, when Chavez was seven years old, the family moved to Albuquerque, where he attended school until he was old enough to get a job. He worked for several years driving a grocery wagon while studying engineering and surveying in the evenings. Eventually, he secured a job with the city engineering department, where he worked until the mid-1910's. He also resided briefly in Belen, New Mexico, where, among other activities, he edited the local newspaper. It was during his school years that his name was changed from Dionisio to Dennis.

During his youth, Chavez read voraciously with a particular focus on history and politics, and by his early twenties, his passion for politics had become apparent. He worked on the political campaigns of several local Democrats and, in 1916, ran for public office himself for the first time, losing by a small margin in a race for county clerk. Later the same year, his work on the U.S. Senate campaign of Andrieus Jones resulted in Jones securing a position for him as a clerk in the Senate. While living and working in Washington during the years that followed, Chavez also took classes at Georgetown University, where he completed a law degree in 1920. Returning to Albuquerque, he set up a law practice there and was elected to a term in the New Mexico Legislature in 1922.

Life's Work

With his eyes fixed on national political office, Chavez ran for New Mexico's seat in the U.S. House of Representatives in 1930, successfully unseating the Republicanincumbent Albert Simms. He was reelected in 1932. During his House career, he served on a number of committees and chaired the House Committee on Indian Affairs. In 1934, he was granted his party's nomination to run for the U.S. Senate against Republican incumbent Bronson Cutting. After he lost by a close margin, Chavez challenged the outcome, claiming fraudulent voting practices by the Republicans. The challenge was still under way when Cutting was killed in a plane crash while traveling to Washington. Democratic Governor Clyde Tingley appointed Chavez to fill the vacant seat. The appointment won the approval of New Mexico voters in 1936 and Chavez remained in the Senate until his death in 1962, winning reelection campaigns in 1940, 1946, 1952, and 1958. He held the distinction of being the first individual of Hispanic descent to be elected to a full term in the U.S. Senate.

Dennis Chavez.
(Harris & Ewing Collection/Library of Congress)

As a Democrat in Washington in the midst of the Great Depression, Chavez was an unabashed supporter of Franklin D. Roosevelt's New Deal, giving his support to its vast array of social programs. He also was highly successful in bringing jobs and projects from the Public Works Administration and Works Progress Administration to his home state, to the extent that the Hatch Bill of 1939 (sponsored by Chavez's fellow senator from New Mexico, Carl Hatch) was in part directed at the system of patronage that Chavez had established. His strong support for Roosevelt also caused him to sign on to the president's doomed "court-packing plan" to reorganize the federal judiciary in 1937. Despite these controversies, Chavez's support among his constituents remained strong. His battle for Indian land rights as a member of the Senate Indian Affairs Committee also was popular with his Native American supporters, although full voting rights were not extended to this group in New Mexico until 1948.

After winning his second Senate term in 1940, Chavez came out briefly as an isolationist in foreign affairs, breaking to some degree with the Roosevelt administration on the issue. After the Japanese attack on Pearl Harbor, however, he fully supported the war effort. Among his initiatives during wartime were his efforts to make permanent the Fair Employment Practices Committee that had been started by the president as an emergency measure in 1941. His efforts in this regard, beginning in 1944, opened him up to vicious attacks from southern senators, who eventually managed to derail the legislation. Chavez also was a strong supporter of legislation to assist American prisoners of war during and after the war. He also was an advocate for improved social and economic conditions in Puerto Rico and the Virgin Islands.

In the 1950's, during Dwight D. Eisenhower's presidency, Chavez served as chair of the powerful Senate

Chavez's Efforts on Behalf of Hispanics and Other Minorities

During his two terms in the U.S. House of Representatives and his twenty-seven years as a member of the U.S. Senate, Dennis Chavez was a strong advocate of Latino rights. To this end, believing that Latino rights were inextricably linked to the rights of other minority groups, he was a strong supporter throughout his career of a wide range of social and civil rights legislation aimed at improving conditions for minorities. One well-known example of this was his battle in the mid-1940's to establish the Fair Employment Practices Committee, begun in 1941 to end discrimination in war-related industries, on a permanent basis. The effort brought on the strong resistance of southern senators such as Theodore G. Bilbo of Mississippi. Although Bilbo and others eventually derailed the legislation, the attempt stands as an important early precursor of what would become the postwar civil rights movement. In addition to generalized legislative efforts, Chavez also offered strong personal encouragement to young Latinos hoping to enter careers in public service, finding jobs for them in Washington that would provide the experience and educational opportunities necessary for advancement. In his legislative efforts and in his exercise of influence on behalf of his Latino constituents, Chavez stands as a major force in Latino rights during the middle years of the twentieth century.

Committee on Public Works and in this capacity played a key role in the creation of the interstate highway system as well as other projects to improve the infrastructure of the country. He also survived a major controversy surrounding his 1952 reelection when his Republican opponent, Patrick Hurley, challenged its outcome. The issue was finally resolved by a vote in the Senate in 1954. As he had been earlier in his career, Chavez remained highly successful during these later years in bringing federal money, especially in the form of defense and technology contracts, to his home state.

Chavez was married to Imelda (nee Espinoza) Chavez for fifty-one years and was the father of three children. He died of a heart attack while still serving in the Senate on November 18, 1962.

SIGNIFICANCE

Serving in the U.S. House of Representatives and the U.S. Senate for a total of more than thirty years, Chavez was the most successful and influential Latino politician of his generation. His presence in national politics spanned the critical periods of the Great Depression, World War II, and the first seventeen years of the postwar era, and his career broke new ground for minorities in national politics. While he worked hard for the rights of Latino people and other minorities, his service extended far beyond that to what was good for the rest of the nation as well.

Scott Wright

FURTHER READING

Baily, Robert J. "Theodore G. Bilbo and the Fair Practices Controversy: A Senator's Reactions to a Changing World." *Journal of Mississippi History* 42, no. 1 (March, 1980): 27-42. Details Chavez' struggle to establish a permanent Fair Employment Practices Committee and the successful blocking of the effort by Mississippi senator Theodore Bilbo.

Jenkins, Jeffery A. "Partisanship and Contested Election Cases in the Senate, 1789-2002." *Studies in American Political Development* 19, no. 1 (April, 2005): 53-74. Includes a detailed discussion of the Chavez-Hurley election dispute in the early 1950's.

Keleher, William A. *Memoirs, Episodes in New Mexico History, 1892-1969*. Santa Fe, N. Mex.: Sunstone Press, 2008. Keleher's memoirs, first published in 1969, include material on Chavez's role in New Mexico politics during the 1930's and especially the 1934 senatorial election and its aftermath.

Maurilio, Virgil, and Roy Lujan. "Parallels in the Careers of Two Hispanic U.S. Senators." *Journal of Ethnic Studies* 13, no. 4 (1986): 1-20. Compares the Senate careers of Chavez and Joseph Montoya (who represented New Mexico in the Senate from 1964 to 1977). Also a good source of basic information on Chavez's life and political career.

See also: Toney Anaya; Jerry Apodaca; Manuel Luján, Jr.; Joseph M. Montoya; Bill Richardson.

Fray Angélico Chávez

American religious leader and writer

Chávez was a Franciscan priest, as well as a noted historical writer, poet, novelist, artist, and archivist. His impact on the religious thought of the American West and on the literary scene in Santa Fe during the 1950's through his death in 1996 was widely felt and acknowledged, as he did much to bring the colonial religious history of New Mexico to public and scholarly attention.

Latino heritage: Mexican

Born: April 10, 1910; Wagon Mound, New Mexico

Died: March 18, 1996; Santa Fe, New Mexico

Also known as: Manuel Ezequiel Chávez

Areas of achievement: Religion and theology; literature

Early Life

Fray Angélico Chávez (fray ahn-JEHL-ih-coh SHAH-vehz) was born Manuel Ezequiel Chávez on April 10, 1910, in the town of Wagon Mound in northern New Mexico, the first of ten children born to Fabián Chávez and María Nicolasa Roybal de Chávez. As if growing up in a Catholic family in New Mexico, a land that had been long dominated by the Order of St. Francis, or Franciscans, was not enough to convince him to take the vows of a religious order, Chávez was exposed at an early age to Franciscan history, most likely when his family lived in San Diego, California, from 1911 until 1916, while his father worked as a carpenter at the Panama-California Exposition. His mother, who had been a teacher and had attended New Mexico Normal University (now called New Mexico Highlands University) in Las Vegas, encouraged him to pursue his education, and he attended a private school in Wagon Mound that was run by Don Zeferino Trujillo, who had the support of New Mexico's famous archbishop, Jean-Baptiste Lamy. Chávez's parents encouraged his literary aspirations, as they both read much, and the young Chávez had cultivated the reading habit by the age of five.

Chávez would later reveal in his writings that he first was attracted to the idea of the Franciscan Order during his family's time in San Diego, and he expressed his desire to join the order during a Franciscan father's visit to his school when he was in fourth or fifth grade. At the age of fourteen, he left his hometown to attend the Saint Francis Seraphic Seminary in Mount Healthy, Ohio, where he studied until he was fully ready to enter his vocation. It was at the seminary that Chávez's academic world expanded with the study of Greek, German, and Latin. He read the classics, but he was also interested in philosophy, poetry, and mysticism. His interest in writing began to take shape, as he was encouraged by the priests who instructed him to express himself artistically through writing and painting. Along with the contributions to the seminary's periodical, he painted historical portraits on the walls of the seminary's new dormitory. It was because of his artistic talents that he was given the nickname "Angélico," after the medieval artist Fra Angelico.

At the age of nineteen, Chávez took his first official vows, and his nickname officially became his Franciscan name. He was ordained in 1937 at Saint Francis Cathedral in Santa Fe, becoming the first native New Mexican to be ordained a Franciscan priest in New Mexico after more than three hundred years of Franciscan presence in the region.

Life's Work

The new friar's first missionary assignment took him to southern New Mexico and the parish of Peña Blanca, which saw to the spiritual needs of three of New Mexico's Native American pueblos: Cochití, Santo Domingo, and San Felipe. During his six years there, he enjoyed an excellent rapport with the region's Pueblo Indians, whose traditions he respected and integrated into his presentations of the Mass. In 1943, he was called into active duty in the U.S. Army, becoming a chaplain serving the 77th Infantry Division in the South Pacific. His service during World War II inspired further writing in which he depicted the horrors of warfare in poignant words. He remained in the Army Reserves and the New Mexico National Guard, serving in Europe during the Korean War and attaining the rank of major. He was able to travel while in Europe, immersing himself in Franciscan and Catholic history and attaining a deeper understanding of the Spanish connection to his own home in New Mexico.

Although he had been active in writing about Hispano (Hispanic New Mexican) history and culture for nearly his entire adult life, Chávez's most productive period began with his return from military service in 1952. He served for eight years at Jémez Pueblo and for five as pastor of Saint Joseph's Parish in Cerrillos, New Mexico. In 1964, he left the pastorate in order to spend all of his time researching and writing. In 1971,

Chávez's Crisis of Faith

In 1967, when the Catholic Church implemented the recommendations of the Second Vatican Council (Vatican II), which not only allowed for and encouraged the use of the common language instead of Latin in the Mass but also profoundly impacted the roles that priests played in their communities, many priests had a difficult time reconciling themselves with their new positions both in the church and in the community. Fray Angélico Chávez was one such priest.

In 1971, although he never formally signed a dispensation from his Franciscan vows, he left active participation in the Order of Saint Francis and the priesthood. For the next eighteen years, Chávez was not seen as a formal member of the order, although he remained active, continuing his intellectual pursuits in Franciscan history. Although some within the order called for his administrative dismissal from the organization, others wanted the order to reach out to their most well-known member and bring him back into the group. In 1974, when Robert Fortune Sánchez became the archbishop of Santa Fe, he appointed Chávez archivist of the archdiocese. Sánchez later allowed Chávez to celebrate Christmas Eve Mass with him, bringing Chávez officially back into communion with the Church. Over the next few years, the leader of the local Franciscan community, Crispin Butz, worked to reinstate Chávez with the order. In 1989, Chávez was allowed to retire to the Saint Francis Friary as an official member of the Order of Saint Francis, where he remained for his final years.

he officially left the priesthood, although he remained consistently active as a scholar of New Mexican history, religion, and culture. In 1989, he moved to Saint Francis Friary in Santa Fe, where he spent the last seven years of his life immersed both in his studies and in the pleasures of daily life in the city. He died on March 18, 1996, after a brief illness and was buried at the Rosario Catholic Cemetery near downtown Santa Fe.

SIGNIFICANCE

Fray Angélico Chávez was a multitalented scholar, artist, and priest. He was the archivist for the Archdiocese of Santa Fe, cataloging and translating many colonial Spanish and Mexican records about the political, cultural, and family history of New Mexico. He traced the genealogy of many of New Mexico's Hispano families all the way back to Juan de Oñate, the first Spanish governor of the region, who arrived in 1598. Among Chávez's most well-received historical writings were *Origins of New Mexico Families: A Genealogy of the Spanish Colonial Period* (1954), *My Penitente Land: A Reflection of Spanish New Mexico* (1974), and *But Time and Chance: The Story of Padre Martinez of Taos, 1793-1867* (1981).

Chávez also wrote poetry and longer fiction, including short stories, such as those found in his *New Mexico Triptych: Being Three Panels and Three Accounts* (1959), and a novel, *The Virgin of Port Lligat* (1959). Seeing folklore as an integral part of New Mexican culture, Chávez collected and edited folk tales in *When the Santos Talked: A Retablo of New Mexico Tales* (1977). As a Hispano priest, poet, artist, and historical scholar, Chávez distinguished himself as one of New Mexico's foremost literary and intellectual figures, occupying an indispensable place in the Santa Fe literary scene throughout much of the late twentieth century, and he has been called the region's most important literary figure of the century.

Steven L. Danver

FURTHER READING

Garcia, Nasarío. Introduction to *Cantares: Canticles and Poems of Youth, 1925-1932*, by Fray Angélico Chávez. Houston: Arte Público Press, 2000. The introduction to this collection of Chávez's early poetry contains an excellent, detailed recounting of his childhood, youth, and early adulthood. .

McCracken, Ellen, ed. *Fray Angélico Chávez: Poet, Priest, and Artist*, Albuquerque: University of New Mexico Press, 2000. This collection of essays analyzes Chávez's literary production but also lends considerable light to his religious views and how they shaped both his personal life and his archival work and writing.

McCracken, Ellen Marie. *The Life and Writing of Fray Angélico Chávez: A New Mexico Renaissance Man*. Albuquerque: University of New Mexico Press, 2009. A literary biography of Chávez, it presents a chronological account of the evolution of Chávez's thought as expressed in his writings, as well as substantial information on his artistic works and religious thought.

Morgan, Phyllis S. *Fray Angélico Chávez: A Bibliography of Published Works (1925-2010) and a Chronology of His Life (1910-1996)*. Los Ranchos de Albuquerque, N.M: Rio Grande Books, 2010. Published on the one hundredth anniversary of his birth, this work, like Chávez himself, integrates literary production with his life events and religious thought.

See also: Nicky Cruz; Antonio José Martínez; José Policarpo Rodríguez; Oscar I. Romo; Yolanda Tarango; Virgilio Elizondo.

Helen Fabela Chávez

American labor activist

As the wife of the United Farm Workers (UFW) organizer and founder César Chávez, Helen Chávez was heavily involved and influential in the union. She balanced her domestic responsibilities with working in the fields and helping other migrant farmworkers.

Latino heritage: Mexican
Born: January 21, 1928; Brawley, California
Also known as: Helen Fabela
Areas of achievement: Activism; social issues

Early Life

Helen Fabela Chávez (fah-BEHL-ah CHAH-vehz) was born Helen Fabela in Brawley, California, on January 21, 1928. Her parents were Mexican immigrants Vidal Fabela and Eloisa Rodriguez, who met in Los Angeles, California, and married in 1923. The Fabela family were migrant farmworkers in the California valleys. Like many Mexican Americans, they worked long hours for low wages in unhealthy conditions. These factors, as well as inadequate housing, took a toll on Chávez's health. She became malnourished and anemic.

Chávez's values of the traditional Mexican familial structure were formed by her mother's dedication to her role as mother and wife. Eloisa would work only temporarily in the fields, focusing most of her attention on the needs of her family, while Vidal was active in the Comisión Mexicana, a group dedicated to maintaining the Mexican community. When Chávez was twelve years old, her father died, leaving the family in a difficult financial situation. To help support her mother and siblings, Chávez and her older sister made the difficult decision to stop attending school and work full time at the DiGiorgio Corporation, a major fruit grower. Chávez also worked for local ranches packing grapes, and when the season ended, she worked in nearby stores as a clerk.

In 1943, the same year she began working full time, Chávez met César Chávez at a malt shop named La Baratita. Although César served in the U.S. Navy from 1944 to 1946 and continued to work seasonally as a migrant field worker with his family, the two dated whenever they could. In October, 1948, the young couple married. César and Helen Chávez had eight children over the next ten years, and Chávez's roles as a mother and wife became central in her life.

Life's Work

Chávez began her activism while living in the "Sal Si Puede" ("Get Out If You Can") barrio of San Jose, California. Her husband became involved in the Community Service Organization (CSO), and Chávez often helped with the bookkeeping and office work, such as writing out daily reports. She often is credited with convincing César to speak with CSO organizer Fred Ross, whom her husband had avoided until Chávez's intervention. Chávez was very supportive of her husband's responsibilities with the CSO. She later began attending local division meetings and conventions, and by the late 1950's, she was participating in civic protests. One protest in particular, devoted to the unemployed local workers, convinced César to form an organization completely dedicated to the struggles of farmworkers.

In 1962, César and Dolores Huerta founded the National Farm Workers Association (NFWA). César worked as an unpaid volunteer when the organization was launched, so Helen had to return to the fields in

Helen Chávez. (Hulton Archive/Getty Images)

order to support her family. She worked long hours and was paid very little. Chávez worked out of necessity, and because of her working-class background and upbringing, she understood that the fight to change the lives of the farmworkers was imperative to the Hispanic community. Over the next few years, Chávez, her children, and her extended family assisted in promoting the ideology and goals of the National Farm Workers Association.

By 1965, Chávez had joined the picket lines while still supporting her family. In October of the same year, she was detained by police for shouting "Huelga" ("Strike") at a protest at the W. B. Camp and Sons farm. César's activism in the farmworkers' struggle had evolved into the formation of the United Farm Workers Organizing Committee through the National Farm Workers Association's mergers with other organizations that had similar goals. The United Farm Workers (UFW) was established in 1966, and Chávez continued to protest the unfair treatment of agricultural laborers with UFW members and her family. Her most public arrest came in 1978 with César at the G & S Produce Company in Yuma, Arizona. Both later were released and given suspended sentences.

César Chávez died in his sleep on April 23, 1993, and more than fifty thousand people attended his funeral in Delano, California. Later that year, César's friends and family founded the César E. Chávez Foundation, an organization that aims to educate people about his life and career and to inspire individuals and communities to carry on his work for civil rights.

In August 8, 1994, Helen Chávez attended a White House ceremony with President Bill Clinton, in which she accepted the posthumous award of the Medal of Freedom to her husband. On May 18, 2011, she and other members of her family joined Secretary of the Navy Ray Mabus to announce that a new naval ship would be named the USNS *César Chávez*. During the announcement, Helen Chávez noted that her husband did not believe he should be singled out for praise because "he knew there were many César Chávezes, so many men and women in the movement who made great sacrifices and achieved great things." For that reason, Helen, her family, and the farmworker movement explained that the USNS *César Chávez* was named in honor of all Latinos who "helped build America and served their country."

Significance

Helen Chávez's role in the fight for migrant farmworkers' rights is defined by her dedication to her family. Her values played an influential part in the onset of her family's involvement in "La Causa." She is often revered for upholding traditional Mexican values and supporting the conventional familial gender roles. While Chávez did value these roles, it is important to remember that at times she was the primary breadwinner while César worked unpaid to form the NFWA. She also protested in the fields and endured multiple arrests and police harassments. Her support, financially and emotionally, helped to change the poor working conditions farm laborers previously had to tolerate.

Monica E. Montelongo

Further Reading

Etulain, Richard W., ed. *César Chávez: A Brief Biography with Documents*. New York: Palgrave, 2002. Chávez's role as a supporter of "La Causa" is shown through her participation and influence in the activism of her husband.

Levy, Jacques E., and César Chávez. *César Chávez: Autobiography of La Causa*, 2d ed. Minneapolis: University of Minn. Press, 2007. A historical account of "La Causa" from César Chávez, including Helen's role and perspective on supporting her husband.

Rose, Margaret Eleanor. "Mujer Valiente: Helen Chávez, the Interdependence of Family Life, Work, and Union Activism." In *Women in the United Farm Workers: A Study of Chicana and Mexicana Participation in a Labor Union, 1950 to 1980*. Los Angeles: University of California, Los Angeles,1988. Includes a formative and substantial biographical chapter on the life of Helen Chávez, including her early childhood and introduction to social activism.

See also: César Chávez; Corky Gonzáles; Dolores Huerta; Antonio Orendain; Reies López Tijerina.

Linda Chavez

American political commentator and activist

A conservative commentator who has been active in politics since the 1970's, Chavez is particularly noted for her active role—and often-controversial views—on issues involving civil rights and immigration.

Latino heritage: Mexican
Born: June 17, 1947; Albuquerque, New Mexico
Areas of achievement: Social issues; government and politics

Early Life

Linda Chavez (CHAH-vehz) was born on June 17, 1947, into an ethnically mixed family. Her mother was an Irish Catholic, while her father was descended from two Mexican American families (Chavez and Armija) of considerable past prosperity that recently had fallen on hard times. Her childhood was turbulent, and she suffered a number of personal tragedies, including the death of her sister. The family moved frequently around New Mexico and Colorado. Despite this, Chavez received a decent education and developed a love of literature.

Chavez met Christopher Gersten, a young socialist Reform Jew, at age eighteen. They married a year later, requiring her to convert to Judaism; she eventually reverted to Catholicism. She had her first son after a difficult pregnancy, and taking care of him while working and studying was very difficult for the young couple. At the University of Colorado, Chavez worked with a Mexican American outreach group but became disenchanted with its increasing militancy and what she saw as a victim mindset. Later, the couple moved to Los Angeles, where she studied and taught at the University of California at Los Angeles. Her experiences with racial militants brought in through quotas profoundly affected her.

Moving to Washington, D.C., Chavez worked briefly at minor political jobs, including staff work at the Democratic National Committee. She went to work for California Democrat Don Edwards as a staffer for the House Judiciary Committee. After a couple of years, she went to work for the National Education Association and then the American Federation of Teachers (AFT).

Life's Work

Chavez started out as an AFT lobbyist, a job she disliked for various reasons, including the fact that her influence reflected the power of the union, not her own effort. In 1977, she served a short stint at the Department of Health, Education, and Welfare, quickly becoming disenchanted by the work habits of career employees and increasingly skeptical about government. When the job of editing the AFT's quarterly opinion magazine, *American Educator*, became available, she happily took it. Albert Shanker, the head of the AFT, held liberal views on economic (especially union) issues but was conservative on many other issues (especially those related to racial preference and foreign policy). Chavez made the magazine into a relatively conservative journal, similar to *Commentary*, which Shanker considered an excellent example to follow. After a year she started editing the union's weekly and monthly newsletters as well. Chavez had two more sons during her stints at the AFT.

By this time, both Chavez and her husband had become conservatives, and in 1983, she joined the administration of President Ronald Reagan as staff director of the Civil Rights Commission. The commission experienced much controversy and infighting over the

Linda Chavez. (AP Photo)

Chavez's Political Views

As a syndicated columnist, Linda Chavez has written on a wide array of subjects, including policy issues and partisan politics. In her books, she makes extensive use of statistical and other data. In general, she can be described as an orthodox but not extreme conservative on social issues (such as abortion and gay and lesbian rights) and the economy. Chavez, however, differs from many conservatives in her support for immigration, especially her support for the rights of illegal immigrants. She supports equal rights for women and racial minorities while opposing radical feminism, policies such as affirmative action (which she finds harmful to all parties), and identity-group politics.

In *Out of the Barrio: Toward a New Politics of Hispanic Assimilation* (1991), Chavez makes her case for assimilation through better education, active citizenship, and economic development over racial separatism. She also argues that English immersion is a better strategy than bilingual education. In *Betrayal: How Union Bosses Shake Down Their Members and Corrupt American Politics* (2004), she details union political corruption at the expense of workers (particularly the use of dues for partisan politics) and the effects this has on politics and the economy.

issue of quotas and other racial preferences, which Chavez opposed; she eventually succeeded in changing some policies but was unable to completely eliminate affirmative-action programs. She was more successful in stopping a feminist effort to replace the policy of equal pay for equal work with one that provided equal pay for work of comparable worth according to abstract formulas. Later, Chavez moved to the White House as director of public liaison; however, she found herself mostly an outsider in the administration, considered too conservative by many staffers. She also was unhappy when an effort to eliminate racial quotas by executive order fell through. She left after less than a year.

In 1986, Chavez decided to run for a Senate seat representing Maryland when liberal Republican incumbent Charles Mathias retired. After performing well on a pop quiz given by a local news station, Chavez won the Republican primary. In the general election, however, she received only 39 percent of the vote.

Chavez next began writing a syndicated column and providing commentary on National Public Radio. She served a stint as president of U.S. English, a group that campaigns for state initiatives to make English the official language of the U.S. government, drawing anger from Latino activist groups. She and several board members later quit the organization when a racist document by its founder was publicized. Chavez wrote her first book, *Out of the Barrio: Toward a New Politics of Hispanic Assimilation* (1991), as a result of these experiences. It generated even more vitriol from Latino activists even though her tone was mostly optimistic. Later, she founded the Center for Equal Opportunity as a conservative think tank on civil rights issues. In 2001, Chavez was nominated for secretary of labor in the George W. Bush administration but removed herself from consideration after a controversy over a former house guest who had been an illegal immigrant. This scandal led Chavez to write two more books. Throughout the 2000's, she remained active as a conservative political commentator.

Significance

Early in her career, Chavez taught remedial English to Mexican American students in Colorado and California. As a House Judiciary Committee staffer, she was involved in the early stages of the impeachment of President Richard Nixon. While editing *American Educator*, she helped introduce intellectuals such as Jeane Kirkpatrick, William Bennett, Robert Bork, and Diane Ravitch to a wider public. She also has been active as a director in a number of major corporations and nonprofit groups, and founded the Center for Equal Opportunity. As a columnist and in many of her government positions, she has addressed issues such as civil rights, labor reform, the rights and assimilation of immigrants (especially Latinos), and education, occasionally having significant influence on policy. The Library of Congress named Chavez a Living Legend in 2000.

Timothy Lane

Further Reading

Barone, Michael, and Grant J. Ujifusa. *Almanac of American Politics 1988*. New York: National Journal, 1987. Covers the political background and major races in each state, including the 1986 Senate race in Maryland.

Chavez, Linda. *Betrayal: How Union Bosses Shake Down Their Members and Corrupt American Politics*. New York: Three Rivers Press, 2004. Chavez catalogs various forms of wrongdoing by unions and offers solutions.

_______. *Out of the Barrio: Toward a New Politics of Hispanic Assimilation*. New York: Basic Books, 1991. A short factual study of Latino politics, arguing for assimilation over identity politics.

_______. *An Unlikely Conservative: The Transformation of an Ex-Liberal*. New York: Basic Books, 2002.

Chavez's autobiography chronicles her early life and describes the evolution of her political views.

See also: Alberto Gonzales; Manuel Luján, Jr.; Maggie Rivas-Rodriguez; Richard Rodriguez.

Guillermo B. Cintron

Puerto Rican-born cardiologist

Cintron is a prominent cardiologist who is best known for his research involving heart function, vessel and valve diseases, heart failure, and transplantation.

Latino heritage: Puerto Rican
Born: March 28, 1942; San Juan, Puerto Rico
Also known as: Guillermo B. Cintron, Jr.; Guillermo Cintron
Areas of achievement: Medicine; science and technology

Early Life

Guillermo (jee-YEHR-moh) B. Cintron (SEEN-trohn), Jr., was born to parents Guillermo Cintron-Ayuso and Rose A. Silve de Cintron in San Juan, Puerto Rico, on March 28, 1942. Cintron was raised in the Caribbean and in the Catholic faith. His bicultural family spoke English and Spanish.

Cintron earned his B.S. degree from the University of Puerto Rico with honors in 1963. He subsequently attended Loyola University-Stritch School of Medicine in Chicago, Illinois. After medical school, Cintron served in the U.S. Navy Medical Corps inVietnam from 1968 to 1970, earning the Vietnam Service Medal. Upon returning from Vietnam, Cintron completed a cardiology internship and residency at George Washington University Hospital and the Veterans Administration Hospital in Washington, D.C. During two of these years, Cintron served as a U.S. Navy primary-care physician in Japan.

Life's Work

After completing his medical education, Cintron went back to San Juan. He was appointed to the faculty at the University of Puerto Rico School of Medicine, where he was an assistant professor from 1975 to 1980 and an associate professor from 1980 to 1983. He was simultaneously director of the first coronary unit at the Veterans Administration Hospital from 1975 to 1983.

Cintron returned to the mainland United States as an associate professor of internal medicine in the division of cardiovascular disease at the University of South Florida, College of Medicine. He later was promoted to a professorship, a position he continued to hold in 2011. Cintron also served as chief of cardiology at the James A. Haley Veterans Administration Hospital in Tampa, Florida, until 2003. While at the college and hospital, Cintron researched cardiology stress testing, specifically the effects of diuretics and other medication on heart rhythm. He also showed the beneficial effects of medication administration during a heart attack. In addition, Cintron conducted research on the effects of obesity on heart disease and the importance of surgery for correction of valvular abnormalities.

Cintron is perhaps best known for is his work on congestive heart failure and heart transplantations. In regard to heart failure, he and his colleagues have demonstrated that vasodilator therapy, which consists of medications to enlarge the blood vessels, increases the function of the heart and improves overall patient outcome. Cintron started the heart transplant program at the University of South Florida in 1985. He has extensively studied heart transplantation, including factors leading to rejection of the transplant. Cintron's research demonstrated that if the first transplantation is rejected, retransplantation with a second heart should not be attempted.

In 2011, Cintron was affiliated with five hospitals in Florida, including Tampa General Hospital and Life Link Healthcare Institute, a nonprofit community service foundation devoted to organ transplantation. He has published the first data showing that portable machines for cardiac catheterization and interventional procedures were limited, but still useful, as alternatives to larger permanent machinery. This finding has global implications, as the use of portable equipment in developing countries with limited access to care could substantially benefit patients.

Cintron has published extensively in peer-reviewed journals, with more than fifteen scientific article publications and a book chapter on cardiology stress testing. He has collaborated in multicenter studies and participated in consortiums, such as the ADHERE (Acute Decompensated Heart Failure National Registry) Scientific Advisory Committee, the Cardiac Transplant Research Database Group, the CHAMP (Combination Hemotherapy and Mortality Prevention) study, and the VA V-HeFT II (Veteran Affairs Cooperative Vasodilator-Heart Failure Trail) Cooperative Studies Group. He is also an editor of the *Journal of Cardiac Failure*.

Cintron has received numerous awards, including a listing as one of *Tampa Bay Metro* magazine's best doctors in America from 2005 to 2010. He is certified by the American Board of Internal Medicine in Cardiology. His professional organizations include membership in the American College of Cardiology and the American Heart Association's Council of Clinical Cardiologists; he was a member of the American College of Physicians from 1976 to 1992. In 1992, he began serving on the Veterans Administration Heart Transplant Board.

SIGNIFICANCE

With more than forty years of clinical work and research, Cintron has established himself as one of the premier cardiologists in the United States. An article published by Cintron and other physicians in *The New England Journal of Medicine,* "A Comparison of Enalapril with Hydralazine-Isosorbide Dinitrate in the Treatment of Chronic Congestive Heart Failure" (1991), has been cited by more than two thousand scientific publications, demonstrating the importance and paramount impact of this research. In 2010, the heart transplant program he began at the University of South Florida had performed more than nine hundred procedures. His scientific publications furthered the medical knowledge of heart disease and paved the way for additional medical breakthroughs.

Janet Ober Berman

FURTHER READING

Fonarow, G. C., et al. "An Obesity Paradox in Acute Heart Failure: Analysis of Body Mass Index and Inhospital Mortality for 108,927 Patients in the Acute Decompensated Heart Failure National Registry." *American Heart Journal* 153, no. 1 (January, 2007): 74-81. Results of multicenter research in which Cintron and colleagues examined the relationship between weight and the risk of dying from heart failure.

Kobashigawa, J. A., et al. "Pretransplantation Risk Factors for Acute Rejection After Heart Transplantation: A Multi-Institutional Study." *Journal of Heart and Lung Transplantation* 12, no.3 (May-June, 1993): 355-366. Cintron was one of the physicians who participated in this twenty-five-institution study that sought to understand factors, such as age and gender, that affect heart transplantation.

Pascual, E. E., et al. "Effects of Diuretic Therapy on the Electrocardiographic Response to Exercise." *Clinical Cardiology* 15, no. 2 (February, 1992): 93-94. Cintron's research disproves the assumption that diuretics caused a false-positive abnormal heart rhythm.

Radovansavec, B., et al. "Retransplantation in 7,290 Primary Transplant Patients: A Ten-Year Multi-Institutional Study." *The Journal of Heart and Lung Transplantation* 22, no. 8 (August, 2003): 862-868. Result of a study by Cintron and collaborators on the success and pitfalls of performing a second heart transplantation after unsuccessful primary transplant.

See also: Richard Henry Carmona; Jose Alberto Fernandez-Pol; Antonia Novello.

EVELYN CISNEROS

American ballerina, educator, and activist

Cisneros was one of the first Latinas to become a prima ballerina with a major American company. She contributes significantly to the Hispanic community as a role model, encouraging young Hispanics to become involved in the arts, and as a social activist.

Latino heritage: Mexican
Born: November 18, 1958; Long Beach, California
Also known as: Evelyn Deanne Cisneros-Legate
Areas of achievement: Dance; education; social issues

EARLY LIFE

Evelyn Deanne Cisneros-Legate (sihs-NEH-rohs) was born in Long Beach, California, in 1958 and lived in Huntington Beach during her childhood. She has one brother. Her grandparents came to the United States from Mexico as migrant workers. Although her family was the only Hispanic family in the neighborhood, her parents placed great importance on their Mexican heritage. They attended a Spanish-speaking church and were involved in the Hispanic community, thus the

Spanish language and Mexican culture were important parts of Cisneros's childhood.

As a child, Cisneros was extremely shy. In an effort to combat her daughter's shyness, Cisneros's mother enrolled her in dance classes when she was seven years old. Although she was the only Hispanic child in her class, the dancing lessons helped her overcome her shyness and soon she was participating in athletics at school. When she was thirteen years old, Cisneros decided that she wanted to study seriously to be a dancer. Preparing to become a ballet dancer, she took lessons at a studio in North Hollywood, which entailed a three-hour round trip five days a week during the school year. During the summers, she attended classes at the San Francisco Ballet School and the American School of Ballet. She was offered an apprenticeship with the San Francisco Ballet at the age of fifteen. Cisneros opted to accept the offer after finishing high school. On February 1, 1976, she began her career as an apprentice at the San Francisco Ballet.

Life's Work

Almost immediately, Cisneros got the opportunity to prove herself as a dancer and her value to the company. Two days after her arrival, one of the company's dancers was unable to perform because of an injury. Cisneros was asked to learn her role. With five hours of work, she mastered the dance and performed with the company. Michael Smuin, artistic director of the ballet company, immediately recognized her talent; Cisneros credits him for being instrumental to her development as a prima ballerina.

In 1977, Cisneros became a member of the San Francisco Ballet. During the twenty-three years that she danced there, Cisneros performed the leading role in classical ballets such as *Swan Lake* (1877), *Sleeping Beauty* (1889), and *La Sylphide* (1832). She also danced the lead role in ballets choreographed specifically for her by Smuin until his dismissal as artistic director in 1985. For a time the new artistic director, Helgi Tomasson, did not cast Cisneros in these roles, even though they had been created for her; however, Tomasson eventually recognized her exceptional talent and allowed her to dance lead roles.

In 1995, Cisneros began performing modern dance as well as ballet. She danced the lead role in *Lambarena*, a dance combining classical ballet and African dance choreographed especially for her by Val Caniparoli. She also worked with Mark Morris and appeared at the Jacob's Pillow Dance Festival. Throughout her career, she made many guest appearances including performances in Spain, Mexico, Cuba, and New Zealand.

In 1996, Cisneros married Stephen Legate, a principal dancer with the San Francisco ballet. Wishing to have a family and sensing that she was ready to leave, she retired from her position as prima ballerina with the San Francisco Ballet in May, 1999. She was honored with a gala performance and a documentary, *Evelyn Cisneros: Moving On*. However, Cisneros did not leave ballet. In 2000, she began teaching intensive summer courses for various ballet companies, including the Boston Ballet. In 2002, she became ballet education coordinator for San Francisco Ballet. She was artistic director for the fortieth anniversary performance of *The Nutcracker* (1892) by Ballet Pacifica. In 2004, with Scott Speck, she wrote *Ballet for Dummies*. In 2010, she accepted the position of principal of the Boston Ballet School's Marblehead Studio. She has two children, Ethan and Sophia.

Cisneros has received many honors for her accomplishments as a dancer and as a leader in the Hispanic community, including the annual Cultural Award of the Mexican American Legal Defense and Educational Fund (1985), a Cyril Magnin Award for outstanding achievement in the arts (1999), two Isadora Duncan Awards (1989, 2000), and honorary doctorates from Mills College and California State University at Monterey Bay. In 1992, she was named one of the One Hundred Most Influential Hispanics by *Hispanic Business* magazine.

Significance

Cisneros has made and continues to make a significant impact on both ballet and the Hispanic community. As a performer, she created memorable roles, enchanted audiences, and contributed to the popularity of ballet with the general public and with Latinos specifically. After retiring, she has continued her affiliation with the San Francisco Ballet and other companies both as a guest teacher and as a liaison with the community in an effort to maintain and enhance the stature of ballet in the United States. In her efforts to promote ballet as an American art form, Cisneros particularly addresses the Hispanic community, encouraging Hispanic girls to dance.

Shawncey Webb

Further Reading

Cisneros, Evelyn. "Ballet Living Legend Brings Talent to Duke City." Interview by Tracy Dingmann. *The Albuquerque Journal*, July 22, 2001, p. F5. Interview in which Cisneros expresses her commitment to passing on a love of ballet to future generations.

Krohn, Katherine E. *Evelyn Cisneros: Prima Ballerina*. Mankato, Minn.: Capstone Press, 2007. Written for younger readers, this book offers a good account of Cisneros's life and career. Includes a time line, a glossary, and a list of Web sites.

Ross, Janice. *San Francisco Ballet at Seventy-Five*. San Francisco, Calif.: Chronicle Books, 2007. A thorough presentation of the history and development of the ballet company to which Cisneros belonged for her entire career.

Steinberg, Cobbett. *San Francisco Ballet: The First Fifty Years*. San Francisco, Calif.: Chronicle Books, 1983. Covers the company from 1933 to 1983, a period that includes Cisneros's collaboration with Michael Smuin.

See also: Fernando Bujones; Royes Fernández; José Arcadio Limón; Rita Moreno; Chita Rivera.

Henry G. Cisneros

American politician

A popular politician until he retired amid scandal in 1997, Cisneros served as mayor of San Antonio and as secretary of Housing and Urban Affairs under President Bill Clinton.

Latino heritage: Mexican

Born: June 11, 1947; San Antonio, Texas

Also known as: Henry Gabriel Cisneros

Areas of achievement: Government and politics; business

Early Life

Henry Gabriel Cisneros (sihs-NEH-rohs) was the son of George Cisneros, an Army colonel and later an employee of the U.S. Civil Service. His mother was the daughter of Romulo Munguia, a dissident Mexican journalist who had sought refuge in the United States in the 1920's. Cisneros was raised in a family that emphasized the importance of hard work, education, and patriotism. Although middle-class, the family remained in the Westside barrio of San Antonio, living among numerous poor families. Like many Chicano children of his generation, Cisneros attended parochial schools, graduating in 1964 from Central Catholic High School. Following graduation, he majored in urban and regional planning at Texas Agricultural and Mechanical University (Texas A&M), where he was the first Chicano student to be commander of the combined Aggie band. He graduated with a bachelor's degree in 1968.

During the following two years, while working on a master's degree at Texas A&M, Cisneros worked in the office of the city manager of Bryan, Texas. At this time, he married his high school sweetheart, Mary Perez. After completing his first graduate degree in 1970, Cisneros was hired as executive vice president of the National League of Cities. He then obtained a prestigious White House Fellowship and served as an assistant to the secretary of the Department of Health, Education, and Welfare. He earned a second master's degree from Harvard University in 1973, followed by a doctorate in public administration from George Washington University in 1976. His dissertation was titled *City Government and Economic Development: A Study of Policy Formulations and Administrative Implementation*.

Life's Work

In 1974, while completing his dissertation, Cisneros returned to his home city with a contract to teach public administration at the University of Texas at San Antonio. The following year, he decided to campaign for election to the city council. During this period, the city was experiencing considerable socioeconomic conflict. Many Mexican Americans believed that they were being neglected by the white-dominated Good Government League (GGL), which had controlled city politics for two decades. Although Cisneros's views were somewhat more liberal than those of most GGL leaders, the group nevertheless endorsed his candidacy. Cisneros conducted an unusually energetic grassroots campaign. The only GGL candidate to prevail without a runoff, he did particularly well among white voters, and at the age of twenty-seven, Cisneros became the youngest councilman in the city's history.

Soon after he took the oath of office, Cisneros announced that he would maintain his independence, a pledge made easier by the GGL's declining power. A proponent of moderately left-of-center positions on most issues, he was particularly supportive of organized labor, education, and public housing. On the controversial issue of economic development, he supported directing growth toward the inner-city neighborhoods, where most unemployed minorities were located, rather than the previous emphasis on developing the northern

Henry Cisneros. (AP Photo)

suburbs, which had tended to increase urban sprawl. Frequently making headlines with his approach to the hands-on study of city government, he participated in garbage collections, helped read electricity meters, and rode along with police officers and firefighters. By forgoing extremist rhetoric and supporting economic development, Cisneros avoided confrontations with the business and political leaders of the city, and he was easily reelected to the council in 1977 and 1979.

In December, 1980, after the incumbent mayor decided not to seek reelection, Cisneros was the first person to announce his candidacy. Supported by many of the city's wealthy elites as well as most minorities and working-class residents, he won the election with more than 60 percent of the vote, becoming the first Chicano major of San Antonio in more than a century. His victory received considerable attention in the national media. An unusually popular mayor, he was reelected to three additional terms, taking 94.2 of the vote in 1983, more than 70 percent in 1985, and 67 percent in 1987.

During his eight-year mayorship, Cisneros supported populist policies that helped the poor and working-class citizens. He directed about $200 million to the neglected Latino Westside for the construction of streets, parks, and libraries. At the same time, a majority of conservative white voters were pleased with his policies because they helped bring unprecedented economic growth to the city. Cisneros successfully obtained federal funds for the expansion of the downtown business district, and he helped attract the capital for the creation of two major tourist attractions, SeaWorld and Fiesta Texas. He also convinced the city to construct the stadium/convention center the Alamodome, which cost $186 million. Cisneros's close ties to the business community allowed him to establish an educational partnership among local schools, community organizations, and local businesses, providing financial assistance to children living in the poorer areas of the city. In 1983, President Ronald Reagan named Cisneros to the Bipartisan Commission on Central America, and in 1985, he was elected president of the National League of Cities. In 1999, *Texas Monthly* named him the Texas Mayor of the Century.

In 1987, Cisneros announced that after completing his term he would not seek reelection in order to work in the private sector. Among his reasons was the low pay he received as mayor; Cisneros's son, John Paul Anthony, suffered from a heart defect that had left the family with large medical bills, and his two daughters were approaching college age. An additional reason Cisneros chose to leave public life was an extramarital affair with his chief fund-raiser, Linda Jones Medlar, who was demanding money to keep the affair secret.

After leaving office in 1989, Cisneros organized and became chairman of the Cisneros Asset Management Company, an investment firm that managed $550 million in fixed-income accounts. He hosted a television show, *Texans*, and a daily Spanish-language radio program, *Adelante*. He also served as a board member of the Rockefeller Foundation and as deputy chair of the Federal Reserve Bank of Dallas. In addition, he was a popular speaker who commanded large fees for appearances at universities and businesses. In 1991, *VISTA* magazine named him the Hispanic Man of the Year.

After winning the presidency in 1992, Bill Clinton nominated Cisneros to be secretary of the Department of Housing and Urban Affairs (HUD). Cisneros accepted, and the U.S. Senate unanimously confirmed the nomination, making him the highest ranking Mexican American official in the U.S. government. He took a special interest in homelessness, even spending one night in a Minneapolis shelter in order to experience the problem firsthand. He spent much time and energy on the HOPE VI program, which attempted to reform public housing by razing dilapidated projects in areas of concentrated poverty, replacing them with newer houses in more prosperous neighborhoods. In addition, he enthusiastically promoted home ownership among persons with low and moderate income through programs that made it easier for them to obtain mortgages. After the Republican victories in the midterm elections of 1994, however, Cisneros spent much of his time in fighting reductions in the HUD budget. Although conservatives disagreed with his moderately liberal perspective, almost all observers gave Cisneros high marks for his administration of HUD.

Cisneros was forced to resign from his HUD position in January, 1997, as a result of the scandal resulting from his earlier relationship with Medlar. In a lawsuit initiated in 1994, she alleged that the discontinuation of promised monthly payments constituted a breach of contract. The most serious problem was that Cisneros had made false statements to Federal Bureau of Investigation (FBI) agents about the amount of money paid to her, actions that constitute a federal crime. The U.S. attorney general appointed a special prosecutor to investigate the matter, and in December, 1997, a grand jury indicted Cisneros on charges of lying to the FBI and obstruction of justice. Sixteen months later, he accepted a plea bargain that required him to plead guilty to a misdemeanor and pay a fine of ten thousand dollars. In January, 2001, Clinton pardoned him for the offense.

After leaving HUD, Cisneros served for three years as president of Univision Communications, the largest Spanish-language broadcaster in the nation. He then established a business organization, American City Vista, with the goal of developing affordable housing in inner-city neighborhoods. He continued, moreover, to be a popular speaker and wrote or contributed to several well-received books, including *Casa y Comunidad: Latino Home and Neighborhood Design* (2006) and *Our Communities, Our Homes: Pathways to Housing and Homeownership in America's Cities and States* (2007).

Cisneros as a Possible Vice Presidential Candidate in 1984

By 1984, Henry G. Cisneros had developed a friendship with former Vice President Walter Mondale, and that year he helped Mondale prevail in the Democratic Party caucus in San Antonio. Once his presidential nomination was assured, Mondale—who wanted either a woman or minority for his running mate—asked Cisneros to travel to Minnesota to discuss the matter. When journalists in Minnesota asked Cisneros about his views, he replied: "If you ever want to know what I'm likely to do on an issue, just remember that I'm never going to stray too far from my Mexican-American base." Despite Cisneros's charisma and communication skills, Mondale chose Congresswoman Geraldine Ferraro as his running mate. Ferraro had more government experience, and Mondale believed that the nomination of a woman would encourage large numbers of female voters to support the Democratic ticket.

At the Democratic National Convention that year, Cisneros was chosen to speak in support of the justice plank of the platform, and he electrified delegates with a speech demanding "fairness in our lives, justice in our system." Despite the Democrats' vigorous efforts, they were unable to defeat President Ronald Reagan, a popular incumbent, at a time when the economy was improving. Appearing on *CBS Morning News* after the election, Cisneros emphasized the need of the Democratic Party to be perceived as a broad national party and not to ignore any region of the country. A party that "becomes the party of the minorities," he cautioned, "will become a minority party nationally."

SIGNIFICANCE

During the late twentieth century, Cisneros was one of the most popular, articulate, and hardworking Latino politicians in the country. Although committed to liberal and pro-Latino policies, he recognized the need for compromise, conciliation, and economic growth, thereby gaining the respect of many moderate and conservative white constituents. Observers consistently gave him high marks for his many achievements while mayor of San Antonio and secretary of the Department of Housing and Urban Development. If his career had not been derailed by scandal, Cisneros seemed set for a bright political future.

Thomas Tandy Lewis

FURTHER READING

Cardona, Rodolfo, and Christopher Henry. *Henry Cisneros: Mexican-American Political Leader*. New York: Facts On File, 1994. Written primarily for young readers, this succinct, compelling account presents the historical context of Cisneros's life and includes many illustrations.

Cisneros, Henry, and Lora Engdahl, ed. *From Despair to Hope: HOPE VI and the New Promise of Pub-*

lic Housing in America's Cities. Washington, D.C.: Brookings Institution Press, 2009. Selection of articles about the housing reforms that Cisneros directed while he was HUD secretary.

Diehl, Kemper, and Jan Jarboe. *Cisneros: Portrait of a New American*. San Antonio: Corona, 1984. Written while Cisneros was San Antonio mayor and presidential candidate Walter Mondale was considering him as a running mate; includes many interesting photographs.

Jones, Tamara. "Henry and Linda: A Painful Story of Public Service and Private Anguish." *The Washington Post Magazine* (February 22, 1998): W11-W13. A detailed analysis of the scandal that forced Cisneros to leave public office.

Rosales, Rodolfo. *The Illusions of Inclusion: The Untold Political Story of San Antonio*. Austin: University of Texas Press, 2000. Despite the election of Cisneros, Rosales argues that inclusion is still largely an illusion for many working-class and poor Chicano residents.

Wolff, Nelson. *Mayor: An Inside View of San Antonio Politics, 1981-1995*. Foreword by Henry Cisneros. San Antonio, Tex.: San Antonio Express-News, 1997. Includes much material about Cisneros as well as racial tensions in the city's politics.

See also: Joaquín Castro; Julián Castro; Manuel Luján, Jr.; Antonio Villaraigosa.

Sandra Cisneros

American writer and activist

Through her poetry and her novels, Cisneros has helped to bring the Mexican American experience to the attention of mainstream American readers. She also serves as a voice for women reared in the patriarchal traditions of her culture, encouraging them to become more independent and to work for change.

Latino heritage: Mexican

Born: December 20, 1954; Chicago, Illinois

Areas of achievement: Literature; poetry; social issues

Early Life

Sandra Cisneros (sihs-NEHR-ohs) was born in Chicago, Illinois, on December 20, 1954. Her father, Alfredo Cisneros del Moral, had left his home in Mexico after dropping out of college. In the United States, he gained legal status and U.S. citizenship by serving in the armed forces during World War II. After the war, he found himself in Chicago, where he met and married Elvira Cordero Anguiano, a Mexican American. They settled on Chicago's North Side, where Alfredo began working as an upholsterer. The death of a baby sister left Cisneros the only girl in the family. Since her six brothers preferred each other's company, she usually was alone; however, with her mother's encouragement, she became a voracious reader and began writing poems and stories.

Cisneros was educated at two Catholic parochial schools, St. Callistus and St. Aloysius. Her father took his family to Mexico for several months each year, so she learned a great deal about traditional life there. She also grew up completely bilingual.

Elvira played a major role in the later success of all her children, as she enrolled them in the public library and took them to museums and free concerts. A turning point for Cisneros came when she was twelve years old and her family finally moved into a house, giving her an assurance of permanence, a collection of interesting friends and neighbors, and, most important, a room of her own where she could think, read, and try her hand at writing.

In 1968, Cisneros entered Josephinum High School, a Catholic school in Chicago, where a teacher's praise impelled her to publish some of her poems and to work on the school literary magazine, eventually becoming its editor. After graduating in 1972, she used a scholarhip she had won to enroll in Chicago's Loyola University, majoring in English. In her junior year Cisneros took a writing workshop, where she received valuable training in the techniques of her profession. At the suggestion of several professors, she applied for the prestigious master of fine arts program in creative writing at the University of Iowa. She was accepted, and upon her graduation from Loyola in 1976, she made her way to the Iowa Writers' Workshop. It was at a seminar there that she had an epiphany: although her definitions of a home and a neighborhood were very different from those of her classmates, she was convinced that her people, too, deserved a place on the printed page. Cisneros had found her subject.

Life's Work

In 1978, with her master's degree in hand, Cisneros was ready to become a professional writer; however, it would be almost two decades before she could support herself by writing. She began working with inner-city youths at the Latino Youth Alternative High School in Chicago. During that time, she became acquainted with Chicano poet Gary Soto, who helped her publish *Bad Boys* (1980), a chapbook containing seven poems. Cisneros then became a recruiter for Loyola University. Meanwhile, she continued to work on her poetry and on the sketches that eventually would become *The House on Mango Street* (1984).

In 1982, Cisneros received a grant from the National Endowment for the Arts that enabled her to spend a year in Europe. By November, she had a manuscript ready to submit to Nicolás Kanellos of Arte Público Press, who had suggested that she compile and publish her stories. After extensive revision, in 1984, *The House on Mango Street* appeared. In 1985, it won the American Book Award of the Before Columbus Foundation, and by 2011 it had sold more than two million copies.

Over the next ten years, Cisneros worked for various institutions. She spent a year as literature director of the Guadalupe Cultural Art Center in San Antonio, Texas, then held teaching positions at California State University at Chico, the University of California at Berkeley, the University of California at Irvine, the University of Michigan at Ann Arbor, and the University of New Mexico at Albuquerque. In 1986, she won a Dobie Paisano Writing Fellowship, which enabled her to complete her first major poetry collection, *My Wicked, Wicked Ways* (1987). The next year, she won another fellowship from the National Endowment for the Arts.

In 1991, Cisneros published *Woman Hollering Creek, and Other Stories*, a collection of stories set in and around San Antonio, Texas. In addition to examining women trapped in a patriarchal culture, Cisneros touches on such issues as poverty, crime, racism, and religious faith. *Woman Hollering Creek* was a best seller and won the PEN Center West Award for Best Fiction of 1991, the Anisfield-Wolf Book Award, and the Lannan Foundation Literary Award.

Two books by Cisneros appeared in 1994: *Hairs* (*Pelitos*), a bilingual picture book for children, and *Loose Woman*, a collection of experimental poems. The following year, she won a MacArthur Foundation fellowship, which at last made her financially secure. Cisneros bought a house in a historic section of San Antonio, infuriated many of her neighbors by painting it bright purple, and began writing a novel, *Caramelo: Or, Puro Cuento* (2002), her most ambitious work to date.

Caramelo is the story of Celaya Reyes, who like Cisneros herself spends her childhood in Mexico and Chicago. Celaya's attempts to disentangle truth from fiction in the extended family histories narrated by her older relatives result in some of the most humorous scenes in what critics agree is an exceptionally vivid, lively novel. *Caramelo* received the 2005 Premio Napoli Award and was nominated for England's Orange Prize. Cisneros was awarded the Texas Medal of the Arts in 2003. In 2009, she became writer-in-residence at Our Lady of the Lake University in San Antonio. Her works have been translated into more than one dozen languages.

Significance

The adoption of *The House on Mango Street* as a text in schools and universities resulted in greater understanding of the problems faced by Chicanos, and when a major publishing house released *Woman Hollering Creek*, fiction by Mexican American women gained a new popularity. Through her works and through personal contacts, as well as through her foundations, Cisneros continues to work actively in support of the rights of immigrants and women.

Rosemary M. Canfield Reisman

Esperanza and *The House on Mango Street*

Sandra Cisneros's best-known work, *The House on Mango Street* (1984), is a collection of vignettes that vary from simple, colloquial narratives to poetic prose, interspersed with poetic meditations. Although it is difficult to categorize, critics agree that the book is unified by the use of a first-person narrator, Esperanza Cordera, a Mexican American girl who observes the action around her, reacts to it, and reflects upon it. Esperanza is both a character participating in the action and an outside observer, drawing conclusions about the flaws in her society, especially in its treatment of women. However, while the book ends with Mango Street essentially unchanged, Esperanza herself has come of age. She has moved from a naïve fascination with boys and sexuality to the realization that marriage and motherhood do not free women but instead condemn them to lifelong imprisonment. By choosing wise women as her advisers, Esperanza enters adulthood committed to her writing, which she sees as her route to freedom.

Further Reading

Calderón, Héctor. "Como México no hay dos": Sandra Cisneros's Feminist Border Stories." In *Narratives of Greater Mexico: Essays on Chicano Literary History, Genre, and Borders*. Austin: University of Texas Press, 2004. Scholarly essay on themes such as gender, culture, and identity in Cisneros's writing. Map, bibliography, and index.

Cisneros, Sandra. "Muy Payasa: Conversation with Sandra Cisneros." Interview by Nancy Sullivan. In *Conversations with Mexican American Writers: Languages and Literatures in the Borderlands*, by Elisabeth Mermann-Jozwiak and Nancy Sullivan. Jackson: University Press of Mississippi, 2009. Cisneros discusses the autobiographical elements in her fiction, the construction of Chicano identity, and other subjects in this interview. Bibliographical references and index.

Eysturoy, Annie O. "*The House on Mango Street*: A Space of Her Own." In *Daughters of Self-Creation: The Contemporary Chicana Novel*. Albuquerque: University of New Mexico Press, 1996. Examines the Chicana's quest for the self in Cisneros's *The House on Mango Street*. Bibliographical references and index.

Kevane, Bridget. "The Fiction of Sandra Cisneros: *The House on Mango Street* (1984) and *Woman Hollering Creek* (1991)." In *Latino Literature in America*. Westport, Conn.: Greenwood Press, 2003. Offers detailed analyses of both *The House on Mango Street* and *Woman Hollering Creek*. Bibliography and index.

Rivera, Carmen Haydée. *Border Crossings and Beyond: The Life and Works of Sandra Cisneros*. Santa Barbara, Calif.: Praeger, 2009. A thorough study of the author and her works. Extensive notes, bibliography, and index.

See also: Isabel Allende; Julia Alvarez; Gloria Anzaldúa; Marie Arana; Ana Castillo; Lorna Dee Cervantes; Denise Chávez; Martha P. Cotera; Carolina Monsivaís; Cherríe Moraga.

Roberto Clemente

Puerto Rican-born baseball player and humanitarian

Clemente was Major League Baseball's first Latin American superstar. During his eighteen-year career, he accumulated 3,000 hits, starred in two World Series, received the National League's most valuable player award, played in eleven All-Star Games, and won multiple batting titles and Gold Glove awards. Immediately after his death, he was inducted into the National Baseball Hall of Fame.

Latino heritage: Puerto Rican

Born: August 18, 1934; Carolina, Puerto Rico

Died: December 31, 1972; at sea, near San Juan, Puerto Rico

Also known as: Roberto Clemente Walker; The Great One; Arriba; Momen

Areas of achievement: Baseball; social issues; philanthropy

Early Life

Roberto Clemente Walker (kleh-MEHN-tay) was the last of eight children born to Melchor and Luisa Clemente, a hardworking couple whose frugal budget did not include buying equipment for their young son's favorite sport, baseball. Undeterred, Clemente and his friends made their own balls and bats, hitting crushed tin cans with tree branches if necessary. When alone, Clemente practiced hitting and throwing in the hours that remained after he had completed the tasks his father assigned him to teach him the value of hard work.

Clemente also worked for others, saving his earnings for a used bicycle that he rode to Puerto Rican Winter League ballgames, and by the time he was eight years old, he was playing organized softball. However, it was as a javelin-throwing high school student that he most distinguished himself as the possessor of an unusually strong and accurate right arm. Clemente was so talented that at age seventeen he had to decide between representing Puerto Rico in the 1952 Olympics and playing professional baseball.

Clemente chose baseball. His first team was the Santurce Cangrejeros, his second the Brooklyn Dodgers' minor-league team in Montreal. Clemente excelled on the field, but he often was benched so that other teams' scouts would not see his burgeoning talent. The unfairness of such platooning infuriated him, but it was nothing compared to the treatment he would later encounter in the major leagues, where spring-training stints in the Deep South would subject him, as a "black" Puerto Rican, to Jim Crow segregation, and insensitive sportswriters seemingly went out of their way to emphasize his difficulty speaking English.

Being benched also kept Clemente from compiling attention-getting statistics. By the end of his season in Montreal, he had hit only 2 home runs and driven in 12 runs, while recording a .257 batting average. Nevertheless, the Dodgers' plan backfired. Branch Rickey, the man who helped break baseball's "color barrier" by bringing Jackie Robinson to the Dodgers in 1947, had since joined the front office of the Pittsburgh Pirates. Based on Rickey's recommendation, the Pirates, whose last-place finish in 1954 guaranteed them the first pick in the 1955 draft, chose Clemente.

Life's Work

Clemente made an immediate impression in Pittsburgh, intimidating baserunners with his strong throws from deep right field and, during his second season, batting an impressive .311 while playing in all but seven games. Although he was irritated by the lack of recognition he received from Pittsburgh's sportswriters and the degree to which he felt like an outsider in the team clubhouse (as a black man who spoke mainly Spanish, he felt doubly oppressed), he became an instant fan favorite.

Despite incurring charges of malingering by missing forty-three games during his third season, occasionally overthrowing Pirate infielders, and a tendency to strike out, Clemente's strengths outweighed his weaknesses. His momentum-generating style of play was recognized as a crucial factor in the Pirates' victory over the New York Yankees in the 1960 World Series. Still, rumors that he exaggerated his injuries persisted, in part because, rather than rest, he spent every winter playing or managing baseball in Puerto Rico. Clemente, however, felt obligated to repay the system that first allowed him to showcase his talents.

Clemente's relationship with the press remained contentious, as writers continued to reproduce his broken English phonetically. At the end of several strong seasons, he finally won the National League most valuable player award (voted on by sportswriters) in 1966. By then, even among the media, he was earning respect. Chief among his admirers was the Pirates' announcer, Bob Prince, who nicknamed him "Arriba." (The regard was mutual. In 1972, Clemente hosted "Bob Prince Day" in Puerto Rico.)

In 1971, the Pirates returned to the World Series, this time facing the Baltimore Orioles. After Pittsburgh lost the first two games, Clemente rallied his team both in the clubhouse (with exhortations worthy of his late-career team-leader status) and on the field (with play that would make him the World Series most valuable player). One year later, in his last regular-season at-bat, he became the eleventh player in Major League Baseball history to record his 3,000th hit.

On December 31, 1972, as Clemente attempted to transport supplies to the survivors of an earthquake in Managua, Nicaragua, the small airplane in which he and four others were traveling crashed into the Atlantic Ocean near San Juan, Puerto Rico. Clemente had known nothing of the pilot's poor safety record; driven by the urgency of the situation, he took no more time to second-guess his mission of mercy than he ever took to second-guess swinging at a pitch outside the strike zone.

Significance

Clemente became a Pittsburgh Pirate in 1955, only eight years after Jackie Robinson had begun baseball's slow march toward racial integration. Already famous in Puerto Rico, Clemente was followed obsessively in his homeland, with his every hit, run batted in, and put-out seen as a victory in the Latino struggle for respect. Clemente embraced this role. At a time when many players of color grudgingly accepted the status quo, he spoke

Roberto Clemente. (Focus on Sport/Getty Images)

Clemente's Induction into the Baseball Hall of Fame

On March 20, 1973, less than three months after his death, the Baseball Writers Association of America (BBWAA) voted to induct Roberto Clemente into the Baseball Hall of Fame. Ordinarily, a player is not eligible for this honor until five years after his retirement. Of the 134 players who previously had been selected, an exception had been made only once, for the beloved and terminally ill New York Yankee Lou Gehrig. By including Clemente in such select company, the BBWAA essentially conferred upon him a double honor.

The writers had good reason to celebrate Clemente. Not only would the on-field accomplishments of the longtime Pirate right fielder have guaranteed his selection under normal circumstances, but also he had died in an act of heroic selflessness: Having learned that relief supplies intended for Nicaraguan earthquake victims were being hoarded by the country's ruling Somoza family, he had decided to accompany an airplane to Nicaragua himself, believing that only his direct intervention would see the supplies through.

At the Hall of Fame induction ceremony, which took place on August 6, 1973, in Cooperstown, New York, Clemente was remembered in speeches by his widow, Vera, and Major League Baseball commissioner Bowie Kuhn. Later, it was recalled Clemente once had felt so unappreciated by the press that he said, "I guess a fellow like me has to die to get voted in by the writers."

out against racism. Eventually, he came to see himself as a representative not only of Latinos but also of all "underdogs," eagerly signing autographs, responding to fan mail, visiting sick children, and befriending strangers of any color in whom he sensed a kindred spirit. When recognition finally came, it brought with it even larger audiences. At these times, Clemente was sure to include encouragement and gratitude to his Latino "family" in Spanish. After his death, he has been memorialized in the many ways. Major League Baseball presents the Roberto Clemente Award each year to a player who exemplifies Clemente's humanitarian spirit. Many public facilities in Puerto Rico bear his name, including a youth center called Sports City, which had long been his dream to establish.

Arsenio Orteza

Further Reading

Maraniss, David: *Clemente: The Passion and Grace of Baseball's Last Hero*. New York: Simon & Schuster, 2006. The definitive account of Clemente's life. Maraniss blends everything of worth from earlier Clemente biographies, corrects previous errors, and adds valuable detail, especially regarding the circumstances of Clemente's death.

Markusen, Bruce: *Roberto Clemente: The Great One*. Champaign, Ill.: Sports Publishing, 2001. An informative biography filled with direct quotations and exhaustive descriptions of individual games.

Wagenheim, Kal: *Clemente!* New York, Praeger, 1973. Published less than one year after Clemente's death, Wagenheim's biography acquainted many fans with Clemente's off-field struggles, quirks, and passions for the first time.

See also: Felipe Alou; Luis Aparicio; Rod Carew; Orlando Cepeda; Juan Marichal; Tony Oliva; Luis Tiant.

Oscar Collazo

Puerto Rican-born radical who attempted to assassinate President Harry S. Truman

Committed to an independent Puerto Rico, Collazo was one of two men who plotted to assassinate President Truman in 1950. His accomplice was killed, and Collazo was captured and sent to prison.

Latino heritage: Puerto Rican
Born: January 20, 1914; Florida, Puerto Rico
Died: February 21, 1994; Vega Baja, Puerto Rico
Area of achievement: Crime; activism

Early Life

Born on a farm, Oscar Collazo (koh-LAH-zoh) was the youngest of fourteen children of a land-owning family in Puerto Rico. When Collazo was four years old, his father sold the family farm and died soon afterward. Collazo grew up working in an elder brother's general store. By 1932, he was out of school, unemployed, and directionless.

In April, 1932, Collazo found himself in a public square in San Juan, listening to a speech by Pedro Albizu Campos, a compelling orator and political agitator. The "supreme leader" of the Nationalist Party of Puerto Rico, Albizu Campos maintained that the incorporation of Puerto Rico into the United States was illegal, financially motivated, and exploitative. Although Albizu Campos and his party were rejected in free elections that year, he won a devoted convert in Collazo. Over time, Collazo personalized Albizu Campos's thesis, believing that predatory North American banking interests had forced his father to sell the family farm.

LIFE'S WORK

Even when he moved to New York to find stable employment, Collazo remained in contact with Puerto Rican radicals. During the 1940's, he served as the president of the New York chapter of the Nationalist Party. At the same time, Collazo gave the outward appearance of a contented family man. He got married, found a good job, had children, and even saved up for a house in the suburbs.

Realizing that he would never win a free election in Puerto Rico, Albizu Campos planned an island-wide revolution sometime in 1950 against the territorial government. It is unclear to what extent violence against the U.S. government was part of this plan, but several historians doubt the likelihood of Collazo plotting an assassination without orders from Albizu Campos.

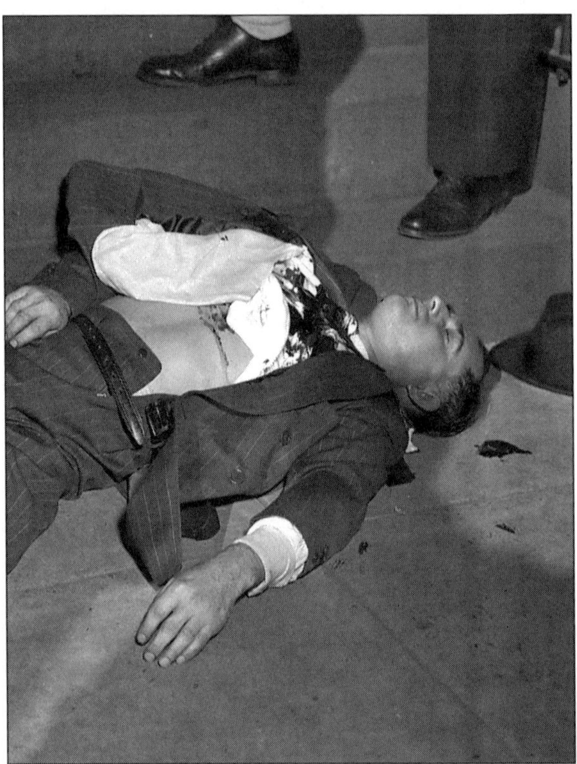

Oscar Collazo. (AP Photo)

In October, 1950, after a series of arrests, the territorial government in Puerto Rico became aware of the planned revolution. In response, the Nationalist Party prematurely launched its revolt; however, because various incidents were poorly coordinated, the uprising was mostly unsuccessful. In the end, a few police stations were burned down and several police officers were murdered. Although an attempt to assassinate the island's governor failed, the party did seize control of a small mountain town, declaring it the capital of a free Puerto Rican republic. Within a week, the uprising was crushed and Albizu Campos was behind bars.

Meanwhile, Collazo and another Puerto Rican assassin, Griselio Torresola, tried to assassinate President Harry S. Truman. At the time, Truman was living in the Blair House, a townhouse on a Washington side street, while the much more secure White House was being renovated. The assassination attempt was a suicide mission that maximized speed and surprise. Collazo approached the house from one direction, carrying a concealed handgun. When he reached the front of the house, he was to draw his weapon and kill any guards on the scene. Although an inept assassin, Collazo was an effective distraction. His pistol jammed when he first tried to shoot, and only after repeatedly striking it was he able to clear the weapon. Alerted to Collazo, the Secret Service and White House police began shooting at him, pinning him down behind a metal railing and eventually wounding him.

With attention drawn to Collazo, Torresola planned to approach the house from the other direction, killing any remaining guards. Afterward, he planned to enter the house, locate the president, and kill him. A trained gunman, Torresola mortally wounded one police officer and seriously wounded two others. In a second-floor bedroom of the Blair House, Truman heard the sound of gunfire and looked out the window. Torresola was only a few dozen feet away. Had he not been killed by a desperate shot from a dying police officer, Torresola might have seen and killed the president.

After a short trial in late 1950, Collazo was sentenced to death. The sentence later was commuted to life in prison. Collazo repeatedly claimed that he had nothing personal against Truman; his goal was to assassinate the president to draw the attention of the world to unfair conditions in Puerto Rico. He just as repeatedly denied that the assassination attempt had any connection to Albizu Campos's failed revolution.

By the late 1970's, after almost thirty years behind bars, Collazo was pardoned by President Jimmy Carter. An unrepentant Collazo returned to Puerto Rico, where he died on February 21, 1994.

Significance

Although unsuccessful in his primary mission, Collazo served as an example for later radicals. In 1954, a group of Puerto Ricans, several of whom personally knew Collazo, attacked the U.S. House of Representatives. Moreover, Collazo signaled a change in would-be presidential assassins. Before 1950, most had been motivated either by personal grudges or by mental illness. After Collazo, most assassins claimed a political motivation—that their murderous actions were designed either to bring about a revolution or to free an imprisoned leader.

Michael R. Meyers

Further Reading

Clarke, James K. *American Assassins: The Darker Side of Politics.* Princeton, N.J.: Princeton University Press, 1982. Surveys the efforts of various historical figures to make political statements through murder.

Collazo, Oscar. *Oscar Collazo: Memorias de un patriota encarcelado.* 2d ed. San Juan, P.R.: Cabrera, 2000. Collazo's Spanish-language autobiography details his political beliefs and motivations.

Hunter, Stephen, and John Bainbridge, Jr. *American Gunfight: The Plot to Kill Harry Truman.* New York: Simon & Schuster, 2005. A skillful reexamination of Collazo and Torresola's tactical plans.

See also: Pedro Albizu Campos; Rubén Berríos; José de Diego; Lolita Lebrón.

Margarita Colmenares

American educator, scientist, and activist

The daughter of Mexican immigrants, Colmenares became a successful and influential engineer who used her position to increase educational opportunities for Latin Americans and women. She also has lent her professional expertise to organizations that help people and companies, and allow organizations to operate in a more environmentally responsible manner.

Latino heritage: Mexican

Born: July 20, 1957; Sacramento, California

Also known as: Margarita Hortensia Colmenares

Areas of achievement: Science and technology; activism; social issues

Early Life

Margarita Hortensia Colmenares (KOHN-meh-NAHR-rehs) was born in Sacramento, California, to Luis Somuano Colmenares and Hortensia O. Colmenares, both of whom were immigrants from Oaxaca, Mexico. She was the oldest of five children. Her father, a migrant worker, later worked at a cannery and a warehouse, and her mother worked part time as a salesperson. At one point, the entire family pitched in to cover the largest newspaper route in downtown Sacramento.

Colmenares's parents instilled in her a strong respect for hard work and education. Despite their tight financial situation, Colmenares's parents sent her to a private, all-girls Catholic school, where she founded a Mexican American student coalition. Even at an early age, she loved to read and showed a strong aptitude for mathematics. Even though she was discouraged from doing so, she took college classes while in high school and excelled at her assigned secretarial courses.

Colmenares began her undergraduate education at California State University, Sacramento, where she studied business, but she soon discovered that she really wanted to study engineering. She transferred to Sacramento City College (SCC) to study chemistry, math, and physics to prepare for an engineering program. As a college sophomore, Colmenares was hired by the California Department of Water Resources as a student aide in Project Surveillance, an engineering unit that made periodic inspections of State Water Project dams, reservoirs, and pumping stations to verify that they operated safely after environmental disruptions such as earthquakes.

After two years at SCC, Colmenares transferred to the School of Engineering at Stanford University. She financed her education with five different scholarships and still found time to direct and perform with the Stanford Ballet Folklorico, a Mexican dance troupe. During her junior and senior years at Stanford, Colmenares worked for Chevron Corporation as a project engineer in El Paso, Texas. In 1981, she earned her B.S. in civil engineering, the same year her mother earned her bachelor's degree in education after twelve years of taking classes part-time.

Life's Work

After graduation, Chevron hired Colmenares to work in the company's San Francisco office as a design and construction engineer. In 1982, while working for Chevron, she founded the San Francisco chapter of the Society of Hispanic Professional Engineers (SHPE). Chevron recognized her talent and steadily promoted her, first to field construction engineer in Salt Lake City; then to a special corporate assignment in management, planning, and development; and then to environmental and safety compliance specialist in Houston, Texas. In 1986, Colmenares was made the lead engineer in an $18 million environmental cleanup project at the Chevron refinery in El Segundo, California. After the completion of this project, she remained in California as an air-quality specialist.

In 1989, the SHPE elected Colmenares as its first woman president, and in 1990, she managed to convince Chevron to grant her a one-year paid leave of absence to work full time as president of the SHPE as an executive on loan. The following year, Chevron granted Colmenares another one-year leave of absence after she won a White House Fellowship; she was the first Hispanic engineer to receive this honor. During her year in Washington, D.C., Colmenares chose to work with the Department of Education (DOE) as a special assistant to deputy secretary David T. Kearns.

Colmenares returned to Chevron in 1992 to work on the company's international operations in Latin America. In 1994, President Bill Clinton's administration hired her to work for the DOE as director of corporate liaison, providing leadership for collaborations between public and private institutions that improved education. Colmenares resigned from Chevron after leaving the DOE in 1998. She spent the following year traveling the world, after which she settled in Guatemala for nearly six years, where she started an education center for very young children.

Eventually, Colmenares returned to Sacramento and, in 2008, founded Think Verde, an organization that consults on sustainable and renewable energy policies and emerging green technologies and policies. She has been a member of the board of directors of the Environmental Council of Sacramento since 2008, and since 2010 has been a member of the Sacramento Greenwise task force, a mayoral initiative to transform Sacramento into the greenest region in the United States. She also continues to advocate for recruitment and retention of minorities in engineering and science careers.

Significance

Colmenares broke down ethnic and gender barriers as one of the first female and first Latino engineers to work for Chevron at such a high level. Even more than her pioneering efforts in engineering, Colmenares has given back to her community. She used her success and influence to help other young Latinos secure better educational opportunities in science and engineering. She was one of the first prominent Hispanic professionals to call national attention to the paucity of Latinos in science and engineering, and she used her position to take steps to help remedy this disparity. She remains a role model for constructive participation by professionals in their civic communities.

Michael A. Buratovich

Further Reading

Ambrose, Susan A., et al. *Journeys of Women in Science and Engineering: No Universal Constants*. Philadelphia: Temple University Press, 1999. A brief profile of Colmenares is part of this work on successful female scientists and engineers.

Cunningham, William, and Mary Cunningham. *Environmental Science: A Global Concern*. New York: McGraw-Hill, 2009. An environmental science textbook that provides a comprehensive overview of environmental science and global awareness and environmental action in plain, easy language.

Mendoza, Sylvia. *The Book of Latina Women: 150 Vidas of Passion, Strength, and Success*. Avon, Mass.: Adams Media, 2004. A collection of inspirational biographies of remarkable Hispanic women that includes a biography of Colmenares.

Olesky, Walter G. *Hispanic American Scientists*. New York: Facts On File, 1998. A series of short biographies of ten successful Mexican American scientists that includes a well-written entry on Colmenares.

See also: Anne Maino Alvarez; France Anne Córdova; Elma González; Eugenia Kalnay; Ellen Ochoa.

Jesús Colón

Puerto Rican-born journalist and labor activist

Colón was an Afro-Puerto Rican writer and labor organizer who chronicled New York's nascent Puerto Rican community from the 1910's through the 1960's. Published in 1961, his seminal collection of personal essays, A Puerto Rican in New York, and Other Sketches, *was the first book written in English to describe the everyday life of a Puerto Rican immigrant to America.*

Latino heritage: Puerto Rican
Born: January 20, 1901; Cayey, Puerto Rico
Died: October 1, 1974; New York, New York
Also known as: Miquis Tiquis; Pericles Espada
Areas of achievement: Journalism; activism; social issues

Early Life

Jesús Colón (koh-LOHN) was born on January 20, 1901, in Cayey, in the heart of tobacco-farming Puerto Rico. He began to form his socialist ideology as a boy, when he went to investigate a voice coming from the cigar factory behind his house and discovered that it belonged to a reader hired by the *tabaqueros* (tobacco workers) to help them pass a tedious day rolling cigars. Although barely able to read and write, the *tabaqueros* were well-informed and sophisticated. Colón later recalled hearing *Germinal* (1885) by Émile Zola, *Le Père Goriot* (1835; *Daddy Goriot*, 1860) by Honoré de Balzac, and Miguel de Cervantes's *Don Quixote de la Mancha* (1605, 1615), as well as political passages by Peter Kropotkin and Karl Marx.

The *tabaqueros* of Cayey had been profoundly affected by the Spanish-American War, which resulted in the American Tobacco Company gaining control of most of the tobacco-producing areas in Puerto Rico. Just after Colón's birth, tobacco production had been transformed from an artisanal craft to a capitalist enterprise with factories that employed hundreds of tobacco rollers at once. With the loss of their autonomy and the compromising of their craft through mass production, the *tabaqueros* became the vanguard of working-class socialist activism in Puerto Rico.

After his family moved to San Juan, Colón emerged as a writer and social activist. He led a student boycott against a teacher and was elected the editor of a political student newspaper, *¡Adelante!* (Forward!). His fervor against social injustice, which had begun in Cayey, was further intensified by a pivotal experience in San Juan in which he and his classmates witnessed mounted policemen brutally suppressing a parade of striking dockworkers and their families.

In 1917, the year that U.S. citizenship was granted to Puerto Ricans, the sixteen-year-old Colón stowed away on a cargo ship to New York City. Joining his older brother Joaquín in Brooklyn, he worked menial jobs while completing his high school education and attending two years at St. John's University. During this time, he also continued advocating for workers' rights, becoming a founding member of the Alianza Obrera Puertorriqueña (Puerto Rican Workers' Alliance) in 1922, the Ateneo Obrero Hispano (Hispanic Workers' Athenaeum) in 1926, and the Liga Puertorriqueña e Hispana (Puerto Rican and Hispanic League) in 1928. These grassroots organizations fostered mutual aid and provided cultural activities for the nascent Puerto Rican community in New York City.

Life's Work

Colón began working as a journalist in 1923 for *Justicia*, the official newspaper of the Federación Libre de Trabajadores (Free Federation of Workers). Early articles also include satiric writing under various pen names for *Gráfico*, edited by Bernardo Vega, who also hailed from Cayey. As Miquis Tiquis, Colón satirized the Puerto Rican community, ridiculing Latina flappers and mocking Spanglish colloquialisms. He also used the pen name Pericles Espada in the short-lived column "Cartas inmorales a mi novia" ("Immoral Letters to My Girlfriend"), which featured editorials on Puerto Rico's social and political situation thinly disguised as fictional letters of advice from Pericles Espada to his beloved, the island of Puerto Rico. Intending at first to write a dozen of these letters, he was cut off after his fifth letter critiqued religion and apparently offended the largely Catholic readers of *Gráfico*.

Mirroring the letters he wrote as Pericles Espada, Colón wrote letters to his fiancée Rufa Concepción Fernández ("Concha"), who had remained in Puerto Rico while he struggled to establish himself. They were married in 1925, after which she joined him in New York City and became his secretary and confidante until her death in 1958.

Colón's disdain as Miquis Tiquis and his lofty tone as Pericles Espada are nowhere in evidence in his later writing, which is marked by a homespun sincerity.

Beginning in 1943, his weekly column "Lo que el pueblo me dice" ("What the People Tell Me") appeared in *Pueblos Hispanos*, a progressive paper that advocated Puerto Rican independence. He also wrote for *Liberación*, a publication created by antifascist Spanish exiles in New York. His articles for these papers were simple and heartfelt appeals that attempted to raise the social consciousness of the Latino community, urging people to register to vote, lobbying on behalf of radical East Harlem politician Vito Marcantonio, and proposing a statue to mark the burgeoning Spanish Harlem community.

In 1955, Colón began writing in English for *The Daily Worker,* a newspaper published by the Communist Party. For fifteen years, his weekly column, "As I See It from Here," provided leftist readers of *The Daily Worker* with a unique insight into the daily life of working-class Puerto Ricans. Many of his columns were what he called "sketches," short anecdotes on his experiences as a young man eking out a living as a laborer and facing discrimination as an Afro-Puerto Rican. In 1961, he complied several of these stories into *A Puerto Rican in New York, and Other Sketches*, a seminal book on the working-class Puerto Rican experience that was all the more revolutionary for being written in English and thus accessible to the general American public.

Colón's open support of the Communist Party led to his investigation by the House Un-American Activities Committee (HUAC) in 1959. In his remarkable testimony, he denounced HUAC for its blatant abuse of constitutional rights and used the opportunity to lobby for Puerto Rican independence.

Colón's involvement in labor rights and Puerto Rican activism led him to run unsuccessfully for public office three times, first for the New York City Council in 1953 on the American Labor Party ticket, a year later as a candidate for the New York State Assembly, and finally in 1969 for New York state comptroller under the Communist Party ticket. His platforms included free daycare for working mothers and an end to the Vietnam War.

At the time of his death in 1974, Colón was working on a second volume of essays. His unfinished manuscript, along with his large collection of papers, photographs, and documents pertaining to the history of Puerto Ricans in America, is housed at the Center for Puerto Rican Studies at Hunter College. Often credited as the intellectual father of Nuyorican literature, he raised awareness of the struggles of Puerto Ricans in America and paved the way for future generations of Latino and Puerto Rican writers.

A Puerto Rican in New York, and Other Sketches

Published in 1961, Jesús Colón's *A Puerto Rican in New York, and Other Sketches* is a collection of autobiographical essays that depict life from the perspective of a working-class Afro-Puerto Rican. The anecdotal stories in this collection depict Colón's political awakening, beginning with "A Voice from the Window," in which he describes his experiences as a boy in Puerto Rico listening with astonishment to the reader at the cigar factory. His most bitter story, "Kipling and I," sees him literally burning his ideals in an effort to survive a cold night. Frigid weather also figures in "On the Docks It Was Cold," in which Colón recalls his time as a dockworker in Depression-era New York. More than just an autobiography, *A Puerto Rican in New York* is marked by a generosity of spirit and a genuine concern for the working poor, offering heartfelt depictions of the fear and isolation experienced by Latinos unable to speak English ("I Heard a Man Crying") and the discrimination Colón faced as a Puerto Rican of African descent ("Hiawatha into Spanish"). Colón's indignation and moral outrage are tempered by his disarming optimism. Many of the sketches end with a fervent appeal for compassion, revealing Colón's socialist sympathies and his faith in the possibility of revolutionary change.

SIGNIFICANCE

Deeply committed to labor rights and social equality, Colón was an ardent multiculturalist and a voice for the working class. His writing helped shape a sympathetic public perception of Puerto Ricans. Colón's articles in *The Daily Worker*, which were compiled into his seminal book, *A Puerto Rican in New York*, offer a rare glimpse into the Puerto Rican community in America before the Great Migration of the 1950's and 1960's. By writing in English, Colón consciously sought to combat the racism inherent in mainstream media by portraying Puerto Ricans as part of the larger community. His heartfelt stories come from many perspectives—he was at once an immigrant who struggled with language barriers, a member of the working poor, and a man of African descent. Through his own experiences, he sought to unite the struggles of disparate oppressed groups.

Victoria Linchong

FURTHER READING

Colón, Jesús. *A Puerto Rican in New York, and Other Sketches.* 2d ed. New York: International Publishers,

1982. Colón's seminal book on his experiences as a Puerto Rican in New York from the 1910's through the 1950's.

_______. *The Way It Was, and Other Writings*. Edited by Edna Acosta-Belén and Virginia Sánchez Korrol. Houston, Tex.: Arte Público Press, 1993. Posthumously published compilation of Colón's late writings. Includes a scholarly essay on Colón's importance as a writer, thinker, and social activist.

James, Winston A., *Holding Aloft the Banner of Ethiopia: Caribbean Radicalism in Early Twentieth Century America*. New York: Verso, 1998. An insightful and intriguing comparison between Arturo Schomberg and Colón. Although both were Puerto Ricans of African descent, Schomberg identified with his African roots, whereas Colón saw himself as working-class and Puerto Rican.

Stanchich, Maritza. "Insular Interventions: Jesús Colón Unmasks Racial Harmonizing and Populist Uplift Discourses in Puerto Rico." In *Hispanic Caribbean Literature of Migration: Narratives of Displacement*, edited by Vanessa Pérez Rosario. New York: Palgrave Macmillan, 2010. Scholarly discussion of Colón's depiction of race and community in his writings.

See also: Luisa Capetillo; César Chávez; Ernesto Galarza; Antonio Orendain; Felisa Rincón de Gautier.

Miriam Colón

Puerto Rican-born actor and founder of the Puerto Rican Traveling Theatre

An actor who has appeared on Broadway and in film and television, Colón also is a trailblazer who established an acting school and theater to foster young talent and introduce audiences to the work of Latino playwrights and performers.

Latino heritage: Puerto Rican

Born: August 20, 1936; Ponce, Puerto Rico

Also known as: Miriam Colón Valle

Areas of achievement: Theater; film; acting; radio and television

Early Life

Miriam Colón (koh-LOHN) was born in Ponce, Puerto Rico, on August 20, 1936. Interested in acting from an early age, she studied drama at the University of Puerto Rico. In 1950, she was cast in the film *Los peloteros* (1951) opposite famous actor Ramón Rivero, known as Diplo, who was forty-two years old. Despite the age difference, she played Diplo's ambitious wife. During the filming in 1950, a major nationalist rebellion ensued in which militants attempted to free Puerto Rico from U.S. control. The U.S. military put down the uprising. The events left an indelible mark on the young actor, and from then on, a patriotic fervor motivated her to pursue lofty goals as an actor while serving her community.

Shortly after the release of her first film and after training with Professor Leo Lavandero, Colón began to accept parts with theater groups in San Juan. Soon thereafter, however, she left her homeland for the United States.

Miriam Colón. (WireImage/Getty Images)

Life's Work

Colón arrived in New York City with a scholarship to attend the Actors Studio. She established herself on Broadway in plays such as *In the Summer House* (1954) and *The Innkeepers* (1956). In 1969, she starred in *The Wrong Way Lightbulb*. She also branched out into film and television, appearing alongside stars such as Charles Bronson, Redd Foxx, Ricardo Montalbán, and Dick Van Dyke. From 1999 to 2002, she had a recurring role on the soap opera *Guiding Light*. Her many film credits include *One-Eyed Jacks* (1961), *The Appaloosa* (1966), *Scarface* (1983), and *Goal!* (2005) and its sequels. She also has appeared in several Spanish-language films.

In addition to her prowess as a performer, Colón has garnered recognition for her work as founder and director of the Puerto Rican Traveling Theatre (PRTT). She established the PRTT in 1967 as an itinerant troupe before it found a permanent home in a restored New York City firehouse. The PRTT is a nonprofit educational corporation operating under an Actors' Equity contract. The theater group consists of a mainstage that produces two new Off-Broadway shows each year at the PRTT's West 47th Street venue; a touring unit that performs for disadvantaged communities; the Raúl Juliá Training Unit, founded in 1969, where youths receive free training in several theater disciplines; and a playwrights unit that offers training for beginners and experienced writers. The group has been successful in producing and nurturing ethnically diverse talent. It has brought the work of Latino playwrights and performers to the attention of the New York theater scene and often mounts bilingual productions.

Significance

Colón has been honored many times for her work as an actor and as founder of the PRTT. In 1978, she was named an Extraordinary Woman of Achievement by the National Council of Christians and Jews. She received an achievement award from the Puerto Rican Legal Defense and Education Fund (now known as LatinoJustice PRLDEF) in 1981 and the Mayor's Award of Honor for the Arts and Culture from New York mayor Ed Koch in 1982. In 1985, she received the Athena Award from the New York Commission on the Status of Women; the next year, she was honored with the Maclovio Barraza Leadership Award from the National Council of La Raza. In 1989, she was awarded an honorary doctorate by the State University of New York.

Colón is a representative of a generation of pioneering Puerto Ricans performers in Broadway productions, film, and television. With Chita Rivera, Rita Moreno, and Priscilla Lopez, she is among the vanguard who paved the way for Latinas in the entertainment industry.

Basilio Serrano

Further Reading

Bonilla-Santiago, Gloria. "Miriam Colón." In *Latinas! Women of Achievement*, edited by Diane Telgen and Jim Kamp. Detroit, Mich.: Visible Ink Press, 1996. Biography placing Colón's achievements in the context of gender and ethnicity.

Fernández, Mayra. *Miriam Colón, Actor and Theater Founder*. Illustrated by Luis Arvelo. Cleveland, Ohio: Modern Curriculum, 1994. A biography aimed at younger readers that chronicles Colón's career and achievements.

Rodríguez, Clara E. *Heroes, Lovers, and Others: The Story of Latinos in Hollywood*. New York: Oxford University Press, 2008. Provides insights into how the entertainment industry has portrayed and employed Latino performers over the years. Includes discussion of Colón's career.

See also: María Conchita Alonso; Linda Cristal; Raúl Juliá; Rita Moreno; Chita Rivera; Elena Verdugo.

Willie Colón

American salsa musician

Colón is a salsero, bandleader, trombonist, composer, arranger, and producer whose own music fuses the styles and rhythms of Puerto Rico, Cuba, the Dominican Republic, Brazil, and other Latin American nations. As a cofounder of the genre dubbed "conscious salsa," Colón also has assumed the role of activist, with much of his music containing social and political themes.

Latino heritage: Puerto Rican

Born: April 28, 1950; South Bronx, New York

Also known as: William Anthony Colón Román; El Malo (the Bad Boy)

Areas of achievement: Music; social issues

EARLY LIFE

William Anthony Colón Román (koh-LOHN) was born to Puerto Rican parents Aracelis Román and Willie Colón in the South Bronx, New York. Growing up, music was ever-present in the barrio as the sound of conga drums, horns, and chanting, and the pulse of Latin rhythms echoed through the streets. Colón's maternal grandmother, Antonia, who had immigrated to the United States in 1923, also was an important musical influence. She came to live with Colón after his grandfather died and bought him his first trumpet from a pawn shop for fifty dollars. He was just twelve years old. Colón's teenage band, the Dandees, was a quartet made up of conga, accordion, clarinet, and Colón's trumpet. He switched to the trombone by age fifteen, in part because it was larger and more difficult to steal.

Established Latin musicians considered Colón an untrained upstart and were bothered by his nontraditional mixing of styles. He had learned his craft on the streets of New York and experimented with styles such as Puerto Rican *aguinaldo*, Cuban *son montuno*, Dominican *merengue*, and Colombian *cumbia*. To Colón, this integration of styles was true salsa—a harmonic blend of all the Latin music in New York.

Willie Colón. (AP Photo)

LIFE'S WORK

Colón's musical career began in earnest when he signed with Fania Records, also known as the "Latin Motown." With singer Héctor Lavoe, Colón released his first album, *El Malo* (1967), about teenage life in the barrio. This album earned Colón the nickname "El Malo" and a bad-boy image that persisted into the mid-1970's. His band played salsa clubs in New York and Puerto Rico and released numerous successful albums: *Cosa nuetra* (1970), *The Big Break* (1971), *El juicio* (1972), and *Lo mato* (1973). Colón also released two Christmas albums, *Asalto Navideño* (1971) and *Asalto Navideño Vol. 2* (1973).

In 1975, Colón met singer Rubén Blades, and from 1977 to 1982, the pair formed a partnership that produced numerous best-selling albums and examples of "conscious salsa." In 1982, Colón left Fania Records to sign with RCA Records, but he continued to produce for a number of Fania musicians including Lavoe and Celia Cruz. Colón also continued to perform throughout Western Europe, the United States, and Latin America. Performance venues ranged from the inaugural balls of presidents Ronald Reagan and Bill Clinton to a concert in the Amazon jungle to which the audience arrived by canoe. In 1995, Colón reunited with Blades to record *Tras la tormenta* (*After the Storm*), and the pair renewed their partnership in November, 1998, for the Amnesty International Concert at La Carlota Airport in Caracas, Venezuela.

Colón's musical success created numerous opportunities to engage in political and social activism. He participated in youth programs, gave speeches at schools, appeared in television advertisements, and took part in cultural events to foster pride in Latino identity and culture. In 1997, Colón became a spokesman for the relief and development organization CARE International. In 2001, he received the Environmental Protection Agency's Environmental Quality Award and Yale University's Chubb Fellowship. Furthermore, Colón helped launch the Sloan-Kettering Campaign and the Covering Kids Program for free or affordable children's medical insurance in 2005.

Colón also was involved in campaigns to end the military occupation of the Puerto Rican island municipality of Vieques, which the U.S. Navy used as a bombing range until 2003. In addition, he ran in the New York State

Seventeenth Congressional District primary in 1994 and in New York City's 2001 Democratic primary as a candidate for the office of public advocate. Trinity College and Lehman College recognized Colón and his contributions with honorary doctorates in 1999 and 2004, respectively.

Significance

Colón has earned numerous Grammy nominations, a Lifetime Achievement Award from the Latin Academy of Recording Arts and Sciences, and many gold and platinum records, making him one of the most celebrated Latin American musicians of the twentieth and early twenty-first centuries. His music was groundbreaking in its fusion of Latin American rhythms, and his social consciousness was evident not only in his lyrics but also in his community involvement. To name just a few of his contributions, Colón has served as chair of the Association of Hispanic Arts, president of the Arthur Schomburg Coalition for a Better New York, a member of the Latino Commission on AIDS, and on the board of the United Nations Immigrant Foundation. In 2004, Colón was inducted into the Bronx Walk of Fame.

Sandra J. Fallon-Ludwig

Further Reading

Colón, Willie. "The Rhythms." In *Low Rent: A Decade of Prose and Photographs from "The Portable Lower East Side,"* edited by Kurt Hollander. New York: Grove Press, 1994. In this autobiographical essay, Colón discusses his family, the influence of his grandmother, and the Latin rhythms he heard growing up in the Bronx and their use in modern music.

_______. "Willie Colón." http://www.williecolon.com. Colón's official Web site includes ample biographical information, photos, music, a calendar of events, and news.

_______. "Willie Colón: The Salsa Kings Don't Just Play Songs of Love." Interview by Leonardo Padura Fuentes. In *Faces of Salsa: A Spoken History of the Music*, by Leonardo Padura Fuentes. Translated by Stephen J. Clark. Washington, D.C.: Smithsonian Books, 2003. In this interview, Colón addresses topics such as the longevity of salsa, growing up in the barrio, commercialism, "conscious salsa," his indebtedness to earlier Cuban performers, and his political views.

Steward, Sue. *Musica!: Salsa, Rumba, Merengue, and More—The Rhythm of Latin America.* Foreword by Willie Colón. San Francisco, Calif.: Chronicle Books, 1999. Offers comprehensive information on Latin American dance music and its history.

See also: Rubén Blades; Paquito D'Rivera; Flaco Jiménez; Eduardo Mata; Poncho Sánchez.

Dave Concepción

Venezuelan-born baseball player

Concepción was a star shortstop in the 1970's and 1980's and a member of Cincinnati's famous "Big Red Machine." He anchored the defense and was a key player on two World Series champion teams.

Latino heritage: Venezuelan

Born: June 17, 1948; Ocumare de la Costa, Aragua, Venezuela

Also known as: David Ismael Concepción Benitez; Davey Concepción; El Rey; Elmer

Area of achievement: Baseball

Early Life

David Ismael Concepción Benitez (kohn-SEHP-see-OHN) was born on June 17, 1948, in Venezuela. He started his baseball career as a pitcher and was drafted into the Cincinnati Reds organization in 1967. Concepción moved from pitcher to shortstop and was called up to the major leagues in 1970. He only played sparingly in his first three years as the Reds competed for the National League pennant; in 1972, the team reached the World Series but lost to the Oakland Athletics.

Life's Work

Concepción became the Reds' everyday shortstop in 1973 and thereafter was an important defensive cog in the team dubbed "the Big Red Machine," which featured stars Ken Griffey, Sr., Johnny Bench, Pete Rose, and Joe Morgan. He was best known for his fielding but also developed into a serviceable hitter and effective base-stealer.

In 1975, the Reds returned to the World Series, where they defeated the Boston Red Sox. Cincinnati repeated as champions the next season, cementing the team's place among the best ever in baseball. Throughout

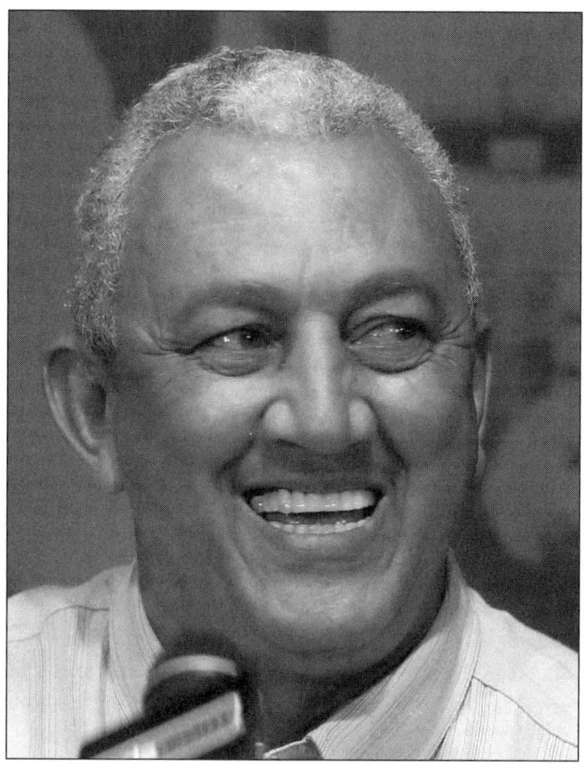

Dave Concepción. (AP Photo)

this span, Concepción was an integral part of the Big Red Machine. He and second baseman Morgan were a dominant double-play combination, and Concepción won four straight Gold Gloves from 1974 to 1977.

After the 1976 World Series, the Big Red Machine was slowly dismantled. In the 1976-1977 offseason, first baseman Tony Perez was traded to Montreal. After the 1978 season, Rose left as a free agent and signed with the Philadelphia Phillies. After the 1979 season, Morgan left. By 1980, only Concepción and Bench were left among the leading players of the Big Red Machine era. The Reds' performance also declined as the 1970's drew to an end. Concepción continued as the team's everyday shortstop and performed admirably. He was not as flashy as fellow shortstop Ozzie Smith, the St. Louis Cardinals star who drew acclaim from the media for his acrobatic plays; Concepción, however, was the better hitter. He won two Silver Slugger Awards as the best hitter at his position and added a fifth Gold Glove in 1979. Concepción also pioneered the one-hop across the artificial turf of Riverfront Stadium, which improved the Reds' defense.

In 1985, his skills declining because of age and nagging injuries, Concepción was replaced as the Reds' everyday shortstop. He continued to play as a utility infielder, covering all four positions admirably. Concepción also dealt with the return of Rose as player-manager. He retired from baseball in 1988.

Significance

When he retired, Concepción was one of the best-known Venezuelan players of his era, second only to fellow shortstop Luis Aparacio, and his success paved the way for future generations of Venezuelan major leaguers. He also was a key member of the Big Red Machine-era Cincinnati teams considered among the best teams in baseball history. A nine-time All-Star, Concepción had his number, 13, retired by the Reds in 2007.

Scott A. Merriman

Further Reading

Honig, Donald. *The Greatest Shortstops of All Time.* New York: Brown & Benchmark, 1992. Offers an overview of Concepción's career and his place among the baseball legends at his position.

Posnanski, Joe. *The Machine: A Hot Team, a Legendary Season, and a Heart-Stopping World Series—The Story of the 1975 Cincinnati Reds.* New York: William Morrow, 2009. Although this book focuses more on the team than on individual players, it offers good insights into the era and teams that made Concepción famous.

Shannon, Mike. *The Good, the Bad, and the Ugly Cincinnati Reds: Heart-Pounding, Jaw-Dropping, and Gut-Wrenching Moments from Cincinnati Reds History.* Chicago: Triumph Books, 2008. As the title suggests, this is a good general history of the Cincinnati Reds, emphasizing the Big Red Machine era and its many stars.

Wendel, Tim. *The New Face of Baseball: The One-Hundred-Year Rise and Triumph of Latinos in America's Favorite Sport.* New York: Philip Lief, 2003. Discusses the movement that Concepción was a significant part of in the 1970's.

See also: Luis Aparicio; Miguel Cabrera; César Cedeño; Tony Fernandez; Ozzie Guillén; Miguel Tejada.

Laura Contreras-Rowe

American author, motivational speaker, and realtor

Contreras-Rowe is a motivational speaker best known for her book Aim High: Extraordinary Stories of Hispanic and Latina Women. *In 2010, she toured the United States, promoting her book and serving as a life coach for young Latinas. A successful realtor, she purchased two successful real-estate franchises during a two-year period.*

Latino heritage: Mexican

Born: March 8, 1966; Dallas, Texas

Also known as: Laura Contreras

Areas of achievement: Business; literature

Early Life

Laura Contreras-Rowe (kohn-TRAY-rehs-roh) was born in Dallas, Texas, in 1966. She grew up along the Mexican border in the city of Laredo, Texas. Her early childhood was marked by her desire to live a better life. She lived in a trailer with her mother and older sister, and the family was poor. To make matters worse, Contreras-Rowe's Laredo neighborhood was plagued with gangs and illegal drugs. Latina role models in her community were not easily identified.

Contreras-Rowe dreamed of getting out of Laredo. One day, she saw golfer Nancy Lopez on television. She began to follow López's golfing career and eventually realized that if golfing afforded Lopez a successful lifestyle, she too could become a successful Latina. For that reason, Contreras-Rowe turned to sports and used athletics to develop her leadership skills. She felt that she finally had the means to escape poverty. Although she was just an average student in high school, Contreras-Rowe managed to complete her college studies at Oral Roberts University, earning a B.S. in broadcast design and telecommunications with a minor in art history, in 1991.

After college, Contreras-Rowe's pursued a successful career as a realtor. In 2006, she purchased her first Keller and Williams Realty franchise in the resort town of Virginia Beach, Virginia. She bought a second Keller and Williams franchise in 2008.

Life's Work

In 2009, Contreras-Rowe lived in an upscale neighborhood in Virginia Beach with her two sons. She owned a fabulous home and luxury cars. That same year, she published her book *Aim High: Extraordinary Stories of Hispanic and Latina Women*, a collection of success stories. Some of the women featured in this book include Minita Ramirez, a dean at Texas A&M International University; Carmen Ramirez-Rathmell, a dentist in Laredo, Texas; Anna Escobeda Cabral, the former U.S. treasurer; television broadcaster Rebecca Gomez Diamond; and drag racer Erica Ann Ortiz. Altogether, thirty-three biographies of Latinas of diverse professional backgrounds are featured in *Aim High*, with five of the women from Laredo, Texas.

The popularity of *Aim High* led Contreras-Rowe to found Why Be Average, a consulting and coaching company that, in her own words, seeks "to educate, motivate and challenge adults, young adults and minority children to aim high and reach their full potential." She speaks to school children on a regular basis about the importance and possibilities of realizing their dreams by earning good educations and developing strong work ethics. In her motivational speaking, Contreras-Rowe tells her audiences that no one should settle for just being average, and everyone should set superior goals in life. To that end, she believes a quality education is the best foundation for a successful life.

In 2010, Contreras-Rowe embarked on a book tour and a series of motivational speaking appearances. She traveled to numerous American cities speaking to more than eighteen thousand people. Audience members included pregnant teens, former gang members, and juveniles recently released from detention centers.

Significance

By 2010, Laura Contreras-Rowe, the woman who sought Latina role models as a child, had herself become a Latina role model, as well as a popular keynote speaker and seminar training consultant. Her speaking and consulting has taken her to many American and international cities. She significantly impacted Latinas through her book *Aim High*, her book tour, and her motivational speeches. *Aim High* received several literary awards, including the Independent Publishers Gold/First Place Book Award for Best Nonfiction Multicultural, Juvenile, Youth, Young Adult books. In 2010, her book garnered three International Latino Book Awards; first place for best gift book, second place for best cover design, and honorable mention/third place for best first book.

Sandra W. Leconte

Further Reading

Contreras-Rowe, Laura, *Aim High: Extraordinary Stories of Hispanic and Latina Women.*http://

aimhighbook.com. Contreras-Rowe's Web site provides a biography, information about her book and consulting company, and other details about her businesses.

Crow, Kirsten. "Author Shoots to Make Latina Role Models Visible in New Book." *Laredo Morning Times*, January 10, 2010. Describes how Contreras-Rowe beat statistical odds to rise from poverty to become a successful realtor and author.

See also: Linda Alvarado; Nancy Lopez; Nina Tassler.

Angel Cordero, Jr.

Puerto Rican-born jockey

The first Puerto Rican inducted into the United States Racing Hall of Fame, Cordero was known as an aggressive jockey who took risks to win. One of only eight jockeys to win three or more Kentucky Derby races, Cordero was foremost a New York jockey, because in eleven straight years, he won more races at New York's famed Saratoga track than any other jockey.

Latino heritage: Puerto Rican

Born: November 8, 1942; Santurce, San Juan, Puerto Rico

Also known as: Ángel Tomás Cordero, Jr.

Area of achievement: Sports

Early Life

Ángel Tomás Cordero, Jr., was born on November 8, 1942, into a horse-racing family in Puerto Rico. His father and grandfather had both been jockeys and later horse trainers. His mother was the daughter of a jockey and a trainer. He had more than twenty uncles and cousins who either rode professionally or trained horses.

In accordance with his mother's wishes, Cordero initially planned to become a dentist. However, he was first placed on a horse at the age of five months, and by the time he was three years old he was sitting in a saddle balanced on a fence, pretending to ride. As a teenager, before he rode in his first professional race, he was a bettor. As a gambler, Cordero could not stand to lose. As a jockey, Cordero reasoned, he would at least have some measure of control over the outcome of a race and get paid for riding.

Cordero recorded his first victory on June 15, 1960, at El Comandante Race Track in Puerto Rico, astride the horse Celador. Cordero moved to the United States to race in 1962 after making a name for himself in his native Puerto Rico. His early races at New York's Belmont Park, Saratoga, and Aqueduct racetracks were disappointing. Cordero spoke little English, and he had difficulty convincing owners and trainers to give him a chance on their horses. He returned to Puerto Rico, improved his English, continued to excel at racing, and then returned to New York in 1965. This time, he became New York's most successful jockey within two years and North America's leading race winner by 1968.

Life's Work

The U.S. champion jockey by number of wins in 1968, Cordero continued racing despite injuries, illness, and suspensions. Despite his perseverance, however, Cordero was unpopular with some racing fans, who resented

Angel Cordero, Jr. (AP Photo)

Cordero's Legacy

When he retired in 1992, Angel Cordero, Jr., had won 7,057 races in 38,646 mounts, a winning percentage of 18.3. Cordero considered his 1976 Belmont Stakes victory aboard Bold Forbes as his greatest win. He referred to himself as the most successful Puerto Rican athlete in any sport and claimed to have won seven of every ten photo finishes in which he was involved. In 1974, he and Laffit Pincay, Jr., became the first two jockeys to each win more than four million dollars in the same year. In one day alone—March 12, 1975—Cordero won six races. Even near the end of his career, which was cut short by injuries, he still was winning regularly. In 1991, the year before his retirement, Cordero rode in 1,341 races, earning 238 wins, 212 second places, and 186 thirds and earning more than nine million dollars in prize money. In that year, Cordero joined Bill Shoemaker and Pincay as the first thoroughbred jockeys to reach 7,000 wins in their careers.

his brash speech and flamboyance. After a victory, Cordero often would leap from his horse and toss his riding crop nonchalantly to a groom. The 5-foot, 3-inch jockey, weighing 113 pounds, inspired passion from racing fans. He often was booed from the grandstands, especially after losing aboard a heavily favored horse.

In 1978, Cordero suffered a fractured vertebra while riding the horse Dr. Johnson at Hollywood Park. He later was thrown off his ride at Aqueduct in 1986 and suffered a lacerated liver and a broken arm. Cordero's worst accident came in January, 1992, when he was involved in a four-horse collision at Aqueduct and suffered a broken arm, three broken ribs, and a damaged kidney and spleen. Cordero had to have his spleen removed and spent several months regaining his health. The collision essentially ended Cordero's career as a top jockey. Although he made a brief comeback in 1995, Cordero was unable to return to winning form.

Although he rode Triple Crown winner Seattle Slew (and called that horse the best he ever rode) during his career, Cordero did not ride any horse to victory in racing's Triple Crown (the Kentucky Derby, the Preakness Stakes, and the Belmont Stakes). Cordero came closest in 1976, when he rode Bold Forbes to victories in both the Kentucky Derby and the Belmont Stakes.

Cordero was the champion jockey by earnings from races won in 1976, a feat he would achieve again in 1982 and 1983, when he also won the Eclipse Award for outstanding jockey. Cordero copied his style of racing from his idol, Eddie Arcaro, who rode low in the stirrups, his eyes looking between the horse's ears.

No stranger to controversy, Cordero was identified as a participant in a New York cheating ring in 1978. One of eleven riders accused, Cordero never was suspended or charged with wrongdoing in the incident. However, race fixing was discovered, and Cordero waited out a ten-year ban on New York-based riders for eligibility into the Racing Hall of Fame. He also drew more than two hundred fines and suspensions for aggressive or reckless riding during his career, thought by many to be a record. "One thing I am always guilty of is trying," Cordero once said.

Upon his retirement, like his father and grandfather before him, Cordero became a trainer. His first win as a trainer came on June 13, 1992, which had been declared "Angel Cordero Day" at Belmont Park. Cordero also served as an agent to fellow Puerto Rican jockey John Velazquez, who was one of the four riders involved in the 1992 collision at Aqueduct.

Despite his injuries and retirement, Cordero made a brief comeback in 1995. He won a race in his native Puerto Rico at El Comandante Race Park, where he had won his first race thirty-five years earlier. Returning to New York, he was winless in ten mounts at Belmont Park. Cordero said, "I want to retire my way and not the other way. I don't want people to remember me going out the other way."

Significance

In his thirty-two years in racing at Saratoga, Cordero was the leader in races won for thirteen of fifteen years, including eleven straight years. He was the state of New York's leader in races won for eight years. With multiple wins in the Kentucky Derby, Preakness Stakes, and the Breeders' Cup, Cordero was known as one of the most strategic and daring jockeys of his day. From 1977 to 1990, his mounts won more than five million dollars each year. Cordero won the Kentucky Derby in 1974 (on Cannonade), 1976 (on Bold Forbes), and 1985 (on Spend a Buck). He won the Preakness Stakes in 1980 (on Codex) and in 1984 (on Gate Dancer). His only Belmont Stakes victory came aboard Bold Forbes in 1976.

Randy L. Abbott

Further Reading

Berkow, Ira. "The Return of Cordero." *The New York Times*, August 29, 1983, p. C4. This article recounts Cordero's return to racing after a two-horse collision left him seriously injured.

Crist, Steven. "Angel Cordero: Jockey the Fans Love to Hate." *The New York Times*, December 12, 1982, p. A1. This article discusses Cordero's alleged role in race-fixing, for which he was never officially charged or suspended.

Durso, Joseph. "Cordero Says His Reluctant Goodbye to Racing." *The New York Times*, May 8, 1992, p. B17. Bowing to the wishes of his family and his doctor, Cordero retired from racing after a four-horse collision in January, 1992, nearly cost him his life.

Platt, Jim, and James Buckley, Jr. "Eddie Arcaro and Angel Cordero." In *Sports Immortals: Stories of Inspiration and Achievement*. Chicago: Triumph Books, 2002. Chronicles the careers of the racing legends and explains how Cordero modeled his racing style on Arcaro's.

See also: Laffit Pincay, Jr.; Ismael Valenzuela.

France Anne Córdova

French-born astrophysicist and university administrator

Córdova is an astrophysicist who has not only done significant studies using traditional methods but also produced new methods to study space. She also has made a major impact on academia as a university administrator devoted to research and diversity.

Latino heritage: Mexican

Born: August 5, 1947; Paris, France

Also known as: France Anne-Dominic Córdova; Françoise Anne-Dominic Córdova

Areas of achievement: Science and technology; education

Early Life

France Anne-Dominic Córdova (KOHR-doh-vah) was the first of twelve children born to a Mexican American father and Irish American mother. She was born in Paris, France, because her father, Frederick, was working there for Cooperative for American Remittances Everywhere (CARE) distributing supplies to the needy. Baptized as Françoise, Córdova later Americanized her name to France. She attended high school in La Puente, California, and was the first person from her high school to be accepted to Stanford University, where she earned an English degree cum laude in 1969. As a sophomore in college, she participated in an anthropological field trip to a Zapotec Indian pueblo in Oaxaca, Mexico. From her experience on this trip, she wrote a novel, *The Women of Santo Domingo* (1969), and a cookbook of Zapotec recipes. The novel won a prize, the opportunity to be a guest editor of *Mademoiselle* magazine. In 1971, Córdova took a job with *The Los Angeles Times* News Service.

Córdova's life changed when a television show on neutron stars led her to seek a job at the Center for Space Research at the Massachusetts Institute of Technology (MIT). From there she was accepted to graduate school and, in 1979, received her doctorate in physics from California Institute of Technology (Caltech). She continued to work for *The Los Angeles Times* News Service during graduate school.

Los Alamos National Laboratory was the site for her first permanent space job as a member of the Space Astronomy and Astrophysics group. Her idea to have hundreds of people—professionals and amateurs—all look at the same events through telescopes changed the way certain phenomena in space are studied. She also did the first measurement of the X-ray radiation from white dwarfs and pulsars. Córdova served as project leader for a group studying unusual astrophysical phenomena, including pulsars, cataclysmic variable stars, dust shells of novae, and X-ray binaries. In 1983, she met Christian Foster, a high school science teacher. They married and had two children: a daughter, Anne-Catherine, and a son, Stephen.

Life's Work

In 1989, Córdova was promoted to deputy group leader for the Space Astronomy and Astrophysics group and accepted the leadership position on the optical monitor digital processing unit on the European Space Agency's X-Ray Multi-Mirror Mission. The satellite studies X-ray spectra from a range of space objects, from black holes to the very hot stars produced when the universe was young. As the United States' principal investigator, she embarked on a long-term commitment to organizing and directing the scientists at University of California at Santa Barbara (UCSB) and at Los Alamos and Sandia National Laboratoriess to build and monitor the satellite. The launch date was 1999.

Córdova's Work at NASA

As chief scientist for the National Aeronautics and Space Administration (NASA), France Ann Córdova served as the scientific adviser to the NASA administrator and the liaison between NASA scientists and scientists at other national agencies and universities. The work involved the evaluation of NASA projects and budgets and working with other agencies, such as the National Science and Technology Council, federal government agencies, and national academies to develop science policy initiatives. Córdova faced one major test when NASA officials suggested combining the nine research centers into two centers. Córdova successfully fought this consolidation, which she thought would be disastrous to the viability of the science programs. Although some programs were lost to cost-cutting, most of the agency's critical programs were saved. One new institute was established at her suggestion, the Institute for Space Biomedical Sciences. She won praise for her unmatched effort, enthusiasm, and understanding of the inner workings of NASA.

Also in 1989, Córdova became professor and head of the Physics Department at Pennsylvania State University. During her tenure at Penn State, she bridged the gap between her writing skills and astrophysics by writing a biography of an outstanding Penn State astrophysicist, Satoshi Matsushima. In 1993, she was appointed chief scientist for the National Aeronautics and Space Administration (NASA), working at Langley Research Center near Washington, D.C.

When she left NASA, Córdova was asked to interview at several universities. Her choice was UCSB, and she became professor of physics and vice chancellor for research. This post allowed her to be closer to her parents and siblings. The research programs, especially interdisciplinary and space programs, at UCSB were molded and promoted during Córdova's term.

The University of California at Riverside (UCR) next named Córdova a distinguished professor of physics and astronomy and chancellor in 2002. At UCR, she worked toward enhancing the university's reputation, research, graduate programs, ranking, and diversity. Other initiatives were aimed at technology transfer and industry startups. In 2007, she was selected as president of Purdue University. The students at UCR picketed, while faculty members sent multiple e-mails to protest her leaving.

By 2010, Córdova already had made an impact at Purdue on student retention and the representation of women and minorities in the undergraduate, graduate, and faculty populations. She helped obtain a National Science Foundation grant to aid in increasing the number of female faculty members in science and math fields at the university. The engineering program also opened a learning lab to decrease class size; the lab's opening led to a decline in class failure rate.

SIGNIFICANCE

As an astrophysicist, Córdova has written several books and more than 150 scientific papers. In 1982, *Science Digest* magazine listed her as one of America's One Hundred Brightest Scientists Under Forty, and in 2008, she was selected as a fellow of the American Academy of Arts and Sciences. NASA honored her work on the Mars Pathfinder Space Program by placing in the spaceship a CD containing a dedication to Córdova.

As Córdova has progressed through the ranks of university administration, she has made a positive effect on each of the four universities she has served, especially in the areas of research and diversity. At each institution, she has been the first Latina and first woman in that position. In 1997, she was awarded an honorary doctorate from Loyola Marymount University in Los Angeles; in 2000, she was named Kilby Prize laureate for contributions to society through science, technology, innovation, invention, and education; and in 2007, she was selected as a California Institute of Technology Distinguished Alumna. Córdova is a true role model for women and minorities.

C. Alton Hassell

FURTHER READING

Córdova, France A. "Breaking Trail: One Path to a University Chancellorship." In *Faculty Career Paths: Multiple Routes to Academic Success and Satisfaction*, edited by Gretchen M.Bataille and Betsy E Brown. Westport, Conn.: Praeger, 2006. Short article in which Córdova describes her career path.

Lum, Lydia. "Upward Mobility." *Diverse Issues in Higher Education* 27, no. 13 (August, 2010): 18-19. Describes Córdova's efforts to improve education for minorities and women.

Medina, Hildy. "It's Not Rocket Science." *Hispanic Business* 29, no. 9 (September, 2007): 30-32. This article describes not only Córdova's career but also her desire for greater diversity at Purdue University.

See also: Franklin Ramón Chang-Díaz; Sidney M. Gutierrez; Ramon E. Lopez; Carlos Noriega; Ellen Ochoa.

Lucha Corpi

Mexican-born writer and educator

Although she began her career as a poet, Corpi soon turned to fiction, penning a remarkable series of lyrical detective novels. Rooted in the personal struggles of young Chicanas, her writings demonstrate a commitment to depicting the challenges that immigrants face and to educating her readers about the history of the Chicano movement.

Latino heritage: Mexican
Born: April 13, 1945; Jáltipan, Veracruz, Mexico
Also known as: Luz del Carmen Corpi Constantino; Luz Corpi
Areas of achievement: Education; literature; poetry; activism

Early Life

Lucha Corpi (LEW-cha KOHR-pee) was born in Jáltipan, Veracruz, Mexico, to Miguel Ángel Corpi and Victoria Constantino de Corpi. Her parents encouraged her to read and do well in school, even though at the time it was uncommon for girls to get such encouragement. When she was seven, she would read the paper to her father, whose vision was limited after a cornea transplant. He would not allow her to read the crime section, but this only sparked her curiosity, which eventually flowered into writing her own crime fiction.

Corpi married at the age of nineteen and moved with her husband to the United States so that he could study at the University of California at Berkeley. Her son, Arturo, was born in 1967 in Berkeley. In 1970, Corpi and her husband divorced, and she considered returning to Mexico but decided to remain in the United States to avoid the stigma on divorced women in the predominantly Catholic nation.

Corpi became a student at UC Berkeley, where she was active in the Chicano movement, taking part in the Third World Strike of the late 1960's. She became a student representative on the executive committee of the newly formed Chicano studies program and was a founding member and president of Aztlán Cultural/Centro Chicano de Escritores. In 1975, Corpi earned a B.A. in comparative literature from UC Berkeley, and in 1979, she earned a M.A. in world and comparative literature from San Francisco State University. After receiving her B.A., she became a teacher in the Oakland Unified School District, where she worked for thirty years, retiring in 2005.

Life's Work

Corpi began writing poetry at the age of twenty-four to express the pain of her divorce and the challenges of being a single mother in a new country. She honed her writing skills through her ongoing studies in literature. Eventually, she began to publish her poems, and in 1980, she published her first solo collection of poetry, *Palabras de mediodía/Noon Words*. This collection includes the much-anthologized "Marina poems," a reformulation of the story of Doña Marina, commonly known as "La Malinche," who was the translator and companion of Hernán Cortés. A second collection of poetry, *Variaciones sobre una tempestad/Variations on a Storm*, appeared in 1990. Many of her poems have been translated into Italian, French, and German.

While Corpi's poetry was written in Spanish and then translated into English for publication, her novels were originally written in English. Corpi's first novel, *Delia's Song*, was published in 1989 and tells the coming-of-age story of Delia, a young Chicana who studies at Berkeley and participates in the Third World Strike. The story follows the protagonist as she becomes involved in the Chicano movement, matures as a poet and novelist, and is confronted with a difficult choice between two men. The novel's experimental style consists of interspersing the third-person narrative with dreams, surreal images, and stream of consciousness.

After her experience of writing *Delia's Song*, Corpi worked to realize her dream of writing detective fiction. Her signature detective, Gloria Damasco, is a speechtherapist turned private eye with an extrasensory awareness she calls her "dark gift." As in *Delia's Song*, dreams and visions form distinct parts of the novels, but in the detective novels they help solve a crime.

The series began with *Eulogy for a Brown Angel* (1992), in which a young child is murdered during the National Chicano Moratorium protest of 1970. *Cactus Blood* (1995), the second novel, is rooted in another major moment in Chicano history, the United Farm Workers' grape boycott. The third novel, *Black Widow's Wardrobe* (1999), tells a modern version of the Doña Marina story through a character who believes she is the reincarnation of Doña Marina. In the fourth detective novel, *Crimson Moon* (2004), two of Gloria's colleagues take center stage as the detectives. This work also includes a cameo by Chicano detective Luis Montez, a character created by writer Manuel Ramos. In

Corpi's "Marina Poems"

The "Marina Poems" were some of Lucha Corpi's first works as an adult writer. First published in English in *The Other Voice: Twentieth Century women's poetry in Translation* (1976), they also appeared in bilingual form in *Palabras de mediodía/Noon Words* (1980). This cycle of four poems tell the story of Doña Marina, translator and companion of the Spanish conquistador Hernán Cortés. Marina is commonly known as "La Malinche," a corruption of her indigenous birth name, Malintzin. Because of her cooperation with Cortés, her name has become synonymous with betraying one's own culture. In Corpi's poems, the story of Marina as a traitor is rewritten to cast her as an unwilling participant who was forced to assist Cortés. Countering the perception of Marina as the instrument of the Aztec empire's downfall, she is described by Corpi as a strong and spiritual woman with a promising future.

Death at Solstice (2009), Gloria returns to the series, this time investigating a crime in the California Gold Country.

In addition to her poetry and detective novels, Corpi has been involved in a variety of creative projects. She has written two bilingual picture books for children: *Where Fireflies Dance* (1997) and *The Triple Banana Split Boy* (2009), and was the editor of *Máscaras* (1997), an anthology of personal essays written by Latinas. She has received numerous awards, among them a National Endowment for the Arts Creative Writing Fellowship (1979) and the PEN Oakland Josephine Miles Literary Prize in fiction (1993). She also was named poet laureate of Indiana University Northwest in 1990.

Significance

Corpi has developed a rich corpus of poetry written in Spanish that expresses the struggles of immigrants, women, and Chicanos. Her novels, which demonstrate a unique and poetic sensibility, are filled with strong and self-aware yet vulnerable Chicana characters. Her vision is at once political, personal, and artistic and has brought fresh life to both the detective fiction genre and Chicano writing. An educator inside and outside the classroom, she continuously educates her readers through her knowledge of the history of Chicanos in California.

Matthew David Goodwin

Further Reading

Baker Sotelo, Susan. *Chicano Detective Fiction: A Critical Study of Five Novelists*. Jefferson, N.C.: McFarland, 2005. A study of five Chicano detective writers that highlights Corpi's relationship to the detective-fiction canon, arguing that the representations of sociopolitical changes in the Chicana community make her novels unique.

Corpi, Lucha. *Eulogy for a Brown Angel*. Houston, Tex.: Arte Público Press, 1992. Corpi's first detective novel, in which her recurring character Gloria Damasco is introduced.

_______. *Palabras de mediodía/Noon Words*. Translated by Catherine Rodriguez-Nieto. 1980. Reprint. Houston, Tex.: Arte Público Press, 2001. Corpi's first solo collection of poetry, containing poems about daily life in Mexico and the joys and sorrows of family. Also includes the "Marina Poems."

Ikas, Karin Rosa. *Chicana Ways: Conversations with Ten Chicana Writers*. Reno, Nev. University of Nevada Press, 2002. Collection of ten interviews with Chicana writers on their work and involvement in the Chicana community (an interview with Corpi is included). Each interview is preceded by a concise introduction and followed by a substantial bibliography.

Libretti, Tim. "Lucha Corpi and the Politics of Detective Fiction." In *Multicultural Detective Fiction: Murder from the "Other" Side*, edited by Adrienne Johnson Gosselin. New York: Garland, 1999. Scholarly analysis of *Eulogy for a Brown Angel* and *Cactus Blood* with an emphasis on social and economic issues in the novels.

Rodriguez, Ralph E. *Brown Gumshoes: Detective Fiction and the Search for Chicana/o Identity*. Austin: University of Texas Press, 2005. This study of five Chicano writers argues that Corpi's work shows an awareness of the fluidity of Chicana identity. The conclusion contains an insightful comparative study of the five writers.

Sanchez, Marta Ester. *Contemporary Chicana Poetry: A Critical Approach to an Emerging Literature*. Berkeley: University of California Press, 1985. A study of four Chicana poets that contains a comprehensive analysis of the "Marina poems."

See also: Julia Alvarez; Ana Castillo; Mary Helen Ponce; Carmen Tafolla; Alma Villanueva; Helena María Viramontes; Bernice Zamora.

GREGORIO CORTEZ

Mexican-born outlaw and folk hero

After killing a Texas sheriff in self-defense, Cortez became both a fugitive from justice and a symbol of resistance against the Anglo occupiers of land that had once belonged to Mexico. As a result, Cortez is a Latino folk hero whose exploits have been celebrated in legends, ballads, and film.

Latino heritage: Mexican
Born: June 22, 1875; near Matamoros, Tamaulipas, Mexico
Died: February 28, 1916; Anson, Texas
Also known as: Gregorio Cortez Lira
Area of achievement: Crime

EARLY LIFE

Gregorio Cortez Lira (greh-GOH-ree-oh cohr-TEHZ LEE-rah) was born on a ranch in the state of Tamaulipas, Mexico, just south of the Rio Grande. He was the seventh of eight children born to Román Cortez Garza and Rosalía Lira Cortinas. When Cortez was twelve years old, he moved with his family to Manor, Texas, east of Austin. Two years later, in 1889, Cortez and his older brother Romaldo began working seasonal jobs on farms and ranches in Karnes and Gonzales counties, east of San Antonio. During this time, Cortez married Leonor Díaz, with whom he raised four children, the eldest born in 1891. Romaldo also married, and the brothers and their families settled in 1900 on rented farm land roughly ten miles west of Kenedy, in Karnes County.

In the late nineteenth and early twentieth centuries, Texas cattle barons and businessmen ruled the borderlands in which Cortez lived and worked. County sheriffs and deputies, as well as the vaunted Texas Rangers, enforced the law, frequently discriminating against Mexican Americans who worked on farms and ranches. Conversely, Mexican Americans often were suspicious of the Anglos who controlled the lands that had not long ago belonged to Mexico. Tensions between the two groups were ever-present, especially when members of one group did not speak the other's language.

LIFE'S WORK

On June 12, 1901, W. T. Morris, the Karnes County sheriff and a former Texas Ranger, came to the farm of Gregorio and Romaldo Cortez in search of a horse thief. Accompanying Morris was one of his deputies, Boone Choate, who spoke some Spanish but apparently did not understand the important difference between *caballo* (horse) and *yegua* (mare). Cortez had recently traded a *yegua*, and thus answered truthfully in Spanish when he denied trading a *caballo*. Hearing only the word *no*, Morris believed Cortez was lying and started to arrest him. In the ensuing struggle, Morris shot Romaldo in the mouth, wounding him critically; Cortez shot and killed Morris in self-defense; and Choate escaped unharmed.

For the next ten days, Cortez crisscrossed roughly five hundred miles of southern Texas, on foot and by horse, skillfully avoiding capture, even though he was pursued by an estimated three hundred lawmen. When a posse of eight men attacked the house where he was hiding on June 14, Cortez shot and killed Gonzales County sheriff Robert M. Glover. Cortez finally was captured on June 22 in a sheep camp just north of the Rio Grande by one Texas Ranger and one former Texas Ranger, who had been informed of Cortez's whereabouts by a Mexican American hoping to receive the reward money.

From July, 1901, to April, 1904, Cortez was tried in court six times. The results were one acquittal, one hung jury, three convictions that were overturned by the Texas Court of Criminal Appeals, and one conviction for the murder of Glover, which the appeals court upheld. Cortez was sentenced to life imprisonment but received a pardon from the state governor on July 7, 1913, after serving just over eight years in the state penitentiary at Huntsville. Cortez then moved to Nuevo Laredo, Mexico, where he fought briefly on the losing side of the Mexican Revolution. Wounded in battle, he returned to Texas to convalesce at the home of one of his three sons. He died three years after his release from prison, probably of natural causes, although some family members contended that he was poisoned by enemies who did not want to see him free.

SIGNIFICANCE

Cortez sought neither fame nor infamy but found both because of misunderstandings and circumstances beyond his control. While many Anglos in southern Texas vilified Cortez as a fiendish desperado, the Mexican population on both sides of the border celebrated him as a folk hero who fought the Anglos skillfully and daringly. Almost immediately after Cortez was captured, various *corridos* (ballads) were composed and sung in his honor. That same tradition continued with the release of the television film *The Ballad of Gregorio Cortez* (1982), featuring Edward James Olmos in the title role.

James I. Deutsch

FURTHER READING

Alonzo, Juan J. *Badmen, Bandits, and Folk Heroes: The Ambivalence of Mexican American Identity in Literature and Film*. Tucson: University of Arizona Press, 2009. Examines several literary and cinematic expressions of Cortez's life, noting how each reflects a different ideological point of view.

Noriega, Chon A. "*No fue mi culpa*, or, You Should be Dead." *Aztlán* 34, no. 2 (Fall, 2009): 1-7. Examines the influence and timeless appeal of the many versions of Cortez's life,including the film, the *corrido*, and even the academic study by Paredes.

Paredes, Américo. *"With His Pistol in His Hand": A Border Ballad and Its Hero*. Austin: University of Texas Press, 1958. This seminal study still is the most authoritative source on Cortez's life and the *corrido* sung about him.

Peña, Manuel H. "Folksong and Social Change: Two Corridos as Interpretive Sources." *Aztlán* 13, nos. 1-2 (Spring-Fall, 1982): 13-42. Places the *corrido* of Gregorio Cortez in the context of other ballads and folk songs that express the reactions of oppressed people to historical events.

Sommer, Doris. *Proceed with Caution, When Engaged by Minority Writing in the Americas*. Cambridge, Mass.: Harvard University Press, 1999. Uses the case of Cortez to explore issues of mistranslation and problems of intercultural communication.

See also: Juan Cortina; Joaquín Murieta; Tiburcio Vásquez.

JUAN CORTINA

Mexican-born criminal and activist

Cortina was a Mexican Texan rancher from a wealthy family. He fought for the rights of poorer Mexicans living in Texas. Cortina also fought for the Mexican army and served as governor of Tamaulipas. He eventually was imprisoned in Mexico without a trial for almost fifteen years.

Latino heritage: Mexican

Born: May 16, 1824; Camargo, Tamaulipas, Mexico

Died: October 30, 1894; Atzcapozalco, Mexico

Also known as: Juan Nepomuceno Cortina; Cheno Cortinas; Red Robber of the Rio Grande

Areas of achievement: Crime; military; activism

EARLY LIFE

Juan Nepomuceno Cortina (NEH-poh-mew-SAY-noh cohr-TEE-nah) was born May 16, 1824, in Camargo, Tamaulipas, Mexico. His parents, Estefana Goseacochea and Trinidad Cortina, both had been married before and each had two sons. In addition to Cortina, Estefana and Trinidad had two more children together, Jose Maria and Maria del Carmen. Cortina, nicknamed Cheno, was slender, with reddish-blond hair and gray eyes.

Cortina's family had been living in the Rio Grande Valley for generations. His great-grandfather was among the first settlers to arrive in the area. Estefana was from a wealthy, aristocratic family. She inherited a large ranch near Brownsville, Texas. The family moved to Matamoros when Cortina was a child. They later moved to his mother's ranch in Santa Rita, Texas.

The Cortina family had several land disputes with Anglo Americans. Cortina also saw and experienced harassment and grew to hate Anglos for their mistreatment of poorer Mexican Texans. At the beginning of the Mexican-American War, Cortina was twenty-two years old. He joined the Mexican army and served under General Mariano Arista. Cortina recruited a group of irregular cavalry of local cowboys and ranch hands. The regiment, known as the Tamaulipas, was placed under Cortina's command. They fought in the battles of Resaca de la Palma and Palo Alto. The war ended February 2, 1848, with the signing of the Treaty of Guadalupe Hildago.

LIFE'S WORK

Cortina's antipathy toward Anglo authority figures soon included local judges and lawyers, whom he saw as corrupt. He felt they were extorting land from the Mexicans who did not understand the American legal system. He gathered and trained a group of followers that functioned as a private army. An incident on July 13, 1859, started the first "Cortina War." Cortina saw a Brownsville marshal brutally arresting Tomas Cabrera, a ranch hand he knew. Cortina intervened and shot the marshal in the shoulder. On September 28, Cortina and his gang rode into Brownsville and seized control of the town, killing five people. On September 30, Cortina issued a proclamation asserting the rights of

Juan Cortina. (Bloomberg via Getty Images)

Mexicans and demanded punishment for anyone violating their rights.

Men from Brownsville formed a posse, the Tigers, and attacked Cortina's ranch with the help of a Mexican militia group. Cortina and his men easily defeated them and demanded Cabrera's release. In early November, the first company of Texas Rangers arrived. Cabrera was hanged the next day, and another attack on Cortina failed. Cortina issued his second proclamation on November 23, asking Governor Sam Houston to defend the Mexicans' rights. A few weeks later, more Rangers and 165 soldiers arrived in Brownsville. Cortina and his four hundred men retreated upriver. They were defeated in battle at Rio Grande City.

After a failed attempt to capture a steamboat, Cortina retreated into the Burgos Mountains. Cortina started his second war in May, 1861, soon after the beginning of the American Civil War. Cortina invaded and attacked the city of Carrizo. He was defeated by Confederate captain Santos Benavides and returned to Mexico. In May, 1862, the French invaded Mexico. Cortina fought against the French at first, then joined them. Later, he gathered an army, defeated the French, and declared himself governor of Tamaulipas in 1864 and 1865.

Cortina returned to Texas in 1870, and while he was accused of running a cattle rustling ring, he was never arrested. He eventually was arrested in 1875 and imprisoned in Mexico City. He was released only to be recaptured the following year. Cortina was held until 1890 without ever standing trial. He died of pneumonia and heart failure October 30, 1894, in Atzcapozalco, Mexico.

Significance

Cortina fought to protect the rights of Mexican-born Texans, whom he felt were being treated unfairly by those in power. He started two small wars to draw attention to these inequalities and show that he was not afraid to commit violence. He issued two proclamations demanding rights for Mexicans. Cortina is widely considered a folk hero for having the courage to protect the Mexicans. The Cortina Wars also drew the attention of the nation and added to the uneasiness of Southerners who felt the Union could not protect those living on the frontier.

Jennifer L. Campbell

Further Reading

Larralde, Carlos, and Jose Rodolfo Jacobo. *Juan N. Cortina and the Struggle for Justice in Texas.* Dubuque, Iowa: Kendall Hunt, 2000. A work focusing on the history of the lower Rio Grande Valley and the struggle of Mexicans along the border for civil rights. The authors portray Cortina as a revolutionary who fought racism.

Thompson, Jerry. *Cortina: Defending the Mexican Name in Texas.* College Station: Texas A&M University Press, 2007. A well-researched biography of Cortina that offers a balanced account of his life. Well-written, suitable for scholars, students, and anyone interested in Texas-Mexican history.

_______. *Juan Cortina and the Texas-Mexico Frontier 1859-1877.* El Paso: Texas Western Press, 1994. Focuses on Cortina and the border area during the mid-1800's, and would be of interest to anyone interested in Texas-Mexican border history. Includes copies of several documents that help shed light on the various and conflicting accounts of Cortina's character.

Thompson, Jerry, and Lawrence T. Jones. *Civil War and Revolution on the Rio Grande Frontier.* Austin: Texas State Historical Association, 2004. A pictorial history of the revolution on the Mexico-Texas border and the American Civil War.

See also: Gregorio Cortez; Joaquín Murieta; Tiburcio Vásquez.

JUAN ESTANISLAO COTERA

American architect and activist

Combined with an outstanding reputation as an architect, Cotera is recognized for his tireless efforts on behalf of those who are less privileged and often excluded. His adopted hometown of Austin, Texas, is a showcase both for his architectural imprint on significant landmarks and for his service at all social and economic levels of the city.

Latino heritage: Mexican

Born: November 13, 1936; El Paso, Texas

Areas of achievement: Architecture; social issues

EARLY LIFE

Juan Estanislao Cotera (WAHN eh-stahn-ees-LAH-oh koh-TEH-rah) was born in El Paso, Texas, the son of Jose Cotera and Maria del Carmen Hospital. He attended El Paso Catholic schools through high school graduation. His ambition to study architecture brought him, in 1961, to Texas Western College (now the University of Texas, El Paso), where he completed three years of study in engineering. In 1963, he and his wife, Martha P. Cotera, who became a prominent Chicana writer, educator, activist and businesswoman in her own right, moved to Austin, Texas, where Juan studied at the University of Texas. Five years later, he received his undergraduate degree in architecture from this university, and he later completed the course work in the university's graduate program in community and regional planning. .

When Cotera first arrived in Austin, he found a city intolerant of diversity, urbanism, and aesthetics, a place deeply divided along white, African American, and Hispanic racial lines, as was most of Texas in the 1960's. Even as a student and young professional, Cotera joined other like-minded students, political activists, architects, and urban planners to volunteer, participate, and lead numerous initiatives dedicated to making the Austin community a more equitable and productive environment for all its citizens. Among his activities, Cotera helped to pass a Fair Housing Ordinance in 1966, and from 1963 to 1967 he served on the Urban Renewal Advocacy Committee, where he worked to halt the displacement of residents through the urban renewal process in historic neighborhoods. He also was a founding member of Texans for the Educational Advancement of Mexican Americans, and his many contributions to this group led to the eventual integration of Austin's public schools. Outside Austin, Cotera in 1971 became a pro bono assistant professor at the University Without Walls at Antioch College in Mercedes, Texas, and in 1972 he became the director of the Urban Renewal Agency in Crystal City, Texas, a newly politically empowered Mexican American community of eight thousand. In his job at the Urban Renewal Agency, Cotera emphasized the need to renew neighborhoods without displacing residents, and he secured Housing and Urban Development (HUD) funds to build more than one hundred new homes in the lowest-income neighborhoods.

LIFE'S WORK

In 1973, Cotera returned to Austin to began his professional career, and two years later he founded the architectural partnership Cotera, Kolar, Negrete & Reed, a firm that endured until 2003, when Cotera formed a new partnership, Cotera+Reed Architects, Inc. Some of the more significant architectural projects that Cotera has undertaken in Austin were a new city hall, on which he collaborated with architect Antoine Predock; St. Edward's University New Residence and Dining Hall, a joint project with Chilean architect Alejandro Aravena; and the Austin-Bergstrom International Airport and Barbara Jordan Passenger Terminal, and the Austin Convention Center and Visitors Bureau, on which he collaborated with architect Lawrence W. Speck. Equally impressive are Cotera's pro bono architectural projects in Austin, such as the Interstate-35 corridor makeover, Cepeda Music Garden, the Center for Mexican American Cultural Arts, and the headquarters of Southwest Key Programs.

Cotera has served on Austin's design commission since 1992, chairing the panel from 1995 to 2002. Two of the many initiatives he led stand out: the drafting of downtown design guidelines, adopted by the Austin City Council in May, 2000, and the drafting of new, expanded urban design guidelines, adopted in 2008, which aim to direct and control the growth and development of inner-city space, as well as the entire urban center.

Cotera has received numerous awards and honors, including the 2007 Award of Appreciation from the Greater Austin Hispanic Chamber of Commerce (Cotera was a cofounder of the organization in 1973 and chaired its board from 1980 until 1982) and the 2008 Fabulous Ten Award from the Austin Lyric Opera. In 2009, his many contributions to Austin were recognized with the John V. Nyfeler FAIA (Fellow of the

American Institute of Architects) Community Service Award. In 2010, after many years of being encouraged by his colleagues to submit his nomination, Cotera complied and was made a fellow of the American Institute of Architects.

Significance

A cornerstone of Cotera's outstanding reputation as an architect has been his commitment to developing a socially responsible, equitable milieu in Austin on a par with the physical design of architecturally significant buildings and spaces. The transformation of downtown Austin into an active, multipurpose, aesthetically pleasing environment, open and welcoming to all the city's people, is a testament to his efforts.

Pilar Cotera Herrera

Further Reading

Cotera+Reed Architects. http://www.coterareed.com. The Web site for Cotera's firm is one of the few accessible sources of information about the architect and his work.

Texas Society of Architects. The Official Blog of the Texas Society of Architects and *Texas Architect* Magazine. http://texasarchitect.blogspot.com/2010/08/2010-tsa-award-for-community-service.html. Reports that Cotera will receive the society's 2010 Community Service Award, providing some background information about Cotera's work. The site contains other references to Cotera.

See also: Eduardo Catalano; Martha P. Cotera; Cesar Pelli.

Martha P. Cotera

Mexican-born activist, educator, and historian

Cotera is an academic who authored groundbreaking studies that defined the pivotal role of women in Chicano political and cultural history in both Mexico and America, She also distinguished herself within Texas's Latino community by her passionate defense of civil rights and her advocacy of expanded educational opportunities for women and minorities.

Latino heritage: Mexican

Born: January 17, 1938; Nuevo Casas Grandes, Chihuahua, Mexico

Also known as: Martha Piña Cotera; Martha Piña

Areas of achievement: Activism; education; scholarship; women's rights

Early Life

Martha Piña Cotera (MAHR-thah PEE-nah koh-TEH-rah) was born Martha Piña in 1938 in Chihuahua, a Mexican state that borders Texas. One of four children, Cotera learned from her grandparents to take pride in her Mexican heritage, especially its politics. Her mother, a strong woman who raised the family, encouraged Cotera in school, where the girl excelled. Indeed, when her family immigrated to El Paso in 1946, Cotera was initially placed in the first grade but quickly tested up to the third grade. Cotera respected the opportunity to obtain an education, and in 1962 she received a B.A. in English, with a minor in history, from Texas Western College (now the University of Texas at El Paso). A year later, she married Juan Estanislao Cotera, who would become an architect, and in 1964 she accepted a position at the Texas State Library in Austin as both librarian and director of its archive of documents central to Texas history.

From the earliest days of her career, Cotera was committed to bettering educational opportunities for young Hispanics. To this end, in 1964 she helped form a collective of Hispanic teachers and school administrators known as Texans for the Educational Advancement of Mexican Americans. Four years later, she was instrumental in tutoring more than two hundred Hispanic students who boycotted classes in Crystal City, Texas, over discriminatory practices. In 1971, she and her husband moved to Mercedes, Texas, where she helped establish Jacinto Trevino College (later Juarez-Lincoln University), a pilot campus designed solely to prepare Hispanic students as teachers in bilingual curricula. Cotera herself completed her master's degree in education there.

Life's Work

Cotera and her husband became increasingly involved in Chicano activism, joining La Raza Unida, a political party founded in 1970 that aimed to offer Texas's large Hispanic population a viable third-party option. It was during this time that Cotera, while serving as director of the Crystal City Memorial Library, noticed what she would later term the entrenched misogyny of the Chicano civil rights movement, and she was moved to organize Muejeres de La Raza Unida (Women of the United Race). Through her activism, Cotera began to investigate the historic role of women in Chicano history.

After moving to Austin in 1974, Cotera worked to establish the first-ever resource bank geared to providing minority women with information about funding for community projects. The next year she accepted a post as a special collections coordinator for the Nettie Lee Benson Latin American Collection at the University of Texas at Austin, one of the nation's largest archives dedicated to a single ethnic group. Her position at the archives allowed her the opportunity to research the role of women in Hispanic culture in both Mexico and the United States. Cotera published dozens of groundbreaking articles and two landmark works: a historic survey of nearly three centuries, *Diosa y Hembra: The History and Heritage of Chicanas in the United States* (1976), and a sampling of her speeches and essays, *The Chicana Feminist* (1977). Her work, grounded in meticulous research into records sometimes centuries old, encouraged a generation of cultural studies programs which reassessed the position of women in a Chicano culture that had long been regarded as patriarchal.

In addition to her scholarly work and political activism, Cotera during two decades spearheaded pioneering causes within the Austin Latino community, organizing funding for arts programs, starting committees aimed at encouraging minority professional women, launching citywide education projects, helping fund programs for battered women and rape victims, and, most notably, establishing a first-of-its-kind database company, Information Systems Development, that focused on providing critical business information for entrepreneurs. In addition, she became a much-sought after speaker at state and national conferences promoting women's rights and minority opportunities. Although she declined to pursue political office herself, her public advocacy of fair housing, improved public transportation, and a wider embrace of cultural diversity in public education curricula, as well as her tireless efforts on behalf of candidates sympathetic to minority rights, made her a fixture in Austin city politics.

In 1997, her twenty-five-year-old son was brutally murdered after a carjacking; he and another man were locked in the trunk of a car by two armed teenagers and subsequently drowned when the teens rolled the car into Town Lake, a reservoir in downtown Austin. Both Cotera and her husband, however, publicly advocated imprisonment rather than capital punishment for the convicted teens.

After leaving her position as archivist and bibliographer for the Benson Collection in 2009, Cotera continued to work for women and minority representation in Austin city politics. In the wake of growing concerns over long-term environmental damage to Texas and its resource-based economy, Cotera, while in her sixties, worked to help minority students who were interested in environmental studies pursue green-based career opportunities. In 2010, she was recognized with a lifetime achievement award by the Veteran Feminists of America.

SIGNIFICANCE

Although her scholarly work in Chicana studies was trailblazing, Martha P. Cotera, in a long and distinguished career of activism and public advocacy of social justice issues, embodied the spirit of politics made local. Within the Austin community, she used her position in numerous advocacy groups and social agencies to encourage cultural development in order to better represent the Chicano arts, increase educational opportunities for minority children (particularly at-risk adolescents), and, perhaps most important, expand business opportunities for women and minority entrepreneurs.

Joseph Dewey

FURTHER READING

Garcia, Alma M. *Chicana Feminist Thought: The Basic Historic Writings*. New York: Routledge, 1997. Brings together the key writings of feminists critical to the Chicano rights movement in the 1960's and 1970's, including Cotera.

Garcia, Juan, ed. *Mexican American Women, Changing Image*. Vol. 5 in *Perspectives in Mexican American Studies*. Tucson: University of Arizona Press, 1996. Wide-ranging collection of scholarly essays that address the role of women in Mexican American culture. Includes an essay by Cotera.

Torres, Eden A. *Chicana Without Apology: The New Chicana Cultural Studies*. New York: Routledge, 2003. A sweeping vision of the role of women in Chicano culture, representing the generation grounded in Cotera's scholarly work.

See also: Pura Belpré; José A. Cárdenas; Juan Estanislao Cotera; María Herrera-Sobek.

Linda Cristal

Argentine-born actor

Cristal succeeded in Hollywood at a time when blond women were preferred and actors were expected to speak perfect American English. Her exotic beauty made her a sensation, though initially her roles were limited to Westerns or other projects that required a Latina actor. Along with films, she was a regular on television, and she is best remembered for her role in The High Chaparral.

Latino heritage: Argentinean

Born: February 23, 1934; Buenos Aires, Argentina

Also known as: Marta Victoria Moya Burges

Area of achievement: Acting; radio and television

Early Life

Linda Cristal (CRIHS-tuhl) was born in Buenos Aries, Argentina, in 1934, one of three children and the only girl. Her father had been a publisher, but he fell out of favor with the ruling political party. The family fled first to Europe and then returned to South America and settled in Uruguay, where they lived in extreme poverty. Her younger brother became ill and died because there was no money for medicine. Her parents both died when Cristal was thirteen, and the deaths were believed to be a suicide pact. Her diabetic mother had no insulin, and her father was deeply ashamed of his inability to provide for his family in exile. Losing all but one member of her birth family could have devastated her forever. Instead, it motivated Cristal to make something of herself. With no one on whom to rely, she was forced to take charge of her life.

Although she had only a third-grade education, Cristal was determined to improve her life. She was a fast learner and studied constantly. Her exotic beauty caught the eye of Mexican film producer Miguelito Alemán, the son of Mexican president Miguel Alemán Valdés. In four years she made four films for Alemán, and she was already a recognized star in that country when actor John Wayne tapped her for a role in *The Alamo* (1960), despite the fact she spoke no English. She worked hard and learned to speak her lines phonetically in just two months.

Life's Work

After her critically well-received *Alamo* debut, Cristal became one of the go-to actors when ethnic roles emerged, joining the ranks of Anna Magnani and Dolores del Río. Those opportunities came often, as this was the golden age of the Western film genre and the Tex-Mex look was in demand. She appeared opposite James Stewart in *Two Rode Together* (1961), among others of the same ilk, and she branched out into light comedy in such films as *The Perfect Furlough* (1959) with Tony Curtis and Janet Leigh. In 1974 she starred with Charles Bronson in *Mr. Majestyk.*

Television beckoned as well, and she enjoyed a long run of roles that included appearances on some of the most popular shows ever made: *Bonanza*, *Fantasy Island*, *Barnaby Jones*, *Police Story*, and *Love Boat*, to name a few. Despite her professional success, a string of broken engagements and failed marriages show that Cristal struggled with her personal life. She had two sons, Gregory and Jordan, with Yale Wexler, whom she married in 1960. This marriage ended in divorce after six years, and Cristal went into semiretirement to raise her sons. Her romantic relationships may have been doomed, but her boys meant everything to her. Cristal was a hands-on mother who made sure her sons had the happy childhood that she had missed.

Linda Cristal. (AP Photo)

She eventually resumed her career, both in film and on television. Cristal will be best remembered for her role of Victoria Montoya Cannon on the hit television series *The High Chaparral.* The show's producers were so impressed with her abilities that they killed off the male lead's wife in the first episode to enable him to marry Cristal's character. Cristal achieved international acclaim with stardom in Mexico and Italy, as well as Hollywood. The uneducated girl from Argentina learned to speak three languages—English, French, and Italian—in addition to her native Spanish. Unlike many stars, she also learned about business. She made sound real estate and other investments and saw her earnings multiply many times over the years. Before retiring for good, she went full circle and starred in a daytime television series in her native Argentina. She returned to California, where she settled in Beverly Hills and doted on her two sons and grandchildren.

Significance

Linda Cristal is significant not only for a show business talent that made her a star in four countries but also for the way she conducted her life. By sheer determination and her own effort, she was able to pull herself out of unimaginable poverty and live the kind of celebrated life of which most people can only dream. Though lacking formal education, she was smart enough to develop her natural talent to its fullest and to not rely solely on her stunning beauty.

Her work has received awards and honors in four countries. Cristal learned to speak fluent English but retained her Argentine accent. She never tried to hide her South American heritage; instead she has used it to her advantage, both in the United States and in the other countries where she worked. Cristal's star shines bright in the international arena.

Norma Lewis

Further Reading

Beltran, Mary C. *Latina/o Stars in the U. S. Eyes: The Making and Meanings of Film and TV Stardom.* Urbana: University of Illinois Press, 2009. The history of Latino contributions to the entertainment industry.

Berg, Charles Ramirez. *Latino Images in Film: Stereotypes, Subversion, and Resistance.* Austin: University of Texas Press, 2002. Discusses the difficulties that Latinos must overcome on the way to success in the entertainment industry.

Rodriguez, Clara. *Heroes, Lovers, and Others: The Story of Latinos in Hollywood.* New York: Oxford University Press, 2008. Traces how how Latino performers have contributed to films from the silent era through the first decade of the twenty-first century.

See also: Miriam Colón; Dolores del Río; Hector Elizondo; Katy Jurado; Elena Verdugo.

Celia Cruz

Cuban-born salsa singer

Cruz was best known for her energetic salsa performances that engaged worldwide audiences and evoked pride in Latino heritage and culture. She was considered a master of the Afro-Cuban popular music art form.

Latino heritage: Cuban

Born: October 21, 1924; Havana, Cuba

Died: July 16, 2003; Fort Lee, New Jersey

Also known as: Úrsula Hilaria Celia Caridad Cruz Alfonso; Queen of Salsa

Areas of achievement: Music; philanthropy

Early Life

Celia Cruz (SEE-lee-uh krewz) was born Úrsula Hilaria Celia Caridad Cruz Alfonso in Santos Suarez, a racially and ethnically diverse working-class neighborhood of Havana, Cuba. One of four children born to Catalina Alfonso ("Ollita") and Simon Cruz, Cruz grew up in a loving and close-knit family. As a youth, Cruz was drawn to the local amateur events and pre-Lenten parades and festivals held throughout Havana during carnival season. As she matured, she frequented the local dances and musical establishments.

Although they recognized her talents, Cruz's parents expected her to lead a traditional Cuban life. In 1947, she enrolled in Havana's Escuela Normal de Maestras (Teachers' College). That same year, Cruz's cousin Serafin signed her up for an amateur talent show; she won first place. Cruz began performing at patriotic events, schools, radio stations, and in contests in and around Havana. The prize money financed her studies

Celia Cruz. (AP Photo/Nick Ut)

as well as other material goods for her family, whom she supported throughout her life.

While still at Teachers' College, Cruz systematically developed her unique performance style. Her aunt Tia Ana, her closest family confidante, encouraged her to sing with emotion and move with the music. Cruz also modeled her performances after her idol, popular Havana singer Paulina Alvarez, and found inspiration in Lucumi, the Santería Afro-Cuban liturgical language she overheard at her neighbor's backyard religious celebrations. Cruz's distinctive dance movements and vocal flourishes took root during these early years.

After graduation, a teacher advised Cruz to pursue a professional singing career. In 1949, she enrolled in the Havana Music Academy. She studied piano, voice, and music theory and also took private lessons. While at the academy, she began her professional career as a bolero, or freelance entertainer, with CMQ Radio Studios. Her father disapproved of her career, but her mother and other family members remained supportive.

Life's Work

In 1950, the widely successful Cuban band La Sonora Matancera hired Cruz as its lead singer. She soon garnered more lucrative work modeling hair-care products and singing commercial jingles for Cuban television. Her affiliation with La Sonora Matancera exposed her to a wider audience, cementing her success in Cuba and laying the foundation for her eventual international profile. The band's international hits included the classics "Guantanamera," "Caramelo," and "El yerbero moderno." In 1962, she married Pedro Knight, La Sonora Matancera's second trumpeter. He eventually left the band and became her manager and devoted partner until her death from brain cancer in 2003.

During Havana's heyday before the Cuban Revolution, Cruz and La Sonora Matancera performed at the world-famous Tropicana and in other popular cabaret shows. Their hit "Burundanga" gained popularity overseas, and the band frequently performed in Venezuela, Colombia, and other Spanish-speaking countries. In the 1950's, Mexico was an important market for Cuban music, and the band developed a loyal Mexican following that later was instrumental in Cruz's worldwide success.

Although she often performed for Cuba's political and social elite, she refused to support Fidel Castro when he assumed power in 1959. She became a Cuban exile while on an extended tour to Mexico in 1960. Castro refused all her requests to return to her homeland to see her mother, a bitter disappointment that fueled Cruz's life-long passion to keep popular Cuban music alive. Through the years, her outspoken opposition to Castro's regime earned her many admiring fans.

Cruz credited her famous stamina and energy to her years in exile in Mexico. La Sonora Matancera and Cruz performed with the popular Mexican touring caravans, and their hard work solidified their success throughout the Spanish-speaking world. In 1961, Cruz applied for U.S. citizenship, later settling in New York City, where there was a solid market for Cuban music. In the late 1960's and early 1970's, La Sonora Matancera's popularity in Mexico and other Spanish-speaking countries sustained the band during the salsa slump in America.

Cruz collaborated with some of the leading musicians of her time. In 1962, she became the first Hispanic woman to perform at Carnegie Hall when she sang with Count Basie and Tito Puente. From 1965 to 1973, Cruz and Puente recorded and toured together. She credited Puente with keeping popular Cuban music alive in the United States during the 1960's. Her 1973 album, *Celia y Johnny*, with Dominican flautist Johnny Pacheco, included their international salsa hit "Quimbara." Pacheco's Fania Records and the Fania All-Stars were at the

The Queen of Salsa

Salsa music is a mixture of cha-cha, cumbia, merengue, *bomba*, rumba, and *guaracha* rhythms from across the Latin American musical spectrum. As the most prominent female performing alongside the male giants of the salsa movement, Celia Cruz came to symbolize Latin America's feminine face to the world. Her powerful stage presence and expressive singing voice helped popularize salsa music at a time when Latino ethnic pride was on the rise. Salsa's enormous crossover appeal was confirmed when the *Sesame Street* muppets performed Cruz's popular hit "Quimbara" in 1994. She was internationally recognized as the Queen of Salsa and had a lasting appeal with generations of fans. Contemporary artists Wyclef Jean and Jeni Fujita have covered her classic "Guantanamera." The 2001 rap hit "La negra tiene tumbao" featured Cruz shouting "Azucar!" a reference to the cries of street vendors who sold sugar and other staples once cultivated by African slaves in Cruz's native Cuba. Cruz sang exclusively in Spanish, popularizing authentic Latin American music and culture. Although she was widely known as the Queen of Salsa, she preferred the title "La Guarachera de Cuba," humble singer of popular Cuban dance music.

vanguard of the burgeoning salsa movement that spread worldwide in the mid-1970's. Cruz's 1975 Madison Square Garden performance of "Cucula" was instrumental in popularizing salsa music in the United States.

As an actor and singer, Cruz made many Cuban, Mexican, and American film and television appearances. She is best known as an actor for her performances in the 1992 film *The Mambo Kings* with Antonio Banderas and 1995's *The Perez Family* with Marisa Tomei. Cruz also was a tireless fund-raiser for the Anti-Cancer League Telethon and founded the nonprofit Celia Cruz Foundation to fund cancer research and help underprivileged youths pursue musical careers.

Cruz received many accolades in her career, including three Grammys, and two Latin Grammys, and numerous gold albums. In 1987, the Latino community successfully campaigned for her star on the Hollywood Walk of Fame. In 1997, she was honored with a Smithsonian Institute Lifetime Achievement Award; in 2001, she received a Smithsonian Institute James Smithson Bicentennial Medal. In 1994, President Bill Clinton presented her with the National Endowment for the Arts Medal. Cruz died on July 16, 2003, in Fort Lee, New Jersey.

Significance

Cruz embodied the spirit of *cubanidad*, or the essence of what it means to be Cuban, for millions of Cuban exiles worldwide. She brought international attention to popular Cuban music and in the process transcended racial and cultural stereotypes. As an Afro-Cuban woman, she was able to dispel misconceptions about women of Latino and African descent. Her song "Latinos en los Estados Unidos" ("Latinos in the United States") illustrates Cruz's vision of a united Latino community, focused on cultural similarities rather than differences. Her popularity coincided with a worldwide trend toward Latino ethnic pride.

Latanya West

Further Reading

Abreu, Christina D. "Celebrity, 'Crossover,' and *Cubanidad*: Celia Cruz as La Reina de la salsa." *Latin American Music Review*, March 22, 2007, pp. 94-124. Critical analysis of the positive and negative social aspects of salsa's "crossover" appeal.

Aparicio, F. R. "The Blackness of Sugar: Celia Cruz and the Performance of (Trans)Nationalism." *Cultural Studies* 13, no. 2 (April 1, 1999): 223-236. Substantive article discussing Cruz's unifying influence on Latin American cultural identity.

"Azucar! The Life and Music of Celia Cruz." http://americanhistory.si.edu/celiacruz. Smithsonian National Museum of American History, Behring Center. 2005. Comprehensive online exhibit exploring Cruz's life and career. Includes sound recordings, photographs, a bibliography, and resource links.

Cruz, Celia, and Ana Cristina Reymundo. *Celia: My Life*. Introduction by Maya Angelou. New York: Saro Entertainment, 2004. Cruz's autobiography was transcribed from more than five hundred hours of recordings.

Hijuelos, Oscar. "A Song for Celia." *The New York Times*, July 23, 2003, pp. 1-3. Revealing tribute to Cruz and the impact of her "pan-Latin" legacy.

Rodriquez-Duarte, Alexis. *Presenting Celia Cruz*. Garden City, N.Y.: Random House, 2004. A behind-the-scenes portrait of Cruz by her friend and fellow Cuban American, photographer Rodriquez-Duarte.

See also: Rubén Blades; Paquito D'Rivera; Lydia Mendoza; Tito Puente; Poncho Sánchez.

Nicky Cruz

Puerto Rican-born religious leader

Cruz founded Nicky Cruz Outreach, a religious organization that evangelizes young people in urban environments worldwide. He has written numerous books, including a best-selling autobiography that has been adapted as a film.

Latino heritage: Puerto Rican
Born: December 6, 1938; San Juan, Puerto Rico
Areas of achievement: Religion and theology; literature

Early Life

Nicky Cruz (NIHK-ee krooz) was one of eighteen children, seventeen boys and one girl, born to Galo Cruz and Aleja Velásquez. Both parents were known for practicing witchcraft. His father was a large man and this, combined with his skills in the occult, resulted in him being called "The Great One." As practicing spiritists, his parents often held séances in their home and were known to perform animal sacrifices. Cruz recalls that once, while in a trance, his mother declared that he was the "son of Satan." This home environment, filled with both mental and physical abuse, produced a child who constantly tried to flee, only to be found by the local police and returned to his parents.

Nicky Cruz. (AP Photo)

By the time Cruz was fifteen, his father could no longer put up with his rebelliousness and sent him to New York to stay with his older brother Frank and his wife. By sixteen, Cruz had fled his brother's home and while living on the streets joined the infamous Brooklyn gang of street toughs known as the Mau Maus. Soon he became their president and found himself involved with drugs, alcohol, and violence with no way out. Unable to sleep and racked by nightmares, Cruz was predisposed to seek something more for his life and open to accepting the gospel message delivered by a street preacher named David Wilkerson. After struggling with the changed lifestyle this message required, Cruz finally accepted the offer of help extended by Wilkerson and eventually went to Bible school in California. It was while studying in La Puente, California, at the Latin America Bible Institute that Cruz met his future wife, Gloria Steffani, and in 1961 they married. The couple would have four daughters: Alicia, Laura, Nicole, and Elena.

When Cruz finished his studies, he went to work as director of Wilkerson's Teen Challenge program in New York City. Married life among the drug addicts and street people he had recently known was not easy, and eventually Cruz decided he needed to leave New York. In 1968, he published his autobiography, *Run Baby Run*, written with the help of Jamie Buckingham. By then he had begun receiving requests to speak before larger and larger groups in various cities, and eventually this would result in the founding of Nicky Cruz Outreach.

Life's Work

When Cruz left the Bible Institute in California to work with Teen Challenge ministry, he already knew that his vocation involved working with people who lived the same kind of life from which he had so recently escaped, but he still did not know how his life's work would develop. He knew that God had called him to be an evangelist, but he was unsure of how to combine his calling with his love for working with teens. He was willing to sacrifice for the cause, but he did not think he had the skills necessary to work with large groups of people. He could talk to one person, but he was apprehensive about standing up and speaking to an audience in English, a language that was not his own.

In 1962, Wilkerson wrote and published *The Cross and the Switchblade*, the story of Cruz. This book was made into a film that premiered in 1970. When Cruz's story became known, people began seeking him out and his speaking career began. He initially participated in evangelist Billy Graham's world-famous crusades, his first opportunity to evangelize. Cruz left Teen Challenge to begin his own ministry and moved to California. However, it was not until 1965, when Cruz's interpreter came down with pneumonia and could not accompany him on a crusade in Seattle, that Cruz began speaking on his own and his ministry began in earnest.

Despite the success he was having through his crusades and rallies, Cruz was still not satisfied. He longed to work with children, knowing that if someone had approached him at an earlier age, he would not have sunk as low as he did. With only three thousand dollars, Cruz began Outreach for Youth with a center for street children in Fresno, California. Cruz and his wife began taking in unwanted and troubled children, placing them in school, and helping them to turn their lives around. This marked the beginning of Nicky Cruz Outreach. The center grew, and so did the number of speaking engagements. Soon Cruz had to turn the center over to others in order to continue with his work as an evangelist. However, his dream of establishing teen centers throughout the country had not died. He later moved his family to Raleigh, North Carolina, to open a center for girls. While that center was successful, Cruz knew that his calling was evangelism and eventually he moved his family to Colorado Springs, Colorado.

Cruz continued his work with rallies, crusades, and a full schedule of meetings in many countries. The focus of NCO ministries since moving to Colorado has been the TRUCE (To Reach Urban Communities Everywhere) program, which operates in cities throughout North America and Europe. TRUCE employs an aggressive ministry, considered unorthodox by many, that sends teams months in advance of a planned event to prepare and train volunteers in local churches and communities. The teams set up free street concerts where attendees hear urban music and see street dancers before receiving a short testimony and hearing an evangelistic message. Finally, an altar call is issued and people are given the opportunity to surrender their lives to Christ. While Cruz's focus has been Europe and North America, his mission is worldwide, and his organization has held rallies as far away as New Zealand.

Cruz and the Pentecostal Movement

Nicky Cruz was trained as a Pentecostal evangelist and has followed that calling his entire adult life. He has held countless crusades and rallies throughout the world. While his message is universally evangelical, his personal preference for the Pentecostal denomination is reflected in his work. According to the Pew Forum on religion and Public Life, 8.5 percent of all Protestants in the United States are Pentecostals. Pentecostals were also the fastest-growing denomination in the world, accounting for about 25 percent of the world's 2 billion Christians in 2006. The popularity of Cruz's autobiography has taken him and his brand of Pentecostalism to all parts of the globe.

Significance

Nicky Cruz Outreach has grown exponentially in the years since Cruz left his job with Teen Challenge to begin his own ministry. Because of his work with troubled youths, Cruz has become known as an authority on youth violence and has spoken to countless state legislatures and on many nationally televised programs. Cruz's work has been instrumental in the growth of Pentecostal congregations throughout the Spanish-speaking world, making this the fastest-growing Protestant denomination among Hispanics. Not only do his rallies and crusades win converts wherever he speaks, but the evangelists he has trained to work in his TRUCE program continue to grow the congregations once Cruz has moved on.

The various books he has written have provided guidance for his evangelical work, and his two autobiographical books, *Run Baby Run* and *Soul Obsession: When God's Primary Pursuit Becomes Your Life's Driving Passion* (2005), serve as examples of how to turn around a life through acceptance of Christ. *Run Baby Run* has been translated into at least forty languages and sold more than fourteen million copies; it is required reading in the secondary school programs of many European nations. The cinematographic version of this book, *Thousand Pieces: The Nicky Cruz Story*, scheduled for release in 2011, could further bring his message to young people.

Norma A. Mouton

Further Reading

Cruz, Nicky, and Jamie Buckingham. *Run, Baby, Run*. New York: Berkley, 1968. This autobiography begins with Cruz's early childhood and takes the reader through the early years of his outreach ministry.

Cruz, Nicky, and Frank Martin. *Soul Obsession: When God's Primary Pursuit Becomes Your Life's Driving Passion*. Colorado Springs, Colo.: WaterBrook Press, 2005. Cruz's second autobiography begins with his conversion to Christianity at the age of nineteen and takes the reader through a series of vignettes about his life as an evangelist.

See also: Fray Angélico Chávez; Virgilio Elizondo; Antonio José Martínez; José Policarpo Rodríguez; Oscar I. Romo; Yolanda Tarango.

Victor Hernández Cruz

Puerto Rican-born poet and essayist

Cruz is a world-renowned poet and the premier member of the Nuyorican poetry movement.

Latino heritage: Puerto Rican

Born: February 6, 1949; Aguas Buenas, Puerto Rico

Areas of achievement: Poetry; literature

Early Life

The son of Severo and Rosa (Hernández) Cruz, Victor Hernández Cruz (hur-NAHN-dehz krewz) was born in Puerto Rico in the small mountain city of Aguas Buenas. His family left the island for the United States five years later in 1954, and although he spent only a brief time in Puerto Rico as a child, he never lost his sense of home; it is this biculturalism that defines Cruz and his work.

Cruz's family lived in a predominantly Puerto Rican neighborhood on the Lower East Side of Manhattan before relocating to the Bronx. Cruz discovered his passion early; instead of finishing his final year of high school in 1966, he self-published *Papo Got His Gun! and Other Poems*, his first chapbook. His family moved soon thereafter, in 1968, to San Francisco, where Cruz continued to form his Puerto Rican American identity through his writing.

Life's Work

At age twenty, Cruz produced his breakthrough work, *Snaps* (1969). Published by Random House, *Snaps* was one of the most highly regarded (and highly criticized) poetry collections of the era. In addition to the ever-present biculturalism in his work, Cruz's greatest influences are the Latin and African American music and dance forms that rose up from the streets of urban neighborhoods in New York City. He has described *Snaps* as "percussion with words" and "choreography, motion, catharsis, finally possession." The term "snaps" evokes the rhythm kept by the doo-wop singers who serenaded the citizens of Harlem from street corners; the hard melodies banged out on marimbas, a Latin American instrument whose ancestor is the West African balafon; and the applause offered to poets who read their works in dimly lit bars and lounges in both New York and San Francisco.

By age twenty-two, Cruz was teaching as a guest lecturer at the University of California at Berkeley when he began to feel the pull of the homeland he left behind as a child. He returned to Puerto Rico that year, a trip that served as the impetus for a collection of poetry, *Mainland* (1973), through which he traversed barrios (neighborhoods) across the nation, including Spanish Harlem in New York. Cruz continued to explore the relationship between Puerto Rico and the United States and the language that many Puerto Ricans had adopted. "Spanglish" is a mixture of English and Spanish, infused with African American street slang. His work introduced a confident new voice to a nation that was struggling with its own identity in the sixties and seventies.

Cruz has contributed more than poetry to the American literary tradition. Both *By Lingual Wholes* (1982) and *Panoramas* (1997) address language and socioeconomic and political issues through prose as well as poetry, all with rawness and honesty. *Red Beans* (1991) is a collection of poems and essays that has been hailed as one of his best works. Describing the Caribbean as a "place of great convergence," Cruz discusses his identity as an immigrant and as a person of Indian, African, and European descent.

His most successful collections include *Snaps*, *Tropicalization* (1976), *Red Beans*, and *Panoramas*. He has received many accolades for his work, including a fellowship from the National Endowment for the Arts, a New York Poetry Foundation Award, and a 1991 Guggenheim Award. He also was elected as chancellor of the Academy of American Poets and served as the editor of *Umbra* magazine and coeditor of an anthology called *Paper Dance: Fifty-five Latin Poets* (1995). He cofounded the Before Columbus Foundation along with Ishmael Reed, among others, in 1976.

Significance

Cruz's work utilizes a literary form that has become known as "Spanglish," an amalgamation of Spanish and English spoken frequently in American Latino neighborhoods. He often is associated with the Beat poets because of his use of jazz rhythms in his work, and he was praised as a poetic innovator by Allen Ginsberg. Cruz also contributed to the popularity of several Latin music forms that emerged in Spanish Harlem during the 1960's, including Latin *bugalú*.

J. Jehriko Turner

Further Reading

Aparicio, Frances R., and Victor Hernández Cruz. "*Salsa*, *Maracas*, and *Baile*: Latin Popular Music in the Poetry of Victor Hernández Cruz." *MELUS* 16, no. 1 (Spring, 1989-Spring, 1990): 43-58. Discusses the influence of Cuban and other Latin American music forms on Cruz's work.

Cruz, Victor Hernández. "The Musical Poet, a Session with Victor Hernández Cruz." Interview by Francisco Cabanillas. *Centro Journal* 16, no. 2 (Fall, 2004): 34-41. Cruz discusses the music that inspired him in New York and California.

_______. *Red Beans*. Minneapolis, Minn.: Coffee House Press, 1991. Poems and essays that address biculturalism and language.

Cruz, Victor Hernández, and Clarence Major. "Work with the Universe: An Interview with Clarence Major and Victor Hernández Cruz." Interview by Walt Sheppard. In *Conversations with Clarence Major*, edited by Nancy L. Bunge. Jackson: University Press of Mississippi, 2002. In this 1969 interview, Cruz and Major, an African American writer and artist, discuss racial and cultural identity in literature.

Esterrich, Carmelo. "Home and the Ruins of Language: Víctor Hernández Cruz and Miguel Algarín's Nuyorican Poetry." *MELUS* 23, no. 3 (Fall, 1998): 43-56. A critical essay that discusses the bicultural nature of Cruz's work and the Nuyorican movement.

See also: Miguel Algarín; Giannina Braschi; Jesús Colón; Esmeralda Santiago; Piri Thomas.

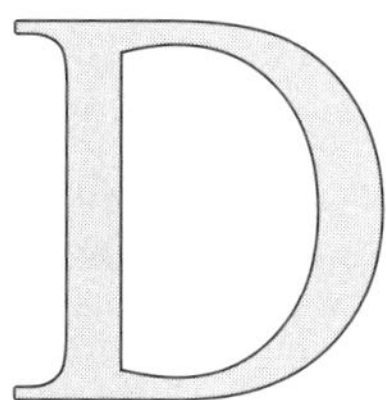

Francisco Dallmeier

Venezuelan-born scientist and environmentalist

Dallmeier has devoted his professional career to the assessment of biodiversity and to educating people about biodiversity and sustainable development. Working at the Smithsonian Institution, he has developed more than three hundred biodiversity monitoring sites throughout the world. He has also written several books and a number of scientific articles on biodiversity.

Latino heritage: Venezuelan

Born: February 15, 1953; Caracas, Venezuela

Also known as: Francisco Gómez-Dallmeier

Area of achievement: Science and technology

Early Life

Francisco Gómez-Dallmeier (frahn-SEES-koh GO-meth DAHL-mee-ehr) was born in Caracas, Venezuela, on February 15, 1953 to Francisco de Sales Gómez Gonzales and Ana Teresa Dallmeier de Gómez. Dallmeier's father's family had lived in Venezuela for generations; his mother's family had emigrated from Germany in the twentieth century. Dallmeier's father was a medical professional and his mother was a special education teacher.

As a child, Dallmeier became interested in insects, birds, and animals. He attended La Salle School and then studied biology at the Central University of Venezuela in Caracas, graduating in 1977. While a student, Dallmeier became a curator of mammals at the Museo de Historia Natural La Salle, and from 1973 to 1977 he served as museum director. During this time he participated in numerous field trips to study birds and wildlife in Venezuela. After attending college Dallmeier worked as a biologist for Ingenieros Electricistas y Mecánicos, C.A., an oil industry engineering consulting firm in Venezuela.

In 1981, he received a Fundacion Gran Mariscal de Ayacucho scholarship to study wildlife ecology at Colorado State University, from which he received a master of science degree in 1984. An Organization of American States scholarship supported him from 1984 to 1986, when he pursued his Ph.D. studies in wildlife biology at Colorado State. Dallmeier married Nancy Joy Parton in 1985 and the couple had two children.

Life's Work

After receiving his doctorate in wildlife ecology in 1986, Dallmeier began a long career in biodiversity assessment at the Smithsonian Institution in Washington, D.C. Biodiversity is an indicator of the status of an ecosystem. When large populations of many different species of plants and animals coexist, an ecosystem is healthy; when an ecosystem experiences stress, populations and species numbers decline. Dallmeier's work has been concentrated on tropical, subtropical, and temperate forest ecosystems, where balancing conservation with resource exploitation is necessary to achieve sustainable development. He has also studied the preservation of biodiversity during stress resulting from climate change.

Dallmeier has supported the creation of numerous monitoring sites within an ecosystem, as he has found considerable variability between sites within ecosystems. He has consistently advocated development of integrated management plans to balance biodiversity conservation with sustainable development. Monitoring of biodiversity can reverse the degradation of an ecosystem that might occur during resource exploitation.

In 2006, Dallmeier became director of the Smithsonian Institution's National Zoological Park Center for Conservation Education and Sustainability. This center oversees the Smithsonian Institution Monitoring and Assessment of Biodiversity Program (MAB), of which Dallmeier become director in 1989. Dallmeier has developed short courses for environmental leaders and business executives, which he has helped teach at the Smithsonian Conservation and Research Center in Front Royal, Virginia. These courses present case studies in conservation management, emphasizing critical thinking and analysis for local and global environmental issues and strategic planning to address specific challenges. Dallmeier has directed the Smithsonian Center for Latino Initiatives since 2002. This center promotes interest and awareness of science among the Latino community.

Significance

Francisco Dallmeier's work on biodiversity, conservation management, and sustainable development is critically important, as natural habitats continue to shrink in the twenty-first century. As director of the MAB, he has sought to promote biodiversity awareness through research, training, education, and outreach. Dallmeier has developed a network of more than three hundred biodiversity monitoring sites in North America, Latin America, Africa, and Asia through the MAB. In the books and scientific papers Dallmeier has coauthored, he has aided the worldwide scientific understanding of biodiversity conservation in temperate and tropical ecosystems.

Anita Baker-Blocker

Further Reading

Abarca, Patricia, and Deanne Kloepfer, *Francisco Dallmeier.* Chicago: Raintree, 2005. Biography aimed at elementary school students.

Dallmeier, Francisco, *Adventures in the Rainforest: Discovering Biodiversity*. Washington, D.C.: Smithsonian Institution, 2002. A short, nontechnical introduction to biodiversity .

Dallmeier, Francisco, et. al. *Climate Change, Biodiversity, and Sustainability in the Americas: Impacts and Adaptations.* Washington, D.C.: Smithsonian Institution Scholarly Press, 2010. Summarizes a 2008 symposium sponsored by the Smithsonian and Environment Canada to examine the effects of climate change on biodiversity.

Dallmeier, Francisco, and J. A. Comiskey, eds. *Forest Biodiversity in North, Central and South America, and the Caribbean: Research and Monitoring*. New York: Parthenon, 1998. In addition to editing this book, Dallmeier and colleagues contributed chapters on the effects of Hurricane Hugo on a Puerto Rican forest, a subtropical dry forest in the Virgin Islands, the use of ethnobotany as a research tool, and a comparison of biodiversity in managed and unmanaged forests in Bolivia.

Herrera-MacBryde, O., et al., eds. *Biodiversidad, Conservación, y Manejo en la Región de la Reserva de la Biosfera Estación Biológica del Beni, Bolivia (Biodiversity, Conservation, and Management in the Region of the Beni Biological Station Biosphere Reserve, Bolivia)*. Washington, D.C.: Smithsonian Instution, SI/MAB Biodiversity Program, 2000. A lengthy scientific report on biodiversity in Bolivia written by Dallmeier and others. Offers a good example of his scientific work on biodiversity.

See also: Walter Alvarez; Arturo Gómez-Pompa; Eugenia Kalnay; Mario Molina.

Nicholas Dante

American playwright and dancer

Drawing on his own experiences as a dancer in theater and television productions, Dante coauthored the book for the groundbreaking Tony Award- and Pulitzer Prize-winning musical A Chorus Line, *which chronicled the struggles and triumphs of aspiring Broadway dancers.*

Latino heritage: Puerto Rican

Born: November 22, 1941; New York, New York

Died: May 21, 1991; New York, New York

Also known as: Conrado Morales; Nikolas Dante

Areas of achievement: Theater; dance; gay and lesbian issues

Early Life

Born Conrado Morales in the Puerto Rican neighborhoods near Spanish Harlem in New York, Nicholas Dante (NIHK-oh-lahs DAHN-tay), an effeminate child who loved to make up fabulous stories about fantasy places, never fit with the machismo culture of his working-class environs. His father loved films and took his son to see motion pictures nearly every week. The boy was entranced by lavish musicals, particularly the films of Cyd Charisse. When he was alone, which was often, he would practice dance moves. In his early teens, when he went alone to motion picture theaters along Forty-second Street and would be propositioned by male patrons, he came to understand that he was gay. He struggled with the realization. Indeed, he left Catholic high school at fourteen because of the atmosphere of intolerance; for example, the principal told him counseling might "fix" the "problem" of his homosexuality.

Dante dreamed of being a journalist but rejected this career because it would require a college degree. For the next decade, he danced when he could in nightclubs and Off-Broadway theaters. It was during this time that he changed his name; he had never felt Puerto Rican and producers had told him he looked Mediterranean. Initially he tried the Greek-sounding Nikolas Dante and then the more Italian Nicholas Dante. He found work in ensemble dance numbers for television productions, most notably a 1968 special featuring Olympic skater Peggy Fleming and several appearances in production numbers for *The Ed Sullivan Show*, as well as in nightclub revues, including drag clubs. In between, he worked in restaurants. His break came in 1970, when he performed in the ensemble of *Applause*, the Tony Award-winning musical starring Lauren Bacall. This show ran for two years.

Life's Work

In 1974, a friend, Michael Bennett, a successful choreographer, invited Dante to participate in informal talk sessions Bennett was conducting with Manhattan dancers struggling to find success in the competitive world of professional theater. Known as gypsies, these gifted dancers worked show to show, performing in choruses and in touring companies, seldom achieving stardom. Bennett had already conceived of a musical based on these dancers and was gathering stories by taping the sessions.

The material, more than twenty-four hours of tape, needed to be shaped into a musical book. Bennett enlisted an enthusiastic Dante. Dante worked for nearly eight months. Later accounts differ as to whether Dante was overwhelmed or whether he requested a fresh perspective, but for whatever reason, James Kirkwood, Jr., who had written a modestly successful novel Dante admired, was enlisted to bring the book to completion. The result was an innovative kind of musical, a montage theater piece without a conventional plot. The play would be an audition among seventeen aspiring dancers competing for eight spots. An autocratic director would elicit from each performer his or her life story, dreams, and struggles. With an accomplished musical score by multiple Oscar-winner Marvin Hamlisch and lyrics by newcomer Edward Kleban, *A Chorus Line* premiered in May, 1975, to lavish critical praise.

Among the most moving moments was a thinly veiled account of Dante's own experience, the monologue of a gay Puerto Rican dancer who calls himself Paul San Marco. Paul had adopted an Italian-sounding name to escape who he was. As he opens up to the director, Paul confesses his struggles with his homosexuality and how he could not bear to tell his parents. The riveting monologue, nearly eight minutes, climaxes with Paul talking about getting work in a drag show. The show was ready to head to Chicago when Paul's parents surprised him by coming to the theater, only to find their son costumed as a showgirl. Expecting a confrontation, Paul is stunned to hear his father, choked with tears, tell the producer to take care of his "son," the first time Paul could remember his father ever calling him that. The monologue was an emotional highlight in the musical, and the actor who played Paul, Sammy Williams, won a Tony Award for Best Featured Actor in a Musical. The musical itself won nine Tonys in 1976, including Best Musical, and that year's Pulitzer Prize for drama, shared by the five men—Bennett, Kirkwood, Dante, Hamlisch, and Kleban—responsible for the show's inception. *A Chorus Line* ran for nearly fifteen years, 6,137 performances, the longest run in Broadway history to that time.

Not surprisingly, Dante never again found the same level of success. He wanted to continue writing but struggled, authoring the book for a musical based on the life of 1920's singer Al Jolson, which had only limited success. In the 1980's, now in his forties, he performed irregularly, playing Paul in productions of *A Chorus Line*. In 1989, he was diagnosed with acquired immunodeficiency syndrome (AIDS). In his last years, thanks in part to an experimental therapy program that involved massive doses of medication, Dante came to peace with himself and even returned to writing. He died from complications from the disease in 1991, at the age of forty-nine.

Significance

Drawing on his own difficult adolescence, Nicholas Dante brought to the collaborative creation of the book for *A Chorus Line* a sense of the lived life of a struggling gypsy, the world of Broadway dancers, and this immediacy ensured that the characters in the ensemble cast emerged as real people with real dreams. With an unerring ear for dialogue, thanks to his own upbringing on the streets of New York, and his keen sense of character, Dante helped give the landmark musical its riveting authenticity.

Joseph Dewey

Further Reading

Kirkwood, James, Jr., Edward Kleban, and Nicholas Dante. *A Chorus Line: The Complete Book of the Musical*. New York: Applause Books, 2000. Commemorative edition to mark the musical's twenty-fifth anniversary. Includes detailed account of the play's inception.

Ramirez, Rafael L. *What It Means to Be a Man: Reflections on Puerto Rican Masculinity*. New Brunswick, N.J.: Rutgers University Press, 1999. Seminal study in the patriarchal culture of machismo that created the pressures and isolation of Dante's formative years.

Viagas, Robert, Baayork Lee, and Thommie Walsh. *On the Line: The Creation of A Chorus Line*. New York: Limelight Editions, 2006. Anecdotal history of the landmark musical through recollections of the seventeen actors who originated the roles.

See also: Miguel Algarín; Giannina Braschi; Victor Hernández Cruz; Rosario Ferré; Rita Moreno; Judith Ortiz Cofer; Chita Rivera; Esmeralda Santiago.

Angela de Hoyos

Mexican-born poet and activist

The "grande dame of Chicano literature," de Hoyos devoted her life to the arts, writing poetry and promoting awareness of the contributions of Chicano artists to the cultural wealth of the United States. Her political activism encompassed both the Chicano and the women's movements of the 1960's and 1970's.

Latino heritage: Mexico

Born: January 23, 1940?;Coahuila, Mexico

Died: September 24, 2009; San Antonio, Texas

Areas of achievement: Poetry; activism; publishing; women's rights

Early Life

Angela de Hoyos (AHN-heel-ah day OY-os) was born in Coahuila, Mexico, on January 23, but the year remains in dispute, reported variously as 1923, 1924, 1940, and 1945. She began writing at the age of four, endowed with, as she herself described it, an insatiable thirst for knowledge. Encouraged by her mother, a talented artist and strong presence in her life, de Hoyos began her literary career reciting an interior monologue of rhymes and verses. As a child her family moved to San Antonio, Texas, where prejudice against her Mexican heritage lay in wait. The wide-ranging variety of her interests, including fine arts and writing, drove her to take various courses at the University of Texas at San Antonio, San Antonio College, Witt Museum, and San Antonio Art Institute. De Hoyos's extensive and diverse list of influences included Emily Dickinson, Gertrude Stein, William Carlos Williams, Rudolfo Anaya, Rolando Hinojosa, Mireya Robles, Rosario Castellanos, Walt Whitman, Jim Sagel, and Simone de Beauvoir. Even before her first book of poetry was published in 1975, her work found a place in various journals, and she had received awards, including those from the National Association of Chicano Studies in 1973 and the San Antonio Poetry Festival in 1974.

Life's Work

De Hoyos did not plan to become a writer per se and was reluctant to consider herself one. She preferred to say that she loved words and needed them to articulate her thoughts, and she remained endlessly surprised at the success and attention her writing received.

De Hoyos's first major book publication came in 1975, with *Arise, Chicano! And Other Poems.* Representing strong Chicano-nationalist "protest" verse, *Arise, Chicano!* established the leading edge of Chicano literary political output. The collection gives voice to multiple perspectives, including that of the migrant worker caught under "the shrewd heel of exploit" and ensnared by the English language, along with audaciously sarcastic treatment of the issues of assimilation and the attendant loss of cultural pride.

Chicano Poems: For the Barrio (1975) followed shortly thereafter, and in it de Hoyos demonstrated an expanding range, with bilingual poems exalting Chicano heritage and incisive treatments of such issues as losing *chicanismo* underneath "Anglo" nationalism. Later work demonstrates de Hoyos's widening areas of concern, reflecting the more universal issues of life and death. *Selecciones* (1976) includes new metaphysical forms and themes, and *Woman, Woman* (1985) offers considered distress at the loss of a close female friendship.

De Hoyos's mode of reader address was often jocular, or as she put it," rogue-ish." In the 1970's, a letter to the editor appeared in a San Antonio newspaper, suggesting that all "Mes'kins" should go home. De Hoyos, in her inimitable spirit, wrote back a letter of her own suggesting she should resurrect the Pinta, the Niña and the Santa María, so everyone can sail back to where they came from. Her roguish poem in a similar vein, "To Walt Whitman," remains one of her most quoted pieces.

De Hoyos and her husband Moises Sandoval established the publishing house M&A Editions, which has published, promoted, and mentored writers like Evangelina Vigil-Piñón, Carmen Tafolla, and Inés Hernández-Ávila. Some of the company's publications have been in the spirit of de Hoyos's concerns, such as *Mi'ja, Never Lend Your Mop . . . and Other Poems* (2000) by Brigid Aileen Milligan. De Hoyos also served as editor of *Huehuetitlan*, a journal of Chicano culture and poetry.

Significance

Inspired by the Texas farm workers' struggle in the late 1960's and early 1970's, de Hoyos's work represents the early literary fruits of the Chicano political movement. In poems like "To Walt Whitman," de Hoyos engages the pillars of the American literary canon, challenging the assumption that writers such as Whitman effectively represented the breadth and depth of literary production in the United States; however, she freely admitted the influence of such authors on her own writing. Internationally renowned, her work has been translated into fifteen languages and continues to be lauded in her hometown of San Antonio.

Jan Voogd

Further Reading

Corpi, Lucha, ed. *Mascaras.* Berkeley, Calif.: Third Woman Press, 1997. A collection of essays by contemporary women writers, including de Hoyos, illuminating their challenges as both Latinas or Chicanas and as Americans.

De Hoyos, Angela. *Arise Chicano! And Other Poems.* Rev. and enlarged ed. San Antonio: M&A Editions, 1980. Probably de Hoyos's most representative and well-known work.

Fernandez, Roberta. *In Other Words: Literature by Latinas of the United States.* Houston: Arte Público Press, 1994. Includes a section devoted to de Hoyos, contextualized within Latin American literature.

Hogeland, Lisa Maria, and Mary Klages. *The Aunt Lute Anthology of U.S. Women Writers.* San Francisco: Aunt Lute Books, 2004. Contains several pages of de Hoyos's work, contextualized more broadly within the spectrum of U.S. women writers.

Milligan, Bryce, and Mary Guerrero Milligan. *Daughters of the Fifth Sun: A Collection of Latina Fiction and Poetry.* New York: Riverhead Books, 1996. Includes work by de Hoyos, referred to within as a godmother of U.S. Latina writing.

Milligan, Bryce, Mary Guerrero Milligan, and Angela De Hoyos, eds. *Floricanto Si! A Collection of Latina Poetry.* New York : Penguin Books, 1998. Contains poems by de Hoyos, contextualized among a broad range of Latina poetry.

See also: Rudolfo Anaya; Gloria Anzaldúa; Rolando Hinojosa; Sara Estela Ramírez; Gary Soto; Carmen Tafolla.

ELIGIO DE LA GARZA II

American politician

De la Garza enjoyed one of the longest and most influential careers of any Latino in national politics in the United States, combining a somewhat conservative approach to American history and political thought with passionate concerns for agriculture, business, free trade, the environment, and the Latino community throughout the country.

Latino heritage: Mexican

Born: September 22, 1927; Mercedes, Texas

Also known as: Kika de la Garza

Area of achievement: Government and politics

EARLY LIFE

Eligio de la Garza II (ay-LEE-hee-oh day lah GAHR-zah) was born in Mercedes, a small town in southernmost Texas in the Rio Grande Valley, and grew up in nearby Mission, Texas, where he attended Our Lady of Guadalupe Catholic School and the local high school.

After graduation, de la Garza began a two-year stint in the U.S. Navy, after which he returned to the Rio Grande Valley and attended a junior college in Edinburg, Texas. De la Garza next joined the U.S. Army and trained at Fort Sill, Oklahoma, at the Army Artillery School. He saw action in Korea as a member of the Thirty-seventh Division Artillery, attaining a rank of second lieutenant.

Upon leaving the Army, de la Garza enrolled at St. Mary's University in San Antonio, Texas, where he obtained a law degree. He practiced law briefly in Mission before deciding to run for a seat in the Texas House of Representatives. He won and held the seat for six terms until he decided to run for national office. In 1964, de la Garza was elected to Congress representing his state's Fifteenth District.

In de la Garza's half-dozen years in the Texas House of Representatives, he became involved with issues that would characterize and define his long career in politics: education, the environment, business, and closer ties between the United States and Mexico. Among his accomplishments as a state representative were the establishment of the Texas Water Commission, a heightened awareness of the importance to the state of coastal wetlands, a reinvigorated English-language program for kindergarten-aged children, and more bridges linking South Texas to Mexico. For his first few years in state office, de la Garza was the only Latino in the Texas House.

LIFE'S WORK

In Congress, de la Garza maintained an agenda identical to that of his days in the Texas House. The Rio Grande Valley region is one in which farming and ranching are paramount, and many of de la Garza's activities in Washington dealt in some form or fashion with the agricultural concerns of his constituents. Within three years of his arrival in Washington, he had assumed the role of chairman of the Subcommittee on Department Operations and Foreign Agriculture. In the early 1980's, de la Garza was named chairman of the House's Committee on Agriculture, making history by becoming the first Latino to chair a standing House committee since World War I.

While serving as chairman of the committee, de la Garza worked diligently to improve the lot of famers throughout the United States, aiding the passage of significant bills that, among other things, helped farmers and ranchers receive federal loans by reforming the Farm Credit System. He also simplified significantly the structure of the federal Department of Agriculture. One of de la Garza's earliest acts as chairman was to help pass the Temporary Emergency Food Assistance Act, which helped deal with surplus agricultural foodstuffs in an efficient and humane way—by seeing to it that such agricultural abundance would be directed to the poor and the homeless. During the late 1980's, lack of rainfall in several key agricultural regions portended catastrophe for many ranching and farming families, so de la Garza was active in the passage of two separate Disaster Assistance Acts for the financial relief of those affected.

A few years later, in the mid-1990's, de la Garza championed the Federal Crop Insurance Reform Act, which set up permanent policies for dealing with disasters in the future. This act also was the primary medium for restructuring the somewhat labyrinthine Department of Agriculture so that it could more easily and speedily deal with threats to American farms and farmers. De la Garza also was influential in the establishment of more stringent laws governing the manufacture and use of insecticides. Among the many acts and bills he either proposed or championed, perhaps the one that most clearly crystallizes his slate of interests and causes is 1990's Food, Agriculture, Conservation, and Trade Act, which created programs to promote better nutrition across the United States, facilitated free trade among

De la Garza and Southern/Tejano Conservatism

Representative Eligio de la Garza II was a Democrat but sometimes voted against the majority of his party on important issues because of his background as a Tejano, a Texan of Mexican ancestry. For example, in 1996, he voted in favor of a resolution to reform welfare and Medicaid that the majority of Democrats opposed; in favor of House Resolution 3752, the American Land Sovereignty Protection Act, which found disfavor with most Democrats; and supported the controversial House Resolution 1883 to ban late-term abortions. Although his vote on HR 1883 can be seen as the result of his staunch Catholic faith, other votes and attitudes spring from the sort of innate conservatism of agricultural societies that Civil War historian Bruce Catton once noted in Robert E. Lee: the strong love of the land and the dedication to preserving it. Although environmentalism typically is associated with liberal political views, many people who grow up in intensely agrarian cultures like that of the Rio Grande Valley embrace concern for the preservation of the land and the water and the air for very practical reasons. In this sense, de la Garza was a conservative politician.

nations, and sought to establish ecologically friendly practices in American farmlands.

Long a friend of international business and trade, especially between the United States and Mexico, de la Garza played a major role in the formulation and passage of the North American Free Trade Agreement (NAFTA), which began the repeal or radical reduction of tariffs and similar fees on imports and exports among the United States, Canada, and Mexico, while at the same time seeking to establish a consensus of practice in maintaining ecologically minded practices in business and industry in the three countries.

Many of de la Garza's efforts in office were specifically directed toward Latino interests. For example, in the mid 1960's, he supported governmental financing of Project SER (Service, Employment, and Redevelopment), a program headquartered in Texas that sought to find jobs and financial stability for Latinos. Later in the 1960's and through the 1970's, he worked with the Mexico-United States Interparliamentary Group, an organization that seeks to foster cooperation between American and Mexican politicians. In late 1976, he joined with four other Latino representatives, including fellow Texan Henry B. González, to form the Congressional Hispanic Caucus, a service organization of Democratic representatives focused on needs and concerns of Latino communities across the United States. From 1989 through 1990, he served as the organization's eighth chairman. Early in 1997, de la Garza retired to McAllen, Texas.

Significance

De la Garza had one of the longest and most impressive careers of any Latino legislator. First elected to the United States House of Representatives in 1964, he retained his seat until 1997 without a serious challenger in any election. His impact on agriculture in the United States and on United States-Mexico relations has been profound and long-lasting.

Thomas Du Bose

Further Reading

De la Garza, Eligio. "Ceiling on Aid Would Hurt Farm Program." *USA Today*, May 18, 1990, p. 12A. This opinion piece offers a good introduction to de la Garza's humanitarian approach to agricultural concerns.

_______. "Linking Trade Growth and the Environment: One Lawmaker's View." *Environmental Law* 23 (1993): 701-702. Shows how de la Garza often synthesized his prime concerns of business, agriculture, and the environment.

Fort, Karen, and the Mission Historical Museum. *Mission*. Chicago: Arcadia, 2009. Well-illustrated introduction to de la Garza's hometown in the Rio Grande Valley and the milieu in which he grew up.

Meier, Matt S. "Eligio "Kika" de la Garza." In *Mexican American Biographies: A Historical Dictionary, 1836-1987*. New York: Greenwood Press, 1988. Contains a concise evaluation of the Representative midway through his long career.

See also: Joe J. Bernal; Joaquín Castro; Julián Castro; Irma Rangel; Leticia Van de Putte.

Oscar De La Hoya

American boxer and boxing promoter

De La Hoya enjoyed great fame and success as a boxer for nearly two decades. He won a gold medal at the 1992 Barcelona Olympics and went on to capture world titles in many different weight divisions into the 2000's. After retiring as a fighter, he achieved success as a boxing promoter with his company Golden Boy Promotions.

Latino heritage: Mexican

Born: February 4, 1973; Los Angeles, California

Also known as: Golden Boy

Areas of achievement: Boxing; business

Early Life

Oscar De La Hoya (day lah HOY-ah) was born in Los Angeles, California, in 1973 and introduced to boxing by his father, Joel, as a child. De La Hoya became an amateur standout, eventually earning a record of 223-5. Highlights of his amateur career included 1989 Golden Gloves national featherweight championship, the 1990 United States amateur featherweight championship, the 1990 gold medal in the featherweight division at the Goodwill Games, the 1991 U.S. amateur lightweight championship, and the gold medal at the 1992 Olympics in Barcelona. De La Hoya dedicated his Olympic gold medal to his mother, who had died from cancer before the Summer Games.

After the 1992 Olympics, De La Hoya turned professional and earned a reputation for a great left hook and left jab. In his first professional fight, on November 23, 1992, he knocked out Lamar Williams in the first round at the Great Western Forum in Inglewood, California. In his twelfth fight, De La Hoya won his first world title, knocking out undefeated Jimmi Bredahl for the World Boxing Organization (WBO) super featherweight title on March 5, 1994. He defended that title once before fighting for the WBO lightweight title, which he won by knocking out Jorge Páez in the second round on July 29, 1994. De La Hoya defended the title six times. During this reign, he unified the International Boxing Federation and WBO titles when he knocked out Rafael Ruelas in the second round in Las Vegas in May, 1995.

In his next fight, that September, De La Hoya forced undefeated Genaro Hernandez to quit on his stool in the sixth round. These victories earned De La Hoya the honor of being *Ring* magazine's fighter of the year for 1995. On June 7, 1996, De La Hoya faced his idol, Julio César Chávez, considered the best Mexican boxer of all time, and earned a technical knockout when the fight was stopped because of a cut suffered by Chávez. With this victory, De La Hoya earned the World Boxing Council (WBC) light welterweight title. He defended that title once and then moved up to the welterweight division to face Pernell Whitaker, at the time widely considered the best fighter in the world. In a closely contested fight, De La Hoya won by unanimous decision. He defended this title five times; these defenses included a victory over Hector Camacho, a former world champion in three weight classes, and a rematch against Chávez.

Life's Work

At this time, the welterweight division was considered the best in boxing, with four men among the top ten pound-for-pound fighters in the world: Félix Trinidad of Puerto Rico, Whitaker, Ike Quartey of Ghana, and De La Hoya. A series of fights similar to the great welterweight-middleweight matches of the late 1970's between Sugar Ray Leonard, Thomas Hearns, Marvin

Oscar De La Hoya. (AP Photo)

Hagler, and Roberto Durán was anticipated. De La Hoya already had defeated Whitaker. Next, he took on Quartey. On February 13, 1999, in Las Vegas, De La Hoya won a twelve-round split decision over the African boxer. This fight showed for the first time De La Hoya's ability to fight tough. He knocked down Quartey in the sixth round, only to be knocked down himself. He managed to survive and knock down Quartey again in the twelfth round, thereby securing the victory. Their sixth round was chosen by *Ring* magazine as the round of the year. After a defense against Oba Carr, De La Hoya took on undefeated Trinidad. Trinidad also already had beaten the aging Whitaker, breaking his jaw in New York City in February, 1999. On September 18, 1999, De La Hoya lost a majority decision to Trinidad. He had built a lead on the scorecards with superior boxing skills through the first eight rounds but refused to engage Trinidad in the later rounds. It was his first loss.

After a comeback fight, De La Hoya took on the undefeated former lightweight champion "Sugar" Shane Mosley in June, 2000. In another closely contested fight, De La Hoya lost a split decision. This fight was so highly anticipated that *Ring* named it the event of the year. After a knockout of rugged Arturo Gatti, De La Hoya defeated Javier Castillejo for the light middleweight title, giving him titles in five different weight classes. He next fought a WBC and World Boxing Association (WBA) unification bout against WBA champion Fernando Vargas. Vargas and De La Hoya were boxing rivals in California. De La Hoya fell behind early but came back to knock Vargas down in the tenth round and then knock him out in the eleventh. Many feel this bout is the crowning achievement of De La Hoya's career.

De La Hoya defended this title once and then lost a unanimous decision to Mosley. He moved up to the middleweight division and won a controversial unanimous decision over Felix Sturm for the WBO belt. This set up a major fight against longtime middleweight champion Bernard Hopkins, a fighter from Philadelphia who had earned respect as a great fighter when he knocked out Trinidad in the fall of 2001. After a close eight rounds, De La Hoya was knocked out after receiving a left hook to the liver. He returned to the ring a year and a half later in May, 2006, knocking out Ricardo Mayorga and winning a junior middleweight title. In May, 2007, De La Hoya fought Floyd Mayweather, Jr., considered the best fighter in the world, but lost by split decision in the most lucrative fight in the history of boxing. This fight was named event of the year by *Ring*. After one more bout, he took on Manny Pacquiao in a welterweight bout. The smaller Pacquiao proved too much for the thirty-six-year-old De La Hoya. The southpaw hit De La Hoya with lefts and pummeled him on the ropes, forcing the Golden Boy to retire on his stool before the ninth round. On April 15, 2009, De La Hoya retired from professional boxing. He left with a record of thirty-nine wins, six losses, and thirty knockouts. All six of those losses came in his final fourteen bouts.

After the end of his fighting days, De La Hoya stayed involved with boxing through his company Golden Boy Promotions, which he established in 2001. Although it has investments in media and other sports, the company focuses on boxing and has become—along with Top Rank and Don King Productions—one of the top promoters in the sport. In 2007, it promoted the most lucrative match in boxing history, the De La Hoya-Mayweather bout. In 2008, it promoted the De La Hoya-Pacquiao fight.

De La Hoya as a Crossover Star

Like fellow Olympic gold medalists Sugar Ray Leonard and Muhammad Ali, Oscar De La Hoya became a celebrity whose fame transcended his accomplishments in the ring and obscured his record. Where Leonard's and Ali's ring records are stellar, De La Hoya's is less impressive. He is not considered as good a fighter as many from his era; Félix Trinidad, Shane Mosley, Bernard Hopkins, Floyd Mayweather, Jr., and Manny Pacquiao—all of whom defeated De La Hoya—are considered better boxers. Even some of De La Hoya's biggest victories came over physically impaired fighters looking to earn the big purse that accompanied a De La Hoya bout: Genaro Hernandez fought De La Hoya with an injured nose that was subsequently broken in their fight, and Julio César Chávez fought De La Hoya with a barely healed cut over his eye—a cut that De La Hoya reopened, leading to a technical knockout. However, despite these blemishes on his record, De La Hoya's fights were consistently big draws with pay-per-view audiences. De La Hoya, a handsome and attractive ambassador of the sport, was able to pique the interest of casual viewers as well as boxing enthusiasts, much like Leonard and Ali.

Significance

With his good looks, facility with both English and Spanish, and titles in six weight divisions, De La Hoya became a crossover celebrity. He earned more than a half-billion dollars as a fighter, a number that indicates his appeal to mainstream audiences, not just hardcore boxing enthusiasts. De La Hoya continued to earn front-page coverage despite long periods of inactivity and losses in many of his biggest fights.

Brett Conway

Further Reading

De La Hoya, Oscar, and Steve Springer. *American Son: My Story*. New York: Harper Collins, 2008. De La Hoya's autobiography traces his rise to stardom and discusses his cultural identity.

Hauser, Thomas. *Chaos, Corruption, Courage and Glory: A Year in Boxing*. Toronto: Sport Classic, 2005. Anthology of essays by the writer on the major boxing storylines of 2003-2004, including coverage of De La Hoya's career during that period.

Kawakami, Tim. *Golden Boy: The Fame, Money, and Mystery of Oscar De La Hoya*. Kansas City, Mo.: Andrews McMeel, 1999. Balanced, journalistic biography of the boxer published around the peak of his career.

Schulberg, Budd. *Ringside: A Treasury of Boxing Reportage*. Chicago: Ivan R. Dee, 2006. Collection of writings on famous fights, including ones involving De La Hoya.

See also: Sixto Escobar; Aurelio Herrera; Félix Trinidad.

Oscar de la Renta

Dominican-born fashion designer and entrepreneur

One of the world's best-known fashion designers, de la Renta began his career as an artist and illustrator. He worked for fashion houses in Spain and France before coming to the United States, where, since the late 1960's, his name has become synonymous with style and glamour.

Latino heritage: Dominican

Born: July 22, 1932; Santo Domingo, Dominican Republic

Also known as: Oscar Aristides Renta Fiallo

Areas of achievement: Fashion; business

Early Life

Oscar de la Renta (OHS-kahr day lah REHN-tah) was born Oscar Aristides Renta Fiallo in Santo Domingo, Dominican Republic. He was the only son among seven children born to a Dominican mother and a Puerto Rican father, who was an American citizen and worked as an insurance agent. After completing high school, de la Renta studied for two years at the National School of Art in his hometown and then continued his education as a painter at the Academia de San Fernando in Madrid, Spain. Because his father did not believe there was any future in art and was reluctant to pay his tuition, de la Renta financed his own studies by working as a newspaper artist, specializing in fashion sketches. This led to further work as an illustrator for Spanish fashion designers who recognized his talent.

In 1956, the wife of John Lodge, the U.S. ambassador to Spain, was captivated by de la Renta's work and asked him to design a dress for her daughter. This job brought him to the attention of designer Cristobal

Oscar de la Renta. (AP Photo)

De la Renta's Style and Clothing Lines

Always in the forefront of fashion, Oscar de la Renta has consistently demonstrated a flair for the dramatic. Though tastes have changed considerably over the half-century since he began to design clothing, certain elements have always been present in de la Renta collections. A specialist in eveningwear, he has earned a reputation for extravagance and painstaking attention to detail. De la Renta is also known for his use of bold colors, rich fabrics, and ornamentation—sequins, buttons, brads, beads, ruffles, fur, feathers, or semiprecious stones—in the creation of figure-flattering garments that often feature cinched waists with wide belts and bust-enhancing scooped or V-shaped necklines that present a totally feminine silhouette.

De la Renta first burst upon the American fashion scene with his 1967 Gypsy evening collection, which is credited with raising awareness of and interest in Russian styling trends. Exotic and eclectic, the collection included a range of clothing that captured the carefree, statement-making essence of the late 1960's and early 1970's. Pieces included jewel-studded hot pants, silk minidresses in abstract patterns, quilted or randomly striped miniskirts with matching jackets, printed denim, and djellabas accented with braids or gems. De la Renta's day wear, by contrast, was much more subdued and appropriate for any occasion.

A force in the evolution of fashion, de la Renta anticipated the rise of professional women with the introduction of his OSCAR line in 1997. A high-end collection of designer sportswear, the OSCAR product line includes knit and woven tops, fleece shirts and blouses, fleece pants, slacks, jeans, and coordinated outerwear, such as jackets, coats, and raincoats. In recognition of the need for a designer label affordable for all working women, de la Renta in 2004 launched O Oscar, a line of sportswear that offers the same cachet as the designer's top lines at a more modest price. Mass-produced for such national department stores as Macy's and Dillard's, O Oscar provides an inexpensive alternative for fashion-conscious women.

Balenciaga, who hired de la Renta as an illustrator. Over the next several years, he advanced to apprentice designer in Madrid. In 1961, Antonio del Castillo lured de la Renta to Paris, France, with a position as an assistant at Lanvin-Castillo, a fashion design house. Two years later, de la Rentae relocated to New York where he was a custom collection designer for Elizabeth Arden.

In 1965, de la Renta went to work for designer Jane Derby, and that same year he launched his first independent ready-to-wear line for Derby's company. De la Renta married for the first time in 1967, becoming the third husband of fashion consultant Françoise de Langland, editor in chief of *French Vogue*. When Derby died in 1969, de la Renta bought her company and gave it his own name.

Life's Work

In 1971, de la Renta became a naturalized American citizen. That same year he was offered the post of Dominican ambassador to the United States, but he turned it down since he had renounced his Dominican citizenship. By then, de la Renta was firmly established in the fashion world, with a reputation for practical, elegant day wear and spectacular, exotic evening clothing drawn from a variety of diverse traditions. In 1973, he was elected president of the Council of Fashion Designers of America (CFDA), a nonprofit organization founded in 1962 and the leading trade association of the fashion and accessory business, which by 2010 included more than 350 of North America's top designers. While serving as president of the organization from 1973 to1976, de la Renta suggested the creation of the prestigious CFDA Awards. In 1984, during his second term as president, CFDA began to bestow honors for lifetime achievement, and the organization later added recognition for menswear, women's wear, international design, and emerging talent in ready-to-wear.

De la Renta began expanding upon his brand name in 1976 with the first of a dozen fragrances he would introduce, which include Pour Lui (1980), Volupte (1992), Oscar for Men (1999), Oscar Tropical (2002), and Rosamor (2004). In 1989, de la Renta married for the second time to Annette Reed, daughter of a German banker and former wife of publisher Samuel P. Reed. De la Renta, who had stepchildren from both his marriages, also adopted a son, Moises, who has become a fashion designer in his own right.

In 1993, the house of Pierre Balmain hired de la Renta as couture collection designer, making him the first Latin American to lead a French high-fashion establishment. De la Renta designed haute couture for Balmain through 2001. He also continued to enhance the reputation of his own fashion house. In 1997, he introduced an exclusive line of sportswear for working women, OSCAR by Oscar de la Renta. In 2001, he added fashion accessories for women, such as handbags, belts, jewelry, cosmetic cases, scarves, and shoes, as well as sleepwear and eyewear. He branched out into home furnishings with brand-name furniture, tableware, crystal stemware, decorative fabrics and accents, wallpaper, bedding, rugs, and other items. He also built upon his menswear line with hosiery, suits, ties, sport coats, and trousers. In 2004, he launched O Oscar, a line of low-priced women's sportswear, with no item selling for more than $100.

In 2004, de la Renta relinquished his position as chief executive officer of his fashion house to his son-in-law Alex Bolen. He retained his title as chairman of the board, continued to design all house collections, and remained extremely active in his multiple enterprises, which include boutiques in New York City; Manhasset, New York; Bal Harbour, Florida; Las Vegas; Los Angeles; and Dallas. By 2011, de la Renta divided his time between two large estates: a fruit plantation called Casa de Madera in the Dominican Republic and a mansion in Connecticut.

SIGNIFICANCE

Throughout his long career as a fashion designer, Oscar de la Renta earned a reputation as a trendsetter. His clothing has been the first choice among many high-profile celebrities, including First Ladies Nancy Reagan, Hillary Clinton, and Laura Bush; model Kate Moss; and actors Marisa Berenson, Claudine Auger, Penelope Cruz, and Sarah Jessica Parker. Recognized for his many contributions to fashion, de la Renta has won multiple industry honors. In 1990, he received the CFDA Lifetime Achievement Award, and in 2000 and 2007 he was named Women's Wear Designer of the Year. He is also a double winner of the American Fashion Critics' Award and was inducted into the organization's Hall of Fame in 1973. In 1995, he received the American Society of Perfumes' Living Legend Award; in 2001, he was honored with a bronze plaque on Seventh Avenue in New York City's fashion center. The country of his birth has likewise honored him, both for his work in fashion and for his philanthropic efforts, such as his contributions to the building of a school in Punta Cana. He was awarded the Dominican Republic's Order of Juan Pablo Duarte and the Order of Cristóbal Colón. De la Renta has also worked for numerous charitable causes in the United States and has served on the boards of the Metropolitan Opera and New Yorkers for Children.

Jack Ewing

FURTHER READING

Booth, Nancy M. *Perfumes, Splashes, and Colognes: Discovering and Crafting Your Personal Fragrances*. North Adams, Mass.: Storey, 1997. A how-to book that discusses the pros and cons of various scents, including the commercial creations of de la Renta.

Darraj, Susan Muaddi. *Oscar de la Renta*. New York: Chelsea House, 2010. This illustrated book is intended for young adults and focuses on the impact of de la Renta's upbringing and outlook on his work.

Lomba, Modesto, Candy Pratts, and Oscar de la Renta. *Geography of Spanish Fashion*. Madrid: T.F. Editores, 2010. This illustrated book with text in English compares and contrasts the creations of more than twenty-five fashion designers of Hispanic heritage.

Mower, Sarah. *Oscar: The Style, Inspiration and Life of Oscar de la Renta*. New York: Assouline, 2002. This lavish book contains a profusion of photographs to illustrate the designer's biography, lifestyle, clothing, and the people who wear his brand.

See also: Carolina Herrera; Narciso Rodriguez.

JANE L. DELGADO

Cuban-born activist, psychologist, and entrepreneur

As the first female president and chief executive officer of the National Alliance for Hispanic Health, Delgado is an outspoken advocate in the Hispanic community on healthcare issues. She was instrumental in leading the first research efforts to study how Hispanic individuals differ in their healthcare needs from people of other ethnic backgrounds.

Latino heritage: Cuban
Born: June 17, 1953; Havana, Cuba
Areas of achievement: Activism; psychology; business

EARLY LIFE

Jane L. Delgado (dehl-GAH-doh) was born to Lucila Aurora Navarro Delgado, a factory worker, on June 17,

1953. Her mother emigrated with Delgado and her sister from Cuba to Brooklyn, New York, in 1955. Delgado credits her mother as a role model who instilled important educational and life lessons. Because she spoke only a little English, Delgado initially struggled in school but was able to learn quickly. She graduated high school two years early and at the age of sixteen enrolled at the State University of New York at New Paltz. Delgado graduated with a bachelor of science degree in 1973.

While still enrolled in school, Delgado began working for the Children's Television Workshop, first as the assistant to the auditor and then as children's talent coordinator on *Sesame Street* (1973-1975). In 1975, Delgado earned master of arts degrees in personality psychology and social psychology from New York University. She then attended the State University of New York at Stony Brook for a doctorate in clinical psychology, which she earned in 1981. She concurrently earned a master of science degree in urban policy sciences from Stony Brook's W. Averell Harriman School for Management and Policy.

Life's Work

During her doctoral work, Delgado joined the U.S. Department of Health and Human Services in 1979. She served as a senior policy analyst and dealt with national health issues. She cowrote a report on minority health in 1985, demonstrating a lack of health data—such as on life expectancy, adult-onset chronic diseases, and birth defects—in the Hispanic population compared with other ethnic groups.

In 1985, Delgado became the first Latina to serve as president and chief executive officer of the National Alliance for Hispanic Health (NAHH), formerly known as the Coalition of Spanish-Speaking Mental Health Organizations. The NAHH is the nation's oldest and largest Hispanic nonprofit organization serving the community's health needs. Delgado oversees the organization's national staff and operations. In 1987, she and the NAHH used the aforementioned report on health data disparities to convince the National Center for Health Statistics to collect health care information on the Hispanic population, specifically Mexican Americans, Puerto Ricans, and Cuban Americans. The Hispanic Health and Nutrition Examination Survey (HHANES) findings were the first published series of scientific journal articles related to Hispanic health, socioeconomic, and demographic data. These articles were of paramount importance in allowing national and community policy and program changes to target Hispanic individuals.

National Coalition of Hispanic Health and Human Services Organization

The mission of the National Alliance for Hispanic Health (NAHH), also known as the National Coalition of Hispanic Health and Human Services Organization, is to improve the health and well-being of the Hispanic community. The NAHH, led by Jane L. Delgado since 1985, provides services to more than 15 million individuals annually. The organization advocates for comprehensive health care, promotes cultural education, and increases public knowledge and awareness of Hispanic health issues. The NAHH conducts research and provides information to individuals through community groups, universities, foundations, and government agencies. Some NAHH programs include Su Familia Helpline, a national bilingual family health information service; Cuidando con Cariño, a phone line to provide information on end-of-life care issues; a Medicare Part D hotline for insurance questions; and ¡Vive to Vida!, an exercise program.

In 2000, Delgado made philanthropy a focus for the NAHH. The organization also emphasizes education in the Hispanic community. In 2008, it announced the NAHH/Merck Ciencia Hispanic Scholars Program, which awards annual scholarships to Hispanic students pursuing science, technology, engineering, or math. The NAHH was named one of the best nonprofit organizations for which to work by *The NonProfit Times* in 2010. Truly committed to health, the NAHH does not accept funding from alcohol or tobacco companies.

Delgado is passionate about improving environmental health. Under the NAHH, Delgado has sponsored programs such as the Health and Environment Action Network, which aims to clean up the nation's dirtiest cities by providing children with environmental monitors that electronically track pollutant data. In 2009, Delgado became the first Latina appointed to the board of directors of the Mickey Leland National Urban Air Toxics Research Center (NUATRC), a research facility focused on air quality. She serves on the Environmental Protection Agency's Clean Air Act advisory council and is a founding board member of the Ocean Awareness Project, which provides community education regarding the ocean and environmental factors affecting it.

In addition to environmental health, Delgado and the NAHH have focused their efforts on health insurance for the uninsured, publicly backing President Barack Obama's health-care reform package. Delgado is a member of the Advisory Panel on Medicare Education and the national advisory council for Rosalynn Carter's Task Force on Mental Health. She is an adviser to the March of Dimes and the American Academy of Family Physicians. She serves on the boards of the Kresge Foundation, Patient Safety Institute, Lovelace Respiratory Research Institute, and the Alaska Native Heritage Center in Anchorage. Delgado also advocates for the use of computers and technology in health care.

Delgado has written several books on Hispanic health. *¡Salud! A Latina's Guide to Total Health* (1997) is the first health book written by and for the Hispanic female population. She also published *The Latina Guide to Health: Consejos and Caring Answers* (2009). Delgado attempts to present medical information in an upbeat and understandable manner when describing conditions that are of particular concern to Hispanic populations.

The numerous awards bestowed to Delgado include the Food and Drug Administration Commissioner's Special Citation (1995), Community Leadership Award from the Puerto Rican Family Institute (1996), and the 2004 National Hispanic Woman of the Year Award. She has twice been named by *Hispanic Business* to its list of One Hundred Most Influential Hispanics in the United States (1998 and 2002). Delgado resides in Washington, D.C., with her husband, Mark A. Steo, and daughter, Elizabeth Ann Steo.

SIGNIFICANCE

Delgado has done groundbreaking work, from her early push to colect health statistics on the Hispanic population to her books that translate this research into advice for the common reader. She works tirelessly on issues for which she has a passion and has dedicated many years to the NAHH. Delgado aims to make inclusiveness a norm by mentoring young individuals of all backgrounds at the organization. She also has reached out to a younger generation by blogging her thoughts and comments on important topics on the NAHH Web site.

Janet Ober Berman

FURTHER READING

Delgado, Jane L. *The Latina Guide to Health: Consejos and Caring Answers*. New York: Newmarket Press, 2009. Focusing on pertinent medical findings in the Hispanic population, such as incidences of mental health disorders and other chronic diseases.

_______. *¡Salud! A Latina's Guide to Total Health*. Rev. ed. New York: HarperCollins, 2002. This new edition of Delgado's first book details the significant health challenges facing Hispanic women, including topics such as pregnancy, menopause, cancer, diabetes, and exercise.

_______, et al. "Hispanic Health and Nutrition Examination Survey: Methodological Considerations." *American Journal of Public Health* 80 Supplement. (December, 1990): 6-10. The first publication of the HHANES findings with the original data regarding health issues specifically related to the Hispanic population.

Metger, Raphael, et al. "Environmental Health and Hispanic Children." *Environmental Health Perspectives* 103, Supplement 6. (1995): 25-32. An NAHH research article on the importance of studying environmental health hazards in the Hispanic population.

See also: Martha Bernal; Richard Henry Carmona; Antonia Novello.

DOLORES DEL RÍO

Mexican-born actor

Del Río was one of the few Latin American film stars to attain success in Hollywood in the early years of filmmaking. She appeared in English- and Spanish-language films from the silent era until the late 1970's without compromising her Mexican identity, her Spanish name, or her personal values.

Latino heritage: Mexican
Born: August 3, 1905; Durango, Mexico
Died: April 11, 1983; Newport Beach, California
Also known as: María de los Dolores Asúnsolo y López Negrete; Lolita; Chatita
Area of achievement: Film

Dolores del Rio. (AP Photo)

Early Life

Dolores del Río (doh-LOH-rehs dehl REEH-oh) was the only daughter of an aristocratic Mexican family of Spanish ancestry. Her father was a banker, and her uncle was Francisco Madero, the president of Mexico. She studied French and took dancing lessons in her youth. However, her family lost its wealth and social position during the Mexican Revolution, and they moved to Mexico City. At this time, del Río was shy and did not appreciate her brown skin. When she was sixteen, she married a friend of the family, Jaime Martínez del Río y Viñen, who took her on a two-year honeymoon to Europe, where she was introduced to dignitaries and Spanish royalty. The couple, however, divorced in 1928 after del Río suffered a miscarriage.

While she was married, del Río and her husband became friends with Edwin Carewe, a Hollywood producer and director, and this relationship launched her acting career. Del Río's goal was to become an actor in both Mexican and Hollywood films. At this time, she acknowledged she could fail to attain this goal, but she would lose nothing if she failed, while if she succeeded "it will be for me the epitome of my artistic endeavors and for Mexico, a small glory."

Life's Work

In 1925, del Río starred in her first American film, *Joanna*, directed by Carewe. Her appearance received good reviews, and she was dubbed the "female Valentino," a reference to actor Rudolph Valentino. She appeared in several other silent films, including *What Price Glory?* (1926), *Resurrection* (1927), and *The Loves of Carmen* (1927). However, her rising career suffered with the introduction of sound because Hollywood executives thought her heavily-accented English would be a detriment to their productions. As a result, she had insignificant roles in many forgettable films of the 1930's. In addition, she refused to participate in *Viva Villa* (1934), because she deemed this film's depiction of Mexican revolutionary general Pancho Villa to be "anti-Mexican."

In 1930, del Río married Cedric Gibbons, an art director and production designer at Metro-Goldwyn-Mayer studios, but this marriage ended in divorce in 1941, in part because of her relationship with actor Orson Welles. (She married her third husband, theater producer Lewis Riley, in 1959, and the couple remained together until her death.)

With her Hollywood career in ruins, del Río returned to Mexico in 1942. The following year, her first Spanish-language film, *Flor silvestre*, was released. This film, made in Mexico and directed by Emilio Fernández, was an unexpected success, making del Río the most famous film star in Mexico. She made several other films with Fernández, cinematographer Gabriel Figueroa, writer Mauricio Magdaleno, and actor Pedro Armendáriz in the 1940's, including *María Candelaria* (1944), *The Abandoned* (1945), and *Bugambilia* (1945). Del Río starred in many other Mexican films during the 1940's and 1950's, for which she received three Silver Ariels, the Mexican equivalent of the Academy Award: in 1946 for *The Abandoned*, in 1952 for *Doña Perfecta* (1951), and in 1954 for *El niño y la niebla* (1953).

In 1954, del Río was cast in the American film *Broken Lance*. However, the U.S. government denied her permission to enter the country because of her alleged support of international communism, and actor Katy Jurado took over her role. Del Río was not allowed to return to the United States until 1956, when she starred in the play *Anastacia.* During the following two years she appeared on American television in the programs *Schlitz Playhouse* and *The United States Steel Hour*. In 1960, she starred with singer Elvis Presley in the film *Flaming Star*. She continued to make both American and Mexican films until the late 1970's.

In 1975, Del Río received a Special Golden Ariel in recognition of her fifty-year acting career. She retired from acting in 1978 and began to paint, write, and manage her financial affairs and real estate. She continued to work occasionally in theater, radio, television, and as a judge at film festivals..

Significance

Dolores del Río's film career spanned six decades. To many who knew her or saw her films, she represented the epitome of Latina beauty, talent, grace, and perseverance.

María Eugenia Trillo

Further Reading

Agrasánchez, Jr., Rogelio. *Mexican Movies in the United States: A History of the Films, Theaters and Audiences, 1920-1960*. Jefferson, N.C.: McFarland, 2006. Discusses the sociopolitical, economic, and historical elements of Mexican films, both films made in Mexico and Hollywood films with Mexican actors.

Carr, Larry. *More Fabulous Faces: The Evolution and Metamorphosis of Dolores del Rio, Myrna Loy, Carole Lombard, Bette Davis and Katharine Hepburn*. New York: Doubleday, 1979. Examines the transformation of five women, including del Río, into superstars, illustrating the changes in both physiognomy and character during their Hollywood careers.

De la Mora, Sergio. *Cinemachismo: Masculinities and Sexuality in Mexican Film*. Austin: University of Texas Press, 2006. A study of iconic, masculine, supermacho figures, as well as more recent representations of masculinity, such as gay men and transvestites.

Hershfield, Joanne. *The Invention of Dolores del Río*. Minneapolis: University of Minnesota Press, 2000. Uses del Río's career to examine Hollywood's racism and how film stars are sold as commodities.

Stock, Ann Marie, ed. *Framing Latin American Cinema: Contemporary Critical Perspectives*. Minneapolis: University of Minnesota Press, 1997. Examines the transnational status of contemporary cinema by focusing on films made in Mexico and Central and South America.

See also: José Ferrer; Katy Jurado; Fernando Lamas; Beatriz Noloesca; Gilbert Roland; César Romero; Lupe Velez.

Daniel DeSiga

American artist

DeSiga, a noted oil painter, muralist, and poster artist, often depicts migrant laborers in the sugar beet and asparagus fields in which he spent much of his childhood in Washington State's agricultural valleys.

Latino heritage: Mexican

Born: December 12, 1948; Walla Walla, Washington

Area of achievement: Art

Early Life

Daniel DeSiga was born on December 12, 1948, in rural Walla Walla, Washington. The son of migrant farmworkers of Mexican and American Indian heritage, he often worked alongside his parents in the fields of eastern Washington. Despite a high school counselor's claims that he was not intelligent enough to attend college, DeSiga earned a bachelor of fine arts degree from the University of Washington. He even later earned a scholarship, the Governor's Award for Academic Excellence.

Life's Work

DeSiga's art records the experiences of farm laborers, the sights, sounds, and smells of his early life: rising early, making tortillas for breakfast, and packing them as meals for work in the fields. One of his earliest murals was painted in the large main hallway of El Centro de la Raza, a social-service center in Seattle. It was installed in the center in the fall of 1972. DeSiga's signature work, the 18-by-45-foot mural spans the east wall. Two windows became Aztec eyes framing memories of stark lives: a farmworker crucified in a beet field; a huge tractor with a dollar sign on its grill and a laughing corpse at the controls; a monstrous harvesting machine with claws and talons; farmworkers laboring over the field, weeding with back-breaking short hoes.

As a young artist and student at the University of Washington in 1972, DeSiga, who had battled multiple sclerosis, found money for paint and scaffolding and went to work on the mural without being paid. Twenty-five years later, he returned as a famous painter and muralist to complete it, adding whales, dolphins, Aztec pyramids, racks of red and green chilies, and several other images, including (at the request of center personnel), the Chinese characters for "crisis," which also mean "opportunity."

DeSiga moved to Santa Fe in 1990, giving up a museum job in Fresno, California, to study for three years under Amado Peña, a Yaqui Indian with a well-known Southwest Native style. DeSiga regarded these as the happiest years of his life. He spent all of his money for the trip, threw his clothes into a corner of a friend's warehouse, and started preparing canvases. Peña discovered that DeSiga, who was starting over in his forties, had talent. Soon they were coproducing an American Indian-inspired version of Wolfgang Amadeus Mozart's *The Magic Flute* (1791) for the San Antonio Festival. Peña designed the sets, while DeSiga made the costumes.

DeSiga later returned to Toppenish, in the Yakima Valley of eastern Washington, where he opened a studio and gallery and cared for his elderly parents before their deaths. One of his largest works, *El Sarape* (2001), painted on a store in Toppenish, Washington, neighboring the Yakima Valley Farm Workers Clinic, depicts these themes. This mural depicts the first Mexican workers who arrived in Toppenish in 1942. He is married to Xochitl Flores.

DeSiga has created more than twenty murals all over the United States. His murals can be seen in several locations around Washington State, including works installed at the Capital Theater in Yakima (2004), the Toppenish Mural Society (2004), the Wa-He-Lut Indian School of Olympia (1998), and the state Employment Security Department in Olympia (1980). His art has been exhibited at the San Francisco Museum of Modern Art, the Wight Art Gallery at the University of California at Los Angeles, and the Denver Art Museum, among other venues. His works also have been shown at the Smithsonian National Museum of Modern Art, the Albuquerque Museum, the San Francisco Museum of Modem Art, the National Museum of American Art, the El Paso Museum of Art, the Bronx Museum of the Arts, and the San Antonio Museum of Art.

Significance

DeSiga's vibrant artwork depicts the lives of farmworkers with dignity and beauty that does not gloss over the bleak and brutal conditions under which they often lived and worked. His achievements are not limited to murals and paintings; he also has designed posters, book covers, and costumes for theater productions.

Bruce E. Johansen

Further Reading

"Daniel DeSiga, The Artist," *Latino Northwest* 3, no. 5 (August-September 2001): 16. A detailed sketch of DeSiga's life as an artist, focusing on his murals in Washington State.

Finch, George. "Well-Known Hispanic Artist Opens Gallery in Toppenish." *Yakima Valley Business Times*, September 10, 2004, p. 6. Offers a profile of DeSiga's life in Washington's Yakima Valley, from youth to his return after age fifty.

Villanueva, Margaret. "*El Sarape* Mural of Toppenish: Unfolding the Yakima Valley's Bracero Legacy." In *Memory, Community, and Activism: Mexican Migration and Labor in the Pacific Northwest*, edited by Jerry García and Gilberto García. East Lansing: Michigan State University Press, 2005. Offers a biography of DeSiga and details the process by which he designed and painted his *El Sarape* mural.

Wan, Tiffany. "Viva la Seattle! A Survey of What Mexican Americans Have Given Seattle—Besides Great Cinco de Mayo Parties." *SeattleMet* (May, 2010). Covers DeSiga's and other artists' roles in Seattle's growing ethnic diversity.

See also: Alfredo M. Arreguín; Judith F. Baca; José Antonio Burciaga; Barbara Carrasco; Leo Tanguma; Jesse Treviño.

Donna de Varona

American swimmer, sportscaster, and activist

De Varona won two Olympic gold medals for swimming and went on to become a successful television sportscaster. She was also an advocate for increased opportunities and equal treatment for women athletes.

Latino heritage: Mexican

Born: April 26, 1947; San Diego, California

Also known as: Donna Elizabeth de Varona-Pinto

Areas of achievement: Sports; journalism; social issues

Early Life

Donna Elizabeth de Varona-Pinto, better known as Donna de Varona (DON-ah deev-ah-ROHN- ah), was born in San Diego, California, on April 26, 1947. She was one of four children born to David de Varona, an insurance agent, and Martha Smith de Varona, a librarian. Her father was a Hall of Fame rower and All American football player at the University of California. De Varona showed an active interest in sports from an early age and was a strong swimmer at the age of three.

When she was six the family moved to Lafayette, California, where she began school. She looked forward to playing Little League with her older brother, but because she was a girl, she was barred from any position except bat girl. Disappointed, de Varona turned to swimming, entering her first competition at the age of nine. Small for her age, de Varona, who was limited by the family's tight budget, was moved from club to club and coach to coach and received only minimal training. As she demonstrated her skill, she advanced to the Berkeley Swim Club and better coaching. She specialized in the four-hundred-meter medley that included freestyle swimming, the butterfly stroke, the sidestroke, and the backstroke. While attending Santa Clara High School, de Varona practiced swimming six hours a day.

De Varona was the youngest player to compete in the 1960 Olympic Games. She won two gold medals at the 1964 Olympics, one in the 400-meter medley and another on the freestyle relay team. That year, the Associated Press and United Press International voted de Varona the most outstanding female athlete in the world.

In 1965, de Varona retired from competitive swimming, having set eighteen world records and thirty-seven individual swimming records. She entered the University of California at Los Angeles, which had no athletic programs for women. There also were no college swimming scholarships for women. Needing work, she used her Olympic experience to become the first female sportscaster, at age seventeen, for ABC's *Wide World of Sports* program.

Life's Work

De Varona began her sportscasting career by providing swimming commentary with broadcaster Jim McKay on *Wide World of Sports.* Her role on the program quickly expanded to include reporting and providing analysis. She joined NBC from 1978 to 1983, appearing on *Sportsworld* and providing sports segements for *Today.* De Varona was the first woman to host the Olympic Games on television, an assignment that continued on a regular basis for twenty years. She covered the 1980 Olympics in Moscow; joined a team of journalists from TNT at the 1998 winter games in Nagano, Japan; and covered the 2000 Olympics from Sydney, Australia, for NBC.

Donna de Varona. (AP Photo)

An outspoken advocate of swimming and its benefits, DeVarona, with Barry Tarshis, wrote *Hydro-Aerobics* (1984). In 1991, she was given an Emmy Award for her coverage of an athlete competing in the Special Olympics. She also wrote, coproduced, and hosted a one-hour ABC Olympics television special, *The Keeper of the Flame,* that was nominated for an Emmy Award.

In 2000, DeVarona sued ABC for $50 million, alleging that the network fired her in 1998 for "failing to appeal to a male demographic of ages eighteen to thirty-nine." DeVarona charged the network with age and gender discrimination, maintaining that older male broadcasters, such as Frank Gifford, were given preferential treatment. She returned to ABC Sports as reporter and analyst after the suit was settled out of court in 2002.

Significance

In addition to being a champion swimmer who set new records in this sport, Donna de Varona was a passionate advocate for equal athletic opportunities for women, as evidenced in her response to the adoption of Title IX in 1972. Title IX of the Higher Education Act is a federal law prohibiting discrimination on the basis of sex in school athletics and other educational activities. After the law's passage, de Varona joined tennis player Billie Jean King in founding the Women's Sports Foundation, an organization dedicated to the advancement of women athletes. Her lawsuit against ABC for its alleged sexism was a significant step toward gender equality.

Mary Hurd

FURTHER READING

Griffin, Pat. *Strong Women, Deep Closets: Lesbian and Homophobia in Sport.* Champaign, Ill.: Human Kinetics, 1998. Meticulously researched book based on extensive interviews with lesbian athletes, coaches, and administrators who attempt to combat the "sexual predator" image promoted by stereotypes and an institutionalized sports system.

Pemberton, Cynthia Lee A. *More than a Game: One Woman's Fight for Gender Equity in Sport.* Foreword by Donna de Varona. Holliston, Mass.: Northeastern Press, 2002. Autobiographical account of Pemberton's six-year ordeal to secure implementation of Title IX at Linfield College in Oregon. The case made national headlines, as Pemberton was charged with intention to destroy the school's football team.

Suggs, Welch. *A Place on the Team: The Triumph and Tragedy of Title IX.* Princeton, N.J.: Princeton University Press, 2006. Detailed history of Title IX of the Higher Education Act (1972), the law that mandated that women athletes be treated the same as men.

Women's Sports Foundation. http://www.womenssportsfoundation.org. Provides information on the organization founded by de Varona and Billie Jean King in the 1970's.

See also: Rosie Casals; Rebecca Lobo; Nancy Lopez; Diana Taurasi.

CAMERON DIAZ

American actor and model

A popular actor who started her career as a model, Diaz has starred in numerous hit films and lent her voice to the animated motion picture Shrek *(2001) and its sequels. She also has appeared alongside actors including Tom Cruise and Julia Roberts.*

Latino heritage: Cuban

Born: August 30, 1972; San Diego, California

Also known as: Cameron Michelle Diaz

Areas of achievement: Acting; fashion

EARLY LIFE

Cameron Michelle Diaz (DEE-ahz) was born on August 30, 1972, in San Diego, California, to Billie and Emilio Diaz. Billie's ancestry is German, English, and Cherokee; while Emilio was a second-generation Cuban American who was born in Los Angeles County and worked as a foreman for an oil company. He died in 2008. Diaz identifies herself as a Cuban American but is not fluent in Spanish. She has two older siblings, a sister and a brother.

Diaz was raised in Southern California. After meeting a modeling talent scout at a party, she joined Elite Model Management at age sixteen. Diaz modeled for Calvin Klein, Coca-Cola, and Levi's and appeared in magazines such as *Mademoiselle.* She was on the cover of *Seventeen* in July, 1990, the year she graduated from Long Beach Polytechnic High School. From ages sixteen to twenty-one, Diaz traveled and lived all around the world, including stops in Paris, Japan, Australia, Mexico, and Morocco. Upon returning to the United States, she turned her attention to acting.

In 1994, Diaz made her film debut as the female lead in the film *The Mask* alongside comedian Jim Carrey. The film was a major commercial success and launched her career as an actor, allowing Diaz to take on a number of roles immediately following its release.

LIFE'S WORK

After starring in *The Mask*, Diaz appeared in a series of independent films, including *The Last Supper* (1995), *Feeling Minnesota* (1996), and *A Life Less Ordinary* (1997). In 1997, she costarred in *My Best Friend's Wedding* as the romantic rival of established star Julia Roberts, a role that burnished her growing reputation. The next year, 1998, she appeared in her largest role to date

Cameron Diaz. (AP Photo)

in *There's Something About Mary*. In the film, a risqué comedy, Diaz starred as a woman ineptly pursued by various suitors. She received a Golden Globe nomination for Best Actress in a Musical or Comedy for the role.

In 1999, Diaz received a second nomination from the Golden Globes and one from the Screen Actors Guild for Best Supporting Actress for her role in *Being John Malkovich*. That year, she also was praised for her performance as the owner and general manager of a professional football team in *Any Given Sunday*. Among other awards, she won an ALMA (American Latino Media Arts) for Outstanding Actress in a Feature Film. In 2000 and 2003, Diaz continued her successful run with starring roles in the film adaptations of the classic television show *Charlie's Angels*. This work was her entry into action films and established her as a sex symbol.

On the heels of her appearance in *Charlie's Angels*, Diaz voiced a lead role in the animated film *Shrek* (2001). The fairy-tale spoof, which spawned several sequels, won international praise from audiences of all ages. She continued to work regularly throughout the 2000's, often in romantic comedies such as *The Holiday* (2006) and *What Happens in Vegas* (2008). However, Diaz also did more ambitious work in films such as *Gangs of New York* (2002) and *My Sister's Keeper* (2009). In 2010, *Forbes* magazine reported that Diaz was tied with Reese Witherspoon as the second-highest paid female actor in Hollywood after Diaz was paid $32 million dollars for her role in *Knight and Day*.

As Diaz's fame has grown, her relationships have become highly publicized. She has been romantically linked to actor Matt Dillon, singer and actor Justin Timberlake, and baseball player Alex Rodriguez.

SIGNIFICANCE

Diaz is a visible representative of the success of the Cuban community in the United States. A popular and versatile actor known for her comic timing as well as her beauty, she has appeared in films in several diverse genres and commands among the highest salaries in the film industry.

Fawn-Amber Montoya

FURTHER READING

Brown, Laura. "Cameron Diaz: Woman on Top." *Harper's Bazaar* (August, 2010). Profile covering Diaz's career, approach to roles, and perception of herself.

Marcovitz, Hal. "Cameron Diaz: Film Star." In *Cuban Americans*. Philadelphia: Mason Crest, 2009. Brief biography and overview of Diaz's career.

Silverman, Stephen. "Cameron Diaz, Something Special." In *Funny Ladies: The Women Who Make Us Laugh*. New York: Abrams, 1999. This short essay highlights Diaz's film work in romantic comedies in the 1990's.

Sullivan, Robert. "Sunshine Superwoman." *Vogue* (June, 2009). Long article offering insights into Diaz's personality, upbringing, and environmentalism.

See also: Jessica Alba; Catherine Bach; Lynda Carter; Eva Longoria; Rosie Pérez; Zoë Saldana; Raquel Welch.

Gwendolyn Díaz

Argentine-born educator and author

Díaz is a professor whose research has focused on Argentine feminist literature, examining the power that Argentine women use to combat the sociopolitical forces in their country. She is also the director of an important annual conference on Latina literature, art, and identity.

Latino heritage: Argentinean

Born: July 25, 1950; Buenos Aires, Argentina

Also known as: Gwendolyn Josie Díaz; Gwendolyn Díaz-Ridgeway

Areas of achievement: Education; literature; women's rights

Early Life

Gwendolyn Josie Díaz (DEE-ahz) was born and raised in Buenos Aires, Argentina. Although she grew up in a traditional patriarchal, religious family, she was offered a lot of encouragement and support, especially when it came to attaining her education. Díaz learned at an early age that education was the key to empowerment and freedom

Díaz received her higher education in the United States, earning a B.A. degree from Baylor University in 1971, She then attended the University of Texas at Austin, receiving a M.A. in 1976 and a Ph.D. in Spanish language and literature, with a concentration on French, in 1981. Díaz initially focused the research for her doctoral dissertation on Argentine women writers. As she was conducting her research, she realized that it was important for women to attain power, especially in Argentina, where women often struggled to retain control as they fought to avoid becoming victims of the Dirty War (1976-1983). Díaz's research stemmed from a desire to empower women, which she believed could be accomplished by writing about the novels of Argentine women writers from various social classes.

After she was teaching at St. Mary's University in San Antonio, Texas, Díaz expanded the focus of her research to include theories of why women write, what they write about, and how their work helps the social status of women. As she continued her research, Latin American women authors and scholars were surprised to discover that someone was focusing their research on them, especially since Argentine scholarship continued to be dominated by machismo in the 1980's.

Life's Work

Díaz is fluent in Spanish, English, French, and Portuguese and publishes her research in both English and Spanish. She has written, cowritten, and edited six books focusing on various aspects of Argentine literature, including *Páginas de Marta Lynch: Seleccionadas por la autora* (1983), *La palabra en vilo: Narrativa de Luisa Valenzuela* (1996), *Luisa Valenzuela sin mascara* (2002), *Women and Power in Argentine Fiction: Stories, Interviews, and Critical Essays* (2009); *Mujer y poder en la literatura Argentina: Relatos, entrevistas y ensayos críticos* (2009); and *Texto, contexto y postexto: Aproximaciones a la obra literaria de Luisa Valenzuela* (2010).

Her own research on empowerment and Argentine women writers led her to develop the Latina Letters Conference on Literature and Identity at St. Mary's University in 1995. The conference provided a forum for Díaz to share her research interests, while also educating students and the community about Latina authors. Some of the authors who have participated in the conference include Sandra Cisneros, Denise Chávez, Ana Castillo, Rosario Ferre, Julia Alvarez, Cristina García, and Gloria Anzaldúa. A decade after its founding, the conference changed its name to the Las Américas Letters Series in the Arts.

The Las Américas Letters conference allowed Díaz to focus her research on Latina writers, artists, community activists, and scholars from all over Central America, South America, and Puerto Rico. She is particularly interested in student involvement in the conference, hoping students will present their own work while meeting and sharing ideas with other writers and activists.

In 2011, Díaz taught world literature and literary theory at St. Mary's University, where she was a professor of English, the director of the English literature and language graduate program, coordinator of Latin American graduate programs, and the director of Las Américas Letters. She was also working on establishing double degree programs to enable students to earn degrees from both St. Mary's University and a university in Argentina.

Díaz has received a Fulbright scholarship, a Carnegie-Mellon fellowship, the St. Mary's University Distinguished Professor Award, and an honorary professorship from the Universidad Católica de Salta, Argentina. She has spoken at conferences in the United States, Latin America, and Europe and has served on the executive committees of the South Central Modern Language Association and the Asociación Internacional de Literatura Femenina Hispánica. In 2011, she began her term as president of the South Central Modern Language Association.

Significance

A noted scholar in the field of Latin American literature, Díaz has furthered the knowledge and understanding of works by women writers from South America, Central America, and the United States. She has given prominence to writers whose voice has often been ignored by the patriarchal attitudes of male writers and critics. As the founder of Las Américas Letters Series in the Arts at St. Mary's University in San Antonio, she has brought together women writers, students, and community members, enabling them to share their works and ideas and to discuss, analyze, and celebrate what it means to be Latina in America and Latin America.

Margaret E. Cantú-Sánchez

Further Reading

Díaz, Gwendolyn. "A Lifelong Passion for Empowering Women." *St. Mary's Blue and Gold* (Fall, 2004): 10-11. In this article, Díaz describes how her initial research led her to develop the Latina Letters conference, which was later transformed and expanded into the Lás Américas Letters conference.

Téllez, Lesley. "Marking a Decade of Latina Letters." *Conexión*, July 7, 2005, p. 7A. Téllez interviews Díaz about the origins of the Latina Letters conference and how it has grown in popularity because of its unique focus on Latina women writers and its ability to adapt and expand.

Villa, Marissa. "Las Américas Series Offers a Week to Tango." *Conexión*, March 5, 2009, p. CX6. Villa interviews Díaz about the Las Américas Letters conference on the tango. Díaz explains that exposure to art forms, including dances like the tango, can ultimately enable students and the community to become aware of a variety of cultures.

See also: Edna Acosta-Belén; Juan Bruce-Novoa; Angela Valenzuela; Patricia Zavella.

Henry F. Díaz

Cuban-born scientist

A research climatologist working for the U.S. National Oceanic and Atmospheric Administration (NOAA), Díaz made fundamental discoveries related to global climate variation and its impact on water resources in the western United States and the Americas.

Latino heritage: Cuban

Born: July 15, 1948; Santiago de Cuba, Cuba

Also known as: Henry Frank Díaz

Area of achievement: Science and technology

Early Life

Henry Frank Díaz (HEHN-ree frank DEE-ahz) was born on July 15, 1948, the son of Francisco Díaz, an attorney, and Maria Vias Díaz. He attended primary school in Santiago de Cuba, Cuba. In 1959, his family moved to Havana, where he attended lower secondary school and began to take an interest in geography and the peculiarities of weather in the tropics. As the impact of Fidel Castro's new Cuban regime became more apparent, Díaz's parents sent him to live with his uncle in New Jersey in 1961. The remaining family members immigrated to Miami in 1965, and Díaz joined them there, graduating from high school in 1967. He then matriculated at Florida State University, where he formally pursued his growing fascination with weather, earning a degree in meteorology in 1971. He obtained an M.S. in atmospheric science at the University of Miami in 1974. That same year he married Marla Cremin.

After earning his master's degree, he landed a meteorological position with the Environmental Data Center at the National Oceanic and Atmospheric Administration (NOAA) in Washington, D.C. In 1975, with his wife and young son, he moved to Asheville, North Carolina, to accept a job as a climate analyst at NOAA's National Climatic Data Center. Working daily with large-scale data sets and searching for weather patterns heightened what would become his lifelong interest in climate variability and the factors that influence it. His interest led him to seek an assignment at NOAA's Climate Research Program in Boulder, Colorado, in 1980, and shortly thereafter NOAA provided a full scholarship and release time for Díaz to pursue a Ph.D. in geography and climatology at the University of Colorado at Boulder. He was appointed acting director of the Climate Research Program in 1984 and earned his Ph.D. from the University of Colorado in 1985.

Life's Work

Already an accomplished and prolific climatological researcher before completing his doctorate, Díaz spent the next twenty-two years primarily at the Climate Diagnostics Center of the Research Laboratories of NOAA in Boulder until his retirement in 2007, enjoying the environment the area provided for an avid outdoorsman. At the same time he was also an adjunct associate professor in the University of Colorado's Department of Geography, as well as an active member of the university's Cooperative Institute for Research in Environmental Sciences. For brief periods he was a visiting scientist at Scripps Institution of Oceanography (summer of 1982), the University of Massachusetts at Amherst (1988-1989), the Swiss Federal Institute of Technology in Zurich (1994), and the University of Arizona (2003).

In his work, Diaz has patiently and thoroughly examined records and markers of climate change, including temperature and weather readings recorded by persons throughout written history, ice core and dendroclimatatological (tree ring) data, evidence from fossils, and massive amounts of information on weather and climate that has accumulated in the modern era through the use of computerized probes and detection devices. He is undoubtedly one of the world's leading authorities on El Niño, the sudden appearance for a few weeks in December of a warm current of water off the Peruvian coast instead of the normally cold waters that rise to the surface; this change alters the entire circulation pattern of the Pacific Ocean, which, in turn, causes global changes in climate. Díaz is also a world-recognized expert on the impact of climate on water resources, focusing on the effects of climate change on the American West. His written works on this subject include the monograph *Climate and Water: Transboundary Challenges in the Americas* (2011), which he coedited with Barbara J. Morehouse.

His painstaking work, conducted in collaboration with colleagues throughout the world, has resulted in the accumulation of reliable records and profiles of climate change for various regions of the world and, ultimately, the entire world. Some of his studies have focused on detailed climatic variability across many years, while others have concentrated on climate change during numerous centuries. Díaz's findings became the basis for long-term studies that furthered scientists' understanding of the world's climate and laid the foundation for the work that solidified scientific concerns about the impact of human-induced climate change and global warming. Díaz wrote numerous works about climate extremes and their radical impacts on society, a theme examined in a book he coedited with Richard J. Murnane, *Climate Extremes and Society* (2008). He has been a frequent speaker at conferences, at which he often discusses the work of other scientists in the field of climate change. He also has collaborated with other scientists to publish numerous papers, and his work is widely cited in his field. Díaz has mentored a host of students and served on various doctoral committees over the years, helping a younger generation of climatologists to master knowledge of his field. He has been a member of the American Meteorological Society, and his work was honored in 2009, when he received NOAA's Distinguished Career Award.

Significance

A prolific, careful, and tenacious climatological researcher, Díaz devoted his professional life to the study of climate fluctuations during various periods of time, with a particular focus on climatic extremes and their effects on past, present, and future societies.

Dennis W. Cheek

Further Reading

Díaz, Henry F., ed. *Climate Variability and Change in the High Elevation Regions: Past, Present, and Future.* New York: Springer, 2010. Collection of papers, many coauthored by Díaz, about a topic that has long drawn his interest. These papers were initially presented at a seminar he organized at Davos, Switzerland.

Díaz, Henry F., and Barbara J. Morehouse, eds. *Climate and Water: Transboundary Challenges in the Americas*. New York: Springer, 2011. Collection of technical essays surveying all major aspects of Díaz's lifelong interest in the relationship between water and climate, with several essays coauthored by Díaz

Díaz, Henry F., and Richard J. Murnane, eds. *Climate Extremes and Society*. New York: Cambridge University Press, 2008. A collection of essays that reflects Díaz's longtime interest in the way climate change affects society in numerous areas, including commerce, agriculture, health, and migration.

See also: Margarita Colmenares; Arturo Gómez-Pompa; Eugenia Kalnay.

JUNOT DÍAZ

Dominican-born writer

Díaz's literary production has made him one of the most prominent contemporary Latino writers. His work has garnered wide-ranging critical and commercial success, and his honors include the Pulitzer Prize for literature in 2008, an achievement accomplished by only one Latino writer before him.

Latino heritage: Dominican

Born: December 31, 1968; Santo Domingo, Dominican Republic

Area of achievement: Literature

EARLY LIFE

Junot Díaz (JEW-noh DEE-ahz) was born on December 31, 1968, in the Villa Juana neighborhood of Santo Domingo, Dominican Republic. When Díaz was six years old, his family moved to Parlin, New Jersey. His mother worked on an assembly line and cleaned homes; his father, who had been a military policeman in the Dominican Republic, drove a forklift in New Jersey. Díaz has described his father's toughness and hypermasculinity as an important influence in his life and work. In interviews, Díaz has called his father a "trigamist" (referring to his father's extramarital relationships) and a "Little League dictator." Díaz was the third of his parents' five children.

As a child, Díaz developed a love of literature, spending a good deal of time in public libraries, although he was also social and encouraged to prove his masculinity by becoming involved in activities such as fighting. After graduating from high school, Díaz attended Kean College (now Kean University) for a year before transferring to Rutgers University, where he honed his creative writing and earned his English degree in 1992. During his college years, Díaz worked various jobs, including at a steel mill and delivering pool tables. He returned to the Dominican Republic for the first time after immigrating at the age of twenty-two, and later he began to visit the country regularly.

Díaz worked for Rutgers University Press before going on to graduate school. He earned his master of fine arts degree in creative writing from Cornell University in 1995. During that time, he began to work on the short stories that would become part of his short story collection *Drown*, which was published in 1996.

LIFE'S WORK

Drown is a collection of short stories unified by nine-year-old narrator Yunior. The stories are characterized by a gritty realism, lucid prose, striking immediacy, and electrifying language that includes both English and Spanish (the latter not differentiated by italics as in many other Latino texts), as well as a range of different registers and stylistic flourishes. Yunior has been described by Díaz as his alter ego and reappears in various incarnations in other short stories by Díaz and in his first novel. The stories are set in both the Dominican Republic and New Jersey and focuses on subjects including migration, poverty, family relationships, and adolescent struggles with belonging and emerging sexuality. Díaz's work met with considerable success and garnered him mainstream recognition as well as a two-book contract with Riverhead Books.

Although Díaz published several short stories in magazines, primarily in *The New Yorker*, after the publication of *Drown*, eleven years elapsed before he published his next book. His first novel, *The Brief and Wondrous Life of Oscar Wao* (2007), became even more successful than *Drown*. Díaz began working on the novel while living in Mexico City in an apartment adjoining

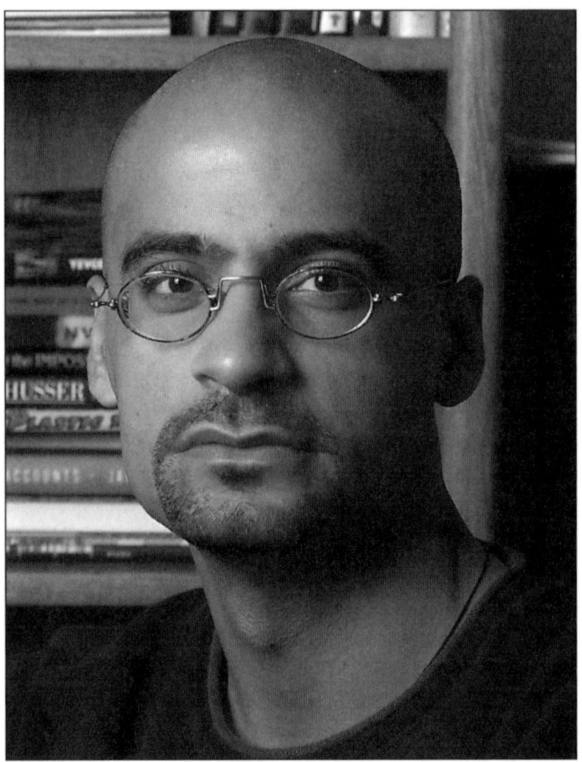

Junot Díaz. (AP Photo)

that of writer Francisco Goldman. At the time, Díaz was working on another novel, *Akira*, that he ultimately left unfinished.

The Brief and Wondrous Life of Oscar Wao began as a short story, published in *The New Yorker* in 2000, containing many of the most important elements of the novel. The 2007 novel marked a stylistic shift from Díaz's earlier work, embracing science fiction and fantasy and making extensive use of humor. The novel also demonstrates an intense focus on history. The central plot of the story focuses on Oscar, an obese Dominican "ghetto nerd" in New Jersey who is socially awkward but also a tragic hero. The narrator, Yunior, describes Oscar and his family, exploring connections between their lives and important elements of Dominican history.

Díaz has won numerous awards and fellowships for his literary work, including a Guggenheim Fellowship in 1999; the PEN/Malamud Award in 2002; the U.S.-Japan Creative Artist Fellowship (National Endowment for the Arts) in 2002; the Radcliffe Institute for Advanced Study Fellowship (Harvard University) in 2003; the Rome Prize from the American Academy of Arts and Letters in 2007; the John Sargent, Sr., First Novel Prize in 2007; the James Beard Foundation M. F. K. Fisher Distinguished Writing Award in 2008; the Dayton Literary Peace Prize for Fiction in 2008; and the Pulitzer Prize in fiction in 2008. Díaz was only the second Latino writer to win the Pulitzer in fiction; the first was Oscar Hijuelos in 1990. He was named one of the thirty-nine best Latin American writers under the age of thirty-nine by the Hay Festival Committee in Colombia. Díaz's books have been translated into at least a dozen languages. *The Brief and Wondrous Life of Oscar Wao* was named one of the best books of 2007 by several publications, including *Time* and *The New York Times*.

Díaz has taught at Syracuse University and joined the faculty at the Massachusetts Institute of Technology in 2002, later becoming the Rudge and Nancy Allen Professor of Writing. He was named distinguished fiction writer in residence with New York University's Creative Writing Department in 2010. Other activities include his work as a founder and participant in the Voices of Our Nations Arts Foundation, which holds summer workshops in San Francisco for developing writers of color; his work as fiction editor for *The Boston Review*; and his election to the Pulitzer Prize board in 2010.

The Brief and Wondrous Life of Oscar Wao

Junot Díaz's 2007 novel *The Brief and Wondrous Life of Oscar Wao* tells the story of Oscar de León (also known as Oscar Wao), an overweight and socially awkward Dominican youth growing up in New Jersey in the 1980's and 1990's. The novel also focuses on several members of Oscar's family: his sister, Lola; his mother, Belicia; and his grandfather, Abelard. Oscar is a tragic hero who seeks to understand and overcome the *fukú*, or curse, that has plagued his family for generations. The narrator of the novel, Yunior, frames the story of the family within the larger national histories of the Dominican Republic and the United States. A particularly important historical figure in the novel is Rafael Trujillo, the Dominican dictator. Trujillo's nefarious power seems to permeate the lives of each of the main characters in the novel, even those who have left the Dominican Republic. In order for Oscar to take on the *fukú*, he must return to his homeland from New Jersey in order to face the evil and violence of his family's history, which his mother had attempted to suppress.

The novel's literary significance derives in part from its style and language. Díaz incorporates various styles and genres in his work, including science fiction, comic books, and fantasy. *The Brief and Wondrous Life of Oscar Wao* also engages with other works—not only in the United States' literary canon but also works of Caribbean writers, including Aimé Césaire, Derek Walcott, Édouard Glissant, and scholar Fernando Ortiz.

Significance

Díaz has produced two influential works of contemporary American literature, written in a unique voice that is rooted in the immigrant experience but resonates much more broadly. The author's work has done a great deal to raise the profile of U.S. Latino literature, particularly since the publication of his popular novel *The Brief and Wondrous Life of Oscar Wao* and his Pulitzer Prize in 2008. Díaz is one of only a handful of Latino writers to garner such widespread mainstream attention and success. He also has championed the work of other writers of color in his capacities as a writer, teacher, editor, and public figure.

Monica Hanna

Further Reading

Di Iorio Sandín, Lyn, and Richard Perez, eds. *Contemporary U.S. Latino/a Literary Criticism*. New York: Palgrave Macmillan, 2007. This collection of critical essays includes two pieces that directly address

Díaz's work and others that place his writing in cultural context.

Díaz, Junot. "Fiction Is the Poor Man's Cinema: An Interview with Junot Díaz." Interview by Diógenes Céspedes and Silvio Torres-Saillant. *Callaloo* 23, no. 3 (Summer, 2000): 892-907. In this interview, Díaz discusses his childhood and education; the relationship between art and politics in his writing; and his literary influences, including Piri Thomas, Toni Morrison, Sandra Cisneros, Ralph Ellison, and Patrick Chamoiseau.

_______. "Junot Díaz." Interview by Edwidge Danticat. *Bomb* 101 (Fall, 2007). In this interview, Haitian writer Danticat and Díaz discuss *The Brief and Wondrous Life of Oscar Wao*, including Díaz's writing process, use of fantasy and science-fiction elements, and writers who have influenced him.

See also: Julia Alvarez; Giannina Braschi; Sandra Cisneros; Rigoberto González; Oscar Hijuelos; Virgil Suárez; Piri Thomas.

Justino Díaz

Puerto Rican-born opera singer

Díaz is considered one of the greatest opera singers from Puerto Rico. His singing career, which spanned four decades, included performances across the United States and throughout Europe.

Latino heritage: Puerto Rican
Born: January 29, 1940; San Juan, Puerto Rico
Area of achievement: Music

Early Life

Justino Díaz (yews-TEE-noh DEE-ahz) was born in San Juan, Puerto Rico, and raised in the small town of Cataño. He began singing as a child in his elementary school and at church and furthered his musical education in the choir at the University of Puerto Rico High School.

Díaz made his operatic debut at the age of seventeen in the role of Ben in Gian Carlo Menotti's opera *The Telephone.* He continued his musical education at the New England Conservatory in Boston, Massachusetts, where he studied with the voice teacher Frederick Jagel and the opera conductor Boris Goldovsky. Díaz made his professional opera debut with the New England Opera Theater in 1961. After graduating from the New England Conservatory, Díaz moved to New York, where he appeared with the American Opera Society. Early in his career, he was represented by the talent agent Hans J. Hoffman. Early symphony appearances include performances with the Rochester Philharmonic and Boston Symphony.

In the spring of 1963, Díaz won the annual voice competition sponsored by the Metropolitan Opera in New York City; he was the first Puerto Rican to win this prestigious prize. He made his Metropolitan Opera debut in October, 1963, in the role of Monterone in Giuseppe Verdi's opera *Rigoletto*. In 1967, Díaz married dancer Anna Aragno, with whom he would have two children. His career continued to flourish with performances at major opera houses throughout the United States and Europe. These performances included productions at La Scala in Milan, Italy, the Royal Opera House at Covent Garden in London, and at the Salzburg Festival in Austria.

Life's Work

One of Díaz's most notable performances was on the opening night of the new Metropolitan Opera House at Lincoln Center in 1966. In this performance, he created the role of Antony in the world-premiere performance of Samuel Barber's opera *Antony and Cleopatra.* He also created the role of Francesco in Alberto Ginastera's *Beatrix Cenci* in 1971. Díaz's wide range and even tone allowed him to sing a variety of bass and baritone roles in the standard operatic repertoire. Early in his career he focused on bass roles including Mephistopheles in Charles Gounod's *Faust*, Escamillo in Georges Bizet's *Carmen*, Raimondo in Gaetano Donizetti's *Lucia di Lammermoor*, and Phillip II in Verdi's *Don Carlo*. In the 1980's Díaz added leading baritone roles to his repertoire. These included Scarpia in Puccini's *Tosca*, Jago in Verdi's *Otello*, and the title roles in Verdi's operas *Rigoletto* and *Macbeth*.

Díaz's attractiveness, charisma, and talents as an actor were praised by critics and secured him the part of Jago in Franco Zeffirelli's film version of *Otello* in 1988. In addition to the previously mentioned opera houses, Díaz sang leading roles at the Paris Opera, Vienna Staatsoper, New York City Opera, Opera of Spoleto, Opera of Rome, Teatro Colón in Buenos Aires, Zarzuela Theater of Madrid, and Barcelona's Gran Teatre del Liceu. Diaz regularly peformed in Puerto Rico as well. He sang in the inaugural concert of the Luis A. Ferré Performing Arts Center in 1994 and made regular appearances at the annual Casals Music Festival in San Juan. In addition to his extensive opera repertoire, Díaz also performed musical theater. He portrayed Luis Muñoz Marín in the 1984 musical *Fela!* and starred in the first full recording of the musical *South Pacific*. He has made numerous recordings for companies such as Deutsche Grammophon, Sony Classics, EMI, and Decca. These recordings include some of his operatic repertoire, as well as oratorios by George Frideric Handel and Luigi Cherubini and a solo album of arias by Wolfgang Amadeus Mozart.

Díaz retired from singing in 2003. He has served for several years as the artistic director of the Casals Music Festival. His talents and service to the arts have been recognized with numerous honors, including an honorary doctorate from New England Conservatory, the Handel Medal from the City of New York, and the National Medal of Culture from the Institute of Puerto Rican Culture.

Significance

During the 1970's and 1980's, Díaz emerged as one of the world's leading bass-baritones. He is one of the most successful classical musicians to emerge from Puerto Rico. The beauty of his voice and his compelling stage presence allowed him to travel around the globe, performing in some of the world's most famous opera houses. During his career, he sang with some of the twentieth century's most celebrated singers and conductors. In addition, he has used his stature to bring talented musicians to Puerto Rico for the annual Casals Music Festival.

Michael Hix

Further Reading

Díaz, Justino. "Song and Dance." Interview by Ralph Zachery. *Opera News* 36, no. 11 (1971-1972): 14-15. In this interview, Díaz discusses his training, early career, and how he juggles his professional and personal lives.

Freeman, J. W. "No Short Cut." *Opera News* 31, no. 9 (1966-1967): 16. Discusses Díaz's early success at the Metropolitan Opera.

Myers, Eric. "Justino Díaz." *Opera News* 70, no. 9 (2006): 14-16. This article highlights Díaz's operatic career. It includes personal anecdotes about other major performers with whom he performed.

See also: Claudio Arrau; Jorge Bolet; Eduardo Mata; Jesús María Sanromá.

José de Diego

Puerto Rican-born politician, writer, and lawyer

A principal figure in the Puerto Rican independence movement, Diego served as undersecretary of the departments of justice and the interior, president of the criminal court in Mayagüez, associate justice of the Puerto Rican supreme court, and a member of the Chamber of Representatives. He is remembered as a great statesman and poet.

Latino heritage: Puerto Rican

Born: April 16, 1866; Aguadilla, Puerto Rico

Died: July 16, 1918; New York, New York

Also known as: José Toribio de Diego y Martínez

Areas of achievement: Government and politics; law; poetry; journalism

Early Life

José Toribio de Diego y Martínez (dee-AY-goh) was born to Felipe de Diego and Elisa Martínez in Aguadilla, Puerto Rico, and received his primary education in Mayagüez. At the age of eleven, he began composing poetic verse.

Diego began his secondary education at the Polytechnical Institute in Logroño, Spain, and joined the Progressive Republican Committee. During these years, he contributed verse and essays, many of which criticized the monarchy, to various publications, including *Comic Madrid*, *The Riojan*, *Progress*, *Sunday Discourses on Free Thought*, and *The Comic Week*. In 1885, Diego published a collection of poems titled *The Highly Despicable*, which reflect his religious confusion and political anxieties. Imprisoned several times from 1885 to 1886, he could not complete his secondary studies in Spain. Under a general amnesty in 1886, he was released and returned to Puerto Rico.

Upon his return, Diego met Carmen Echevarría Acevedo, with whom he fell in love. In 1887, he joined the Autonomist Party, published the poem "Sor Ana," a vitriolic attack on religion, and returned to Spain to study law at the University of Barcelona. He discontinued his relationship with Echevarría in 1888 and composed his anguished and embittered poem "A Laura." Plagued by illness, Diego returned to Puerto Rico in 1889, where he continued the study of law on his own. He eventually went to the University of Havana, where he was awarded a licentiate (1891) and doctorate (1892) in law. In 1892, he returned to Puerto Rico and married Petra Lucila de la Torre, but they divorced in 1896.

Life's Work

After Puerto Rico was granted political autonomy, Diego was named undersecretary of justice and the interior by the autonomous government and served as a member of the Chamber of Representatives. After Puerto Rico became an American protectorate in 1898, Diego was named an associate justice of the supreme court. In 1899, he became the president of the criminal court in Mayagüez and participated in the Constitutive Assembly of the new Federal Party. Serving as the representative from Mayagüez to the Chamber of Deputies from 1902 to 1917, Diego published the first complete edition of *Pomarrosas: Poesías* in 1904.

American officials advocated closer ties with Puerto Rico and proposed to grant American citizenship. Diego and Luis Muñoz Rivera formed the new Union of Puerto Rico Party to challenge increasing American control, with Diego presenting independence as a viable solution. In 1907, he was elected president of the Chamber of Deputies, a position he would keep until his death. In *Ciudadanía a de los Puertorriqueños* (1913; *Citizenship of Puerto Ricans*), Diego argued for the establishment of a "Republic of Puerto Rico," which he advocated as president of the Union Party from 1914 to 1916.

Diego opposed the use of English, and, in 1915, founded the José de Diego Institute to foment the study of the law and Spanish culture. The next year, he published more literary works: a second edition of *Pomarrosas;* a collection of poems he had written in his childhood, *Jovillos;* a collection of poetry with a political bent, *Cantos de rebeldia* (*Songs of Rebellion*); and a collection of political essays, *Nuevas campañas* (*New Campaigns*). He also was elected president of the Antillean Academy of Language and returned to Spain to deliver speeches in major cities. Diego fell gravely ill and had a leg amputated in 1917. He was moved to New York City for treatment but died on July 16, 1918. His last collection of poems, *Cantos de pitirre* (*Songs of the Kingbird*), was published posthumously in 1950.

Significance

One of the most influential figures of Puerto Rican history, Diego was an illustrious jurist, legislator, orator, and defender of the democratic process who led his people from the oppression of the dying Spanish empire to limited self-determination under the hegemony of the United States. Diego's tireless struggle for Puerto Rican political and cultural independence inspired his impassioned defense of the Spanish language and the traditional Hispanic culture of Puerto Rico, and culminated in his election as the president of the Ateneo Puertorriqueño (Puerto Rican Athenaeum), the island's most illustrious cultural body. Responsible for drafting countless laws and working to establish lasting political structures that would bring justice and social stability, Diego embodies the Puerto Rican search for identity and the commonweal. Perhaps more lasting are his many poetic works and essays, which are stylistic masterpieces of the Spanish language that also capture the deepest of human emotions.

Mark T. DeStephano

Further Reading

Bejel, Emilio. "Poetry." In *A History of Literature in the Caribbean*, edited by A. James Arnold. Amsterdam, Pa.: J. Benjamins, 1994-2001. Discusses Diego's work in the context of Latin American poetry and literature of the period.

Picó, Fernando. *History of Puerto Rico: A Panorama of Its People*. Princeton, N.J.: Markus Wiener, 2006. Picó explains the ways in which Diego was instrumental in the construction of the new Puerto Rican political order through his interactions with American military and civilian authorities.

Wagenheim, Kal, and Olga Jiménez de Wagenheim. *The Puerto Ricans: A Documentary History*. Princeton, N.J.: Markus Wiener, 2008. Although treated indirectly, Diego's central role in Puerto Rican politics and government under the United States is here chronicled in primary documents.

See also: Pedro Albizu Campos; Luis A. Ferré; Lolita Lebrón; Luis Muñoz Marín; Luis Muñoz Rivera.

Paquito D'Rivera

Cuban-born musician and writer

A virtuoso on the saxophone and clarinet, D'Rivera by the 1970's was known as one of the world's most versatile musicians, equally comfortable in jazz, Western classical, and Latin American vernacular styles. He also is a composer, arranger, bandleader, and prominent figure in the Cuban American community.

Latino heritage: Cuban

Born: June 4, 1948; Havana, Cuba

Also known as: Francisco D'Rivera; El Paq-Man

Areas of achievement: Music; literature

Early Life

Paquito D'Rivera (pah-KEE-toh dee-rih-VEH-rah) was born on June 4, 1948, to Tito D'Rivera, a professional classical saxophonist, and Maura D'Rivera, a teacher. From early childhood, he was immersed in a musical environment; his father gave him his first saxophone, a curved soprano instrument, when D'Rivera was only five years old. He learned so quickly that after just a year he was playing solos in public. Recognizing his son's talent, Tito taught him privately, arranged for him to be featured in concerts, and encouraged him to attempt the most challenging repertoire. Although Tito did not improvise, he was a great admirer of American jazz, and his collected recordings of Benny Goodman and other musicians left a deep impression on D'Rivera. The young musician's early promise continued to bear fruit when, at the age of ten, he began performing at the National Theater in Havana. Two years later, he was accepted into the Havana Conservatory.

After playing in a military band for two years, D'Rivera became a soloist with the Cuban National Symphony Orchestra. He was active in modern music circles and grew increasingly impatient with the aesthetically conservative government of Cuba, which discouraged jazz and experimental forms of Western classical music. D'Rivera and Chucho Valdés established the Orquestra Cubana de Musica Moderna, with D'Rivera as the conductor. He later joined with some of these musicians to form a fusion group that blended Cuban styles with jazz, rock, and Western classical music. This group, Irakere, was very successful and attracted a great deal of attention outside of Cuba. In 1979, the group's self-titled album, released by CBS Records, won a Grammy Award for the Best Latin Recording. During the band's European tour, D'Rivera defected and began working extensively in the United States.

Life's Work

Although he sacrificed time with his wife and son, who eventually were able to join him in the United States after years of effort, D'Rivera's artistic career flourished. One of the most prominent American musicians who engaged D'Rivera during this period was trumpeter Dizzy Gillespie, who for decades had been incorporating Afro-Caribbean elements into jazz. D'Rivera also found work playing for recordings, and in 1981, he recorded *Paquito Blowin'*, his first solo album, which was well-received. While continuing a busy schedule of performing and recording in the improvisatory, polyrhythmic styles of Latin-jazz fusion, D'Rivera also devoted a good deal of professional time to building his reputation as a master of Western classical music, both as a performer (primarily on clarinet in these cases) and as a composer, writing pieces commissioned for the National Symphony Orchestra, the

Paquito D'Rivera. (AP Photo)

New Jersey Chamber Music Society, the Rotterdam Philharmonic, and others.

In 1988, D'Rivera joined Gillespie in an exciting new project: the United Nations Orchestra, a large and eclectic ensemble that included instruments and styles from diverse musical traditions. D'Rivera and trombonist Slide Hampton were the founding music directors. After Gillespie died in 1993, the group continued to perform. D'Rivera also joined the Caribbean Jazz Project in 1994 with Dave Samuels and Andy Narell. Several of D'Rivera's recordings earned Grammy Awards, including *Portraits of Cuba* (1996), *Paquito D'Rivera Quintet: Live at the Blue Note* (2000), *Historia del Soldado* (2002), and *Brazilian Dreams* (2002). In 2007, he won his ninth Grammy, in the Best Latin Jazz Album category for *Funk Tango*.

In the 2000's, D'Rivera received increasing international acclaim for his work as a soloist, composer, and director. His work with other musicians continued to expand into new genres. Collaborators included cellist Yo-Yo Ma and the Assad Brothers guitar duo. D'Rivera also was active as a writer, penning scathing criticisms of Cuba's government under Fidel Castro, liner notes for albums, editorials, and fiction. His humor-laden novel *¡Oh, La Habana!*, published in 2004, explored the environment of Havana in the 1940's and 1950's.

Significance

In spite of his political opposition to the government of his homeland, D'Rivera has played the role of a cultural ambassador, introducing audiences to diverse musical styles. By continuing the work of Dizzy Gillespie, he often is credited with helping to bring together two major streams of African-influenced music. As a composer and performer, he also bridges the worlds of jazz and Western classical music.

John E. Myers

Further Reading

D'Rivera, Paquito. *My Sax Life: A Memoir.* Evanston, Ill.: Northwestern University Press, 2005. Complete, detailed autobiography covering D'Rivera's life and multifaceted career. Photos, index.

Panken, Ted. "Paquito D'Rivera—Honoring...Himself!" *DownBeat* 72, no. 4 (April, 2005): 50-55. In-depth coverage of a Carnegie Hall concert celebrating D'Rivera's fiftieth year of professional music-making.

Roberts, John Storm. *Latin Jazz: The First of the Fusions, 1880's to Today*. New York: Schirmer Books, 1999. This history of Latin jazz includes coverage of D'Rivera and his impact on the genre. Photos, bibliography, discography, glossary, index.

Yanow, Scott. *Afro-Cuban Jazz*. San Francisco, Calif.: Miller Freeman, 2000. General history that includes interviews and biographic entries on many of the pioneering musicians in the genre, including D'Rivera, with comprehensive discography. Photos, index, bibliography.

See also: Ray Barretto; Willie Colón; Paul Gonsalves; Tito Puente; Poncho Sánchez.

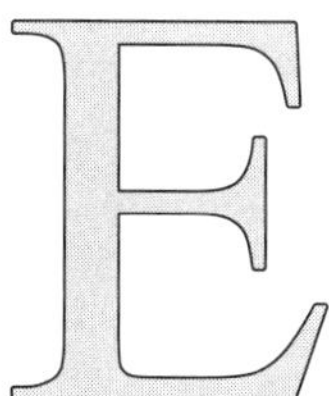

Sheila E.

American drummer and singer

One of the most prominent percussionists in Latin jazz, pop, and rock music, Sheila E. is particularly known for her collaborations with Prince in the 1980's, for her solo recordings and tours, and for numerous recordings and performances with other popular music artists.

Latino heritage: Mexican

Born: December 12, 1959; Oakland, California

Also known as: Sheila Cecilia Escovedo; Sheila Escovedo

Area of achievement: Music

Early Life

Sheila Cecilia Escovedo (SHEE-luh seh-SEE-lee-uh EH-skoh-VAY-doh) was born December 12, 1959, in Oakland, California to a Mexican America father, Pete, and a Creole mother, Juanita. Sheila E. was the first of four children (with two brothers, Juan and Peter Michael, and one sister, Zina), and her father was the leader and timbale player of the Latin jazz band Azteca. When Sheila E. was young, money was limited for the Escovedo family; they lived in a tough neighborhood on the east side of Oakland. Sheila E.'s mother worked the night shift at dairy factories, while her father took Sheila E. to his performances at local clubs.

With her father as her mentor and teacher, Sheila E. began playing percussion instruments at age three. She imitated her father as he practiced and rehearsed, and she was exposed to the rehearsals and performances of his group. Her unusual left-handed conga technique is the result of mirroring her father's playing. She also took part in some performances of the group from an early age. In the hope that she would become a symphonic musician, her father started her playing the violin when she was ten years old. Sheila E.'s adolescent years also included exposure to the gangs of Oakland and winning awards as a track and field athlete.

Life's Work

After dropping out of high school at age seventeen, Sheila E. toured Europe and Asia with Azteca. Later, she toured with the George Duke Band and continued to play with a wide variety of musicians, including Tito Puente, Stevie Wonder, Billy Cobham, and Gloria Estefan. While touring as part of Lionel Richie's band in 1983 she met Prince, who suggested she change her name and helped her record her first album, *The Glamorous Life*, in 1984. After touring Europe, Sheila E. joined Prince's *Purple Rain* tour in 1985 as the opening act.

In several ways, Prince gave Sheila E. significant opportunities to develop an audience of her own. Prince encouraged her to sing on his recording of "Erotic City" and he helped her get a recording contract with Warner Brothers. In the mid-1980's, she quickly built international acclaim with the release of

Sheila E. (AP Photo)

her second and third albums, *Romance 1600* (1985) and *Sheila E* (1987), and by acting in her first film, *Krush Groove* (1986).

Sheila E. continued to perform as drummer with Prince in 1987 for the *Sign O' the Times* recording and tour. In 1989, she released the live recording *La Familia*, featuring her father, Pete Escovedo, and Latin jazz legend Tito Puente. In 1990, she also appeared in the film *The Adventures of Ford Fairlane*. In 1991, she released *Sex Cymbal*, which had more commercial success than her other recordings of the late 1980's.

In the early 1990's, health problems resulting from continuous work forced Sheila E. to take several years off. In 1994, she started the E-Train, a band playing a mixture of styles including soul, funk, gospel, and Latin jazz. In 1998, she became the bandleader for Magic Johnson's short-lived television talk show, *The Magic Hour*. After touring and recording with a variety of musicians in the late 1990's early 2000's, she returned to collaboration with Prince on his *Musicology* tour in 2004.

Sheila E. works with the Toca Drum company in the design of signature percussion instruments and a line of Latin percussion instruments for children. She also founded and volunteers her time to the philanthropic activities of the Elevate Hope Foundation, which is focused on helping abused and abandoned children.

SIGNIFICANCE

Although she began her performing career as a percussionist, Sheila E. became internationally known as a singer, drummer, and bandleader. Her long musical partnership with Prince and early training from her father gave her the skills and the opportunity to become one of the best-known Latina musicians of her generation. At a time when men dominated drumming, as well as the rock and popular music fields, Sheila E. became widely recognized as one of the most talented and popular drummers and pop singers, regardless of gender. She was the first female bandleader for a late-night television talk show. In later years, she used her fame and wealth to bring attention to social issues, including child abuse and neglect.

David Steffens

FURTHER READING

Granados, Christine. *Sheila E: A Real-Life Reader Biography*. Childs, Md.: Mitchell Lane, 2000. This brief biography of Sheila E. is written for young readers.

Hahn, Alex. *Possessed: The Rise and Fall of Prince*. New York: Billboard Books, 2003. This extensive biography of Prince includes details about Sheila E.'s performances and recordings with Prince.

Sheila E. http://www.sheilae.com. The official Sheila E. Web site includes an extensive biography, discography, photo gallery, performance schedule, merchandise, ministry information, and contact information.

See also: Paquito D'Rivera; Gloria Estefan; Jennifer Lopez; Tito Puente; Poncho Sánchez.

Hector Elizondo

American actor and activist

Elizondo has established himself as a formidable and prolific actor whose career has spanned Broadway, film, and television. He also is active in philanthropic and cultural causes.

Latino heritage: Puerto Rican and Spanish

Born: December 22, 1936; New York, New York

Areas of achievement: Acting; radio and television; theater; social issues

Early Life

Hector Elizondo (EH-lih-ZAHN-doh) was born to Carmen Medina Reyes Elizondo and Martin Echevarria Elizondo in New York City on December 22, 1936. He grew up with traditions from both his Puerto Rican mother and his father, a Basque who had emigrated from Spain years before.

Elizondo sang with the Frank Murray Boys Choir while still in elementary school, which led to paying work. He briefly worked on a radio show and television variety program before deciding that he would rather play after school. As a high school student, Elizondo exhibited his athleticism in sports, warranting attention from baseball scouts. He planned on becoming a teacher and attended City College in New York for one year before leaving the program to support his new wife and son, Rodd. Although the marriage quickly failed, Elizondo retained custody of his son. He remarried twice, the third marriage coming in 1969 to Carolee Campbell, an actor and book binder.

After leaving college, Elizondo worked in jobs outside the entertainment industry for several years before he was able to begin his acting career. He took dance lessons to hone his skills while waiting for his break.

Life's Work

Elizondo began performing in Off-Broadway theater productions in 1963, launching a successful long-term career in show business that encompassed theater, television, and film. Elizondo has managed to stay involved in each genre, deftly scheduling his work so that he remained active in each form.

In 1969, Elizondo won an Obie Award for his part in the play *Steambath*. He also performed in *The Price* and *The Great White Hope* on Broadway. Elizondo's first film was the comedy *Young Doctors in Love* in 1982, beginning a fruitful collaboration with director Garry Marshall. Elizondo also appeared in Marshall's *Runaway Bride* (1999), *Valentine's Day* (2010), *The Princess Diaries* (2001), and its 2004 sequel.

Elizondo played what perhaps was his most high-profile role in Marshall's *Pretty Woman* (1990), starring Julia Roberts and Richard Gere. Elizondo originally intended his role to remain uncredited but Marshall opted to credit his work. As a result of his portrayal of the sympathetic manager of an upscale hotel, Elizondo received nominations for a Golden Globe and an American Comedy Award. Proving that he also could perform drama in film, Elizondo accepted roles in *The Taking of Pelham One Two Three* (1974), *American Gigolo* (1980), and *Love in the Time of Cholera* (2007), each of which contained weighty subject matter and gave Elizondo an opportunity to show his range.

In 1994, Elizondo was cast as a series regular on the television medical drama *Chicago Hope*, remaining on the show throughout its run. His portrayal of Dr. Phillip Watters garnered him an Emmy in 1997. He later played supporting roles on television shows such as *Grey's Anatomy* and *Monk*. In 2007, he costarred in the short-lived television series *Cane*, a family drama featuring a primarily Latino cast.

While Elizondo's television and film credits have garnered him the most public recognition, he also has done voice work for projects as diverse as PBS documentaries and children's cartoons. Elizondo narrated PBS's *The American Experience*, *NOVA*, and the English version of *The Borinqueneers*, a documentary recounting the experience of the U.S. Army's 65th Infantry, which was composed of Puerto Rican soldiers. His voiceover work also includes children's programming such as the animated film *Batman: Mystery of the Batwoman* (2003) and episodes of animated series such as *Avatar: The Last Airbender*. Elizondo also volunteered his time and talent to L.A. Theatre Works, which provides traditional radio dramas to National Public Radio for widespread broadcast.

The recipient of several Emmy nominations and other entertainment-industry awards, Elizondo also has been honored by cultural organizations. The Multicultural Motion Picture Association presented Elizondo its Integrity Award for his work in film, and the Nosotros Foundation, an organization dedicated to furthering the work of Hispanics in the entertainment industry, gave Elizondo a Lifetime Achievement Award.

Throughout his career, Elizondo's family has remained central to his life, and he parlayed his extended family's devastating experience with Alzheimer's disease into activism on behalf of the Alzheimer's Association. Because four of his aunts suffered from the disease, Elizondo took its impact very seriously and used his fame to help raise awareness and funding for research.

Significance

A prolific performer, Elizondo has more than one hundred credits in film and television in addition to his work on stage. He has portrayed wildly diverse characters in projects representing many genres, showing his broad range and ample talent.

Bonnye Busbice Good

Further Reading

Otfinoski, Steven. "Hector Elizondo." In *Latinos in the Arts*. New York: Facts On File, 2007. Career overview and brief biography of Elizondo. Bibliography.

Reyes, Luis, and Peter Rubie. *Hispanics in Hollywood: A Celebration of 100 Years in Film and Television.* Hollywood, Calif.: Lone Eagle, 2000. Discusses Elizondo's contributions in the context of Hispanic performers' overall success in the entertainment industry.

Rodriguez, Claire. *Heroes, Lovers, and Others: The Story of Latinos in Hollywood.* 2d ed. New York: Oxford University Press, 2008. Rodriguez examines Elizondo's success in several entertainment genres and how he presents positive images of Latin Americans.

See also: Andy Garcia; Raúl Juliá; Cheech Marín; Esai Morales; Edward James Olmos; Freddie Prinze; Martin Sheen; Danny Trejo.

Virgilio Elizondo

American religious leader and scholar

Elizondo, a Catholic priest, is a prominent Mexican American theologian and scholar who is considered the "father of U.S. Latino theology." His major contributions are in the development of mestizo theology, which relies on Mexican American experiences of oppression, poverty, and cultural and religious mestizaje (racial mixture) as a locus for theological reflection. As a scholar, he has published extensively and has been the recipient of numerous awards and honorary degrees.

Latino heritage: Mexican

Born: August 26, 1935; San Antonio, Texas

Also known as: Virgilio P. Elizondo; Virgil P. Elizondo

Areas of achievement: Religion and theology; scholarship; social issues

Early Life

Virgilio P. Elizondo (vehr-HIHL-ee-o ehl-ee-ZON-doh) was born in San Antonio, Texas, on August 26, 1935. His father, Virgilio Elizondo, was originally from the small town of Rosales in the Mexican state of Chihuahua and his mother, Ana María Peimbert Elizondo, was from Mexico City. His parents immigrated to the United States, where they and his grandparents, Antonio Elizondo and María Manuela Petra Paula Ester Fernández del Castillo, settled in the predominantly Mexican barrio located on the west side of San Antonio. The family had a small grocery store in the barrio, and they owned a small house with no hot water that was shared by Elizondo's siblings, grandparents, parents, three canaries, two cats, and two German shepherd dogs named Kaiser and Tarzan. Elizondo's parents faced the hardships of acculturation, long working hours, poor living conditions, harsh treatment, and language difficulties, which were commonly experienced by many Mexican immigrants.

Elizondo attended a Catholic elementary school run by German nuns, where he was discriminated against and forbidden to speak Spanish. Feeling alienated and rejected in his own country while a student at this school, Elizondo experienced the beginning of his consciousness as a mestizo, a person of biologically and culturally mixed background. Given the hardship he endured, his parents eventually transferred him to another German-run school located in downtown San Antonio, where his academic experience was more positive. He received his high school education at Peacock Military Academy, where he continued to be pejoratively singled out as Mexican. Throughout his childhood, he was often the target of commonplace racist indignities, including hostile, derogatory insults and ethnic epithets.

Elizando attended Saint Mary's University in San Antonio, from which he graduated in 1957 with a B.S. degree in chemistry, an area of study he temporarily pursued because of his interest in becoming a medical doctor or psychiatrist. Inspired by Archbishop Robert Emmet Lucey's ministry for poor, uneducated, and unemployed Mexican Americans residing in the Archdiocese of San Antonio, Elizondo decided to follow Lucey's path of ministry and advocacy for the needs of others. Elizondo entered the seminary to explore his calling to the Catholic priesthood. He completed his seminary studies and was ordained a diocesan priest in 1963. In 1968, he spent a year in Manila at the East Asian Pastoral Institute, where he studied culture and evangelization and earned a diploma in pastoral catechesis. He also completed a master's degree in pastoral studies in 1969 at Ateneo de Manila University, a Jesuit private university in the Philippines. He pursued doctoral studies in Paris at the Institut Catholique, from which he obtained a Ph.D. and a doctoral degree in sacred theology in June, 1978. His doctoral training included exposure to some of the most influential theological figures of the twentieth century. He was taught historical theology by the prominent Dominican theologian Marie-Dominique Chenu and ecclesiology by Yves Congar, one of the most well-known and respected Catholic scholars and experts on the study of the church.

Under the mentorship and guidance of his dissertation advisor, French sociologist Jacques Audinet, Elizondo titled his dissertation "Mestissage, violence culturelle, annonce de l évangile: La dimension interculturelle de l évangélisation" ("*Mestizaje*, Cultural Violence, According to the Gospel: The Intercultural Dimension of Evangelization"). His dissertation developed a theology of *mestizaje* and explored the sociohistorical process of this two-fold *mestizaje* based on the double conquest of the Mexican people, first under the Spanish rule in Mexico and then under the United States' conquest of the Mexican American Southwest.

Life's Work

In 1972, Elizando founded the Mexican American Cultural Center in San Antonio, an institution dedicated to Mexican American cultural and theological studies. He served as the center's first president from 1972 to 1987. In addition, from 1977 to 1979 he was an an editor of *Concilium,* a worldwide Catholic journal which promotes theological reflection and discussion in the spirit of the Second Vatican Council.

Elizondo was rector of the San Fernando Cathedral from 1983 to 1995, and he presided over a Sunday Spanish Mass that was broadcast to more than one million households. During his tenure as rector, he focused on social justice causes, while advocating for immigration reform and just wages for underpaid and exploited Mexican American laborers. In 2010, he was a professor of pastoral and Hispanic theology and a fellow of the Institute for Latino Studies at the University of Notre Dame, where he specialized in the study of Our Lady of Guadalupe, pastoral and Hispanic theology, and inculturation,

Elizondo has published several influential theological books, and he is widely admired for these contributions to Latino theological reflection. These books include *The Human Quest: A Search for Meaning Through Life and Death* (1978), *The Mexican-American Promise* (1983), *Way of the Cross: The Passion of Christ in the Americas* (1992), *Guadalupe: Mother of the New Creation* (1997), *A God of Incredible Surprises: Jesus of Galilee* (2003), and *Galilean Journey* (2003). He has also been the recipient of some of the most prestigious awards in the Catholic theological community, including the John Courtney Murray Award for his distinguished work in theology, which he received from the Catholic Theological Society of America in 2007. In addition, he has been awarded honorary doctoral degrees by Sienna Heights College (1979), the Jesuit School of Theology at Berkeley, California (1984), St. Mary's University of San Antonio (1998), and the Christian Theological Seminary (2002), among others. In 1995, the city of San Antonio named the park located between City Hall and the San Fernando Cathedral the Elizondo Plaza.

Significance

Elizondo's significance as a Mexican American religious leader and scholar is evidenced by his rise from a life of poverty, prejudice, and hatred to his becoming an internationally renowned author, theologian, and advocate for the poor. His theological studies are extensively cited and referenced by scholars, and his work will continue to inspire future generations of Mexican Americans who seek to better understand their faith from the perspective of the oppressed and rejected Galilean Jesus Christ.

Fernando A. Ortiz

Further Reading

Elizondo, Virgilio. *The Future Is Mestizo: Life Where Cultures Meet.* Rev. ed. Boulder: University Press of Colorado, 2000. Comprehensive autobiographical resource that traces Elizondo's childhood and most of his adult life in great detail. The narrative of his humble background and his dedicated scholarly development as a Mexican American theologian enables the reader to more fully understand the theme of the "Galilean journey," which pervades most of his theological reflection and work.

_______. *Guadalupe: Mother of the New Creation.* Maryknoll, N.Y.: Orbis Books, 1997. Elizondo notes the importance of Our Lady of Guadalupe in his *mestizo* theology, and he discusses how she represents the creation of a new culture that brings intersecting people and their identities together.

_______. "Jesus the Galilean Jew in Mestizo Theology." *Theological Studies* 70, no. 2 (June, 2009): 262-280. Elizondo recounts the Mexican American journey that led to his biblical and theological exploration of Jesus of Galilee. He describes the development of his theological method, frequently referencing his ethnic minority background and identity, while simultaneously drawing meaningful comparisons to Jesus' own identity and conscious development as a marginal Galilean Jew.

See also: Fray Angélico Chávez; Antonio José Martínez; José Policarpo Rodríguez; Oscar I. Romo; Yolanda Tarango.

Gaspar Enríquez

American artist

Enríquez is an accomplished Chicano artist who has produced mixed-media collages, acrylic and air-brushed works, metal sculptures, and murals depicting the Mexican American subculture found in the barrios along the U.S.-Mexico border. His diverse and intense portrayals capture the essence of what it means to identify oneself as Chicano or Chicana.

Latino heritage: Mexican

Born: July 18, 1942; El Paso, Texas

Area of achievement: Art

Early Life

Gaspar Enríquez (gahs-PAHR ehn-REE-kehz) was born in El Paso, Texas, which is also the setting of his artwork. When he was eighteen years old, he left El Paso's Segundo Barrio and went to California, where he worked as a machinist. While there earning money to support his family, he enrolled in art classes at East Los Angeles Junior College. After returning to El Paso in the late 1960's, Enríquez continued to work full time while pursuing a B.A. in art education, which he received from the University of Texas at El Paso in 1970. In 1985, he earned an M.A. in metals from New Mexico State University.

Enríquez has cited the support of his mother, sisters, fifth-grade teacher, and deceased wife as motivations for pursuing a career as an artist. He taught art for thirty-four years at Bowie High School until his retirement, inspiring countless students, many of whom have served as the backdrop for his works. He has also been cited as a having a major impact on nationally renowned Chicano artists José "Match" Fernández, Mauricio Olague, Alex Rubio, and Vincent Valdez, among others.

Life's Work

Enríquez has received widespread acclaim for his art, which offers an intense portrayal of Mexican Americans along the U.S.-Mexico border who are often ignored or forgotten by mainstream chroniclers of the region. His works do not admonish or glamorize the choice to identify oneself as Chicano or Chicana. Instead, he depicts the unique beliefs and attitudes of the subcultures that have developed and transformed since the World War II era, including *pachucos*, *tirilones*, *cholos*, and gangsters. His most identifiable art captures the quintessential Chicano identity, and to this end Enríquez portrays his subjects as they appear, most of them staring directly at their observers and proudly displaying their dual Mexican American heritage. Influenced by the folk and religious art prevalent during his childhood, Enríquez has used these elements in his own works, along with traditional *retablo* and icon painting. He has also cited the influence of his mentor, sculptor Luis Alfonso Jiménez, Jr., who died in a tragic studio accident in 2006.

Among Enríquez's most recognizable works are *Cholos,* which is exhibited in the San Antonio Convention Center; *History of the Mission Valley,* a silo mural that he created with Olague in 1994; *Tirando Rollo*, which centers on a young Chicana communicating in *caló*, a form of slang that was sometimes used by women to sign messages to their incarcerated loved ones; and *La Rosa Dolorosa de Mi Vida Loca,* a mixed-media installation portraying a young Chicano's death, with his girlfriend holding his limp body as a modern Madonna offers a rose.

Enríquez has participated in countless exhibitions, both solo and group shows, throughout the United States. His work has been exhibited in galleries, on tours, in public spaces, and in museums every year from 1987 to 2008. His art was displayed in the national exhibitions *CARA: Chicano Art: Resistance and Affirmation* (1990-1993) and *Chicano Visions,* a showcase that toured various American museums. In addition, in 2000 he illustrated Rudolfo Anaya's children's book *Elegy on the Death of César Chávez.*

Enríquez has served on art advisory panels, and in 1994, he received a Mid-Americarts Alliance Fellowship. His works have been routinely purchased by private collectors and museums, such as the Albuquerque Museum of Art, the El Paso Museum of Art, and the Lyndon Baines Johnson Library. His ability to raise funds for community projects has been indispensable in assisting numerous organizations and individual artists.

Significance

Enríquez's distinctive style, versatile use of various techniques, and choice of subject matter contribute to his standing in the Chicano movement, which challenges the traditional European definition of art. His intense artworks depict the unique characteristics of the Mexican American subculture that has developed along the border. Though his art does not glorify the Chicano lifestyle, his portrayals do offer a realistic and respectful view of individuals living along the border who are cross-cultural. As a result, he has become a prominent voice for those inhabitants who struggle to create identities within a dominant Anglo culture while honoring their Mexican heritage.

Alyson F. Lerma

Further Reading

Anaya, Rudolfo. *Elegy on the Death of César Chávez.* El Paso, Tex.: Cinco Puntos Press, 2000. Children's book features Enríquez's mixed-media collages, watercolors, and paintings portraying the aftermath of Chávez's death.

Enríquez, Gaspar. *Gaspar Enríquez.* http://www.gasparenriquez.com. Enríquez's official website offers essential, detailed, and updated information on his life, art, and influences, as well as images of his artwork.

Keller, Gary D. *Contemporary Chicana and Chicano Art: Artists, Works, Culture, and Education.* Tempe, Ariz.: Bilingual Press/Editorial Bilingüe, 2002. Discusses various Chicano and Chicana artists and their unique styles, as well as Enríquez's works and his role in the Chicano movement.

Marín, Cheech. *Chicano Visions: American Painters on the Verge.* Boston: Little Brown, 2002. Catalog from a national exhibition that discusses various artists' works and their unique places in the Chicano art movement.

Vargas, George. *Contemporary Chicano Art: Color and Culture for a New America.* Austin: University of Texas Press, 2010. Chronicles the history and uniqueness of Chicano art as an expression of dual heritage. Discusses Enríquez's contributions to the development of Chicano art.

See also: Judith F. Baca; Barbara Carrasco; Daniel DeSiga; Carmen Lomas Garza; Yolanda M. López; Leo Tanguma; Jesse Treviño.

Jaime Escalante

Bolivian-born math teacher

As a high school math teacher in East Los Angeles, Escalante encouraged Latino students to enroll in upper-level math courses and to take Advanced Placement examinations. His influence resulted in many of them going on to college and attaining advanced degrees. His success was documented in the film Stand and Deliver *(1988).*

Latino heritage: Bolivian

Born: December 31, 1930; La Paz, Bolivia

Died: March 30, 2010; Roseville, California

Also known as: Jaime Alfonso Escalante Gutierrez

Area of achievement: Education

Jaime Escalante. (AP Photo)

Early Life

Jaime Alfonso Escalante Gutierrez (HI-may EHS-kah-LAHN-tay) was born in La Paz, Bolivia in 1930. He was the son of two teachers. Escalante developed an interest in science and mathematics, which he studied in Bolivia before immigrating to the United States in the 1960's. He did not speak English when he arrived in the United States, and he began taking classes, mostly at night, while working at Burroughs Corporation. Escalante earned a mathematics degree at Pasadena City College and then went to California State University, Los Angeles (CSULA), for more in-depth study.

Escalante began his teaching career at Garfield High School in East Los Angeles. He initially was appalled at the lack of preparation of his students, but he persevered, challenging the students to take algebra and then continuing to prod them to take increasingly difficult courses. He believed that if he helped Latino students excel in mathematics, they could obtain good jobs in computer and engineering fields.

Escalante's methods were unusual for Garfield High School. Many teachers there had given up on the struggling students, while Escalante continued to push them to achieve. He ran afoul of some school administrators, who disapproved of his style and his focus on higher-level mathematics. Finally, an administrator came to Garfield who agreed with his methods, and with that administrator's support, Escalante had some very successful years.

Life's Work

In 1979, Escalante taught his first calculus course at the high school level. Only five students remained in the class until the end of the school year, two of whom passed the Advanced Placement (AP) calculus test. In 1980, he had nine students, and seven of them passed. The next year, fourteen of his fifteen students passed the AP calculus test. In 1982, eighteen of his students achieved passing grades. However, the Educational Testing Service (which designs the AP tests) became suspicious of the Garfield students' success. Escalante believed that the only reason the students' scores were questioned was that they had Hispanic names.

Fourteen of Escalante's eighteen students were asked to take the test over. Twelve of them did so and passed again. The success of these students led more students to enroll in Escalante's classes. In 1983, thirty-three students took the test and thirty passed. The number of students taking his classes and passing the calculus AP exam continued to increase until 1987.

In the mid 1980's, Escalante gained national attention for his approach to teaching inner-city youths. A book was written documenting his career, and a film, *Stand and Deliver*, which depicted the events surrounding the 1982 AP test, was released in 1988. Observers asked to sit in on his classes to learn his techniques. Escalante continually claimed that he had no secrets—that both teacher and student simply had to work hard.

Escalante also spoke often to his students about *ganas* which translates loosely as "determination" or "the drive to work unceasingly." This, he said, was the secret to his (and his students') success.It is possible that Escalante's fame hurt his effectiveness at Garfield High. He reportedly received death threats and hate mail in the late 1980's and early 1990's. His class sizes increased beyond the limits set by the local teachers' union, which undermined his popularity with other teachers. He left Garfield, mentioning politics and jealousy as reasons, in the early 1990's.

Escalante continued to teach in high schools in Sacramento, California, and also became involved in a movement to discontinue bilingual education in the state. Escalante's position on this issue was controversial, especially among Latinos. He also hosted a PBS series, *Futures*, which introduced students to math- and science-based careers. It became one of the most popular educational programs in public broadcasting history and received more than fifty awards, including the George Foster Peabody Award, one of the highest honors in the broadcasting field.

In 2001, Escalante moved back to Bolivia and taught in a university in Cochabamba. He developed bladder cancer and returned to the United States for treatment. He lived in various places, including Sacramento and Roseville, California, during his last years. Escalante died on March 30, 2010, in Roseville.

Institutions of higher learning honored Escalante for his success with his students. Boston College, for example, named a tutoring program in his honor. Escalante was a 1999 inductee into the National Teachers Hall of Fame and holds honorary degrees from CSULA, the University of Massachusetts, Concordia University, Wittenberg University, and University of Northern Colorado. He was awarded the Presidential Medal for Excellence in Education in 1988. He also received the Andres Bello Prize from the Organization of American States and a Hispanic Heritage Award.

Significance

Escalante used mathematics to inspire poor Latino students to transcend their bleak lives in the inner city and aspire to greatness. He knew from experience that the language of mathematics transcended other language barriers. Once they had experienced achievement, he believed, the students could continue to climb the educational ladder. Many of Escalante's former pupils went on to achieve in fields including law and architecture.

M. C. Ware

Further Reading

Byers, Ann. *Jaime Escalante: Sensational Teacher*. Berkeley Heights, N.J.: Enslow, 1996. This young adult biography is one of a series highlighting successful Latinos.

Mathews, Jay. *Escalante: The Best Teacher in America*. New York: Henry Holt, 1989. This book was written when Escalante was at his peak and, along with the film *Stand and Deliver*, helped to make him famous.

Woo, Elaine. "Jaime Escalante Dies at Seventy-nine; Math Teacher Who Challenged East L.A. Students to *Stand and Deliver*." *The Los Angeles Times*, March 31, 2010. Lengthy obituary chronicling Escalante's career and legacy.

See also: Joseph A. Fernández; Julian Nava; Edward James Olmos.

Achievements of Escalante's Students After Graduation

Jaime Escalante was successful in giving his students a "ticket" out of crime-ridden East Los Angeles. His students won acceptance to top colleges including Harvard, Stanford, Dartmouth, Wellesley, Occidental, and the Massachusetts Institute of Technology (MIT). Some notable alumni of Escalante's math classes include Daniel Castro, who graduated from MIT with a degree in electrical engineering and then received a law degree from the University of California at Berkeley; Mark Baca, an employee of a Los Angeles nonprofit organization; lawyers Sandra Muñoz, Araceli Lerma, Angel Navarro, and Jeannie Moreno; Angela Fajardo, a teacher and administrator; Jema Estrella, an architect; elementary school teacher Elsa Bolado, who was one of the students involved in the 1982 Advanced Placement test scandal; Thomas Valdez, an engineer for the National Aeronautics and Space Administration, who now speaks to students about the importance of science and math; and Erika Camacho, a mathematics professor at Arizona State University. They would not have achieved their success without the influence and guidance of Jaime Escalante.

Sixto Escobar

Puerto Rican-born boxer

Escobar was the first world boxing champion from Puerto Rico. By the end of his career, he had held the title three times from 1934 to 1939, never being knocked down or knocked out. His success paved the way for later Puerto Rican champions such as Wilfred Benítez, José Torres, and Félix Trinidad.

Latino heritage: Puerto Rican

Born: March 23, 1913; Barceloneta, Puerto Rico

Died: November 17, 1979; Barceloneta, Puerto Rico

Also known as: El Gallito

Area of achievement: Boxing

Early Life

Sixto Escobar (SEES-toh EHS-koh-bahr) was born to Jacinto Escobar and Adela Vargas in Barceloneta, Puerto Rico, on March 23, 1913. He attended school until the eighth grade but decided to end his formal education and concentrate on sports. He was involved in boxing in and around his neighborhood; however, at that time, the sport was illegal in Puerto Rico, prompting boxers to fight clandestinely on rooftops and in backyards. When boxing became legal in February, 1927, Escobar registered as an amateur. He finished his amateur career with a record of twenty-one wins, one loss, and one draw.

Escobar won a decision in his first professional fight in the summer of 1930. With boxing losing popularity in Puerto Rico, he moved to Venezuela, thinking he could get more fights in the bantamweight division there. He won six fights in a row and was matched against Enrique Chaffardet for the Venezuelan featherweight title, but he lost a ten-round decision on points. Escobar fought ten more times in Venezuela, including twice more against Chaffardet, suffering a draw and a loss. After a brief stop in Puerto Rico, Escobar went to the United States, where he was handled by legendary trainers Whitey Bimstein and Ray Arcel.

Stepping in for Midget Wolgast, Escobar fought Bobby Leitham, the Canadian bantamweight champion, on May 7, 1934, in Massachusetts. The bout with Escobar was supposed to be a tune-up fight for Leitham, who was scheduled for a bantamweight title eliminator. Escobar knocked him out in the seventh round. The fighters met again in Montreal, Canada, in June, 1934. Escobar again knocked Leitman out, sending him into retirement. Less than three weeks later, Escobar returned to Montreal to face Rodolfo Casanova for the Montreal Athletic Commission bantamweight title and the vacant National Boxing Association (NBA) title. After dominating his Mexican opponent for eight rounds, Escobar knocked him out in the ninth, becoming the first Puerto Rican and third Latin American to win a world title.

Life's Work

On August 8, 1934, Escobar fought his first full fifteen-round fight, defeating Eugene Huat in Montreal. In December, Escobar hurt his ankle and had to spend months recuperating. He went to Puerto Rico, where he was treated like a king. After a trio of fights in Mexico and the United States, Escobar returned to Montreal to defend his title against Pete Sanstol on August 7, 1935. He pummeled the challenger, who refused to quit. This bout broke the record for gate receipts in a Montreal fight. Less than three weeks later, Escobar was in New York City, where he lost a fifteen-round decision and his world title to Lou Salica. Two and a half months later, they met at Madison Square Garden, and Escobar regained his title with a fifteen-round decision. On August 31, 1936, he won by knockout in the thirteenth round over Tony Marino in New York City to unify the NBA and New York State Athletic Association titles.

In October and December, Escobar dropped a pair of non-title decisions to Harry Jeffra, a fighter to whom he would later lose his title. In February, 1937, he traveled to Puerto Rico and defended his title against Salica, with former heavyweight champion Jack Dempsey as the referee. On September 23, 1937, Escobar lost his title in a one-sided fight against Jeffra. They had a rematch in February, 1938, in Puerto Rico. This time, Escobar knocked down Jeffra three times to regain his title, the only time he would defeat Jeffra in their five bouts. In April, 1939, Escobar defended his title against K. O. Morgan, a fighter to whom he had lost the previous April.

The fight against Morgan was the last time Escobar defended his title. He could no longer make the bantamweight limit and finished with 1 win, 5 losses, and 1 draw in his final 7 bouts. He retired with a record of 36-22-3 with 15 knockouts, although this record is in dispute given that some fights have not been recorded. No other Puerto Rican held a world title until Carlos Ortiz won the junior welterweight title in 1959. Sixto Escobar Stadium in San Juan, Puerto Rico, was named in Escobar's honor. Escobar worked as a beer salesman after his boxing career. He suffered from the effects of diabetes until his death in 1979.

Significance

Escobar was the first Puerto Rican world champion and only the third world champion from Latin America. Although he lost the title to Jeffra and Salica, he was able to regain it, the mark of a true champion. Many boxing observers consider him the best Puerto Rican fighter of all time. Escobar was inducted into the Madison Square Garden Hall of Fame in 1950, the *Ring* Magazine Boxing Hall of Fame in 1975, and the International Boxing Hall of Fame in 2002, the fourth Puerto Rican to be so honored.

Brett Conway

Further Reading

Friedman, Ian C. "Sixto Escobar." In *Latino Athletes*. New York: Facts On File, 2007. This reference source offers a useful overview of Escobar's achievements.

Gems, Gerald R. *The Athletic Crusade: Sport and American Cultural Imperialism*. Lincoln: University of Nebraska Press, 2006. This publication discusses Sixto Escobar and other Puerto Rican athletes whose success helped build national identity and pride

Mullan, Harry, and Bob Mee. *The Ultimate Encyclopedia of Boxing*. London: Carlton, 2007. Includes information about Escobar's career.

See also: Art Aragon; Oscar De La Hoya; Aurelio Herrera; Félix Trinidad.

Martín Espada

American poet and writer

Through his poetry, essays, teaching, and activism, Espada has attempted to speak for the downtrodden. He always has been an advocate for the less privileged in society, especially minorities who have not been allowed to become full participants.

Latino heritage: Puerto Rican

Born: August 7, 1957; Brooklyn, New York

Areas of achievement: Poetry; literature; education; activism

Early Life

Martín Espada (mahr-TEEN ehs-PAH-dah) was born on August 7, 1957, in Brooklyn, New York, to a Jewish mother and a Puerto Rican father. Growing up in Brooklyn, Espada learned from his father the plight of the Puerto Rican community. The family lived in public housing. It was not easy growing up in the neighborhood; to survive it was necessary to have an inner toughness. Several decades later, Espada would put his experiences in the streets of Brooklyn into his poetry.

Martín's father, Frank Espada, was born in Puerto Rico and felt a strong affinity to his homeland. Believing that is was appropriate to speak up for his culture, the elder Espada was a leading voice in New York City for the cause of civil rights. The young Espada learned from his father that it was a struggle for the minority communities to make a decent living in the United States. In addition to being a community leader, his father became a powerful photographer. Espada witnessed that circumstances would not change for the better without racial minorities standing up against injustice at every turn. He even attended rallies with his father at which he saw the political fervor first hand.

As a teenager, Espada became an avid writer of poetry. The writing of poetry became the center of his world, and it gave him an outlet to express his observations, his concerns, and his true self. As he got older, it was necessary to find employment. Espada worked at various jobs, including a stint as a bouncer at a bar, a bindery worker, and a groundskeeper at a minor league baseball park. This eclectic set of experiences helped him to truly comprehend what it is like to make ends meet as a working-class American and also helped him to hone his skills as an observer.

Espada earned a bachelor's degree in history from the University of Wisconsin at Madison in 1981. He decided to continue his education by attending law school

Martín Espada. (AP Photo)

at Northeastern University in Boston. Remaining focused, Espada earned his law degree from Northeastern in 1985. With a law degree in hand, he set out to help those individuals living in the Boston area as a tenant lawyer. At the legal-aid office, Su Clinica Legal, Espada tirelessly worked for several years to make the law lend support to the Spanish-speaking clients who visited the clinic.

Life's Work

Espada's first collection of poetry, *The Immigrant Iceboy's Bolero*, was published in 1982. The poet thought it appropriate to include several of his father's photographs in this volume. Espada speaks of his father's journey to the United States as a boy of nine years old. Influenced by the great Chilean poet Pablo Neruda, Espada decided to write poetry that challenged the status quo, to make a political statement in his poetry without it becoming mere propaganda. As with Neruda's approach to writing, Espada wished to shine a light on a situation or historical event. He believed poetry could serve as a "teaching moment" for both the reader and the poet. In 1984, Espada received a Massachusetts Artists Foundation Fellowship. Over the years, the poet has been given several other honors. In 1986 and again in 1992, he received a National Endowment for the Arts (NEA) Fellowship. His 1990 poetry collection *Rebellion Is the Circle of a Lover's Hands* won the prestigious Paterson Poetry Prize in 1991.

In 1993, Espada began teaching English, Latino poetry, and creative writing at the University of Massachusetts at Amherst, where he has lived with his wife, Katherine, and their son, who was born in 1991. With each new volume of poetry, Espada has continued to confirm himself as one of the leading poets of his generation. The Before Columbus Foundation's 1997 American Book Award for poetry was given to his fifth poetry collection, *Imagine the Angels of Bread* (1996). While Espada primarily is considered a poet, he has also excelled as both an editor and a translator. In 1998, he published *Zapata's Disciple*, a collection of essays. Never losing faith in the power of poetry, Espada published *The Republic of Poetry* in 2006 and *Trouble Ball* in 2011.

Significance

Through his writing and activism, Martín Espada has attempted to be a voice for the voiceless, the forgotten, and those who have been left behind. While never strident, the poet forcefully speaks for his causes. First and foremost, he believes in poetry as an art form. He has refused to sacrifice a poem merely to further a point of view. It speaks to the brilliance of Espada as a poet that he is able to incorporate the political into his work and in so doing the work only is enhanced by the effort.

Jeffry Jensen

Further Reading

Dowdy, Michael. "Spaces for Congregation and Creative Play: Martín Espada and Victor Hernández Cruz's Poetic Plazas." *College Literature* 37, no. 2 (Spring, 2010): 1-24. Dowdy has written a fascinating study of how both of these poets have employed the plaza as a symbolic space that can stand up against the corporate mentality that has attempted to bombard every public space throughout the world.

Espada, Martín. "Jésus Colón's Truth-Seeking Disciple: An Interview with Martín Espada." Interview by José B. Gonzalez. *Latino Studies* 5 (Spring, 2007): 123-128. Examines the poet's process of writing. Espada speaks about his influences and how important historical events are woven into the fabric of his poetry. There also is a discussion of his role as a bilingual poet, and it is pointed out that in everything he writes it is crucial to be truthful.

_______. "Poetry and the Burden of History: An Interview with Martín Espada." Interview by Steven Ratiner. *The Christian Science Monitor*, March 6, 1991, p. 16-17. The poet makes it clear that it is important for him to add perspective to historical events in his poetry.

Fink, Thomas. "Visibility and History in the Poetry of Martín Espada." *Americas Review* 25 (1999): 202-221. It is pointed out how Espada's Puerto Rican background has influenced his poetry and social activism. Fink makes it clear that Espada always strives to be honest and forthright in everything he writes.

Meehan, Kevin. "Martín Espada." In *Contemporary American Poets: Lives, Works, Sources*, edited by Linda Cullum. Westport, Conn.: Greenwood Press, 2004. Meehan has written a solid portrait of Espada's achievements as a political poet, educator, and social activist.

Salgado, Cesar A. "About Martín Espada." *Ploughshares* 31, no. 1 (Spring, 2005): 203-206. A strong portrait of what makes Espada one of the most important poets writing in contemporary America.

See also: Miguel Algarín; Alurista; Judith Ortiz Cofer; Lola Rodríguez de Tió; Clemente Soto Vélez.

Gloria Estefan

Cuban-born singer

Estefan was one of the first Latin American performers to be successful in both the Latin American and U.S. music markets simultaneously. Known for her interpretations of tropical music, Latin pop, and American dance music and ballads, Estefan was instrumental in turning the city of Miami into the capital of Latin music.

Latino heritage: Cuban

Born: September 1, 1957; Havana, Cuba

Also known as: Gloria María Milagrosa Fajardo García Estefan; Gloria María Milagrosa Fajardo García

Area of achievement: Music

Early Life

Gloria María Milagrosa Fajardo García Estefan (eh-STEH-fahn) was born in Havana, Cuba, to José Manuel Fajardo, a member of the Cuban army and bodyguard to president Fulgencio Batista, and Gloria Fajardo, a teacher and talented singer who encouraged her daughter's musical talents from an early age.

The family immigrated to the United States after the Cuban revolution led by Fidel Castro and settled in Miami, Florida. A participant in the Bay of Pigs invasion in 1960, José spent more than a year imprisoned in Cuba. Estefan's mother used music as a way to comfort her daughter, filling their home with the sounds of traditional and contemporary Cuban music. For her ninth birthday, Estefan's mother got her a guitar, which she used to accompany her singing and compose her own songs.

After his release, José enlisted in the U.S. Army and served in the Vietnam War. He received a diagnosis of multiple sclerosis shortly after his return, forcing his wife to support the family. Because her teaching credential was not valid in the United States, Estefan's mother worked during the day while attending college at night to earn her teaching certificate. Meanwhile, Estefan took care of her younger sister and household chores.

Having received a partial scholarship to the University of Miami, Estefan embarked on a degree in education in 1975, supplementing her income by working as an interpreter at the Miami International Airport. Singing at a relative's birthday party, she was spotted by Emilio Estefan, keyboardist and manager of the band the Miami Latin Boys. Later that year, while attending a wedding at which the band was performing, Gloria Estefan was invited to join them for a song. Emilio was so impressed that he asked her to join the band. Estefan initially refused, preferring to focus on her studies, but soon decided to join the band with her cousin Merci. The group was renamed the Miami Sound Machine. In 1978, after graduating college, Estefan married Emilio and began performing with the band full time.

Life's Work

With the success of the dance song "Dr. Beat" from the album *Eyes of Innocence* (1984), the Miami Sound Machine extended its reach from the Miami scene to the national level. The band followed with the album *Primitive Love* (1985), which contained the song "Conga," an unprecedented mix of English-language lyrics set to a Cuban beat. Despite the doubts of record company executives, the song became the first in history to appear simultaneously on *Billboard* charts in four categories.

Gloria Estefan.
(Albert L. Ortega/PictureGroup.com via AP Images)

The Miami Sound Machine

Formed in Miami in 1973, the band in which Gloria Estefan rose to stardom originally was known as the Miami Latin Boys. The band performed mainstream pop and rock songs, as well as Cuban and other Latin American music, in English and Spanish. The group initially was a trio comprising Emilio Estefan (keyboards), Juan Avila (bass), and Enrique "Kiki" Garcia (drums); all had been born in Cuba and raised in Miami. Emilio met Gloria Estefan while playing a wedding reception and invited her to join the band. With the addition of Estefan and her cousin, the band was renamed the Miami Sound Machine (MSM). Their first self-titled album was released locally in 1978 and included English songs on one side, Spanish on the other. The success of this recording led to the production of two more albums.

In 1980, CBS Records signed the MSM, and Emilio quit his job to become the band's full-time manager. In 1981, their first all-Spanish-language album, *Otra vez*, was released, followed by extensive touring throughout Latin America and Europe. Their first English-language single, "Dr. Beat," was released in 1984. The band achieved its first Top 10 song on the U.S. pop chart with the infectious "Conga." In preparation for their next album, *Primitive Love* (1985), Emilio hired three new musicians who called themselves the Three Jerks. As Estefan's fame grew, the band was relegated to the background. After the tour to promote their album *Let It Loose* (1987), the last remaining member of the original Miami Latin Boys, Kiki Garcia, and the Three Jerks quit the band. The musicians claimed they had not been properly credited or compensated for their work.

While touring around the world with the Miami Sound Machine, Estefan quickly became the main attraction. The band's name was changed to Gloria Estefan and the Miami Sound Machine in 1987; the following year, the band's name was dropped entirely, and Estefan was billed as a solo artist.

After recovering from a devastating accident in 1990 in which she fractured her spine, Estefan returned to the stage stronger than ever. At this time, she became part of President George H. W. Bush's campaign against drugs, as well as a public delegate and working member of the United Nations. In 1993, Estefan's first all-Spanish-language album *Mi tierra*, was released. It contained songs written by her and inspired by traditional Cuban music. The album became a commercial and critical success, earning Estefan her first Grammy Award.

Estefan continued touring and recording throughout the 1990's, releasing a Christmas album; an album of covers of American songs from her youth; another Spanish-language album, *Abriendo puertas* (1995), for which she earned her second Grammy Award; and the pop albums *Destiny* (1996) and *Gloria!* (1998). Important performances included halftime shows at Super Bowls XXIX and XXXIII and the closing ceremony of the 1996 Atlanta Summer Olympics, for which her song "Reach" served as official theme. She also performed alongside Celine Dion, Mariah Carey, Shania Twain, and Aretha Franklin on the VH1 1998 concert special *Divas Live*.

While continuing to record and tour in the 2000's, Estefan and Emilio moved into other business ventures, including the ownership of restaurants, hotels, and a stake in the Miami Dolphins football team. Estefan also has appeared in films and television shows and written children's books and a cookbook. Along with her seven Grammy Awards, Estefan has received the Ellis Island Heritage Award and an American Music Award for Lifetime Achievement. She also holds honorary degrees from the University of Miami and the Berklee College of Music; in 2005, she received a star on the Hollywood Walk of Fame.

SIGNIFICANCE

Estefan is one of the most successful Latin music crossover artists, thriving in both the United States and Latin markets. Her success with the Miami Sound Machine and in her solo career paved the way for the boom of Latin music in the late 1990's. Along with Emilio, who is a successful music producer, she is responsible for the wider reach of Latin artists such as Jon Secada, Shakira, Celia Cruz, and Jennifer Lopez through championing their work, composing songs for their albums, and collaborating with them. Refusing to participate in projects that she felt would cast Latinos in a negative light (such as the television show *Miami Vice*), Estefan has worked toward providing a positive role model for Hispanic immigrants to the United States. She continues to be a key figure for the Cuban American community and the Latino community at large through her political and charitable enterprises, as well as her continued appearances on national media outlets.

Georgina Chinchilla-Gonzalez

Further Reading

Gonzales, Doreen. *Gloria Estefan: Singer and Entertainer.* New Jersey: Enslow, 1998. This biography traces Estefan's life and career emphasizing her difficulties as a Cuban immigrant in Miami.

Guevara, Gema. "La Cuba de Ayer/La Cuba de Hoy: The Politics of Music and Diaspora." In *Musical Migrations: Transnationalism and Cultural Hybridity in Latin/o America*, edited by Frances R. Aparicio and Cándida F. Jáquez. New York: Palgrave Macmillan, 2003. This essay explores the connections between the politics of Cuban exiles and the modern use of traditional Cuban tropes in music, focusing particularly on Estefan's album *Mi tierra.*

Ortiz, Ricardo. *Cultural Erotics in Cuban America.* Minneapolis: University of Minnesota Press, 2007. This scholarly exploration of cultural identity in the Cuban American diaspora presents close readings of works by writers and performers, including Estefan's *Destiny* tour.

See also: Mariah Carey; Vikki Carr; Celia Cruz; Sheila E.; Jennifer Lopez; Jon Secada.

Luis R. Esteves

Puerto Rican-born military leader

Known as the founder of the Puerto Rico National Guard, Esteves used his experience in World War I to efficiently organize his fellow Puerto Ricans into a well-trained unit that served in World War II, the Korean War, and other missions throughout the world.

Latino heritage: Puerto Rican

Born: April 30, 1893; Aguadilla, Puerto Rico

Died: March 12, 1958; San Juan, Puerto Rico

Also known as: Luis Raul Esteves Völckers

Area of achievement: Military

Early Life

Luis Raul Esteves Völckers (eh-STEH-vehs) was the sixth child of eight born to Francisco Esteves Soriano and Enedina Völckers Van der Dijs in Aguadilla, Puerto Rico. Esteves's interest in the military was a family tradition, as his father had previously served in the Spanish military.

As a boy, Esteves attended school in Aguadilla and Mayagüez, entering the United States Military Academy at West Point after his high school graduation. At West Point, he became the first Puerto Rican to graduate from the well-regarded military academy. Esteves graduated in June, 1915, while Europe was embroiled in World War I and the United States unsuccessfully sought to maintain neutrality. Esteves's graduating class of 164 students became known as the "Class of Generals" because more than 50 of his peers earned that rank. Esteves was the first of his classmates to achieve the rank of general and was followed by four-star generals Dwight D. Eisenhower and Omar Bradley, among others. While at West Point, Esteves befriended future president Eisenhower, forging a friendship that lasted for decades and helped give Puerto Ricans a voice in the military hierarchy during World War II.

On May 19, 1917, Esteves married Guadalupe Navarro in El Paso, Texas. The couple had four sons and one daughter between 1918 and 1930, and the family primarily lived in Puerto Rico.

Life's Work

Esteves devoted most of his adult life serving his country and creating new ways to help other Puerto Ricans. His military career began with his assignment to the Twenty-third Infantry as a second lieutenant under General John J. Pershing, whose objective was to contain Pancho Villa on the United States-Mexico border. Villa, later immortalized in American and Mexican popular culture, reacted to the United States' support of his political opponent by attacking towns on the American side of the border. During Esteves's service in Texas, Pershing and Villa continued their series of violent skirmishes. While stationed in El Paso, Esteves used his proficiency in Spanish to act as a liaison between the two countries. He later served as mayor of Polvo, Mexico, for a brief period.

The tensions between Mexico and the United States soon were overshadowed by the escalation of World War I. Moving to Syracuse, New York, Esteves's regiment splintered into the existing Twenty-third Infantry and the newly created Thirty-fourth Infantry. Esteves, by then a captain, became second in command of the Twenty-third Infantry. Many of these soldiers later served in the Panama Canal Zone.

Shortly before the United States entered the war in 1917, the U.S. government granted citizenship to Puerto Ricans; this declaration meant that Esteves finally was recognized as a citizen of the country he served. Esteves returned to Puerto Rico to oversee multiple officer training camps and was promoted to major.

After World War I ended, Esteves resigned his commission in the Army but continued to advance his career. Working with Puerto Rican and American government and military officials, Esteves organized the Puerto Rico National Guard, reshaping what was known as the "Porto Rico Regiment" into the Sixty-fifth Infantry. This special unit of the United States Army was the only one to be composed entirely of Hispanic soldiers. The Sixty-fifth Infantry was nicknamed "the Borinqueneers," a term that alluded to Puerto Rico's moniker of "the land of the brave lord," and later earned the respect of General Douglas MacArthur.

In 1937, Esteves became adjutant general of Puerto Rico, a post to which he would later return and from which he retired after the end of World War II. After returning to active status in the Army, Esteves was posted in North Africa and Europe during World War II, ultimately fighting in central Europe.

After World War II ended, Esteves returned to the Puerto Rico National Guard, where he served as adjutant general until his retirement in 1957. Throughout his years of service, Esteves earned several medals, including the Legion of Merit, victory medals for World War I and World War II, and the National Defense Service Medal.

While Esteves concentrated on his military career, he also wrote several books, including one on dominoes and others about his Puerto Rican childhood. Reflecting on his military experience, he wrote about his life as a soldier and also penned training manuals for the Puerto Rico National Guard. Esteves died on March 12, 1958, in San Juan, Puerto Rico.

Significance

Esteves excelled in the United States military, using his innate and learned abilities to work within the hierarchy to create tangible ways for Puerto Ricans to demonstrate their capability while earning international respect for Puerto Rico by their service.

Bonnye Busbice Good

Further Reading

Esteves, Luis R. *Notes on Combat Training for Infantry Officers*. San Juan, P.R.: Bureau of Supplies, Printing and Transportation, 1942. Esteves explains the methods that he refined over decades of training officers for the Puerto Rico National Guard.

Fernandez, Virgil. "The Borinqueneers." In *Hispanic Military Heroes*, edited by Virgil Fernandez. Austin, Tex.: VFJ, 2006. Describes the role of Esteves's Sixty-fifth Infantry, the Borinqueneers, during the major wars of the twentieth century.

Welsome, Eileen. *The General and the Jaguar: Pershing's Hunt for Pancho Villa—A True Story of Revolution and Revenge*. New York: Little, Brown, 2006. Recounts the tense skirmishes along the Mexican border between General Pershing and Pancho Villa during Esteves's assignment in Texas under Pershing.

See also: Santos Benavides; Roy Benavidez; Richard E. Cavazos; Guy Gabaldon; Horacio Rivero, Jr.; Pedro del Valle.

Emilio Estevez

American actor and filmmaker

Part of a family well-known in the entertainment industry, Estevez is a popular actor who starred in several successful films in the 1980's and 1990's. He also has written and directed films such as Bobby *(2006), which centers on the assassination of Robert F. Kennedy.*

Latino heritage: Spanish

Born: May 12, 1962; New York, New York

Areas of achievement: Acting; filmmaking; screenwriting

Early Life

Emilio Estevez (EH-steh-vehz) is the oldest of four children born to actor Martin Sheen (who was born Ramon Estevez, son of Spanish and Irish immigrants) and Janet Templeton Sheen on May 12, 1962, in New York. The family lived on Manhattan's Upper West Side until 1968, when Sheen moved his family to Malibu, California.

At the age of seven, Estevez began writing short stories and poems, and, at eight, wrote and submitted an

Emilio Estévez. (AP Photo)

original episode of Rod Serling's *Night Gallery* television series that was understandably rejected. Soon, he was writing, directing, and producing his own material. By age thirteen, Estevez had begun utilizing advanced sound equipment and writing for small productions with friends Rob Lowe and Sean Penn. When his father was cast in Francis Ford Coppola's *Apocalypse Now* (1979), Estevez accompanied him to Manila, Philippines, where the motion picture was filmed. Estevez was given a small role, but the scene in which he appeared was later cut.

Based on his meeting with a Vietnam veteran in Manila, Estevez penned a play, *Echoes of an Era*, directed by Penn and acted in by his classmates. The play concerns a soldier who is left for dead on a battlefield and later struggles to adjust to life back in the United States. Estevez also participated in a short anti-nuclear-war film, *Meet Mr. Bomb*, that parodied the duck-and-cover films of the 1950's.

After graduating from Santa Monica High School, Estevez landed his first feature-film role in *Tex* (1982), based on a novel by S. E. Hinton. Directed by Tim Hunter, the film concerns two teenage boys (played by Estevez and Matt Dillon) essentially raising themselves. The film received excellent reviews and was followed by *The Outsiders*, based on another novel by Hinton and directed by Coppola. The film featured several young actors who went on to achieve enormous success and were dubbed the "Brat Pack."

Estevez next starred in *Repo Man*, a well-reviewed cult film directed by Alex Cox. In 1984, Estevez was cast by director John Hughes as one of the five main characters in *The Breakfast Club* (1985), a role that made him a star. He plays a high school jock who gradually bonds with four diverse classmates during a day of detention.

LIFE'S WORK

After the success of *The Breakfast Club*, Estevez wrote the screenplay for *That Was Then . . . This Is Now* (1985), in which he starred as a young man who becomes emotionally disturbed when his longtime friend finds a girlfriend. Directed by Christopher Cain and distributed by Paramount, the film failed to find a large audience.

Looking to escape his teen-idol image, Estevez took a part in *Maximum Overdrive* (1986), a horror film written and directed by Stephen King that disappointed critically and financially. Estevez then turned to directing in *Wisdom* (1986), making him the youngest person to direct and star in a feature film. Also starring his then-girlfriend Demi Moore, the film was unsuccessful.

Undaunted, Estevez proceeded to *Stakeout* (1987), a comedy in which he shared top billing with Richard Dreyfuss. An accomplished comedic duo, Estevez and Dreyfuss reteamed in a sequel that also was very popular. Estevez then joined an ensemble cast in the Western *Young Guns* (1988). Featuring Estevez's brother Charlie Sheen, Kiefer Sutherland, and other young actors, the film also spawned a sequel, *Young Guns II* (1990). In the same year, Estevez directed *Men at Work*, teaming with his brother again in the lowbrow comedy.

In 1992, Estevez starred in the Disney family film *The Mighty Ducks*. He plays an arrogant lawyer who is sentenced to coach a struggling youth hockey team. Estevez played the role through two sequels, *D2: The Mighty Ducks* (1994) and *D3: The Mighty Ducks* (1996). The trilogy was enormously successful.

In 2006, Estevez released *Bobby*, a film project he had worked on for years. A great admirer of Robert F. Kennedy, Estevez wrote the script, directed, and acted in the film. The film uses a large ensemble cast to represent people who were present in the Ambassador Hotel's ballroom and kitchen on June 4, 1968, and illustrates the interaction of their stories with the historic events of that day. Estevez also makes extensive use of Kennedy's speech and actual recordings made at the time of his assassination.

The Brat Pack

The term "Brat Pack" was popularized by David Blum in a *New York Magazine* profile of a group of young, successful actors. Blum depicted these young actors—mostly young men in their late teens and twenties—as a 1980's equivalent of the Rat Pack of the 1950's and 1960's. The actors were young, talented, and often appeared together in films. Emilio Estevez was their leader. Other members included Estevez's childhood friends Sean Penn and Rob Lowe, Tom Cruise, C. Thomas Howell, Matt Dillon, and Judd Nelson. Many of these actors first appeared together in *The Outsiders* (1983), but the films most associated with the Brat Pack are 1985's *The Breakfast Club* and *St. Elmo's Fire.* Actors such as Anthony Michael Hall and Molly Ringwald, who appeared in director John Hughes's *The Breakfast Club* and *Sixteen Candles,* and Ally Sheedy also became associated with the group. The Brat Pack films often concerned teenagers or young adults struggling with alienation, peer pressure, communication problems with their parents, and anxieties about the future. These issues resonated with young audiences, making the Brat Pack wildly popular.

In 2010, Estevez went to Spain with his father to make *The Way*, which he wrote, directed, and acted in. The film follows the pilgrimage of Tom (Martin Sheen), a bereaved father carrying his dead son's ashes in a box (Estevez plays the son in flashbacks) as he walks the Camino de Santiago. The story invokes many significant Christian themes.

Significance

Estevez showed creative talent early in his life, and although he benefited from his father's support and connections, he was determined to make his own way in the entertainment industry.

He became a highly successful actor, notably in several films that spoke to the anxieties and aspirations of a generation. However, he continues to challenge himself through writing and directing ambitious projects of his own.

Mary Hurd

Further Reading

Blum, David. "Hollywood's Brat Pack." *New York Magazine* 18, no. 23 (June 10, 1985): 40-48. This lengthy profile of Estevez and his contemporaries popularized the term "Brat Pack."

Fleeman, Michael. "Emilio Estevez the History Boy." *People* 66, no. 23 (December 4, 2006). Describes Estevez's long struggle to make *Bobby*, his film about the assassination of Robert F. Kennedy, and his interest in the story.

Riley, Lee, and David Schumacher. *The Sheens: Martin, Charlie, and Emilio Estevez.* London: Robson Books, 1991. Detailed biography of the Sheen/Estevez family, their difficulties, careers, spirituality, and social activism.

See also: Benjamin Bratt; Andy Garcia; John Leguizamo; Esai Morales; Charlie Sheen; Martin Sheen; Jimmy Smits.

Leobardo Estrada

American sociologist

A well-respected career academic in sociology—specifically in the burgeoning field of urban planning—Estrada has contributed his expertise to countless regional and national blue-ribbon panels investigating the impacts of economics and social policy on the size, movement, and integrity of the Latino immigrant population, particularly in the southwestern United States since World War II.

Latino heritage: Mexican
Born: May 6, 1945; El Paso, Texas
Areas of achievement: Sociology; scholarship; education

Early Life

Leobardo Estrada (lee-oh-BAHR-doh eh-STRAH-duh), born in El Paso, Texas, was raised in a comfortable middle-class home with a keen awareness of his Mexican heritage. Early on, success in school came easily, but Estrada lacked motivation. Interested generally in Latino culture in Texas, he matriculated at Baylor University in Waco to study sociology. Years later, he recalled how nonchalantly he approached academics at Baylor until he met the woman he would eventually marry. His prospective father-in-law agreed to the engagement on the condition that Estrada commit to attending graduate school. That led Estrada to apply to Florida State University.

At Florida State, Estrada focused on demography, the discipline within sociology geared to analyzing and describing the dimensions and movements of specific population groups—in his case the Latino population in the Southwest. Unlike social theorists, demographers gather a wide variety of empirical data—such as economic information, census data, birth and death records, employment numbers, housing and education statistics—and extrapolate from it a reading of the activity of a specific population group. Estrada discovered the challenge of gathering information on a significant population that had, to that point, attracted little academic interest.

Life's Work

Certain that he would dedicate his career to academics, Estrada completed his doctorate and accepted an appointment at the University of Michigan. However, because his field of interest required that he work closer to the culture he was studying, he returned to Texas, accepting teaching positions first at the University of Texas at El Paso and then at the University of North Texas. Estrada became known not only for his dynamic classroom presentations but also for his advocacy of often-controversial causes related to the Hispanic community. He clashed occasionally with university administrators over his public political activism. In 1977, Estrada accepted a position as associate professor of urban planning in the School of Public Affairs at the University of California at Los Angeles (UCLA). The university proved a good fit for Estrada: It encouraged faculty members to extend their expertise beyond the limits of the classroom to benefit the wider community.

Over the next three decades, Estrada gathered data on the Latino population in the Los Angeles area with particular attention to the role of economics and the environment. As an ethnic demographer, Estrada published widely in the most prestigious journals in the field. His interest was in tracking developing trends within the city's Latino population (during those years, Latinos accounted for aroud 45 percent of the city's total population): its movements within and between neighborhoods, shifts in job opportunities and career selection, business startups, housing, birth and death rate fluctuations, and changes in education levels and family net income. His expertise was sought by educators, hospital administrators, business leaders, public transportation executives, and politicians. Estrada was asked twice by the U.S. Census Bureau to develop methodologies for accurately analyzing and gathering census data on the Hispanic population. He served as a special assistant to the chief of the bureau's Population Division and later as staff assistant to the deputy director of the bureau. He published seminal material in the field of demography, most notably *The Changing Profile of Mexican America: A Sourcebook for Policy Making* (1986).

While maintaining his dedication to the classroom, Estrada served as consultant to public foundations (most notably the Ford Foundation), hospitals, charities (particularly those concerned with youths and education), and a variety of international corporations. He also made two notable contributions to the Los Angeles area. In 1990, given his familiarity with the census, he was called upon to lend his expertise in the controversial redistricting of the powerful Los Angeles Board of Supervisors, an effort designed to make the board better reflect the city's diversity. The redistricting led directly to the election of the first Latino city supervisor since Reconstruction. A year later, Estrada was named to the city's Christopher Commission, a blue-ribbon independent committee chaired by Warren Christopher (later President Bill Clinton's secretary of state) that was impaneled in response to the national outcry over the videotaped beating of Rodney King. The committee was asked to review more than two thousand allegations of excessive force by officers of the Los Angeles Police Department and set an agenda for the reform of the department.

Into his sixties, Estrada maintained his public profile, promoting a range of public issues involving the Latino community, focusing specifically on entrepreneurial opportunities and wealth creation for urban families. In November, 2008, he was named to the transition team for President Barack Obama's incoming administration.

Significance

Estrada earned a national reputation for the integrity of his research methodologies and for reaching conclusions that were grounded in and shaped by hard data rather than driven by personal agendas or biases. His measure of trends in the Latino immigrant population in Southern California influenced local government policy, research funding, and community development projects. He epitomized the academic whose work finds significant application in the world outside the classroom.

Joseph Dewey

Further Reading

Cannon, Lou. *Official Negligence: How Rodney King and the Riots Changed Los Angeles and the*

LAPD. New York: Basic Books, 1999. Careful and exhaustive review of the controversial case and the Christopher Commission, which brought Estrada national attention.

Ochoa, Enrique C., and Gilda L. Ochoa. *Latino Los Angeles: Transformations, Communities, and Activism*. Tucson: University of Arizona Press, 2005. Wide-ranging study that gives context to the specific analyses Estrada completed on the demographics of the Los Angeles Latino population.

Poston, Dudley L., Jr., and Leon F. Bouvier. *Population and Society: An Introduction to Demography*. New York: Cambridge University Press, 2010. A helpful and accessible introduction to the science of population study, census analysis, and cultural sociology, with particular emphasis on the sort of racial and ethnic demography Estrada pioneered.

See also: Rodolfo F. Acuña; Corky Gonzáles; José Ángel Gutiérrez.

Tomás Estrada Palma

Cuban-born Cuban president (1902-1906), military leader, and activist

Estrada Palma was the first president of the Cuban republic and played an important role in that country's struggle for independence from Spain. A general in the Liberation Army, he later headed the Cuban Revolutionary Party in the United States and secured U.S. support for the second war of independence.

Latino heritage: Cuban

Born: July 9, 1835; Bayamo, Cuba

Died: November 4, 1908; Santiago de Cuba, Cuba

Areas of achievement: Government and politics; military

Early Life

Tomás Estrada Palma (toh-MAHS ehs-TRAH-dah PAHL-mah) was born in Bayamo in eastern Cuba to Maria Candelaria de Palma y Tamayo and Andrés Duque de Estrada y Palma. His father died when Estrada Palma was still a boy. After attending schools in Havana, he was sent to Spain in 1852 to study law at the University of Seville. He left before graduating and returned to Cuba to take over the family estate following the death of his guardian.

In 1868, Oriente landowner Carlos Manuel de Céspedes proclaimed the island's independence, calling on his compatriots to fight against the Spaniards. Estrada Palma was part of a delegation sent to persuade the rebels to lay down arms. Instead, he joined them and fought in the Ten Years' War (1868-1878). Rapidly rising to the rank of general, Estrada Palma also was elected president of the "Republic in Arms." In October, 1877, he was captured by Spanish forces and imprisoned in Havana and then in Spain, where he remained until the war ended.

Upon his release, Estrada Palma refused to accept the terms of the peace agreement and return to Cuba. Instead, he went to France, the United States, and Central America. He met and married the daughter of the Honduran president, Genoveva Guardiola y Arbizu, with whom he would have six children. He was appointed postmaster general, but in 1883, the family left Honduras and moved to the United States. They settled in

Tomás Estrada Palma. (Library of Congress)

Estrada Palma and the United States

When Tomás Estrada Palma became president of Cuba, he was sixty-seven years of age and had spent almost three decades in exile, mainly in the United States. A naturalized U.S. citizen, Estrada Palma identified strongly with his adopted country. He spoke English, converted to Quakerism, and had acquired American tastes and views. After the end of the 1898 Spanish-American War, he was reluctant to return to Cuba and would have preferred to remain in the United States. Like other naturalized Cuban Americans, Estrada Palma had a divided loyalty. He approved of U.S. democracy and favored a close relationship with that country, convinced that its guidance was necessary to maintain order in an independent Cuba emerging from centuries of colonial rule. This ideology placed him at odds with José Martí, a fellow revolutionary who feared U.S. dominance of independent Cuba, and also with insurgents on the island who felt that he placed too much emphasis on gaining U.S. assistance in winning the war. Estrada Palma and other naturalized Cuban Americanss of the New York junta were successful in building U.S. support for their cause because of their familiarity with North American ways. Estrada Palma also was well-known to the U.S. government and highly regarded. He campaigned for the Cuban presidency from New York, only renouncing his U.S. citizenship when he returned to Cuba to take office.

Central Valley, New York, where Estrada Palma established a school for Latin American boys.

LIFE'S WORK

The exiled Cuban writer and revolutionary José Martí had made New York a center of operations for the independence struggle. Martí appointed Estrada Palma adviser to the Cuban Revolutionary Party, which they founded in 1892. Plans for another war were laid in Central Valley, and in April, 1895, Martí returned to Cuba to fight. After Martí's death in battle in May, Estrada Palma assumed leadership of the party. In September, he formed the Cuban Junta, an association of naturalized Cuban Americans, to garner support for the revolutionary cause. Leaving his family in Central Valley, Estrada Palma moved to New York City and then to Washington, D.C. There, he opposed Spanish attempts to grant autonomy to the island, successfully lobbying Congress to pass the Joint Resolution—a bill that led the United States to declare war on Spain in April, 1898.

The Spanish were quickly defeated, but Cuban independence did not immediately follow. The island experienced a period of U.S. occupation, and the first republican elections were only called at the end of 1901. There were two candidates: Estrada Palma and General Bartolomé Masó. Masó was more popular, as Estrada Palma was almost unknown in Cuba; however, Estrada Palma had the support of prominent figures such as Máximo Gomez, former commander of the Liberation Army. More importantly, he had the backing of the U.S. government. When the outgoing U.S. governor Leonard Wood appointed supporters of Estrada Palma to the electoral commission, Masó withdrew his candidacy. Estrada Palma won the election unopposed and returned to Cuba to take office in May, 1902.

Estrada Palma's administration began well. An honest and well-intentioned man, he continued programs initiated under U.S. occupation, including public education and improvements in public services. His prudent personal financial habits carried over into government policy, producing a budget surplus. However, his administration disappointed the former freedom fighters who had imagined a very different independent Cuba. None of the ministers Estrada Palma chose was a war veteran or revolutionary émigré. Spanish colonial legislation remained in place because of his failure to mobilize his congress to approve the new constitution. He sought foreign investment to promote the island's economic recovery, but this resulted in U.S. control of land and the sugar industry and Spanish domination of commerce.

Estrada Palma was most heavily criticized for introducing legislation that placed independent Cuba under the protection of the United States. He supported the Platt Amendment, an appendix to the Cuban Constitution that gave the United States the right to intervene militarily if order or stability was threatened. It also leased areas of Cuban territory, including Guantánamo Bay, to the United States for military bases.

In 1905, Estrada Palma sought reelection, this time as the candidate of the Moderate Party. His opponent was General José Miguel Gomez, the popular candidate of the Liberal Party. Estrada Palma was not expected to win the election, but government resources were used to ensure his victory. He might not have been aware of the scale of the fraud, but Estrada Palma was keen to win a second term in order to continue his program to develop Cuba. The Liberals withdrew their campaign in protest and Estrada Palma was reelected in December.

In August, 1906, the Liberals organized an armed uprising in protest of the corrupt election. Estrada Palma attempted unsuccessfully to crush the revolt, and fighting spread throughout the island. In September, he appealed to President Theodore Roosevelt to intervene. Rather than send troops, Roosevelt appointed a commission headed by Secretary of War William H. Taft to investigate. Taft recommended a compromise that would recognize some of the Liberal demands, but Estrada Palma refused to negotiate. He resigned as president on September 28, leaving the country with no government and forcing the United States to intervene. Estrada Palma left Havana on October 2 and returned to his family estate at Bayamo. He remained there, living in reduced circumstances, until his death on November 4, 1908.

Significance

Estrada Palma dedicated much of his life to obtaining independence for Cuba, the last Spanish colony. He held high-ranking military and civilian positions in the revolutionary movement. After the death of José Martí, Estrada Palma was responsible for managing the movement from outside of Cuba and, importantly, obtaining U.S. involvement in the final war against Spain. His correspondence with Cuban and American military men and politicians is an important chronicle of events of the time. Don Tomás, as he was affectionately known, was regarded as the most honest president of the republican era. However, his reputation suffered because he approved legislation that ensured Cuban political and military dependence on the United States.

Christine Ayorinde

Further Reading

Hernández, José M. *Cuba and the United States: Intervention and Militarism, 1868-1933*. Austin: University of Texas Press, 1993. A good analysis of Estrada Palma's time in the United States and how this influenced his adminstration.

Keenan, Jerry. "Tomás Estrada Palma." In *Encyclopedia of the Spanish-American and Philippine-American Wars*. Santa Barbara, Calif.: ABC-CLIO, 2001. Brief entry on Estrada Palma that discusses his role in the run-up to the Spanish-American War.

Millett, Allan Reed. *The Politics of Intervention: The Military Occupation of Cuba, 1906-1909*. Columbus: Ohio State University Press, 1968. Covering the background to the second U.S. intervention in Cuba, this book provides a detailed account of Estrada Palma, the man and the president.

Pérez, Louis A., Jr. *Cuba Under the Platt Amendment, 1902-1934*, Pittsburgh, Pa.: University of Pittsburgh Press, 1986. A history of U.S.-Cuba relations in the early years of the republic that discusses Estrada Palma's presidency.

Thomas, Hugh. *Cuba or the Pursuit of Freedom*, New York: Da Capo Press, 1998. This wide-ranging study of Cuban history has a detailed chapter on Estrada Palma's time as President.

See also: Lourdes Casal; José Martí; Jorge Mas Canosa.